THE PERSONALITY READER

SECOND EDITION

Edited and with Commentary by

MIRIAM W. SCHUSTACK

California State University, San Marcos

HOWARD S. FRIEDMAN

University of California, Riverside

PEARSON

Boston • New York • San Francisco
Mexico City • Montreal • Toronto • London • Madrid • Munich • Paris
Hong Kong • Singapore • Tokyo • Cape Town • Sydney

Editor-in-Chief: Susan Hartman
Sponsoring Editor: Michelle Limoges
Editorial Assistant: Allison Rowland
Marketing Manager: Karen Natale
Editorial Production Service: Omegatype Typography, Inc.
Composition Buyer: Linda Cox
Manufacturing Buyer: JoAnne Sweeney
Electronic Composition: Omegatype Typography, Inc.
Cover Administrator: Joel Gendron

For related titles and support materials, visit our online catalog at www.ablongman.com.

Copyright © 2008 Pearson Education, Inc.

All rights reserved. No part of the material protected by this copyright notice may be reproduced or utilized in any form or by any means, electronic or mechanical, including photocopying, recording, or by any information storage and retrieval system, without written permission from the copyright owner.

To obtain permission(s) to use material from this work, please submit a written request to Allyn and Bacon, Permissions Department, 75 Arlington Street, Boston, MA 02116 or fax your request to 617-848-7320.

A previous edition was published under the title of *Readings in Personality: Classic Theories and Modern Research*, copyright © 2001 by Allyn and Bacon.

ISBN-13: 978-0-205-48551-2   ISBN-10: 0-205-48551-0

Library of Congress Cataloging-in-Publication Data

The personality reader / edited and with commentary by Miriam W. Schustack,
Howard S. Friedman. — 2nd ed.
       p.   cm.
  Includes bibliographical references and index.
  ISBN 0-205-48551-0
 1. Personality—Textbooks.   I. Schustack, Miriam W.   II. Friedman, Howard S.
  BF698.R346   2008
  155.2—dc22

                                                    2006052476

Printed in the United States of America

10   9   15

CONTENTS

UNIT FOUR
BEHAVIORIST AND LEARNING ASPECTS OF PERSONALITY

UNIT FIVE
COGNITIVE ASPECTS OF PERSONALITY

UNIT SIX
TRAIT AND SKILL ASPECTS OF PERSONALITY

UNIT SEVEN
HUMANISTIC AND EXISTENTIAL ASPECTS OF PERSONALITY

UNIT EIGHT
PERSON-SITUATION INTERACTIONIST ASPECTS OF PERSONALITY

UNIT NINE
APPLICATIONS TO INDIVIDUAL DIFFERENCES

PREFACE

In many ways, the best introduction to the brilliance of influential personality theorists and researchers is through their own words. A verbal and eloquent group, personality theorists are not shy about stating their views of human nature in a forceful and direct manner. In the context of a course that provides orientation and framework to students, excerpts from theorists' writings can be a powerful tool for learning.

We have selected articles and excerpts that give the student a taste of the perspective offered by key theorists from the major traditions. The articles provide an excellent sampling of the core concepts with which any well-educated personality psychologist is familiar. More basically, the selections provide a set of answers to the question, What does it mean to be a person? *The Personality Reader* can thus be used in a wide variety of courses.

Each selection begins with a brief description of the author and the author's theoretical perspective, and provides some context for the specific work to follow. The selection is followed by a set of Questions to Think About to help the student think critically about the concepts presented in the selection.

The book is organized into nine units, which correspond to nine basic perspectives on personality. Although this reader is designed to stand on its own, the units are also set up to correspond loosely to our personality textbook, *Personality: Classic Theories and Modern Research* (Allyn and Bacon). That textbook is coordinated with a website with quizzes, links, and other resources for student learning.

We want to thank Kathleen Clark, Paavai Jayaraman, Aarti Kulkami, Joya Paul, and Sophia Rath for their assistance in preparing the first edition of this book. We also thank the authors of the selected contributions.

M.W.S.

H.S.F.

1

The Origin and Development
of Psychoanalysis

SIGMUND FREUD

Sigmund Freud (1856–1939) was the son of Jacob Freud and his third wife, the young and attractive Amalie. Sigmund and his two adult half brothers adored her. He was trained as a physician and neurologist. Like many scientists of his time, Freud saw himself as discarding old superstitions (including religion) and developing a science of the mind. Building on Charles Darwin's ideas of evolution, Freud saw the sex drive as fundamental.

When the 26-year-old Freud fell in love with Martha Bernays, he had to wait four long years to marry her. Around that time, Freud began developing his psychosexual theories of the human psyche, which had a profound influence on twentieth-century thought, as they popularized notions of repressed psychosexual conflict. The following reading, given as a lecture (in German) at Clark University in 1909, during Freud's only visit to America, lays out one of the core ideas of the psychoanalytic perspective—that sexuality lies at the heart of people's psychological problems.

[P]sychoanalytic investigations trace back the symptoms of disease with really surprising regularity to impressions from the sexual life, show us that the pathogenic wishes are of the nature of erotic impulse-components (*Triebkomponente*), and necessitate the assumption that to disturbances of the erotic sphere must be ascribed the greatest significance among the etiological factors of the disease. This holds of both sexes.

I know that this assertion will not willingly be credited. Even those investigators who gladly follow my psychological labors, are inclined to think that I overestimate the etiological share of the sexual moments. They ask me why other mental excitations should not lead to the phenomena of repression and surrogate-creation which I have described. I can give them this answer; that I do not know why they should not do this, I have no objection to their doing it, but

experience shows that they do not possess such a significance, and that they merely support the effect of the sexual moments, without being able to supplant them. This conclusion was not a theoretical postulate; in the *Studien über Hysterie*, published in 1895 with Dr. Breuer, I did not stand on this ground. I was converted to it when my experience was richer and had led me deeper into the nature of the case. Gentlemen, there are among you some of my closest friends and adherents, who have travelled to Worcester with me. Ask them, and they will tell you that they all were at first completely sceptical of the assertion of the determinative significance of the sexual etiology, until they were compelled by their own analytic labors to come to the same conclusion.

The conduct of the patients does not make it any easier to convince one's self of the correctness of the

Source: Freud, S. (1912). The origin and development of psychoanalysis. *American Journal of Psychology,* 21(2), 181–218. (Selection is from the Fourth Lecture.)

view which I have expressed. Instead of willingly giving us information concerning their sexual life, they try to conceal it by every means in their power. Men generally are not candid in sexual matters. They do not show their sexuality freely, but they wear a thick overcoat—a fabric of lies—to conceal it, as though it were bad weather in the world of sex. And they are not wrong; sun and wind are not favorable in our civilized society to any demonstration of sex life. In truth no one can freely disclose his erotic life to his neighbor. But when your patients see that in your treatment they may disregard the conventional restraints, they lay aside this veil of lies, and then only are you in a position to formulate a judgment on the question in dispute. Unfortunately physicians are not favored above the rest of the children of men in their personal relationship to the questions of the sex life. Many of them are under the ban of that mixture of prudery and lasciviousness which determines the behaviour of most *Kulturmenschen* in affairs of sex.

Now to proceed with the communication of our results. It is true that in another series of cases psychoanalysis at first traces the symptoms back not to the sexual, but to banal traumatic experiences. But the distinction loses its significance through other circumstances. The work of analysis which is necessary for the thorough explanation and complete cure of a case of sickness does not stop in any case with the experience of the time of onset of the disease, but in every case it goes back to the adolescence and the early childhood of the patient. Here only do we hit upon the impressions and circumstances which determine the later sickness. Only the childhood experiences can give the explanation for the sensitivity to later traumata and only when these memory traces, which almost always are forgotten, are discovered and made conscious, is the power developed to banish the symptoms. We arrive here at the same conclusion as in the investigation of dreams—that it is the incompatible, repressed wishes of childhood which lend their power to the creation of symptoms. Without these the reactions upon later traumata discharge normally. But we must consider these mighty wishes of childhood very generally as sexual in nature.

Now I can at any rate be sure of your astonishment. Is there an infantile sexuality? you will ask. Is

childhood not rather that period of life which is distinguished by the lack of the sexual impulse? No, gentlemen, it is not at all true that the sexual impulse enters into the child at puberty, as the devils in the gospel entered into the swine. The child has his sexual impulses and activities from the beginning, he brings them with him into the world, and from these the so-called normal sexuality of adults emerges by a significant development through manifold stages. It is not very difficult to observe the expressions of this childish sexual activity; it needs rather a certain art to overlook them or to fail to interpret them.

As fate would have it, I am in a position to call a witness for my assertions from your own midst. I show you here the work of one Dr. Sanford Bell, published in 1902 in the *American Journal of Psychology*. The author was a fellow of Clark University, the same institution within whose walls we now stand. In this thesis, entitled "A Preliminary Study of the Emotion of Love between the Sexes," which appeared three years before my "Drei Abhandlungen zur Sexualtheorie," the author says just what I have been saying to you: "The emotion of sex love . . . does not make its appearance for the first time at the period of adolescence as has been thought." He has, as we should say in Europe, worked by the American method, and has gathered not less than 2,500 positive observations in the course of fifteen years, among them 800 of his own. He says of the signs by which this amorous condition manifests itself: "The unprejudiced mind, in observing these manifestations in hundreds of couples of children, cannot escape referring them to sex origin. The most exacting mind is satisfied when to these observations are added the confessions of those who have as children experienced the emotion to a marked degree of intensity, and whose memories of childhood are relatively distinct." Those of you who are unwilling to believe in infantile sexuality will be most astonished to hear that among those children who fell in love so early not a few are of the tender ages of three, four, and five years.

It would not be surprising if you should believe the observations of a fellow-countryman rather than my own. Fortunately a short time ago from the analysis of a five-year-old boy who was suffering from anxiety, an analysis undertaken with correct technique by his own father, I succeeded in getting a fairly complete picture of the bodily expressions of the impulse and the mental productions of an early stage of childish sexual life. And I must remind you that my friend, Dr. C. G. Jung, read you a few hours ago in this room an observation on a still younger girl who from the same cause as my patient—the birth of a little child in the family—betrayed certainly almost the same secret excitement, wish and complex-creation. Accordingly I am not without hope that you may feel friendly toward this idea of infantile sexuality that was so strange at first. I might also quote the remarkable example of the Zürich psychiatrist, E. Bleuler, who said a few years ago openly that he faced my sexual theories incredulous and bewildered, and since that time by his own observations had substantiated them in their whole scope. If it is true that most men, medical observers and others, do not want to know anything about the sexual life of the child, the fact is capable of explanation only too easily. They have forgotten their own infantile sexual activity under the pressure of education for civilization and do not care to be reminded now of the repressed material. You will be convinced otherwise if you begin the investigation by a self-analysis, by an interpretation of your own childhood memories.

Lay aside your doubts and let us evaluate the infantile sexuality of the earliest years. The sexual impulse of the child manifests itself as a very complex one, it permits of an analysis into many components, which spring from different sources. It is entirely disconnected from the function of reproduction which it is later to serve. It permits the child to gain different sorts of pleasure sensations, which we include, by the analogues and connections which they show, under the term sexual pleasures. The great source of infantile sexual pleasure is the auto-excitation of certain particularly sensitive parts of the body; besides the genitals are included the rectum and the opening of the urinary canal, and also the skin and other sensory surfaces. Since in this first phase of child sexual life the satisfaction is found on the child's own body and has nothing to do with any other object, we call this phase after a word coined by Havelock Ellis, that of "auto-erotism." The parts of the body significant in giving sexual pleasure we call "erogenous zones." The thumb-

sucking (*Ludeln*) or passionate sucking (*Wonnesaugen*) of very young children is a good example of such an auto-erotic satisfaction of an erogenous zone. The first scientific observer of this phenomenon, a specialist in children's diseases in Budapest by the name of Lindner, interpreted these rightly as sexual satisfaction and described exhaustively their transformation into other and higher forms of sexual gratification. Another sexual satisfaction of this time of life is the excitation of the genitals by masturbation, which has such a great significance for later life and, in the case of many individuals, is never fully overcome. Besides this and other auto-erotic manifestations we see very early in the child the impulse-components of *sexual pleasure*, or, as we may say, of the *libido*, which presupposes a second person as its object. These impulses appear in opposed pairs, as active and passive. The most important representatives of this group are the pleasure in inflicting pain (sadism) with its passive opposite (masochism) and active and passive exhibition-pleasure (*Schaulust*). From the first of these later pairs splits off the curiosity for knowledge, as from the latter the impulse toward artistic and theatrical representation. Other sexual manifestations of the child can already be regarded from the view-point of object-choice, in which the second person plays the prominent part. The significance of this was primarily based upon motives of the impulse of self-preservation. The difference between the sexes plays, however, in the child no very great rôle. One may attribute to every child, without wronging him, a bit of the homosexual disposition.

The sexual life of the child, rich, but dissociated, in which each single impulse goes about the business of arousing pleasure independently of every other, is later correlated and organized in two general directions, so that by the close of puberty the definite sexual character of the individual is practically finally determined. The single impulses subordinate themselves to the overlordship of the genital zone, so that the whole sexual life is taken over into the service of procreation, and their gratification is now significant only so far as they help to prepare and promote the true sexual act. On the other hand, object-choice prevails over auto-erotism, so that now in the sexual life all components of the sexual impulse are satisfied in the loved person. But not all the original impulse-components are given a share in the final shaping of the sexual life. Even before the advent of puberty certain impulses have undergone the most energetic repression under the impulse of education, and mental forces like shame, disgust and morality are developed, which, like sentinels, keep the repressed wishes in subjection. When there comes, in puberty, the high tide of sexual desire it finds dams in this creation of reactions and resistances. These guide the outflow into the so-called normal channels, and make it impossible to revivify the impulses which have undergone repression.

The most important of these repressed impulses are koprophilism, that is, the pleasure in children connected with the excrements; and, further, the tendencies attaching themselves to the persons of the primitive object-choice.

Gentlemen, a sentence of general pathology says that every process of development brings with it the germ of pathological dispositions in so far as it may be inhibited, delayed, or incompletely carried out. This holds for the development of the sexual function, with its many complications. It is not smoothly completed in all individuals, and may leave behind either abnormalities or disposition to later diseases by the way of later falling back or *regression*. It may happen that not all the partial impulses subordinate themselves to the rule of the genital zone. Such an impulse which has remained disconnected brings about what we call a perversion, which may replace the normal sexual goal by one of its own. It may happen, as has been said before, that the auto-erotism is not fully overcome, as many sorts of disturbances testify. The originally equal value of both sexes as sexual objects may be maintained and an inclination to homosexual activities in adult life result from this, which, under suitable conditions, rises to the level of exclusive homosexuality. This series of disturbances corresponds to the direct inhibition of development of the sexual function, it includes the perversions and the general *infantilism* of the sex life that are not seldom met with.

The disposition to neuroses is to be derived in another way from an injury to the development of the sex life. The neuroses are related to the perversions as the negative to the positive; in them we find the same impulse-components as in perversions, as bearers of the complexes and as creators of the symptoms; but here they work from out the unconscious. They have

undergone a repression, but in spite of this they maintain themselves in the unconscious. Psychoanalysis teaches us that overstrong expression of the impulse in very early life leads to a sort of fixation (*Fixirung*), which then offers a weak point in the articulation of the sexual function. If the exercise of the normal sexual function meets with hindrances in later life, this repression, dating from the time of development, is broken through at just that point at which the infantile fixation took place.

You will now perhaps make the objection: "But all that is not sexuality." I have used the word in a very much wider sense than you are accustomed to understand it. This I willingly concede. But it is a question whether you do not rather use the word in much too narrow a sense when you restrict it to the realm of procreation. You sacrifice by that the understanding of perversions; of the connection between perversion, neurosis and normal sexual life; and have no means of recognizing, in its true significance, the easily observable beginning of the somatic and mental sexual life of the child. But however you decide about the use of the word, remember that the psychoanalyst understands sexuality in that full sense to which he is led by the evaluation of infantile sexuality.

Now we turn again to the sexual development of the child. We still have much to say here, since we have given more attention to the somatic than to the mental expressions of the sexual life. The primitive object-choice of the child, which is derived from his need of help, demands our further interest. It first attaches to all persons to whom he is accustomed, but soon these give way in favor of his parents. The relation of the child to his parents is, as both direct observation of the child and later analytic investigation of adults agree, not at all free from elements of sexual accessory-excitation (*Miterregung*). The child takes both parents, and especially one, as an object of his erotic wishes. Usually he follows in this the stimulus given by his parents, whose tenderness has very clearly the character of a sex manifestation, though inhibited so far as its goal is concerned. As a rule, the father prefers the daughter, the mother the son; the child reacts to this situation, since, as son, he wishes himself in the place of his father, as daughter, in the place of the mother. The feelings awakened in these relations between parents and children, and, as a resultant of them, those among the children in relation to each other, are not only positively of a tender, but negatively of an inimical sort. The complex built up in this way is destined to quick repression, but it still exerts a great and lasting effect from the unconscious. We must express the opinion that this with its ramifications presents the *nuclear complex* of every neurosis, and so we are prepared to meet with it in a not less effectual way in the other fields of mental life. The myth of King Œdipus, who kills his father and wins his mother as a wife is only the slightly altered presentation of the infantile wish, rejected later by the opposing barriers of incest. Shakespeare's tale of Hamlet rests on the same basis of an incest complex, though better concealed. At the time when the child is still ruled by the still unrepressed nuclear complex, there begins a very significant part of his mental activity which serves sexual interest. He begins to investigate the question of where children come from and guesses more than adults imagine of the true relations by deduction from the signs which he sees. Usually his interest in this investigation is awakened by the threat to his welfare through the birth of another child in the family, in whom at first he sees only a rival. Under the influence of the partial impulses which are active in him he arrives at a number of "infantile sexual theories," as that the same male genitals belong to both sexes, that children are conceived by eating and born through the opening of the intestine, and that sexual intercourse is to be regarded as an inimical act, a sort of overpowering.

But just the unfinished nature of his sexual constitution and the gaps in his knowledge brought about by the hidden condition of the feminine sexual canal, cause the infant investigator to discontinue his work as a failure. The facts of this childish investigation itself as well as the infant sex theories created by it are of determinative significance in the building of the child's character, and in the content of his later neuroses.

It is unavoidable and quite normal that the child should make his parents the objects of his first object-choice. But his *libido* must not remain fixed on these first chosen objects, but must take them merely as a prototype and transfer from these to other persons in the time of definite object-choice. The breaking loose (*Ablösung*) of the child from his parents is thus a problem impossible to escape if the social virtue of the young individual is not to be impaired. During the time that the repressive activity is making its choice among the partial sexual impulses and later, when the influence of the parents, which in the most essential way has furnished the material for these repressions, is lessened, great problems fall to the work of education, which at present certainly does not always solve them in the most intelligent and economic way.

Gentlemen, do not think that with these explanations of the sexual life and the sexual development of the child we have too far departed from psychoanalysis and the cure of neurotic disturbances. If you like, you may regard the psychoanalytic treatment only as a continued education for the overcoming of childhood-remnants (*Kindheitsresten*).

Questions to Think About

1. What are some alternatives to Freud's focus on childhood sexuality that might also explain adult psychological difficulties?

2. Freud's view was that normal sexual behavior in adults could develop only if many aspects of the child's "polymorphously perverse" sexual predispositions were repressed. How else could the development of healthy adult sexuality be explained, with alternative theoretical perspectives?

3. How might Freud's focus on a central role for sexuality be related to the sexually repressed culture of his time and place? Does the approach seem to fit as well when applied to environments that are less prudish than Vienna at the turn of the twentieth century?

2

Psychoanalytic "Evidence": A Critique Based on Freud's Case of Little Hans

JOSEPH WOLPE AND STANLEY RACHMAN

In this classic response to Freud's classic case of Little Hans, Joseph Wolpe (1915–1997) and Stanley Rachman used learning theory to present an alternative explanation of Hans's phobia. This in turn launched a dispute with psychoanalytic psychotherapists about whether it is necessary to search for deep, hidden conflicts when attempting to help people with anxiety and related dysfunctions. This dispute continues to this day. Further explanation of the behaviorist and learning approaches to personality is found later in this book in the selections by Watson and Rayner and by B. F. Skinner.

Wolpe and Rachman are best known for using behaviorist principles (of learning) to treat anxiety. For example, they helped develop systematic desensitization, a technique for treating anxiety in which people learn relaxation techniques, and then learn to relax in situations of steadily increasing provocation. In the selection that follows, they claim that their approach is more scientific than Freud's and suggest that psychoanalysts and their patients search for evidence to support their theories (and thus are biased).

Beginning with Wohlgemuth's trenchant monograph, the factual and logical bases of psychoanalytic theory have been the subject of a considerable number of criticisms. These have generally been dismissed by psychoanalysts, at least partly on the ground that the critics are oblivious of the "wealth of detail" provided by the individual case. One way to examine the soundness of the analysts' position is to study fully-reported cases that they themselves regard as having contributed significantly to their theories. We have undertaken to do this, and have chosen as our subject matter one of Freud's most famous cases, given in such detail that the events of a few months occupy 140 pages of the *Collected Papers*.

In 1909, Freud published "The Analysis of a Phobia in a Five-year old Boy." This case is commonly referred to as "The case of Little Hans." Ernest Jones, in his biography of Freud, points out that it was "the first published account of a child analysis," and states that "the brilliant success of child analysis" since then was "indeed inaugurated by the study of this very case." The case also has special significance in the development of psychoanalytic theory because Freud believed himself to have found in it "a more direct and less roundabout proof" of some fundamental psychoanalytic theorems. In particular, he thought that it provided a direct demonstration of the essential role of sexual urges in the development of phobias. He felt his position to have been greatly strengthened by this case and two generations of analysts have referred to

Source: Wolpe, J., & Rachman, S. (1960). Psychoanalytic "evidence": A critique based on Freud's case of Little Hans. *Journal of Nervous & Mental Disease, 131,* 135–148. Reprinted by permission.

Editor's note: Citations in the text of this selection and the sources to which they point have been edited to leave only those that are the most relevant and important. Readers wishing to see the full reference list can consult the original work.

the evidence of Little Hans as a basic substantiation of psychoanalytic theories. As an example, Glover may be quoted.

> *In its time the analysis of Little Hans was a remarkable achievement and the story of the analysis constitutes one of the most valued records in psychoanalytical archives. Our concepts of phobia formation, of the positive Oedipus complex, of ambivalence, castration anxiety and repression, to mention but a few, were greatly reinforced and amplified as the result of this analysis.*

In this paper we shall re-examine this case history and assess the evidence presented. We shall show that although there are manifestations of sexual behavior on the part of Hans, there is no scientifically acceptable evidence showing any connection between this behavior and the child's phobia for horses; that the assertion of such connection is pure assumption; that the elaborate discussions that follow from it are pure speculation; and that the case affords no factual support for any of the concepts listed by Glover above. Our examination of this case exposes in considerable detail patterns of thinking and attitudes to evidence that are well-nigh universal among psychoanalysts. It suggests the need for more careful scrutiny of the bases of psychoanalytic "discoveries" than has been customary; and we hope it will prompt psychologists to make similar critical examinations of basic psychoanalytic writings.

The case material on which Freud's analysis is based was collected by Little Hans's father, who kept Freud informed of developments by regular written reports. The father also had several consultations with Freud concerning Little Hans's phobia. During the analysis, Freud himself saw the little boy only once.

The following are the most relevant facts noted of Hans's earlier life. At the age of three, he showed "a quite peculiarly lively interest in that portion of his body which he used to describe as his widdler." When he was three and a half, his mother found him with his hand to his penis. She threatened him in these words, "If you do that, I shall send for Dr. A. to cut off your widdler. And then what will you widdle with?" Hans replied, "With my bottom." Numerous further remarks concerning widdlers in animals and humans were made by Hans between the ages of three and four, including questions directed at his mother and father asking them if they also had widdlers. Freud attaches importance to the following exchange between Hans and his mother. Hans was "looking on intently while his mother undressed."

MOTHER: "What are you staring like that for?"
HANS: "I was only looking to see if you'd got a widdler, too."
MOTHER: "Of course. Didn't you know that?"
HANS: "No, I thought you were so big you'd have a widdler like a horse."

When Hans was three and a half his sister was born. The baby was delivered at home and Hans heard his mother "coughing," observed the appearance of the doctor and was called into the bedroom after the birth. Hans was initially "very jealous of the new arrival" but within six months his jealousy faded and was replaced by "brotherly affection." When Hans was four he discovered a seven-year-old girl in the neighborhood and spent many hours awaiting her return from school. The father commented that "the violence with which this 'long-range love' came over him was to be explained by his having no play-fellows of either sex." At this period also, "he was constantly putting his arms round" his visiting boy cousin, aged five, and was once heard saying, "I *am* so fond of you" when giving his cousin "one of these tender embraces." Freud speaks of this as the "first trace of homosexuality."

At the age of four and a half, Hans went with his parents to Gmunden for the summer holidays. On holiday Hans had numerous playmates including Mariedl, a fourteen-year-old girl. One evening Hans said, "I want Mariedl to sleep with me." Freud says that Hans's wish was an expression of his desire to have Mariedl as part of his family. Hans's parents occasionally took him into their bed and Freud claims that, "there can be no doubt that lying beside them had aroused erotic feelings in him; so that his wish to sleep with Mariedl had an erotic sense as well."

Another incident during the summer holidays is given considerable importance by Freud, who refers to it as Hans's attempt to seduce his mother. It must be quoted here in full.

Hans, four and a quarter. This morning Hans was given his usual daily bath by his mother and afterwards dried and powdered. As his mother was powdering round his penis and taking care not to touch it, Hans said, "Why don't you put your finger there?"

MOTHER: "Because that'd be piggish."
HANS: "What's that? Piggish? Why?"
MOTHER: "Because it's not proper."
HANS (laughing): "But it's great fun."

Another occurrence prior to the onset of his phobia was that when Hans, aged four and a half, laughed while watching his sister being bathed and was asked why he was laughing, he replied, "I'm laughing at Hanna's widdler." "Why?" "Because her widdler's so lovely." The father's comment is, "Of course his answer was a disingenuous one. In reality her widdler seemed to him funny. Moreover, this is the first time he has recognized in this way the distinction between male and female genitals instead of denying it."

In early January, 1908, the father wrote to Freud that Hans had developed "a nervous disorder." The symptoms he reported were: fear of going into the streets; depression in the evening; and a fear that a horse would bite him in the street. Hans's father suggested that "the ground was prepared by sexual overexcitation due to his mother's tenderness" and that the fear of the horse "seems somehow to be connected with his having been frightened by a large penis." The first signs appeared on January 7th, when Hans was being taken to the park by his nursemaid as usual. He started crying and said he wanted to "coax" (caress) with his mother. At home "he was asked why he had refused to go any further and had cried, but he would not say." The following day, after hesitation and crying, he went out with his mother. Returning home Hans said ("after much internal struggling"), *"I was afraid a horse would bite me"* (original italics). As on the previous day, Hans showed fear in the evening and asked to be "coaxed." He is also reported as saying, "I know I shall have to go for a walk again tomorrow," and "The horse'll come into the room." On the same day he was asked by his mother if he put his hand to his widdler. He replied in the affirmative. The following day his mother warned him to refrain from doing this.

At this point in the narrative, Freud provided an interpretation of Hans's behavior and consequently arranged with the boy's father "that he should tell the boy that all this nonsense about horses was a piece of nonsense and nothing more. The truth was, his father was to say, that he was very fond of his mother and wanted to be taken into her bed. The reason he was afraid of horses now was that he had taken so much interest in their widdlers." Freud also suggested giving Hans some sexual enlightenment and telling him that females "had no widdler at all."

"After Hans had been enlightened there followed a fairly quiet period." After an attack of influenza which kept him in bed for two weeks the phobia got worse. He then had his tonsils out and was indoors for a further week. The phobia became "very much worse."

During March, 1908, after his physical illnesses had been cured, Hans apparently had many talks with his father about the phobia. On March 1, his father again told Hans that horses do not bite. Hans replied that white horses bite and related that while at Gmunden he had heard and seen Lizzi (a playmate) being warned by her father to avoid a white horse lest it bite. The father said to Lizzi, *"Don't put your finger to the white horse"* (original italics). Hans's father's reply to this account given by his son was, "I say, it strikes me it isn't a horse you mean, but a widdler, that one mustn't put one's hand to." Hans answered, "But a widdler doesn't bite." The father: "Perhaps it does, though." Hans then "went on eagerly to try to prove to me that it was a white horse." The following day, in answer to a remark of his father's, Hans said that his phobia was "so bad because I still put my hand to my widdler every night." Freud remarks here that, "Doctor and patient, father and son, were therefore at one in ascribing the chief share in the pathogenesis of Hans's present condition to his habit of onanism." He implies that this unanimity is significant, quite disregarding the father's indoctrination of Hans the previous day.

On March 13, the father told Hans that his fear would disappear if he stopped putting his hand to his widdler. Hans replied, "But I don't put my hand to my widdler any more." Father: "But you still want to." Hans agreed, "Yes, I do." His father suggested that he should sleep in a sack to prevent him from wanting to touch his widdler. Hans accepted this view and on the following day was much less afraid of horses.

Two days later the father again told Hans that girls and women have no widdlers. "Mummy has none, Anna has none and so on." Hans asked how they managed to widdle and was told "They don't have widdlers like yours. Haven't you noticed already when Hanna was being given her bath." On March 17 Hans reported a phantasy in which he saw his mother naked. On the basis of this phantasy and the conversation related above, Freud concluded that Hans had not accepted the enlightenment given by his father. Freud says, "He regretted that it should be so, and stuck to his former view in phantasy. He may also perhaps have had his reasons for refusing to believe his father at first." Discussing this matter subsequently, Freud says that the "enlightenment" given a short time before to the effect that women really do not possess a widdler was bound to have a shattering effect upon his self-confidence and to have aroused his castration complex. For this reason he resisted the information, and for this reason it had no therapeutic effect.

For reasons of space we shall recount the subsequent events in very brief form. On a visit to the Zoo Hans expressed fear of the giraffe, elephant and all large animals. Hans's father said to him, "Do you know why you're afraid of big animals? Big animals have big widdlers and you're really afraid of big widdlers." This was denied by the boy.

The next event of prominence was a dream (or phantasy) reported by Hans. "In the night there was a big giraffe in the room and a crumpled one; and the big one called out because I took the crumpled one away from it. Then it stopped calling out; and then I sat down on the top of the crumpled one."

After talking to the boy the father reported to Freud that this dream was "a matrimonial scene transposed into giraffe life. He was seized in the night with a longing for his mother, for her caresses, for her genital organ, and came into the room for that reason. The whole thing is a continuation of his fear of horses." The father infers that the dream is related to Hans's habit of occasionally getting into his parents' bed in the face of his father's disapproval. Freud's addition to "the father's penetrating observation" is that sitting down on the crumpled giraffe means taking possession of his

mother. Confirmation of this dream interpretation is claimed by reference to an incident which occurred the next day. The father wrote that on leaving the house with Hans he said to his wife, "Good-bye, big giraffe." "Why giraffe?" asked Hans. "Mummy's the big giraffe," replied the father. "Oh, yes," said Hans, "and Hanna's the crumpled giraffe, isn't she?" The father's account continues, "In the train I explained the giraffe phantasy to him, upon which he said 'Yes, that's right.' And when I said to him that I was the big giraffe and that its long neck reminded him of a widdler, he said 'Mummy has a neck like a giraffe too. I saw when she was washing her white neck'."

On March 30, the boy had a short consultation with Freud who reports that despite all the enlightenment given to Hans, the fear of horses continued undiminished. Hans explained that he was especially bothered "by what horses wear in front of their eyes and the black round their mouths." This latter detail Freud interpreted as meaning a moustache. "I asked him whether he meant a moustache," and then, "disclosed to him that he was afraid of his father precisely because he was so fond of his mother." Freud pointed out that this was a groundless fear. On April 2, the father was able to report "the first real improvement." The next day Hans, in answer to his father's inquiry, explained that he came into his father's bed when he was frightened. In the next few days further details of Hans's fear were elaborated. He told his father that he was most scared of horses with "a thing on their mouths," that he was scared lest the horses fall, and that he was most scared of horse-drawn buses.

HANS: "I'm most afraid too when a bus comes along."
FATHER: "Why? Because it's so big?"
HANS: "No. Because once a horse in a bus fell."
FATHER: "When?"

Hans then recounted such an incident. This was later confirmed by his mother.

FATHER: "What did you think when the horse fell down?"
HANS: "Now it will always be like this. All horses in buses'll fall down."
FATHER: "In all buses?"

HANS: "Yes. And in furniture vans too. Not often in furniture vans."

FATHER: "You had your nonsense already at that time?"

HANS: "*No* (italics added). I only got it then. When the horse in the bus fell down, it gave me such a fright really: That was when I got the nonsense."

The father adds that, "all of this was confirmed by my wife, as well as the fact that *the anxiety broke out immediately afterwards*" (italics added).

Hans's father continued probing for a meaning of the black thing around the horses' mouths. Hans said it looked like a muzzle but his father had never seen such a horse "although Hans asseverates that such horses do exist." He continues, "I suspect that some part of the horse's bridle really reminded him of a moustache and that after I alluded to this the fear disappeared." A day later Hans observing his father stripped to the waist said, "Daddy you are lovely! You're so white."

FATHER: "Yes. Like a white horse."

HANS: "The only black thing's your moustache. Or perhaps it's a black muzzle."

Further details about the horse that fell were also elicited from Hans. He said there were actually two horses pulling the bus and that they were both black and "very big and fat." Hans's father again asked about the boy's thoughts when the horse fell.

FATHER: "When the horse fell down, did you think of your daddy?

HANS: "Perhaps. Yes. It's possible."

For several days after these talks about horses Hans's interests, as indicated by the father's reports, "centered upon lumf (feces) and widdle, but we cannot tell why." Freud comments that at this point "the analysis began to be obscure and uncertain."

On April 11 Hans related this phantasy. "I was in the bath and then the plumber came and unscrewed it. Then he took a big borer and stuck it into my stomach." Hans's father translated this phantasy as follows: "I was in bed with Mamma. Then Pappa came and drove me away. With his big penis he pushed me out of my place by Mamma."

The remainder of the case history material, until Hans's recovery from the phobia early in May, is concerned with the lumf theme and Hans's feelings towards his parents and sister. It can be stated immediately that as corroboration for Freud's theories all of this remaining material is unsatisfactory. For the most part it consists of the father expounding theories to a boy who occasionally agrees and occasionally disagrees. The following two examples illustrate the nature of most of this latter information.

Hans and his father were discussing the boy's slight fear of falling when in the big bath.

FATHER: "But Mamma bathes you in it. Are you afraid of Mamma dropping you in the water?"

HANS: "I am afraid of her letting go and my head going in."

FATHER: "But you know Mummy's fond of you and won't let you go."

HANS: "I only just thought it."

FATHER: "Why?"

HANS: "I don't know at all."

FATHER: "Perhaps it was because you'd been naughty and thought she didn't love you any more?"

HANS: "Yes."

FATHER: "When you were watching Mummy giving Hanna her bath perhaps you wished she would let go of her so that Hanna should fall in?"

HANS: "Yes."

On the following day the father asks, "Are you fond of Hanna?"

HANS: "Oh, yes, very fond."

FATHER: "Would you rather that Hanna weren't alive or that she were?"

HANS: "I'd rather she weren't alive."

In response to close, direct questioning Hans voiced several complaints about his sister. Then his father proceeded again:

FATHER: "If you'd rather she weren't alive, you can't be fond of her, at all."

HANS (assenting): "Hm, well."

FATHER: "That's why you thought when Mummy was giving her her bath if only she'd let go, Hanna would fall in the water . . ."

HANS (taking me up): ". . . and die."

FATHER: "and then you'd be alone with Mummy. A good boy doesn't wish that sort of thing, though."

On April 24, the following conversation was recorded.

FATHER: "It seems to me that, all the same, you do wish Mummy would have a baby."

HANS: "But I don't want it to happen."

FATHER: "But you wish for it?"

HANS: "Oh, yes, *wish*."

FATHER: "Do you know why you wish for it? It's because you'd like to be Daddy."

HANS: "Yes. How does it work?"

FATHER: "You'd like to be Daddy and married to Mummy; you'd like to be as big as me and have a moustache; and you'd like Mummy to have a baby."

HANS: "And Daddy, when I'm married I'll have only one if I want to, when I'm married to Mummy, and if I don't want a baby, God won't want it either when I'm married."

FATHER: "Would you like to be married to Mummy?"

HANS: "Oh yes."

THE VALUE OF THE EVIDENCE

Before proceeding to Freud's interpretation of the case, let us examine the value of the evidence presented. First, there is the matter of selection of the material. The greatest attention is naturally paid to material related to psychoanalytic theory and there is a tendency to ignore other facts. The father and mother, we are told by Freud, "were both among my closest adherents." Hans himself was constantly encouraged, directly and indirectly, to relate material of relevance to the psychoanalytic doctrine.

Second, we must assess the value to be placed on the testimony of the father and of Hans. The father's account of Hans's behavior is in several instances suspect. For example, he twice presents his own interpretations of Hans's remarks as observed facts. This is the father's report of a conversation with Hans about the birth of his sister Hanna.

FATHER: "What did Hanna look like?"

HANS (hypocritically): "All white and lovely. So pretty."

On another occasion, despite several clear statements by Hans of his affection for his sister (and also the voicing of complaints about her screaming), the father said to Hans, "If you'd rather she weren't alive, you can't be fond of her at all." Hans (assenting): "Hm, well." (See above.)

The comment in parenthesis in each of these two extracts is presented as observed fact. A third example has also been quoted above. When Hans observes that Hanna's widdler is "so lovely" the father states that this is a "disingenuous" reply and that "in reality her widdler seemed to him funny." Distortions of this kind are common in the father's reports.

Hans's testimony is for many reasons unreliable. Apart from the numerous lies which he told in the last few weeks of his phobia, Hans gave many inconsistent and occasionally conflicting reports. Most important of all, much of what purports to be Hans's views and feelings is simply the father speaking. Freud himself admits this but attempts to gloss over it. He says, "It is true that during the analysis Hans had to be told many things which he could not say himself, that he had to be presented with thoughts which he had so far shown no signs of possessing and that his attention had to be turned in the direction from which his father was expecting something to come. This detracts from the evidential value of the analysis but the procedure is the same in every case. For a psychoanalysis is not an impartial scientific investigation but a therapeutic measure." To sum this matter up, Hans's testimony is subject not only to "mere suggestion" but contains much material that is not his testimony at all!

From the above discussion it is clear that the "facts of the case" need to be treated with considerable caution and in our own interpretation of Hans's behavior we will attempt to make use only of the testimony of direct observation.

FREUD'S INTERPRETATION

Freud's interpretation of Hans's phobia is that the boy's oedipal conflicts formed the basis of the illness which "burst out" when he underwent "a time of privation and the intensified sexual excitement." Freud says, "These were tendencies in Hans which had already been suppressed and which, so far as we can tell, had never been able to find uninhibited expression: hostile and jealous feelings against his father, and sadistic impulses (premonitions, as it were, of copulation) towards his mother. These early suppressions may perhaps have gone to form the predisposition for his subsequent illness. These aggressive propensities of Hans's found no outlet, and as soon as there came a time of privation and of intensified sexual excitement, they tried to break their way out with reinforced strength. It was then that the battle which we call his 'phobia' burst out."

This is the familiar oedipal theory, according to which Hans wished to replace his father "whom he could not help hating as a rival" and then complete the act by "taking possession of his mother." Freud refers for confirmation to the following: "Another symptomatic act, happening as though by accident, involved a confession that he had wished his father dead; for, just at the moment that his father was talking of his death-wish Hans let a horse that he was playing with fall down—knocked it over, in fact." Freud claims that, "Hans was really a little Oedipus who wanted to have his father 'out of the way' to get rid of him, so that he might be alone with his handsome mother and sleep with her." The predisposition to illness provided by the oedipal conflicts is supposed to have formed the basis for "the transformation of his libidinal longing into anxiety." During the summer prior to the onset of the phobia, Hans had experienced "moods of mingled longing and apprehension" and had also been taken into his mother's bed on occasions. Freud says, "We may assume that since then Hans had been in a state of intensified sexual excitement, the object of which was his mother. The intensity of this excitement was shown by his two attempts at seducing his mother (the second of which occurred just before the outbreak of his anxiety); and he found an incidental channel of discharge for it by masturbating.... Whether the sudden exchange of this excitement into anxiety took place spontaneously, or as a result of his mother's rejection of his advances, or owing to the accidental revival of earlier impressions by the 'exciting cause' of his illness... this

we cannot decide. The fact remains that his sexual excitement suddenly changed into anxiety."

Hans, we are told, "transposed from his father on to the horses." At his sole interview with Hans, Freud told him "that he was afraid of his father because he himself nourished jealous and hostile wishes against him." Freud says of this, "In telling him this, I had partly interpreted his fear of horses for him: the horse must be his father—whom he had good internal reasons for fearing." Freud claims that Hans's fear of the black things on the horses' mouths and the things in front of their eyes was based on moustaches and eye-glasses and had been "directly transposed from his father on to the horses." The horses "had been shown to represent his father."

Freud interprets the agoraphobic element of Hans's phobia thus. "The content of his phobia was such as to impose a very great measure of restriction upon his freedom of movement, and that was its purpose... After all, Hans's phobia of horses was an obstacle to his going into the street, and could serve as a means of allowing him to stay at home with his beloved mother. In this way, therefore, his affection for his mother triumphantly achieved its aim."

Freud interprets the disappearance of the phobia as being due to the resolution by Hans of his oedipal conflicts by "promoting him (the father) to a marriage with Hans's grandmother... instead of killing him." This final interpretation is based on the following conversation between Hans and his father.

On April 30, Hans was playing with his imaginary children.

FATHER: "Hullo, are your children still alive? You know quite well a boy can't have any children."

HANS: "I know. I was their Mummy before, *now I'm their Daddy*" (original italics).

FATHER: "And who's the children's Mummy?"

HANS: "Why, Mummy, and you're their *Grandaddy*" (original italics).

FATHER: "So then you'd like to be as big as me, and be married to Mummy, and then you'd like her to have children."

HANS: "Yes, that's what I'd like, and then my Lainz Grandmamma" (paternal side) "will be their Grannie."

CRITIQUE OF FREUD'S CONCLUSIONS

It is our contention that Freud's view of this case is not supported by the data, either in its particulars or as a whole. The major points that he regards as demonstrated are these: (1) Hans had a sexual desire for his mother, (2) he hated and feared his father and wished to kill him, (3) his sexual excitement and desire for his mother were transformed into anxiety, (4) his fear of horses was symbolic of his fear of his father, (5) the purpose of the illness was to keep near his mother and finally (6) his phobia disappeared because he resolved his Oedipus complex.

Let us examine each of these points:

1. That Hans derived satisfaction from his mother and enjoyed her presence we will not even attempt to dispute. But nowhere is there any evidence of his wish to copulate with her. Yet Freud says that, "if matters had lain entirely in my hands . . . I should have confirmed his instinctive premonitions, by telling him of the existence of the vagina and of copulation." The "instinctive premonitions" are referred to as though a matter of fact, though no evidence of their existence is given.

The only seduction incident described (see above) indicates that on *that particular occasion* Hans desired contact of a sexual nature with his mother, albeit a sexual contact of a simple, primitive type. This is not adequate evidence on which to base the claim that Hans had an Oedipus complex which implies a sexual desire for the mother, a wish to possess her and to replace the father. The most that can be claimed for this "attempted seduction" is that it provides a small degree of support for the assumption that Hans had a desire for sexual stimulation by some other person (it will be recalled that he often masturbated). Even if it is assumed that stimulation provided by his mother was especially desired, the two other features of an Oedipus complex (a wish to possess the mother and replace the father) are not demonstrated by the facts of the case.

2. Never having expressed either fear or hatred of his father, Hans was told by Freud that he possessed these emotions. On subsequent occasions Hans denied the existence of these feelings when questioned by his father. Eventually, he said "Yes" to a statement

of this kind by his father. This simple affirmative obtained after considerable pressure on the part of the father and Freud is accepted as the true state of affairs and all Hans's denials are ignored. The "symptomatic act" of knocking over the toy horse is taken as further evidence of Hans's aggression towards his father. There are three assumptions underlying this "interpreted fact"—first, that the horse represents Hans's father; second, that the knocking over of the horse is not accidental; and third, that this act indicates a wish for the removal of whatever the horse symbolized.

Hans consistently denied the relationship between the horse and his father. He was, he said, afraid of horses. The mysterious black around the horses' mouths and the things on their eyes were later discovered by the father to be the horses' muzzles and blinkers. This discovery undermines the suggestion (made by Freud) that they were transposed moustaches and eye-glasses. There is no other evidence that the horses represented Hans's father. The assumption that the knocking over of the toy horse was meaningful in that it was prompted by an unconscious motive is, like most similar examples, a moot point. Freud himself (3) does not state that *all* errors are provoked by unconscious motives and in this sense "deliberate." This is understandable for it is easy to compile numerous instances of errors which can be accounted for in other, simpler terms without recourse to unconscious motivation or indeed motivation of any kind. Despite an examination of the literature we are unable to find a categorical statement regarding the frequency of "deliberate errors." Furthermore, we do not know how to recognize them when they do occur. In the absence of positive criteria the decision that Hans's knocking over of the toy horse was a "deliberate error" is arbitrary.

As there is nothing to sustain the first two assumptions made by Freud in interpreting this "symptomatic act," the third assumption (that this act indicated a wish for his father's death) is untenable; and it must be reiterated that there is no independent evidence that the boy feared or hated his father.

3. Freud's third claim is that Hans's sexual excitement and desire for his mother were transformed into anxiety. This claim is based on the assertion that "theoretical considerations require that what is today the object of a phobia must at one time in the past have been the source of a high degree of pleasure." Certainly such a transformation is not displayed by the facts presented. As stated above, there is no evidence that Hans sexually desired his mother. There is also no evidence of any change in his attitude to her before the onset of the phobia. Even though there is some evidence that horses were to some extent previously a source of pleasure, in general the view that phobic objects must have been the source of former pleasures is amply contradicted by experimental evidence. Apart from the numerous experiments on phobias in animals which disprove this contention, the demonstrations of Watson and Rayner and Jones have clearly shown how phobias may be induced in children by a simple conditioning process. The rat and rabbit used as the conditioned stimuli in these demonstrations can hardly be regarded as sources of "a high degree of pleasure," and the same applies to the generalized stimulus of cotton wool.

4. The assertion that Hans's horse phobia symbolized a fear of his father has already been criticized. The assumed relationship between the father and the horse is unsupported and appears to have arisen as a result of the father's strange failure to believe that by the "black around their mouths" Hans meant the horses' muzzles.

5. The fifth claim is that the purpose of Hans's phobia was to keep him near his mother. Aside from the questionable view that neurotic disturbances occur for a purpose, this interpretation fails to account for the fact that Hans experienced anxiety even when he was out walking *with his mother.*

6. Finally, we are told that the phobia disappeared as a result of Hans's resolution of his oedipal conflicts. As we have attempted to show, there is no adequate evidence that Hans had an Oedipus complex. In addition, the claim that this assumed complex was resolved is based on a single conversation between Hans and his father (see above). This conversation is a blatant example of what Freud himself refers to as Hans having to "be told many things he could not say himself, that he had to be presented with thoughts which he had so far *shown* no signs of possessing, and that his attention had to be turned in the direction that his father was expecting something to come."

There is also no satisfactory evidence that the "insights" that were incessantly brought to the boy's attention had any therapeutic value. Reference to the facts of the case shows only occasional coincidences between interpretations and changes in the child's phobic reactions. For example, "a quiet period" early followed the father's statement that the fear of horses was a "piece of nonsense" and that Hans really wanted to be taken into his mother's bed. But soon afterwards, when Hans became ill, the phobia was worse than ever. Later, having had many talks without effect, the father notes that on March 13 Hans, after agreeing that he still *wanted* to play with his widdler, was "much less afraid of horses." On March 15, however, he was frightened of horses, after the information that females have no widdlers (though he had previously been told the opposite by his mother). Freud asserts that Hans resisted this piece of enlightenment because it aroused castration fears, and therefore no therapeutic success was to be observed. The "first real improvement" of April 2 is attributed to the "moustache enlightenment" of March 30 (later proved erroneous), the boy having been told that he was "afraid of his father precisely because he was so fond of his mother." On April 7, though Hans was constantly improving, Freud commented that the situation was "decidedly obscure" and that "the analysis was making little progress."

Such sparse and tenuous data do not begin to justify the attribution of Hans's recovery to the bringing to consciousness of various unacceptable unconscious repressed wishes. In fact, Freud bases his conclusions entirely on deductions from his theory. Hans's latter improvement appears to have been smooth and gradual and unaffected by the interpretations. In general, Freud infers relationships in a scientifically inadmissible manner: if the enlightenments or interpretations given to Hans are followed by behavioral improvements, then they are automatically accepted as valid. If they are not followed by improvement we are told the patient has not accepted them, and not that they are invalid. Discussing the failure of these early enlightenments, Freud says that in any event therapeutic success is not the primary aim of the analysis, thus sidetracking the issue; and he is not deflected from claiming an improvement to be due to an interpretation even when the latter is erroneous, *e.g.,* the moustache interpretation.

No systematic follow-up of the case is provided. However, fourteen years after the completion of the analysis, Freud interviewed Hans, who "declared that he was perfectly well and suffered from no troubles or inhibitions" (!). He also said that he had successfully undergone the ordeal of his parents' divorce. Hans reported that he could not remember anything about his childhood phobia. Freud remarks that this is "particularly remarkable." The analysis itself "had been overtaken by amnesia!"

AN ALTERNATIVE VIEW OF HANS'S PHOBIA

In case it should be argued that, unsatisfactory as it is, Freud's explanation is the only available one, we shall show how Hans's phobia can be understood in terms of learning theory, in the theoretical framework provided by Wolpe. This approach is largely Hullian in character and the clinical applications are based on experimental findings.

In brief, phobias are regarded as conditioned anxiety (fear) reactions. Any "neutral" stimulus, simple or complex, that happens to make an impact on an individual at about the time that a fear reaction is evoked acquires the ability to evoke fear subsequently. If the fear at the original conditioning situation is of high intensity or if the conditioning is many times repeated, the conditioned fear will show the persistence that is characteristic of *neurotic* fear; and there will be generalization of fear reactions to stimuli resembling the conditioned stimulus.

Hans, we are told, was a sensitive child who "was never unmoved if someone wept in his presence" and long before the phobia developed became "uneasy on seeing the horses in the merry-go-round being beaten." It is our contention that the incident to which Freud refers as merely the exciting cause of Hans's phobia was in fact the cause of the entire disorder. Hans actually says, "No. I only got it [the phobia] then. When the horse in the bus fell down, it gave me such a fright, really! That was when I got the nonsense." The father says, "All of this was confirmed by my wife, as well as the fact that the anxiety broke out immediately afterwards." The evidence obtained in studies on experimental neuroses in animals and the studies by Watson and Rayner, Jones and Woodward on phobias in children indicate that it

is quite possible for one experience to induce a phobia.

In addition, the father was able to report two other unpleasant incidents which Hans had experienced with horses prior to the onset of the phobia. It is likely that these experiences had sensitized Hans to horses or, in other words, he had already been partially conditioned to fear horses. These incidents both occurred at Gmunden. The first was the warning given by the father of Hans's friend to avoid the horse lest it bite, and the second when another of Hans's friends injured himself (and bled) while they were playing horses.

Just as the little boy Albert (in Watson's classic demonstration) reacted with anxiety not only to the original conditioned stimulus, the white rat, but to other similar stimuli such as furry objects, cotton wool and so on, Hans reacted anxiously to horses, horse-drawn buses, vans and features of horses, such as their blinkers and muzzles. In fact he showed fear of a wide range of generalized stimuli. The accident which provoked the phobia involved two horses drawing a bus and Hans stated that he was more afraid of large carts, vans or buses than small carts. As one would expect, the less close a phobic stimulus was to that of the original incident the less disturbing Hans found it. Furthermore, the last aspect of the phobia to disappear was Hans's fear of large vans or buses. There is ample experimental evidence that when responses to generalized stimuli undergo extinction, responses to other stimuli in the continuum are the less diminished the more closely they resemble the original conditional stimulus.

Hans's recovery from the phobia may be explained on conditioning principles in a number of possible ways, but the actual mechanism that operated cannot be identified, since the child's father was not concerned with the kind of information that would be of interest to us. It is well known that especially in children many phobias decline and disappear over a few weeks or months. The reason for this appears to be that in the ordinary course of life generalized phobic stimuli may evoke anxiety responses weak enough to be inhibited by other emotional responses simultaneously aroused in the individual. Perhaps this process was the true source of Little Hans's recovery. The interpretations may have been irrelevant, or may even have retarded recovery by adding new threats and new fears to those already present. But since Hans does not seem to have been greatly upset by the interpretations, it is perhaps more likely that the therapy was actively helpful, for phobic stimuli were again and again presented to the child in a variety of emotional contexts that may have inhibited the anxiety and in consequence diminished its habit strength. The *gradualness* of Hans's recovery is consonant with an explanation of this kind.

CONCLUSIONS

The chief conclusion to be derived from our survey of the case of Little Hans is that it does not provide anything resembling direct proof of psychoanalytic theorems. We have combed Freud's account for evidence that would be acceptable in the court of science, and have found none. In attempting to give a balanced summary of the case we have excluded a vast number of interpretations but have tried not to omit any material facts. Such facts, and they alone, could have supported Freud's theories. For example, if it had been observed after Gmunden that Hans had become fearful of his father, and that upon the development of the horse phobia the fear of the father had disappeared, this could reasonably have been regarded as presumptive of a displacement of fear from father to horse. This is quite different from observing a horse phobia and then asserting that it must be a displaced father-fear without ever having obtained any direct evidence of the latter; for then that which needs to be demonstrated is presupposed. To say that the father-fear was repressed is equally no substitute for evidence of it.

Freud fully believed that he had obtained in Little Hans a direct confirmation of his theories, for he speaks towards the end of "the infantile complexes that were revealed behind Hans's phobia." It seems clear that although he wanted to be scientific Freud was surprisingly naive regarding the requirements of scientific evidence. Infantile complexes were not *revealed* (demonstrated) behind Hans's phobia: they were merely hypothesized.

It is remarkable that countless psychoanalysts have paid homage to the case of Little Hans, without being offended by its glaring inadequacies. We shall not here attempt to explain this, except to point to one probable major influence—a tacit belief among analysts that Freud possessed a kind of unerring insight that absolved him from the obligation to obey rules

applicable to ordinary men. For example, Glover, speaking of other analysts who arrogate to themselves the right Freud claimed to subject his material to "a touch of revision," says, "No doubt when someone of Freud's calibre appears in our midst he will be freely accorded...this privilege." To accord such a privilege to anyone is to violate the spirit of science.

It may of course be argued that some of the conclusions of Little Hans are no longer held and that there is now other evidence for other of the conclusions; but there is no evidence that in general psychoanalytic conclusions are based on any better logic than that used by Freud in respect of Little Hans. Certainly no analyst has ever pointed to the failings of this account or disowned its reasoning, and it has continued to be regarded as one of the foundation stones on which psychoanalytic theory was built.

SUMMARY

The main facts of the case of Little Hans are presented and it is shown that Freud's claim of "a more direct and less roundabout proof" of certain of his theories is not justified by the evidence presented. No confirmation by direct observation is obtained for any psychoanalytic theorem, though psychoanalysts have believed the contrary for 50 years. The demonstrations claimed are really interpretations that are treated as facts. This is a common practice and should be checked, for it has been a great encumbrance to the development of a science of psychiatry.

REFERENCES

Freud, S. (1950). *Collected papers,* Vol. 3. London: Hogarth Press.

Glover, E. (1956). *On the early development of mind.* New York: International Universities Press.

Glover, E. (1952). Research methods in psychoanalysis. *International Journal of Psychoanalysis 33,* 403–409.

Jones, E. (1955). *Sigmund Freud: Life and work,* Vol. 2. London: Hogarth Press.

Watson, J. B., and Rayner, P. (1920). Conditioned emotional reactions. *Journal of Experimental Psychology 3,* 1–14. [Editor's note: This article is included as Reading 21 of this reader.]

Wohlgemuth, A. (1923). *A critical examination of psychoanalysis.* London: Allen Unwin.

Questions to Think About

1. Freud has proposed a deep, complex theory of human nature. What do we lose by discarding it and turning instead to simple notions of conditioning? What do we gain?

2. Given Wolpe and Rachman's views about the biases involved in Freud's collection of evidence to support a psychoanalytic interpretation of Little Hans's phobia, what kind of evidence might they accept to support a psychoanalytic interpretation?

3. Freud believed that underlying most human conflicts and distresses are issues of unresolved, repressed sexuality and aggression. Behaviorists view such notions as unscientific. How can Freud's theories best be tested, since by their very nature the repressed sexual conflicts are difficult to access?

3

The Interpretation of Dreams

SIGMUND FREUD

Sigmund Freud made sure to publish his exciting new book, *The Interpretation of Dreams,* in the year 1900, hoping that it would have a great influence on his new science of the mind in the new century. Although dream interpretation was well established by biblical times, several thousand years ago, Freud viewed dream interpretation based on his new theories as a scientific tool, a royal road to the unconscious. He began interpreting his own dreams as well as those of other people to figure out what was going on in the hidden recesses of a person's psyche. As a biologist, Freud saw himself as well acquainted with the biological structures and laws that underlie his psychological views.

According to Freud, a pointed object like a clarinet could represent a phallus, and a fur bag could represent a vagina. In dreams, hidden thoughts that we cannot normally access can slip out, represented by symbols.

I shall, therefore, select one of my own dreams and use it to elucidate my method of interpretation. Every such dream necessitates a preliminary statement. I must now beg the reader to make my interests his own for a considerable time and to become absorbed with me in the most trifling details of my life, for an interest in the hidden significance of dreams imperatively demands such transference.

Preliminary statement: In the summer of 1895 I had psychoanalytically treated a young lady who stood in close friendship to me and those near to me. It is to be understood that such a complication of relations may be the source of manifold feelings for the physician, especially for the psychotherapist. The personal interest of the physician is greater, his authority is less. A failure threatens to undermine the friendship with the relatives of the patient. The cure ended with partial success, the patient got rid of her hysterical fear, but not of all her somatic symptoms. I was at that time not yet sure of the criteria marking the final settlement of a hysterical case, and expected her to accept a solution which did not seem acceptable to her. In this disagreement, we cut short the treatment on account of the summer season. One day a younger colleague, one of my best friends, who had visited the patient—Irma—and her family in their country resort, came to see me. I asked him how he found her, and received the answer: "She is better, but not altogether well." I realise that those words of my friend Otto, or the tone of voice in which they were spoken, made me angry. I thought I heard a reproach in the words, perhaps to the effect that I had promised the patient too much, and rightly or wrongly I traced Otto's supposed siding against me to the influence of the relatives of the patient, who, I assume, had never approved of my treatment. Moreover, my disagreeable impression did not become clear to me, nor did I give it expression. The very same evening, I wrote down the history of

Source: Freud, S. (1915). *The interpretation of dreams.* (Translation by A. A. Brill of 3rd edition.) London: George Allen & Unwin, Ltd. (Selection is from Dream of July 23–24, 1895, pp. 88–102.)

Irma's case, in order to hand it, as though for my justification, to Dr. M., a mutual friend, who was at that time a leading figure in our circle. During the night following this evening (perhaps rather in the morning) I had the following dream, which was registered immediately after waking:—

DREAM OF JULY 23–24, 1895

A great hall—many guests whom we are receiving—among them Irma, whom I immediately take aside, as though to answer her letter, to reproach her for not yet accepting the "solution." I say to her: "If you still have pains, it is really only your own fault." She answers: "If you only knew what pains I now have in the neck, stomach, and abdomen; I am drawn together." I am frightened and look at her. She looks pale and bloated; I think that after all I must be overlooking some organic affection. I take her to the window and look into her throat. She shows some resistance to this, like a woman who has a false set of teeth. I think anyway she does not need them. The mouth then really opens without difficulty and I find a large white spot to the right, and at another place I see extended grayish-white scabs attached to curious curling formations, which have obviously been formed in the turbinated bone—I quickly call Dr. M., who repeats the examination and confirms it. . . . Dr. M.'s looks are altogether unusual; he is very pale, limps, and has no beard on his chin. . . . My friend Otto is now also standing next to her, and my friend Leopold percusses her small body and says: "She has some dulness on the left below," and also calls attention to an infiltrated portion of the skin on the left shoulder (something which I feel as he does, in spite of the dress). . . . M. says: "No doubt it is an infection, but it does not matter; dysentery will develop too, and the poison will be excreted. . . .We also have immediate knowledge of the origin of the infection. My friend Otto has recently given her an injection with a propyl preparation when she felt ill, propyls. . . . Propionic acid. . . . Trimethylamine (the formula of which I see printed before me in heavy type). . . . Such injections are not made so rashly. . . . Probably also the syringe was not clean.

This dream has an advantage over many others. It is at once clear with what events of the preceding day it is connected, and what subject it treats. The

preliminary statement gives information on these points. The news about Irma's health which I have received from Otto, the history of the illness upon which I have written until late at night, has occupied my psychic activity even during sleep. In spite of all this, no one, who has read the preliminary report and has knowledge of the content of the dream, has been able to guess what the dream signifies. Nor do I myself know. I wonder about the morbid symptoms, of which Irma complains in the dream, for they are not the same ones for which I have treated her. I smile about the consultation with Dr. M. I smile about the nonsensical idea of an injection with propionic acid, and at the consolation attempted by Dr. M. Towards the end the dream seems more obscure and more terse than at the beginning. In order to learn the significance of all this, I am compelled to undertake a thorough analysis.

ANALYSIS

The hall—many guests, whom we are receiving.

We were living this summer at the Bellevue, in an isolated house on one of the hills which lie close to the Kahlenberg. This house was once intended as a place of amusement, and on this account has unusually high, hall-like rooms. The dream also occurred at the Bellevue, a few days before the birthday of my wife. During the day, my wife had expressed the expectation that several friends, among them Irma, would come to us as guests for her birthday. My dream, then, anticipates this situation: It is the birthday of my wife, and many people, among them Irma, are received by us as guests in the great hall of the Bellevue.

I reproach Irma for not having accepted the solution. I say: "If you still have pains, it is your own fault."

I might have said this also, or did say it, while awake. At that time I had the opinion (recognised later to be incorrect) that my task was limited to informing patients of the hidden meaning of their symptoms. Whether they then accepted or did not accept the solution upon which success depended—for that I was not responsible. I am thankful to this error, which fortunately has now been overcome, for making life easier for me at a time when, with all my unavoidable ignorance, I was to produce successful cures. But I see in the speech which I make to Irma in the dream, that above all things I do not want to be to blame for the pains which she still feels. It is Irma's own fault, it cannot be mine. Should the purpose of the dream be looked for in this quarter?

Irma's complaints; pains in the neck, abdomen, and stomach; she is drawn together.

Pains in the stomach belonged to the symptom-complex of my patient, but they were not very prominent; she complained rather of sensations of nausea and disgust. Pains in the neck and abdomen and constriction of the throat hardly played a part in her case. I wonder why I decided upon this choice of symptoms, nor can I for the moment find the reason.

She looks pale and bloated.

My patient was always ruddy. I suspect that another person is here being substituted for her.

I am frightened at the thought that I must have overlooked some organic affection.

This, as the reader will readily believe, is a constant fear with the specialist, who sees neurotics almost exclusively, and who is accustomed to ascribe so many manifestations, which other physicians treat as organic, to hysteria. On the other hand, I am haunted by a faint doubt—I know not whence it comes—as to whether my fear is altogether honest. If Irma's pains are indeed of organic origin, I am not bound to cure them. My treatment, of course, removes only hysterical pains. It seems to me, in fact, that I wish to find an error in the diagnosis; in that case the reproach of being unsuccessful would be removed.

I take her to the window in order to look into her throat. She resists a little, like a woman who has false teeth. I think she does not need them anyway.

I had never had occasion to inspect Irma's oral cavity. The incident in the dream reminds me of an examination made some time before, of a governess who at first gave an impression of youthful beauty, but who upon opening her mouth took certain measures for concealing her teeth. Other memories of medical examinations and of little secrets which are discovered by them, unpleasantly for both examiner and examined, connect themselves with the case. "She does not need them anyway," is at first perhaps a compliment

for Irma; but I suspect a different meaning. In careful analysis one feels whether or not the "background thoughts" which are to be expected have been exhausted. The way in which Irma stands at the window suddenly reminds me of another experience. Irma possesses an intimate woman friend, of whom I think very highly. One evening on paying her a visit I found her in the position at the window reproduced in the dream, and her physician, the same Dr. M., declared that she had a diphtheritic membrane. The person of Dr. M. and the membrane return in the course of the dream. Now it occurs to me that during the last few months, I have been given every reason to suppose that this lady is also hysterical. Yes, Irma herself has betrayed this to me. But what do I know about her condition? Only the one thing, that like Irma she suffers from hysterical choking in dreams. Thus in the dream I have replaced my patient by her friend. Now I remember that I have often trifled with the expectation that this lady might likewise engage me to relieve her of her symptoms. But even at the time I thought it improbable, for she is of a very shy nature. *She resists,* as the dream shows. Another explanation might be that *she does not need it;* in fact, until now she has shown herself strong enough to master her condition without outside help. Now only a few features remain, which I can assign neither to Irma nor to her friend: *Pale, bloated, false teeth.* The false teeth lead me to the governess; I now feel inclined to be satisfied with bad teeth. Then another person, to whom these features may allude, occurs to me. She is not my patient, and I do not wish her to be my patient, for I have noticed that she is not at her ease with me, and I do not consider her a docile patient. She is generally pale, and once, when she had a particularly good spell, she was bloated. I have thus compared my patient Irma with two others, who would likewise resist treatment. What can it mean that I have exchanged her for her friend in the dream? Perhaps that I wish to exchange her; either the other one arouses in me stronger sympathies or I have a higher opinion of her intelligence. For I consider Irma foolish because she does not accept my solution. The other one would be more sensible, and would thus be more likely to yield. *The mouth then really opens without difficulty;* she would tell more than Irma.

What I see in the throat; a white spot and scabby nostrils.

The white spot recalls diphtheria, and thus Irma's friend, but besides this it recalls the grave illness of my eldest daughter two years before and all the anxiety of that unfortunate time. The scab on the nostrils reminds me of a concern about my own health. At that time I often used cocaine in order to suppress annoying swellings in the nose, and had heard a few days before that a lady patient who did likewise had contracted an extensive necrosis of the nasal mucous membrane. The recommendation of cocaine, which I had made in 1885, had also brought grave reproaches upon me. A dear friend, already dead in 1895, had hastened his end through the misuse of this remedy.

I quickly call Dr. M., who repeats the examination.

This would simply correspond to the position which M. occupied among us. But the word "quickly" is striking enough to demand a special explanation. It reminds me of a sad medical experience. By the continued prescription of a remedy (sulfonal) which was still at that time considered harmless, I had once caused the severe intoxication of a woman patient, and I had turned in great haste to an older, more experienced colleague for assistance. The fact that I really had this case in mind is confirmed by an accessory circumstance. The patient, who succumbed to the intoxification, bore the same name as my eldest daughter. I had never thought of this until now; now it seems to me almost like a retribution of fate—as though I ought to continue the replacement of the persons here in another sense; this Matilda for that Matilda; an eye for an eye, a tooth for a tooth. It is as though I were seeking every opportunity to reproach myself with lack of medical conscientiousness.

Dr. M. is pale, without a beard on his chin, and he limps.

Of this so much is correct, that his unhealthy appearance often awakens the concern of his friends. The other two characteristics must belong to another person. A brother living abroad occurs to me, who wears his chin clean-shaven, and to whom, if I remember aright, M. of the dream on the whole bears some resemblance. About him the news arrived some days before that he was lame on account of an arthritic disease in the hip. There must be a reason why I fuse the two persons into one in the dream. I remember that in fact I was on bad terms with both of them for similar reasons. Both of them had

rejected a certain proposal which I had recently made to them.

My friend Otto is now standing next to the sick woman, and my friend Leopold examines her and calls attention to a dulness on the left below.

My friend Leopold is also a physician, a relative of Otto. Since the two practise the same specialty, fate has made them competitors, who are continually being compared with each other. Both of them assisted me for years, while I was still directing a public dispensary for nervous children. Scenes like the one reproduced in the dream have often taken place there. While I was debating with Otto about the diagnosis of a case, Leopold had examined the child anew and had made an unexpected contribution towards the decision. For there was a difference of character between the two similar to that between Inspector Brassig and his friend Charles. The one was distinguished for his brightness, the other was slow, thoughtful, but thorough. If I contrast Otto and the careful Leopold in the dream, I do it, apparently, in order to extol Leopold. It is a comparison similar to the one above between the disobedient patient Irma and her friend who is thought to be more sensible. I now become aware of one of the tracks along which the thought association of the dream progresses; from the sick child to the children's asylum. The dulness to the left, below, recalls a certain case corresponding to it, in every detail in which Leopold astonished me by his thoroughness. Besides this, I have a notion of something like a metastatic affection, but it might rather be a reference to the lady patient whom I should like to have instead of Irma. For this lady, as far as I can gather, resembles a woman suffering from tuberculosis.

An infiltrated portion of skin on the left shoulder.

I see at once that this is my own rheumatism of the shoulder, which I always feel when I have remained awake until late at night. The turn of phrase in the dream also sounds ambiguous; something which I feel . . . in spite of the dress. "Feel on my own body" is intended. Moreover, I am struck with the unusual sound of the term "infiltrated portion of skin." "An infiltration behind on the upper left" is what we are accustomed to; this would refer to the lung, and thus again to tuberculosis patients.

In spite of the dress.

This, to be sure, is only an interpolation. We, of course, examine the children in the clinic undressed; it is some sort of contradiction to the manner in which grown-up female patients must be examined. The story used to be told of a prominent clinician that he always examined his patients physically only through the clothes. The rest is obscure to me; I have, frankly, no inclination to follow the matter further.

Dr. M. says: "It is an infection, but it does not matter. Dysentery will develop, and the poison will be excreted.

This at first seems ridiculous to me; still it must be carefully analysed like everything else. Observed more closely, it seems, however, to have a kind of meaning. What I had found in the patient was local diphtheritis. I remember the discussion about diplitheritis and diphtheria at the time of my daughter's illness. The latter is the general infection which proceeds from local diphtheritis. Leopold proves the existence of such general infection by means of the dulness which thus suggests a metastatic lesion. I believe, however, that just this kind of metastasis does not occur in the case of diphtheria. It rather recalls pyæmia.

It does not matter, is a consolation. I believe it fits in as follows: The last part of the dream has yielded a content to the effect that the pains of the patient are the result of a serious organic affection. I begin to suspect that with this I am only trying to shift the blame from myself. Psychic treatment cannot be held responsible for the continued presence of diphtheritic affection. But now, in turn, I am disturbed at inventing such serious suffering for Irma for the sole purpose of exculpating myself. It seems cruel. I need (accordingly) the assurance that the result will be happy, and it does not seem ill-advised that I should put the words of consolation into the mouth of Dr. M. But here I consider myself superior to the dream, a fact which needs explanation.

But why is this consolation so nonsensical?

Dysentery:

Some sort of far-fetched theoretical notion that pathological material may be removed through the intestines. Am I in this way trying to make fun of Dr. M.'s great store of far-fetched explanations, his habit of finding curious pathological relationships? Dysentery suggests something else. A few months ago I had in charge a young man suffering from remarkable

pains during evacuation of the bowels, a case which colleagues had treated as "anæmia with malnutrition." I realized that it was a question of hysteria; I was unwilling to use my psychotherapy on him, and sent him off on a sea voyage. Now a few days before I had received a despairing letter from him from Egypt, saying that while there he had suffered a new attack, which the physician had declared to be dysentery. I suspect, indeed, that the diagnosis was only an error of my ignorant colleague, who allows hysteria to make a fool of him; but still I cannot avoid reproaching myself for putting the invalid in a position where he might contract an organic affection of the bowels in addition to his hysteria. Furthermore, dysentery sounds like diphtheria, a word which does not occur in the dream.

Indeed it must be that, with the consoling prognosis; "Dysentery will develop, etc.," I am making fun of Dr. M., for I recollect that years ago he once jokingly told a very similar story of another colleague. He had been called to consult with this colleague in the case of a woman who was very seriously ill and had felt obliged to confront the other physician, who seemed very hopeful, with the fact that he found albumen in the patient's urine. The colleague, however, did not let this worry him, but answered calmly: "That does not matter, doctor; the albumen will without doubt be excreted." Thus I can no longer doubt that derision for those colleagues who are ignorant of hysteria is contained in this part of the dream. As though in confirmation, this question now arises in my mind: "Does Dr. M. know that the symptoms of his patient, of our friend Irma, which give cause for fearing tuberculosis, are also based on hysteria? Has he recognised this hysteria, or has he stupidly ignored it?"

But what can be my motive in treating this friend so badly? This is very simple: Dr. M. agrees with my solution as little as Irma herself. I have thus already in this dream taken revenge on two persons, on Irma in the words, "If you still have pains, it is your own fault," and on Dr. M. in the wording of the nonsensical consolation which has been put into his mouth.

We have immediate knowledge of the origin of the infection.

This immediate knowledge in the dream is very remarkable. Just before we did not know it, since the infection was first demonstrated by Leopold.

My friend Otto has recently given her an injection when she felt ill.

Otto had actually related that in the short time of his visit to Irma's family, he had been called to a neighbouring hotel in order to give an injection to some one who fell suddenly ill. Injections again recall the unfortunate friend who has poisoned himself with cocaine. I had recommended the remedy to him merely for internal use during the withdrawal of morphine, but he once gave himself injections of cocaine.

With a propyl preparation … propyls … propionic acid.

How did this ever occur to me? On the same evening on which I had written part of the history of the disease before having the dream, my wife opened a bottle of cordial labelled "Ananas," (which was a present from our friend Otto. For he had a habit of making presents on every possible occasion; I hope he will some day be cured of this by a wife.) Such a smell of fusel oil arose from this cordial that I refused to taste it. My wife observed: "We will give this bottle to the servants," and I, still more prudent, forbade it, with the philanthropic remark: "They mustn't be poisoned either." The smell of fusel oil (amyl…) has now apparently awakened in my memory the whole series, propyl, methyl, &c., which has furnished the propyl preparation of the dream. In this, it is true, I have employed a substitution; I have dreamt of propyl, after smelling amyl, but substitutions of this kind are perhaps permissible, especially in organic chemistry.

Trimethylamin. I see the chemical formula of this substance in the dream, a fact which probably gives evidence of a great effort on the part of my memory, and, moreover, the formula is printed in heavy type, as if to lay special stress upon something of particular importance, as distinguished from the context. To what does this trimethylamin lead, which has been so forcibly called to my attention? It leads to a conversation with another friend who for years has known all my germinating activities, as I have his. At that time he had just informed me of some of his ideas about sexual chemistry, and had mentioned, among others, that he thought he recognized in trimethylamin one of the products of sexual metabolism. This substance thus leads me to sexuality, to that factor which I credit with the greatest significance for the origin of the nervous affections which I attempt to cure. My patient Irma is a young widow; if I am anxious to excuse the failure of her cure, I suppose I shall best do so by referring to this condition, which her admirers would be glad to change. How remarkably too, such a dream is fashioned! The other woman, whom I take as my patient in the dream instead of Irma, is also a young widow.

I suspect why the formula of trimethylamin has made itself so prominent in the dream. So many important things are gathered up in this one word: Trimethylamin is not only an allusion to the overpowering factor of sexuality, but also to a person whose sympathy I remember with satisfaction when I feel myself forsaken in my opinions. Should not this friend, who plays such a large part in my life, occur again in the chain of thoughts of the dream? Of course, he must; he is particularly acquainted with the results which proceed from affections of the nose and its adjacent cavities, and has revealed to science several highly remarkable relations of the turbinated bones to the female sexual organs (the three curly formations in Irma's throat). I have had Irma examined by him to see whether the pains in her stomach might be of nasal origin. But he himself suffers from suppurative rhinitis, which worries him, and to this perhaps there is an allusion in pyæmia, which hovers before me in the metastases of the dream.

Such injections are not made so rashly. Here the reproach of carelessness is hurled directly at my friend Otto. I am under the impression that I had some thought of this sort in the afternoon, when he seemed to indicate his siding against me by word and look. It was perhaps: "How easily he be can be influenced; how carelessly he pronounces judgment." Furthermore, the above sentence again points to my deceased friend, who so lightly took refuge in cocaine injections. As I have said, I had not intended injections of the remedy at all. I see that in reproaching Otto I again touch upon the story of the unfortunate Matilda, from which arises the same reproach against me. Obviously I am here collecting examples of my own conscientiousness, but also of the opposite.

Probably also the syringe was not clean. Another reproach directed at Otto, but originating elsewhere.

The day before I happened to meet the son of a lady eighty-two years of age whom I am obliged to give daily two injections of morphine. At present she is in the country, and I have heard that she is suffering from an inflammation of the veins. I immediately thought that it was a case of infection due to contamination from the syringe. It is my pride that in two years I have not given her a single infection; I am constantly concerned, of course, to see that the syringe is perfectly clean. For I am conscientious. From the inflammation of the veins, I return to my wife, who had suffered from emboli during a period of pregnancy, and now three related situations come to the surface in my memory, involving my wife, Irma, and the deceased Matilda, the identity of which three persons plainly justifies my putting them in one another's place.

I have now completed the interpretation of the dream. In the course of this interpretation I have taken great pains to get possession of all the notions to which a comparison between the dream content and the dream thoughts hidden behind it must have given rise. Meanwhile, the "meaning" of the dream has dawned upon me. I have become conscious of a purpose which is realized by means of the dream, and which must have been the motive for dreaming. The dream fulfills several wishes, which have been actuated in me by the events of the preceding evening (Otto's news, and the writing down of the history of the disease). For the result of the dream is that I am not to blame for the suffering which Irma still has, and that Otto is to blame for it. Now Otto has made me angry by his remark about Irma's imperfect cure; the dream avenges me upon him by turning the reproach back upon him. The dream acquits me of responsibility for Irma's condition by referring it to other causes, which indeed furnish a great number of explanations. The dream represents a certain condition of affairs as I should wish it to be; *the content of the dream is thus the fulfilment of a wish; its motive is a wish.*

This much is apparent at first sight. But many things in the details of the dream become intelligible when regarded from the point of view of wish-fulfilment. I take revenge on Otto, not only for hastily taking part against me, in that I accuse him of a careless medical operation (the injection), but I am also avenged on him for the bad cordial which smells like fusel oil, and I find an expression in the dream which unites both reproaches; the injection with a preparation of propyl. Still I am not satisfied, but continue my revenge by comparing him to his more reliable competitor. I seem to say by this: "I like him better than you." But Otto is not the only one who must feel the force of my anger. I take revenge on the disobedient patient by exchanging her for a more sensible and more docile one. Nor do I leave the contradiction of Dr. M. unnoticed, but express my opinion of him in an obvious allusion, to the effect that his relation to the question is that of an *ignoramus* (*"dysentery will develop,"* etc.).

It seems to me, indeed, as though I were appealing from him to someone better informed (my friend, who has told me about trimethylamin); just as I have turned from Irma to her friend, I turn from Otto to Leopold. Rid me of these three persons, replace them by three others of my own choice, and I shall be released from the reproaches which I do not wish to have deserved! The unreasonableness itself of these reproaches is proved to me in the dream in the most elaborate way. Irma's pains are not charged to me, because she herself is to blame for them, in that she refuses to accept my solution. Irma's pains are none of my business, for they are of an organic nature, quite impossible to be healed by a psychic cure. Irma's sufferings are satisfactorily explained by her widowhood (trimethylamin!); a fact which, of course, I cannot alter. Irma's illness has been caused by an incautious injection on the part of Otto, with an ill-suited substance—in a way I should never have made an injection. Irma's suffering is the result of an injection made with an unclean syringe, just like the inflammation of the veins in my old lady, while I never do any such mischief with my injections. I am aware, indeed, that these explanations of Irma's illness, which unite in acquitting me, do not agree with one another; they even exclude one another. The whole pleading—this dream is nothing else—recalls vividly the defensive argument of a man who was accused by his neighbour of having returned a kettle to him in a damaged condition. In the first place, he said, he had returned the kettle undamaged; in the second, it already had holes in it when he borrowed it; and thirdly, he had never borrowed the kettle from his neighbour at all. But so much the better; if even one of these three methods of defence is recognized as valid, the man must be acquitted.

Still other subjects mingle in the dream, whose relation to my release from responsibility for Irma's illness is not so transparent: the illness of my daughter and that of a patient of the same name, the harmfulness of cocaine, the illness of my patient travelling in Egypt, concern about the health of my wife, my brother, of Dr. M., my own bodily troubles, and concern about the absent friend who is suffering from suppurative rhinitis. But if I keep all these things in view, they combine into a single train of thought, labelled perhaps: concern for the health of myself and others—professional conscientiousness. I recall an undefined disagreeable sensation, as Otto brought me the news of Irma's condition. I should like to note finally the expression of this fleeting sensation which is part of this train of thought that is mingled into the dream. It is as though Otto had said to me: "You do not take your physicians's duties seriously enough, you are not conscientious, do not keep your promises." Thereupon this train of thought placed itself at my service in order that I might exhibit proof of the high degree in which I am conscientious, how intimately I am concerned with the health of my relatives, friends, and patients. Curiously enough, there are also in this thought material some painful memories, which correspond rather to the blame attributed to Otto than to the accusation against me. The material has the appearance of being impartial, but the connection between this broader material, upon which the dream depends, and the more limited theme of the dream which gives rise to the wish to be innocent of Irma's illness, is nevertheless unmistakable.

I do not wish to claim that I have revealed the meaning of the dream entirely, or that the interpretation is flawless.

I could still spend much time upon it; I could draw further explanations from it, and bring up new problems which it bids us consider. I even know the points from which further thought associations might be traced; but such considerations as are connected with every dream of one's own restrain me from the work of interpretation. Whoever is ready to condemn such reserve, may himself try to be more straightforward than I. I am content with the discovery which has been just made. If the method of dream interpretation here indicated is followed, it will be found that the dream really has meaning, and is by no means the expression of fragmentary brain activity, which the authors would have us believe. *When the work of interpretation has been completed the dream may be recognised as the fulfilment of a wish.*

Questions to Think About

1. According to Freud's interpretation of his dream, what were his feelings for Irma? What conclusions did Freud reach about her diagnosis? Why did Freud say, "If you still get pains, it's your own fault"?

2. Freud continually stresses the fact that dreams fulfill certain wishes and desires. What are some of the wishes and motives that Freud fulfilled through his dream?

3. To what extent did this dream interpretation depend on Freud knowing the personal history of the dreamer in great detail? Could the interpretation been done as thoroughly if Freud had more limited access to the actual life of the dreamer?

4. Recall a dream you have had recently. Try to use Freud's psychoanalytic approach to interpret your dream. Describe the manifest and, more importantly, the *latent* content of your dream.

4

The Assault on Truth:
Freud's Suppression of the Seduction Theory

JEFFREY MOUSSAIEFF MASSON

J. M. Masson (1941–) was the provisional Projects Director of the Freud Archives. He undertook the responsibility of putting together a complete record of all of Freud's letters and other materials. It was during this task that he found correspondence and papers on the seduction theory that Freud had proposed and then abandoned. Masson tried to expose this theory and the controversy surrounding it to the public, but he was met with disapproval from the psychoanalytic establishment and was soon dismissed from his position at the Freud Archives.

In classic Freudian theory, personality is formed as the child struggles with unconscious sexual urges. For example, little boys feel sexual attraction to their mothers and little girls feel sexual attraction to their fathers, but these dangerous desires cannot be realized. Psychological tension results. According to Freud, adult neuroses result from unresolved sexual conflicts in childhood. Psychoanalysis was built on the idea that children's memories and perceptions are unreliable conglomerations, influenced by struggles between unacceptable impulses and the demands of society. However, what if many adult neuroses arise not from imagined sexual conflicts but from real sexual abuse? That is, what if sexual abuse of young children is common and is really the cause of many neuroses? Masson asserts in this introductory chapter that Freud considered this possibility but was pressured to abandon the idea because it would cause public outrage that would threaten the position of psychoanalysis.

In 1970, I became interested in the origins of psychoanalysis and in Freud's relationship with Wilhelm Fliess, the ear, nose, and throat physician who was his closest friend during the years Freud was formulating his new theories.

For some time I had been corresponding with Anna Freud about the possibility of preparing a complete edition of Freud's letters to Fliess, an abridged version of which had been published in 1950 in German and in 1954 in English as *The Origins of Psychoanalysis* (New York: Basic Books).

This edition had been edited by Anna Freud, Ernst Kris, and Marie Bonaparte. In 1980, I met with Dr. K. R. Eissler, the head of the Freud Archives and Anna Freud's trusted adviser and friend, and with Anna Freud in London, and Miss Freud agreed to a new edition of the Freud/Fliess letters. As a result, I was given access to this sealed correspondence (the originals are in the Library of Congress), which constitutes our most important source of information concerning the beginnings of psychoanalysis.

Source: Masson, J. M. (1984). *The assault on truth: Freud's suppression of the seduction theory.* New York: Farrar. Straus and Giroux. Reprinted with permission of Ballantine Books, a division of Random House. Copyright © 1984, 1985, 1992, 1998, 2003 by Jeffrey Moussaieff Masson. (Selection is from Introduction, pp. xv–xxiii.)

In addition to including all the letters and passages which previously had been omitted (which amounted to more than half the text), I thought it necessary to annotate the book fully. I would thus need access to other relevant material. Anna Freud offered her complete cooperation, and I was given the freedom of Maresfield Gardens, where Freud spent the last year of his life.

Freud's magnificent personal library was there, and many of the volumes, especially from the early years, were annotated by Freud. In Freud's desk I discovered a notebook kept by Marie Bonaparte after she purchased Freud's letters to Fliess in 1936, in which she comments on Freud's reactions to these letters, which he had written years before. I also found a series of letters concerned with Sándor Ferenczi, who was in later years Freud's closest analytic friend and colleague, and with the last paper Ferenczi delivered to the 12th International Psycho-Analytic Congress in Wiesbaden. This paper dealt with the sexual seduction of children, a topic that had engrossed Freud during the years of his friendship with Fliess.

In a large black cupboard outside Anna Freud's bedroom, I found many original letters to and from Freud written during this same period, letters that were previously unknown—a letter from Fliess to Freud, letters from Charcot to Freud, letters from Freud to Josef Breuer, to his sister-in-law Minna Bernays, to his wife Martha, and to former patients.

A short time later, Dr. Eissler asked me if I would be willing to succeed him as director of the Freud Archives. I agreed and was appointed provisional Projects Director. The Archives had purchased Freud's house in Maresfield Gardens, and I was to convert the house into a museum and research center. Anna Freud gave me access to the restricted material she had already donated to the Library of Congress, to enable me to prepare a catalogue of all the Freud material at the Library (most of it from the Archives), which came to nearly 150,000 documents. The Library agreed to supply copies of these documents to the projected museum. I also became one of the four directors of Sigmund Freud Copyrights, which allowed me to negotiate with Harvard University Press for the publication of Freud's letters in scholarly, annotated, complete editions.

As I was reading through the correspondence and preparing the annotations for the first volume of the series, the Freud/Fliess letters, I began to notice what appeared to be a pattern in the omissions made by Anna Freud in the original, abridged edition. In the letters written after September 1897 (when Freud was supposed to have given up his "seduction" theory), all the case histories dealing with sexual seduction of children were excised. Moreover, every mention of Emma Eckstein, an early patient of Freud and Fliess who seemed connected in some way with the seduction theory, was deleted. I was particularly struck by a section of a letter written in December 1897 that brought to light two previously unknown facts: Emma Eckstein was herself seeing patients in analysis (presumably under Freud's supervision); and Freud was inclined to lend credence, once again, to the seduction theory.

I asked Anna Freud why she had deleted this section from the December 1897 letter. She said she no longer knew why. When I showed her an unpublished letter from Freud to Emma Eckstein, she said that she could well understand my interest in the subject, as Emma Eckstein had indeed been an important part of the early history of psychoanalysis, but the letter should nevertheless not be published. In subsequent conversations, Miss Freud indicated that, since her father eventually abandoned the seduction theory, she felt it would only prove confusing to readers to be exposed to his early hesitations and doubts. I, on the other hand, felt that these passages not only were of great historical importance, they might well represent the truth. Nobody, it seemed to me, had the right to decide for others, by altering the record, what was truth and what was error. Moreover, whatever Freud's ultimate decision, it was evident that he was haunted by this theory all his life.

I showed Miss Freud the 1932 correspondence I found in Freud's desk concerning his close friend Sándor Ferenczi's last paper, which dealt with this very topic. Clearly, I thought, it was her father's continued preoccupation with the seduction theory that explained his otherwise mysterious turning away from Ferenczi. Miss Freud, who was very fond of Ferenczi, found these letters painful reading and asked me not to publish them. But the theory, I insisted, was not one that Freud had dismissed lightly as an early and insignificant error, as we had been led to believe.

Anna Freud urged me to direct my interests elsewhere. In conversations with other analysts close to the Freud family, I was given to understand that I had stumbled upon something that was better left alone. Perhaps, if the seduction theory had really been only a detour along the road to truth, as so many psychoanalysts believe, it would have been possible for me to turn my attention to other matters. But the seduction hypothesis, in my opinion, was the very cornerstone of psychoanalysis. In 1895 and 1896 Freud, in listening to his women patients, learned that something dreadful and violent lay in their past. The psychiatrists who had heard these stories before Freud had accused their patients of being hysterical liars and had dismissed their memories as fantasy. Freud was the first psychiatrist who believed his patients were telling the truth. These women were sick, not because they came from "tainted" families, but because something terrible and secret had been done to them as children.

Freud announced his discovery in a paper which he gave in April 1896 to the Society for Psychiatry and Neurology in Vienna, his first major public address to his peers. The paper—Freud's most brilliant, in my opinion—met with total silence. Afterwards, he was urged never to publish it, lest his reputation be damaged beyond repair. The silence around him deepened, as did his loneliness. But he defied his colleagues and published "The Aetiology of Hysteria," an act of great courage. Eventually, however, for reasons which I will attempt to elucidate in this book, Freud decided that he had made a mistake in believing his women patients. This, Freud later claimed, marked the beginning of psychoanalysis as a science, a therapy, and a profession.

It had never seemed right to me, even as a student, that Freud would not believe his patients. I did not agree that the seduction scenes represented as memories were only fantasies, or memories of fantasies. But I had not thought to doubt Freud's historical account (often repeated in his writings) of his motives for changing his mind. Yet, when I read the Fliess letters without the omissions (of which Freud, by the way, would undoubtedly have approved), they told a very different, agonizing story. Moreover, wherever I turned, even in

Freud's later writing, I encountered cases in which seduction or abuse of children played a role.

Muriel Gardiner, a psychoanalyst and a friend of both Anna Freud and Kurt Eissler, supported my work both financially and by giving me every possible encouragement. She asked me to go through the unpublished material she had in her home concerning the Wolf-Man, one of Freud's most famous later patients, who had been financially supported by Dr. Gardiner and Dr. Eissler. There I found some notes by Ruth Mack Brunswick for a paper she never published. At Freud's request, she had re-analyzed the Wolf-Man and was astonished to learn that as a child he had been anally seduced by a member of his family—and that Freud did not know this. She never told him. Why? Did Freud not know because he did not want to know? And did Ruth Mack Brunswick not tell him because she sensed this?

In my search for further data, I tried to learn more about Freud's trip to Paris in 1885–1886. I visited the library of his early teacher, Charcot, in the Salpêtriére, and that led me to the Paris morgue, for I knew that Freud had attended autopsies performed there by a friend and collaborator of Charcot's, Paul Brouardel. Hints dropped by Freud indicated that he had seen something at the morgue "of which medical science preferred to take no notice." At the morgue, I learned that a whole literature of legal medicine existed in French devoted to the topic of child abuse (especially rape), and Freud had this material in his personal library, though he did not refer to it in his writings. I discovered, moreover, that some of the autopsies attended by Freud may have been autopsies done on children who had been raped and murdered.

I found myself in a strange position. When I became a psychoanalyst, I believed that Freud had fearlessly pursued truth, that he wanted to help his patients face their personal histories, and the wrongs inflicted on them, no matter how unpleasant. My analytic training taught me early on that these ideals were not shared by the profession at large. But I did not think they had altogether vanished from the science; surely there were still people who uncompromisingly sought out truth. That is why, I argued to myself, I had been encouraged in my research; no restrictions had been placed on it.

The information I was uncovering, I felt, was vital to an understanding of how psychoanalysis had developed, and I reported the results of my research to those responsible for it in the first place, Anna Freud, Dr. Eissler, and Dr. Gardiner. I thought that although they might not agree with my interpretations, they would not discount the significance of my discoveries.

My disappointment with psychoanalysis as I knew it was well known, and in fact it was shared by many of my colleagues. In this connection, one meeting with Anna Freud seems to me important enough to merit recounting. Generally, my relations with Miss Freud were formal, confined to discussions of research matters. One afternoon, however, we both began to talk more personally. I told her how disillusioned I was with my training in Toronto, and said that I had not found much improvement in San Francisco and I doubted it would be different anywhere else. I asked her whether, if her father were alive today, he would want to be part of the psychoanalytic movement, or even would want to be an analyst. "No," she replied, "he would not." Anna Freud, then, understood my criticism of psychoanalysis as it is practiced today, and seemed to support me in this criticism. However, when my research carried me further back, to Freud himself, this support ceased.

Indeed, what I was finding pointed back to Freud's early period, 1897–1903, as the time when fundamental changes set in that would, in my opinion, undermine psychoanalysis. With the greatest reluctance, I gradually came to see Freud's abandonment of the seduction hypothesis as a failure of courage. If I was wrong in my view, surely I would meet with intelligent rebuttal and serious criticisms of my interpretation of the documents. Wherever it lay, the truth had to be faced, and the documents I found had to be brought out into the open.

At the invitation of Anna Freud, I presented a preliminary account of my findings to a meeting of psychoanalysts at the Hampstead Clinic in London in 1981. The participants had been invited by Anna Freud to a conference on "Insight in Psychoanalysis," and many of the leading analysts from around the world were present. The negative response to my paper alerted me to the political overtones of my research, to the possibility that it would have an adverse effect on the profession. But I dismissed such considerations as not worthy of attention by a serious researcher.

In June 1981 I was asked to make a more detailed presentation of the documents and their implications before a closed meeting of the Western New England Psychoanalytic Society in New Haven. The paper I gave was entitled "The Seduction Hypothesis in the Light of New Documents." The anger aroused by this paper, most of it directed at me rather than focused on the documents I had uncovered, brought home the realization that my views would not be treated simply as one man's attempt to come closer to the historical truth behind Freud's abandonment of the seduction theory. The truth or falsity of my research was not questioned, only the wisdom of making the material available to the public. My interpretations, the critics seemed to feel, put in jeopardy the very heart of psychoanalysis.

It was my conviction that what Freud had uncovered in 1896—that, in many instances, children are the victims of sexual violence and abuse within their own families—became such a liability that he literally had to banish it from his consciousness. The psychoanalytic movement that grew out of Freud's accommodation to the views of his peers holds to the present day that Freud's earlier position was simply an aberration. Freud, so the accepted view goes, had to abandon his erroneous beliefs about seduction before he could discover the more basic truth of the power of internal fantasy and of spontaneous childhood sexuality. Every first-year resident in psychiatry knew that simple fact, yet I seemed incapable of understanding it. And I now claimed that this accepted view actually represented a travesty of the truth. The prevalent opinion in psychotherapy was that the victim fashioned his or her own torture. In particular, violent sexual crimes could be attributed to the victim's imagination, a position held by Freud's pupil Karl Abraham and enthusiastically accepted by Freud himself. It was a comforting view for society, for Freud's interpretation—that the sexual violence that so affected the lives of his women patients was nothing but fantasy—posed no threat to the existing social order. Therapists could thus remain on the side of the successful and the powerful, rather than of the miserable victims of family violence. To question the basis of that accommodation was seen as something more than a historical investigation; it threatened to call into question the very fabric of psychotherapy.

When a series of articles in *The New York Times* in August 1981 reported on my findings, the resulting wave of protest culminated in a demand for my removal from the Archives. I was dismissed, to the evident relief of the analytic community; the reason

offered was that I had shown "poor judgment" in expressing opinions before a non-professional audience.

Here, then, is the story of Freud's abandonment of the seduction theory, including the documents and my interpretations. My pessimistic conclusions may possibly be wrong. The documents may in fact allow a very different reading. However they are evaluated, I believe that anybody who reads them will come away with a new understanding of psychoanalysis.

_____ Questions to Think About _____

1. Why did Freud initially develop his seduction theory and why did he later drop it? Was it social pressure that forced him to drop the theory or did he find solid evidence to the contrary?

2. What would happen to psychoanalytic theory and practice if neuroses were found to be mostly caused by actual sexual abuse rather than by sexual conflict and repression?

3. How do the experiences of the author, Masson, in dealing with the psychoanalytic establishment over the issue of the seduction theory compare to the experiences Freud had in dealing with the medical establishment of his time?

5

What Should Psychologists Do about Psychoanalysis?

HENRY A. MURRAY

Henry Murray (1893–1988) was an American psychologist who spent most of his career at Harvard University. He was originally trained as a physician and as a biochemist, but was so profoundly influenced by the ideas of Carl Jung when the two met in Switzerland that he moved into psychology. Murray underwent psychoanalysis under Jung, and then later under Franz Alexander, a leader in psychosomatic medicine. One of Murray's best known contributions to personality psychology is the Thematic Apperception Test (TAT), which was developed by Murray and Christiana Morgan (although the role of Morgan, Murray's long-time collaborator and mistress, is often overlooked). Murray blended psychoanalytic and neo-analytic ideas into a basis for empirical research. Murray preferred the term "personology" to personality, because he felt it better reflected the richness of the life of each individual. The selection included here presents Murray's thoughtful evaluation of psychoanalytic theory.

. . . In many people the word "psychoanalysis" is the nucleus of a complex, a fighting word, a cat-o'-nine-tails to flog the culpable, or the password to an esoteric cult. It stands for something that must be accepted wholly or rejected, as a suitor before a woman. When the Harvard Clinic was brought to the bar of judgment recently, I was asked: "Is this a psychoanalytic clinic or is it not?" Could anything be more benighted? I cannot see it as a hate affair, or as a love affair in which every fault is transformed into an endearing quality like the mole on my wife's cheek. Psychoanalysis means many things. It means a procedure and a large number of therapeutic rules, many of which are matters of debate among the analysts. Some of these rules I accept as the best available guides, others I follow occasionally and tentatively, others I ignore. Psychoanalysis also means a vast collection of unusual and important facts, among which a personologist cannot fail to find a great deal

that is pertinent to his problems. Finally, psychoanalysis stands for a conceptual system which explains, it seems to me, as much as any other. But this is no reason for going in blind and swallowing the whole indigestible bolus, cannibalistically devouring the totem father in the hope of acquiring his genius, his authoritative dominance, and thus rising to power in the psychoanalytic society, that battle-ground of Little Corporals. No; I, for one, prefer to take what I please, suspend judgment, reject what I please, speak freely.

In advocating psychoanalysis—as I do constantly—I have been thwarted by the absence of any satisfactory textbook on the subject. I have found nothing that I could heartily recommend to a student or indeed to any moderately critical inquirer. Analytic authors have not yet learnt to sort out facts from theories, probabilities from improbabilities; with but fugitive impressions of the requirements of scientific proof,

Source: Murray, H. A. (1940). What should psychologists do about psychoanalysis? *Journal of Abnormal and Social Psychology, 35,* 150–175. (Selection is excerpted from the article.)

they are boyish in their readiness to dogmatize. There is, nevertheless, so much precious ore amid the slag that a personologist, I think, should persevere—tolerant of intellectual frailities and foibles—until he finds it. What the analysts know is hard—especially for them—to say; and the psychologists who might be competent to say—they do not yet know.

It would take—it *did* take—a long book to encompass everything that I consider relatively true or promising in psychoanalysis. Here there is space only for a brief synopsis of the concepts that seem most essential to a scheme of personology. First of all—and here my prejudice leaps out—psychoanalysis is dynamic in the special sense that it is founded on a theory of directional forces, forces which, if unimpeded, usually produce, in one way or another, results that are satisfying, positively or negatively, to the organism. The principle of adaptation rests upon this concept. Logically, you cannot assent to one and deny the other. But the argument makes a long story which cannot be gone into now. At the moment I am mentally unfit to accept as fundamental any system of psychology which does not include a theory of drives, needs, conations (or what have you).

The psychoanalysts distinguish only two drives, sex and aggression; but these have been studied closely, and much that has been discovered about their modes (fixation, conflict, fusion, sublimation) applies equally well to other tendencies. Psychoanalysis is worth reading if only for what it teaches us about sex. For it is now clear that this instinct—punished and guilt-laden, veiled by shame and twisted by hypocrisy, turned back upon itself and driven into ugly alleys—is not only the chief factor in psychogenic illness but has been for centuries the source of unspeakable mental torment, the veritable plague spot of human personality. This was the price of innocence. As a corollary to the instinct theory is Freud's notion of cathexis, which describes the degree of positive or negative valence with which each object (individual, group, cause) that concerns the subject is endowed. Through such cathexes each general tendency becomes specific.

The *sine qua non* of psychoanalysis is the theory of unconscious processes, which affirms that activities quite similar to those distinguishable introspectively (perceptions, emotions, intellections, intentions) occur continually in us without our knowledge. (In order to establish this point, the misunderstanding about words that commonly arises must be first dispelled by defining such psychic entities as "intention" and "emotion" *both* according to their natures as directly experienced subjectively and according to their discernible effects.) Closely related to this theory is the division of the mind into structured, partly conscious *ego* processes, and less structured, unconscious *id* processes; the ego being, so to speak, separated from the id by a layer of selective and inhibitive functions. Here the concept of repression is indispensable in accounting for the habitual exclusion of certain unacceptable tendencies and traces. Besides repression, Freud has described a number of other mechanisms (projection, sublimation, rationalization) whereby the ego partially succeeds in veiling, transforming, or excusing some of the active components of the id. Of course to speak of "the id" or "the unconscious" is a mere makeshift, but it is too early to imprison in tidy operational definitions the myriad varieties of noted facts. The ego is an elusive being which has not yet been caught in any conceptual corral; as a first approximation, however, the notion of a discriminating semi-conscious entity, standing between two environments—signs and pressures from within and from without—is a convenient one. Hinting of the nature of id processes we have dreams and fantasies, and the mental life of children, savages, and psychotics. Their thought, primitive and prelogical, is marked by more emotive and symbolic imagery (fewer abstract words) and exhibits a greater number of instinctive, lower-order tendencies than does that of normal adults.

The theory of the unconscious (of the *alter ego* or shadow-self) helps to explain contrasting phases of behavior, ambivalence, sudden explosions, regressions, conversions. ("He was not himself"; "I would not have known him.") It throws light on fixed and refractory frames of reference, settled sentiments and beliefs. It is essential to an understanding of illusions, delusions, morbid anxiety, compulsions, and insanity. It is invaluable in interpreting neurotic accidents and illness. The unconscious is an historical museum of the breed and of the individual, exhibiting tableaux of development. But also, in a sense, it is the womb of fate, the procreating source of new directions, of art, and of religion. It is here that one must seek for novelty, for the incubating complex that will govern the next move. No creator can afford to disrespect the twilight stirrings of the mind, since out of these arise the quickening ideas that are his life.

Psychoanalysis stresses the primacy of the *body*, the chemistry of its essential organs, its endocrines and appetites. The brain and central nervous system are its instruments (its president and officials) with power to coordinate and satisfy its needs. The self-consciousness acquired in the brain is like a tiny coral isle growing in a sea of dreams (containing representatives of the body) which influence its every waking moment and sweep over it in sleep. To understand the mind, therefore, one must search for much that lies beyond the range of consciousness. What a man does and says in public is but a fraction of him. There is what he does in private, and the reasons he gives for doing it. But even this is not enough. Beyond what he says there is what he will not say but knows, and, finally, what he does not know. Only a depth psychologist can reach the latter.

Among other useful psychoanalytic concepts, some are so eminently suitable to everyday experience that they have been accepted widely as self-evident. One wonders why these things were never said before in scientific language. It seems incredible, for example, that no pre-Freudian psychologist ever conceptualized in full relief the eternal conflict between man and men, between personal desires and social sanctions. Freud's concept of the superego (conscience) as the internalization of parental and cultural demands organizes many facts; and serves, by the way, to make a bridge between psychology and sociology. The moral man carries society within him.

The analysts have also contributed a great deal to our understanding of children. They have taught us to take stock of the infant's reactions to certain well-nigh universal situations—birth, weaning, bowel training, advent of younger sibling, withdrawal of support—all of which are potentially traumatic. We now know that fantasies are almost as influential as actual events, that the contemporary concerns (dilemmas and anxieties) of the child give to occurrences special meanings which determine their effects, and, finally, that some events leave permanent impressions which modify development. Complexes arising out of the child's relations to its mother and to its father are of signal import. In addition to these and other general theories, the analysts have proposed specific formulations to account for a great variety of conditions and reactions, too numerous to mention here.

I can hardly think myself back to the myopia that once so seriously restricted my view of human nature, so natural has it become for me to receive impressions of wishes, dramas and assumptions that underlie the acts and talk of everyone I meet. Instead of seeing merely a groomed American in a business suit, travelling to and from his office like a rat in a maze, a predatory ambulating apparatus of reflexes, habits, stereotypes, and slogans, a bundle of consistencies, conformities, and allegiances to this or that institution— a robot in other words—I visualize (just as I visualize the activity of his internal organs) a flow of powerful subjective life, conscious and unconscious; a whispering gallery in which voices echo from the distant past; a gulf stream of fantasies with floating memories of past events, currents of contending complexes, plots and counterplots, hopeful intimations and ideals. To a neurologist such perspectives are absurd, archaic, tender-minded; but in truth they are much closer to the actualities of inner life than are his own neat diagrams of reflex arcs and nerve anastomoses. A personality is a full Congress of orators and pressure-groups, of children, demagogues, communists, isolationists, warmongers, mugwumps, grafters, log-rollers, lobbyists, Caesars and Christs, Machiavels and Judases, Tories and Promethean revolutionists. And a psychologist who does not know this in himself, whose mind is locked against the flux of images and feelings, should be encouraged to make friends, by being psychoanalyzed, with the various members of his household.

Figurative language, such as I am using here, is widely condemned as rank anthropomorphism, but what sin could be more pardonable than this when talking about *men*—not about vegetables, minerals, and sewing machines? Anyhow, such talk is pragmatically effective in dealing with most patients; and hence by this token scientific. Technical language, on the other hand, is ineffective and therefore "illogical" in the Paretian sense. For this reason, emotive speech will always have its place—resistant to certain poisons in "scientific" psychology—even after it is found that some complex of chemicals is mostly responsible for the rebel in us, another for the pacifist, still another for the lecher.

I have been speaking chiefly of Freudian concepts; but among the theories which I consider necessary or fruitful I should certainly place some of those proposed by Jung, Adler, and Rank. So much contentious blood has been spilt in the guerilla war that still rages between the schools founded by these pioneers that now it is quite impossible for the protagonists of one dogma to appreciate the values and validities of others. Semi-blindness is a residuum as well as a cause of combat. To an impartial eye, however, the one-sidedness of each of these divergent creeds is as obvious as a paralytic limb. Freudian psychology, for example, is clearly limited to certain spheres of functioning and is more applicable to some types and some conditions of men than to others. It is chiefly designed to interpret what a man says when he lies on a couch and his memories are canalized by his desire to appease an analyst's consuming and insatiable interest in sexual adventures. It does not fit all of the people all of the time. Consequently it will have to be expanded to encompass much that up to now has been neglected. Freud denied that anything had entirely evaded his watchful eye when he said: "If psychoanalysis has not yet duly appreciated certain matters, this has never been because it overlooked them or underrated their importance, but simply because it was following a certain course which had not yet led to them." In other words, psychoanalysis must discover everything for itself, borrowing nothing from others, and stamp it with its private seal; and since life is a prodigious nut for a few unaided men to crack, psychoanalysis is destined (if it pursues this course) not to appreciate certain matters for a long, long time. . . .

Freud's theory, I submit, is an utterly analytic instrument which reduces a complex individual to a few primitive ingredients and leaves him so. It has names—and the most unsavoury—for parts, but none for wholes. It dissects but does not bind up the wounds that it has made. Unconcerned with psychosynthesis and its results, it is of little use either in formulating progress in personality development or in helping a patient—after the transference neurosis and the leveling that an analysis produces—to gather up his forces and launch out on a better way of life. This is the flaw which Jung was quickest to detect and remedy, by directing his therapeutic efforts to an understanding of the forward, rather than to the backward, movements of the psyche. The unconscious, in his opinion, is more than an asylum of but-half-relinquished infantile desires; it is the breeding ground of enterprise. One cannot live by laparotomies alone, or by disinfectants or deodorants, as even Freud admitted when he said: "Men are strong as long as they represent a strong idea." The truth will out; though it proves to be a waif excluded from its father's house.

This is not the place to examine the probing, disintegrating and deflating tendency in psychoanalytic practice. Well might someone write a treatise on the subject, fixing his eye on the intention that designed it, that decided what data should be chosen for consideration, what aspects exhibited in concepts, how the whole dissection should proceed. It would be noted first of all that the patient, who in the end almost invariably seeks, and needs, advice—since it is as hard for him to synthesize as to analyze himself—gets none; gets none from the only man—his analyst—who knows him well enough to judge his powers, the man who has reasons to be much concerned, selfishly and unselfishly, in his future welfare, the man whose business it is to know not only what makes for illness but what makes for health. An inquirer into such matters would listen skeptically to the analyst's rationalizations of his refusal to give positive suggestions. He would note his lack of interest and talent for just this, and his sharply contrasting eagerness to impose the dogma of analysis—more and more analysis, reversing the life process. The direction of the will that underlies all this, the theory and therapy, is fairly obvious. One might have thought the Freudians, so quick to see perverted streaks in other men, would have been polite enough to tell us frankly what sublimated promptings were back of their scientific labors. It would then have been unnecessary for some rude unmasker like myself to speak of voyeurism, depreciating sadism, and the id's revenge on culture, the superego, and the ego. Why not expose and prove the value of these motives? Being sociable with the id myself, I cannot but sympathize with its efforts to get on to a new Declaration of Independence. But the question is, have the Freudians allowed the id enough creativeness and the ego enough will to make any elevating declaration? What is Mind today? Nothing but the butler and procurer of the body. The fallen angel theory of the soul has been put to rout by the starker theory of the soulless fallen man, a result—as Adam, the father of philosophy, demonstrated for all time—of experiencing and viewing love as a mere cluster of sensations. Little man, what now? Freud's pessimism, his conviction that happiness was impossible, his melancholy patronage of the death instinct, should put us on our guard. But then, on second thought, this yielding of the ego to the id, this devotion to its savage depths may be the harbinger of what Henry James, the Swedenborgian, called "creative Love, all whose tenderness *ex vi termini* must be reserved only for what intrinsically is most bitterly hostile and negative to itself"—a sentence, by the way, which the originator of pragmatism said, "discloses for the problem of evil its everlasting solution."

For our day it was Freud, the modern Alberich, who made off with the Rhinemaiden's gold, the *leuchtende Lust,* the shining eye, as Wagner wrote, "that wakes and sleeps in the depths, and fills the waves with its light"; and if his disciples, the present Nibelungs, have been among the few (with Hitler) to escape the world-wide deflation of the ego, it is because the ring that Freud fashioned from the ravished gold has the power of casting long rays into the heretofore mysterious and appalling regions of the psyche, the mind's dark halls of Eblis. Testifying to the master's genius is the fact that a mediocrity who has learnt to use his instruments acquires the powers of a sorcerer, and his consultation room becomes the house of magic to his patients. No wonder Freud is idolized! But let analysts keep their heads. No greater disservice can be done their founder's cause than by making scripture of his utterances, holding his flimsiest conjectures sacred as his profoundest insights. "Genius is full of trash," said Melville. It is out of the germy soil of foolishness that new truths are born. To cling slavishly to *all* of Freud is a mockery to the example of his life, the history of his independently creative mind. Science is a passing fable that sets us free when it arrives and when it leaves.

Questions to Think About

1. In this article, Murray refers to himself as a "rude unmasker" of psychoanalytic theory. What aspects of his discussion seem to merit such a strongly negative characterization?

2. Murray is critical of Freud's view that the important drives are limited to sex and aggression. What is lost by not incorporating other human drives into the theory?

3. Paradoxically, Freud's psychoanalytic theory is criticized for being overly "analytic" in the sense of breaking down and dissecting, but not sufficiently synthetic and integrative and constructive. Is this a well-founded criticism, and is it fair to criticize an analytic theory for being too analytic?

4. Why might Murray, while acknowledging that his own understanding had been broadened by the psychoanalytic approach, nevertheless disparage the psychoanalytic community as dogmatic and closed?

6

The Conception of the Unconscious

CARL G. JUNG

Carl Gustav Jung (1875–1961) grew up in a religious home in Switzerland. His father, the Reverend Paul Jung, was a country minister, and his mother, Emilie, was a minister's daughter. Jung's theories of personality were focused on the more mystical and spiritual aspects of personality and the roots of his approach can be traced to thoughts and experiences from his own childhood.

Jung was interested in the deepest universal aspects of personality. He expanded ideas of the unconscious to include emotionally charged images and quasi-instincts that seem characteristic of all generations. In particular, he was interested in beliefs that we all share and in how our many similarities develop. Jung described personality as being comprised of competing forces, pulling one against another to reach equilibrium. According to the Jungian theory, the mind or psyche is divided into three parts: the conscious ego, the personal unconscious, and the collective (or universal, impersonal) unconscious. Jung introduced the concepts of archetypes (powerful emotional symbols) and complexes (emotionally charged thoughts and feelings on a particular theme). Most significantly, it was Jung who challenged Freud and broke new conceptual ground about motivation and the ego, allowing other approaches to flourish.

Since the breach with the Viennese school upon the question of the fundamental explanatory principle of analysis—that is, the question if it be sexuality or energy—our concepts have undergone considerable development. After the prejudice concerning the explanatory basis had been removed by the acceptance of a purely abstract view of it, the nature of which was not anticipated, interest was directed to the concept of the unconscious.

According to Freud's theory the contents of the unconscious are limited to infantile wish-tendencies, which are repressed on account of the incompatibility of their character. Repression is a process which begins in early childhood under the moral influence of environment; it continues throughout life. These repressions are done away with by means of analysis, and the repressed wishes are made conscious. That should theoretically empty the unconscious, and, so to say, do away with it; but in reality the production of infantile sexual wish-fantasies continues into old age.

According to this theory, the unconscious contains only those parts of the personality which might just as well be conscious, and have really only been repressed by the processes of civilisation. According to Freud the essential content of the unconscious would therefore be *personal*. But although, from such a view-point the infantile tendencies of the unconscious are the more prominent, it would be a mistake to estimate or define the unconscious from this alone, for it has another side.

Not only must the repressed materials be included in the periphery of the unconscious, but also all the psychic material that does not reach the threshold of consciousness. It is impossible to explain all

Source: Jung, C. G. (1917). The conception of the unconscious. In C. G. Jung, *Collected papers on analytical psychology.* New York: Moffat Yard & Company. (Selection is excerpted from pp. 445–474.)

these materials by the principle of repression, for in that case by the removal of the repression a phenomenal memory would be acquired, one that never forgets anything. As a matter of fact repression exists, but it is a special phenomenon. If a so-called bad memory were only the consequence of repression, then those persons who have an excellent memory should have no repression, that is, be incapable of being neurotic. But experience teaches us that this is not the case. There are, undoubtedly, cases with abnormally bad memories, where it is clear that the main cause must be attributed to repression. But such cases are comparatively rare.

We therefore emphatically say that the unconscious contains all that part of the psyche that is found under the threshold, including subliminal sense-perceptions, in addition to the repressed material. We also know—not only on account of accumulated experience, but also for theoretical reasons—that the unconscious must contain all the material that has *not yet* reached the level of consciousness. These are the germs of future conscious contents. We have also every reason to suppose that the unconscious is far from being quiescent, in the sense that it is inactive, but that it is probably constantly busied with the formation and re-formation of so-called unconscious phantasies. Only in pathological cases should this activity be thought of as comparatively autonomous, for normally it is coordinated with consciousness.

It may be assumed that all these contents are of a personal nature in so far as they are acquisitions of the individual life. As this life is limited, the number of acquisitions of the unconscious must also be limited, wherefore an exhaustion of the contents of the unconscious through analysis might be held to be possible. In other words, by the analysis of the unconscious the inventory of unconscious contents might be completed, possibly in the sense that the unconscious cannot produce anything besides what is already known and accepted in the conscious. Also, as has already been said, we should have to accept the fact that the unconscious activity had thereby been paralysed, and that by the removal of the repression we could stop the conscious contents from descending into the unconscious. Experience teaches us that is only possible to a very limited extent. We urge our patients to retain

their hold upon repressed contents that have been brought to consciousness, and to insert them in their scheme of life. But, as we may daily convince ourselves, this procedure seems to make no impression upon the unconscious, inasmuch as it goes on producing apparently the same phantasies, namely, the so-called infantile-sexual ones, which according to the earlier theory were based upon personal repressions. If in such cases analysis be systematically continued, an inventory of incompatible wish-phantasies is gradually revealed, whose combinations amaze us. In addition to all the sexual perversions every conceivable kind of crime is discovered, as well as every conceivable heroic action and great thought, whose existence in the analysed person no one would have suspected. . . .

We now come to a problem the overlooking of which would cause the greatest confusion.

As I said before, the immediate result of the analysis of the unconscious is that additional personal portions of the unconscious are incorporated into the conscious. I called those parts of the unconscious which are repressed but capable of being made conscious, *the personal unconscious.* I showed moreover that through the annexation of the deeper layers of the unconscious, which I called the *impersonal unconsciousness,* an extension of the personality is brought about which leads to the state of God-Almightiness ("Gottähnlichkeit"). This state is reached by a continuation of the analytical work, by means of which we have already reintroduced what is repressed to consciousness. By continuing analysis further we incorporate some distinctly impersonal universal basic qualities of humanity with the personal consciousness, which brings about the aforesaid enlargement, and this to some extent may be described as an unpleasant consequence of analysis.

From this standpoint, the conscious personality seems to be a more or less arbitrary excerpt of the collective psyche. It appears to consist of a number of universal basic human qualities of which it is *a priori* unconscious, and further of a series of impulses and forms which might just as well have been conscious, but were more or less arbitrarily repressed, in order to attain that excerpt of the collective psyche, which we call personality. The term *persona* is really an excellent one, for persona was originally the mask which an actor wore, that served to indicate the character in which he appeared. For if we really venture to undertake to decide what psychic material must be accounted personal and what impersonal, we shall soon reach a state of great perplexity; for, in truth, we must make the same assertion regarding the contents of the personality as we have already made with respect to the impersonal unconscious, that is to say that it is *collective,* whereas we can only concede *individuality to the bounds of the persona,* that is to the particular choice of personal elements, and that only to a very limited extent. It is only by virtue of the fact that the persona is a more or less accidental or arbitrary excerpt of the collective psyche that we can lapse into the error of deeming it to be *in toto* individual, whereas as its name denotes, it is only a mask of the collective psyche *a mask which simulates individuality,* making others and oneself believe that one is individual, whilst one is only acting a part through which the collective psyche speaks.

If we analyse the persona we remove the mask and discover that what appeared to be individual is at bottom collective. We thus trace "the Little God of the World" back to his origin, that is, to a personification of the collective psyche. Finally, to our astonishment, we realise that the persona was only the mask of the collective psyche. Whether we follow Freud and reduce the primary impulse to sexuality, or Adler and reduce it to the elementary desire for power, or reduce it to the general principle of the collective psyche which contains the principles of both Freud and Adler, we arrive at the same result; namely, the dissolution of the personal into the collective. Therefore in every analysis that is continued sufficiently far, the moment arrives when the aforesaid God-Almightiness must be realised. This condition is often ushered in by peculiar symptoms; for instance, by dreams of flying through space like a comet, of being either the earth, the sun, or a star, or of being either extraordinarily big or small, of having died, etc. Physical sensations also occur, such as sensations of being too large for one's skin, or too fat; or hypnagogic feelings of endless sinking or rising occur, of enlargement of the body or of dizziness. This state is characterised psychologically

by an extraordinary loss of orientation about one's personality, about what one really is, or else the individual has a positive but mistaken idea of that which he has just become. Intolerance, dogmatism, self-conceit, self-depreciation, contempt and belittling of "not analysed" fellow-beings, and also of their opinions and activities, all very frequently occur. An increased disposition to physical disorders may also occasionally be observed, but this occurs only if pleasure be taken therein, thus prolonging this stage unduly.

The wealth of the possibilities of the collective psyche is both confusing and dazzling. The dissolution of the persona results in the release of phantasy, which apparently is nothing else but the functioning of the collective psyche. This release brings materials into consciousness of whose existence we had no suspicion before. A rich mine of mythological thought and feeling is revealed. It is very hard to hold one's own against such an overwhelming impression. That is why this phase must be reckoned one of the real dangers of analysis, a fact that should not be concealed.

As may easily be understood, this condition is hardly bearable, and one would like to put an end to it as soon as possible, for the analogy with a mental derangement is too close. The essence of the most frequent form of derangement—dementia praecox or schizophrenia—consists, as is well known, in the fact that the unconscious to a large extent ejects and replaces the conscious. The unconscious is given the value of reality, being substituted for the reality function. The unconscious thoughts become audible as voices, or visible as visions, or perceptible as physical hallucinations, or they become fixed ideas of a kind that supersede reality. In a similar, although not in the same way, by the resolution of the persona of the collective psyche, the unconscious is drawn into the conscious. The difference between this state of mind and that of mental derangement consists in the fact that the unconscious is brought up by the help of the conscious analysis; at least that is the case in the beginning of analysis, when there are still strong cultural resistances against the unconscious to be overcome. Later on, after the removal of the barriers erected by time and custom, the unconscious usually proceeds, so to say, in a peremptory manner, sometimes even discharging itself in torrents into the consciousness. In this phase the analogy with mental derangement is very close. But it would only be a real mental disorder should the content of the unconscious *take the place of the conscious reality,* that is, in other words, if the contents of the unconscious were believed absolutely and without reserve. . . .

SUMMARY

A. *Psychological Material must be divided into* CONSCIOUS *and* UNCONSCIOUS *Contents.*

1. The *conscious contents* are partly *personal,* in so far as their universal validity is not recognised; and partly *impersonal,* that is, collective, in so far as their universal validity is recognised.

2. The *unconscious contents* are partly *personal,* in so far as they concern solely repressed materials of a personal nature, that have once been relatively conscious and whose universal validity is therefore not recognised when they are made conscious; partly *impersonal,* in so far as the materials concerned are recognised as *impersonal* and of purely universal validity, of whose earlier even relative consciousness we have no means of proof.

B. *The Composition of the Persona.*

1. The conscious personal contents constitute the conscious personality, the conscious ego.

2. The unconscious personal contents constitute the *self,* the unconscious or subconscious ego.

3. The conscious and unconscious contents of a personal nature constitute the persona.

C. *The Composition of the Collective Psyche.*

1. The conscious and unconscious contents of an *impersonal* or collective nature compose the psychological *non-ego,* the *image of the object.* These materials can appear analytically as projections of feeling or of opinion, but they are *a priori* collectively identical with the object-imago, that is they appear as qualities of the object, and are only *a posteriori* recognised as subjective psychological qualities.

2. The persona is that grouping of conscious and unconscious contents which is opposed as ego to the non-ego. The general comparison of personal contents of different individuals establishes their far-reaching similarity, extending even to identity, by which the *individual* nature of personal contents, and therewith of the persona, is for the most part suspended. To this extent the persona must be considered an excerpt of the collective psyche, and also a component of the collective psyche.

3. The collective psyche is therefore composed of the object-imago and the persona.

D. *What is Individual.*

1. What is individual appears partly as the principle that decides the selection and limitation of the contents that are accepted as personal.

2. What is individual is the principle by which an increasing differentiation from the collective psyche is made possible and enforced.

3. What is individual manifests itself partly as an impediment to collective accomplishment, and as a resistance against collective thinking and feeling.

4. What is individual is the uniqueness of the combination of universal (collective) psychological elements.

E. *We must divide the Conscious and Unconscious Contents into Individualistic and Collectivistic.*

1. A content is individualistic whose developing tendency is directed towards the differentiation from the collective.

2. A content is collectivistic whose developing tendency aims at universal validity.

3. There are insufficient criteria by which to designate a given content as simply individual or collective, for uniqueness is very difficult to prove, although it is a perpetually and universally recurrent phenomenon.

4. The life-line of an individual is the resultant of the individualistic and collectivistic tendency of the psychological process at any given moment.

Questions to Think About

1. Both Freud and Jung acknowledged an important association between repressed thoughts and psychological analysis. How did their views of repression differ?

2. How is the "impersonal unconscious" an extension of the personality?

3. Jung says that the "persona" is only a mask of the collective psyche suggesting a lack of individuality. Discuss the existence of a universal, collective personality and whether or not individual differences are merely a result of masks people wear to simulate individuality.

4. Jung suggests that schizophrenia may result when the unconscious ejects and replaces the conscious, hence the unconscious is given the value of reality. What might Freud say about this explanation for schizophrenia?

5. In Jung's view, what is the relationship between the "self" and conscious versus unconscious personal content?

7

The Neurotic Constitution: The Origin and Development of the Feeling of Inferiority

ALFRED ADLER

Alfred Adler (1870–1937) was born in Vienna, and was frail as a child, coming close to death on several occasions. Adler felt powerless and fearful due to his childhood frailty and his flirtations with death. He decided to become a physician to learn to defeat death. He studied medicine at the University of Vienna, graduated in 1895, and started his own practice soon thereafter. In 1902, Adler was a member of the Vienna Psychoanalytic Society and he attended some small, informal seminars with Freud. However, by 1911, disagreements between Adler and Freud became so intense that Adler resigned from his position as president of the society and began his own society, called the Society for Free Psychoanalysis. The debates with Freud and other Freudian psychoanalysts helped Adler to think through his own emerging theory of personality.

Adler titled his theory *Individual Psychology* because he firmly believed in the unique motivations of individuals and the importance of each person's perceived niche in society. Adler believed that striving for superiority is a central core of personality. He coined the terms *inferiority complex* and *superiority complex,* claiming that physical problems in early life engender feelings of inferiority that lead to later neurosis. Adler also developed a personality typology based loosely on ancient Greek notions of the bodily humors, but he is perhaps best known as someone who firmly believed in the positive, goal-oriented nature of humankind.

The facts established through my study of somatic inferiority concerned themselves with the causes, the behavior, the manifestations and altered mode of activity of inferiorily developed organs and has led me to assume the idea of "compensation through the central nervous system" with which were linked certain discussions of the subject of psychogenesis.

There came to light a remarkable relationship between somatic inferiority and psychic overcompensation, so that I gained a fundamental viewpoint, namely, that the realization of somatic inferiority by the individual becomes for him a permanent impelling force for the development of his psyche. . . .

The psychic phase of this compensation and overcompensation can only be disclosed by means of psychologic investigation and analysis.

As I have given a detailed description of organ-inferiority as the etiology of the neuroses in my former contributions, . . . I may in the present description confine myself to those points which promise a further elucidation of the relationship between somatic-inferiority and psychic compensation and which are of importance in the study of the neurotic character.

Summarizing, I lay stress on the fact that organ-inferiority, as described by me, includes the incompleteness in such organs, the frequently demonstrable

Source: Adler, A. (1917). The origin and development of the feeling of inferiority. In A. Adler, *The neurotic constitution* (pp. 1–34), (B. Glueck & J. E. Lind, Trans.). New York: Moffat, Yard and Co. (Selection is excerpted from the chapter.)

arrests of development or functional maturity, the functional failure in the post-fetal period and the fetal character of organs and systems of organs; on the other hand the accentuation of their developmental tendency in the presence of compensatory and coördinating forces and the frequent bringing about of increased functional activity. One may easily detect in every instance from observation of the child and from the anamneses of the adult that the possession of definitely inferior organs is reflected upon the psyche—and in such a way as to lower the self-esteem, to raise the child's psychological uncertainty; but it is just out of this lowered self-esteem that there arises the struggle for self-assertion which assumes forms much more intense than one would expect. As the compensated inferior organ gains in the scope of activity both qualitatively and quantitatively and acquires protective means from itself as well as from the entire organism, the predisposed child in his sense of inferiority selects out of his psychic resources expedients for the raising of his own value which are frequently striking in nature and among which may be noted as occupying the most prominent places those of a neurotic and psychotic character. . . .

Concerning the nature of the predisposition to disease dependent upon organ-inferiority there exists a unanimity of opinion. The standpoint assumed by me emphasizes more strongly than does that of other authors, the assurance of an adjustment through compensation. With the release from the maternal organism there begins for these inferior organs or systems of organs the struggle with the outside world, which must of necessity ensue and which is initiated with greater vehemence than in the more normally developed apparatus. This struggle is accompanied by greater mortality and morbidity rates. This fetal character, however, at the same time furnishes the increased possibility for compensation and over-compensation, increases the adaptability to ordinary and extraordinary resistances and assures the attainment of new and higher forms, new and higher accomplishments.

Thus the inferior organs furnish the inexhaustible material by means of which the organism continuously seeks to reach a better accord with the altered conditions of life through adaptation, repudiation, and improvement. Its hypervalency is deeply rooted in the compulsion of a constant training, in the variability and greater tendency to growth, frequently associated with inferior organs, and in the more facile evolution of the appertaining nervous and psychic complexes, on account of the introspection and concentration bestowed on them. The evils of constitutional inferiority manifest themselves in the most varied diseases and predispositions to disease. . . .

The inferior organ constantly endeavors to make a very special demand upon the interest and attention. I was able to prove in this and other contributions to what extent inferiority of an organ constantly shows its influence on the psyche in action, in thought, in dreams, in the choice of a vocation and in artistic inclinations and capabilities.

The existence of an inferior organ demands a kind of training on the part of the appertaining nerve tracts and on the part of the psychic superstructure which would render the latter active in a compensatory manner when a possibility for compensation exists. In such an event, however, we must likewise find a reënforcement in the psychic superstructure of certain allied points of contact which the inferior organ has with the outside world. . . .

The neurotic individual is derived from this sphere of uncertainty and in his childhood is under the pressure of his constitutional inferiority. In most cases this may be easily detected. In other cases the patient behaves as if he were inferior. In all cases, however, his striving and thinking are built upon the foundation of the feeling of inferiority. This feeling must always be understood in a relative sense, as the outgrowth of the individual's relation to his environment or to his strivings. He has constantly been drawing comparisons between himself and others, at first with his father, as the strongest in the family, sometimes with his mother, his brothers and sisters, later with every person with whom he comes into contact. Upon closer analysis, one finds that every child, especially the one less favored by nature, has made a careful estimate of his own value. The constitutionally inferior child, the unattractive child, the child too strictly reared, the pampered child, all of whom we may align as being predisposed to the development of a neurosis, seek more diligently than does the normal child to avoid the evils of their existence. They soon long to banish into a distant future the fate which confronts them. In order to bring this about, he, the defective child, requires an expedient which enables him to keep before his eyes a fixed picture in the vicissitudes of life and the uncertainty of his existence. He turns to the construction of this expedient. He sums up in his self-estimation all evils, considers himself incompetent, inferior, degraded, insecure. And in order to find a guiding principle he takes as a second fixed point his father or mother who endowed him with all the attributes of life.

And in adjusting this guiding principle to his thinking and acting, in his endeavors to raise himself to the level of his (all-powerful) father, even to the point of surpassing the latter, he has quite removed himself with one mighty bound from reality and is suspended in the meshes of a fiction.

Similar observations may also be made in a lesser degree among normal children. They too desire to be great, to be strong, to rule as the father, and are guided by this objective. Their conduct, their psychical and physical attitude is constantly directed towards this goal, so that one may almost detect a true imitation, an identical psychic gesture.

Example becomes the guide to the "masculine" goal, so long as the masculinity is not doubted. Should the idea of "the masculine goal" become unacceptable to girls, then there takes place a change of form of this "masculine" guiding principle. One can scarcely evaluate this phenomenon in a more correct way than by assuming that the necessary denial of the gratification of certain organic functions forces the child from the first hour of his extrauterine life into assuming a combative attitude towards his environment. . . .

In the temporary denials and discomforts which the first years of childhood bring with them, one must seek the impulse for the development of a host of common traits of character. Above all the child learns in his weakness and helplessness, in his anxiety and manifold shortcomings to value an expedient which assures him of the help and support of his relatives and guarantees their concern. In his negativistic behavior, in his obstinacy and refractoriness he often finds a gratification of his consciousness of his own powers, thus ridding himself of the painful realization of his inferiority. Both mainsprings of the child's behavior,

obstinacy and obedience, guarantee to him an accentuation of his feeling of ego-consciousness and assist him in groping his way towards the masculine goal or, as we wished to adduce before, towards the equivalent of this. The awakening self-consciousness is always being suppressed in constitutionally inferior children, their self-esteem is lowered because their capacity for gratification is much more limited. . . .

The child usually explains his difficulty by the assumption of a neglect, a slight by the parents, especially as it occurs in later children or in the youngest, occasionally even in the first born. This hostile aggression, reinforced and accentuated in constitutionally inferior children, becomes confluent with his effort to become as great and strong as the strongest and thrusts forward activities which lie at the bottom of the infantile ambition. All later trains of thought and activities of the neurotic are constructed similarly with his childhood wish phantasy. The "recurrence of the identical" (Nietzsche) is nowhere so well illustrated as in the neurotic. His feeling of inferiority in the presence of men and things, his uncertainty in the world force him to an accentuation of his guiding principles. To these he clings throughout life in order to orient himself in existence by means of his beliefs and superstitions, in order to overcome his feeling of inferiority, in order to rescue his sense of ego-consciousness, in order to possess a subterfuge to avoid a much-dreaded degradation. Never has he succeeded so well in this as during his childhood. His guiding fiction which makes him behave as if he surpassed all others may therefore, also bring about a form of conduct identical with that of the child. . . .

An individual of this type will as a rule manifest a carefully adjusted mode of behavior, exactness and pedantry, first of all, in order not to increase the great difficulties of life and secondly and principally, in order to distinguish himself from others in dress, in work, in morals, and thus acquire for himself a feeling of superiority. . . .

The egoism of neurotics, their envy, their greed, frequently unconscious, their tendency to undervalue men and things, originate in their feeling of uncertainty and serve the purpose of assuring them, of guiding them and of spurring them on. . . .

Therefore from constitutional inferiority there arises a feeling of inferiority which demands a compensation in the sense of a maximation of the ego-consciousness. From this circumstance the fiction which serves as a final purpose acquires an astonishing influence and draws all the psychic forces in its direction. Itself an outgrowth of the striving for secu-

rity, it organizes psychic preparatory measures for the purpose of guaranteeing security, among which the neurotic character as well as the functional neurosis are noticeable as prominent devices.

The guiding fiction has a simple, infantile scheme, and influences the apperception and the mechanism of memory.

_____ Questions to Think About _____

1. Are people who suffer from various physical problems in childhood doomed to suffer from psychological difficulties throughout their lives as well? How would Adler's view affect our treatment of those who are handicapped or disabled?

2. To what extent do notions of superiority as an overcompensation for inferiority apply to people in general rather than just to the physically impaired people on whom Adler focuses?

3. Other than the inferiority complex, are there other explanations that account for the behavior of people who are consistently overbearing, hostile, greedy, and egoistic?

8

The Goals of Analytic Therapy

KAREN HORNEY

Karen Horney (1885–1952) was a leading neo-analyst who challenged many of Freud's views about a world centered around the male. She proposed a theory of womb envy, which stated that rather than females' being envious of the male penis, males were unconsciously envious of the female's ability to give birth. She also put much more emphasis than Freud had on the role of culture and society in shaping personality.

Karen Danielson Horney grew up in Hamburg, Germany, at the end of the nineteenth century. Her world was filled with interpersonal struggles. She believed that her father did not love her as he loved his sons. She felt that she was unattractive and spent her life becoming intelligent instead. She grew up at a time when women had limited opportunities and yet she was one of the first women admitted into medical school. In 1901 she married Oskar Horney and had three daughters. She was always distant with her daughters, because she wanted to instill in them a sense of independence, but her child-rearing style might have lacked appropriate warmth and interest. It is now generally accepted that children struggle with their social worlds to develop their identities, but the ideal paths to self-realization are still a subject of great debate.

The goals of psychoanalysis have changed in recent years. When Freud made the astonishing discovery that symptoms, such as the paralysis of an arm or anxiety, could be eliminated by calling back to mind the traumatic experience the patient had forgotten, or, as we say, had not gotten over at the time, it was of course the aim of therapy to remove the symptoms. The next discovery Freud made was that this simple method of removing symptoms did not always work. In some cases, no individual experience could be found that was responsible for a specific physical disorder, and it seemed necessary to make a long detour and learn a great deal about the patient's life and his entire personality in order to understand the symptom and help the patient to overcome it. Freud gradually realized the fact that symptoms do not simply vanish but can only be removed if we understand the human

personality, and especially neurosis. The goal was therefore redefined as removing symptoms through an understanding of the personality. But the emphasis was still on the symptom.

The next development was that several progressive analysts noticed with surprise that there are neuroses without symptoms. It was Franz Alexander who rather naively named this discovery "character neurosis," a formulation we feel to be totally wrong today, since every neurosis is a character neurosis; but at the time, the discovery was a considerable advance. What Alexander was trying to say was that neurosis is not only a matter of symptoms but is a disorder of the personality.

We have still not overcome the focus on the symptom, however. Because an enormous number of people suffer from neuroses, it is only natural that the

Source: Horney, K. (1991). The goals of analytic therapy. *American Journal of Psychoanalysis, 51*(3), 219–226. (Translation by Andrea Dlaska of Horney's 1951 paper published in German in *Psyche*.) Reprinted by permission.

doctor should look for a short way to free patients from desperate situations, from depression, insomnia, alcoholism, or whatever the symptom may be. It gives him the feeling, justified to a certain extent, that at least he did help. The fact that short-term therapy plays such an enormous role is due to a genuine need, but it reflects a widespread ignorance among both doctors and patients.

I can illustrate this with an example. A patient who started an analysis at age 40 told me that she was engaged at the age of 21 and had suffered from such severe symptoms of fatigue that she was unable to do anything at all. It was quite natural that her doctor told her that she was simply weak and needed some rest, although this did not improve her exhaustion. Then a friend appeared who had just become acquainted with analysis, was full of enthusiasm, and said, "This is all psychological; your tiredness has to do with your doubts about your fiancé. You have some reservations with regard to marriage." Her fatigue ceased instantly, and she could climb a mountain.

This is impressive, of course, and, like short-term therapy, it helped the patient to master an obstacle. But it ignored a great many questions. Where did the ambivalent feelings toward her fiancé come from? Why was she not aware of them? Why did she never raise the question of whether she should marry that man? These would have been reasonable questions at the time. Or the question of whether her reservations only related to this specific man or would arise with every man or with every human being.

When I later analyzed this patient, deep traits of self-denial emerged behind the reservations, which appeared to have been produced by a current situation. After her marriage was dissolved, she took up a relationship of typical morbid dependence, a self-denying relationship in which she had deep feelings of being sacrificed.

This example shows that a symptom cannot be understood unless one enters more deeply into the personality. As soon as one starts asking very simple questions—Why didn't she become conscious of the conflict right away? What was the conflict? Why did she want to get married at all? Why didn't she have any doubts?—as soon as one does this one gets involved in the deep entanglements of the personality.

When we understand that the hidden traits of the overall structure contribute to this patient's symptoms, we realize that symptoms are not isolated but that a neurosis is a disorder of the personality as a whole. The goal of therapy increasingly shifts to an embracing of the entire personality.

In other areas of medicine the doctor is usually not contented with the removal of a symptom. He will hardly be satisfied to get rid of a cough without trying to cure its cause. Therefore, the objection that the personality is not the concern of analysis cannot really be sustained, unless one clearly contends that the task of the doctor and of modern psychoanalytic therapy merely lies in achieving a symptomatic cure. We realize that our conception of the goals of therapy depends on our understanding not only of neurosis but also on our Weltanschauung, i.e., our conception of our profession.

When we realized that neurosis basically is a process in which human relationships are disturbed, the goal of therapy emerged as the improvement of human relationships. This was a much more complex goal than relieving symptoms, since human relationships are decidedly the most important part of life. But what does improvement of human relationships mean? We can say, for instance, that a person who is either too dependent, or too dominating, or too aggressive, or who exploits other people can be considered improved if we can help him to view relationships with others on a basis of mutual respect and to learn to give something. Similarly, a patient who is defensively aggressive toward others and to whom we open the possibility of friendly feelings and common goals can be considered improved. It would be an improvement if a person whose relationships are mainly determined by habitual intimidation of others, habitual friendliness, habitual praise, or distancing through politeness—all compulsive strategies—could be helped again to spontaneous feelings. By improvement we mean, then, turning such relationships into something more constructive.

Probing deeper, we realize that such disorders in human relationships are more or less determined by conflicts. A person feels a strong need to distance himself from others but he may also desire affection. Or, a person feels that he has to fight and subject everybody, but he also needs warmth. We see the goal of therapy as helping people to resolve conflicts of this kind and to achieve a harmony of feelings and a sense of inner integration. If we try to help a person to have direct and wholehearted feelings for others, to replace deliberate or automatic strategies with spontaneity, we say that we are helping the person to find himself.

We end up with three objectives: reorientation, constructive integration, and finding oneself. This leads to the fourth concern, which is a person's relationship with himself. In a way, of course, this was included when we talked of a person's relationships with others, since no dividing line can be drawn between a person's relationships with others and with himself. They are connected with each other and inseparable, but the emphasis may lie on the one side or the other. We are gradually beginning to examine intrapsychic processes more closely. I have to condense here considerably.

What we see on the surface are a person's feelings toward himself, which usually vary considerably. At times, someone may feel that he is the most brilliant and generous person ever, but at other times he may feel just as profoundly that he is a complete idiot. He can consider himself the most glorious lover and feel it to be the utmost cruelty to reject a woman who approaches him because it deprives her of the unique experience of himself; but he may also feel that a girl who loves him can only be despicable, or he may feel safe only with strumpets. Such waverings may be conscious with some people, hidden with others, but they are always there.

In neurosis a process sets in regularly in which a person despairs because he feels lost, divided, inferior, and takes refuge in fantasy. He begins to glorify himself and feels that, like a personified god, he is, or should be, equipped with infinite power and perfection, that he is as good as St. Francis or has absolute courage. If he does not possess absolute courage, he considers himself a downright coward. In other words, by building his pedestal so high, by idealizing himself in such a fantastic way, by raising his standard to an impossible level, he is beginning to turn against himself as he really is. He begins to hate and despise himself the way he happens to be. If this self-hate and self-contempt get the upper hand, he does indeed feel

guilty, stupid, depraved, hopeless, whereas the minute the self-glorification gets the upper hand he feels on top of the world.

We can summarize this process with the titles of two books: *Man Against Himself* by Menninger, and *Man for Himself* by Fromm. Man turns against himself with the whole bitterness of his worst enemy. If I am not capable of writing a brilliant article on a subject I haven't even thought about, I am simply good for nothing. If my child is ill and I do not devote every minute to him without thinking of anything else, I am simply a miserable mother. As Rashkolnikov says, "If I am not as ruthless as Napoleon who could kill without qualms, if I cannot slay one poor pawnbroker, I am good for nothing and a damned coward."

One might expect that at this point the goals of therapy should be to help a person surrender such illusions and realize that, in reality, he is claiming to be like god, and at the same time, to make him aware of his self-hate, so that he finally can see and accept himself as the person he is. One cannot simply attack the patient's illusions, however. If one treated a patient in this way, showed him outright where his illusions lay, and told him that he had to surrender them in order to be happy, he might say, if he is the more arrogant type, "I don't know, are you crazy or am I?" There would even be some validity in this question, for if he really accepted what the doctor told him, he might break down immediately and fall into an abyss of self-contempt. If he takes the suggestions of the analyst seriously there is also the possibility that the patient will fall prey to something I call "insincere resignation." "All right, I realize I'm not exactly a genius, at least not without effort; it seems I have to accept myself on a lower level." This means, in effect, that he is settling for a "swallow the bitter pill" attitude. "Of course I would like to live these wonderful ideals, but since you tell me that they are not realistic, well, I'll simply give them up."

We should ask ourselves why a direct approach is not possible. I found an answer to this question in O'Neill's play *The Ice Man Cometh,* in which a man meets some drunks in an inn and tells them, "These are all illusions, you would like to give them up yourselves; show us what you can do, lead an active life." But they cannot do it and only feel even more miserable. For these illusions are not simply phantoms. The patient cannot give them up before he has become much stronger without doing damage to himself.

I would like to cite an old German fairytale to illustrate this process from a slightly different angle. It describes a little fir tree who wants to have golden leaves. It gets them, but in the night they are stolen by robbers. The tree thinks that his idea was no good and wishes for glass leaves. He gets them, but a storm breaks them all. This wasn't right either, says the tree, and now I wish for leaves like a maple's, but in no event my own. So he gets the green leaves, but a goat eats them all. Finally, the little tree decides that it was best to simply be a fir tree.

Here you have a glorification of the gold and glass leaves, which the tree believes he wants to have because they are something better. He wants to be something different from what he really is, for in reality he happens to be a fir tree, and only as a fir tree can he grow. Even without the robbers, the goats, the storms, a fir tree with golden leaves would perish as a fir tree. His real self would be destroyed in the process.

In our own words, this means that if we begin to idealize ourselves, if we consider ourselves outstanding, godlike, more important than befits us, if we want to be something we are not, without knowing it, we lose our own self. From the perspective of this understanding of the neurotic process, it is the goal of therapy to help a person to find his own self, to rediscover his own feelings, his wishes, what he really believes—to help him to make his own decisions; for only if he finds himself has he a chance to grow and fulfill himself.

If we suggest this to the patient in general terms, he will probably say, "Right, that's exactly what I want, to be myself." But this would again be a deception. Remember Peer Gynt who constantly talks about being "himself," while in reality he is only chasing the phantom of his self-glorification. He becomes emperor of the Sahara, where he solves the enigmas of the Sphinx, but he ends up in the madhouse, having destroyed his whole life. It is right that one should wish to be oneself, but one has to wish for the right thing. Initially no neurotic can achieve that; he mainly lives on his neurotic pride and his illusions. The way to his real self is painful, for it is not only full of

obstacles and disruptions but is also full of confusing and diverting delusions.

The neurotic has to do a number of things simultaneously in order to gradually reach himself. First, he has to experience and understand all the false values on which his pride is founded. Then he has to realize what he can and cannot do. He has to understand, for instance, that he has talents for real achievements, but that he has to develop his abilities before he can do very much with them. In the past, he has neglected to recognize his real capacities and to develop them, but now their discovery and development must become genuinely desirable for him.

He must also realize through analysis that he does not recognize his own feelings and never has recognized them, that he only feels what he thinks he ought to feel, and that this has made him insecure, has deprived him of vitality, and has robbed his feelings of intensity and depth. He must come to understand that nothing in life is more desirable than genuinely experiencing his real feelings in all their intensity. He has only believed what others believed and has never asked himself, "What do I really believe?" He must discover that finding out what he really believes is an important part of his growth. He may also realize that he was too proud ever to ask for anything. He may originally have called that modesty, but he now understands that this was not a good method, since this way one never learns from one's experiences. To profit from one's experiences it is necessary to admit to one's needs and imperfections. He may have believed that he only reproached himself, condemned himself, and had guilty feelings in order to demonstrate the loftiness of his moral standards. But now he has to realize that he has not really recognized his imperfections and that he has never attempted to overcome them in a constructive way.

This process gradually undermines false pride while making clear what the self lacked so far: real emotions, real beliefs, and personal decisions. The patient recognizes that real emotions or the effort to achieve them are the really desirable thing. False positions are slowly surrendered and a genuine insight into the self takes their place; there is now strength of feeling, a knowledge of what he wants, and the ability to take responsibility. The patient no longer considers it a loss to detach himself from his illusions, for now he knows that striving to be his real self is the only productive way of living.

I would like to illuminate the same issue from another perspective. One may ask whether one should really say with Socrates that the goal of analysis is to know yourself. I would argue that this depends on what one means by self-knowledge. We can shed some light on this, if we differentiate between the actual self and what William James calls the real self. The actual self is everything I am, my aggressions, my false pride, my vindictiveness. At first, the patient cannot see this, since he will admit to certain traits he is proud of, according to his type, while he will deny others. An arrogant person will admit to his vindictiveness, which he will call a sense of justice, while he will deny his need for sympathy or affection and his great vulnerability. The dependent type will admit to self-denying traits with comparative ease, will gladly take the part of a martyr, a victim, or assume the dependent attitude in a love relationship; but he will refuse to own up to vindictiveness, pride, ambition, or competitive feelings: "Oh no, that's not like me." Some patients do this on a large scale. What they like is their self, and the rest is their neurosis. One patient said, "The idealized image is I, the rest is unconscious."

The patient must learn to recognize what he is really like, but it is *not* enough to know about oneself without taking a firm viewpoint or reorienting oneself. In reality, this never happens anyway, for the more a person knows about himself, the more he is forced to differentiate between good and evil. The more he knows, the more unconditionally he has to decide for the constructive forces of his real self. One might say in brief, "For the patient, the goal of analysis is to learn to know himself as he is (actual self) in order to reorient himself and to make finding his real self a possibility." It is difficult to describe the nature of the real self. It is something one can only describe from experience; something within us that can decide, accept, and discard, that can want something, have spontaneous feelings, and exercise willpower. We can call it constructive energy—something that holds us together.

Every neurotic is aware of certain aspects of himself and unaware of others. Because he denies certain parts of himself, according to the nature of his disease,

he only lives a part of himself. One patient expressed it as follows: "I might be compared to a person whose one lung does not function at all, while three quarters of the other is ill." It is always surprising to see with how little a person can still function—but only as long as things go smoothly. Any situation that taxes the patient can lead to a severe and unexpected breakdown.

A neurotic does not perceive himself as a whole organism, as a unity, but tends to feel painfully divided. He manages, in one way or other, to create a pseudosolution in order not to feel this division constantly, a pseudofeeling of unity that allows him to live. Pseudosolutions can be of very different kinds. One solution is seclusion—I am thinking here of people who live tolerably well, who seem to lack nothing as long as they keep their distance from others and, I would like to add, from themselves. This is one of the neurotic solutions that allows a partial functioning without the person being aware of how divided he really is. Others find their neurotic solution in "love," which in this case means a dependent relationship. The person expects love to provide all the answers to his problems and worries, to provide an integration through merger with another. Others look for their solution in ambition, yet others simply in fantasy. We must not make light of these solutions, for while they lead the person deeper and deeper into neurosis, they at least allow him to function. The fact that such pseudosolutions can develop also shows that a constructive force is at work that aims at integration. It is not very useful in this form, since it leaves the neurotic divided into compulsive traits; but it is there and is a powerful drive that we can use in therapy. If we try again to define the goals of our work when we have realized that the neurotic lives only in a divided way and not with his whole self, we may say, "The goal of psychoanalysis is integration and unity."

Integration, finding oneself, and the ability for growth are constructive forces. They are extremely strong drives in our selves, maybe the strongest, the only ones that really count. Therapy depends on these strong constructive drives, and even the most skilled analyst would get nowhere without them. It is a goal and a means of therapy to mobilize and strengthen these forces, for only with their help can a person overcome the retarding forces within himself. If the analyst tries to bring the patient closer to himself, he is basically doing no more and, in a way, even less than the somatic doctor, who has the means of the clinic at his disposal, while in analysis the actual healing forces lie in the patient himself. This is a fact of which by no means every analyst is aware. I cannot bring about the growth of the patient myself, any more than he can bring about mine. The analyst can make suggestions here and there, he can make the patient aware of things, he can foster the patient's wish to be himself, but the patient must do the growing.

In conclusion, let us return to Ibsen's Peer Gynt, a man who shouts from every roof top that he is "himself," that he wants to be "himself" all his life. But Peer Gynt only wants to be self-sufficient, which, to him, implies a godlike self-sufficiency, a perfection without any needs. Ibsen shows very clearly that this is not human. Peer Gynt never was himself, for in that case he would have had another goal. "Be true to yourself" does not mean "be self-sufficient," for self-sufficiency is at once too much and too little for a human being.

Questions to Think About

1. Horney states that her goal in therapy and Freud's goal in therapy have different objectives. What are the modern implications?

2. How does Horney's view of neurosis as a disturbance in human relationships compare with Freud's view of neurosis?

3. Is there any empirical evidence or can there be any empirical evidence showing that all neurotic behavior stems from a person's loss of the real self?

4. What might be gained and what might be lost when a patient undergoing therapy rejects the idealized self in favor of the real self?

5. What are the implications for women of viewing psychological development as centered around the penis, as Freud asserted? What are the implications for understanding personality of focusing more on the culture, as Horney suggests?

9

The Life Cycle: Epigenesis of Identity

ERIK H. ERIKSON

With his focus on identity, Erik Erikson (1902–1994) worked squarely within the neo-analytic (ego) perspective on personality. Erikson faced his own identity challenges in childhood. His Scandinavian birthfather abandoned Erik before he was born, and Erik was raised by his mother and Jewish stepfather. His stepfather was a physician and hoped that Erik would follow in his footsteps, but Erik first became an artist, and then became interested in psychoanalysis. He underwent psychoanalytic training with Sigmund Freud's daughter, Anna Freud. When the Nazis came to power in Germany, Erik moved to the United States and changed his name from Erik Homburger to Erik H. Erikson.

Building on certain psychoanalytic views but rejecting others, Erikson believed that each of us must struggle with the demands of our emotions and the pressures of the environment. Erikson was among the first to propose a life long, developmental theory of self-identity. He thus moved psychoanalytic thought beyond childhood, and opened the theoretical possibility of identity crises in adulthood. In this selection, Erikson describes his idea that Identity emerges in stages through the successful negotiation of a series of conflicts or crises.

Among the indispensable co-ordinates of identity is that of the life cycle, for we assume that not until adolescence does the individual develop the prerequisites in physiological growth, mental maturation, and social responsibility to experience and pass through the crisis of identity. We may, in fact, speak of the identity crisis as the psychosocial aspect of adolescing. Nor could this stage be passed without identity having found a form which will decisively determine later life.

Let us, once more, start out from Freud's far-reaching discovery that neurotic conflict is not very different in content from the "normative" conflicts which every child must live through in his childhood, and the residues of which every adult carries with him in the recesses of his personality. For man, in order to remain psychologically alive, constantly re-resolves these conflicts just as his body unceasingly combats the encroachment of physical deterioration. However,

since I cannot accept the conclusion that just to be alive, or not to be sick, means to be healthy, or, as I would prefer to say in matters of personality, *vital,* I must have recourse to a few concepts which are not part of the official terminology of my field.

I shall present human growth from the point of view of the conflicts, inner and outer, which the vital personality weathers, re-emerging from each crisis with an increased sense of inner unity, with an increase of good judgment, and an increase in the capacity "to do well" according to his own standards and to the standards of those who are significant to him. The use of the words "to do well" of course points up the whole question of cultural relativity. Those who are significant to a man may think he is doing well when he "does some good" or when he "does well" in the sense of acquiring possessions; when he is doing well in the sense of learning new skills and new

Source: Erikson, E. (1968). The life cycle: Epigenesis of identity. In E. Erikson, *Identity, youth, and crisis.*
New York: W. W. Norton. Copyright © 1968 by W. W. Norton & Company, Inc. Used by permission of
W. W. Norton & Company, Inc. (Selection is pp. 91–96.)

knowledge or when he is not much more than just get-ting along; when he learns to conform all around or to rebel significantly; when he is merely free from neu-rotic symptoms or manages to contain within his vi-tality all manner of profound conflict.

There are many formulations of what constitutes a "healthy" personality in an adult. But if we take up only one—in this case, Marie Jahoda's definition, according to which a healthy personality *actively mas-ters* his environment, shows a certain *unity of person-ality,* and is able to *perceive* the world and himself *correctly*—it is clear that all of these criteria are rela-tive to the child's cognitive and social development. In fact, we may say that childhood is defined by their initial absence and by their gradual development in complex steps of increasing differentiation. How, then, does a vital personality grow or, as it were, accrue from the successive stages of the increasing capacity to adapt to life's necessities—with some vital enthu-siasm to spare?

Whenever we try to understand growth, it is well to remember the *epigenetic principle* which is derived from the growth of organisms *in utero.* Somewhat gen-eralized, this principle states that anything that grows has a ground plan, and that out of this ground plan the parts arise, each part having its time of special ascen-dancy, until all parts have arisen to form a functioning whole. This, obviously, is true for fetal development where each part of the organism has its critical time of ascendance or danger of defect. At birth the baby leaves the chemical exchange of the womb for the so-cial exchange system of his society, where his gradu-ally increasing capacities meet the opportunities and limitations of his culture. How the maturing organism continues to unfold, not by developing new organs but by means of a prescribed sequence of locomotor, sen-sory, and social capacities, is described in the child-development literature. As pointed out, psychoanalysis has given us an understanding of the more idiosyn-cratic experiences, and especially the inner conflicts, which constitute the manner in which an individual be-comes a distinct personality. But here, too, it is impor-tant to realize that in the sequence of his most personal experiences the healthy child, given a reasonable amount of proper guidance, can be trusted to obey inner laws of development, laws which create a suc-cession of potentialities for significant interaction with those persons who tend and respond to him and those institutions which are ready for him. While such inter-action varies from culture to culture, it must remain within "the proper rate and the proper sequence" which governs all epigenesis. Personality, therefore, can be said to develop according to steps predetermined in the human organism's readiness to be driven toward, to be aware of, and to interact with a widening radius of sig-nificant individuals and institutions.

It is for this reason that, in the presentation of stages in the development of the personality, we employ an epi-genetic diagram analogous to the one employed in *Childhood and Society* for an analysis of Freud's psy-chosexual stages. It is, in fact, an implicit purpose of this presentation to bridge the theory of infantile sexuality (without repeating it here in detail) and our knowledge of the child's physical and social growth.

The diagram is presented [on p. 53]. The double-lined squares signify both a sequence of stages and a gradual development of component parts; in other words, the diagram formalizes a progression through time of a differentiation of parts. This indicates (1) that each item of the vital personality to be discussed is sys-tematically related to all others, and that they all depend on the proper development in the proper sequence of each item; and (2) that each item exists in some form before "its" decisive and critical time normally arrives.

If I say, for example, that a sense of basic trust is the first component of mental vitality to develop in life, a sense of autonomous will the second, and a sense of initiative the third, the diagram expresses a number of fundamental relations that exist among the three com-ponents, as well as a few fundamental facts for each.

Each comes to its ascendance, meets its crisis, and finds its lasting solution in ways to be described here, toward the end of the stages mentioned. All of them exist in the beginning in some form, although we do not make a point of this fact, and we shall not confuse things by calling these components different names at earlier or later stages. A baby may show something like "autonomy" from the beginning, for example, in the particular way in which he angrily tries to wriggle his hand free when tightly held. How-ever, under normal conditions, it is not until the sec-ond year that he begins to experience the whole

	1	2	3	4	5	6	7	8
VIII								INTEGRITY vs. DESPAIR
VII							GENERATIVITY vs. STAGNATION	
VI						INTIMACY vs. ISOLATION		
V	Temporal Perspective vs. Time Confusion	Self-Certainty vs. Self-Consciousness	Role Experimentation vs. Role Fixation	Apprenticeship vs. Work Paralysis	IDENTITY vs. IDENTITY CONFUSION	Sexual Polarization vs. Bisexual Confusion	Leader- and Followership vs. Authority Confusion	Ideological Commitment vs. Confusion of Values
IV				INDUSTRY vs. INFERIORITY	Task Identification vs. Sense of Futility			
III			INITIATIVE vs. GUILT		Anticipation of Roles vs. Role Inhibition			
II		AUTONOMY vs. SHAME, DOUBT			Will to Be Oneself vs. Self-Doubt			
I	TRUST vs. MISTRUST				Mutual Recognition vs. Autistic Isolation			

critical alternative between being an autonomous crea-ture and being a dependent one, and it is not until then that he is ready for a specifically new encounter with his environment. The environment, in turn, now feels called upon to convey to him its particular ideas and concepts of autonomy in ways decisively contributing to his personal character, his relative efficiency, and the strength of his vitality.

It is this encounter, together with the resulting cri-sis, which is to be described for each stage. Each stage becomes a crisis because incipient growth and aware-ness in a new part function go together with a shift in instinctual energy and yet also cause a specific vulner-ability in that part. One of the most difficult questions to decide, therefore, is whether or not a child at a given stage is weak or strong. Perhaps it would be best to say that he is always vulnerable in some respects and com-pletely oblivious and insensitive in others, but that at the same time he is unbelievably persistent in the same respects in which he is vulnerable. It must be added that the baby's weakness gives him power; out of his very dependence and weakness he makes signs to which his environment, if it is guided well by a re-sponsiveness combining "instinctive" and traditional patterns, is peculiarly sensitive. A baby's presence ex-erts a consistent and persistent domination over the outer and inner lives of every member of a household. Because these members must reorient themselves to accommodate his presence, they must also grow as in-dividuals and as a group. It is as true to say that babies control and bring up their families as it is to say the converse. A family can bring up a baby only by being brought up by him. His growth consists of a series of challenges to them to serve his newly developing po-tentialities for social interaction.

Each successive step, then, is a potential crisis be-cause of a radical change in perspective. Crisis is used here in a developmental sense to connote not a threat of catastrophe, but a turning point, a crucial period of increased vulnerability and heightened potential, and therefore, the ontogenetic source of generational strength and maladjustment. The most radical change of all, from intrauterine to extrauterine life, comes at the very beginning of life. But in postnatal existence, too, such radical adjustments of perspective as lying relaxed, sitting firmly, and running fast must all be ac-complished in their own good time. With them, the in-terpersonal perspective also changes rapidly and often radically, as is testified by the proximity in time of such opposites as "not letting mother out of sight" and "wanting to be independent." Thus, different capaci-ties use different opportunities to become full-grown components of the ever-new configuration that is the growing personality.

REFERENCES

Jahoda, M. (1950). Toward a social psychology of mental health. In M. J. E. Benn (Ed.), *Symposium on the healthy personality.* New York: Josiah Macy, Jr. Foun-dation.

Erikson, Erik H. (1963). *Childhood and society* (2nd ed.). New York: W. W. Norton.

Questions to Think About

1. How important are inner motivations compared to environmental factors in the successful movement through the stages of life? For example, would a child be able to develop an autonomous self if the caregiver was very protective and controlling?

2. Is it possible for a person to move on to start a new stage of development without having completed a prior stage?

3. Erikson claimed that people who are mentally healthy or "normal" go through conflicts and inner crises as they develop. If this is the case, then how can we tell if a teenager or young adult is going through a normal developmental challenge or is facing a crisis that requires intervention?

4. What are some key factors that promote or signify the completion of one stage and the starting of a new one?

10

The Trouble with Change:
Self-Verification and Allegiance to the Self

WILLIAM B. SWANN, JR.

William B. Swann, Jr. (1952–) was trained as a social psychologist, and has had a long-standing interest in identity and the self. Much of his work straddles the fields of personality and social psychology, focused on how aspects of the self influence interpersonal relationships. He has been on the faculty at the University of Texas for many years, and his work has been very heavily cited by researchers in social psychology, personality psychology, and organizational behavior. The selection below describes and explains a paradoxical phenomenon—a person will often prefer negative feedback and unfavorable evaluations over positive ones, if the negative information better matches the person's view of him- or herself.

For Ms. W suffering and victimization were in some respects preferable to kindness and concern. Ms. W not only misperceived that Mr. S was unfaithful but also resisted any information that contradicted her misperception and actively sought verification that he was unfaithful. The better he treated her the more depressed and pessimistic she became [for] she was threatened by a caring and loving partner. She accepted her past abuse as an appropriate reflection of her worth. A challenge to this self-image was a challenge to how she adapted and coped with her victimization (Widiger, 1988, p. 821).

The responses of Ms. W seem paradoxical because they defy the widespread conviction that all people possess a deep-seated need for praise and adulation. It turns out that although people with negative self-views do at some level desire praise and adoration, they also want *self-verification* in the form of evaluations that confirm and validate their self-views. This desire for self-confirmation appears to be an exceedingly general one, one that shapes the lives of all of us, whether we have high or low self-esteem. In fact, it does not matter whether people's self-views are positive or negative, well-founded or misplaced, or based on something that happened during the previous year or in the distant past. Once people become confident of their self-views, they rely on these self-views to predict the reactions of others, to guide behavior, and to organize their conceptions of reality (e.g., Mead, 1934). Because self-views must be stable to serve these vital functions, people work to verify and confirm them (e.g., Aronson, 1968, Secord & Backman, 1965, Swann, 1983, 1996). These self-verification strivings may operate consciously or nonconsciously and may take several distinct forms.

FORMS OF SELF-VERIFICATION

An especially important form of self-verification occurs when people choose partners who see them as

Source: Swann, W. B., Jr. (1997). The trouble with change: Self-verification and allegiance to the self. *Psychological Science, 8*(3), 177–180. Reprinted by permission.

Editor's note: All citations in the text of this selection have been left intact from the original, but the list of references includes only those sources that are the most relevant and important. Readers wishing to follow any of the other citations can find the full references in the original work or in an online database.

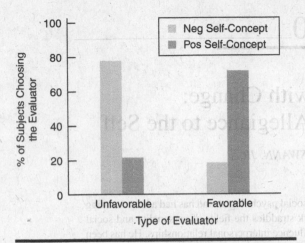

FIGURE 1   Preferences for favorable versus unfavorable interaction partners among people with positive (pos) versus negative (neg) self-concepts. The data on which this figure is based are from Swann, Stein-Seroussi, and Giesler (1992).

they see themselves, thereby creating social environments that are likely to support their self-views. In one study, for example, we asked people with positive and negative self-views whether they would prefer to interact with evaluators who had favorable or unfavorable impressions of them. As can be seen in Figure 1, people with positive self-views preferred favorable partners, and people with negative self-views preferred unfavorable partners (e.g., Swann, Stein-Seroussi, & Giesler, 1992).

More than a dozen replications in different laboratories using diverse methodologies have left little doubt that people with negative self-views seek unfavorable feedback and partners (e.g., Hixon & Swann, 1993, Robinson & Smith-Lovin, 1992, Swann, Hixon, Stein-Seroussi, & Gilbert, 1990, Swann, Pelham, & Krull, 1989, Swann, Wenzlaff, Krull, & Pelham, 1992). Males and females display this propensity to an equal degree, irregardless of the degree to which the self-views are changeable or whether they are associated with specific qualities (intelligence, sociability, dominance) or global self-worth (self-esteem, depression). Similarly, people prefer to interact with self-verifying partners even if presented with the alternative of participating in a different experiment (Swann,

Wenzlaff, & Tafarodi, 1992). Finally, people are particularly likely to seek self-verifying evaluations if their self-views are extreme and firmly held (e.g., Pelham & Swann, 1994, Swann, Pelham, & Chidester, 1988, Swann & Ely, 1984). Clinically depressed persons, for example, are more likely to seek negative evaluations than people with low self-esteem, presumably because depressives are thoroughly convinced that they are worthless (Giesler, Josephs, & Swann, 1996).

People's efforts to verify their negative self-views should not be confused with masochism. For example, rather than savoring unfavorable evaluations (as one might expect masochists to do), people with negative self-views are intensely ambivalent about such evaluations. In choosing a negative evaluator in one study (Swann, Stein-Seroussi, & Giesler, 1992), one person with low esteem noted

I like the [favorable] evaluation but I am not sure that it is ah, correct. Maybe it sounds good but [the unfavorable evaluator] seems to know more about me. So I'll choose [the unfavorable evaluator]

The thoughts that give rise to such ambivalence emerge sequentially. Upon receiving and categorizing positive feedback, people are immediately drawn to it, regardless of their self-views. A preference for self-confirming feedback emerges later when people access their self-views and compare these self-views to feedback (for a further discussion of the mechanisms that seem to underlie self-verification effects, see Swann, 1996, pp. 55–69).

The foregoing analysis implies that any procedure that prevents people from engaging in the comparison process that gives rise to self-verification strivings should cause people with negative self-views to prefer favorable appraisals. In support of this proposition, when my colleagues and I (Swann et al., 1990) had some people choose an interaction partner while they were deprived of cognitive resources (by rushing their decision or having them rehearse a phone number), we found that people with negative self-views were less inclined to self-verify (i.e., choose a partner who appraised them unfavorably). Furthermore, after participants were no longer deprived of cognitive resources, they repudiated their earlier choices in favor of self-verifying ones. Such findings suggest that when people with negative self-views choose unfavorable feedback over favorable feedback, it is because their desire for self-verifying unfavorable feedback overrides their desire for favorable feedback.[1]

Recent work indicates that if, despite their attempts to acquire self-verifying feedback, people receive doses of self-discrepant feedback that cannot be readily dismissed, they become anxious (Pinel & Swann, 1996). In extreme cases, people may experience what Kohut (1984) referred to as disintegration anxiety, a sinking feeling that something is terribly wrong accompanied by severe disorientation and a sense of emptiness, incoherence, and worthlessness.

In light of the obvious aversiveness of disintegration anxiety, it is not surprising that people who receive disconfirming feedback take steps to counter it. For example, when people suspect that others perceive them as being more or less likable than they perceive themselves to be, they strive to bring the partners' evaluations into harmony with their self-views, even if (in the case of people with low self-esteem) this means lowering the partners' evaluations (e.g., Swann & Read, 1981, Study 2). Such compensatory activity, in turn, stabilizes people's self-views against self-discrepant feedback. In one study, for instance, people who had an opportunity to resist a challenge to their self-views by "setting the evaluator straight" were less likely to experience change in their self-views than those who had no opportunity to correct the evaluator (e.g., Swann & Hill, 1982).

Should the foregoing strategies fail to produce self-confirming social worlds, people may withdraw from the relationships in which they are receiving disconfirming feedback. For example, if people wind up in marriages in which their spouses perceive them more (or less) favorably than they perceive themselves,

they become less intimate with those spouses (Ritts & Stein, 1995, Swann, De La Ronde, & Hixon, 1994).

If self-discrepant feedback is unavoidable, people may construct the illusion of self-confirming worlds by "seeing" more support for their self-views than actually exists. For example, just as people with positive self-views spend the longest time scrutinizing what someone says about them when they expect the remarks will be favorable, those with negative self-views spend the longest time scrutinizing when they expect the remarks will be unfavorable (e.g., Swann & Read, 1981, Study 1). A parallel phenomenon emerges when researchers examine what people remember about the evaluations they receive. Just as people with positive self-views remember more favorable than unfavorable statements that have been made about them, people with negative self-views remember more unfavorable than favorable statements (e.g., Swann & Read, 1981, Study 3).

And if these attentional and memorial processes are not enough to insulate people against evaluations that challenge their self-views, people may nullify discrepant evaluations by selectively dismissing incongruent feedback. For example, people express more confidence in the perceptiveness of evaluators whose appraisals confirm their self-conceptions (e.g., Shrauger & Lund, 1975).

In conjunction with the processes already outlined, such selective dismissal of challenging feedback may systematically skew people's perceptions of reality, encouraging them to conclude that their social worlds are far more supportive of their self-views than is warranted. Although these processes may stabilize people's self-views and foster feelings of coherence and predictability, they are also likely to impede positive psychological change.

IMPLICATIONS OF SELF-VERIFICATION PROCESSES FOR THERAPY

Imagine a woman who seeks therapy in the hope of removing the self-doubt that has plagued her since her youth. Although the therapist may succeed to bringing her to acknowledge and derive a feeling of pride from her strengths, she may also discover that these positive self-views are undone when she returns home to a husband who is contemptuous of her. Such a scenario

---

[1.]The second stage that gives rise to self-verification strivings may later be overridden during a third stage in which people's responses are based on a cost-benefit analysis of characteristics of the feedback, their self-views, and the social context. Hence there appear to be at least three distinct phases in people's reactions to feedback: an initial phase characterized by a preference for positive feedback, a second phase characterized by a preference for congruent feedback, and a final phase during which people systematically analyze the options available to them and behave so as to maximize their benefits and minimize their costs. For a further discussion, see Swann and Schroeder (1995).

is not just hypothetical. In one study, Predmore and I invited couples to the laboratory and seated partners in a room together. Some intimates perceived their partner congruently and some perceived their partner less congruently. At a key point in the procedure, we gave one member of each couple incongruent feedback. When we later measured how much people's self-views changed in the direction of the feedback, we found that participants were relatively impervious to the feedback if they were sitting with an intimate who saw them congruently. This tendency for congruent relationship partners to insulate one another against challenging feedback was equally apparent whether their self-views were positive or negative (Swann & Predmore, 1985).

Such evidence suggests an important addendum to Mark Twain's adage "A man cannot be comfortable without his own approval." To establish and sustain positive self-views, people must not only gain their own approval, they must also gain the approval and support of certain key interaction partners, including friends, co-workers, lovers, and relatives. In this sense, self-views are not merely psychological structures that exist inside people, as their hearts, lungs, or livers do; rather, through people's interactions, their self-views become externalized into the social worlds that they construct around themselves. As a result, when patients enter therapy in the hope of improving their self-views, their therapists' efforts to convince them that they are lovable and competent may be undone when they return home to lovers or family members who dismiss them. And if therapists do manage to instill a sense of self-worth that is resilient against challenges, patients' partners may respond by encouraging the patients to revert back to their former selves, withdraw from therapy, or both (e.g., Kerr, 1981, Wachtel & Wachtel, 1986).

But intimates who have unfavorable impressions of their partners may do more than stabilize their partners' negative self-views. Because intimates tend to assume that their partners' shortcomings reflect on *them,* they may be highly intolerant of such shortcomings and actively reject partners whom they perceive to suffer from such short-comings (e.g., Swann et al., 1994). This means that when people with negative self-views choose intimates who see them as they

see themselves, they increase the chance that their intimates will reject them in a general way. Such rejecting intimates may even go so far as to verbally and physically abuse them. Women with low self-esteem seem to be particularly apt to marry men who are high in negative instrumentality (i.e., who are hostile, egotistical, dictatorial, arrogant). Women involved with such men are especially apt to report being physically abused (Buckner & Swann, 1995).

The therapeutic context may provide one way out of this conundrum. Because therapists do not feel that the shortcomings of their patients reflect on them, therapists are in a good position to validate their patients' shortcomings (i.e., provide negative feedback) in a supportive and accepting context. When administered in such a context, negative feedback may actually be beneficial. Finn and Tonsager (1992), for example, established warm and supportive relationships with patients and then gave those patients feedback that confirmed their self-views. Two weeks later, patients who had received congruent feedback displayed better psychological functioning and higher self-esteem than a no-feedback control group—despite the fact that the congruent feedback was sometimes decidedly negative (e.g., "you are depressed, thought disordered, angry, obsessional"). Patients seemed to benefit enormously from the perception that "you seem to know all my shortcomings but still like me."

Why are confirming, negative evaluations beneficial? One reason is that congruent feedback may increase people's perceptions that they are competent in at least one sphere, knowing themselves. This realization may foster a feeling of psycho-epistemological competence, a sense of mastery and heightened perceptions of predictability and control—perceptions that may reduce anxiety. In addition, being understood by a therapist may reduce feelings of alienation, for it tells patients that someone thought enough of them to learn who they are. For these and related reasons, when provided in a supportive context, self-verifying feedback may have beneficial effects, even when it is negative (see also Linehan, [1997]).

Another approach that therapists may use is to employ the self-verification strivings of patients in the service of changing their self-views. In one study, for instance, my colleagues and I capitalized on the tendency for people to resist feedback that disconfirms their self-views. We asked people questions that were so conservative (e.g., "Why do you think men always make better bosses than women?") that even staunch conservatives resisted the premises inherent in the questions. Upon observing themselves take a somewhat liberal position, these conservative participants adjusted their attitudes in a liberal direction (Swann et al., 1988). This effect is conceptually related to *paradoxical* techniques in which therapists impute to patients qualities that are more extreme than the patients' actual qualities (e.g., characterizing an unassertive person as a complete doormat) in the hope that the patients will behaviorally resist the innuendo (e.g., become more assertive) and adopt corresponding self-views (e.g., Watzlawick, Weakland, & Fisch, 1974).

There are, of course, additional strategies that may be exploited in attempting to change people's self-views. The more general point here, however, is that therapists who are interested in changing self-views should recognize that people's desire for positive evaluations may sometimes be overridden by a desire for self-verification. The desire for self-verification may compel people to work to maintain their positive—and negative—self-views by embracing confirming feedback, eschewing disconfirming feedback, and surrounding themselves with friends, intimates, and associates who act as accomplices in maintaining their self-views. Research on the nature, underpinnings, and boundary conditions of such self-verification strivings may thus provide insight into the widely reported phenomenon of *resistance*—the tendency for patients in therapy to resist positive change. In so doing, such research may pave the way for the development of intervention strategies that accommodate or exploit self-verification strivings rather than being sabotaged by them.

REFERENCES

Aronson, E. (1968). A theory of cognitive dissonance. A current perspective. In L. Berkowitz (Ed.), *Advances in experimental social psychology* (Vol. 4, pp. 1–34). New York: Academic Press.

Hixon, J. G., & Swann, W. B., Jr. (1993). When does introspection bear fruit? Self-reflection, self-insight, and interpersonal choices. *Journal of Personality and Social Psychology, 64*, 35–43.

Linehan, M. M. (1997). Validation and psychotherapy. In A. C. Bohart & L. S. Greenberg (Eds.), *Empathy reconsidered: New directions in psychotherapy*. Washington, DC: American Psychological Association.

Secord, P. F., & Backman, C. W. (1965). An interpersonal approach to personality. In B. Maher (Ed.), *Progress in experimental personality research* (Vol. 2, pp. 91–125). New York: Academic Press.

Swann, W. B., Jr. (1996). *Self traps: The elusive quest for higher self-esteem*. New York: Freeman.

Swann, W. B., Jr., Pelham, B. W., & Krull, D. S. (1989). Agreeable fancy or disagreeable truth? How people reconcile their self-enhancement and self-verification needs. *Journal of Personality and Social Psychology, 57*, 782–791.

Swann, W. B., Jr., Wenzlaff, R. M., & Tafarodi, R. W. (1992). Depression and the search for negative evaluations: More evidence of the role of self-verification strivings. *Journal of Abnormal Psychology, 101*, 314–371.

Questions to Think About

1. Under what conditions will people tend to prefer negative over positive evaluations of themselves?

2. Should it be a goal of therapy to change a client's self-image, or it is enough to have the goal of improving the person's adjustment while maintaining his or her existing view of the self?

3. Could this research be characterized as supporting abusive relationships by showing that both parties in such a relationship may prefer that the abuser treat the victim badly? Why or why not?

11

Recent Developments
in Psychoanalytic Theorizing

STEPHEN A. MITCHELL

Stephen A. Mitchell (1946–2000) was a psychologist trained in psychoanalysis at the William Alanson White Institute in New York, a rival to the more strictly Freudian New York Psychoanalytic Society. His views on psychoanalysis thus reflected not only Freud, but also Erich Fromm and Harry Stack Sullivan, who had founded the alternative psychoanalytic training institute. Mitchell coauthored an influential book that clarified the contribution of the object relations approach (which focuses on interpersonal relationships) to psychoanalysis (which is primarily focused on drives of sexuality and aggression). The selection here reflects Mitchell's long-standing interest in how the relationship between therapist and patient in psychoanalysis influences the course of the analysis in ways that go beyond the Freudian ideal in which the primary role of the analyst is limited to providing the patient with interpretations of the patient's free associations and dreams.

The last decade or so has been a time of extraordinary change within psychoanalytic thinking. Since psychoanalysts often tend to be very conservative by nature, speaking of revolutionary changes in psychoanalysis might sound to many of you like a contradiction in terms, but I think this is just what has happened. There have been many sorts of changes that can be characterized in many different ways: changes in theory; changes in technique; major political, generational, and institutional shifts; and so on.

The change that I want to focus on is the movement toward a more interactional view of the analytic process, because I think this has had the most impact on the ways psychoanalysts are thinking about their work, and because it has the greatest importance for the exploration of the interface between psychoanalysis and other psychotherapies.

In this paper, I want to do three things: to describe some clinical material as a point of reference, to examine the logic of the classical model of the analytic situation and why it necessarily led to an inattention to interaction, and to consider some of the different traditions of psychoanalytic thought that are moving in this direction today.

George, a 35-year-old architect, makes an appointment for a consultation. He is interested in beginning an analysis and is seeing several different analysts so that he can decide with whom he feels he can best work. He enters the office for the first appointment with a jaunty air and a twinkle in his eye and, without requiring an invitation, launches into a brisk, well-organized and entertaining narrative of his life.

George is seeking treatment because he feels the approach of middle age and has a sense that there is

Source: Mitchell, S. A. (1994). Recent developments in psychoanalytic theorizing. *Journal of Psychotherapy Integration, 4*(2), 93–103. Reprinted by permission.

Editor's note: All citations in the text of this selection have been left intact from the original, but the list of references includes only those sources that are the most relevant and important. Readers wishing to follow any of the other citations can find the full references in the original work or in an online database.

considerable unfinished business left over from his childhood that he has never dealt with. Although quite successful in his career, there are ways in which he feels he holds himself back from being fully creative. Also, the history of his relationships with women has been problematic. He has had a series of intense, romantic involvements lasting six or seven years, always ending with his gradually losing interest in and abandoning the woman. He has a sense that this pattern with women is related to the unfinished childhood business.

George comes from a large southern city; his mother was descended from a long line of wealthy southern aristocracy and father was a very successful businessman. He was an only child, the object of devotion by his mother, who spent a great deal of time with him while her husband was away on business activities and trips. When he was 6, his mother was inflicted with a debilitating illness of which she died two years later. He thinks he was with her a good deal of the time during her decline, but has only sketchy, "postcard" memories. George's father, very much in love with his wife, was devastated by the loss and went into a deep depression that lasted years. He spent some time with his son, but they never spoke of the boy's mother. He became preoccupied with his work. George was taken care of, almost adopted by, an older sister of the mother's who herself had several children.

George moved from this tragic beginning to recount highlights from his later childhood and an adventurous, rather romantic young adulthood. He had traveled a great deal, trying several vocations before settling on architecture, in which he had been extremely successful. Yet he felt he held himself back from taking the risks entailed in fully exploring his own creative potential. He was more comfortable in the role of a challenging and provocative prodigy of a famous mentor than in fully stepping out on his own. He finished his account with thumbnail sketches of the most important women in his life and his intense but ill-fated romances with each.

Toward the end of that first hour, I asked George whether he had any ideas about possible connections between his adult difficulties with commitment, both in terms of work and in terms of relationships with women, and his early childhood history. He thought a moment and then said that perhaps the early loss of

his mother left him feeling that all relationships were doomed, as if he were on a train sure to crash, which he himself abandons before he himself is left precipitously once again. I responded that that sounded like a useful speculation and suggested another consultation to explore further the possibility of beginning an analysis.

George replied that he actually had pretty much decided to begin treatment with another analyst, a woman, whom he had seen twice before scheduling this appointment. Some friends of his, knowledgeable about the world of psychoanalysis, had urged him to consult with several analysts before making his decision. He felt comfortable with me, but thought he felt more comfortable somehow with the woman analyst. He would think about it and let me know if he thought it useful to schedule a second appointment. I felt somewhat disappointed; George seemed as if he would be an interesting man to work with, and it felt as if the rug had been pulled out from under me.

After about two weeks, during which time I assumed that George had begun treatment with the other analyst, I received another phone call asking for an appointment. George seemed quite different as he entered the session for the second consultation, more muted, a bit depressed, no twinkle in his eye. He sat down, sighed, and said, "Well, I've been jilted."

He'd gone back for his third session with the other analyst to inform her of his commitment to working with her. Before he could do that, she told him that she had decided that it would be impossible for them to work together. He then filled in the details.

He had been given this analyst's name by a friend of his who was also a friend of the analyst. At that time he and his friend discussed the possible complications of such a referral, and they both agreed that it was extremely unlikely they would run into each other socially and that the connection was distant enough so as to not preclude the commencement of an analysis. George, however, had enough doubt about it that he raised it at the beginning of the first consultation with her. George and the analyst also ended up agreeing that their mutual friend, whom neither of them saw with great frequency, did not pose enough of a problem to preclude their working together. Two consultations then followed, which led George to his decision to work with her. It was because he felt sure they had talked through this potential problem that George felt quite stunned by her announcement that they could not work together. She had reconsidered, she said, and had come to the conclusion that he ought to begin his analysis without such unnecessary complications. He tried to talk her out of her decision, but it appeared quite non-negotiable. He had the suspicion that she might have spoken to a colleague about the question, because she repeated her reasoning in precisely the same words she had used the first time.

I felt the emotional tone of this second meeting was quite depressive, very different from the first consultation. I noted that George seemed quite upset about what had happened. George agreed and had noted that he had trouble getting up out of bed most mornings since. He was usually quite buoyant; he'd been somewhat depressed and it took him almost two weeks to get around to calling me. But now he had decided he definitely wanted to work with me and was ready to commence.

I suggested that something quite powerful had happened between him and the other analyst, and that he seemed to be experiencing a deep sense of loss. George filled in more details about the meaning of this loss to him. He had felt very comfortable with the woman analyst, whose office was decorated in a fashion quite different from mine, in softer tones, more comfortable and relaxing furniture. She herself had seemed to him a bit tense, not as comfortable in her role as analyst, but that seemed endearing to him. He felt that there was a hint of flirtation in their exchanges, that she probably liked him. "It sounds very cozy," I said. "That's just the word I was thinking of," George said. The coziness made him feel more comfortable beginning an analysis, the prospect of which was frightening to him. He felt some sense of dread about digging around in the remote recesses of his childhood experiences; he didn't know where it would lead him. Somehow he felt he would be more in control with the woman analyst, and that reassurance had contributed to his choice to work with her.

"I take it you find little coziness here?" I asked. "Right," George chuckled. He found me a very attentive, sharp listener. He had no question about the value of the work to which he had now committed himself.

But there was little of the reassuring control he felt he would have in the other office. I asked about his thoughts about her reversal. The issue of the mutual friend seemed bogus to him now; perhaps she had also felt this flirtatious connection between them and had been scared off.

I become aware of feeling a growing sense of bleakness, a mournful, forlorn sort of feeling. I asked George whether he had considered consulting with another woman analyst. George said he had briefly considered that possibility, but decided against it. He felt confident in me and committed to begin the work.

As I let my thoughts drift, I began to feel that George had, in fact, lost something profound and irreplaceable. I would never be able to provide George with the help that he felt he could find with the other analyst. My own office, which I usually experience as quite a comfortable, even cozy place, now seemed quite empty and barren. I felt I could offer George only the prospect of hard, tedious work, and that, contrary to my usual experience of myself, there was nothing nurturing about me. My thoughts drifted between George's early loss of his mother and my own loss of my mother (much later than George, in my early adulthood). I thought of my own feelings of being left, motherless, with my father as only parent, and then of George's probable experience at having been left with his father, absorbed with his own grief and unable to offer George much sense of consolation or renewal.

"So, it is just the two of us left alone together," I said. George thought for a moment and smiled sadly. I went on to note that the train had crashed before he had even gotten a chance to settle comfortably in his seat. We both marveled at the way in which his early experiences seemed, somehow, to have been reenacted in these consultations.

Let us step back from the reality of the clinical situation for a moment and consider the way in which Freud thought about what the patient and analyst are supposed to be doing, which is a bit different from what my patient and I found ourselves involved in.

The patient's participation in the analytic situation might be crudely divided into things the patient does on the one hand, and things the patient thinks and says on the other.

Ultimately, in Freud's way of thinking about the analytic situation, *all* the things the patient does, all actions (acting out and acting in), operate as resistances to the analytic process, which requires that the patient think and speak rather than act. The locus of change for Freud is *inside the patient's head,* in the lifting of repression barriers and the overcoming of amnesias. It is the analyst's words and ideas, in interpretations, that effect this internal change in the patient; it is the patient's words, in reporting free associations, that makes it possible for the analyst to interpret.

What the analyst is supposed to be thinking about are the patient's free associations; what the analyst is supposed to be saying are interpretations. In its purest form (in Freud's theory, although certainly not in his practice), no other speech is required, because talk other than interpretation (e.g., questions or observations) is likely to effect and alter the flow of the patient's free associations. (Glover, 1955, terms questions by the analyst "crypto-interpretations.") The analyst should be thinking about the patient's associations and shaping and delivering interpretations when the time is right. Actions by the analyst, acting out (e.g., by forgetting a session) or acting in (by drifting off and letting his attention wander), are pieces of countertransference that operate as counterresistances, obstacles to the analytic process.

Therefore, in the traditional model of the analytic situation, actions on the part of both the patient and the analyst, are regarded as, at best, preludes to thought and speech. The patient is expected to stop acting and, instead, speak about his conflictual feelings and thoughts about the analyst. The analyst is expected to stop acting and, instead, use his or her experience to fashion appropriate interpretations. To the extent to which patient and analyst together continue to act rather than to think and speak, they are *enacting* the patient's crucial conflictual material and/or *reenacting* the patient's important historical configurations, rather than thinking and speaking, remembering and interpreting them.

According to the standards of the classical model, George and both of the two consulting analysts have been conducting themselves in a problematic fashion, since, in their joint efforts, they have managed to reenact some central features of George's early history and current dynamic conflicts. George began the treatment

with me by creating a powerful set of impressions. He conveyed his sense that he would have preferred treatment with the other analyst, a woman, who could offer something very precious to him, which was missing with me. She, however, abruptly and arbitrarily abandoned him. He conveyed the impression that he himself may depart at a moment's notice, despite whatever sense the analyst has of important connections being made.

I, for my part, felt deficient in my ability to help, experiencing myself as a caricature of a male analyst, and felt disconnected from my own internal sources of nurturance. This shaping of my internal experience was very closely connected with the activation of my grief in relation to the loss of my own mother (and, perhaps, a disconnection from my maternal introject). I was aware of some of this as it was happening and tried to express some of it in my remark, "So it is now just the two of us alone together." I also in some sense acted out aspects of the countertransference in my question about whether the patient had considered consulting another woman analyst.

Because of recent revolutions in psychoanalytic thought, many contemporary clinicians would approach the kinds of enactments and reenactments represented in these consultations not as aberrations or departures from analysis, but as the very stuff of analysis. The relationship between enactment and interpretation is now not assumed to be inversely proportional. Thought is no longer regarded as generated through the inhibition of action, but rather thought and action are considered to be independently generated, simultaneous, and continually interpenetrating realms of experience. One might, for example, regard enactments and reenactments as not detracting from interpretation, but rather as providing powerful examples upon which interpretations can be based. One might regard interpretations not as alternatives to enactments, but as forms of enactments themselves.

In virtually every major current psychoanalytic school, the extraordinarily complex interactive features of the analytic relationship are being increasingly accepted and struggled with conceptually. In the remainder of this paper, I would like to illustrate some of the ways that interaction is being approached, and note some of the advantages and constraints of the different analytic traditions in their efforts.

Consider this description of the analytic process by a leading contemporary Freudian, Martin Silverman:

> If the analyst is indeed immersed in the intense emotional interchange that the analytic situation is designed to provoke, he is subjected to powerful pressures to abandon his analytic neutrality. He is bombarded by a stream of complaints, supplications, subtle seductions, bitter accusations, and ingenious bits of blackmail from his patients. He is also subjected to an intense pull from within his own being to ease his burden by obtaining some measure of instinctual gratification from the analytic experience to make up for the deprivation and abuse to which he has given himself up. The analyst is continually drawn to do more than analyze, and his very humanness makes it difficult for him to invariably resist all the temptations. (Silverman, 1985, pp. 176–177)

This description of the work of the psychoanalyst, reminiscent of Ulysses tied to the mast, is a far cry from Freudian writing of 20 years ago. The analyst is now seen as embedded in the relational field, and the pulls on the analyst are regarded as related to the patient's dynamics and providing potentially useful information. Thus, even within contemporary mainstream Freudian thought, the analyst's role is no longer portrayed as one of lofty, cerebral detachment.

There are still serious constraints within this line of thought, in my view. Countertransference is still regarded, ultimately, as a contaminant, even if unavoidable and natural. The newsstand around the corner from my office used to sell buttons that said "Shit happens." For the contemporary Freudian, countertransference happens; in the implicit anal metaphor within which it is discussed, countertransference is to be controlled and eliminated as quickly as possible. Nevertheless, there has been important movement in the direction of regarding the analyst as a fuller participant in the process.

There has also been a great deal of revolutionary rethinking in the Kleinian tradition. Contemporary Kleinian writers (e.g., Joseph, 1989) have made important contributions to the study of interaction in the development of the concept of projective identification and in the exploration of what they call the patient's "relations with the interpretation." Projective identification points to the importance of both the analyst's emotional experience of the patient in the here-and-now and the patient's awareness of the analyst's affectivity.

Consider this quote from Betty Joseph, which illustrates the increased sensitivity to the analyst's participation in the process and the way in which the analyst's experience can often be used as a guide to important dynamics in the patient:

> Our understanding of the nature and the level of anxiety is interlinked, and depends, in large part, on our correct assessment of the use that the patient is making of us . . . frequently the guide in the transference, as to where the most important anxiety is, lies in an awareness that, in some part of oneself, one can feel an area in the patient's communications that one wishes not to attend to—internally in terms of the effect on oneself, externally in terms of what and how one might interpret. (Joseph, 1989, p. 111)

A problem in the way that the concept of projective identification is sometimes used is that it can suggest that the analyst functions as a smooth or clean container for the projected features of the patient's experience. What is often not figured into the equation is the complex, often indeterminate mix between the patient's issues and affective experience and those of the analyst.

While addressing themselves increasingly to interactional dimensions, both Freudian and Kleinian authors maintain a powerful faith in the transformative power of the correct interpretation. In the work of Betty Joseph, for example, there is an intricate and elegant examination of the way in which the patient experiences the analyst's interpretations within his or her own psychic organization, as an assault, for example, or as a seduction. Interpretations are not getting through, because they are not being experienced as interpretations. What is the way out of this dilemma? The analyst must interpret the patient's relationship to the interpretation, the way in which they experience it as an assault or a seduction. But there is a problem here. Is not the interpretation of the patient's relation to the interpretation also an interpretation? On what grounds are we to assume that the interpretation of the patient's relationship to the interpretation gets through any more constructively than any other interpretation? It is here that the traditional belief in the transformative power of the correct interpretation impedes the study of the ways in which analysts manage, often by creating a different sort of emotional presence, to get patients to hear them in a different way.

Consider the following excerpt from an important paper by Grossman and Stewart (1976) involving a contemporary Freudian critique of the traditional concept of "penis envy." They show how the interpretation of penis envy in a destructive, previous analysis, collusively fed into and aggravated the patient's most difficult problems:

> It became apparent that she had taken the interpretation of her "penis envy" in the first analysis simply as the "proof" of her worthlessness. She had not seen it as an interpretation, but rather as an accusation and a confirmation of her worst fears that she was in fact hopeless and worthless. . . . Indeed, the "helpless acceptance" of the penis envy interpretation in the first analysis seemed masochistically gratifying. (1976, p. 293)

But Grossman and Stewart make it clear that an awareness of the problems does not make the second analysis a day at the beach. The difficulties are still there:

> Even to interpret her masochism posed the threat that the interpretation would be experienced as a "put down" and gratify her masochistic impulse; all interpretations, if not narcissistically gratifying, gratified masochistic wishes. They were felt as attacks in which her worthlessness, her defectiveness, and her aggression were unmasked. The analysis threatened to become interminable, one in which the relationship to the analyst was maintained, but only at the price of an analytic stalemate. (1976, pp. 293–294).

I really like this description, because it depicts what for me is the heart of every analysis—the point where interpretations fail because it becomes apparent that they are being swallowed up by the transference–countertransference dynamics. How is this worked past? This is the challenge of every analysis, and it is always individually crafted. The analyst has to somehow create a different emotional presence; to get the patient to hear and experience him or her in a different way. What do Grossman and Stewart say?

> Over many years the patient was able to recognize her need to be a mistreated little girl, rather than to face her disappointments as a grown woman. (1976, p. 294)

I had to read this passage over several times, because I was convinced that either I had missed some-

thing or that there was actually a paragraph missing. Having depicted so clearly the futility of interpretations themselves with this patient, the authors imply that just throwing more and more interpretations, "over many years," solved the problem. I think this illustrates the limitations of analytic traditions that still rely conceptually on the content of interpretations alone to account for the therapeutic action.

The two traditions that have made advances in thinking about therapeutic impacts outside the content of interpretations have been interpersonal psychoanalysis and more recent developmental models.

The developmental traditions inspired by the work of Winnicott (1958, 1965) and Kohut (1971, 1977) have made important contributions to precisely this problem. They call for a malleability on the analyst's part, a willingness to allow themselves to be shaped by the patient's subjectivity, to be created by the patient's need for new, developmentally necessary objects. They also call for a genuine appreciation of the patient's painful disillusionment in the face of the inevitable failure to completely provide those experiences.

The limitation of the developmental contribution lies in an overestimation of the extent to which analysts *can* remove themselves as subjects from the interactional field. The vision of the analyst merely holding or containing the patient's experience in order to facilitate new growth lends itself to a revised version of the myth of the generic analyst and casts a cloud over the idiosyncratic features of the analyst's participation in the process. It is along these lines that Carol Gilligan (1986, p. 492) has suggested that mirroring, a favorite metaphor for both Winnicott and Kohut, is not as suited to represent the development of the self in a relational context as is the metaphor of dialogue. Yet dialogue sounds a bit too adultomorphic. We need other metaphors to depict reciprocal interactions and also the way in which both good parenting and good analysis create spaces for self-development that maximize potentials and minimize constraints.

Finally, for several decades, the interpersonal tradition has been on the cutting edge of thinking about the implications of analytic interaction. Unburdened by the struggle to preserve a one-person framework, interpersonal authors from Sullivan onward have emphasized the importance of here-and-now enactments and various dimensions of the analyst's participation in the analytic process. For Thompson (1964) and Fromm, the analyst's countertransference was regarded as an invaluable source of information about the patient's character and difficulties in living.

The constraints in the interpersonal tradition stem from Sullivan's early dialectical reaction to the Freudian intrapsychic model. Theorists should not speculate about invisible psychic forces and places, Sullivan (1953) argued (anticipating some of Schafer's 1976, later contributions). Useful theory stays close to what can be observed, to what actually takes place between people. Unfortunately, Sullivan's operationalism led to his avoidance of a systematic study of the patterns of subjective experience, the structures of the internal object world, and the ways in which they bridge past and present. This left interpersonal authors with a poverty of concepts for bridging interaction with its intrapsychic roots. Too much emphasis was placed on the analyst's immediate affective reaction. In my view, there has been a tendency to overuse the concept of authenticity in the contemporary interpersonal literature, as if one could quickly and easily decide what in the experience of both analysand and analyst was truly authentic. The analysand is to be demystified, as if an unambiguous rendering of both past and present reality is so simply revealed. These constraints within the interpersonal tradition are part of what has interested many contemporary interpersonal authors and clinicians in object relations theories, because the latter provide a palette of concepts for painting a vision of an inner world much richer than Sullivan's cautious sketches, structured not out of drives and defenses but from the internalization of interpersonal interaction.

I would like to conclude by suggesting that what has been happening in psychoanalysis in recent years is a sweeping, progressive reconceptualization and reintegration of fundamental assumptions and principles, the radical nature of which is often masked by the deference to tradition in psychoanalytic writing and politics. These developments within psychoanalysis should make it a more suitable and constructive participant in explorations involving the integration of psychoanalysis with other psychotherapies.

REFERENCES

Glover, E. (1955). *The technique of psycho-analysis.* New York: International Universities Press.

Kohut, H. (1971). *The analysis of the self.* New York: International Universities Press.

Kohut, H. (1977). *The restoration of the self.* New York: International Universities Press.

Schafer, R. (1976). *A new language for psychoanalysis.* New Haven, CT: Yale University Press.

Silverman, M. (1985). Countertransference and the myth of the perfectly analyzed analyst. *Psychoanalytic Quarterly, 54,* 175–199.

Sullivan, H. S. (1953). *The interpersonal theory of psychiatry.* New York: Norton.

Thompson, C. (1964). *Interpersonal psychoanalysis.* New York: Basic Books.

Questions to Think About

1. The primary content of this article is the author's report and reflections about his interactions with one patient. What are the strengths and limitations of using a single, concrete, personal experience as the basis for discussing more general issues of psychoanalytic practice?

2. To what extent is Mitchell's main point a prescription for how psychoanalysts should behave in conducting an analysis versus a description of how they do behave in that role?

3. In Mitchell's final point in the article, he claims that psychoanalysis had already been greatly changed during the latter part of the twentieth century by the incorporation of interpersonal and object relations approaches, but that the psychoanalytic establishment preferred not to draw attention to these changes. How might a strict Freudian try to explain why many contemporary psychoanalysts prefer the fiction that they are following the rules originally set down by their "founding father"?

12

Measurement of Character

FRANCIS GALTON

In the latter half of the nineteenth century, the British scientist Sir Francis Galton (1822–1911) began the study of genetic influences on personality, inspired by the work of his cousin Charles Darwin. Galton drew family trees of blood relatives of famous and eminent people and found that eminence seemed to run in families. For example, a son might succeed his father as a professor at a university chair (professorship). Galton also noticed that among the lower classes in nineteenth-century Britain, hardly anyone achieved eminence. Of course, genetic factors are not the only possible explanation of why the son of a wealthy, well-educated professor would be more likely to achieve prominence in a hierarchical society than would the son of poor, illiterate parents. To his credit (given the tenor of the times), Galton recognized this possibility, and he suggested that adopted children be studied, including adoptive twins. So it was Galton who began the study of adoptive twins. Galton wished to develop a scientific approach to the measurement of what he termed "character," just as scientific measurement was beginning to be applied to intelligence and to physical characteristics.

I do not plead guilty to taking a shallow view of human nature, when I propose to apply, as it were, a foot-rule to its heights and depths. The powers of man are finite, and if finite they are not too large for measurement. Those persons may justly be accused of shallowness of view, who do not discriminate a wide range of differences, but quickly lose all sense of proportion, and rave about infinite heights and unfathomable depths, and use such like expressions which are not true and betray their incapacity. Examiners are not, I believe, much stricken with the sense of awe and infinitude when they apply their foot-rules to the intellectual performances of the candidates whom they examine; neither do I see any reason why we should be awed at the thought of examining our fellow creatures as best we may, in respect to other faculties than intellect. On the contrary, I think it anomalous that the art of measuring intellectual faculties should have become highly developed, while that of dealing with other qualities should have been little practised or even considered.

The use of measuring man in his entirety, is to be justified by exactly the same arguments as those by which any special examinations are justified, such as those in classics or mathematics; namely, that every measurement tests, in some particulars, the adequacy of the previous education, and contributes to show the efficiency of the man as a human machine, at the time it was made. It is impossible to be sure of the adequacy in every respect of the rearing of a man, or of his total efficiency, unless he has been measured in character and physique, as well as in intellect. A wise man desires this knowledge for his own use, and for the same reason that he takes stock from time to time of his finances. It teaches him his position among his fellows, and whether he is getting on or falling back, and he shapes his ambitions and conduct accordingly. "Know thyself" is an ancient phrase of proverbial philosophy, and I wish to discuss ways by which its excellent direction admits of being better followed.

Source: Galton, F. (1884). Measurement of character. *Fortnightly Review, 36,* 179–185.

The art of measuring various human faculties now occupies the attention of many inquirers in this and other countries. Shelves full of memoirs have been written in Germany alone, on the discriminative powers of the various senses. New processes of inquiry are yearly invented, and it seems as though there was a general lightening up of the sky in front of the path of the anthropometric experimenter, which betokens the approaching dawn of a new and interesting science. Can we discover landmarks in character to serve as bases for a survey, or is it altogether too indefinite and fluctuating to admit of measurement? Is it liable to spontaneous changes, or to be in any way affected by a caprice that renders the future necessarily uncertain? Is man, with his power of choice and freedom of will, so different from a conscious machine, that any proposal to measure his moral qualities is based upon a fallacy? If so, it would be ridiculous to waste thought on the matter, but if our temperament and character are durable realities, and persistent factors of our conduct, we have no Proteus to deal with in either case, and our attempts to grasp and measure them are reasonable.

I have taken pains, as some of my readers may be aware, to obtain fresh evidence upon this question, which, in other words, is, whether or no the actions of men are mainly governed by cause and effect. On the supposition that they are so governed, it is as important to us to learn the exact value of our faculties, as it is to know the driving power of the engine and the quality of the machine that does our factory-work. If, on the other hand, the conduct of man is mainly the result of mysterious influences, such knowledge is of little service to him. He must be content to look upon himself as on a ship, afloat in a strong and unknown current, that may drift her in a very different direction to that in which her head is pointed.

My earlier inquiries into this subject had reference to the facts of heredity, and I came across frequent instances in which a son, happening to inherit somewhat exclusively the qualities of his father, had been found to fail with his failures, sin with his sins, surmount with his virtues, and generally to get through life in much the same way. The course of his life had, therefore, been predetermined by his inborn faculties, or, to continue the previous metaphor, his ship had not drifted, but pursued the course in which

her head was set until she arrived at her predestined port.

The second of my inquiries was into the life-histories of twins, in the course of which I collected cases where the pair of twins resembled each other so closely, that they behaved like one person, thought and spoke alike, and acted similar parts when separated. Whatever spontaneous feeling the one twin may have had, the other twin at the very same moment must have had a spontaneous feeling of exactly the same kind. Such habitual coincidences, if they had no common cause, would be impossible; we are therefore driven to the conclusion that whenever twins think and speak alike, there is no spontaneity in either of them, in the popular acceptation of the word, but that they act mechanically and in like ways, because their mechanisms are alike. I need not reiterate my old arguments, and will say no more about the twins, except that new cases have come to my knowledge which corroborate former information. It follows, that if we had in our keeping the twin of a man, who was his "double," we might obtain a trustworthy forecast of what the man would do under any new conditions, by first subjecting that twin to the same conditions and watching his conduct.

My third inquiry is more recent. It was a course of introspective search into the operations of my own mind, whenever I caught myself engaged in a feat of what at first sight seemed to be free-will. The inquiry was carried on almost continuously for three weeks, and proceeded with, off and on, for many subsequent months. After I had mastered the method of observation a vast deal of apparent mystery cleared away, and I ultimately reckoned the rate of occurrence of perplexing cases, during the somewhat uneventful but pleasant months of a summer spent in the country, to be less than one a day. All the rest of my actions seemed clearly to lie within the province of normal cause and consequence. The general results of my introspective inquiry support the views of those who hold that man is little more than a conscious machine, the larger part of whose actions are predicable. As regards such residuum as there may be, which is not automatic, and which a man, however wise and well informed, could not possibly foresee, I have nothing to say, but I have found that the more carefully I inquired, whether it was into hereditary similarities of conduct, into the life-histories of twins, or now introspectively into the processes of what I should have called my own Free-Will, the smaller seems the room left for the possible residuum.

I conclude from these three inquiries that the motives of the will are mostly normal, and that the character which shapes our conduct is a definite and durable "something," and therefore that it is reasonable to attempt to measure it. We must guard ourselves against supposing that the moral faculties which we distinguish by different names, as courage, sociability, niggardness, are separate entities. On the contrary, they are so intermixed that they are never singly in action. I tried to gain an idea of the number of the more conspicuous aspects of the character by counting in an appropriate dictionary the words used to express them. Roget's *Thesaurus* was selected for that purpose, and I examined many pages of its index here and there as samples of the whole, and estimated that it contained fully one thousand words expressive of character, each of which has a separate shade of meaning, while each shares a large part of its meaning with some of the rest.

It may seem hopeless to deal accurately with so vague and wide a subject, but it often happens that when we are unable to meet difficulties, we may evade them, and so it is with regard to the present difficulty. It is true that we cannot define any aspect of character, but we can define a test that shall elicit *some* manifestation of character, and we can define the act performed in response to it. Searchings into the character must be conducted on the same fundamental principle as that which lies at the root of examinations into the intellectual capacity. Here there has been no preliminary attempt to map out the field of intellect with accuracy; but definite tests are selected by which the intellect is probed at places that are roughly known but not strictly defined, as the depth of a lake might be sounded from a boat rowing here and there. So it should be with respect to character. Definite acts in response to definite emergencies have alone to be noted. No accurate map of character is required to start from.

Emergencies need not be waited for, they can be extemporised; traps, as it were, can be laid. Thus, a great ruler whose word can make or mar a subject's fortune, wants a secret agent and tests his character during a single interview. He contrives by a few min-

utes' questioning, temptation, and show of displeasure, to turn his character inside out, exciting in turns his hopes, fear, zeal, loyalty, ambition, and so forth. Ordinary observers who stand on a far lower pedestal, cannot hope to excite the same tension and outburst of feeling in those whom they examine, but they can obtain good data in a more leisurely way. If they are unable to note a man's conduct under great trials for want of opportunity, they may do it in small ones, and it is well that those small occasions should be such as are of frequent occurrence, that the statistics of men's conduct under like conditions may be compared. After fixing upon some particular class of persons of similar age, sex, and social condition, we have to find out what common incidents in their lives are most apt to make them betray their character. We may then take note as often as we can, of what they do on these occasions, so as to arrive at their statistics of conduct in a limited number of well-defined small trials.

One of the most notable differences between man and man, lies in the emotional temperament. Some persons are quick and excitable; others are slow and deliberate. A sudden excitement, call, touch, gesture, or incident of any kind evokes, in different persons, a response that varies in intensity, celerity, and quality. An observer watching children, heart and soul at their games, would soon collect enough material to enable him to class them according to the quantity of emotion that they showed. I will not attempt to describe particular games of children or of others, nor to suggest experiments, more or less comic, that might be secretly made to elicit the manifestations we seek, as many such will occur to ingenious persons. They exist in abundance, and I feel sure that if two or three experimenters were to act zealously and judiciously together as secret accomplices, they would soon collect abundant statistics of conduct. They would gradually simplify their test conditions and extend their scope, learning to probe character more quickly and from more of its sides.

It is a question by no means to be decided off-hand in the negative, whether instrumental measurements of the magnitude of the reflex signs of emotion in persons who desire to submit themselves to experiment, are not feasible. The difficulty lies in the more limited range of tests that can be used when the freedom of movement is embarrassed by the necessary mechanism. The exciting cause of emotion whatever it be, a fright, a suspense, a scold, an insult, a grief, must be believed to be genuine, or the tests would be worthless. It is not possible to sham emotion thoroughly. A good actor may move his audience as deeply as if they were witnessing a drama of real life, but the best actor cannot put himself into the exact frame of mind of a real sufferer. If he did, the reflex and automatic signs of emotion excited in his frame would be so numerous and violent, that they would shatter his constitution long before he had acted a dozen tragedies.

The reflex signs of emotion that are perhaps the most easily registered, are the palpitations of the heart. They cannot be shammed or repressed, and they are visible. Our poet Laureate has happily and artistically exemplified this. He tells us that Launcelot returning to court after a long illness through which he had been nursed by Elaine, sent to crave an audience of the jealous queen. The messenger utilises the opportunity for observing her in the following ingenious way like a born scientist.

> *"Low drooping till he well nigh kissed her feet*
> *For loyal awe, saw with a sidelong eye*
> *The shadow of a piece of pointed lace*
> *In the Queen's shadow, vibrate on the wall*
> *And parted, laughing in his courtly heart."*

Physiological experimenters are not content to look at shadows on the wall, that depart and leave no mark. They obtain durable traces by the aid of appropriate instruments. Maret's pretty little pneumo-cardiograph is very portable, but not so sure in action as the more bulky apparatus. It is applied tightly to the chest in front of the heart, by a band passing round the body. At each to-and-fro movement, whether of the chest as a whole, or of the portion over the heart, it sucks in or blows out a little puff of air. A thin india-rubber tube connects its nozzle with a flat elastic bag under the short arm of a lever. The other end of the lever moves up and down in accordance with the part of the chest to which the pneumo-cardiograph is applied, and scratches light marks on a band of paper which is driven onwards by clockwork. This little instrument can be worn under the buttoned coat without being noticed. I was anxious to practise myself in its use, and wore one during the formidable ordeal of delivering the Rede Lecture in the Senate House at Cambridge, a month ago (most of this very memoir forming part of that lecture). I had no connection established between my instrument and any recording apparatus, but wore it merely to see whether or no it proved in any way irksome. If I had had a table in front of me, with the recording apparatus stowed out of sight below, and an expert assistant near at hand to turn a stop-cock at appropriate moments, he could have obtained samples of my heart's action without causing me any embarrassment whatever. I should have forgotten all about the apparatus while I was speaking.

Instrumental observers of the reflex signs of emotion have other means available besides this, and the sphygmograph that measures the pulse. Every twitch of each separate finger even of an infant's hand is registered by Dr. Warner's ingenious little gauntlet. Every movement of each limb of man or horse is recorded by Dr. Maret. The apparatus of Mosso measures the degree in which the blood leaving the extremities rushes to the heart and head and internal organs. Every limb shrinks sensibly in volume from this withdrawal of the blood, and the shrinkage of any one of them, say the right arm, is measured by the fall of water in a gauge that communicates with a long bottleful of water, through the neck of which the arm has been thrust, and in which it is softly but effectually plugged.

I should not be surprised if the remarkable success of many persons in "muscle-reading" should open out a wide field for delicate instrumental investigations. The poetical metaphors of ordinary language suggest many possibilities of measurement. Thus when two persons have an "inclination" to one another, they visibly incline or slope together when sitting side by side, as at a dinner-table, and they then throw the stress of their weights on the near legs of their chairs. It does not require much ingenuity to arrange a pressure gauge with an index and dial to indicate changes in stress, but it is difficult to devise an arrangement that shall fulfil the threefold condition of being effective, not attracting notice, and being applicable to ordinary furniture. I made some rude experiments, but being busy with other matters, have not carried them on, as I had hoped.

Another conspicuous way in which one person differs from another is in temper. Some men are easily provoked, others remain cheerful even when affairs go very contrary to their liking. We all know specimens of good and bad-tempered persons, and all of us could probably specify not a few appropriate test conditions to try the temper in various ways, and elicit definite responses. There is no doubt that the temper of a dog can be tested. Many boys do it habitually, and learn to a nicety how much each will put up with, without growling or showing other signs of resentment. They do the same to one another, and gauge each other's tempers accurately.

It is difficult to speak of tests of character without thinking of Benjamin Franklin's amusing tale of the "Handsome and the Deformed Leg," and there is no harm in quoting it, because, however grotesque, it exemplifies the principle of tests. In it he describes two sorts of people; those who habitually dwell on the pleasanter circumstances of the moment, and those who have no eyes but for the unpleasing ones. He tells how a philosophical friend took special precautions to avoid those persons who being discontented themselves, sour the pleasures of society, offend many people, and make themselves everywhere disagreeable. In order to discover a pessimist at first sight, he cast about for an instrument. He of course possessed a thermometer to test heat, and a barometer to tell the air-pressure, but he had no instrument to test the characteristic of which we are speaking. After much pondering he hit upon a happy idea. He chanced to have one remarkably handsome leg, and one that by some accident was crooked and deformed, and these he used for the purpose. If a stranger regarded his ugly leg more than his handsome one he doubted him. If

he spoke of it and took no notice of the handsome leg, the philosopher determined to avoid his further acquaintance. Franklin sums up by saying, that every one has not this two-legged instrument, but every one with a little attention may observe the signs of a carping and fault-finding disposition.

This very disposition is the subject of the eighteenth "character" of Theophrastus, who describes the conduct of such men under the social conditions of the day, one of which is also common to our own time and countrymen. He says that when the weather has been very dry for a long time, and it at last changes, the grumbler being unable to complain of the rain, complains that it did not come sooner. The British philosopher has frequent opportunities for applying weather tests to those whom he meets, and with especial fitness to such as happen to be agriculturists.

The points I have endeavoured to impress are chiefly these. First, that character ought to be measured by carefully recorded acts, representative of the usual conduct. An ordinary generalisation is nothing more than a muddle of vague memories of inexact observations. It is an easy vice to generalise. We want lists of facts, every one of which may be separately verified, valued and revalued, and the whole accurately summed. It is the statistics of each man's conduct in small every-day affairs, that will probably be found to give the simplest and most precise measure of his character. The other chief point that I wish to impress is, that a practice of deliberately and methodically testing the character of others and of ourselves is not wholly fanciful, but deserves consideration and experiment.

Questions to Think About

1. Why did Galton propose that measurement tools should be developed for assessing "character" (personality)?

2. In what ways does Galton's approach reflect his world view as a member of the highly educated upper class?

3. What is the relationship between Galton's proposal that character should be measured by observing and recording a person's usual behaviors and the type of modern personality test that primarily relies on self-report?

13

The Intelligence Quotient
of Francis Galton in Childhood

LEWIS M. TERMAN

Lewis Terman (1877–1956) was a central figure in the development of intelligence testing in the United States. He was on the faculty of Stanford University from 1910 until his death, and it was Terman's work at Stanford in refining the work of Binet and Simon that led to the "Stanford-Binet" test first published by Terman in 1916. Terman initiated a large-scale longitudinal study of a sample of bright children in California that continues to this day. (Readings 29 and 46 of this book report on data gathered as part of that project.) Terman believed that genetic factors were important determinants of intelligence; he was involved with the eugenics movement which sought to improve the human species by encouraging those deemed genetically fit to produce more offspring and by discouraging or preventing those deemed unfit from reproducing. In this article, Terman assesses the IQ of Francis Galton (who was by then dead) by interpreting records of Galton's childhood abilities in light of tasks normally used in IQ testing, concluding that Galton had an IQ of about 200 (in the range of genius).

The writer does not remember to have seen Francis Galton classed among boy prodigies. Indeed, Galton's main contributions to science were given to the world at so late a date in his life that he is not infrequently mentioned as an illustration of late maturing genius. *Hereditary Genius* was published in the author's fiftieth year; *Natural Inheritance* in his sixty-eighth year; and on the practical side the most important work of his life was not accomplished until he was more than eighty years of age.

In the recently published Volume I of Karl Pearson's *Life, Letters and Labors of Galton,* there is ample evidence that Galton was a boy of unusual attainments and that he was extraordinarily precocious. The biography in question departs radically from the usual type of biography by presenting documentary evidence regarding the more important events in the life of its subject, and that concerning Galton's childhood is especially full and significant. From the evidence given, one is justified in concluding that between the ages of three and eight years, at least, Francis Galton must have had an intelligence quotient not far from 200; that is, his mental age at that time was not far from double his actual age.

The significance of this will be apparent when we say that after diligent search in several cities and several counties in California—a search including many thousand of children in scope—the highest intelligence quotient we have yet found is 170. The number that we have found going above 150 can be counted on the fingers of one hand.

From early childhood Galton was under the instruction of his sister, Adèle, herself a mere child. "She taught him his letters in play, and he could point

Source: Terman, L. M. (1917). The intelligence quotient of Francis Galton in childhood. *American Journal of Psychology, 28*(2), 209–215.

to them all before he could speak. Adèle had a wonderful power of teaching and gaining attention without fatiguing. She taught herself Latin and Greek that she might teach him. She never had him learn by heart, but made him read his lesson, bit by bit, eight times over, when he could say it. He could repeat much of Scott's *Marmion* and understood it all by the time he was five." (Quoted by Pearson from Elizabeth Anne Galton's *Reminiscences*).

Pearson further informs us that Francis knew his capital letters by twelve months and both his alphabets by eighteen months; that he could read a little book, *Cobwebs to Catch Flies,* when two and a half years old, and could sign his name before three years. The following letter has survived from his fourth year, a letter which has been endorsed by his mother, saying that Francis wrote and spelled it entirely himself:

> "My
> dear
> Uncle
> we have
> got Ducks.   I know
> A Nest.   I mean
> to make a
> Feast."

The day before his fifth birthday he wrote the following letter to his sister:

"MY DEAR ADÈLE,

I am 4 years old and I can read any English book. I can say all the Latin Substantives and Adjectives and active verbs besides 52 lines of Latin poetry. I can cast up any sum in addition and can multiply by 2, 3, 4, 5, 6, 7, 8, [9], 10, [11]

I can also say the pence table. I read French a little and I know the clock.

FRANCIS GALTON,
Febuary 15, 1827."

The only misspelling is in the date. The numbers 9 and 11 are bracketed above, because little Francis, evidently feeling that he had claimed too much, had scratched out one of these numbers with a knife and pasted some paper over the other!

This document should have great interest for those who have worked with mental tests. That Francis at less than five years could read any English book demonstrates beyond any possible doubt that he was as far advanced at this time as the *average* English or American child at nine or ten years. It is an accomplishment which we do not believe is possible to a mental age of less than nine years with any amount of formal instruction. It is certain that our subject's accomplishments did not include merely the ability to pronounce words mechanically, for there is ample evidence from other sources that at this early age he read with understanding.

Again, at this age Francis had learned to do any sum in addition, and had learned all but the hardest part of the multiplication table. This indicates, at least, nine-year intelligence, for we have found that, however old a child and however much school instruction he may have had, the multiplication table is seldom mastered thoroughly much below the nine-year level. Further, his knowledge of the "pence table" indicates an acquaintance with the coins and their values such as children ordinarily do not have before something like eight years.

Besides informing us that Francis had, at this tender age, gotten quite a start in French and Latin, the above letter also tells us that he "knows the clock"; that is, presumably, he was able to tell the time of day by the clock. This performance has been definitely standardized at the mental age of 9 to 10 years, and it is almost never passed before the mental age of eight years.

The reader may raise the question whether it is safe to accept a child's own statements with regard to the above points. It would not be, of course, if there were no corroborative evidence. The fact that there is such evidence from many sources, and the fact that little Francis was known to be as remarkably conscientious as he was intelligent, justifies us in accepting the above statements without the slightest discount.

The fact that Francis' reading at the age of five years was intelligent and not of the mechanical kind, is demonstrated by his ability at that age to offer quotations which would fit a given situation. For example, when he was five years old, a boy friend asked his advice as to what he ought to say in a letter to his father, who, it seems, was in danger of being shot for some political affair. Little Francis replied immediately from Walter Scott:

> *"And if I live to be a man,*
> *My father's death revenged shall be."*

Again at the age of five, he was found holding a group of tormenting boys at arm's length, shouting meanwhile,

> *"Come one, come all. This rock shall fly*
> *From its firm base, as soon as I."*

By six, under the tutelage of Adèle, he had become thoroughly conversant with the Iliad and the Odyssey. At this age, a visitor at the Galton home made Francis weary by cross-questioning him about points in Homer. Finally, the boy replied, "Pray, Mr. Horner, look at the last line in the 12th book of the Odyssey" and then ran off. The line in question reads, "But why rehearse all this tale, for even yesterday I told it to thee and to thy noble wife in thy house; and it liketh me not twice to tell a plain told tale."

It seems that Adèle also taught Francis a good deal about entomology, and at six and seven years he was active and persistent in collecting insects and minerals, which he is said to have classified and studied in more than a childish way. It has been shown by Mrs. Burk that collections of an analytical and classificatory type are not common before twelve or thirteen years. Here, again, we find evidence of an intelligence quotient not far from 200.

Pearson quotes the following letter written by a visitor at the Galton home on December 28, 1828:

> "The youngest child, Francis, is a prodigy. He is seven next February and reads 'Marmion', 'The Lady of the Lake', Cowper's, Pope's and Shakespeare's works for pleasure, and, by reading a page twice over, repeats it by heart. He writes a beautiful hand, is in long division, and has been twice through the Latin Grammar; all taught by Adèle."

At the age of eight, Francis was taken away from home to attend a boarding school. Here he was placed in a high class, although the boys in it ranged up to fifteen years. Since this was a private school attended by children of a superior social class, it is altogether likely that his fourteen and fifteen-year-old classmates were themselves above the average mental level of that age; hence Francis must by this time have reached a mental level of not far from that which is median for sixteen years.

In his first year at this school, we find Francis writing to his father in these words: "I am very glad that you have left off being a banker, for you will have more time to yourself and better health." This little quotation certainly betokens a degree of filial solicitude by no means common to children of this age. Such altruism does not ordinarily develop so early. The words fit sixteen-year much better than eight-year intelligence.

Francis' interests at the age of ten are indicated by the following letter:

December 30, 1832.

My Dearest Papa:
  It is now my pleasure to disclose the most ardent wishes of my heart, which are to extract out of my boundless wealth in compound, money sufficient to make this addition to my unequaled library.

The Hebrew Commonwealth by John . . . 9
A Pastor Advice 2
Hornne's commentaries on the Psalms . . 4
Paley's Evidence on Christianity 2
Jones Biblical Cyclopedia 10
—————
27

It is hardly necessary to comment on the above letter as an indication of the boy's mental maturity. It speaks for itself.

Francis' interests, however, were not wholly literary, for at the age of thirteen he gave us "Francis Galton's Aerostatic Project." It seems this was a series of drawings representing a flying machine. It was to work by large, flapping wings with a sort of revolving steam engine, and was supposed to carry five passengers, a pilot and an engineer.

At the age of fifteen, we find the youth Galton expressing in his letters to his father serious opinions on mind training, the relative value of classics and English, and other matters of educational theory. These opinions were voiced by him again some sixty years later, substantially without change.

At the age of fifteen Francis was admitted to the general hospital at Birmingham as a medical student.

It is well known that, in general, a high correlation obtains between favorable mental traits of all kinds; that, for example, children superior in intelligence also tend to be superior in moral qualities. Francis Galton was no exception to this rule, as indicated by the following letter written by his mother when the boy was only eight years old: "Francis from his earliest age showed highly honorable feelings. His temper, although hasty, brought no resentment, and his little irritations were soon calmed. His open-minded disposition, with great good nature and kindness to those boys younger than himself, made him beloved by all his school fellows. He was very affectionate and even sentimental in his manners. His activity of body could only be equalled by the activity of his mind. He was a boy never known to be idle. His habit was always to be doing something. He showed no vanity at his superiority over other boys, but said it was a shame that their education should have been so neglected."

After Mr. Pearson has given us all the above significant information, it is astonishing to find him commenting upon it as follows: "The letters we have quoted from these early years may appear to the reader to contain little of note. They are, indeed, just what a healthy normal child would write, but it is that very fact that makes them essential human documents and gives them their fundamental interest. . . .

"Need we attempt to see signs of exceptional ability or to discover foreshadowings of future achievement in these outpourings of healthy childhood? I do not think we can say more than that Francis Galton was a normal child with rather more than average ability", etc.

Mr. Pearson's error is of a kind which is now coming to be generally recognized by those who work with mental tests; that is, an error due to the failure to take into account the significance of a mental performance *in terms of the mental age to which it corresponds.*

Pearson did not know, and the average teacher does not fully appreciate, that a child of four years who is able to do the things characteristic of a child of seven or eight years is a genius of the first order. It is hard to get people to understand that what a child is able to do has no significance unless we take age into account.

The opposite error is no less common; that is, for a mentally retarded child in a grade far below his age to be considered perfectly normal and average in intelligence. Only recently we were consulted by a teacher regarding a child who was described as "slow to learn". The child in question was twelve years old and in the first grade, and we suggested to the teacher that in all probability the child was feeble-minded. We were met, however, with the most positive assurance that the little girl in question could not possibly be feeble-minded, that she was actually learning the work of the first grade, and that her normal mentality was shown by her motherly interest in her little six-year-old classmates. Without arguing the matter further, we urged the teacher to bring the child for a Binet test, with the result that she was found to have a mental age of a little less than 6 years by the Stanford Revision. This child had been in school several years and had had every opportunity to learn, except the advantage of endowment. Experience has taught us that such a subject will never reach the mental level of seven years, however long she may live.

This teacher's error may seem to some almost incredible. In reality it is an error of about the same degree as that made by Mr. Pearson, though in the opposite direction. Similar errors, though perhaps not quite as great, are abundant even in the writings of psychologists on mental tests. They are to be found over and over, for example, in Professor Holmes' recent book "The Backward Child."

Studies are now in progress at Stanford University on exceptionally intelligent children, and we should especially like to receive information about children who test much above 150 by the Stanford-Binet scale. As already stated, the highest intelligence quotient that we have found is 170. We need accurate case descriptions and follow-up work on cases testing 150 to 200.

Questions to Think About

1. Terman explains several times in his analysis that Francis Galton's older sister Adèle taught him much of what he knew (and even taught herself Latin and Greek in order to teach these languages to Francis). Francis Galton's biographer Karl Pearson also notes that all the impressive skills Francis showed in early childhood had been taught to him by Adèle. Why, then, might both Pearson and Terman focus on Francis as a child prodigy, and not even mention the obvious intellect and maturity of his sister?

2. To what extent does current research and/or your personal experience support Terman's claim that high IQ is correlated with positive qualities of character (honor, morality, kindness, and so on)?

3. How might the many parallels between Galton and Terman himself (especially their interest in the genetic basis of intelligence—Galton wrote a book titled "Hereditary Genius" and Terman wrote one titled "Genetic Studies of Genius") have influenced Terman's evaluation of Galton?

14

Dimensions of Personality:
The Biosocial Approach to Personality

HANS J. EYSENCK

Some of the most interesting evidence for the effects of biological temperament on personality comes from this British psychologist. Eysenck (1916–1997) developed a nervous system–based theory of personality. The basic idea of Eysenck's theory is that extroverts have a relatively low level of brain arousal that leads them to seek stimulation. Conversely, introverts are thought to have a higher level of central nervous system arousal, so they tend to shy away from stimulating social environments.

Eysenck's research led him to believe that the basis of personality was accounted for by three personality dimensions. He viewed all traits as deriving from three biological systems: extraversion, neuroticism, and psychoticism. Psychoticism includes a tendency toward psychopathology involving impulsivity and cruelty, tough-mindedness, shrewdness, low agreeableness, and low conscientiousness. Neuroticism is an emotional instability.

Eysenck, born in Germany, fled to England in 1934 where he became an important voice in psychology. Eysenck's parents were actors and he himself became an extremely passionate and outspoken psychologist and intellectual. Thus, it is not surprising Eysenck asked intriguing questions such as whether extraversion runs in families.

A PARADIGM OF PERSONALITY DESCRIPTION

It would seem difficult to doubt the truth of the proposition that man is a biosocial animal (Eysenck, 1980b). There is no longer any doubt about the strong determination of individual differences in personality by genetic factors (Eaves, Eysenck, & Martin, 1989), and much progress has been made in the study of physiological, neurological, and biochemical-hormonal factors in mediating this influence (Eysenck, 1981; Zuckerman, Ballenger, & Post, 1984; Stelmack, 1981). It has been suggested that the biological aspects of personality should be identified with the concept of

temperament (Strelau, 1983) and this may prove an acceptable use, although the dictionary defines the term as equivalent to personality ("the characteristic way an individual behaves, especially towards other people"). What is not in doubt is the importance of considering individual differences as an important part of scientific psychology (Eysenck, 1984) and, indeed, it has been fundamental for any proper understanding of human behavior (Eysenck, 1983). Personality is more than superficial behavioral characteristics, easily acquired and easily abandoned; it is an indispensable part of any meaningful scientific investigation in

Source: Eysenck, H. J. (1991). Dimensions of personality: The biosocial approach to personality. In J. Strelau & A. Angleitner (Eds.), *Explorations in temperament* (pp. 87–103). New York: Plenum. Reprinted by permission. (Selection is excerpted from pp. 87–99.)

Editor's note: All citations in the text of this selection have been left intact from the original, but the list of references includes only those sources that are the most relevant and important. Readers wishing to follow any of the other citations can find the full references in the original work or in an online database.

educational, industrial, clinical, social or experimental psychology (Eysenck & Eysenck, 1985).

Concepts like values, interests, and attitudes are related to personality but do not usually form part of its central core. Undoubtedly they too are influenced by biological factors as shown, for instance, by the high heritabilities for social attitudes and interests (Eaves *et al.,* 1989); but too little work has been published on such determinants to deserve extended treatment here.

The multiplicity of approaches to the descriptive analysis of personality should not mislead psychologists into thinking there is no agreement; Eysenck (1983) has argued that there is a paradigm in personality research, and Royce and Powell (1983), in a re-analysis of all large-scale psychometric analyses of personality to date have found that there are three major dimensions in this field. They appear again and again, and are very similar to the three major dimensions suggested by Eysenck, namely Psychoticism (P), Extraversion (E), and Neuroticism (N). There are several reasons for asserting that these three dimensions are firmly linked with biological determinants. These reasons are as follows:

1. As already noted, regardless of instrument of measurement or method of analysis, these three dimensions emerge from practically all large-scale investigations into personality, a result unlikely if environmental factors alone determined a person's position on these dimensions (Eysenck & Eysenck, 1985; Royce & Powell, 1983).

2. These same three dimensions are found cross-culturally in all parts of the world where studies have been carried out to investigate this universality (Barrett & Eysenck, 1984). Using the Eysenck Personality Questionnaire (EPQ; Eysenck & Eysenck, 1975), these authors analyzed results from 25 countries as diverse as Nigeria and Uganda in Africa, mainland China and Japan, European and Scandinavian countries, South American countries, Socialist countries like the USSR, Hungary, and Poland, as well as the former British colonies (USA, Canada, and Australia), testing 500 males and 500 females in each country with a translation of the EPQ, and carrying out factor analyses separately for males and

females. It was found that, overall, practically identical factors emerged, showing indices of factor comparison which averaged .98. This identity of personality dimensions in fundamentally different cultures suggests a biological foundation.

3. Individuals tend to retain their position on these three dimensions with remarkable consistency (Conley, 1984a, b, 1985). This suggests that the events of everyday life have little influence on a person's temperament, and that biological causes are predominant in determining disposition.

4. Work on the genetics of personality (Eaves *et al.,* 1989) has powerfully reinforced this argument, as already pointed out; genetic factors determine at least half the phenotypic variance of the major dimensions of personality, and there is little if any evidence for between family environmental variance. This finding alone would seem to contradict all the major theories of personality advanced in psychological textbooks!

Clearly, genetic factors cannot act directly on behavior; there must be an intervening link between genes and chromosomes on the one hand, and social behavior on the other. This intervening link may be looked for in physiological factors, neurological structure, biochemical and hormonal determinants or other biological features of the organism. The proper theory of personality requires some knowledge of the relationships between social behavior, on the one hand, which gives rise to the descriptions of the major dimensions of personality, based on patterns of behavior, and specific biological features of the organism on the other. It is unlikely that simple heuristic findings will establish a convincing link; what is needed clearly is a set of theories relating the various dimensions of personality. Eysenck (1990) has given a detailed review of the theories and studies available to date in this very large and complex field; here we can only discuss some of the issues in question, with particular reference to the theory of "arousal" in relation to extraversion-introversion.

BIOLOGICAL THEORIES OF PERSONALITY

Eysenck (1967) originally suggested a link between cortical arousal and extraversion-introversion. This was based essentially on the findings of Moruzzi and Magoun (1949) of the ascending reticular activating system (ARAS), the system activation of which elicited a general activation pattern in the cortical EEG. Collaterals from the ascending sensory pathways produce activity in the ARAS, which subsequently relays the excitation to numerous sites in the cerebral cortex. It was this excitation which produced the EEG synchronization observed by Moruzzi and Magoun. Much research has since shown that the reticular formation is implicated in the initiation and maintenance of motivation, emotion, and conditioning by way of excitatory and inhibitory control of autonomic and postural adjustments, and by way of cortical coordination of activity serving attention, arousal, and orienting behavior.

The link suggested by Eysenck (1967) between personality and the ARAS amounted to the suggestion that the extraversion-introversion dimension is identified largely with differences in level of activity in the cortico-reticular loop, introverts being characterized by higher levels of activity than extroverts, and thus being chronically more cortically aroused. In addition, Eysenck suggested that neuroticism was closely related to the activity of the visceral brain, which consists of the hippocampus-amygdala, singulum, septum, and hypothalamus. These two systems are independent, hence we have an orthogonal relation between extraversion-introversion and neuroticism-stability. However, this independence is only partial. One of the ways in which cortical arousal can be produced is through activity in the visceral brain which reaches the reticular formation through collaterals. Activity in the visceral brain produces autonomic arousal, and Eysenck has used the term *activation* to distinguish this form of arousal from that produced by reticular activity. Thus in a condition of high activation, we would expect high arousal; a person who is strongly affected by anger, or fear, or some other emotion will certainly also be in a state of high cortical arousal. Fortunately, such states of strong emotional involvement are relatively rare, but they do indicate that the independence of the two systems is only relative (Routtenberg, 1966).

A detailed discussion of the concept of arousal by many authors is given in a book edited by Strelau

and Eysenck (1987). Clearly, the concept of general physiological arousal that was a core construct in Duffy's (1957) early theory and Hebb's (1955) optimal arousal approach does not seem viable any longer. The reticulo-cortical system of Moruzzi and Magoun (1949) now appears to be only one of several arousal systems (Zuckerman & Como, 1983), probably including the limbic arousal system, suggested by recent work (Aston-Jones & Bloom, 1981), as well as a monoamine oxidase system, the diffuse thalamocortical system and the pituitary-adrenocortical system (Zuckerman, 1983). This apparent diversity may not prevent the systems from operating in a relatively unitary fashion. Clearly, the way from the "conceptual nervous system" of Hebb to the "central nervous system" of the neurosciences is a hard one!

PROBLEMS IN THEORIES TESTING

At first sight it may seem relatively easy to test theories of this kind by taking groups of extroverts and introverts, or high and low N scorers, and submitting them to physiological tests of one kind or another. However, note the following:

1. There is no single measure of arousal or excitation in the neurophysiological field. As Lacey and Lacey (1958) have emphasized repeatedly, the underlying systems show *response specificity*, in that different systems are primarily activated by suitable stimulation in different people. Thus one person may react to emotional stimuli primarily through an increase in heart rate, another through increase in the conductivity of the skin, a third through more rapid breathing, etc. No single measure is adequate to portray the complexity of reactions; the recommended solution is to take measures of as many systems as possible, and score changes in the system maximally involved. But few experimenters have followed this advice, so that failure to support the theory may be due to faulty or too restricted choice of measuring instrument.

2. There is also *stimulus specificity*, in the sense that different people may be sensitive to different stimuli. Saltz (1970) has shown that failure, or the threat of failure, produces more anxiety among N+ subjects, whereas shocks generate greater anxiety among N– than N+ subjects. Genetic factors predispose individuals to condition anxiety responses to quite specific stimuli (Eysenck & Martin, 1987). Thus the usual stimuli chosen by experimenters, e.g., shocks, may result in quite different relationships between stimulus and response than some other stimuli.

3. Relations between stimulus and response are usually nonlinear. Both the Yerkes-Dodson Law (1908) and Pavlov's (1927) Law of Transmarginal Inhibition show that as stimuli get stronger, responses at first increase in strength, then they decline, producing a curvilinear regression. This leads to complex theoretical formulation which makes precise prediction difficult. We can predict that the high arousal of introverts will lead to a reversal of the stimulus-response correlation at a lower point of stimulus intensity than would be true of extroverts, but the precise point is difficult to establish. Nevertheless, the Law has shown impressive predictive powers in relation to a variety of behavioral responses (Eysenck, 1976; Eysenck & Eysenck, 1985).

4. Threshold and ceiling effects may make choice of measure difficult. Looking at the electrodermal response (EDR) as a measure of N, we could use as our response measure: (a) Size of response; (b) latency of response; or (c) duration of response, i.e., time to return to base-line. Only (c) seems to give useful correlations, but that could not have been predicted from what little we know of the EDR.

5. Resting levels are ill-defined, and are influenced powerfully by uncontrolled preexperimental variables. Subjects coming into our laboratories may have suffered an emotional shock quite recently, may have smoked or drunk alcohol heavily, have been frightened by rumors about the experiments to be performed, or may have been annoyed by being kept waiting; these and many other factors may determine decisively their reactions in the test. Eysenck (1981) has discussed in detail how anticipation in subjects produced quite contradictory results in two series of experiments. Spence had postulated, and found, that eyeblink conditioning was correlated with N, not with E. Eysenck had postulated, and found, that eyeblink conditioning was correlated with E, but not N. Kimble visited both laboratories and discovered that while

Eysenck reassured his subjects, told them explicitly that they would not receive electric shock, hid all the threatening apparatus, and avoided mechanical links with the eyelid, Spence went to the opposite extreme and thoroughly frightened his subjects. As a consequence, N played an important part in Spence's experiments, differences in activation drowning out differences in arousal, while activation played no part in Eysenck's experiment, allowing arousal to determine the observed correlations. Note that these pre-experimental conditions were not discussed in the presentation of the experiments in question!

6. Neurological and hormonal systems interact in complex ways, and so do the dimensions of personality; it is never safe to assume that E+ and E– subjects are not influenced in their reactions by differences in P, or N, or intelligence, or whatever. At best these extraneous influences balance out, but they obviously constitute a goodly background of noise against which the signal may not be all that strong. The effects of such interactions deserve more detailed study than they have received hitherto. These difficulties are particularly critical in relation to neuroticism, because of the added complication that it is very difficult to manipulate experimentally states of depression, anxiety, guilt feelings, etc. Laboratory experiments are very restricted in what can and cannot be done ethically, and the very minor and weak manipulations of mood possible in the laboratory pay little relation to the very strong feelings elicited in a normal life. Cortical arousal, on the other hand, is much more manipulable, and hence work with the arousal theory of extraversion has been much more successful.

EEG STUDIES AND PERSONALITY

Of the many different ways in which cortical arousal has been studied in relation to extraversion-introversion, the most prominent and indeed also the most obvious has of course been that of using electroencephalography. High levels of arousal are linked with low-amplitude, high-frequency activity in the alpha range of the EEG, and if it were found that extroverts showed low-amplitude and high-frequency alpha activity, this would certainly speak very strongly against the theory. It can of course be objected that the EEG, being recorded from the outside of the skull, represents a kind of composite amalgam of electrical energy generated from different parts of the cortex, and may thus produce a misleading impression of the actual activity in any specific area of the brain. In spite of this complication, evidence has consistently tended to support the hypothesis.

Gale (1983) has reviewed 33 studies containing a total of 38 experimental comparisons. Results are far from uniform, but nevertheless on this criterion extroverts were less aroused than introverts in 22 comparisons, while introverts were less aroused than extroverts in only five comparisons, no significant effects being reported in the remaining studies. The ratio of 22 to 5 in favor of the hypothesis is certainly a very positive finding, but one would like to be able to account for the 5 studies failing to show the predicted relationship.

Gale suggested that the effects of extraversion of the EEG were influenced by the level of arousal induced by the experimental conditions; in particular, he suggested that introverts are most likely to be more aroused than extroverts in moderately arousing conditions, with the differences between introverts and extroverts either disappearing or being reversed with conditions producing either very low or very high levels of arousal. These suggestions follow from the general theory, with high levels of arousal and introversion producing the paradoxical lowering of arousal postulated by Pavlov's Law of Transmarginal Inhibition. Conditions of very low arousal would paradoxically produce strong feelings of boredom in extroverts, which have been shown to lead to attempts at disinhibition.

Gale classified all the relevant EEG studies according to whether the test conditions were minimally, moderately, or highly arousing; he found that introverts appeared to be more aroused than extroverts in all eight of the studies using moderately arousing conditions that reported significant effects of extraversion; but the expected result was found in only 9 out of 12 significant studies using low-arousal conditions, and 5 out of 7 using high-arousal conditions. This result certainly suggests that in testing the hypothesis we should avoid extreme low arousal and high arousal situations, although even under such conditions likely to produce failure of the hypothesis,

we still have 14 experiments supporting it, and only 5 giving the opposite result.

Later studies (O'Gorman & Mallise, 1984; O'Gorman & Lloyd, 1987; and Venturini, Pascalis, Imperiali, & Martini, 1981) found results which on the whole were in confirmity with the hypothesis. They also added new measures, such as the alpha attenuation response, which demonstrated that extroverts sometimes reacted to the auditory stimuli, while introverts did not. This greater responsivity to stimulation of introverts is of course in line with the theory.

Cortical evoked potentials furnish us with another possible way of testing the theory. Stelmack, Achorn, and Michaud (1977) found that introverts obtained greater amplitude of the average evoked response (AER) than extroverts with low-frequency stimulation, both with 55 dB and with 80 dB, while observing no differences between groups with high-frequency stimulation. This finding is explicable in terms of the known tendency of greater interindividual variability of the AER at low-frequency than at high-frequency levels (Davis & Zerlin, 1966; Rothman, 1970), as an increase in variance would obviously increase the possibility of obtaining significant covariance. The study is instructive in demonstrating the need to control details of the experimental manipulation, and pay attention to known features of the variables in question.

Another approach using evoked potentials is the augmenting/reducing effect, which relies on the assessment of cortical responses to stimuli of varying intensities. Increasing intensity of stimulation may produce corresponding increases or decreases in the amplitude of particular EP components recorded from different subjects. Augmenters are called such because increased stimulation produces increased amplitude, while for reducers increased stimulation produces decreased amplitude. The theory would predict an increase in amplitude with increases in stimulus intensity, up to a point where transmarginal inhibition would set in to lead to a reduction in amplitude. The point where reduction would be expected to set in would be expected to occur at *lower* levels of stimulus intensity for introverts than for extroverts. Thus introverts should be reducers, extroverts augmenters. This, indeed, has been the pattern in earlier studies (Friedman & Mears, 1979; Soskis & Shagass, 1974), and in studies using sensation-seeking measures, especially disinhibition, which is most closely related to extraversion (von Knorring, 1980; Zuckerman, Murtaugh, & Siegel, 1974). The only study out of line is one published by Haier, Robinson, Braden and Williams (1984). This only dealt with 11 augmenters and 10 reducers, which is a very small number, but nevertheless the results were significant and counter to the theory. Clearly, what is needed are more analytical studies to give us more information. . . .

ELECTRODERMAL STUDIES OF PERSONALITY

Studies of electrodermal responses are almost as numerous as those using the EEG. In particular, relations have been studied to the orienting response (Lynn, 1966; Sokolov, 1963). Eysenck's theory would predict that introverts would show a stronger OR, and slower habituation. A large number of studies has been referenced by Eysenck (1990), most supporting the hypothesis, but many giving insignificant or contrary results. It can be noted that greater intensity of stimulation tends to produce differences where less intense stimulation does not. Thus, as far as auditory stimulation is concerned, which has been most widely used, studies using sounds in the region of 60–75 dB typically fail to differentiate introverts and extroverts, whereas stimuli in the 75–90 dB range tend to do so. As mentioned, interindividual variability of the auditory-evoked response has been found to be greater under low-frequency conditions, which also favor the differentiation of extroverts and introverts; similarly, low-frequency stimulation seems to be more effective in differentiating extroverts and introverts in the OR paradigm. . . .

MISCELLANEOUS MEASURES OF PERSONALITY

In addition to EEG and electrodermal studies, there are a number of miscellaneous measures which ought at least to be mentioned. The first of these concerns stimulated salivation in its relation to extraversion. Eysenck's theory predicts that introverts would react more strongly than extroverts to stimulation, such as drops of lemon juice on the tongue, producing a greater flow of saliva. Deary, Ramsay, Wilson, and

Riad (1988) have summarized details on nine studies; they abstract their results as follows:

> *The negative relation between extraversion and acid-stimulated salivation holds: for both male and female Ss with different saliva collection procedures; whether fresh or synthetic lemon juice or citric acid is used as a stimulus, (although fresh lemon juice appears the most reliable); whether the stimulus is dropped or swabbed onto the tongue and whether the saliva is collected for ten seconds or ten minutes. There is, however, some evidence that the correlation is more robust when testing is performed in the morning when arousal differences are at their greatest. Swallowing the stimulus also appears to reduce the correlation. (p. 906)*

S. P. G. and H. J. Eysenck (1967), tested the hypothesis that swallowing the stimulus, and thus increasing its intensity, would evoke transmarginal inhibition preferentially in introverts, and found that it in fact reversed the correlation. Overall results are certainly favorable to the hypothesis. In their own study, Deary, *et al.* (1988) used 24 subjects, and reported replication of the findings outlined above.

Pupillometry is the next topic to be discussed in this section. In recent years there has been an increased interest in the use of the pupillary response as a psychophysiological measure relating to personality. Pupillary dilation is due primarily to sympathetic activity, whereas constriction reflects parasympathetic activity. We can thus use pupillometry to measure individual differences in responsiveness to stimulation, and tonic pupil size in the absence of specific stimulation can provide an index of general or autonomic arousal. In the first of this line of studies, Holmes (1967) measured speed of pupillary constriction to the onset of a light. The fast dilators tended to be extraverted, whereas the fast constrictors were introverted. Holmes argued that the rapid pupillary constriction of introverts indicated that they had greater amounts of acetylcholine at cholinergic synapses than extroverts.

Frith (1977) confirmed some of Holmes' findings, reporting that high scorers of the impulsivity component of extraversion showed less pupillary constriction than low impulsives in responses to a light flash, perhaps because they were less reactive to stimulation. He also found that impulsivity was negatively correlated with pupil size during an initial interval of no stimulation. This suggests that the more impulsive subjects (high P?) were less aroused than the less impulsive subjects.

The most important study in this field was reported by Stelmack and Mandelzys (1975); they also found that introverts had larger pupils than extroverts in the absence of specific stimulation, suggesting that the introverted subjects were more aroused throughout the experiment. As regards phasic pupillary responses to auditorily presented neutral, affective, and taboo words, they found that introverts showed significantly more pupillary dilation to these stimuli than extroverts, especially in response to taboo words. In other words, introverts responded more strongly than extroverts to the auditory stimuli. Altogether this line of research seems promising, and should be pursued in the future.

Studies of physique and constitution, as reviewed by Eysenck (1990), are also relevant to the concept of extraversion, although, because of a failure to link theoretically the work on body build, blood groups, etc. with the concept of arousal, these data will not be discussed in detail here. Suffice it to say that extroverts tend to be relatively broad, introverts elongated in body build (Eysenck, 1970; Rees, 1973), and that introversion is found to be significantly more frequent among persons having the AB blood group (Angst & Maurer-Groeli, 1974; Maurer-Groeli, 1974a, b). Eysenck (1977) has reported on national differences in personality as related to ABO blood group polymorphism.

BIOCHEMICAL DETERMINANTS OF PERSONALITY

As a final group of studies relating biological mechanisms to personality we must turn to biochemical influences, a group of determinants which have been studied more and more frequently in recent years, and work which has been surveyed in some detail by Zuckerman, Ballenger, and Post (1984). Of the more obvious hormones here we may mention the gonadal hormones, particularly testosterone. It is of course *prenatal* androgenization which has been shown to be particularly effective in producing masculine-type behaviors (Eysenck & Wilson, 1979), and there are obvious problems with correlational studies of testosterone and

behavior, as well as with other biochemicals that show day-to-day fluctuations in level. Nevertheless, Daitzman, Zuckerman, Sammelwitz, and Ganjam (1978) found significant correlations between plasma androgen levels and the Disinhibition subscale of the Sensation-Seeking Scale, i.e., the scale most closely related to extraversion. In their later and more comprehensive study, Daitzman and Zuckerman (1980) again found high scorers on the Disinhibition scale to have higher levels of testosterone, and of estradiol and estrogen, than those with lower scores. They also used other indices of hormonal influence, and carried out a factor analysis too complex to be discussed here.

Another important biochemical agent is the enzyme MAO, which is present in all tissues including brain, with highest brain concentrations being found in the hypothalamus. MAO plays a role in the degradation of the monoamines norepinephrine, dopamine, and serotonin. The review by Zuckerman *et al.* (1984) indicates that MAO levels relate *negatively* to extraversion and sensation-seeking; these findings are consistent with behavioral observations of high- and low-MAO monkeys, and humans (Coursey, Buchsbaum, & Murphy, 1979). High-MAO monkeys in colony tended to be solitary, inactive, and passive; low-MAO monkeys tended to be active, to make many social contacts, and engage frequently in play. In rodents, too, MAO inhibitors produce hyperactivity and increase activity in a novel environment. Later studies by Schalling, Edman, Asberg, and Oreland, (1988), Calhoon (1988), Klinteberg, Schalling, Edman, Oreland, and Asberg (1987), and von Knorring, Oreland, and Wimblad (1984) bear out these major findings. Correlations have also been found between measures of impulsivity and CSF levels of the serotonin metabolite, 5-HIAA (Schalling, Asberg, Edman, & Levander, 1984), which is interesting in view of the associations assumed to exist between low-platelet MAO activity and central serotonergic hyperactivity. These results form a fairly congruent whole centering on the concept of impulsivity, and hence implicating P as well as E. Others have used the monoamine system (e.g., Ballenger, Post, Jimmerson, Lake, Murphy, Zuckerman, & Cronin, 1983), showing that CSF calcium correlated positively with extraversion and negatively with neurotic introversion and general neuroticism. Another interesting finding is that cortisol assayed from CSF correlated negatively with the Disinhibition scale from the Sensation-Seeking Scale.

Finally, we must mention the sedation threshold (Krishnamoorti & Shagass, 1963; Shagass & Jones, 1958; Shagass & Kerenyi, 1958). In these studies we start out with a group of introverts, ambiverts and extraverts who are administered some form of depressant or sedative, usually one of the barbiturates; also defined is a "sedation threshold," i.e., a point at which qualitative differences in behavior occur as a function of drug administration. Extraverts being characterized by lower arousal (or higher inhibition) than introverts, according to the theory, should require less of the drug to reach this threshold. The early studies certainly supported the hypothesis quite strongly, but later studies (e.g., Claridge, Donald, & Birchall, 1981) found that differences in neuroticism disturbed this clear-cut picture. The highest drug tolerance was shown by introverts with smallest neuroticism, and the lowest drug tolerance occurred among neurotic extraverts. Thus the hypothesis that introverts have higher sedation thresholds than extraverts was supported among those of medium neuroticism, whereas the opposite tendency was present among those of low neuroticism. While on the whole the data supports the hypothesis, it clearly requires amplification.

This rapid overview will suffice to show that there are meaningful and significant relationships between biological features of the organism and observable behavior patterns in social life. No doubt the arousal theory is simplistic, not sufficiently detailed, and certainly oversimplified; nevertheless it has given rise to large numbers of positive findings. Making a rough-and-ready calculation of all the available studies in this field, we may say that the ratio of successes to failures is roughly 4 or 5 to 1. This would seem to argue that while the theory is clearly along the right lines, it requires a good deal of modification, amplification, and explication, particularly with respect to the details of experimental manipulation. Predictions from the personality theory to behavioral indices and laboratory studies of memory, conditioning, vigilance, reminiscence, perception, and many other areas, have on the whole been somewhat more successful than predictions in the physiological, neuro-

logical, and hormonal fields (Eysenck, 1976, 1981), for reasons already given. Nevertheless, at the moment there is no alternative theory which could account for the facts anything like as well as that of cortical arousal.

It should perhaps be noted, if only as a final comment, that the arrow of causality does not necessarily always go from the biological to the behavioral side. Taking testosterone as an example, aggressive and sexual behavior can significantly change the level of testosterone, as well as being itself influenced by that level (Eysenck, 1990). This is not true of all the variables discussed (e.g., blood type polymorphisms are not affected by behavior), but it would be simple-minded to assume that the relationship is completely one-sided. The biosocial approach to human behavior, and to personality in particular, must take all possibilities into account. Nevertheless, it is clear that in the majority of cases genetic factors determine physiological, neurological and hormonal patterns, and these in turn affect behavior. This simple lesson is absolutely fundamental to an understanding of personality differences in particular, and behavior in general.

REFERENCES

Eysenck, H. J. (1967). *The biological basis of personality.* Springfield, IL: Thomas.

Eysenck, H. J. (1990). Biological dimensions of personality. In L. A. Pervin (Ed.), *Handbook of personality theory and research.* New York: Guilford Press.

Haier, R. J., Robinson, D. L., Braden, W., & Williams, D. (1984). Evoked potential augmenting-reducing and personality differences. *Personality and Individual Differences, 5,* 293–301.

Klinteberg, B., Schalling, D. Edman, G., Oreland, L., & Asberg, H. E. (1987). Personality correlates of platelet monamine oxidase (MAO) activity in female and male subjects. *Neuropsychology, 18,* 89–96.

Stelmack, R. M. (1981). The psychophysiology of extraversion and neuroticism. In H. J. Eysenck (Ed.), *A model for personality.* New York: Springer.

Strelau, J., & Eysenck, H. J. (Eds.). (1987). *Personality dimensions and arousal.* New York: Plenum.

Zuckerman, M. (Ed.). (1983). *Biological bases of sensation seeking, impulsivity and anxiety.* Hillsdale, NJ: Erlbaum.

_____ Questions to Think About _____

1. What are some of the advantages of considering both the biology and environment of an individual when assessing personality?

2. Could a person's personality be biologically designed by altering biochemical and/or biological functions? What are some possible consequences of creating an "artificial personality"?

3. How useful are such biological measures as heart rate, blood, pupil dilation, and physique to personality assessment?

15

My Genes Made Me Do It

STANTON PEELE AND RICHARD DEGRANDPRE

Stanton Peele is a psychologist who is an expert on research on addiction. He received his Ph.D. from the University of Michigan, and has spent many years talking to the public about the bases of drug use and social compulsions. Richard DeGrandpre, who worked with Peele on this article, is known for his opposition to the overuse of drugs, especially Ritalin, to treat Attention Deficit Disorder.

Peele has been forceful in arguing that people increasingly have a tendency to over-attribute and overexplain their behavior in terms of genetic and other biological causes. As this selection points out, growing interest in the biological bases of behavior raises many old issues of freedom versus determinism, and blame versus responsibility, that are so important for understanding personality psychology and are often hidden or embedded within the theories.

Just about every week now, we read a newspaper headline about the genetic basis for breast cancer, homosexuality, intelligence, or obesity. In previous years, these stories were about the genes for alcoholism, schizophrenia, and manic-depression. Such news stories may lead us to believe our lives are being revolutionized by genetic discoveries. We may be on the verge of reversing and eliminating mental illness, for example. In addition, many believe, we can identify the causes of criminality, personality, and other basic human foibles and traits.

But these hopes, it turns out, are based on faulty assumptions about genes and behavior. Although genetic research wears the mantle of science, most of the headlines are more hype than reality. Many discoveries loudly touted to the public have been quietly refuted by further research. Other scientifically valid discoveries—like the gene for breast cancer—have nonetheless fallen short of initial claims.

Popular reactions to genetic claims can be greatly influenced by what is currently politically correct.

Consider the hubbub over headlines about a genetic cause for homosexuality and by the book *The Bell Curve,* which suggested a substantial genetic basis for intelligence. Many thought the discovery of a "gay gene" proved that homosexuality is not a personal choice and should therefore not lead to social disapproval. *The Bell Curve,* on the other hand, was attacked for suggesting differences in IQ measured among the races are inherited.

The public is hard pressed to evaluate which traits are genetically inspired based on the validity of scientific research. In many cases, people are motivated to accept research claims by the hope of finding solutions for frightening problems, like breast cancer, that our society has failed to solve. At a personal level, people wonder about how much actual choice they have in their lives. Accepting genetic causes for their traits can relieve guilt about behavior they want to change, but can't.

These psychological forces influence how we view mental illnesses like schizophrenia and depression,

Source: Peele, S., & DeGrandpre, R. (1995). My genes made me do it! *Psychology Today, 28*(4), (July/August), 50–53, 62, 64, 66, 68. Reprinted by permission.

social problems like criminality, and personal maladies like obesity and bulimia. All have grown unabated in recent decades. Efforts made to combat them, at growing expense, have made little or no visible progress. The public wants to hear that science can help, while scientists want to prove that they have remedies for problems that eat away at our individual and social well-being.

Meanwhile, genetic claims are being made for a host of ordinary and abnormal behaviors, from addiction to shyness and even to political views and divorce. If who we are is determined from conception, then our efforts to change or to influence our children may be futile. There may also be no basis for insisting that people behave themselves and conform to laws. Thus, the revolution in thinking about genes has monumental consequences for how we view ourselves as human beings.

THE HUMAN GENOME PROJECT

Today scientists are mapping the entire genome—the DNA contained in the 23 human chromosomes. This enterprise is enormous. The chromosomes of each person contain 3 billion permutations of four chemical bases arrayed in two interlocking strands. This DNA may be divided into between 50,000 and 100,000 genes. But the same DNA can function in more than one gene, making the concept of individual genes something of a convenient fiction. The mystery of how these genes, and the chemistry underlying them, cause specific traits and diseases is a convoluted one.

The Human Genome Project has, and will continue to, advance our understanding of genes and suggest preventive and therapeutic strategies for many diseases. Some diseases, like Huntington's, have been linked to a single gene. But the search for single genes for complex human traits, like sexual orientation or antisocial behavior, or mental disorders like schizophrenia or depression, is seriously misguided.

Most claims linking emotional disorders and behaviors to genes are *statistical* in nature. For example, differences in the correlations in traits between identical twins (who inherit identical genes) and fraternal twins (who have half their genes in common) are examined with the goal of separating the role of environment from that of genes. But this goal is elusive. Research finds that identical twins are treated

more alike than fraternal twins. These calculations are therefore insufficient for deciding that alcoholism or manic-depression is inherited, let alone television viewing, conservatism, and other basic, everyday traits for which such claims have been made.

THE MYTH OF MENTAL ILLNESS

In the late 1980s, genes for schizophrenia and manic-depression were identified with great fanfare by teams of geneticists. Both claims have now been definitively disproved. Yet, while the original announcements were heralded on TV news and front pages of newspapers around the country, most people are unaware of the refutations.

In 1987, the prestigious British journal *Nature* published an article linking manic-depression to a specific gene. This conclusion came from family linkage studies, which search for gene variants in suspect sections on the chromosomes of families with a high incidence of a disease. Usually, an active area of DNA (called a genetic marker) is observed to coincide with the disease. If the same marker appears only in diseased family members, evidence of a genetic link has been established. Even so, this does not guarantee that a gene can be identified with the marker.

One genetic marker of manic-depression was identified in a single extended Amish family. But this marker was not apparent in other families that displayed the disorder. Then, further evaluations placed several members of the family without the marker in the manic-depressive category. Another marker detected in several Israeli families was subjected to more detailed genetic analysis, and a number of subjects were switched between the marked and unmarked categories. Ultimately, those with and without the putative markers had similar rates of the disorder.

Other candidates for a manic-depression gene will be put forward. But most researchers no longer believe a single gene is implicated, even within specific families. In fact, genetic research on manic-depression and schizophrenia has rekindled the recognition of the role of environment in emotional disorders. If distinct genetic patterns can't be tied to the disorders, then personal experiences are most likely crucial in their emergence.

Epidemiologic data on the major mental illnesses make it clear that they can't be reduced to purely genetic causes. For example, according to psychiatric epidemiologist Myrna Weissman, Ph.D., Americans born before 1905 had a 1 percent rate of depression by age 75. Among Americans born a half century later, 6 percent become depressed *by age 24!* Similarly, while the average age at which manic-depression first appears was 32 in the mid 1960s, its average onset today is 19. Only social factors can produce such large shifts in incidence and age of onset of mental disorders in a few decades.

GENES AND BEHAVIOR

Understanding the role of our genetic inheritance requires that we know how genes express themselves. One popular conception is of genes as templates stamping out each human trait whole cloth. In fact, genes operate by instructing the developing organism to produce sequences of biochemical compounds.

In some cases, a single, dominant gene *does* largely determine a given trait. Eye color and Huntington's disease are classic examples of such Mendelian traits (named after the Austrian monk, Gregor Mendel, who studied peas). But the problem for behavioral genetics is that complex human attitudes and behavior—and even most disease—are not determined by single genes.

Moreover, even at the cellular level, environment affects the activity of genes. Much active genetic material does not code for any kind of trait. Instead it regulates the speed and direction of the expression of other genes; it modulates the unfolding of the genome. Such regulatory DNA reacts to conditions inside and outside the womb, stimulating different rates of biochemical activity and cellular growth. Rather than forming a rigid template for each of us, most genes form part of a lifelong give-and-take process with the environment.

The inextricable interplay between genes and environment is evident in disorders like alcoholism, anorexia, or overeating that are characterized by abnormal behaviors. Scientists spiritedly debate whether such syndromes are more or less biologically driven. If they are mainly biological—rather than psycholog-ical, social, and cultural—then there may be a genetic basis for them.

Therefore, there was considerable interest in the announcement of the discovery of an "alcoholism gene" in 1990. Kenneth Blum, Ph.D., of the University of Texas, and Ernest Noble, M.D., of the University of California, Los Angeles, found an allele of the dopamine receptor gene in 70 percent of a group of alcoholics—these were cadavers—but in only 20 percent of a non-alcoholic group. (An allele is one form of gene.)

The Blum-Noble discovery was broadcast around the country after being published in the *Journal of the American Medical Association* and touted by the AMA on its satellite news service. But, in a 1993 *JAMA* article, Joel Gelernter, M.D., of Yale and his colleagues surveyed all the studies that examined this allele and alcoholism. Discounting Blum and Noble's research, the combined results were that 18 percent of nonalcoholics, 18 percent of problem drinkers, and 18 percent of severe alcoholics *all* had the allele. There was simply no link between this gene and alcoholism!

Blum and Noble have developed a test for the alcoholism gene. But, since their own data indicate that the majority of people who have the target allele are not alcoholics, it would be foolhardy to tell those who test positive that they have an "alcoholism gene."

The dubious state of Blum and Noble's work does not disprove that a gene—or set of genes—could trigger alcoholism. But scientists already know that people do not inherit loss-of-control-drinking whole cloth. Consider this: Alcoholics do not drink uncontrollably when they are unaware that they are drinking alcohol—if it is disguised in a flavored drink, for example.

A more plausible model is that genes may affect how people experience alcohol. Perhaps drinking is more rewarding for alcoholics. Perhaps some people's neurotransmitters are more activated by alcohol. But although genes can influence reactions to alcohol, they cannot explain why some people continue drinking to the point of destroying their lives. Most people find orgasms rewarding, but hardly any engage in sex uncontrollably. Rather, they balance their sexual urges against other forces in their lives.

Jerome Kagan, Ph.D., a Harvard developmental psychologist, was speaking about more than genes when he noted, "we also inherit the human capacity for restraint."

OF (FAT) MICE AND MEN

Public interest was aroused by the 1995 announcement by Rockefeller University geneticist Jeffrey Friedman, M.D., of a genetic mutation in obese mice. The researchers believe this gene influences development of a hormone that tells the organism how fat or full it is. Those with the mutation may not sense when they have achieved satiety or if they have sufficient fatty tissue, and thus can't tell when to stop eating.

The researchers also reported finding a gene nearly identical to the mouse obesity gene in humans. The operation of this gene in humans has not yet been demonstrated, however. Still, professionals like University of Vermont psychologist Esther Rothblum, Ph.D., reacted enthusiastically. "This research indicates that people really are born with a tendency to have a certain weight, just as they are to have a particular skin color or height."

Actually, behavioral geneticists believe that less than half of total weight variation is programmed in the genes, while height is almost entirely genetically determined. Whatever role genes play, America is getting fatter. A survey by the Center for Disease Control found that obesity has increased greatly over the last 10 years. Such rapid change underlines the role of environmental factors, like the abundance of rich foods in America's overeating. The CDC has also found that teens are far less physically active than they were even a decade ago.

Certainly people metabolize food differently and some gain weight more easily than others. Nonetheless, anyone placed in a food-rich environment that encourages inactivity will gain weight, whatever fat genes the person has. But, in nearly all environments, highly motivated people can maintain lower weight levels. We thus see that social pressure, self-control, specific situations—even seasonal variations—combine with physical make-up to influence diet and determine weight.

Accepting that weight is predetermined can relieve guilt for overweight people. But people's belief that they cannot control their weight can itself contribute to obesity. No test will ever be performed that can tell you how much you must weigh. Personal choices will always influence the equation. And anything that inspires positive efforts at weight control can help people lose weight, or avoid gaining more.

The case of obesity—along with schizophrenia, depression, and alcoholism—raises a striking paradox. At the same time that we now view these conditions as diseases that should be treated medically, their prevalence is growing precipitously. The very reliance on drugs and other medical treatments has created a cultural milieu that seeks external solutions for these problems. Relying on external solutions may itself be exacerbating matters; it may be teaching us a helplessness that is at the root of many of our problems. Instead of reducing the incidence of these problems, this seems to have fueled their growth.

HARNESSING DISCOVERIES

In 1993, the gene that determines the occurrence of Huntington's disease, an irreversible degeneration of the nervous system, was discovered. In 1994, a gene was identified that leads to some cases of breast cancer. Utilizing these discoveries, however, is proving more difficult than anticipated.

Finding a gene for breast cancer was cause for elation. But of all the women with breast cancer, only a tenth have family histories of the disease. Furthermore, only half of this group has the gene mutation. Scientists also hoped that breast cancer victims without family histories would show irregularities at this same site on the DNA. But only a small minority do.

The section of the DNA involved in inherited breast cancer is enormously large and complex. There are probably several hundred forms of the gene. The task of determining which variations in the DNA cause cancer, let alone developing therapies to combat the disease, is tremendous. Right now, women who learn that they have the gene defect know they have a high (85 percent) likelihood of developing the disease. But the only decisive response available to them is to have their breasts removed before the disease appears. And even this does not eliminate the possibility of cancer.

The failure to translate genetic discoveries into treatments has also been true for Huntington's disease. Scientists have been unable to detect how the flawed gene switches on dementia and palsy. These difficulties with a disease created by an individual gene show the monumental complexity involved in unraveling how genes determine human traits.

When a distinct gene is not involved, linking genes to traits may well be an absurdity. Any possible link between genes and traits is exponentially more complex with elaborate behavior patterns like overdrinking, personality characteristics like shyness or aggressiveness, or social attitudes such as political conservatism and religiousness. Many genes might be involved in all such traits. It is impossible to separate the contributions environment and DNA make to attitudes and behaviors.

BEHAVIORAL GENETICS: METHODS AND MADNESS

The research discussed so far searches for genes implicated in specific problems. But research relating behavior and genetics rarely involves actual examination of the genome. Instead, psychologists, psychiatrists, and other nongeneticists calculate a heritability statistic by comparing the similarity in behaviors among different sets of relatives. This statistic expresses the old nature–nurture division by representing the percentage of a behavior due to genetic inheritance versus the percentage due to environmental causes.

Such research purports to show a substantial genetic component to alcoholism. For example, some studies have compared the incidence of alcoholism in adopted children with that of their adoptive parents and with their natural parents. When the similarities are greater between the offspring and absent biologic parents, the trait is thought to be highly heritable.

But children are often adopted by relatives or people from the same social background as the parents. The very social factors related to placement of a child—particularly ethnicity and social class—are also related to drinking problems, for example, thus confusing efforts to separate nature and nurture. A team led by University of California sociologist Kaye Fillmore, Ph.D., incorporated social data on adoptive families in the reanalysis of two studies claiming a large genetic inheritance for alcoholism. Fillmore found that the educational and economic level of the receiving families had the greater influence, statistically erasing the genetic contribution from the biological parents.

Another behavioral genetics methodology compares the prevalence of a trait in monozygotic (identical) twins and dizygotic (fraternal) twins. On average, fraternal twins have only half their genes in common. If the identical twins are more alike, it is believed that genetic inheritance is, more important, because the two types of twins are supposedly brought up in identical environments. (To eliminate the confounding influence of gender differences, only same-sex fraternal twins are compared.)

But if people treat identical twins more similarly than they treat fraternal twins, the assumptions of the heritability index dissolve. Much research shows that physical appearance affects how parents, peers, and others react to a child. Thus, identical twins—who more closely resemble one another—will experience a more similar environment than fraternal twins. University of Virginia psychologist Sandra Scarr, Ph.D., has shown that fraternal twins who resemble one another enough to be *mistaken* for identical twins have more similar personalities than other such twins.

Heritability figures depend upon a number of factors, such as the specific population being studied and where. For example, there will be less variation in weight in a food-deprived environment. Studying the inheritance of weight in deprived settings rather than an abundant food environment can greatly influence the heritability calculation.

Heritability figures in fact vary widely from study to study. Matthew McGue, Ph.D., and his colleagues at the University of Minnesota calculated a zero heritability of alcoholism in women, while at the same time a team led by Kenneth Kendler, M.D., at Virginia Medical College calculated a 60 percent heritability with a different group of female twins! One problem is that the number of female alcoholic twins is small, which is true of most abnormal conditions we study. As a result, the high heritability figure Kendlier's team found would be reduced to nothing with a shift in the diagnoses of as few as four twins.

Shifting definitions also contribute to variations in the heritability measured for alcoholism. Alcoholism may be defined as any drinking problems, or only physiological problems such as DTs, or various combinations of criteria. These variations in methodology explain why heritability figures for alcoholism in different studies vary from zero to almost 100 percent!

THE INHERITANCE OF HOMOSEXUALITY

In the debate over homosexuality, the data supporting a genetic basis are similarly weak. One study by Michael Bailey, Ph.D., a Northwestern University psychologist, and Richard Piliard, M.D., a psychiatrist at Boston University, found that about half the identical twins (52 percent) of homosexual brothers were homosexual themselves, compared with about a quarter (22 percent) of fraternal twins of homosexuals. But this study recruited subjects through ads in gay publications. This introduces a bias toward the selection of overtly gay respondents, a minority of all homosexuals.

Moreover, other results of their study do not support a genetic basis for homosexuality. Adopted brothers (11 percent) had as high a "concordance rate" for homosexuality as ordinary brothers (9 percent). The data also showed that fraternal twins were more than twice as likely as ordinary brothers to share homosexuality, although both sets of siblings have the same genetic relationship. These results suggest the critical role of environmental factors.

One study that focused on a supposed homosexual gene was conducted by Dean Hamer, Ph.D., a molecular biologist at the National Cancer Institute. Hamer found a possible genetic marker on the X chromosome in 33 of 40 brothers who were both gay (the number expected by chance was 20). Earlier Simon LeVay, M.D., a neurologist at the Salk Institute, noted an area of the brain's hypothalamus that was smaller among gay than heterosexual men.

Although both these findings were front-page stories, they provide quite a slender basis for the genetics of homosexuality. Hamer did not check for the frequency of the supposed marker in heterosexual brothers, where it could conceivably be as prevalent as in gay siblings. Hamer has noted that he doesn't know how the marker he found could cause homo-

sexuality, and LeVay likewise concedes he hasn't found a brain center for homosexuality.

But for many, the politics of a homosexual gene outweigh the science. A genetic explanation for homosexuality answers bigots who claim homosexuality is a choice that should be rejected. But to accept that nongenetic factors contribute to homosexuality does not indicate prejudice against gays. David Barr, of the Gay Men's Health Crisis, puts the issue this way: "It doesn't really matter why people are gay. . . . What's really important is how they're treated."

EVERYDAY PSYCHOLOGICAL TRAITS

By assigning a simple percentage to something very complex and poorly understood, behavioral geneticists turn heritability into a clear-cut measurement. Behavioral geneticists have employed these same statistical techniques with ordinary behaviors and attitudes. The resulting list of traits for which heritability has been calculated extends from such well known areas as intelligence, depression, and shyness to such surprising ones as television viewing, divorce, and attitudes like racial prejudice and political conservatism.

Such heritability figures may seem quite remarkable, even incredible. Behavioral geneticists report that half of the basis of divorce, bulimia, and attitudes about punishing criminals is biologically inherited, comparable to or higher than the figures calculated for depression, obesity, and anxiety. Almost any trait seemingly yields a minimum heritability figure around 30 percent. The heritability index acts like a scale that reads 30 pounds when empty and adds 30 pounds to everything placed on it!

Believing that basic traits are largely predetermined at birth could have tremendous implications for our self conceptions and public policies. Not long ago, an announcement of a government conference, for example, suggested that violence could be prevented by treating with drugs children with certain genetic profiles. Or parents of children with an alcoholic heritage may tell the children never to drink because they're destined to be alcoholics. But such children, in expecting to become violent or drink excessively, may enact a self-fulfilling prophecy. Indeed, this is known to be the case. People who believe they are alcoholic drink more when told a beverage contains alcohol—even if it doesn't.

Believing the heritability figures developed by behavioral geneticists leads to an important conclusion: Most people must then be overestimating how much daily impact they have on important areas of children's development. Why ask Junior to turn off the TV set if television viewing is inherited, as some claim? What, exactly, can parents accomplish if traits such as prejudice are largely inherited? It would not seem to matter what values we attempt to convey to our children. Likewise, if violence is mostly inbred, then it doesn't make much sense to try to teach our kids to behave properly.

FROM FATALISM TO DEPRESSION

The vision of humanity generated by statistical research on behavioral genetics seems to enhance the passivity and fatalism many people are already saddled with. Yet evidence gathered by University of Pennsylvania psychologist Martin Seligman, Ph.D., and others indicates that "learned helplessness"—or believing one can't influence one's destiny—is a major factor in depression. The opposite state of mind occurs when people believe they control what happens to them. Called self-efficacy, it is a major contributor to psychological well-being and successful functioning.

Is there a connection between the increase in depression and other emotional disorders in 20th-century America and our outlook as a society? If so, then the growing belief that our behavior is not ours to determine could have extremely negative consequences. As well as attacking our own sense of personal self-determination, it may make us less able to disapprove of the misbehavior of others. After all, if people are born to be alcoholic or violent, how can they be punished when they translate these dispositions into action?

Jerome Kagan, whose studies provide a close-up of the interaction of nature and nurture and how it plays out in real life, worries that Americans are too quick to accept that behavior is predetermined. He has studied the temperaments of infants and children and found distinctive differences from birth—and even before. Some babies are outgoing, seemingly at home in the world. And some recoil from the environment;

their nervous systems are overly excitable in response to stimulation. Do such findings mean children born with a highly reactive nervous system will grow into withdrawn adults? Will extremely fearless children grow into violent criminals?

In fact, less than half of the reactive infants (those who more frequently fret and cry) are fearful children at the age of two. It all depends on the actions parents take in response to their infant.

Kagan fears people may read too much into children's supposedly biological dispositions, and make unwarranted predictions about how they will develop: "It would be unethical to tell parents that their three-year-old son is at serious risk for delinquent behavior." People who are more fearful or fearless than average have choices about the paths their lives will take, like everyone else.

NATURE, NURTURE: LET'S CALL THE WHOLE THING OFF

How much freedom each person has to develop returns us to the issue of whether nature and nurture can be separated. Thinking of traits as being either environmentally or genetically caused cripples our understanding of human development. As Kagan puts it, "To ask what proportion of personality is genetic rather than environmental is like asking what proportion of a blizzard is due to cold temperature rather than humidity."

A more accurate model is one in which chains of events split into further layers of possible paths. Let's return to alcoholism. Drinking produces greater mood change for some people. Those who find alcohol to serve a strong palliative function will be more likely to use it to calm themselves. For example, if they are highly anxious, alcohol may tranquilize them. But even this tranquilizing effect, we should recognize, is strongly influenced by social learning.

Among drinkers who are potentially vulnerable to alcohol's addictive effects, most will nonetheless find alternatives to drinking to deal with anxiety. Perhaps their social group disapproves of excessive drinking, or their own values strongly rule out drunkenness. Thus, although people who find that alcohol redresses their anxiety are more likely to drink addictively than others, they are not programmed to do so.

MIRROR, MIRROR

The goal of determining what portion of behavior is genetic and environmental will always elude us. Our personalities and destinies don't evolve in this straightforward manner. Behavioral genetics actually shows us how the statistical plumbing of the human spirit has reached its limits. Claims that our genes cause our problems, our misbehavior, even our personalities are more a mirror of our culture's attitudes than a window for human understanding and change.

_____ Questions to Think About _____

1. Why are so many people and so many counselors eager to explain alcoholism, obesity, and mental disturbances in terms of genetic endowment?

2. People clearly vary in certain biological temperaments. Think about more complex models that explain how these temperaments unfold in different environments.

3. Why does it matter if a tendency to overeat and gain weight is 31-percent influenced by our biological makeup or 46-percent so influenced?

4. Given that conditions like depression or obesity vary dramatically across time and subpopulations, is it reasonable to think that some gene or group of genes plays a straightforward role in producing them?

16

Violence against Stepchildren

MARTIN DALY AND MARGO WILSON

Martin Daly (1944–) and Margo I. Wilson (1942–) take a Darwinian view of parental love. They specialize in researching the evolutionary psychology of violence. Within this field of research, they have studied family homicide, child abuse, and step-relationships. They thus view complex human behaviors as having been selected for by eons of survival pressures.

Working for a while at the University of California, Riverside, and then for many years at McMaster University in Canada, Daly and Wilson use human epidemiological data (the distribution of disease and health in populations), but they also study animal ecosystems, including desert rodents. Daly is a past-president of the Human Behavior and Evolution Society.

On February 20th, 1992, 2-year-old Scott M. died in a Montreal hospital of massive internal injuries caused by one or more abdominal blows. At the manslaughter trial of his mother's 24-year-old live-in boyfriend, doctors testified that Scott's body displayed "all the symptoms of a battered child," mainly because of "numerous bruises of varying ages." The accused, who portrayed himself as Scott's primary caretaker, admitted assaulting the mother and other adults, but "I don't hurt kids." According to an acquaintance, however, the accused had admitted striking the child with his elbow because Scott was "bothering him while he was trying to watch television." The trial outcome was conviction.

A reader of any major newspaper is likely to have encountered similar stories, and may even have noticed that the victims are often the progeny of their killers' predecessors. Is step-relationship really a significant risk factor for lethal assaults on children? (Persons who reside with a partner and the partner's child or children of prior unions are here deemed stepparents regardless of marital registration.)

This issue has been obscured by a scarcity of relevant information in official records. In the United States, for example, the census has not distinguished between genetic parenthood and stepparenthood, and the national archive of homicide cases (the Federal Bureau of Investigation's *Supplementary Homicide Reports*) is also incomplete in this regard. But local data sets can be more informative. We examined the Chicago police department's homicide records, for example, and found that 115 children under 5 years of age were killed by their putative fathers in 1965 through 1990, while 63 were killed by stepfathers or (more or less co-resident) mothers' boyfriends. Most of these children were less than 2 years old, and because very few babies reside with substitute fathers, the numbers imply greatly elevated risk to such children. Just how great that risk might be cannot be determined, however, without better information on the living arrangements of Chicago children.

Canadian data permit somewhat more precise comparisons. A national homicide archive maintained by Statistics Canada from 1974 to 1990 included the

Source: Daly, M., & Wilson, M. I. (1996). Violence against stepchildren. *Current Directions in Psychological Science, 5,* 77–81. Reprinted by permission.

Editor's note: Citations in the text of this selection and the sources to which they point have been edited to leave only those that are the most relevant and important. Readers wishing to see the full reference list can consult the original work.

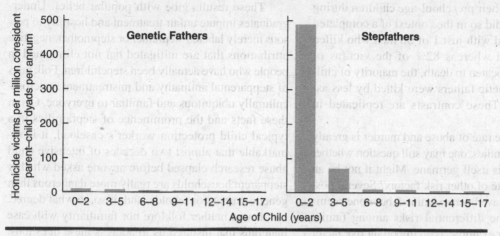

FIGURE 1   Estimated rates of homicide by genetic fathers versus stepfathers in Canada, 1974–1990. Rate numerators are based on a Statistics Canada national archive of all homicides known to Canadian police. Denominators are age-specific estimates of the numbers of Canadian children residing with each type of father, based on census information on the numbers of Canadian children in each age class in each year and age-specific proportions living with genetic fathers versus stepfathers averaged across two national surveys, conducted in 1984 (Statistics Canada's *Family History Survey*) and 1990 (Statistics Canada's *General Social Survey*). Homicide rates for stepfathers are probably underestimates, for reasons explained in the text.

relevant distinctions among parental relationships, and recent national probability sample surveys provide estimates of the age-specific distribution of such relationships in the population at large. Estimated rates of homicide by stepfathers versus genetic fathers in Canada are portrayed in Figure 1. Because step-relationships were in fact increasing from 1974 to 1990, the use of recent surveys for population-at-large estimation ensures a conservative comparison: It is virtually certain that estimated numbers of stepfathers in the population are higher than actually prevailed over the 17-year period, and that the estimated homicide rates by stepfathers are therefore low. Nevertheless, the differential is immense.

VIOLENCE IN STEPFAMILIES

Research on child abuse proliferated after Henry Kempe and colleagues' 1962 proclamation of a battered-child syndrome. However, no study addressed the incidence of child maltreatment in step- versus genetic-parent homes until 1980, when we reported

that stepchildren constituted a much higher proportion of U.S. child abuse cases than their numbers in the population at large would warrant. This excess could not be dismissed as an artifact of biased detection or reporting because it was most extreme in the fatal cases, for which such biases should be minimal: Whereas young children incurred about seven times higher rates of physical abuse in step-plus-genetic-parent homes than in two-genetic-parent homes, the differential in fatal abuse was on the order of 100-fold. Canadian and British data tell much the same story, with a large excess of stepchildren among reported child abuse victims and an even larger excess among children fatally abused.

Genetic parents kill children, too, but recent analyses indicate that the motives in these cases tend to be different. Whereas filicidal parents are often deeply depressed and may even construe murder-suicide as a humane act of rescue, homicidal step-parents are seldom suicidal and typically manifest their antipathy to their victims in the relative brutality of their lethal acts. In Canada, 44 of 155 men

(28%) who slew their preschool-age children during a 17-year period did so in the context of a completed suicide, compared with just 1 of 66 men who killed stepchildren, and whereas 82% of the victims of stepfathers were beaten to death, the majority of children slain by genetic fathers were killed by less assaultive means. These contrasts are replicated in British cases.

Given that the rate of abuse and murder is greatly elevated in stepfamilies, one may still question whether step-relationship is itself germane. Might it not be an incidental correlate of other risk factors? Several possible confounds have been examined, but none seems to account for the differential risks among family types. Poverty, for example, is an important risk factor in its own right, but is virtually uncorrelated with the incidence of step-relationship in two-parent families in the United States or Canada and thus cannot explain away the family composition effects. Large family size and maternal youth are additional factors with effects on abuse risk that are apparently distinct from the effects of step-relationship.

Finally, excess risk in stepfamilies might be due to excess numbers of violent personalities among remarried persons, but this hypothesis is refuted by evidence that abusive stepparents typically spare their own children. Step-relationship itself remains the single most important risk factor for severe child maltreatment yet discovered.

DISCRIMINATIVE PARENTAL SOLICITUDE AND STEPPARENTAL INVESTMENT

Elevated risk at the hands of stepparents has been abundantly confirmed, in a range of societies and with respect to the gamut of forms of child maltreatment. But conflict in stepfamilies is not confined to these extremes. Research on nonviolent stepfamilies is a growth industry with a single focus: how people cope with the problems characteristic of step-relationships. It is important to emphasize that many people do indeed cope very well. Nevertheless, the research consistently indicates that step-relationships are, on average, less investing, more distant, more conflictual, and less satisfying than the corresponding genetic parent–child relationships.

These results gibe with popular belief. Undergraduates impute unfair treatment and hostility to persons merely labeled stepfather or stepmother, negative attributions that are mitigated but not eliminated in people who have actually been stepchildren. Folk tales of stepparental antipathy and mistreatment are cross-culturally ubiquitous and familiar to everyone. Given these facts and the prominence of stepfamilies in a typical child protection worker's caseload, it is remarkable that almost two decades of intensive child abuse research elapsed before anyone asked whether stepparent households are really more dangerous than genetic-parent households, and, if so, to what degree.

It was neither folklore nor familiarity with case materials that inspired us to address these questions. We were stimulated by evolutionary logic and by the results of research on nonhuman animals. Current theory implies that natural selection shapes social motives and behavior to function nepotistically on behalf of blood kin, and animals have demonstrably evolved a variety of psychological mechanisms functioning to protect parents against parasitism by unrelated young. Parental care is costly, and animals usually avoid expending it on behalf of young other than their own. But then why is the human animal so willing to enter into step-relationships that may entail prolonged, costly pseudoparental investments?

One hypothesis is that stepparenthood was simply not a recurring adaptive problem for ancestral humans, so people never evolved any psychological defenses against it. Nonnutritive saccharin, an evolutionarily unforeseen component of novel environments, tickles an evolved system for the recognition of nutritive sugars. Might substitute parenthood constitute a sort of social saccharin: an evolutionarily novel circumstance in which the evolved psychology of parenthood is activated in a context slightly different from that for which it evolved? We consider this hypothesis implausible because step-relationship is assuredly not a modern novelty. Mortality levels in contemporary tribal foragers suggest that remarriage and stepparenthood must have been common for as long as people have formed marital bonds with biparental care. Moreover, the available evidence indicates that half-orphans who entered the perilous status of stepchild in a nonstate society faced a major diminution in the quality and quantity of parental care, and an elevated risk of death. In one study of a contemporary South American foraging people, for example, 43% of children raised by a mother and stepfather died before their 15th birthdays, compared with just 19% of those raised by two genetic parents.

An alternative explanation for stepparental investment that is more plausible than the social-saccharin hypothesis derives from comparative studies. Although animals usually avoid caring for their mates' offspring of prior unions, exceptions have been observed in certain species of fish, birds, and mammals. In each case, stepparental investment has been interpreted as *mating effort,* that is, as part of the cost of courting a single parent who, despite the burden of dependent young, remains an attractive prospective mate in a limited mating market. This explanation fits the human case, too. Stepparents assume their obligations in the context of a web of reciprocities with the genetic parent, who is likely to recognize more or less explicitly that stepparental tolerance and investment constitute benefits bestowed on the genetic parent and the child, entitling the stepparent to reciprocal considerations.

In this light, the existence of stepparental investment is not so surprising. But the fact of such investment cannot be taken to imply that stepparents ordinarily (or indeed ever) come to feel the sort of commitment commonly felt by genetic parents. Evolutionary thinking suggests that stepparental affection will tend to be restrained. Indulgence toward a mate's children may have had some social utility for many millennia, but it must rarely have been the case that a stepchild's welfare was as valuable to one's expected fitness as one's own child's welfare. We would therefore expect evolved mechanisms of parental feeling to be buffered against full activation when one merely assumes a parental role, and the empirical literature on stepfamily life confirms this expectation.

PARENTAL LOVE IS MORE THAN JUST A ROLE

Even within the history of Western nations, step-relationships are no novelty. In fact, they were more prevalent in Europe in recent centuries than they are now, thanks to higher death rates of parents whose children were still dependent. In premodern Germany, the age-specific mortality of children was elevated if one parent died and, more remarkably, was further elevated if the surviving parent remarried. It seems that Cinderella was more than a fairy tale.

The cross-cultural ubiquity of Cinderella stories reflects basic, recurring tensions in human society. Stepparental obligations are seldom attractive, and dependent children decrease a widowed or forsaken parent's value in the marriage market. In remarriages, pre-existing children remain a focus and a source of marital conflict, including marital violence. People in all societies face these problems, and they deal with them in various ways. One solution is for remarrying parents to leave children in the care of postmenopausal female relatives. Another is for a widow to retain her children and marry her dead husband's brother, a practice widely perceived as reducing the likelihood or severity of exploitation and mistreatment, because the stepfather is an uncle who may be expected to have some benevolent interest in his brother's children. In the absence of such practices, children have been obliged to tag along as best they can, hoping that their welfare will remain a high priority of the surviving genetic parent. Sometimes the genetic parent has to choose between the new mate and the child, and may even become complicit in the exploitation and abuse of the latter.

American social scientists have interpreted stepparenthood as a role, only partly coincident with that of genetic parenthood. The role concept has usefully directed attention to the importance of socialization and scripts, but it is at best a limited metaphor that has diverted attention away from motivational and emotional aspects of the social psyche. There is more to social action than mere familiarity with the relevant roles. Why are people motivated to embrace certain roles and to shun others? Parents are profoundly concerned for their children's well-being and future prospects, but human concerns have no part in role theorists' explanations of human action.

As Donald Symons has argued, it is especially in the domain of social motives and feelings that psychology needs Darwinism. Some aspects of human physiological and mental adaptations may be elucidated without consideration of how natural selection works, but the investigation of social motives and feelings gains crucial guidance from the recognition that it is genetic posterity, rather than happiness or life span or self-esteem, that has been the arbiter of their evolution. As any evolutionist might have anticipated, it appears that stepparents do not typically experience the same child-specific love and commitment, nor reap the same emotional rewards from unreciprocated parental investment, as genetic parents. Enormous differentials in the risk of violence are one particularly dramatic result of this predictable difference in feelings.

REFERENCES

Daly, M., & Wilson, M. I. (1996). Evolutionary psychology and marital conflict: The relevance of stepchildren. In D. M. Buss & N. Malamuth (Eds.), *Sex, power, conflict: Feminist and evolutionary perspectives*. New York; Oxford.

Lightcap, J. L., Kurland, J. A., & Burgess, R. L. (1982). Child abuse: A test of some predictions from evolutionary theory. *Ethology and Sociobiology, 3,* 61–67.

Symons, D. (1987). If we're all Darwinians, what's the fuss about? In C. Crawford, M. Smith, & D. Krebs (Eds.), *Sociobiology and psychology*. Hillsdale, NJ: Erlbaum.

Questions to Think About

1. How and why might child homicides differ between genetic parents and stepparents?
2. What factors may promote solidarity or discord within stepfamilies?
3. How might stepparenthood serve as a mating effort?
4. When do stepparents experience the same child-specific love and commitment, and reap the same emotional rewards from unreciprocated parental investment, as genetic parents? Why would many stepparents give their lives for their stepchildren?
5. What are the dangers of an oversimplified, evolutionary view of stepparenthood?
6. What are the limits of generalizing from the social behavior of rodents to the social behavior of humans?

17

Sex Differences in Jealousy:
Evolution, Physiology, and Psychology

DAVID M. BUSS, RANDY J. LARSEN, DREW WESTEN,
AND JENNIFER SEMMELROTH

Although basic evolutionary theory has been known to psychologists since the late 1800s, few direct applications to personality psychology have been attempted until recent years. In part, this is due to new developments in the theory. Evolutionary approaches to personality represent one of the few new "grand," wide-ranging approaches to personality to emerge in a long time. This approach has encountered a substantial amount of criticism as well.

David Buss, Randy Larsen, Drew Westen, and Jennifer Semmelroth are active and influential modern-day personality researchers, whose work has ranged over a variety of important topics. In this article, they make an interesting and provocative argument about how and why men and women may differ in what makes them jealous.

In species with internal female fertilization and gestation, features of reproductive biology characteristic of all 4,000 species of mammals, including humans, males face an adaptive problem not confronted by females—uncertainty in their paternity of offspring. Maternity probability in mammals rarely or never deviates from 100%. Compromises in paternity probability come at substantial reproductive cost to the male—the loss of mating effort expended, including time, energy, risk, nuptial gifts, and mating opportunity costs. A cuckolded male also loses the female's parental effort, which becomes channeled to a competitor's gametes. The adaptive problem of paternity uncertainty is exacerbated in species in which males engage in some postzygotic parental investment (Trivers, 1972). Males risk investing resources in putative offspring that are genetically unrelated.

These multiple and severe reproductive costs should have imposed strong selection pressure on males to defend against cuckoldry. Indeed, the literature is replete with examples of evolved anticuckoldry mechanisms in lions (Bertram, 1975), bluebirds (Power, 1975), doves (Erickson & Zenone, 1976), numerous insect species (Thornhill & Alcock, 1983), and nonhuman primates (Hrdy, 1979). Since humans arguably show more paternal investment than any other of the 200 species of primates (Alexander & Noonan, 1979), this selection pressure should have operated especially intensely on human males. Symons (1979); Daly, Wilson, and Weghorst (1982); and Wilson and Daly [1992] have hypothesized that male sexual jealousy evolved as a solution to this adaptive problem (but see Hupka, 1991, for an alternative view). Men who were indifferent to sexual

Source: Buss, D. M., Larsen, R. J., Westen, D., & Semmelroth, J. (1992). Sex differences in jealousy: Evolution, physiology, and psychology. *Psychological Science, 3,* 251–255. Reprinted by permission.

Editor's note: All citations in the text of this selection have been left intact from the original, but the list of references includes only those sources that are the most relevant and important. Readers wishing to follow any of the other citations can find the full references in the original work or in an online database.

contact between their mates and other men presumably experienced lower paternity certainty, greater investment in competitors' gametes, and lower reproductive success than did men who were motivated to attend to cues of infidelity and to act on those cues to increase paternity probability.

Although females do not risk maternity uncertainty, in species with biparental care they do risk the potential loss of time, resources, and commitment from a male if he deserts or channels investment to alternative mates (Buss, 1988; Thornhill & Alcock, 1983; Trivers, 1972). The redirection of a mate's investment to another female and her offspring is reproductively costly for a female, especially in environments where offspring suffer in survival and reproductive currencies without investment from both parents.

In human evolutionary history, there were likely to have been at least two situations in which a woman risked losing a man's investment. First, in a monogamous marriage, a woman risked having her mate invest in an alternative woman with whom he was having an affair (partial loss of investment) or risked his departure for an alternative woman (large or total loss of investment). Second, in polygynous marriages, a woman was at risk of having her mate invest to a larger degree in other wives and their offspring at the expense of his investment in her and her offspring. Following Buss (1988) and Mellon (1981), we hypothesize that cues to the development of a deep emotional attachment have been reliable leading indicators to women of potential reduction or loss of their mate's investment.

Jealousy is defined as an emotional "state that is aroused by a perceived threat to a valued relationship or position and motivates behavior aimed at countering the threat. Jealousy is 'sexual' if the valued relationship is sexual" (Daly et al., 1982, p. 11; see also Salovey, 1991; White & Mullen, 1989). It is reasonable to hypothesize that jealousy involves physiological reactions (autonomic arousal) to perceived threat and motivated action to reduce the threat, although this hypothesis has not been examined. Following Symons (1979) and Daly et al. (1982), our central hypothesis is that the events that activate jealousy physiologically and psychologically differ for men and women because of the different adaptive problems they have faced over human evolutionary history in mating contexts. Both sexes are hypothesized to be distressed over both sexual and emotional infidelity, and previous findings bear this out (Buss, 1989). However, these two kinds of infidelity should be weighted differently by men and women. Despite the importance of these hypothesized sex differences, no systematic scientific work has been directed toward verifying or falsifying their existence (but for suggestive data, see Francis, 1977; Teismann & Mosher, 1978; White & Mullen, 1989).

STUDY 1: SUBJECTIVE DISTRESS OVER A PARTNER'S EXTERNAL INVOLVEMENT

This study was designed to test the hypothesis that men and women differ in which form of infidelity—sexual versus emotional—triggers more upset and subjective distress, following the adaptive logic just described.

Method

After reporting age and sex, subjects ($N = 202$ undergraduate students) were presented with the following dilemma:

> Please think of a serious committed romantic relationship that you have had in the past, that you currently have, or that you would like to have. Imagine that you discover that the person with whom you've been seriously involved became interested in someone else. What would distress or upset you more (*please circle only one*):
>
> **(A) Imagining your partner forming a deep emotional attachment to that person.**
>
> **(B) Imagining your partner enjoying passionate sexual intercourse with that other person.**

Subjects completed additional questions, and then encountered the next dilemma, with the same instructional set, but followed by a different, but parallel, choice:

> **(A) Imagining your partner trying different sexual positions with that other person.**

(B) Imagining your partner falling in love with that other person.

Results

Shown in Figure 1 (upper panel) are the percentages of men and women reporting more distress in response to sexual infidelity than emotional infidelity. The first empirical probe, contrasting distress over a partner's sexual involvement with distress over a partner's deep emotional attachment, yielded a large and highly significant sex difference (χ^2 5 47.56, $df = 3$, $p < .001$). Fully 60% of the male sample reported greater distress over their partner's potential sexual infidelity; in contrast, only 17% of the female sample chose that option, with 83% reporting that they would experience greater distress over a partner's emotional attachment to a rival.

This pattern was replicated with the contrast between sex and love. The magnitude of the sex difference was large, with 32% more men than women reporting greater distress over a partner's sexual involvement with someone else, and the majority of women reporting greater distress over a partner's falling in love with a rival ($\chi^2 = 59.20$, $df = 3$, $p < .001$).

STUDY 2: PHYSIOLOGICAL RESPONSES TO A PARTNER'S EXTERNAL INVOLVEMENT

Given the strong confirmation of jealousy sex linkage from Study 1, we sought next to test the hypotheses using physiological measures. Our central measures of autonomic arousal were electrodermal activity (EDA), assessed via skin conductance, and pulse rate (PR). Electrodermal activity and pulse rate are indicators of autonomic nervous system activation (Levenson, 1988). Because distress is an unpleasant subjective state, we also included a measure of muscle activity in the brow region of the face—electromyographic (EMG) activity of the *corrugator supercilii* muscle. This muscle is responsible for the furrowing of the brow often seen in facial displays of unpleasant emotion or affect (Fridlund, Ekman, & Oster, 1987). Subjects were asked to image two scenarios in which a partner became involved with someone else—one

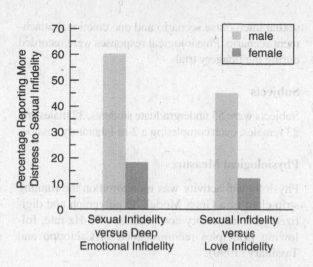

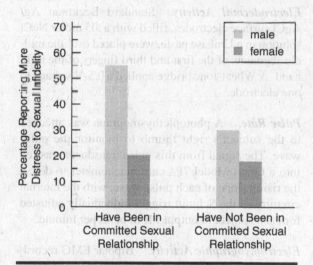

FIGURE 1   Reported comparisons of distress in response to imagining a partner's sexual or emotional infidelity. The upper panel shows results of Study 1— the percentage of subjects reporting more distress to the sexual infidelity scenario than to the emotional infidelity (left) and the love infidelity (right) scenarios. The lower panel shows the results of Study 3—the percentage of subjects reporting more distress to the sexual infidelity scenario than to the emotional infidelity scenario, presented separately for those who have experienced a committed sexual relationship (left) and those who have not experienced a committed sexual relationship (right).

sexual intercourse scenario and one emotional attachment scenario. Physiological responses were recorded during the imagery trials.

Subjects

Subjects were 55 undergraduate students, 32 males and 23 females, each completing a 2-hr laboratory session.

Physiological Measures

Physiological activity was monitored on the running strip chart of a Grass Model 7D polygraph and digitized on a laboratory computer at a 10-Hz rate, following principles recommended in Cacioppo and Tassinary (1990).

Electrodermal Activity. Standard Beckman Ag/AgCl surface electrodes, filled with a .05 molar NaCl solution in a Unibase paste, were placed over the middle segments of the first and third fingers of the right hand. A Wheatstone bridge applied a 0.5-V voltage to one electrode.

Pulse Rate. A photoplethysmograph was attached to the subject's right thumb to monitor the pulse wave. The signal from this pulse transducer was fed into a Grass Model 7P4 cardiotachometer to detect the rising slope of each pulse wave, with the internal circuitry of the Schmitt trigger individually adjusted for each subject to output PR in beats per minute.

Electromyographic Activity. Bipolar EMG recordings were obtained over the *corrugator supercilii* muscle. The EMG signal was relayed to a wide-band AC-preamplifier (Grass Model 7P3), where it was band-pass filtered, full-wave rectified, and integrated with a time constant of 0.2 s.

Procedure

After electrode attachment, the subject was made comfortable in a reclining chair and asked to relax. After a 5-min waiting period, the experiment began. The subject was alone in the room during the imagery session, with an intercom on for verbal communication. The instructions for the imagery task were written on a form which the subject was requested to read and follow.

Each subject was instructed to engage in three separate images. The first image was designed to be emotionally neutral: "Imagine a time when you were walking to class, feeling neither good nor bad, just neutral." The subject was instructed to press a button when he or she had the image clearly in mind, and to sustain the image until the experimenter said to stop. The button triggered the computer to begin collecting physiological data for 20 s, after which the experimenter instructed the subject to "stop and relax."

The next two images were infidelity images, one sexual and one emotional. The order of presentation of these two images was counterbalanced. The instructions for sexual jealousy imagery were as follows: "Please think of a serious romantic relationship that you have had in the past, that you currently have, or that you would like to have. Now imagine that the person with whom you're seriously involved becomes interested in someone else. *Imagine you find out that your partner is having sexual intercourse with this other person.* Try to feel the feelings You would have if this happened to you."

The instructions for emotional infidelity imagery were identical to the above, except the italicized sentence was replaced with *"Imagine that your partner is falling in love and forming an emotional attachment to that person."* Physiological data were collected for 20 s following the subject's button press indicating that he or she had achieved the image. Subjects were told to "stop and relax" for 30 s between imagery trials.

Results

Physiological Scores. The following scores were obtained: (a) the amplitude of the largest EDA response occurring during each 20-s trial; (b) PR in beats per minute averaged over each 20-s trial; and (c) amplitude of EMG activity over the *corrugator supercilii* averaged over each 20-s trial. Difference scores were computed between the neutral imagery trial and the jealousy induction trials. Within-sex *t* tests revealed no effects for order of presentation of the sexual jealousy image, so data were collapsed over this factor.

Jealousy Induction Effects. Table 1 shows the mean scores for the physiological measures for men and

TABLE 1 Means and Standard Deviations on Physiological Measures during Two Imagery Conditions

MEASURE	IMAGERY TYPE	MEAN	SD
	Males		
EDA	Sexual	1.30	3.64
	Emotional	−0.11	0.76
Pulse	Sexual	4.76	7.80
rate	Emotional	3.00	5.24
Brow	Sexual	6.75	32.96
EMG	Emotional	1.16	6.60
	Females		
EDA	Sexual	−0.07	0.49
	Emotional	0.21	0.78
Pulse	Sexual	2.25	4.68
rate	Emotional	2.57	4.37
Brow	Sexual	3.03	8.38
EMG	Emotional	8.12	25.60

Note. Measures are expressed as changes from the neutral image condition. EDA is in microsiemen units, pulse rate is in beats per minute, and EMG is in microvolt units.

women in each of the two imagery conditions. Differences in physiological responses to the two jealousy images were examined using paired-comparison t tests for each sex separately for EDA, PR, and EMG. The men showed significant increases in EDA during the sexual imagery compared with the emotional imagery ($t = 2.00$, $df = 29$, $p < .05$). Women showed significantly greater EDA to the emotional infidelity image than to the sexual infidelity image ($t = 2.42$, $df = 19$, $p < .05$). A similar pattern was observed with PR. Men showed a substantial increase in PR to both images, but significantly more so in response to the sexual infidelity image ($t = 2.29$, $df = 31$, $p < .05$). Women showed elevated PR to both images, but not differentially so. The results of the *corrugator* EMG were similar, although less strong. Men showed greater brow contraction to the sexual infidelity image, and women showed the opposite pattern, although results with this nonautonomic measure did not reach significance ($t = 1.12$, $df = 30$, $p < .14$, for males; $t = −1.24$, $df = 22$, $p < .12$, for females). The

elevated EMG contractions for both jealousy induction trials in both sexes support the hypothesis that the affect experienced is negative.

STUDY 3: CONTEXTS THAT ACTIVATE THE JEALOUSY MECHANISM

The goal of Study 3 was to replicate and extend the results of Studies 1 and 2 using a larger sample. Specifically, we sought to examine the effects of having been in a committed sexual relationship versus not having been in such a relationship on the activation of jealousy. We hypothesized that men who had actually experienced a committed sexual relationship would report greater subjective distress in response to the sexual infidelity imagery than would men who had not experienced a high-investing sexual relationship, and that women who had experienced a committed sexual relationship would report greater distress to the emotional infidelity image than women who had not been in a committed sexual relationship. The rationale was that direct experience of the relevant context during development may be necessary for the activation of the sex-linked weighting of jealousy activation.

Subjects

Subjects for Study 3 were 309 undergraduate students, 133 men and 176 women.

Procedure

Subjects read the following instructions:

> Please think of a serious or committed romantic relationship that you have had in the past, that you currently have, or that you would like to have. Imagine that you discover that the person with whom you've been seriously involved became interested in someone else. What would distress or upset you more (*please circle only one*):
>
> **(A) Imagining your partner falling in love and forming a deep emotional attachment to that person.**
>
> **(B) Imagining your partner having sexual intercourse with that other person.**

Alternatives were presented in standard forced-choice format, with the order counterbalanced across subjects. Following their responses, subjects were asked: "Have you ever been in a serious or committed romantic relationship? (yes or no)" and "If yes, was this a sexual relationship? (yes or no)."

Results

The results for the total sample replicate closely the results of Study 1. A much larger proportion of men (49%) than women (19%) reported that they would be more distressed by their partner's sexual involvement with someone else than by their partner's emotional attachment to, or love for, someone else ($\chi^2 = 38.48$, $df = 3, p < .001$).

The two pairs of columns in the bottom panel of Figure 1 show the results separately for those subjects who had experienced a committed sexual relationship in the past and those who had not. For women, the difference is small and not significant: Women reported that they would experience more distress about a partner's emotional infidelity than a partner's sexual infidelity, regardless of whether or not they had experienced a committed sexual relationship ($\chi^2 = 0.80, df = 1$, ns).

For men, the difference between those who had been in a sexual relationship and those who had not is large and highly significant. Whereas 55% of the men who had experienced committed sexual relationships reported that they would be more distressed by a partner's sexual than emotional infidelity, this figure drops to 29% for men who had never experienced a committed sexual relationship ($\chi^2 = 12.29, df = 1, p < .001$). Sexual jealousy in men apparently becomes increasingly activated upon experience of the relevant relationship.

DISCUSSION

The results of the three empirical studies support the hypothesized sex linkages in the activators of jealousy. Study 1 found large sex differences in reports of the subjective distress individuals would experience upon exposure to a partner's sexual infidelity versus emotional infidelity. Study 2 found a sex linkage in autonomic arousal to imagined sexual infidelity versus emotional infidelity; the results were particularly strong for the EDA and PR. Study 3 replicated the

large sex differences in reported distress to sexual versus emotional infidelity, and found a strong effect for men of actually having experienced a committed sexual relationship.

These studies are limited in ways that call for additional research. First, they pertain to a single age group and culture. Future studies could explore the degree to which these sex differences transcend different cultures and age groups. Two clear evolutionary psychological predictions are (a) that male sexual jealousy and female commitment jealousy will be greater in cultures where males invest heavily in children, and (b) that male sexual jealousy will diminish as the age of the male's mate increases because her reproductive value decreases. Second, future studies could test the alternative hypotheses that the current findings reflect (a) domain-specific psychological adaptations to cuckoldry versus potential investment loss or (b) a more domain-general mechanism such that any thoughts of sex are more interesting, arousing, and perhaps disturbing to men whereas any thoughts of love are more interesting, arousing, and perhaps disturbing to women, and hence that such responses are not specific to jealousy or infidelity. Third, emotional and sexual infidelity are clearly correlated, albeit imperfectly, and a sizable percentage of men in Studies 1 and 3 reported greater distress to a partner's emotional infidelity. Emotional infidelity may signal sexual infidelity and vice versa, and hence both sexes should become distressed at both forms (see Buss, 1989). Future research could profitably explore in greater detail the correlation of these forms of infidelity as well as the sources of within-sex variation. Finally, the intriguing finding that men who have experienced a committed sexual relationship differ dramatically from those who have not, whereas for women such experiences appear to be irrelevant to their selection of emotional infidelity as the more distressing event, should be examined. Why do such ontogenetic experiences matter for men, and why do they appear to be irrelevant for women?

Within the constraints of the current studies, we can conclude that the sex differences found here generalize across both psychological and physiological methods—demonstrating an empirical robustness in the observed effect. The degree to which these sex-linked elicitors correspond to the hypothesized sex-linked adaptive problems lends support to the evolutionary psychological framework from which they were derived. Alternative theoretical frameworks, including those that invoke culture, social construction, deconstruction, arbitrary parental socialization, and structural powerlessness, undoubtedly could be molded post hoc to fit the findings—something perhaps true of any set of findings. None but the Symons (1979) and Daly et al. (1982) evolutionary psychological frameworks, however, generated the sex-differentiated predictions in advance and on the basis of sound evolutionary reasoning. The recent finding that male sexual jealousy is the leading cause of spouse battering and homicide across cultures worldwide (Daly & Wilson, 1988a, 1988b) offers suggestive evidence that these sex differences have large social import and may be species-wide.

REFERENCES

Daly, M., & Wilson, M. (1988a). Evolutionary social psychology and family violence. *Science, 242,* 519–524.

Daly, M., & Wilson, M. (1988b). *Homicide.* Hawthorne, NY: Aldine.

Hrdy, S. B. G. (1979). Infanticide among animals: A review, classification, and examination of the implications for the reproductive strategies of females. *Ethology and Sociobiology, 1,* 14–40.

Hupka, R. B. (1991). The motive for the arousal of romantic jealousy: Its cultural origin. In P. Salovey (Ed.), *The psychology of jealousy and envy* (pp. 252–270). New York: Guilford Press.

Salovey, P. (Ed.). (1991). *The psychology of jealousy and envy.* New York: Guilford Press.

Trivers, R. (1972). Parental investment and sexual selection. In B. Campbell (Ed.), *Sexual selection and the descent of man, 1871–1971* (pp. 136–179). Chicago: Aldine.

Wilson, M., & Daly, M. (1992). The man who mistook his wife for a chattel. In J. Barkow, L. Cosmides, & J. Tooby (Eds.), *The adapted mind: Evolutionary psychology and the generation of culture.* New York: Oxford University Press.

_____ Questions to Think About _____

1. Derive some predictions and hypotheses for future experiments about jealousy. Using these predictions and hypotheses, propose some new experiments.

2. What are alternative explanations for the findings? What are the limits of an evolutionary approach in drawing strong inferences about human behavior?

3. What does this paper tell us about jealousy in sexually experienced individuals?

4. If sex differences in jealousy were adaptive in human evolutionary history, should these patterns change over the long term in an environment where contraception and paternity testing are widely available?

18

Exaptation: A Crucial Tool
for an Evolutionary Psychology

STEPHEN JAY GOULD

A paleontologist focused on evolutionary theory, Stephen Jay Gould (1941–2002) has examined the existence of racism in science. In his book, *The Mismeasure of Man,* Gould tells how even the most eminent scientists were blinded by prejudices while claiming to be engaged in purely scientific assessments. One example of such a prejudice is using skull size to "prove that men are smarter than women and Caucasians are smarter than African Americans." Such biases were especially dangerous because, though many well-intentioned scientists of the nineteenth and twentieth centuries were not conscious of distortions in their data, the fact was that their biases led to inaccurate and incorrect results. Politicians then used these biased findings to help justify racist and sexist social policies.

In the following excerpt, Gould warns against concluding that, just because some characteristic is helpful in today's world, it must have been selected for through natural selection. Rather, he points out that many characteristics that have previously been selected for a specific purpose are now taken over for, that is co-opted for, a new use. It is therefore very difficult to know the selection pressures that have allowed for complex human behaviors, and it is dangerous to assume that people behave the way they do simply because of "natural selection."

In his classic treatise, "On the Nature of Limbs," published in 1849, Richard Owen presented a conundrum for biologists committed to the principle of adaptations—a word and concept of ancient pedigree, long antedating Darwin's later explanation in terms of evolution by natural selection. Mammals, and humans especially, must begin life with a tight squeeze—the passage of the relatively large fetal head through the narrow birth canal. The bones of the skull are not yet fully ossified or sutured together. Consequently, the nonrigid head can be "molded" as the bones alter their positions to allow this first essential adjustment to extrauterine life. If this molding could not occur, birth

with such a large head would be impossible. Thus, we seem to have a *prima facie* case for a *vitally important adaptation* in this delayed ossification of skull bones. After all, big heads are a key to human success, and delayed ossification permits big heads. (With limited brain growth after birth, small neonatal heads and later expansion may not represent an option for an alternative pathway.)

Yet Owen, Britain's greatest vertebrate anatomist and first director of the independent natural history branch of the British Museum, denied that delayed ossification could rank as a mammalian adaptation— for the excellent reason that "lower" vertebrates (and

Source: Gould, S. J. (1991). Exaptation: A crucial tool for an evolutionary psychology. *Journal of Social Issues, 47,* 43–65. Reprinted by permission. (Selection is excerpted from the original.)

Editor's note: All citations in the text of this selection have been left intact from the original, but the list of references includes only those sources that are the most relevant and important. Readers wishing to follow any of the other citations can find the full references in the original work or in an online database.

mammalian ancestors), which need only to break free from an egg, share this feature with us. Owen wrote, linking the case to a general critique of adaptationism by way of Sir Francis Bacon's famous simile about the barrenness of teleology in general:

> Such a final purpose is indeed readily perceived and admitted in regard to the multiplied points of ossification of the skull of the human fetus, and their relation to safe parturition. But when we find that the same ossific centers are established, and in similar order, in the skull of the embryo kangaroo, which is born when an inch in length, and in that of the callow bird that breaks the brittle egg, we feel the truth of Bacon's comparison of "final causes" to the Vestal Virgins, and perceive that they would be barren and unproductive of the fruits we are laboring to attain. (1849, p. 40)

Charles Darwin, whose strongly adaptationist theory set the problem (by imposing limits to thought) that this paper addresses, took Owen's point and example to heart, and repeated the case in a cautionary note on overindulgence in adaptationist explanation (Darwin, 1859, p. 197):

> The sutures in the skull of young mammals have been advanced as a beautiful adaptation for aiding parturition, and no doubt they facilitate, or may be indispensable for this act; but as sutures occur in the skulls of young birds and reptiles, which have only to escape from a broken egg, we may infer that this structure has arisen from the laws of growth, and has been taken advantage of in the parturition of the higher animals.

This case raises some of the deepest issues in evolutionary theory but, for now, let me pose a question almost laughably trivial in comparison (yet deceptively profound as an opening to the generalities): If the term "adaptation" be inappropriate for reasons given by Owen and Darwin, what shall we call this eminently useful delay of ossification in the human embryo? We cannot maintain a clear concept if we have no name for the primary phenomenon so illustrated.

We might honor the fact that delayed ossification did not arise "for" its current role in parturition by calling it a "nonadaptation" or a "nonaptation" (and such cumbersome terms are in frequent use, by yours truly among others—see Gould, 1984). But such a resolution would be unsatisfactory for at least two

reasons beyond infelicity: (a) active concepts should not be defined negatively by what they are not, and (b) "nonaptation" would not get at the heart of the evolutionary meaning of the phenomenon—that a useful structure may arise for other reasons and then be coopted for its present role.

I can imagine two solutions to this terminological problem:

1. We might extend "adaptation"—the great warhorse term of Darwinian evolution—to cover this phenomenon. Delayed ossification is useful in parturition, and "adaptation" is about use—so why not extend a term for a *process of building utility* into a general description for the *state of utility*, whatever its origin? (Insofar as evolutionary biologists have considered the issue at all, they have favored this extension. Nonetheless, most extensions of "adaptation" from process to state do not represent an active decision, consciously devised and defended, but rather a passive oozing forth of a favored term beyond a logical border into a defenseless territory. Many biologists have not even considered the crucial difference between historical origin and current utility. In a thoughtless analog of the contemporary motto "if it feels good, do it," they have simply taken the line, "if it works, call it adaptation.") But this extension should be rejected for two reasons:

(a) *Historical.* Adaptation, throughout the history of English usage in biology, has been a "process term," not a "state term." This definition inheres in etymology, for an adaptation is, literally, something fit (*aptus*) by active construction for (*ad*) its usage. The process meaning conforms with vernacular use; we can adapt a bicycle for a young beginner by installing training wheels, but no one would call a credit card an adaptation for opening certain kinds of locked doors, even though the card works as well for this purpose as does the altered bike for a stable ride. Moreover, and most importantly, the process definition affirms a long tradition of professional usage within evolutionary biology. The previous quotation from Darwin himself clearly supports the "process" definition—for Darwin states that some colleagues have called delayed ossification an adaptation, but they are wrong because this eminently useful feature has been coopted, rather than built for, successful parturition. This usage enjoys an unbroken pedigree, and is explicitly defended in the most important modern work on adaptation—for Williams (1966, p. 6) argues that we should speak of adaptation only if we can "attribute the origin and perfection of this design to a long period of selection for effectiveness in this particular role."

(b) *Conceptual and utilitarian.* For a historical scientist, no conceptual tool can be more important than the clear separation of *historical origin* and *current utility.* The false conceptual passage from present function to initial construction ranks with the post hoc fallacy and the confusion of correlation with cause as primary errors of reasoning about temporal sequences. We all understand this principle in the case of human artifacts: No one would claim that the U.S. Mint made dimes thin so that all Americans could carry surrogate screwdrivers in their change purses. And we all laugh at Voltaire's Dr. Pangloss when he exclaims: "Everything is made for the best purpose. Our noses were made to carry spectacles, so we have spectacles. Legs were clearly intended for breeches, and we wear them."

2. We might recognize a lacuna (favorite fancy word of scholars, though the vernacular "gap" will do nicely) in current terminology and coin a new term for the important phenomenon illustrated by the case of delayed ossification—i.e., vital current utility based on cooptation of structures evolved in other contexts and for other purposes (or perhaps for no purpose at all). We who dwell in the jargon-polluted groves of academe should propose new words only with the greatest cau-

tion, in the direst of circumstances, and in the absence of any other reasonable solution to a problem. The most compelling justification for a new term resides in conceptual gaps and persistent errors in thought reasonably connected with the absence of a category in the taxonomy of ideas. For a concept without a name often lies hidden from identification and use.

Elisabeth Vrba and I struggled with this issue in our attempts to formulate theories of large-scale evolutionary change. We finally decided that the absence of a term for "useful structures not evolved for their current function, but coopted from other contexts" had produced a sufficiently long-standing and serious muddle to warrant a new term by the criteria suggested above. We therefore proposed the term "exaptation" for "features that now enhance fitness, but were not built by natural selection for their current role" (Gould & Vrba, 1982, p. 4). The extent of immediate commentary (Lewin, 1982) and later usage and debate (Endler & McLellan, 1988; Gans, 1988; Pierce, 1988; Chatterton & Speyer, 1989; and many others) convinces us that, at the very least, we identified a conceptual weakness not sufficiently appreciated by evolutionary biologists in the past.

In our "taxonomy of fitness" (see Table 1), process, state (character), and usage must be distinguished. In the realm of process, traditional adaptation (Darwin's usage) occurs when natural selection shapes a feature for its current use. If characters are built for other reasons, and then "seized" for an altered utility, we speak (using a vernacular term) of "cooptation." Coopted characters may have been built by natural selection for

TABLE 1 A Taxonomy of Fitness

PROCESS	CHARACTER		USAGE	
Natural selection shapes the character for a current use—adaptation	Adaptation		Function	
A character, previously shaped by natural selection for a particular function (an adaptation), is coopted for a new use—cooptation		Aptation		Effect
A character whose origin cannot be ascribed to the direct action of natural selection (a nonaptation) is coopted for current use—cooptation	Exaptation		Effect	

a different function (e.g., the proto-wing, initially evolved as an adaptation for thermoregulation and later coopted for flight, according to the standard, classic conjecture), or may have arisen for no adaptive purpose at all (e.g., as a sequel or consequence of another adaptation, in what Darwin called "correlation of growth"). In either case, coopted structures will probably undergo some secondary modification—counting as superimposed, true adaptation—for the newly seized function. (The feather, for example, will need some redesign for efficient flight—as we can scarcely imagine that a structure evolved for thermoregulation would be accidentally and optimally suited for something so different as aerial locomotion.) But such secondary tinkering does not alter the primary status of such a structure as coopted rather than adapted.

For current state, we reluctantly permit *stare decisis* in retaining "adaptation" for characters built by selection for their current use. (We assume, for example, that the elaborate plumages and behavioral displays of male birds of paradise are true adaptation for mating success.) We do regret the retention of the same word—adaptation—for both a process and a utility arising by the process, but we bow to entrenched convention here. We then fill the previous gap by coining *exaptation* for useful structures coopted from other contexts—for such structures are fit (*aptus*) not by explicit molding for (*ad*) current use, but as a consequence of (*ex*) properties built for other reasons.

We recognize, of course, that distinction of adaptation from exaptation requires knowledge of historical sequences—and that such evidence is often, probably usually, unavailable. In such cases, we may only know that a structure is currently useful—and we may be unable to identify the source of utility. In such cases, we urge that the neutral term "aptation" (encompassing both ad- and ex-aptation) be used in place of the conventional and falsely inclusive "adaptation." (Vrba and I are delighted that since publication of our revised taxonomy in 1982, this recommendation has been followed by many biologists—see Vermeij, 1987, and Allmon, in press—whatever their feeling about our term "exaptation.")

In the final category of usage, adaptations have functions, but "function" cannot describe the utility of an exaptation. To cite Williams' (1966) amusing but profound example, flying fishes fall back into the water by virtue of gravity, and this descent is essential to their continued existence. But weight, as an inevitable property of matter in Newton's world, is an exaptation for falling back, clearly not an adaptation. In ordinary English usage, we would not call falling back a function of weight. We therefore, following Williams, designate the utility of an exaptation as an "effect" (again choosing vernacular English—falling back is an effect of weight).

One final point on terminology: Evolutionists have always recognized that some currently useful structures must be coopted rather than adapted—if only because cooptation provides the classical solution to the famous "problem of the incipient stages of useful structures." In plain English and concrete form, how can wings evolve for flight if 5% of a wing confers no conceivable aerodynamic benefit? The classical solution argues that wings evolved for something else (thermoregulation, in the most common scenario) and were then coopted.

In standard terminology, the proto-wing is called a "preadaptation" for flight. I doubt that any other evolutionary term has been so widely viewed as misleading and problematical. All teachers introduce "preadaptation" with an apology, disavowing the explicit etymological claim for foreordination, and explaining that the term really does not mean what it plainly says. But we did not decide to coin "exaptation" as a mere etymological nicety. If "preadaptation" had included all that "exaptation" now supplies, we would not have suggested our revision. As its major inadequacy, "preadaptation" covers only one of the two styles of cooptation, and therefore cannot subsume all exaptations. Preadaptations are built for one purpose, and then coopted for another (e.g., wings built for thermoregulation are coopted for flight). But what about the second category?—structures not built as adaptations at all, but later coopted for utilities just as vital (e.g., weight existing by virtue of the physics of matter, is then coopted for falling back into the water). Preadaptation does not cover the large domain of nonaptations later coopted for utility—and "exaptation" is therefore needed to fill a substantial lacuna. I argue in the next section that the concept of coopted nonaptation is the key to a proper evolutionary psychology for the human brain—and exaptation is therefore especially vital in human affairs.

I need hardly mention—for it forms the underlying theme of this paper—that the conceptual incubus of this entire tale is the overreliance on adaptation so characteristic of English evolutionary thought, and the insufficiently critical acceptance of this bias in cognate fields that, however properly, have borrowed evolutionary concepts for their own explanations. . . .

THE HUMAN BRAIN

As the primary point of this paper, I wish to present an argument for regarding the human brain as, *prima facie,* the best available case for predominant exaptation—in other words, for a near certainty that exaptations must greatly exceed adaptations in number and importance (the proper criterion of relative frequency). Based on this argument, exaptation becomes a crucial concept for an evolutionary psychology. Much of our cultural tradition has been devoted to defining human uniqueness, particularly in terms of brain power and action. We may epitomize the evolutionary version of this massive interdisciplinary effort by stating that the human brain is, *par excellence,* the chief exemplar of exaptation.

The case can be best developed by recalling a famous episode from the history of evolutionary theory. Charles Darwin drew no boundaries in applying his theory of natural selection to organic nature. He specifically included the human brain—the structure that he had called "the citadel itself" in an early notebook—and he wrote two books (Darwin, 1871, 1872) on the evolution of human bodies, brains, and emotional expressions.

Alfred Russel Wallace, codiscoverer of natural selection, applied the theory (far more rigidly than Darwin, as we shall see) to everything else, but stopped short at the human brain. Our intellect and morality, Wallace argued, could not be the result of natural evolution. Some higher power must have intervened to construct this latest and greatest of evolutionary innovations—natural selection for absolutely everything else; God for the human brain.

Darwin was aghast at his colleague's *volte face* right at the finish line itself. He wrote to Wallace in

1869: "I hope you have not murdered too completely your own and my child" (Marchant, 1916, p. 197). A month later, he added ruefully: "If you had not told me, I should have thought that [your remarks on the brain] had been added by some one else. As you expected, I differ grievously from you, and I am very sorry for it" (Marchant, 1916, p. 199). Wallace, sensitive to the rebuke, thereafter referred to his theory of the human brain as "my special heresy."

The outlines of this tale are well known, but the usual interpretation of Wallace's motives is not only wrong, but backwards. Sources cite Wallace's interest in spiritualism, or simply suggest intellectual cowardice in failing to extend an argument to its most threatening limit. I do not claim to have any insight into Wallace's psyche (where such factors may be relevant), but I can at least report that his explicit logical argument for cerebral uniqueness flowed not from reticence or active theological belief, but (ironically) from a fierce and opposite commitment to the exclusive power of natural selection as an evolutionary agent.

Darwin viewed natural selection as a dominant but not exclusive force. Wallace, ironically, was the hyper-Darwinian of his age. He held that all forms and behaviors, including the most trivial, must be directly built by natural selection for utility. He wrote in 1867 (reprinted in Wallace, 1890):

> No special organ, no characteristic form or marking, no peculiarities of instinct or of habit, no relations between species or between groups of species, can exist but which must now be, or once have been, useful to the individuals or races which possess them.

Wallace would not admit the existence of spandrels [Ed. note: spandrels are coopted nonaptations, or nonadaptation side consequences], or of any nonaptations correlated with features built by natural selection:

> The assertion of "inutility" in the case of any organ is not, and can never be, the statement of a fact, but merely an expression of our ignorance of its purpose or origin.

Paradoxically, this very hyperadaptationism led Wallace to deny that natural selection could have built the human brain—for the following interesting and idiosyncratic reason. Wallace, almost uniquely among 19th-century Western natural scientists, was a genuine nonracist who believed in at least the near intellectual equality of all peoples. Yet he was a cultural chauvinist, who asserted a massive superiority of Western ways over "savage" practices. Consequently, under his hyperadaptationism, an insoluble paradox arises: natural selection can only build for immediate use; savages (surrogates for ancestors) have brains as good as ours but do not employ them to nearly their full capacity in devising complex culture. Hence, natural selection did not construct the human brain.

To cite just one example, Wallace argued that the human ability to sing beautifully must have arisen long before any call upon this capacity, and cannot therefore be a product of natural selection. He wrote:

> *The habits of savages give no indication of how this faculty could have been developed by natural selection, because it is never required or used by them. The singing of savages is a more or less monotonous howling. . . . This wonderful power . . . only comes into play among civilized people. It seems as if the organ had been prepared in anticipation of the future progress in man, since it contains latent capacities which are useless to him in his earlier condition. (Wallace, 1895, p. 198)*

Darwin was dumbfounded, primarily because he did understand the concept of spandrels (and also because he had more appreciation for the complexities of "savage" cultures). Wallace's illogic can be illustrated by the following anachronistic metaphor: If I put a computer in the business office of my small company, its capacities are not limited by the purposes of my installation. My computer, by virtue of its structural complexity and flexibility, maintains latent and unused capacities that must vastly outnumber the explicit reasons for my design or purchase. And the more complex the computing device, the greater the disparity between its field of potential and my explicit purposes (e.g., the calculator attached to my Casio watch may not perform much beyond my needs; but a Cray supercomputer can do more than I could ever even imagine).

Similarly for the evolution of the human brain. For the sake of argument, I will accept the most orthodox of Darwinian positions—that the human brain achieved its enlarged size and capacity by natural selection for some set of purposes in our ancestral state. Large size is therefore an adaptation. Does this mean that everything the enlarged brain can do must be a direct product of the natural selection that built the structure? Wallace certainly thought so, in arguing that "latent capacities" must imply preparation in "anticipation of future progress"—and therefore indicated intelligent design by God. But the principle of exaptation and the concept of spandrels expose Wallace's dilemma as a non-problem. Natural selection built the brain; yet, by virtue of structural complexities so engendered, the same brain can perform a plethora of tasks that may later become central to culture, but that are spandrels rather than targets of the original natural selection—singing Wagner (to cite Wallace's example, though some, even today, regard the *Ring* as monotonous howling), not to mention reading and writing. . . .

THE EXAMPLE OF RELIGION

To choose just one overly broad and oversimplified example, much sociobiological effort has been expended in devising adaptive scenarios for the origin of religion (most center on the importance of tribal order and cohesion). But consider Freud's alternative, an argument based on spandrels. The origin of consciousness in our enlarged brain forced us to deal explicitly with the most frightening of all conceivable facts—the certainty of our personal mortality. To assuage this fear, we devised a great cultural variety of concepts with a central theme of mitigation—from metempsychosis (transmigration of souls), to resurrection of the body, to eternal realms for immaterial souls. These concepts form the core of religion as a cultural institution.

I am not so naive as to imagine that anything so complex and so multifaceted as religion could be fully rendered by either of these monistic propositions, but they do provide alternative approaches to a basis. The recognition of personal mortality is clearly a spandrel of our large brains, for surely no one would seek the adaptive advantage of increased brain size in achievement of this knowledge! If Freud is right, this focal and organizing concept of religion is a spandrel of a brain enlarged for other reasons; and religion did not arise as an adaptation (whatever its current function, and despite the cogency of a claim that all societies need institutions to promote and maintain group cohesion—for religion need not supply this function).

Go down the list of what you regard as human universals and cultural predictabilities. How many would you putatively assign to adaptation, and therefore view as amenable to sociobiological explanation? Incest avoidance? Such universal gestures as eyebrow flashing? Fine—but how long is your list and how much of our human essence, how much of what really makes culture, will you find? On the other side of the scale place the basis of religion as exaptation; add anything that relies on reading, writing, or any form of mental expression not in the initial repertoire of large-brained populations; add most of the fine and practical arts, the norms of commerce, the practices of war. Exaptation may be historically subsequent to adaptation, and may only coopt the structures and capacities built by adaptation. (But do not be so sure that the brain necessarily became large as an adaptation for more complex conceptualization; other alternatives exist, and consciousness itself may be exaptive.) No matter; the list of exaptations is a mountain to the adaptive molehill. Structural consequences have outstripped original bases. Human uniqueness, human power, human nature itself, lies in the consequences. . . .

FUNDAMENTAL ATTRIBUTES

Those characteristics that we share with other closely related species are most likely to be conventional adaptations. (For example, I accept my colleague Steve Pinker's (1985) argument for the basic mechanics of the visual system, while rejecting his extensions to special properties of human consciousness.) But attributes unique to our species, and constituting the essence of what we call *human* consciousness, are likely to be exaptations by the arguments of the last section.

As an obvious prime candidate, consider the greatest and most contentious of all subjects embodying claims for our uniqueness: human language. The adaptationist and Darwinian tradition has long advocated a gradualistic continuationism—constructing scenarios that language "grew" from gestural and calling systems

of other species; trying to teach chimpanzees the rudiments of human linguistic structure, etc. Noam Chomsky, on the other hand, has long advocated a position corresponding to the claim that language is an exaptation of brain structure. (Chomsky, who has rarely written anything about evolution, has not so framed his theory, but he does accept my argument as a proper translation of his views into the language of my field—Chomsky, personal communications.) Many adaptationists have so misunderstood Chomsky that they actually suspect him of being an odd sort of closet creationist. For them, evolution means adaptive continuity, and they just cannot grasp the alternative of exaptive seizure of latent capacity that is present for other reasons.

The spectacular collapse of the chimp language experiments, and their exposure as some combination of wishful thinking and the Clever Hans effect, have made Chomsky's alternative all the more plausible. Cross-species continuity must exist, of course, in the growth of conceptual powers, but why should our idiosyncratic capacity for embodying much of this richness in the unique and highly peculiar mental structure called language be seen as an expression of this continuity? The traits that Chomsky (1986) attributes to language—universality of the generative grammar, lack of ontogeny (for language "grows" more like a programmed organ than like memorizing the kings of England), highly peculiar and decidedly nonoptimal structure, formal analogy to other attributes, including our unique numerical faculty with its concept of discrete infinity—fit far more easily with an exaptive, rather than an adaptive, explanation. The brain, in becoming large for whatever adaptive reasons, acquired a plethora of cooptable features. Why shouldn't the capacity for language be among them? Why not seize this possibility as something discrete at some later point in evolution, grafting upon it a range of conceptual capacities that achieve different expression in other species (and in our ancestry)?

EVOLUTIONARY SCENARIOS

Consider everyone's favorite game in evolutionary reconstruction—the spinning of behavioral and ecological scenarios for human origins. We usually consider these efforts as exercises in adaptationism. But, given the cardinal property of adaptation as usually limiting and restricting, and given the need to posit structures that permit flexibility and opportunity in conceptualizing human origins, these scenarios almost always make a claim for *exaptation* at crucial junctions (not, perhaps, in the radical mode of spandrels, but at least in the more conventional style of quirky functional shifts from an original reason to a very different consequence).

As just one example, recently subject to much discussion and debate, consider Falk's (1990) "radiator theory" (so close to Aristotle's old idea that the brain cools the blood). In her theory, gracile (slender) and robust (heavy-boned) australopithecines evolved different adaptations for adequate cranial blood flow in bipedal creatures—robusts via a greatly enlarged occipital/marginal sinus system, graciles via a widespread network of veins becoming more elaborate with time. This network system, an efficient cooling device, may have arisen as an adaptive response to the more intense solar radiation of savanna habitats favored by graciles. But this "radiator" then released a thermal constraint on brain size—allowing a larger brain to cool adequately. The graciles could evolve into the large brained *Homo* lineage; the robusts were stuck. Thus, the radiator system, arising as an ecological adaptation in initially small-brained graciles, became an exaptation for cooling the enlarged brain of their descendants. If Falk is right, we would not be here today but for this crucial exaptation.

CURRENT UTILITY

If you doubt all the other arguments for exaptation, just make a list of the most important current uses of consciousness. Start with reading, writing, and arithmetic. How many can even be plausibly rendered as adaptations?

Even so committed a hereditarian (and adaptationist) as Bouchard (of the Minnesota twin study) has seen the point, at least for the variability underlying human cognitive differences. Bouchard et al. (1990) write:

Whatever the ancient origins and functions of genetic variability, its repercussions in contemporary society are pervasive and important. A human species whose members did not vary genetically with respect to significant cognitive and motivational attributes ... would have created a very different society than the one we know. (p. 228)

They even recognize that most of this variability, in ancestral contexts, might have been "evolutionary debris, unimportant to fitness and perhaps not expressed in prehistoric environments" (p. 228). Bravo, for this is a radical exaptive hypothesis with a vengeance (and almost surely correct)—describing a trait now vital to our social constitution, but so nonaptive at its origin that it achieved no phenotypic expression.

Yet just as these erstwhile adaptationists see the light, they retrogress with a knee-jerk assertion of the orthodox position that they denied in their primary specific interpretation!

Evolutionary psychologists or sociobiologists attempt to delineate species-typical proclivities or instincts and to understand the relevant evolutionary developments that took place in the Pleistocene epoch and were adaptive in the lives of tribal hunter-gatherers. The genes sing a prehistoric song that today should sometimes be resisted but which it would be foolish to ignore. (1990, p. 228)

And yet, the authors just told us that these particular genes probably were not singing at all back then, despite their crucial role in framing human society today. I interpret this inconsistency as a lovely example of working through the logic of a specific argument correctly (the claim for exaptation of a spandrel), but then missing the implication and spouting a contradictory orthodoxy. Clearly, we need to make the notion of exaptation explicit and available.

An evolutionary psychology properly grounded in the centrality of exaptation would be a very different, and less threatening, construct (for those feeling the breath of biological imperialism) than the conventional Darwinian account of continuity in adaptation, with its implications of gradualism, predictability, and simple transfer from overt cultural expression to underlying biological basis. Exaptation, with its quirky and unpredictable functional shifts (e.g., thermoregulation to flight) and its recruitment of nonadaptive, even invisible structures (e.g., repeated copies of genes providing for future flexibility; the "debris" of unexpressed genetic variability leading to later cultural diversity), produces a cultural history with unanticipated changes in direction, potentially abrupt transitions, and no simply derived status of cultural expressions (for the path from biological substrate to overt manifestation passes through the switches of exaptive shift). The concept of exaptation honors the contingency of history, the unpredictable discontinuity of change in complex systems, and the plurality of legitimate sources of insight from biological substrate through quirky shift to social expression. We can therefore recall Haldane's dictum that "the universe is not only queerer than we suppose, but queerer than we *can* suppose." And lest we be tempted to read this (as Haldane most surely did not) as nihilism or pessimism (rather than as joy for being in such a fascinating place), we should also remember Einstein's equally famous remark that the Lord God is subtle, but not malicious (*Raffiniert ist der Herr Gott, aber boshaft ist er nicht*).

REFERENCES

Bouchard, T. J., Lykken, D. T., McGue, M., Segal, N. L., Jr., & Tellegen, A. (1990). Sources of human psychological differences: The Minnesota study of twins reared apart. *Science, 250,* 223–228.

Darwin, C. (1859). *On the origin of species.* London: John Murray.

Darwin, C. (1871). *The descent of man and selection in relation to sex.* London: John Murray.

Darwin, C. (1872). *On the expression of the emotions in man and animals.* London: John Murray.

Gould, S. J. (1980). *The panda's thumb.* New York: Norton.

Gould, S. J. (1989). A developmental constraint in *Cerion,* with comments on the definition and interpretation of constraint in evolution. *Evolution, 43,* 516–539.

Gould, S. J., & Vrba, E. S. (1982). Exaptation—a mission term in the science of form. *Paleobiology, 8,* 4–15.

Lewin, R. (1982). Adaptation can be a problem for evolutionists. *Science, 216,* 212–213.

Vrba, E. S., & Gould, S. J. (1986). The hierarchical expansion of sorting and selection: Sorting and selection cannot be equated. *Paleobiology, 12,* 217–228.

Questions to Think About

1. How do exaptations differ from adaptations?

2. Why can delayed ossification of the human skull be considered an exaptation? Why is the human brain an ideal example of exaptation?

3. What are the dangers of seeing culture-based practices such as the dominance of men (rather than women) in political office as due to the natural way of the world?

19

Genetics and Experience

ROBERT PLOMIN AND JENAE NEIDERHISER

Robert Plomin is a well known researcher in the field of behavior genomics, seeking to identify genes that influence complex behavioral systems. Since the time that this article was published, he has begun to use molecular genetics as a technique to identify specific genes that are linked to psychological traits. Jenae Neiderhiser, now a professor at George Washington University, looks at family relationships and DNA in twins, siblings and adoptees in an effort to understand how children and their families influence each other. Although some assumptions in the early days of this type of research were overly simplistic, the field has developed a sophisticated understanding of the relationships between genes and environment, and we have finally gone beyond the primitive question of nature versus nurture.

During the 1980s, the tide of antipathy in psychology toward genetic research changed to acceptance. Rarely now does it raise blood pressures to report evidence for genetic influence on personality, psychopathology, and cognitive abilities, the three domains that have been investigated most thoroughly. Results of family, twin, and adoption studies converge on the conclusion that these domains show significant and substantial genetic influence. Genetic differences among individuals often account for as much as half of the observed differences for dimensions and disorders within these domains. It is difficult to find psychological traits that reliably show no genetic influence [Plomin, DeFries, & McClearn, 1990].

Asking whether genetic differences contribute to observed differences among individuals for a particular behavior is a reasonable first step toward understanding the origins of individual differences. This

basic nature-nurture question has scarcely been broached for some major domains of psychology, such as perception, learning, language, social cognition, and even neuro-science. Nonetheless, it is reasonable to expect that genetic factors will be found to be important for these domains as well.

Genetic research has begun to move beyond the question of whether genetic factors are important in psychology. One direction for research could be called *environmental genetics*. This new field investigates genetic influence on ostensible measures of the psychological environment. At first, this approach sounds paradoxical because behaviorism has conditioned psychologists to think of the environment as something "out there" independent of the individual. To the contrary, measures of the psychological environment usually involve behavior.

For example, in developmental psychology, environmental measures typically assess parental behavior.

Source: Plomin, R., & Neiderhiser, J. (1992). Genetics and experience. *Current Directions in Psychological Science, 1*(5), 160–163. Reprinted by permission.

Editor's note: All citations in the text of this selection have been edited so that bracketed citations with author names replace numbered citations. The list of references includes only those sources that are the most relevant and important. Readers wishing to follow any of the other citations can find the full references in the original work or in an online database.

Differences among parents in their behavior to their children could in part be due to genetically influenced characteristics of the parents, such as their personality. Parental behavior might also reflect genetically influenced characteristics of their children. As another example, the stress of life events is an environmental construct assessed in thousands of psychological studies. However, not all life events happen capriciously, and it is possible that genetic characteristics are involved in the likelihood of experiencing certain life events.

Thus, measures of the psychological environment assess experience in both dictionary definitions of the word: direct participation in an event and apprehension of an event. Considered from this perspective, the possibility of a genetic contribution to the process of participating in and apprehending events seems plausible.

Genetic differences among individuals can contribute to differences in their experiences. To the extent that environmental measures are measures of experience, it is possible to conceptualize them as extended phenotypes and to apply the usual methods of quantitative genetics. For example, twin and adoption studies can be used to provide empirical tests of the importance of genetic effects. The key is to treat the environmental measure as a dependent measure and to ask whether genetic factors contribute to the observed variance on the environmental measure, as illustrated in the path diagram in Figure 1. For example, if identical twins' scores on a particular measure of the environment are no more similar than the scores of fraternal twins, genetic influence cannot be important.

EVIDENCE FOR GENETIC EFFECTS ON "ENVIRONMENTAL" MEASURES

A dozen twin and adoption studies show significant genetic effects when measures of the environment are treated as dependent measures in genetic analyses [Plomin & Bergeman, 1991]. On average, environmental measures yield heritability estimates of about .30, suggesting that more than a quarter of the variance of environmental measures can be accounted for by genetic differences. For example, adult identical twins are more similar than fraternal twins in their scores on a widely used measure of life events.

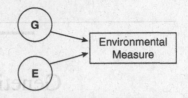

FIGURE 1   An environmental measure can be analyzed as a dependent measure in quantitative genetic analyses that decompose observed variance into genetic (G) and environmental (E) components of variance. Following conventions of path analysis, the rectangle signifies a measured variable and circles represent latent traits.

Genetic influence has been documented for such diverse measures as videotaped observations of parents' behavior toward their children, ratings by parents and children of their family environment, and ratings of peer groups, social support, and life events. Evidence for significant genetic effects has emerged for some of the most widely used measures of environment, such as the Home Observation for Measurement of the Environment (HOME), the Family Environment Scales, and the Social Readjustment Rating Scale of life events.

A review of this literature [Plomin & Bergeman, 1991] concluded:

> In summary, it is remarkable that research reported to date, using diverse measures and methods, so consistently converges on the conclusion that genetic influence is significant and substantial on widely used measures of the environment. (p. 386)

This review appeared with 30 commentaries and a response to the commentaries. Of the 30 commentaries, 19 explicitly agreed with the major conclusion and 6 implicitly agreed. Only 5 explicitly disagreed, and these denied that it is possible to detect genetic influence on anything, let alone measures of the environment.

The genetic studies described in this review each included just one or two environmental measures. A recent genetic study, the Nonshared Environment in Adolescent Development project, focused on the systematic examination of diverse measures of the family environment [Plomin, Reiss, Hetherington, & Howe, 1992].

The design involved a national sample of 719 two-parent families with same-sex adolescent siblings; the sample included nondivorced families with identical twins, fraternal twins, and full siblings and stepfamilies with full siblings, half-siblings, and genetically unrelated siblings. In a report of scores of interview and questionnaire measures, three quarters of the measures showed significant genetic effects in model-fitting analyses, and the average heritability estimate was about .25. As in previous studies, measures of parental behavior generally showed genetic effects, whether rated by parents or by children. In addition, the social environment provided by siblings showed genetic effects. In summary, this first systematic genetic exploration of diverse measures of the family environment confirmed the hypothesis of genetic involvement in widely used measures of the environment.

Much more research is needed to spell out the details of the role of genetics in environmental measures. For example, how does the finding play out in terms of other measures, especially naturalistic, ethological, and ecological observational measures? Do some environmental measures show greater genetic influence than others? Nonetheless, the basic phenomenon—that genetic factors contribute to variance on widely used environmental measures—is reasonably well documented, especially considering the novelty of this discovery.

DIRECTIONS FOR FUTURE RESEARCH

These research findings raise several questions for future research. Three obvious questions involve generalization, gender differences, and development. The major question about generalization is whether the extant results based on middle-class U.S. and Swedish samples will generalize to other cultures or to the extremes of children's environments, such as abusive families. Next to nothing is known about gender differences or developmental changes in the contribution of genetics to measures of the environment.

Two programmatic directions for research can be categorized as investigation of the antecedents and the consequences of genetic involvement in environmental measures. The question of *antecedents* asks what genetically influenced characteristics of individuals lead to genetic involvement in measures of the environment. In other words, the term antecedents refers to the mechanisms or predictors of the genetic contribution to environmental measures. For example, genetically influenced dimensions of personality such as extraversion may contribute to genetic influence on environmental measures such as parental affection and characteristics of peer groups.

The question of *consequences* asks the extent to which associations between environmental measures and outcome variables emerge for genetic reasons. That is, if environmental measures as well as outcome measures show genetic influence, this raises the possibility that associations between environmental measures and outcomes can be explained genetically. For example, although it seems almost self-evident that negative life events lead to depression, it is possible that genetic factors contribute to this association. Genetic effects on a measure of life events may overlap with genetic effects on a measure of depression, thus producing a correlation between the two measures that is genetic in origin.

Investigations of both the antecedents and the consequences of genetic involvement in environmental measures can profit from advances in multivariate genetic analysis during the past decade. Most genetic analyses have been univariate, analyzing the genetic contribution to the variance of a single measure considered by itself. The gist of multivariate genetic analysis is to analyze the genetic contribution to the covariance between two measures rather than to the variance of each measure considered separately.

Antecedents

Figure 2 is a path diagram that illustrates a bivariate genetic analysis between an antecedent measure (such as personality) and a measure of the environment. The bivariate analysis decomposes genetic influence on the environmental measure into two components. One component (the latent variable G in Figure 2) represents genetic effects on the environmental measure that overlap with genetic effects on the antecedent measure. The other component (the latent variable g in Fig. 2) represents residual genetic influence on the environmental measure that is not shared with the antecedent measure.

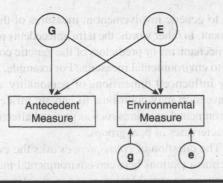

FIGURE 2 The extent to which genetic effects on an environmental measure can be explained by genetic effects on an antecedent measure, such as personality, can be assessed by a bivariate genetic analysis. In this bivariate path model, the latent variable G represents genetic effects that the environmental measure and the antecedent measure have in common. The latent variable g represents residual genetic effects on the environmental measure that are not shared with the antecedent measure. Similarly, E and e are latent variables that represent common and unique environmental influences, respectively. Because the focus of this analysis is on genetic contributions to environmental measures, the environmental latent variables are not subdivided into components representing shared and nonshared environment, as is usually done in such analyses.

In other words, the path from the residual genetic latent variable represents the extent to which genetic effects on the environmental measure are independent of genetic effects on the antecedent measure.

One report of this type considered the extent to which genetic influence on extraversion and neuroticism contributes to genetic effects on adults' perceptions of their current family environments [Chipuer, Plomin, Pederson, McClearn, & Nesselroade, 1993]. The genetic design combined the twin and adoption methods, using identical and fraternal twins reared apart and matched twins reared together. Although genetic influence on both extraversion and neuroticism contributed slightly to genetic effects on the environmental measures, more than 80% of the genetic variance of the environmental measures was independent of genetic influence on these two major dimensions of personality.

Other analyses in progress seem to be telling a similar story: Standard trait measures such as personality or cognitive abilities do not appear to be able to account for the genetic contribution to environmental measures. If this tentative conclusion proves to be correct, what are the genetic mechanisms? Our working hypothesis is that trait measures attempt to assess behavior across situations and across time, whereas measures of the environment are by definition measures of specific contexts—often intense and engaging contexts such as family interactions. For this reason, we suggest that measures of the environment might assess genetically influenced characteristics of individuals that are not usually assessed by psychological trait measures. Research in this direction might bring to light context-specific aspects of behavior that have not been scrutinized previously from a genetic perspective.

Consequences

Consequences of the genetic contribution to environmental measures can be examined in a similar manner using a multivariate genetic approach. As shown in the path diagram in Figure 3, a multivariate genetic analysis can investigate the extent to which the association between an environmental measure (e.g., life events) and an outcome measure (e.g., depression) is mediated genetically. The phrase *genetic mediation* refers to the product of the paths from the latent variable G, which represents the genetic contribution to the association between the environmental measure and the outcome measure.

One report of this type, from the Colorado Adoption Project, investigated associations between a measure of the home environment (the HOME, mentioned earlier) and mental development in infancy [Braungart, Fulker, & Plomin, 1992]. A sibling adoption design was employed; resemblance was compared for nonadoptive siblings (who are 50% similar genetically) and pairs of genetically unrelated children adopted into the same adoptive families. Substantial genetic influence was found for both the environmental measure and the measure of mental development when each child was 12 months old and again when each child was 24 months old. These findings raise the

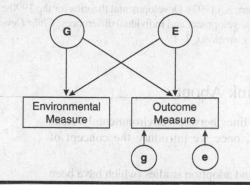

FIGURE 3   The extent to which the phenotypic correlation between an environmental measure and an outcome measure is mediated genetically can also be investigated by a bivariate genetic analysis. The variables in this bivariate path model are explained in the legend to Figure 2. Genetic mediation is represented by the product of the two path coefficients leading from the latent variable G.

question whether genetic factors contribute to associations between the environmental measure and mental development. When the path model shown in Figure 3 was applied to these data, no evidence of genetic mediation was found at 12 months. At 24 months, however, genetic factors accounted for half of the association between the environmental measure and the measure of mental development.

Other analyses in progress suggest that other environment-outcome associations may involve genetic factors. For example, in the Swedish Adoption/Twin Study of Aging, the association between life events and later depression is substantially due to genetic factors.

In summary, two major directions for research in environmental genetics involve investigating the antecedents and consequences of the genetic contribution to measures of the environment. Preliminary research in these two directions hints at the exciting possibilities that await further exploration.

IMPLICATIONS

Research in environmental genetics, like any genetic research, does not imply genetic determinism. Nor does it suggest that nongenetic factors are unimportant. What this research does indicate is that measures

widely used in psychology as measures of the environment show a significant and substantial contribution of genetic variability. Labeling a measure "environmental" does not make it a pure measure of the environment. People make their own environments [Scarr, 1992].

Demonstrating that genetic factors are involved in experience represents an important first step in research in environmental genetics. One might think that the implicit message from such research is that current measures of the environment have been mistakenly tinged with genetic influence and simply need to be cleaned up. To the contrary, there is a larger issue that lies at the heart of the interface between nature and nurture: The ways in which people interact with their environments—their experiences—are influenced by genetic differences. Understanding how genetic factors are involved in experience is bound to help psychologists understand how nature and nurture transact to affect development.

Although genetic factors can affect the environments that people receive passively, genetic influence seems most likely to occur to the extent that individuals actively select, modify, and create the environments they experience. In this sense, research in environmental genetics might help to take psychology beyond the passive model of the environment inherited from behaviorism. Psychologists need to investigate the reactive and active organism-environment transactional processes by which genotypes become phenotypes.

REFERENCES

Braungart, J. M., Fulker, D. W., & Plomin, R. (1992). Genetic mediation of the home environment during infancy: A sibling adoption study of the HOME. *Developmental Psychology, 28*(6), 1048–1055.

Chipuer, H. M., Plomin, R., Pedersen, N. L., McClearn, G. E., & Nesselroade, J. R. (1993). Genetic influence on family environment: The role of personality. *Developmental Psychology, 29*(1), 110–118.

Plomin, R., & Bergeman, C. S. (1991). The nature of nurture: Genetic influences on "environmental" measures. *Behavioral and Brain Sciences, 14*, 373–386.

Plomin, R., DeFries, J. C., & McClearn, G. E. (1990). *Behavioral Genetics* (2nd ed.). New York: Freeman.

Plomin, R., Reiss, D., Hetherington, E. M., & Howe, G. W. (1994). Nature and nurture: Genetic contributions to measures of the family environment. *Developmental Psychology, 30*(1), 32–43.

Scarr, S. (1992). Developmental theories for the 1990s: Development and individual differences. *Child Development, 63*, 1–19.

Questions to Think About

1. Is it helpful or merely confusing that the lines between environmental versus genetic influences are less clearly drawn, once we introduce the concept of "environmental genetics"?

2. Why is the field still so dependent on twin and adoption studies (which have been used since the days of Sir Francis Galton in the nineteenth century), given the plethora of sophisticated measurement tools available for both genetic and behavioral analysis?

3. Plomin and Neiderhiser make the point that if some measure of environmental similarity for twin pairs shows no differential similarity for identical versus fraternal twins, we can conclude that genetic influence is not important. What is the range of possible conclusions when similarity is reliably higher for identical twins?

20

The Child Is Father of the Man: Personality Continuities from Childhood to Adulthood

AVSHALOM CASPI

Avshalom Caspi is a contemporary psychologist who crosses disciplinary and national boundaries. He was born in Israel, trained in the United States, holds academic appointments at the University of Wisconsin and Kings College, London, and does field research in New Zealand. His work overlaps with the "life-course approach," in which personality is understood as unfolding over time, with patterns of behavior influenced not only by internal drives, motives, abilities, and traits, but also subject to change as a function of age, culture, social groups, life events, and so on. An important feature of this approach is the idea that situations can be influential, but that situations and individuals are not randomly paired—individuals create their own person-situation interactions by creating, selecting, and interpreting the situations of their lives. Therefore, situational influences can act to reinforce or maintain personality rather than necessarily changing it.

My heart leaps up when I behold
A rainbow in the sky:
So was it when my life began;
So is it now I am a man;
So be it when I shall grow old, Or let me die!
The Child is father of the Man;
And I could wish my days to be
Bound each to each by natural piety.

—William Wordsworth,
"My Heart Leaps Up When I Behold"

Behavioral differences among children are apparent very early in life. Some children squirm and fuss when they are picked up; others like to be cuddled. Some children approach new situations with great zeal; others shrink from novelty. Are such behavioral differences, or temperamental styles, evanescent qualities or do they presage the life patterns to follow? Although many psychological theories subscribe to the view that what is past is prologue, this conjecture has been surprisingly difficult to substantiate empirically because it requires costly and time-consuming longitudinal studies that track people over time and across multiple developmental settings. As such, scientists, clinicians, and parents continue to wonder, is the child really the father of the man?

Contemporary interest in the developmental study of early emerging temperamental differences is largely due to the insightful work of Thomas and Chess (see Kagan, 1998). These pediatric psychiatrists

Source: Caspi, A. (2000). The child is father of the man: Personality continuities from childhood to adulthood. *Journal of Personality and Social Psychology, 78*(1), 158–172. Copyright © 2000 by the American Psychological Association. Reprinted by permission.

Editor's note: All citations in the text of this selection have been left intact from the original, but the list of references includes only those sources that are the most relevant and important. Readers wishing to follow any of the other citations can find the full references in the original work or in an online database.

found that a majority of children could be grouped into one of three temperamental types which they labeled *easy, difficult,* and *slow to warm up*. Repeated assessments of a group of 141 children, studied from the first few years of life to young adulthood, showed that these temperamental profiles were fairly stable over the short run, but in the long run it proved difficult to predict specific adult outcomes for the different groups of children (Chess & Thomas, 1987, 1990; Thomas, Chess, & Birch, 1970). Chess and Thomas's observations spawned a great deal of interest among psychiatrists and psychologists, who have since conducted larger studies to inquire about the origins of personality (Rothbart & Bates, 1998). These subsequent studies have confirmed the existence of the three temperamental types originally identified by Chess and Thomas, but these studies also show that temperamental types, identified in the first 3 years of life, do offer important clues about specific adult outcomes. Some of the most remarkable evidence about continuities in behavioral development comes from the Dunedin Multidisciplinary Health and Development Study, one of the largest longitudinal studies of human development carried out over the past 30 years (Silva & Stanton, 1996). The purpose of the present article is to summarize these findings about continuities in behavioral development, which have been uncovered by following a cohort of children from age 3 to 21.

The goal of the research we have conducted in the Dunedin study has been to determine whether there are continuities across the first two decades of life. Some, although not all, of the findings reported in this article have appeared previously, in specialty journals (e.g., criminology, psychiatry, sociology) according to the outcome, and serially as new follow-up data have been collected. (Citations to earlier publications that offer more measurement and statistical detail are provided throughout this article.) To evaluate the strength of continuity, in this article I focus less on the effect size for any particular outcome variable (although I report these too) and more on the pervasive influence of early appearing temperamental differences for life-course development. By pervasive influence I refer to whether temperamental qualities shape behavior in multiple settings and across many domains of social

and psychological functioning. As such, I review evidence about the links between children's temperamental qualities at age 3 and their behavior problems at home as well as at school, their personality styles at age 18, and their interpersonal relationships, work histories, psychiatric disorders, and criminal behavior at age 21. An empirical demonstration that the influence of early temperamental differences is pervasive and affects multiple outcomes underscores the importance of early intervention efforts.

THE DUNEDIN STUDY

The Dunedin study is an investigation of the health, development, and behavior of a complete cohort of children born during a 1-year period (between April 1, 1972, and March 31, 1973) in Dunedin, New Zealand's fourth largest city. Perinatal data were obtained at delivery and when the children were later traced for follow-up at age 3; 1,037 individuals (52% males and 48% females; 91% of the eligible births) participated in the assessment, forming the base sample for the longitudinal study. Since then the participants have been reassessed at ages 5, 7, 9, 11, 13, 15, 18, and 21. Although by now the participants are living throughout New Zealand, as well as in Australia, Europe, and North America, the basic procedure for data collection has remained the same: At each assessment wave, we bring each participant back to the Dunedin research unit within 60 days of his or her birthday for a full day of interviews and examinations in which various data (e.g., physical examinations, psychological tests, psychiatric interviews) are collected by different trained examiners. These data are supplemented by questionnaires that are mailed, as developmentally appropriate, to parents, teachers, and peers nominated by the participants themselves.

The Dunedin study is a unique resource for the study of behavioral development because it combines five ingredients. First, it is a prospective-longitudinal study in which information is obtained about the same persons as they are assessed repeatedly over time. In the absence of prospective studies, some researchers use retrospective studies and ask people to report about their past. Unfortunately, most people are inefficient and inaccurate processors of information about their past. There is little agreement between how people recollect themselves and what is known about them from concurrent data sources. As such, developmental researchers can ill afford to assume that retrospective reports are valid and veridical accounts of the past (Rutter, Maughan, Pickles, & Simonoff, 1998). The only alternative is to conduct prospective studies in which people are followed and assessed repeatedly in real time.

Second, the Dunedin study is an epidemiological study of a birth cohort. All walks of life are represented in this developmental-longitudinal study. The participants were born to college professors, carpenters, and clerks, as well as to adolescent parents who had not yet entered the labor force. By the time they reached adulthood, some of the participants were already on their way to successful careers as scientists, athletes, and musicians, whereas others were in prisons and mental hospitals. It is a misunderstanding of epidemiology for one to think that it is solely concerned with obtaining prevalence rates or that it is only concerned with describing pathology. The real importance of epidemiology lies in its ability to yield an unbiased understanding of associations between variables, which is especially important for describing and explaining developmental continuity and change across the life course (Costello & Angold, 1995; Rutter, 1982). The importance of a general population sample is that it avoids those distortions in associations between variables that are very common in volunteer samples or in selected samples of various kinds (e.g., Newman, Moffitt, Caspi, & Silva, 1998).

Third, the Dunedin study has suffered very little attrition; over 97% of the individuals in the original study participated in the most recent assessment, which we conducted in 1993–1994, when they were 21 years old. In contrast, many longitudinal studies lose 25–40% of their initial samples, and attrition is seldom random. When select individuals are lost from a longitudinal study, the validity and generalizability of conclusions about continuities in behavioral development are compromised (Magnusson & Bergman, 1990).

Fourth, the Dunedin study involves a multidisciplinary team of researchers who have collectively measured a wide variety of outcomes about the study members. This enables us to evaluate the pervasiveness of continuities in personality development across many domains of functioning.

Fifth, the Dunedin study is large enough and has the available data to control for confounding explanations of continuity, including sex differences in prevalence rates, differences in social class background, and differences in intelligence. All analyses described in this article included these controls and, as detailed in the original publications, the continuity effects hold above and beyond these potential artifacts.

TEMPERAMENTAL QUALITIES OBSERVED AT AGE 3

Numerous methods are available today for assessing temperament, but in 1975, when the Dunedin children were 3 years old, there were fewer and less well-developed measures (see Rothbart & Bates, 1998), with the notable exception of techniques being introduced by Chess and Thomas (1987) and their colleagues (e.g., Graham, Rutter, & George, 1973). However, child development professionals and clinicians were long ago impressed by the applied importance of ascertaining early emerging temperamental differences, and the absence of standard tools did not deter them from conceiving and modifying various means for assessing such individual differences. Such was the case in the Dunedin study.

At 3 years of age, each study child participated in a 90-min testing session involving cognitive and motor tasks, such as a picture vocabulary test and tests of fine and gross motor coordination. The children were tested by examiners who had no knowledge of their behavioral history. Following the testing, each child's examiner rated the child on 22 different behavioral characteristics (see Table 1) using ratings that were derived from the collaborative Study on Cerebral Palsy, Mental Retardation, and Other Neurological Disorders of Infancy and Childhood (see Goldsmith & Gottesman, 1981) and that are similar in scope to the behavior ratings contained in Bayley's infant behavior record (e.g., Matheny, 1980). Principal-components analyses of the examiners' ratings revealed three replicable factors, labeled *Lack of Control, Approach,* and *Sluggishness* (Caspi, Henry, McGee,

TABLE 1   Behavioral Characteristics Assessed by Examiners in the Dunedin Study

ITEM	DESCRIPTION
Emotionally labile	Extreme instability and overreactivity of emotional responses
Restless	Extreme overactivity, inability to sit still, constantly in motion
Impulsive	Explosive, uncontrolled behavior
Willful	Extremely assertive, rough, aggressive behavior lacking in reserve
Task withdrawal	Refusal to continue or attempt tasks that appear difficult
Requires attention	Constant need for attention or help
Fleeting attention	Lacks concentration, brief attention to tasks
Lacks persistence	Little effort to reach a goal, inability to keep goal or question in mind
Negativism	Resistance to directions or to demands of the situation and the examiner
Self-critical	Lacks self-confidence in attempting new tasks
Easy separation	Little or no concern around a new person or setting
Quick adjustment	Absence of wariness in a novel situation
Friendly	Extreme case in social interaction
Self-confidence	Pride in performance and willingness to tackle presented tasks
Self-reliance	Overt confidence and absorption in test material
Flat affect	Little change in emotional tone, responding to all activities in the same way
Passivity	Placid, sluggish behavior with slow, infrequent movement
Limited communication	Limited verbal responses, relative absence of verbal initiations
Shy	Withdrawn, unresponsive social behavior
Malleable	Passivity and acquiescence to examiner and test demands
Upset by strangers	Clinging toward mother, inability to separate even with reassurances
Fearful	Acute discomfort and apprehension that interferes with test performance

Moffitt, & Silva, 1995). Cluster analyses of these three factors revealed five homogeneous types of children at age 3. Reliability of the clusters was established by replicating the cluster solution on two randomly selected thirds of the available pool of 1,023 children who had complete temperament data at age 3 (for details, see Caspi & Silva, 1995).

This "typological" or person-centered approach focuses on the configuration of multiple variables within each child rather than on the relative standing of children across single variables; it is concerned with how different variables are organized within the child and how this organization defines different types of children. The well-adjusted type ($n = 405$; 48% male), resembling the Chess–Thomas (Chess & Thomas, 1987) easy type, included children who were capable of self-control when it was demanded of them, who were adequately self-confident, and who did not become unduly upset when confronting new people and situations. The undercontrolled type ($n = 106$; 62% male), resembling the Chess–Thomas difficult type, included children who were impulsive, restless, negativistic, distractible, and labile in their emotional responses. The inhibited type ($n = 80$ 40% male), resembling the Chess–Thomas slow-to-warm-up type, included children who were socially reticent, fearful, and easily upset by strangers. Thus, like Chess and Thomas before us, we found that approximately 40% of the children could be placed in the easy category and another 10% of the children could be placed in the difficult and slow-to-warm-up groups, respectively. In fact, research on personality development has identified these three types of children using different sources of information (e.g., parent reports, observations) and different statistical methods in different parts of the world (e.g., Iceland, Netherlands, Germany, New Zealand, United States), suggesting that these three types are the best candidates for inclusion in a generalizable typology of temperament (Robins, John, Caspi, Moffitt, & Stouthamer-Loeber, 1996).

We also found two types of children not anticipated by Chess and Thomas (1987). The confident type ($N = 281$; 52% male) were zealous, somewhat impulsive, eager to explore the testing materials, and adjusted to the testing situation quickly; however, unlike undercontrolled children they were not impersistent or negativistic. The reserved type ($n = 151$; 48% male) were timid and somewhat uncomfortable in the testing session; however, unlike inhibited children their response disposition was not extreme and their caution did not interfere with their task orientation. In this article, I limit my review to our results from comparisons of the well-adjusted, undercontrolled, and inhibited children because these groups replicate across cultures and they also provide an interpretive fit with previous studies about the structure of temperament. In contrast, the generality of additional types, such as the reserved and confident groups, has yet to be replicated in other samples, and it is unclear whether they constitute independent types or whether they can be subsumed within the three replicable types (Robins, John, & Caspi, 1998). I turn now to evidence of the connection between temperamental qualities observed at age 3 and psychosocial outcomes gathered using multiple methods in multiple settings from childhood to adulthood.

TEMPERAMENTAL QUALITIES AT AGE 3 PREDICT CHILDREN'S BEHAVIOR PROBLEMS

Because clinical concerns have historically inspired a great deal of interest in the measurement of temperament, it is not surprising that most longitudinal studies have set out to identify links between temperamental styles and behavior problems in childhood and adolescence (Rothbart & Bates, 1998). The results from some such studies have been difficult to interpret because they are based on reports of temperament and behavior problems obtained from the same rater at different ages, most often on reports provided over time by mothers. Using such reports to estimate behavioral continuity is problematic because observed continuities may reflect not only continuities in children's characteristics but also, to some unknown extent, continuities in maternal characteristics (Bates, 1994). To examine the links between children's temperamental

style and their behavior problems without this artifact, we relied on independent data sources.

From ages 5 to 11, teachers and parents completed the Rutter Child Scale on a biennial basis (for a review see Elander & Rutter, 1996; McGee, Williams, & Silva, 1985 for Dunedin details). This questionnaire inquires about the major areas of a child's behavioral and emotional functioning during the previous year and provides scale scores that index externalizing problems (e.g., fighting, bullying, lying, disobeying) and internalizing problems (e.g., worrying, crying easily, fussing). To examine the associations between children's temperamental styles and their later behavior problems, we standardized (z scores) the scales within each age period and estimated multiple regression models in which the undercontrolled and inhibited groups were represented by dummy-coded variables and the well-adjusted group served as the reference group. The results showed that undercontrolled children were repeatedly and independently rated as exhibiting more externalizing problems at ages 5, 7, 9, and 11, both by their parents ($bs = .52, .29, .43, .55$, respectively; all $ps < .01$) and by their teachers ($bs = .35, .32, .22, .37$, respectively; all $ps < .01$). As these findings show, the associations between undercontrolled behavior and externalizing problems were not attenuated by the passage of time and were robust across home and school settings. There was no evidence pointing to comparable links with internalizing problems; neither the undercontrolled nor the inhibited children were likely to suffer significantly more internalizing problems during childhood.

In adolescence, when the participants were 13 and 15 years old, their parents filled out the Revised Behavior Problem Checklist (Quay, 1983), which contains extensive and age-appropriate items tapping both externalizing and internalizing problems. Undercontrolled children continued to exhibit significantly more externalizing behavior problems at this point in the life course ($bs = .31$ and $.40$, respectively; $ps < .01$), and they also showed evidence of suffering from internalizing problems ($bs = .27$ and $.24$, respectively; $ps < .05$). In contrast, inhibited children suffered significantly from internalizing problems during adolescence ($bs = .41$ and $.33$, respectively; $ps < .01$). These findings fit with what is known from other cross-sectional and longitudinal studies: Measures of undercontrolled temperament are related to both externalizing and internalizing problems, and measures of inhibition are more clearly related to internalizing problems (Bates, Wachs, & Emde, 1994).

TEMPERAMENTAL QUALITIES AT AGE 3 PREDICT PERSONALITY STRUCTURE AT AGE 18

Whereas individual differences in temperament refer to stylistic differences between how children approach and respond to the world, adult personality traits represent the social and cognitive elaborations of these early styles; they index how adults relate to and think about the world around them (Rutter, 1987). To examine the links between behavioral styles in childhood and personality traits in young adulthood, we assessed the participants' personalities at age 18 using the Multidimensional Personality Questionnaire (MPQ; Tellegen et al., 1988; Tellegen & Waller, in press), one of the best known contemporary structural models of personality (Church & Burke, 1994). As summarized in Table 2, the MPQ provides for each person a comprehensive profile of scores on 10 distinct personality traits that define three general superfactors of personality. *Constraint* is a combination of the Traditionalism, Harm Avoidance and Self-Control scales. Individuals high on this factor tend to endorse social norms, act in a cautious and restrained manner, and avoid thrills. *Negative Emotionality* is a combination

of the Aggression, Alienation, and Stress Reaction scales. Individuals high on this dimension have a low general threshold for the experience of negative emotions such as fear, anxiety, and anger and tend to be involved in antagonistic relationships. *Positive Emotionality* is a combination of the Achievement, Social Potency, Well-Being, and Social Closeness scales. Individuals high on this dimension tend to view life as being essentially a pleasurable experience. (The MPQ Absorption scale was not included in the MPQ version administered in the Dunedin study.)

Figure 1 shows that the age-18 personality profiles of the three groups of children are very different. At age 18, the undercontrolled children scored low on traits indexing Constraint. They described themselves as reckless and careless (low self-control) and said they enjoyed dangerous and exciting activities (low harm avoidance). They scored high on traits indexing Negative Emotionality. They said that they enjoyed causing discomfort to other persons (high aggression), yet they also reported feeling mistreated, deceived, and betrayed by others (high alienation). In contrast, inhibited children scored high on traits indexing Constraint and low on traits indexing Positive Emotionality. They reported being cautious rather than impulsive (high self-control), they preferred safe activities over dangerous ones (high harm avoidance), they said they refrained from trying to take advantage of others, and they were unlikely to favor aggressive behavior (low aggression). Finally, they were lacking in social potency —they were submissive, not fond of leadership roles,

TABLE 2   Multidimensional Personality Questionnaire (MPQ) Scale Descriptions

MPQ SCALE	DESCRIPTION OF A HIGH SCORER
Traditionalism	Desires a conservative social environment; endorses high moral standards
Harm avoidance	Avoids excitement and danger; prefers safe activities even if they are tedious
Control	Is reflective, cautious, careful, rational, planful
Aggression	Hurts others for own advantage: will frighten and cause discomfort for others
Alienation	Feels mistreated, victimized, betrayed, and the target of false rumors
Stress reaction	Is nervous, vulnerable, sensitive, prone to worry
Achievement	Works hard; enjoys demanding projects and working long hours
Social potency	Is forceful and decisive; fond of influencing others; fond of leadership roles
Well-being	Has a happy, cheerful disposition; feels good about self and sees a bright future
Social closeness	Is sociable, likes people, and turns to others for comfort

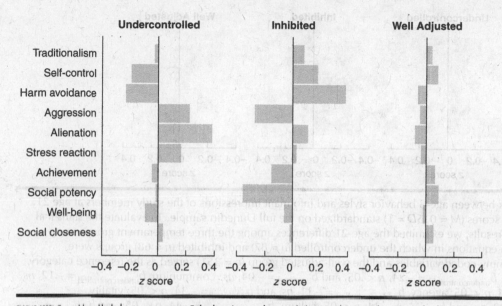

FIGURE 1 The link between age-3 behavior styles and the study members' Multidimensional Personality Questionnaire (MPQ) profiles at age 18. The figure shows z scores ($M = 0$, $SD = 1$) standardized on the full Dunedin sample. To evaluate the statistical significance of the results, we examined the age-18 differences among the three temperament groups using multiple regression equations in which the undercontrolled ($n = 92$) and inhibited ($n = 72$) groups were represented by dummy-coded variables and the well-adjusted group ($n = 366$) served as the reference category. Traditionalism, $b_{undercontrolled} = -.06$, ns, and $b_{inhibited} = .04$, ns; self-control, $b_{undercontrolled} = -.27$, $p < .05$, and $b_{inhibited} = .09$, ns; harm avoidance, $b_{undercontrolled} = -.17$, ns, and $b_{inhibited} = .48$, $p < .001$; aggression, $b_{undercontrolled} = .25$, $p < .05$, and $b_{inhibited} = -.25$, $p < .05$; alienation, $b_{undercontrolled} = .46$, $p < .001$, and $b_{inhibited} = .14$, ns; stress reaction, $b_{undercontrolled} = .21$, ns, and $b_{inhibited} = .05$, ns; achievement, $b_{undercontrolled} = -.10$, ns, and $b_{inhibited} = -.24$, ns; social potency, $b_{undercontrolled} = -.08$, ns, and $b_{inhibited} = -.44$, $p < .001$; well-being, $b_{undercontrolled} = -.06$, ns, and $b_{inhibited} = -.03$, ns; social closeness, $b_{undercontrolled} = -.09$, ns, and $b_{inhibited} = -.06$, ns.

and had little desire to influence others (low social potency). In summary, as young adults, inhibited children were characterized by an overcontrolled personality and a nonassertive style. The final panel of Figure 1 shows the personality profile of well-adjusted children, whose behavior at age 3 was characterized as age and situation appropriate; their style of approach and response to the testing session was regarded as expectable by the examiners and made for smooth testing. This style was still discernible at age 18: Statistically, well-adjusted children defined normal, average young adults.

Three years later, when the study members were 21 years old, we asked them to nominate someone who knew them well. We mailed questionnaires to

these "informants" and asked them to describe the study members using a checklist of adjectives; 95% of the informants returned completed questionnaires. A factor analysis of this checklist revealed that informant ratings could be grouped into five salient dimensions, which correspond roughly to the five-factor model of personality (McCrae & Costa, 1997). These informant ratings tend to corroborate the participants' self-reported personality profiles. As shown in Figure 2, undercontrolled children were rated by people who knew them well as low on Conscientiousness (e.g., not "reliable" or "trustworthy"). In contrast, inhibited children were rated low on Communion (e.g., not "affectionate"), Agency (e.g., not "outgoing" or "confident"), and Vitality (e.g., not "popular" or "healthy").

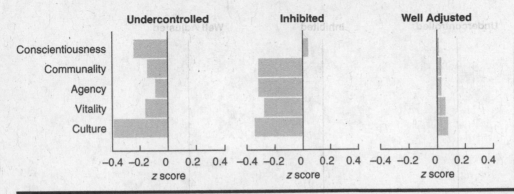

FIGURE 2 The link between age-3 behavior styles and informant impressions of the study members at age 21. The figure shows z scores ($M = 0$, $SD = 1$) standardized on the full Dunedin sample. To evaluate the statistical significance of the results, we examined the age-21 differences among the three temperament groups using multiple regression equations in which the undercontrolled ($n = 87$) and inhibited ($n = 68$) groups were represented by dummy-coded variables and the well-adjusted group ($n = 351$) served as the reference category. Conscientiousness, $b_{undercontrolled} = -.24$, $p < .05$, and $b_{inhibited} = -.04$, ns; communion, $b_{undercontrolled} = -.12$, ns, and $b_{inhibited} = -.24$, $p < .05$; agency, $b_{undercontrolled} = -.11$, ns, and $b_{inhibited} = -.34$, $p < .05$; vitality, $b_{undercontrolled} = -.22$, ns, and $b_{inhibited} = -.34$, $p < .05$; culture, $b_{undercontrolled} = -.44$, $p < .05$, and $b_{inhibited} = -.40$, $p < .001$.

In addition, undercontrolled and inhibited children were both described as low on Culture (e.g., not "creative" or "good at art").

In combination, these results constitute convergent evidence about the preservation of individual differences in personality style from ages 3 to 21 across three different data sources: from (a) observer ratings at age 3 to (b) self reports at age 18 to (c) informant descriptions at age 21.

TEMPERAMENTAL QUALITIES AT AGE 3 PREDICT THE QUALITY OF INTERPERSONAL RELATIONSHIPS AT AGE 21

Young adulthood is associated with a unique set of relational challenges, which Erikson (1950) aptly summarized by calling this developmental period the stage of "intimacy versus isolation." Would temperamental styles observed at age 3 relate to the negotiation of this life stage? On the basis of our personality findings, we expected that undercontrolled children would experience more conflicted interpersonal relationships, whereas inhibited children would have restricted interpersonal relationships. We examined the study members' interpersonal lives by looking at their relationships with (a) members of their household (including households they set up after leaving their parents' homes) and (b) a romantic partner (Newman, Caspi, Moffitt, & Silva, 1997).

By age 21, 79% of the participants had left their parents' home. We thus defined *home* as the study members' current residence and asked them to appraise the quality of interpersonal relationships in their household using the family relations index (Moos & Moos, 1981). This index assesses the extent of cohesion (e.g., "There is a feeling of togetherness"), expressiveness (e.g., "We tell each other about our personal problems"), and conflict (e.g., "We fight a lot" [reversed]) between members of a household. Figure 3 shows that undercontrolled children had significantly lower scores on the household relations index, reflecting conflict and tension with members of their household in young adulthood.

In addition to interviewing the study members about the general atmosphere of their home environment, we also interviewed them about their love lives. For the purposes of this study, an intimate relationship was defined as a relationship with a romantic partner

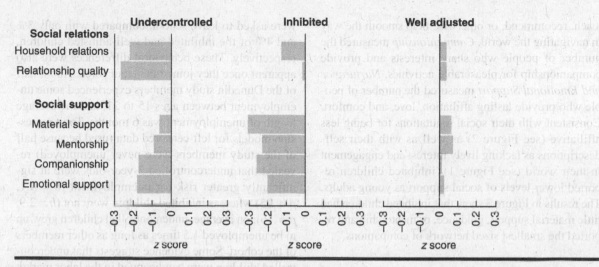

FIGURE 3   The link between age-3 behavior styles and the study members' interpersonal relations at age 21. The figure shows z scores ($M = 0$, $SD = 1$) standardized on the full Dunedin sample. To evaluate the statistical significance of the results, we examined the age-21 differences among the three temperament groups using multiple regression equations in which the undercontrolled ($n = 72–93$) and inhibited ($n = 62–73$) groups were represented by dummy-coded variables and the well-adjusted group ($n = 307–373$) served as the reference category. The lower-bound range on the sample sizes is due to the fact that not all study members had a romantic partner about whom to report. Household relations index, $b_{undercontrolled} = -.25$, $p < .05$, and $b_{inhibited} = -.14$, ns; relationship quality, $b_{undercontrolled} = -.26$, $p < .05$, and $b_{inhibited} = -.01$, ns; material support, $b_{undercontrolled} = -.13$, ns, and $b_{inhibited} = -.36$, $p < .01$; mentorship, $b_{undercontrolled} = -.17$, ns, and $b_{inhibited} = -.30$, $p < .05$; companionship, $b_{undercontrolled} = -.19$, ns, and $b_{inhibited} = -.27$, $p < .05$; emotional nurturance, $b_{undercontrolled} = -.21$, ns, and $b_{inhibited} = -.19$, ns.

during the past 12 months that had lasted at least 1 month; 83% of the study members reported that they were involved in such an intimate relationship. We found no evidence that the three temperament groups differed in their likelihood of being in an intimate relationship, χ^2 (2, $N = 539$) = 1.66, ns. We interviewed those study members who were involved with a romantic partner about their relationship. This structured interview yielded a global measure of relationship quality with items that reflect shared activities and interests (e.g., "We like to spend our free time with each other"), balance of power (e.g., "We are flexible in how we handle differences"), respect and fairness, emotional intimacy and trust, and open communication (e.g., "We are supportive of each other in difficult times"). Figure 3 shows that as young adults, undercontrolled children were involved in more conflicted

relationships, as expressed in significantly fewer mutual interests shared with their partners, more unequal balance of power in the relationship, and less intimacy and trust.

TEMPERAMENTAL QUALITIES AT AGE 3 PREDICT THE AVAILABILITY OF SOCIAL SUPPORT IN YOUNG ADULTHOOD

When the participants were at age 21, we also obtained information about social-support networks by asking them to specify the number of people who could provide them with different types of support (Newman et al., 1997). *Material or Practical Assistance* measured the number of people who would help with financial or physical assistance when needed. *Mentorship and Guidance* measured the number of people who advise, teach, recommend, or otherwise help smooth the way in navigating the world. *Companionship* measured the number of people who share interests and provide companionship for pleasurable activities. *Nurturance and Emotional Support* measured the number of people who provide lasting affiliation, love, and comfort. Consistent with their social reputations for being less affiliative (see Figure 2) as well as with their self-descriptions as lacking lively interest and engagement in their world (see Figure 1), inhibited children reported lower levels of social support as young adults. The results in Figure 3 show that inhibited children had little material support, guidance, or mentorship and reported the smallest sized network of companions.

TEMPERAMENTAL QUALITIES AT AGE 3 PREDICT UNEMPLOYMENT IN THE TRANSITION TO ADULTHOOD

Entering the labor force and finding employment is one of the most significant role transitions of young adulthood (Petersen & Mortimer, 1994). Employment yields income, grants training opportunities, and contributes to skill acquisition. It also provides young people a source of vocational identity, a sense of mastery and purpose, and a "stake" in adult institutions. How individuals develop such human capital is of growing interest to psychologists, and the Dunedin results show that early temperamental qualities may play a role in this process (Caspi, Wright, Moffitt, & Silva, 1998).

We obtained reliable monthly educational and employment histories from the Dunedin study members using a life history calendar that covered the period from their 15th birthday to age 21. We chose age 15 because it was the end of compulsory schooling for this birth cohort; turning 15 thus offered Dunedin study members the first opportunity to enter the labor force. The Dunedin study members left secondary school at the median age of 17 years 8 months. Both the undercontrolled and the inhibited children left secondary school significantly earlier, on average 3–4 months before the well-adjusted children, but they did so for different reasons. Among those who did not complete 5 years of high school (the maximum number of years), 21% of the undercontrolled children

were asked to leave school, compared with only 3% and 4% of the inhibited and well-adjusted children, respectively. These behavioral differences were also apparent once they joined the labor force. About half of the Dunedin study members experienced some unemployment between ages 15 to 21, and the average length of unemployment was 6 months. Tobit regression models for left-censored data (used because half of the study members were never unemployed) revealed that undercontrolled 3-year-olds were at significantly greater risk for unemployment ($b = 4.1$, $p < .05$) whereas inhibited children were not ($b = 2.9$, $p = .16$); on average, undercontrolled children grew up to be unemployed 1.5 times as long as other members of the cohort. Some evidence suggests that undercontrolled children were handicapped in the labor market because they continued to bring an aversive interpersonal style to bear on their dealings with others in the workplace; for example, they were 2.5 times (95% confidence interval: 1.2–5.5) as likely to be fired from a job compared with well-adjusted children. Not surprisingly, by age 21, undercontrolled children ($b = .33$, $p < .01$), but not inhibited children ($b = .16$, $p = .17$), also reported that they relied on benefits from multiple types of governmental support to make ends meet. It is still too early in their lives for us to assess the study members' occupational attainments, but these results about the transition to adulthood suggest that early temperamental qualities may be implicated in different socioeconomic trajectories.

TEMPERAMENTAL QUALITIES AT AGE 3 PREDICT PSYCHIATRIC DISORDERS IN YOUNG ADULTHOOD

Young adulthood is the peak risk period for the development of mental illness (Institute of Medicine, 1994), begging the question Can we foretell who is at risk for psychiatric problems during the transition from adolescence to adulthood? When the study members were 21 years old, we administered to them the Diagnostic Interview Schedule (DIS, version III–R) to obtain diagnoses of mental disorder following criteria established in the *Diagnostic and Statistical Manual of Mental Disorders* (DSM–III–R) of the American Psychiatric Association (1987). Forty percent of the

Dunedin study members met criteria for a psychiatric disorder (Newman et al., 1996), an estimate that is consistent with the prevalence rate of psychiatric disorders for this age group (37%) as revealed in the U.S. National Comorbidity Survey (Kessler et al., 1994). Mental health problems did not randomly afflict study members. As young adults, undercontrolled (46%) and inhibited (53%) children were more likely than well-adjusted children (38%) to be diagnosed with a psychiatric disorder. However, the more important question, clinically and theoretically, is whether age-3 behavior styles foretell specific adult psychiatric outcomes (McDevitt, 1986).

We focused on the most prevalent disorders of this age period to determine whether temperament could foretell who is at risk for different types of mental health problems during the transition to adulthood (Caspi, Moffitt, Newman, & Silva, 1996). We examined the following groupings of psychiatric disorders: (a) anxiety disorders, comprising generalized anxiety disorder, obsessive–compulsive disorder, panic disorder, agoraphobia, social phobia, simple phobia, or any combination of these disorders; (b) mood disorders, including separate diagnoses of major depression–dysthymia versus manic episode; (c) antisocial personality disorder; and (d) alcohol dependence. . . .

The prevalence rates (i.e., cohort base rates) of specific disorders in the Dunedin sample as a whole as well as the rates for well-adjusted, undercontrolled, and inhibited children [were analyzed]. . . . Age-3 behavior styles could not distinguish young adults at risk for developing an anxiety disorder. We also tested whether age-3 behavior could predict specific subtypes of anxiety disorders (e.g., social phobia, agoraphobia), but the results were not significant. . . . [There was a] link between age-3 behavior styles and mood disorders at age 21. Inhibited children were significantly more likely to be diagnosed with depression at age 21, whereas undercontrolled children were not. Although manic depression could not be predicted from age-3 behavior styles, it is of interest that none of the inhibited children had experienced an episode of mania, which is characterized by symptoms of increased activity, inflated self-esteem, and impulsivity. Thus, inhibition showed predictive specificity within the family of mood disorders. . . . [There was an]

association between age-3 behavior styles and antisocial personality disorder at age 21. Undercontrolled children were significantly more likely to meet diagnostic criteria for this disorder, which is characterized by predatory, callous, and exploitative behavior that is refractory to contingencies. . . . Undercontrolled children were also significantly more likely to be diagnosed with alcohol dependence at age 21. Inhibited children had elevated rates of alcoholism as well, but this result did not attain statistical significance. Finally, . . . [there was an] association between age-3 behavior styles and suicide attempts at age 21. As part of the mental health interview, study members were asked about suicide attempts they had made during the past 12 months. Attempts were counted whether or not they had required medical attention. Suicide attempts were significantly more concentrated among former undercontrolled and inhibited children. In summary, our longitudinal data suggest that early emerging behavioral differences not only act as a persisting risk factor for later psychiatric problems but also can sometimes confer risk for specific forms of psychopathology.

TEMPERAMENTAL QUALITIES AT AGE 3 PREDICT CRIMINAL BEHAVIOR AT AGE 21

We assessed illegal behavior at age 21 using the Self-Report Delinquency Interview, which is used to study delinquent behavior among young people throughout the Western world (see Moffitt, Silva, Lynam, & Henry, 1994). Using a reporting period of the previous 12 months, this interview asks the study members whether they engaged in each of 48 different illegal and antisocial behaviors including acts of theft, assault, vandalism, drug trafficking, and fraud. Following standard practice, we created a "variety" index that sums the number of different types of illegal behaviors in which each study member engaged. Variety scores such as these are endorsed by criminologists, as "it appears that the best available operational measure of the propensity to offend is a count of the number of distinct problem behaviors engaged in by a youth (that is, a variety scale)" (Hirschi & Gottfredson, 1995, p. 134). . . . Undercontrolled children, as young adults, were significantly more likely to be involved in a life of crime.

Official records corroborate these self-reported data. We obtained records of study members' cumulative court convictions at all courts in New Zealand and Australia by searching the central computer systems of the New Zealand police. Conviction records did not include traffic offenses with the exception of driving under the influence of alcohol or criminally negligent driving; 14% of the study members had been convicted of a crime by age 21, accounting for a total of 895 convictions. Of special interest are repeat offenders, who have been convicted of two or more offenses. . . . Undercontrolled children were significantly more likely to have been convicted of multiple crimes than were inhibited or well-adjusted children.

Our longitudinal data also reveal that early emerging temperamental differences are linked to social attitudes about crime. According to perceptual deterrence theory, individuals may be deterred from crime if they perceive legal consequences as certain, swift, and severe (Williams & Hawkins, 1986). We thus measured *perceived risk of arrest* by asking each study member, at age 21, to indicate how often they thought they would get caught for a specific crime committed on 10 different days (e.g., "If you shoplifted from a store on 10 different days, how many times do you think you would probably get caught for shoplifting?"). We inquired about seven different crimes, including shoplifting, drug use, car theft, assault, burglary, drunk driving, and fraud (Moffitt, Caspi, Dickson, Stanton, & Silva, 1996). On the whole, the participants thought they would get caught an average of 5 times out of 10 ($SD = 1.7$). But not all children grew up to perceive the same risks $F(2, 533) = 5.8$, $p < .05$. Interestingly, it was the inhibited children who in adulthood most feared getting caught. On average, they thought they would be caught 5.7 times out of 10, significantly more often than undercontrolled and well-adjusted children, who thought they would get caught 4.7 and 5.1 times out of 10, respectively. Perceptual deterrence theory also argues that informal social sanctions, such as censure by friends and family, may deter individuals from crime. We measured such *perceived informal social sanctions* by asking the participants to indicate whether they would

lose the respect of close friends and family members if those persons knew about their involvement in each of seven illegal behaviors: shoplifting, drug use, car theft, assault, burglary, drunk driving, and fraud. The results showed significant attitudinal differences at age 21 between the three temperament groups, $F(2, 539) = 2.84$, $p = .05$. Consistent with their personality profile as alienated young adults, undercontrolled children perceived fewer social deterrents to crime (Mean z score $= -.20$) than did the inhibited ($-.05$) and well-adjusted ($.06$) children.

CONCLUSION

A fundamental assumption guiding the study of personality development is that early emerging temperamental differences shape the course of development, its problematic presentations and healthful outcomes (Rutter, 1987). The Dunedin study instantiates this assumption by offering the most comprehensive evidence to date of personality continuities from the first 3 years of life to adulthood.

Assertions about personality continuity are often ambiguous. For example, the boy who has daily temper tantrums when he is 3 years old but weekly tantrums when he is 9 years old has increased his level of emotional control; he has changed in absolute terms. But if he ranks first in temper tantrums among his peers at both ages, he has not changed in relative terms. Further ambiguity arises because the surface manifestations of personality undergo profound transformations with development. For example, the undercontrolled child who has daily temper tantrums in early childhood may refrain from this behavior as an adult. But if he emerges into adulthood as a man who is irritable and moody, we may grant that the surface behavior has changed but claim that the underlying personality type has not. Although the form of behavior changes over time, the course of personality development is said to evidence coherence if the qualities of behavior are preserved over time: "The notion of coherence refers to a pattern of findings where a construct, measured by several different methods, retains its psychological meaning as revealed in relationships to a variety of other measures" across time and in different contexts (Ozer, 1986, p. 83).

We have seen evidence of coherence by following a cohort of children from age 3 to age 21. When observed at age 3, children classified as undercontrolled (10% of the sample) were described as irritable, impulsive, emotionally labile, and impersistent on tasks. Throughout childhood, their parents and teachers found them difficult to manage. In terms of their personality structure at age 18, undercontrolled children were characterized not only by high levels of impulsivity and thrill seeking but also by aggression and interpersonal alienation. By age 21, undercontrolled children reported more employment difficulties and higher levels of interpersonal conflict at home and in their romantic relationships. They had extensive brushes with the law, and their successful assumption of adult roles was compromised by their abuse of alcohol. People who knew them well corroborated this profile of conflicted interpersonal adjustment in describing undercontrolled children grown up as unreliable and untrustworthy.

When observed at age 3, children classified as inhibited (8% of the sample) were notably shy, fearful, and socially ill-at-ease. As adolescents they suffered from internalizing problems of distress. At age 18, they were characterized by overcontrolled, cautious, and nonassertive personality styles, expressing little desire to take on leadership roles or to exert influence over others. By age 21, they reported lower levels of social support, and their mental health was compromised by depression. People who knew them well corroborated this profile in describing inhibited children grown up as less affiliative, low on social agency, and lacking lively interest and engagement in their worlds.

Finally, the well-adjusted type (40% of the sample) included children whose style of approach and response at age 3 was regarded as age and situation normative; they overcame their initial wariness to the examiner in the testing session and became friendly as the session went on, they displayed appropriate self-control, and although they attempted to cope with challenging tasks, they did not become too upset if the tasks proved too difficult. This style was still discernible in adulthood; statistically, well-adjusted children defined normal, average young adults.

These three groups of children did not behave in the same way in every situation. Instead, we saw pre-dictable and meaningful ways of relating to the environment in different social settings at different ages. The results suggest the hypothesis that the continuities of personality are expressed not in the constancy of behavior across time and diverse circumstances but through the consistency over time in the ways persons characteristically modify their changing contexts as a function of their behavior.

Are These Connections Meaningful?

From childhood to adulthood, each of the empirical connections uncovered in the Dunedin study represents only a small to medium effect size. Recall, however, that the sources of these connections are behavioral observations of children's temperamental qualities that were made after a 90-min testing session by an examiner who was otherwise unacquainted with the child. It is also true that age-3 temperamental qualities explained only a meager amount of the variance in any single adult outcome. However, the importance of the reported findings lies not in the prediction of a single outcome but rather in the pervasive association between temperamental qualities at age 3 and multiple, independently ascertained indexes of psychosocial functioning at different ages and in different settings. Moreover, because the effects of personality differences accumulate over a lifetime, a focus on a single outcome variable measured at a single point in time will result in an underestimate of the extent of continuity in behavioral development (Caspi, Bem, & Elder, 1989; Rutter & Rutter, 1993). Abelson (1985) makes this point in noting that differences between baseball players are trivial if considered on the basis of a single at bat but become meaningful over the course of a game, a season, and a career. So it is on the playing field of life.

Small effect sizes have been defended as important elsewhere (e.g., Ahadi & Diener, 1989; Prentice & Miller, 1992; Rosenthal & Rubin, 1982), but another way to think about the consequences of continuity is to abandon traditional metrics of social science research and examine the real-world implications of early emerging behavioral differences. Consider antisocial behavior. Crimes impose costs on victims and entail costs to society. To obtain estimates of the cost of crime, I relied on the work of economists who have quantified in dollar terms the cost of each type of crime committed. These estimates take into account costs to the criminal justice system as well as to victims (e.g., reduced productivity, out-of-pocket expenses). Be- · cause an economic analysis of the costs of crime is not available for New Zealand per se, I used estimates calculated for the United States to assign a dollar value to crimes (e.g., assault, drunk driving, burglary, car theft) for which Dunedin study members have been convicted on a per crime basis (see Cohen, Miller, & Rossman, 1994, especially Tables 16 and 17, p. 128; Miller, Cohen, & Wiersema, 1996, especially Table 2, p. 9). Assuming that the relative costs of crime are fairly comparable across nations, the results show that undercontrolled children imposed more costs to society ($M = $24,722$) than did the inhibited ($M = $3,093$) or well-adjusted ($M = 720) children. A test of group differences is statistically significant at conventional levels, but that misses the point: Developmental continuities are pervasive; they have consequences not only for the welfare of the individual but also for the welfare of the wider community.

It is important to place evidence from the Dunedin study about developmental connectedness in historical perspective. Throughout the 20th century, professional opinion and public advice have been swayed by claims and counterclaims about the extent of continuity and discontinuity in human development (Block, 1984). Only 20 years ago, one of the century's leading child psychologists assailed what he believed was a misguided "faith in connectedness" and suggested instead that early psychological characteristics and experiences have few implications for later behavior (Kagan, 1980). The fact that Dunedin data chart connections from the first few years of life (as early as age 3) to young adulthood is thus a significant achievement, for this was and remains a contested claim (Lewis, 1999).

How Early Can We Tell?

The Dunedin study's behavioral data were first collected only at age 3, after a lot of development already occurred. Can we foretell adult life patterns from psychological characteristics at even earlier ages? The

second year of life may be the crucial dividing line for predicting adult personality differences because of the intercorrelated cognitive–emotional changes that take place during this period. During the second year of life, perceptual and cognitive changes enable children to master object permanence and engage in symbolic play (Kagan, 1981). Self-conscious emotions such as embarrassment and shame also begin to appear at this time (Astington, 1993). These capacities may be necessary for children to form mental representations of their social world and to develop beliefs and expectations that are then affirmed by an expanding and reactive social environment (Kagan, 1984). It is possible that continuity or predictability may not emerge until infants experience these major developmental reorganizations during the second year of life.

There are other reasons to doubt the feasibility of prediction prior to the second year of life. It is possible that much of the observed variation in infant . behavior is due to transient conditions, such as temporary allergies. As these conditions disappear with growth, so may their associated behavioral tendencies (Kagan, 1984). It is also possible that predictability may not emerge until a later age because early psychological differences are especially likely to be modified by the child's subsequent experiences with the environment (Chess & Thomas, 1987). Temperamental dimensions in infancy are the "personality" of the newborn, but whether they show continuity depends on the degree of "fit" between the child's temperamental characteristics and the socialization context (Wachs, 1994).

But before giving up on predicting later personality from infant temperament, one should consider the parallel case of predicting IQ. For many years, psychologists argued that intellectual performance scores obtained in the earliest years of life correlated poorly with IQ scores at later ages, implying that infancy and toddlerhood may be especially plastic developmental periods for intellectual status. But new evidence challenges this claim, as studies have shown that assessments of habituation and recognition memory in the first year of life predict later IQ quite well (McCall & Carriger, 1993). What implications do these findings have for the prediction of personality? According to Asendorpf (1992), these findings highlight the distinction between the stability of individual differences and the continuity of psychological constructs. Correlations across time may be low either because the rank order of individuals has changed over time or because the construct intelligence is indexed by different behaviors at different ages. Thus, it may be that, compared with previous measures of infant intelligence, habituation and recognition paradigms tap an information processing mechanism that is more similar to those skills tapped by later IQ tests. With regard to the prediction of personality differences, it may be that behavioral indicators in early childhood and those in adulthood have unequal validity coefficients; that is, they do not adequately reflect the behavioral expression of the same personality construct. Further advances in prediction will be made only if researchers are able to operationalize the same trait construct at different ages.

From Prediction to Explanation

The goal of this article has been to summarize evidence from one study about continuities in personality development, from early childhood to adulthood. It was beyond the objective of this summary to test hypotheses about processes that maintain continuity or prompt change. Ultimately, a complete developmental approach to the study of personality also must explain how continuities emerge and document what processes promote change. It is important to bear in mind that in the study of personality continuity and change, the twin goals of prediction and explanation are not always best served by the same types of data collection methods and designs. Longitudinal studies that gather repeated data on persons across the life course are the lifeblood of research on personality development because they can demonstrate the extent of continuity and change in behavioral development, document the consequences for later development of early emerging personality features, and identify the changing expressions of early emerging personality types across age and in diverse developmental settings (Block, 1993). However, the social, cognitive, and behavioral processes underlying continuity do not merely unfold across swaths of time. Rather, according to theories now dominant, these processes take place in the context of new interpersonal interactions with different people in different developmental settings; parents, siblings, peers, coworkers, and partners are variously drawn in at different points in the life course as accomplices in the maintenance of continuity (Wachtel, 1994). This has two implications for research on processes underlying personality continuity. First, to the extent that the most important sources of continuity (and change) are to be found in interpersonal settings, the ideal study of individual development ought to be conceived of as a study of social relationships, one in which longitudinal participants are successively studied alongside their significant others at different points in the life course (e.g., Kandel, Davies, & Baydar, 1990). Second, the study of continuity and change must include both global ratings of individual differences (to document connections across time and circumstance) and minute-to-minute assessments of social interactions (to document how behavior patterns are sustained and potentially altered) (Patterson & Bank, 1990). Each strategy provides different but crucial information about continuity and change in personality development. The Dunedin study design is strong for documenting connections across time, but other designs are needed to explore how social transactions maintain continuity or prompt change.

I have discussed in previous works how early temperamental differences become elaborated over time to shape multiple outcomes (Caspi, 1998). The process of developmental elaboration refers to the mechanisms by which those temperamental attributes that are part of each individual's genetic heritage accumulate response strength through their repeated reinforcement and become elaborated into cognitive structures strongly primed for accessibility. There are many kinds of person–environment transactions, but three play particularly important roles both in promoting the continuity of personality and in controlling the trajectory of the life course itself. Reactive transactions occur when different individuals exposed to the same environment experience it, interpret it, and react to it differently. Evocative transactions occur when an individual's personality evokes distinctive responses from others. Proactive transactions occur when individuals select or create environments of their own. These person–environment transactions represent probabilistic connections that strengthen response dispositions across the age-graded life course as individuals assume new roles and relationships and interpret and modify their experiences in corresponding social settings.

The key word in the previous sentence was *probabilistic*. Longitudinal studies of the natural history of personality development underscore that continuity is more likely than change. But the fact that natural-development studies point to the connectedness of behavioral development across the life course does not preclude the possibility of planned interventions, nor does it negate the possibility of naturally occurring change. In part, some change comes about because the course of personality development resembles a "random walk," a series of stochastic events, or fortuitous chance encounters, that collectively and cumulatively contribute to differences between individuals and that also have the capacity to deflect life paths (Bandura, 1982; Meehl, 1978, p. 811). Other change comes about because the intersection of psychological dispositions and social-structural or ecological characteristics creates differential opportunities for the expression of individual differences (Laub & Sampson, 1993). For example, undercontrolled boys are significantly less likely to become involved in crime if they stay in school (Henry, Caspi, Moffitt, Harrington, & Silva, [1999]). And finally, some change in the natural history of development comes about because people do respond to reinforcers and punishers, whether delivered as explicit or implicit contingencies. For example, inhibited children respond differently than noninhibited children to different parenting practices (Kochanska, 1997), and parental interventions can generate "lawful" or predictable discontinuities in early development (Park, Belsky, Putnam, & Crnic, 1997). Responsivity to new contingencies is not limited to the childhood years and to formative relationships with parents. New relationships in adulthood also offer the potential for turning points, as suggested by the finding that marital attachment is associated with change in the criminal behavior of antisocial youth and may thus help

to explain emergent discontinuities in adult development (Laub, Nagin, & Sampson, 1998).

Why, then, against this background of potential change, are both maladaptive and adaptive patterns of behavior sustained across the life course? For the most part, it is because the course of behavioral development is shaped and elaborated in environments that covary with personality differences (Scarr & McCartney, 1983). In the early years of life, person–environment covariation occurs because of the joint transmission of genes and culture from parents to offspring. Given that parents and children resemble each other in temperamental qualities, children whose difficult temperament might be curbed by firm discipline will tend to have parents who are inconsistent disciplinarians, and the converse is also true: Warm parents tend to have infants with an easy temperament. Later in life, person–environment covariation occurs because people choose situations and select partners who resemble them, reinforcing their earlier established interactional styles. Across the life course—from one's family of origin to one's family of destination—behavioral development takes place in environments that are correlated with individual differences in personality. And even though it is not possible to predict chance encounters, personality differences influence how even these fortuitous events are subjectively experienced. The child thus becomes the father of the man (at $p < .05$).

REFERENCES

Block, J. (1993). Studying personality the long way. In D. Funder, R. D. Parke, C. Tomlinson-Keasey, & K. Widaman (Eds.), *Studying lives through time: Personality and development* (pp. 9–41). Washington, DC: American Psychological Association.

Caspi, A. (1998). Personality development across the life course. In W. Damon (Series Ed.) & N. Eisenberg (Vol. Ed.), *Handbook of child psychology: Vol. 3. Social, emotional, and personality development* (pp. 311–388). New York: Wiley.

Chess, S., & Thomas, A. (1990). Continuities and discontinuities in temperament. In L. Robins & M. Rutter (Eds.), *Straight and devious pathways from childhood to adulthood* (pp. 205–220). New York: Cambridge University Press.

Kagan, J. (1980). Perspectives on continuity. In O. G. Brim, Jr. & J. Kagan (Eds.), *Constancy and change in human development* (pp. 26–74). Cambridge, MA: Harvard University Press.

Lewis, M. (1999). On the development of personality. In Pervin & O. P. John (Eds.), *Handbook of personality theory and research* (2nd ed., pp. 327–346). New York: Guilford Press.

Rothbart, M., & Bates, J. E. (1998). Temperament. In W. Damon (Series Ed.) & N. Eisenberg (Vol. Ed.),

Handbook of child psychology: Vol. 3. Social, emotional, and personality development (pp. 105–176). New York: Wiley.

Rutter, M. (1987). Temperament, personality, and personality disorder. *British Journal of Psychiatry, 150,* 443–458.

Scarr, S., & McCartney, K. (1983). How people make their own environments: A theory of genotype→environment effects. *Child Development, 54,* 424–435.

Questions to Think About

1. How does the observation that temperament at age 3 can be a good predictor of personality and social relations in young adulthood support or undermine a strongly genetic view of personality?

2. If potential adoptive parents are introduced to a three-year-old who appears to match the undercontrolled or "difficult" temperament pattern, should they feel discouraged at the prospect of bringing that child into their family? Why or why not?

3. What kinds of interventions might have improved the young-adulthood outcomes for the undercontrolled 3-year-olds, and are those different from the interventions that might have improved outcomes for the inhibited children?

21

Conditioned Emotional Reactions

JOHN B. WATSON AND ROSALIE RAYNER

John B. Watson (1878–1958) was a dominant figure in establishing a key learning approach in psychology called *behaviorism.* Behaviorism emphasizes the study of observable behavior rather than internal thoughts or traits. The environment is key to understanding a person.

A professor at Johns Hopkins University from 1908 to 1919, Watson's basic theories about studying observable behavior were proclaimed in his 1914 book, *Behavior.* Additionally, in 1919, he wrote *Psychology from the Standpoint of a Behaviorist,* which condemned introspectionists and psychoanalysts. Watson's basic perspective on personality was that personality is a function of the environment in which a child is raised; that is, personality is conditioned (learned). In the following selection, Watson and his assistant Rosalie Rayner (1899–1936) show that emotional problems can be conditioned (learned) and, thus, are not necessarily due to any internal conflicts or neuroses.

In recent literature various speculations have been entered into concerning the possibility of conditioning various types of emotional response, but direct experimental evidence in support of such a view has been lacking. If the theory advanced by Watson and Morgan to the effect that in infancy the original emotional reaction patterns are few, consisting so far as observed of fear, rage and love, then there must be some simple method by means of which the range of stimuli which can call out these emotions and their compounds is greatly increased. Otherwise, complexity in adult response could not be accounted for. These authors without adequate experimental evidence advanced the view that this range was increased by means of conditioned reflex factors. It was suggested there that the early home life of the child furnishes a laboratory situation for establishing conditioned emotional responses. The present authors have recently put the whole matter to an experimental test.

Experimental work has been done so far on only one child, Albert B. This infant was reared almost from birth in a hospital environment; his mother was a wet nurse in the Harriet Lane Home for Invalid Children. Albert's life was normal: he was healthy from birth and one of the best developed youngsters ever brought to the hospital, weighing twenty-one pounds at nine months of age. He was on the whole stolid and unemotional. His stability was one of the principal reasons for using him as a subject in this test. We felt that we could do him relatively little harm by carrying out such experiments as those outlined below.

At approximately nine months of age we ran him through the emotional tests that have become a part of our regular routine in determining whether fear reactions can be called out by other stimuli than sharp noises and the sudden removal of support. Tests of this type have been described by the senior author in another place. In brief, the infant was confronted suddenly and for the first time successively with a white rat, a rabbit, a dog, a monkey, with masks with and without hair, cotton wool, burning newspapers, etc. A permanent record of Albert's reactions to these objects

Source: Watson, J. B., & Rayner, R. (1920). Conditioned emotional reactions. *Journal of Experimental Psychology, 3,* 1–14.

and situations has been preserved in a motion picture study. Manipulation was the most usual reaction called out. *At no time did this infant ever show fear in any situation.* These experimental records were confirmed by the casual observations of the mother and hospital attendants. No one had ever seen him in a state of fear and rage. The infant practically never cried.

Up to approximately nine months of age we had not tested him with loud sounds. The test to determine whether a fear reaction could be called out by a loud sound was made when he was eight months, twenty-six days of age. The sound was that made by striking a hammer upon a suspended steel bar four feet in length and three-fourths of an inch in diameter. The laboratory notes are as follows:

One of the two experimenters caused the child to turn its head and fixate her moving hand; the other, stationed back of the child, struck the steel bar a sharp blow. The child started violently, his breathing was checked and the arms were raised in a characteristic manner. On the second stimulation the same thing occurred, and in addition the lips began to pucker and tremble. On the third stimulation the child broke into a sudden crying fit. This is the first time an emotional situation in the laboratory has produced any fear or even crying in Albert.

We had expected just these results on account of our work with other infants brought up under similar conditions. It is worth while to call attention to the fact that removal of support (dropping and jerking the blanket upon which the infant was lying) was tried exhaustively upon this infant on the same occasion. It was not effective in producing the fear response. This stimulus is effective in younger children. At what age such stimuli lose their potency in producing fear is not known. Nor is it known whether less placid children ever lose their fear of them. This probably depends upon the training the child gets. It is well known that children eagerly run to be tossed into the air and caught. On the other hand it is equally well known that in the adult fear responses are called out quite clearly by the sudden removal of support, if the individual is walking across a bridge, walking out upon a beam, etc. There is a wide field of study here which is aside from our present point.

The sound stimulus, thus, at nine months of age, gives us the means of testing several important factors. I. Can we condition fear of an animal, *e.g.,* a white rat, by visually presenting it and simultaneously striking a steel bar? II. If such a conditioned emotional response can be established, will there be a transfer to other animals or other objects? III. What is the effect of time upon such conditioned emotional responses? IV. If after a reasonable period such emotional responses have not died out, what laboratory methods can be devised for their removal?

I. The establishment of conditioned emotional responses. At first there was considerable hesitation upon our part in making the attempt to set up fear reactions experimentally. A certain responsibility attaches to such a procedure. We decided finally to make the attempt, comforting ourselves by the reflection that such attachments would arise anyway as soon as the child left the sheltered environment of the nursery for the rough and tumble of the home. We did not begin this work until Albert was eleven months, three days of age. Before attempting to set up a conditioned response we, as before, put him through all of the regular emotional tests. *Not the slightest sign of a fear response was obtained in any situation.*

The steps taken to condition emotional responses are shown in our laboratory notes.

11 Months 3 Days

1. White rat suddenly taken from the basket and presented to Albert. He began to reach for rat with left hand. Just as his hand touched the animal the bar was struck immediately behind his head. The infant jumped violently and fell forward, burying his face in the mattress. He did not cry, however.

2. Just as the right hand touched the rat the bar was again struck. Again the infant jumped violently, fell forward and began to whimper.

In order not to disturb the child too seriously no further tests were given for one week.

11 Months 10 Days

1. Rat presented suddenly without sound. There was steady fixation but no tendency at first to reach for it. The rat was then placed nearer, whereupon tentative reaching movements began with the right hand. When the rat nosed the infant's left hand, the hand was immediately withdrawn. He started to reach for the head of the animal with the forefinger of the left hand, but withdrew it suddenly before contact. It is thus seen that the two joint stimulations given the previous week were not without effect. He was tested with his blocks immediately afterwards to see if they shared in the process of conditioning. He began immediately to pick them up, dropping them, pounding them, etc. In the remainder of the tests the blocks were given frequently to quiet him and to test his general emotional state. They were always removed from sight when the process of conditioning was under way.

2. Joint stimulation with rat and sound. Started, then fell over immediately to right side. No crying.

3. Joint stimulation. Fell to right side and rested upon hands, with head turned away from rat. No crying.

4. Joint stimulation. Same reaction.

5. Rat suddenly presented alone. Puckered face, whimpered and withdrew body sharply to the left.

6. Joint stimulation. Fell over immediately to right side and began to whimper.

7. Joint stimulation. Started violently and cried, but did not fall over.

8. Rat alone. *The instant the rat was shown the baby began to cry. Almost instantly he turned sharply to the left, fell over on left side, raised himself on all fours and began to crawl away so rapidly that he was caught with difficulty before reaching the edge of the table.*

This was as convincing a case of a completely conditioned fear response as could have been theoretically pictured. In all seven joint stimulations were given to bring about the complete reaction. It is not unlikely had the sound been of greater intensity or of a more complex clang character that the number of joint stimulations might have been materially reduced. Experiments designed to define the nature of the sounds that will serve best as emotional stimuli are under way.

II. When a conditioned emotional response has been established for one object, is there a transfer? Five days later Albert was again brought back into the laboratory and tested as follows:

11 Months 15 Days

1. Tested first with blocks. He reached readily for them, playing with them as usual. This shows that there has been no general transfer to the room, table, blocks, etc.

2. Rat alone. Whimpered immediately, withdrew right hand and turned head and trunk away.

3. Blocks again offered. Played readily with them, smiling and gurgling.

4. Rat alone. Leaned over to the left side as far away from the rat as possible, then fell over, getting up on all fours and scurrying away as rapidly as possible.

5. Blocks again offered. Reached immediately for them, smiling and laughing as before.

The above preliminary test shows that the conditioned response to the rat had carried over completely for the five days in which no tests were given. The question as to whether or not there is a transfer was next taken up.

6. Rabbit alone. The rabbit was suddenly placed on the mattress in front of him. The reaction was pronounced. Negative responses began at once. He leaned as far away from the animal as possible, whimpered, then burst into tears. When the rabbit was placed in contact with him he buried his face in the mattress, then got up on all fours and crawled away, crying as he went. This was a most convincing test.

7. The blocks were next given him, after an interval. He played with them as before. It was observed by four people that he played far more energetically with them than ever before. The blocks were raised high over his head and slammed down with a great deal of force.

8. Dog alone. The dog did not produce as violent a reaction as the rabbit. The moment fixation occurred the child shrank back and as the animal came nearer he attempted to get on all fours but did not cry at first. As soon as the dog passed out of his range of vision he became quiet. The dog was then made to approach the infant's head (he was lying down at the moment). Albert straightened up immediately, fell over to the opposite side and turned his head away. He then began to cry.

9. The blocks were again presented. He began immediately to play with them.

10. Fur coat (seal). Withdrew immediately to the left side and began to fret. Coat put close to him on the left side, he turned immediately, began to cry and tried to crawl away on all fours.

11. Cotton wool. The wool was presented in a paper package. At the end the cotton was not covered by the paper. It was placed first on his feet. He kicked it away but did not touch it with his hands. When his hand was laid on the wool he immediately withdrew it but did not show the shock that the animals or fur coat produced in him. He then began to play with the paper, avoiding contact with the wool itself. He finally, under the impulse of the manipulative instinct, lost some of his negativism to the wool.

12. Just in play W. put his head down to see if Albert would play with his hair. Albert was completely negative. Two other observers did the same thing. He began immediately to play with their hair. W. then brought the Santa Claus mask and presented it to Albert. He was again pronouncedly negative.

11 Months 20 Days

1. Blocks alone. Played with them as usual.

2. Rat alone. Withdrawal of the whole body, bending over to left side, no crying. Fixation and following with eyes. The response was much less marked than on first presentation the previous week. It was thought best to freshen up the reaction by another joint stimulation.

3. Just as the rat was placed on his hand the rod was struck. Reaction violent.

4. Rat alone. Fell over at once to left side. Reaction practically as strong as on former occasion but no crying.

5. Rat alone. Fell over to left side, got up on all fours and started to crawl away. On this occasion there was no crying, but strange to say, as he started away he began to gurgle and coo, even while leaning far over to the left side to avoid the rat.

6. Rabbit alone. Leaned over to left side as far as possible. Did not fall over. Began to whimper but reaction not so violent as on former occasions.

7. Blocks again offered. He reached for them immediately and began to play.

All of the tests so far discussed were carried out upon a table supplied with a mattress, located in a small, well-lighted dark-room. We wished to test next whether conditioned fear responses so set up would appear if the situation were markedly altered. We thought it best before making this test to freshen the reaction both to the rabbit and to the dog by showing them at the moment the steel bar was struck. It will be recalled that this was the first time any effort had been made to directly condition response to the dog and rabbit. The experimental notes are as follows:

8. The rabbit at first was given alone. The reaction was exactly as given in test (6) above. When the rabbit was left on Albert's knees for a long time he began tentatively to reach out and manipulate its fur with forefingers. While doing this the steel rod was struck. A violent fear reaction resulted.

9. Rabbit alone. Reaction wholly similar to that on trial (6) above.

10. Rabbit alone. Started immediately to whimper, holding hands far up, but did not cry. Conflicting tendency to manipulate very evident.

11. Dog alone. Began to whimper, shaking head from side to side, holding hands as far away from the animal as possible.

12. Dog and sound. The rod was struck just as the animal touched him. A violent negative reaction appeared. He began to whimper, turned to one side, fell over and started to get up on all fours.

13. Blocks. Played with them immediately and readily.

On this same day and immediately after the above experiment Albert was taken into the large well-lighted lecture room belonging to the laboratory. He was placed on a table in the center of the room immediately under the skylight. Four people were present. The situation was thus very different from that which obtained in the small dark room.

1. Rat alone. No sudden fear reaction appeared at first. The hands, however, were held up and away from the animal. No positive manipulatory reactions appeared.

2. Rabbit alone. Fear reaction slight. Turned to left and kept face away from the animal but the reaction was never pronounced.

3. Dog alone. Turned away but did not fall over. Cried. Hands moved as far away from the animal as possible. Whimpered as long as the dog was present.

4. Rat alone. Slight negative reaction.

5. Rat and sound. It was thought best to freshen the reaction to the rat. The sound was given just as the rat was presented. Albert jumped violently but did not cry.

6. Rat alone. At first he did not show any negative reaction. When rat was placed nearer he began to show negative reaction by drawing back his body, raising his hands, whimpering, etc.

7. Blocks. Played with them immediately.

8. Rat alone. Pronounced withdrawal of body and whimpering.

9. Blocks. Played with them as before.

10. Rabbit alone. Pronounced reaction. Whimpered with arms held high, fell over backward and had to be caught.

11. Dog alone. At first the dog did not produce the pronounced reaction. The hands were held high over the head, breathing was checked, but there was no crying. Just at this moment the dog, which had not barked before, barked three times loudly when only about six inches from the baby's face. Albert immediately fell over and broke into a wail that continued until the dog was removed. The sudden barking of the hitherto quiet dog produced a marked fear response in the adult observers!

From the above results it would seem that emotional transfers do take place. Furthermore it would seem that the number of transfers resulting from an experimentally produced conditioned emotional reaction may be very large. In our observations we had no means of testing the complete number of transfers which may have resulted.

III. The effect of time upon conditioned emotional responses. We have already shown that the conditioned emotional response will continue for a period of one week. It was desired to make the time test longer. In view of the imminence of Albert's departure from the hospital we could not make the interval longer than one month. Accordingly no further emotional experimentation was entered into for thirty-one days after the above test. During the month, however, Albert was brought weekly to the laboratory for tests upon right and left-handedness, imitation, general de-

velopment, etc. No emotional tests whatever were given and during the whole month his regular nursery routine was maintained in the Harriet Lane Home. The notes on the test given at the end of this period are as follows:

1 Year 21 Days

1. Santa Claus mask. Withdrawal, gurgling, then slapped at it without touching. When his hand was forced to touch it, he whimpered and cried. His hand was forced to touch it two more times. He whimpered and cried on both tests. He finally cried at the mere visual stimulus of the mask.

2. Fur coat. Wrinkled his nose and withdrew both hands, drew back his whole body and began to whimper as the coat was put nearer. Again there was the strife between withdrawal and the tendency to manipulate. Reached tentatively with left hand but drew back before contact had been made. In moving his body to one side his hand accidentally touched the coat. He began to cry at once, nodding his head in a very peculiar manner (this reaction was an entirely new one). Both hands were withdrawn as far as possible from the coat. The coat was then laid on his lap and he continued nodding his head and whimpering, withdrawing his body as far as possible, pushing the while at the coat with his feet but never touching it with his hands.

3. Fur coat. The coat was taken out of his sight and presented again at the end of a minute. He began immediately to fret, withdrawing his body and nodding his head as before.

4. Blocks. He began to play with them as usual.

5. The rat. He allowed the rat to crawl towards him without withdrawing. He sat very still and fixated it intently. Rat then touched his hand. Albert withdrew it immediately, then leaned back as far as possible but did not cry. When the rat was placed on his arm he withdrew his body and began to fret, nodding his head. The rat was then allowed to crawl against his chest. He first began to fret and then covered his eyes with both hands.

6. Blocks. Reaction normal.

7. The rabbit. The animal was placed directly in front of him. It was very quiet. Albert showed no avoiding reactions at first. After a few seconds he puckered up his face, began to nod his head and to look intently at the experimenter. He next began to push the rabbit away with his feet, withdrawing his body at the same time. Then as the rabbit came nearer he began pulling his feet away, nodding his head, and wailing "da da." After about a minute he reached out tentatively and slowly and touched the rabbit's ear with his right hand, finally manipulating it. The rabbit was again placed in his lap. Again he began to fret and withdrew his hands. He reached out tentatively with his left hand and touched the animal, shuddered and withdrew the whole body. The experimenter then took hold of his left hand and laid it on the rabbit's back. Albert immediately withdrew his hand and began to suck his thumb. Again the rabbit was laid in his lap. He began to cry, covering his face with both hands.

8. Dog. The dog was very active. Albert fixated it intensely for a few seconds, sitting very still. He began to cry but did not fall over backwards as on his last contact with the dog. When the dog was pushed closer to him he at first sat motionless, then began to cry, putting both hands over his face.

These experiments would seem to show conclusively that directly conditioned emotional responses as well as those conditioned by transfer persist, although with a certain loss in the intensity of the reaction, for a longer period than one month. Our view is that they persist and modify personality throughout life. It should be recalled again that Albert was of an extremely phlegmatic type. Had he been emotionally unstable probably both the directly conditioned response and those transferred would have persisted through-out the month unchanged in form.

IV. "Detachment" or removal of conditioned emotional responses. Unfortunately Albert was taken from the hospital the day the above tests were made. Hence the opportunity of building up an experimental technique by means of which we could remove the conditioned emotional responses was denied us. Our own view, expressed above, which is possibly not very well grounded, is that these responses in the home environment are likely to persist indefinitely, unless an accidental method for removing them is hit upon. The importance of establishing some method must be apparent to all. Had the opportunity been at hand we should have tried out several methods, some of which

we may mention. (1) Constantly confronting the child with those stimuli which called out the responses in the hopes that habituation would come in corresponding to "fatigue" of reflex when differential reactions are to be set up. (2) By trying to "recondition" by showing objects calling out fear responses (visual) and simultaneously stimulating the erogenous zones (tactual). We should try first the lips, then the nipples and as a final resort the sex organs. (3) By trying to "recondition" by feeding the subject candy or other food just as the animal is shown. This method calls for the food control of the subject. (4) By building up "constructive" activities around the object by imitation and by putting the hand through the motions of manipulation. At this age imitation of overt motor activity is strong, as our present but unpublished experimentation has shown.

INCIDENTAL OBSERVATIONS

(a) Thumb sucking as a compensator device for blocking fear and noxious stimuli. During the course of these experiments, especially in the final test, it was noticed that whenever Albert was on the verge of tears or emotionally upset generally he would continually thrust his thumb into his mouth. The moment the hand reached the mouth he became impervious to the stimuli producing fear. Again and again while the motion pictures were being made at the end of the thirty-day rest period, we had to remove the thumb from his mouth before the conditioned response could be obtained. This method of blocking noxious and emotional stimuli (fear and rage) through erogenous stimulation seems to persist from birth onward. Very often in our experiments upon the work adders with infants under ten days of age the same reaction appeared. When at work upon the adders both of the infants arms are under slight restraint. Often rage appears. They begin to cry, thrashing their arms and legs about. If the finger gets into the mouth crying ceases at once. The organism thus apparently from birth, when under the influence of love stimuli is blocked to all others.[1] This resort to sex stimulation when under the influence of noxious and emotional situations, or when the individual is restless and idle, persists throughout adolescent and adult life. Albert, at any rate, did not resort to thumb sucking except in the presence of such stimuli. Thumb sucking could immediately be checked by offering him his blocks. These invariably called out active manipulation instincts. It is worth while here to call attention to the fact that Freud's conception of the stimulation of erogenous zones as being the expression of an original "pleasure" seeking principle may be turned about and possibly better described as a compensatory (and often conditioned) device for the blockage of noxious and fear and rage producing stimuli.

(b) Equal primacy of fear, love and possibly rage. While in general the results of our experiment offer no particular points of conflict with Freudian concepts, one fact out of harmony with them should be emphasized. According to proper Freudians sex (or in our terminology, love) is the principal emotion in which conditioned responses arise which later limit and distort personality. We wish to take sharp issue with this view on the basis of the experimental evidence we have gathered. Fear is as primal a factor as love in influencing personality. Fear does not gather its potency in any derived manner from love. It belongs to the original and inherited nature of man. Probably the same may be true of rage although at present we are not so sure of this.

The Freudians twenty years from now, unless their hypotheses change, when they come to analyze Albert's fear of a seal skin coat—assuming that he comes to analysis at that age—will probably tease from him the recital of a dream which upon their analysis will show that Albert at three years of age attempted to play with the pubic hair of the mother and was scolded violently for it. (We are by no means denying that this might in some other case condition it). If the analyst has sufficiently prepared Albert to accept such a dream when found as an explanation of

his avoiding tendencies, and if the analyst has the authority and personality to put it over, Albert may be fully convinced that the dream was a true revealer of the factors which brought about the fear.

It is probable that many of the phobias in psychopathology are true conditioned emotional reactions either of the direct or the transferred type. One may possibly have to believe that such persistence of early conditioned responses will be found only in persons who are constitutionally inferior. Our argument is meant to be constructive. Emotional disturbances in adults cannot be traced back to sex alone. They must be retraced along at least three collateral lines—to conditioned and transferred responses set up in infancy and early youth in all three of the fundamental human emotions.

ENDNOTE

1. The stimulus to love in infants according to our view is stroking of the skin, lips, nipples and sex organs, patting and rocking, picking up, etc. Patting and rocking (when not conditioned) are probably equivalent to actual stimulation of the sex organs. In adults of course, as every lover knows, vision, audition and olfaction soon become conditioned by joint stimulation with contact and kinaesthetic stimuli.

REFERENCES

Watson, J. B. (1919). *Psychology, from the standpoint of a behaviorist.* Philadelphia and London: J. B. Lippincott.

Watson, J. B., & Morgan, J. J. (1917). Emotional reactions and psychological experimentation. *American Journal of Psychology, 28,* 163–174.

Questions to Think About

1. What are conditioned emotional responses? How can they be established?

2. Why was the fear response to the rat by Albert B. transferred to the dog and the rabbit, but not to the blocks or the table?

3. What do these tests on Albert imply about human emotional disturbances in adults? To what might adult emotional disturbances be attributed?

4. How does Watson's explanation of emotional disturbance differ from Freud's? What are the implications for therapy (treatment)?

22

Intellectual Self-Management in Old Age

B. F. SKINNER

B. F. Skinner was by no means a personality psychologist; indeed, he thought the term *personality* to be meaningless. Notions of internal, nonobservable psychological characteristics were an anathema to him. Rather, Skinner theorized, personality can be located in the environment; the responses that have been rewarded are the ones that are most likely to appear again. For example, to Skinner, a neurotic is someone who has been reinforced for overly emotional behavior.

Skinner (1904–1990) worked for many years at Harvard University, constantly criticizing the idea of internal states and generally being a thorn in the side of traditional personality theorists. Studying rats and pigeons, Skinner deduced laws about the most effective schedules of reinforcement. In this selection, Skinner shows how one can deal with old age by focusing on changing the external environment, rather than worrying about internal biological deterioration.

A quarter of a century ago I presented a paper at the Eastern Psychological Association meeting called "A Case History in Scientific Method." In it I pointed out that my life as a behavioral scientist did not seem to conform to the picture usually painted by statisticians and scientific methodologists. The present article is also a case history but in a very different field. I have heard it said that G. Stanley Hall, one of our founding fathers, wrote a book on each of the stages of his life as he passed through it. I did not have the foresight to begin early enough to do that, but I can still talk about the last stage, and so I now present myself to you behaving verbally in old age as I once presented those pigeons playing Ping-Pong.

Developmentalism is a branch of structuralism in which the form or topography of behavior is studied as a function of time. At issue is how behavior changes as one grows older. *Aging* should be the right word for this process, but it does not mean developing. In accepted usage, *to develop* is not simply to grow

older but to unfold a latent structure, to realize an inner potential, to become more effective. *Aging,* on the other hand, usually means growing less effective. For Shakespeare the "ages of man" ranged from the infant mewling and puking, to the schoolboy "creeping like snail unwillingly to school," to lovers sighing and soldiers seeking the bubble reputation, to the justice full of wise saws and modern instances, to a stage in which the "big manly voice . . . pipes and whistles in his sound" and then at last to second childishness and mere oblivion—"sans teeth, sans eyes, sans taste," and in the end, of course, "sans everything." The aged are old people. Aging is growing not merely older but old.

In developmentalism the horticultural metaphor is strong. There are stages of *growth,* and *maturity* is hailed as a desirable state of completion. But the metaphor then becomes less attractive, for there is a point at which we are glad to stop developing. Beyond maturity lie decay and rot. Fortunately, the developmental account is incomplete, and what is missing is

Source: Skinner, B. F. (1983). Intellectual self-management in old age. *American Psychologist, 38,* 239–244. Copyright © 1983 by the American Psychological Association. Reprinted with permission.

particularly important if we want to do anything about aging. There is no doubt an inexorable biological process, a continuation of the growth of the embryo, which can be hindered or helped but not stopped. In speaking of the development of an *organism,* growth is no metaphor, but *persons* develop in a different way and for different reasons, many of which are not inexorable. Much of what seems to be the unfolding of an inner potential is the product of an unfolding environment; a person's *world* develops. The aging of a person, as distinct from the aging of an organism, depends upon changes in the physical and social environments. We recognize the difference when we say that some young people are old for their years or when, as Shakespeare put it, old people return to childishness. Fortunately, the course of a developing environment can be changed. That kind of aging can be retarded.

If the stages in our lives were due merely to the passage of time, we should have to find a fountain of youth to reverse the direction of change, but if many of the problems of old people are due to shortcomings in their environments, the environments can be improved.

Organism and person do not, of course, develop independently; the biological changes interact with the environmental contingencies. As the senses grow dull, the stimulating environment becomes less clear. As muscles grow slower and weaker, fewer things can be done successfully. Changes in sensory and motor capacities are conspicuous in games and other forms of competition, and athletes retire young just because of aging.

Many remedial steps are, of course, well-known. Eyeglasses compensate for poor vision and hearing aids for poor hearing. These are conspicuous prosthetic devices, but what is needed is a *prosthetic environment* in which, in spite of reduced biological capacities, behavior will be relatively free of aversive consequences and abundantly reinforced. New repertoires may be needed as well as new sources of stimulation. If you cannot read, listen to book recordings. If you do not hear well, turn up the volume on your phonograph (and wear headphones to protect your neighbors). Foods can be flavored for aging palates. Paul Tillich, the theologian, defended pornography on the ground that it extended sexuality into old age. And there is always the possibility, secondhand though it

may be, of living the highly reinforcing lives of others through literature, spectator sports, the theater and movies, and television.

There is nothing particularly new in all this, but there is a special problem to which little attention has, I think, been given. One of the inexorable effects of biological aging is particularly important for those engaged in intellectual work—in writing, inventing, composing, painting, having ideas—in a word, thinking. It is characteristic of old people not to think clearly, coherently, logically, or, in particular, creatively. In physiological terms we should have to say that deterioration occurs not only in sense organs and effectors but in central processes. The changes are certainly central if we are talking about the nervous system, but changes in behavior are changes in the body as a whole.

Forgetting is a classical problem. It is most conspicuous in forgetting names because names have so little going for them by way of context. I have convinced myself that names are very seldom wholly forgotten. When I have time—and I mean something on the order of half an hour—I can almost always recall a name if I have already recalled the occasion for using it. I work with thematic and formal prompts, in the latter case going through the alphabet, testing for the initial letter. But that will not work in introducing your wife to someone whose name you have forgotten. My wife and I use the following strategy: If there is any conceivable chance that she could have met the person, I simply say to her, "Of course, you remember . . . ?" and she grasps the outstretched hand and says, "Yes, of course. How are you?" The acquaintance may not remember meeting my wife, but is not sure of his or her memory, either.

The failure to produce a name at the right moment, as in making an introduction, can be especially punishing, and the punishment is part of the problem. Stutterers are all the more likely to stutter because they have failed to speak fluently in the past, and an emotional state called "anxiety" has been conditioned. Similarly, we may fail to recall a name when making an introduction in part because of past failings. We are, as we say, afraid we are going to forget. Some help may come from making such situations as free from aversive consequences as possible. Graceful ways of explaining your failure may help. Appeal to your age. Flatter your listener by saying that you have noticed that the more important the person, the easier it is to forget the name. Recall the amusing story about forgetting your own name when you were asked for it by a clerk. If you are skillful at that sort of thing, forgetting may even be a pleasure. Unfortunately, there is no similar strategy when you are suffering from a diminished access to verbal behavior while writing a paper. Nevertheless, a calm acceptance of deficiencies and a more careful observance of good intellectual self-management may have a comparable effect.

The problem is raised by the way in which we make use of past experience, the effects of which seem to fade too quickly. A special set of techniques is needed for its solution. Practical examples may be helpful before turning to comparable intellectual behavior.

Ten minutes before you leave your house for the day you hear a weather report: It will probably rain before you return. It occurs to you to take an umbrella (the sentence means quite literally what it says: The behavior of taking an umbrella occurs to you), but you are not yet able to execute it. Ten minutes later you leave without the umbrella. You can solve that kind of problem by executing as much of the behavior as possible when it occurs to you. Hang the umbrella on the doorknob, or put it through the handle of your briefcase, or in some other way start the process of taking it with you.

Here is a similar intellectual problem: In the middle of the night it occurs to you that you can clarify a passage in the paper you are writing by making a certain change. At your desk the next day you forget to make the change. Again, the solution is to make the change when it occurs to you, using, say, a notepad or tape recorder kept beside your bed. The problem in old age is not so much how to have ideas as how to have them when you can use them. A written or dictated record, consulted from time to time, has the same effect as the umbrella hung on the doorknob. A pocket notebook or recorder helps to maximize one's intellectual output by recording one's behavior when it occurs. The practice is helpful at any age but particularly so for the aging scholar. In place of memories, memoranda.

Another symptom of the same failing is to forget what you were going to say. In a conversation you wait politely until someone else finishes, and your own clever comment has then vanished. One solution is to keep saying it to yourself; another is to appeal to the privilege of old age and interrupt the speaker; another is to make a note (perhaps pretending it is about what the other person is saying). The same problem arises when *you* are speaking and digress. You finish the digression and cannot remember why you embarked on it or where you were when you did so. The solution is simply not to digress—that is, not to interrupt yourself. A long sentence always raises that kind of problem: The last part is not likely to agree with the first because the first has passed out of reach. The effect is especially clear in speaking a language you do not speak well, where it is always a mistake to embark upon complex sentences. You will do much better if you speak only simple sentences, and the same remedy is available to the aging scholar who is giving an impromptu address in his or her own language. Short sentences are also advisable when you are talking to yourself—in other words, thinking.

A different kind of problem is solved by skillful prompting. You are going to attend a class reunion and are taking someone with you whom you must introduce to old friends. How can you remember their names? Before you go, look in your alumni register for a list of those who will be there, visualizing them if you can. The textual stimuli will prompt names that must otherwise be emitted, if at all, simply in response to the appearances of your friends.

Forgetting a name is only a conspicuous example of the essential failing. In writing a paper or thinking about a problem, there are relevant responses that would occur sooner or in greater abundance to a younger person. Their absence is not as conspicuous as a forgotten name, but it must be acknowledged and dealt with. One way to increase the probability that relevant responses will occur while you are writing a paper or solving a problem is to read relevant material and reread what you have written. Reference books within easy reach will supply prompts for names, dates, and other kinds of information. A thesaurus can be used, not to find a new word, but to prompt an old one. Even in extemporaneous speaking it is possible to prepare yourself in advance. You may "put yourself in better possession" of the verbal behavior you will be emitting by rehearsing your speech just one more time.

Old age is like fatigue, except that its effects cannot be corrected by relaxing or taking a vacation. Particularly troublesome is old age *plus* fatigue, and half of that can be avoided. It may be necessary to be content with fewer good working hours per day, and it is particularly necessary to spend the rest of the time in what the Greeks called *eutrapelia*—the productive use of leisure. Leisure should be relaxing. Possibly you like complicated puzzles, or chess, or other intellectual games. Give them up. If you want to continue to be intellectually productive you must risk the contempt of your younger acquaintances and freely admit that you read detective stories or watch Archie Bunker on TV.

The kind of fatigue that causes trouble has been called mental, perhaps because it has so little to do with the physical fatigue of labor. You can be fully rested in a physical sense yet tired of what you are doing intellectually. To take appropriate steps one needs some measure of fatigue. Curiously enough, Adolf Hitler can be of help. In a report to the Nieman Foundation, William Lederer has called attention to relevant documents in the Harvard library. Toward the end of the Second World War, Hitler asked the few social scientists left in Germany to find out why people made bad decisions. When they reported that it was when they were mentally exhausted, he asked them for a list of the signs of mental fatigue. Then he issued an order: Any officer showing signs of mental fatigue should immediately be sent on vacation. Fortunately for the world, he did not apply the order to himself.

Among the signs on Hitler's list are several I find helpful. One is an unusual use of profanity or blasphemy. According to that principle, at least two of our recent presidents must have been mentally exhausted. When I find myself saying "damn," I know it is time to relax. (That mild expletive is a sign of my age as well as of my fatigue; I have never felt right about the scatological language of young people.) Other signs on Hitler's list include an inclination to blame others for mistakes, procrastinating on making decisions, an inclination to work longer hours than normally, an inclination to feel sorry for oneself, a reluctance to take exercise and relax, and dietary extremes—either gluttonous appetite or almost none at all. Clues not on

Hitler's list that I have found useful are especially bad handwriting and mistakes in playing the piano.

Effects on my thinking are much harder to spot, but I have learned to watch for a few of them. One is verbal padding. The ancient troubador sang or spoke standard lines that allowed time to remember what to say next. Phrases like "At this point it is interesting to note . . ." or "Let us now turn to another aspect of the problem . . ." serve the same function. They hold the floor until you have found something to say. Fatigued verbal behavior is also full of clichés, inexact descriptions, poorly composed sentences, borrowed sentences, memorized quotations, and Shakespeare's "wise saws." These are the easy things to say and they come out when you are tired. They can be avoided, if at all, only by avoiding fatigue.

I could have doubled my audience by calling my article "Cognitive Self-Management in Old Age." *Cognitive* means so many things that it could scarcely fail to apply here. But I could have described the field much more accurately by speaking of *verbal* self-management, because the problems are primarily verbal. I have discussed some of them in an article called "How to Discover What You Have to Say," recently published in the *Behavior Analyst.* At any given moment we are in possession of a latent repertoire of verbal behavior, every item of which presumably has a resting probability of "occurring to us." As a layperson might put it, there are lots of ideas waiting to be had. Some of them have occurred many times, are strengthened by common features of our daily life, and hence are the ideas that it is easiest to have as we think about or write about a problem, but they generally yield hackneyed, shopworn stuff. What is worth saying—the idea that is possibly unique to us because of the uniqueness of our experience and hence more likely to be called original—is least likely to occur. In short, in old age special difficulties arise because verbal behavior becomes less and less accessible. Perhaps we can do nothing about the accessibility, but we can improve the conditions under which verbal behavior occurs.

It helps to make the behavior as easy as possible; there are no crutches or wheelchairs for the verbally handicapped, but some prosthetic support is available—convenient pens, pencils, and paper, a good typewriter (a word processor, if possible), dictating equipment, and a convenient filing system.

I find it harder to "think big thoughts" in the sense of moving easily from one part of a paragraph to another or from one part of a chapter to another. The intraverbal connections are weak, and inconsistencies are therefore likely. The prosthetic remedy is to use outlines—spatial arrangements of the materials of a paragraph, chapter, or book. Decimal notation is helpful, with successive digits indicating chapter, section, paragraph, and sentence, in that order. This may look like constraint, but it is constraint against senile nattering and inconsistencies and repetition. You remain free to change the outline as a paragraph or chapter develops. An index, constructed as you write, will help in answering questions like "Now where did I take *that* up?" or "Have I already said that?"

It is commonly believed that those who have passed their prime can have nothing new to say. Jorge Luis Borges exclaimed, "What can I do at 71 except plugiarize myself!" Among the easiest things to say are things that have already been said, either by others or, especially, by ourselves. What we have already said most closely resembles what we now have to say. One of the more disheartening experiences of old age is discovering that a point you have just made—so significant, so beautifully expressed—was made by you in something you published a long time ago.

But one *can* say something new. Creative verbal behavior is not produced by exercising creativity; it is produced by skillful self-management. The creation of behavior raises the same issues as the creation of species. It is a selective process, and the appearance of something new—the *origin* of Darwin's title—can be promoted by introducing variations. You are also less likely to plagiarize yourself if you move into a new field or a new style.

One problem is often called a lack of motivation. Aging scholars lose interest; they find it hard to get to work; they work slowly. It is easy to attribute this to a change in *them,* but we should not overlook a change in their world. For *motivation* read *reinforcement.* In old age, behavior is not so strongly reinforced. Biological aging weakens reinforcing consequences. Behavior is more and more likely to be followed by aches and pains and quick fatigue. Things tend to become "not worth doing" in the sense that the aversive consequences exact too high a price. Positive reinforcers become less common and less powerful. Poor vision closes off the world of art, faulty hearing the enjoyment of highly fidelitous music. Foods do not taste as good, and erogenous tissues grow less sensitive. Social reinforcers are attenuated. Interests and tastes are shared with a smaller and smaller number of people.

In a world in which our behavior is not generously reinforced we are said to lack zest, joie de vivre, interest, ambition, aspirations, and a hundred other desirable "states of mind" and "feelings." These are really the by-products of changed contingencies of reinforcement. When the occasion for strong behavior is lacking or when reinforcing consequences no longer follow, we are bored, discouraged, and depressed. But it is a mistake to say that we suffer from such feelings. We suffer from the defective contingencies of reinforcement responsible for the feelings. Our environment is no longer maintaining strong behavior.

Our culture does not generously reinforce the behavior of old people. Both affluence and welfare destroy reinforcing contingencies, and so does retirement. Old people are not particularly important to younger people. Cicero made the point in his *De Senectute:* "Old age is honored only on condition that it defends itself, maintains its rights, is subservient to no one, and to its last breath rules over its own domain." We neglect that sage advice when we turn things over to another generation; we lose our position in the world and destroy important social reinforcers. Parents who turn their fortunes over to their children and then complain of neglect are the classical example, and aging scholars often do something of the same as they bring their work to an end in the expectation that they will be satisfied with well-deserved kudos. They find themselves out of date as the world moves forward.

A common reinforcer affects old age in a different, though equally destructive way. Aging scholars come into possession of a unique stock-in-trade—their memories. They learn that they can hold a restless audience with personal reminiscences. "Thorndike? Oh, I knew him well." I have been guilty of a bit of that name-dropping myself when other reinforcers were in short supply, and I have been wallowing in reminiscence lately in writing my autobiography. The trouble is that it takes you backward. You begin to live your life in the wrong direction.

There are other things than memories to be exploited by the aged, and a careful assessment of one's possessions may be helpful. Harvey Lehman found that in certain fields—theoretical physics, for example—the best work was done well before the age of 40. What should theoretical physicists do with the rest of their lives? Some 20 years ago I asked Lehman that question about myself (I trust that my personal reference to Lehman has gripped you). I felt that my science was fairly rigorous, and perhaps I was near the end of a productive life as an experimentalist. What should I do with myself? "Administration," Lehman said. But I had been a department chairman, and that was not an attractive alternative. I turned instead to broader issues in the design of a culture, culminating in the publication of *Beyond Freedom and Dignity*.

Something more than subject matter is involved. The whole repertoire we call intellectual is acquired when one is young. It survives as a lifestyle when one grows old, when it is much harder to execute. If intellectual behavior were as conspicuous as baseball, we would understand the problem. The solution may simply be to replace one repertoire with another. People who move from one city to another often suffer a brief depression, which appears to be merely the result of an old repertoire of behavior having become useless. The old stores, restaurants, theaters, and friends are no longer there. The depression is relieved by acquiring a new repertoire. It may be necessary in old age to acquire new ways of thinking, to adopt a new intellectual style, letting the size of the repertoire acquired in a long life offset the loss of skill in making use of it.

We should ask what we have written papers or books *for*. In the world of scholarship the answer is seldom money (if we exclude writers of pot-boiling textbooks), and in any case, economic circumstances in old age are not easily improved. If the answer is commendation or fame, the problem may be extinction if commendation no longer follows, or satiation if there is a surfeit of commendation. Not much can be done about that, but a more likely explanation, and

one which suggests helpful action, is that the scholar at his or her desk is not receiving the previously accustomed, immediate reinforcements: Sentences are not saying what they should say; solutions to problems remain out of reach; situations are not being effectively characterized; sequences are not in the right order; *sequiturs* are too often *non*. Something can be done about that, as I have suggested in the article mentioned earlier.

Reinforcers need not occur too frequently if we are fortunate enough to have been reinforced on a good schedule. A "stretched variable-ratio schedule" refers to a process you have all experienced as you acquired a taste for good literature, in which the reinforcing moments occur much less often than in cheap literature. In a comic strip you laugh at the end of every four frames, and in cheap literature something interesting happens on almost every page. Learning to enjoy good literature is essentially learning to read for longer and longer periods of time before coming upon a moving passage—a passage all the more moving for having required a long preparation. Gambling is reinforced on a variable-ratio schedule, and pathological gamblers show the effect of a history in which they began with reasonable success and only later exhausted their resources. Many of the reinforcers in old age tend to be on a stretched variable-ratio schedule. The Marquis de Sade described many interesting examples. The same process may explain the persistence of the aging scholar. If your achievements as a thinker have been spaced on a favorable schedule, you will have no difficulty in remaining active even though current achievements are spaced far apart. Like the hooked gambler, you will enjoy your life as a thinker in spite of the negative utility.

An audience is a neglected, independent variable. What one says is determined in a very important way by whom one is talking to. But the retired teacher no longer talks with students, the retired scientist no longer discusses work with colleagues. Old people find themselves spending time with others who are not interested in their fields. They may receive fewer invitations to speak or find it harder to accept them. Those who will read the papers or books they are writing are much too far removed in time to serve as an audience. An appropriate measure of intellectual self-management is to organize discussions, if only in groups of two. Find someone with similar interests. Two heads together are better than both apart. In talking with another person we have ideas that do not occur when we are alone at our desks. Some of what we say may be borrowed from what the other says, but the mere effect of having someone to say it to is usually conspicuous.

In searching for an audience, beware of those who are trying to be helpful and too readily flatter you. Second childishness brings you back within range of those kindergarten teachers who exclaim, "But *that* is very *good!*" Except that now, instead of saying, "My, you are really growing up!" they will say, "You are not really getting old!" As I have pointed out elsewhere, those who help those who can help themselves work a sinister kind of destruction by

making the good things in life no longer properly contingent on behavior. If you have been very successful, the most sententious stupidities will be received as pearls of wisdom, and your standards will instantly fall. If you are still struggling to be successful, flattery will more often than not put you on the wrong track by reinforcing useless behavior.

Well, there you have it. I have been batting that Ping-Pong ball back and forth long enough. I have reported some of the ways in which I have tried to avoid growing old as a thinker, and in addition I have given you a sample of the result. You may wish to turn to another comparison with a different species and conclude, if I may so paraphrase Dr. Johnson, "Sir, an aged lecturer is like a dog walking on his hinder legs. It is not done well; but you are surprised to find it done at all."

Questions to Think About

1. Does aging occur mostly as a result of deteriorating environmental contingencies rather than deteriorating biological abilities?

2. Why is positive reinforcement in a stretched variable-ratio schedule favored over constant reinforcement?

3. Could Skinner's tools for intellectual self-management apply for young people and middle-aged people, as well as for the aged?

23

Some Issues Concerning the Control
of Human Behavior: A Symposium

CARL R. ROGERS AND B. F. SKINNER

It is hard to imagine two theorists more different from one another than Carl Rogers and B. F. Skinner. Skinner referred to himself as a "radical behaviorist," meaning, among other things, that he believed that all behavior was a function of the reinforcement history of the organism. He saw no scientific legitimacy in concepts such as identity, the self, goals, human spirituality, or free will. As an empiricist, he claimed that observable behavior was the only acceptable subject matter for scientific theory. Carl Rogers (1902–1987), a major figure of the humanistic movement in psychology, believed that people had an inherent tendency to grow toward fulfilling their potential—that "becoming one's self" was a natural maturational process that moved in a positive direction unless thwarted by external forces. Rogers supported a phenomenological approach, in which important issues are defined and experienced from the perspective of the individual, what he termed "the experiencing person." This article is based on remarks made by each of the theorists in a symposium held at the American Psychological Association annual meeting in 1956.

I [SKINNER]

Science is steadily increasing our power to influence, change, mold—in a word, control—human behavior. It has extended our "understanding" (whatever that may be) so that we deal more successfully with people in nonscientific ways, but it has also identified conditions or variables which can be used to predict and control behavior in a new, and increasingly rigorous, technology. The broad disciplines of government and economics offer examples of this, but there is special cogency in those contributions of anthropology, sociology, and psychology which deal with individual behavior. Carl Rogers has listed some of the achievements to date in a recent paper. Those of his examples which show or imply the control of the single organism are primarily due, as we should expect, to psychology. It is the experimental study of behavior which carries us beyond awkward or inaccessible "principles," "factors," and so on, to variables which can be directly manipulated.

It is also, and for more or less the same reasons, the conception of human behavior emerging from an experimental analysis which most directly challenges traditional views. Psychologists themselves often do not seem to be aware of how far they have moved in this direction. But the change is not passing unnoticed by others. Until only recently it was customary to deny the possibility of a rigorous science of human behavior by arguing, either that a lawful science was impossible because man was a free agent, or that merely statistical predictions would always leave

Source: Reprinted with permission from Rogers, C. R., & Skinner, B. F. (1956). Some issues concerning the control of human behavior: A symposium. *Science, 124,* Number 3231, 1057–1066. Copyright 1956 AAAS.

Editor's note: Numbered references and in-text citations have been deleted. The list of references includes only those sources that are the most relevant and important.

room for personal freedom. But those who used to take this line have become most vociferous in expressing their alarm at the way these obstacles are being surmounted.

Now, the control of human behavior has always been unpopular. Any undisguised effort to control usually arouses emotional reactions. We hesitate to admit, even to ourselves, that we are engaged in control, and we may refuse to control, even when this would be helpful, for fear of criticism. Those who have explicitly avowed an interest in control have been roughly treated by history. Machiavelli is the great prototype. As Macaulay said of him, "Out of his surname they coined an epithet for a knave and out of his Christian name a synonym for the devil." There were obvious reasons. The control that Machiavelli analyzed and recommended, like most political control, used techniques that were aversive to the controllee. The threats and punishments of the bully, like those of the government operating on the same plan, are not designed—whatever their success—to endear themselves to those who are controlled. Even when the techniques themselves are not aversive, control is usually exercised for the selfish purposes of the controller and, hence, has indirectly punishing effects upon others.

Man's natural inclination to revolt against selfish control has been exploited to good purpose in what we call the philosophy and literature of democracy. The doctrine of the rights of man has been effective in arousing individuals to concerted action against governmental and religious tyranny. The literature which has had this effect has greatly extended the number of terms in our language which express reactions to the control of men. But the ubiquity and ease of expression of this attitude spells trouble for any science which may give birth to a powerful technology of behavior. Intelligent men and women, dominated by the humanistic philosophy of the past two centuries, cannot view with equanimity what Andrew Hacker has called "the specter of predictable man." Even the statistical or actuarial prediction of human events, such as the number of fatalities to be expected on a holiday weekend, strikes many people as uncanny and evil, while the prediction and control of individual behavior is regarded as little less than the work of the devil. I am not so much concerned here with the

political or economic consequences for psychology, although research following certain channels may well suffer harmful effects. We ourselves, as intelligent men and women, and as exponents of Western thought, share these attitudes. They have already interfered with the free exercise of a scientific analysis, and their influence threatens to assume more serious proportions.

Three broad areas of human behavior supply good examples. The first of these—*personal control*—may be taken to include person-to-person relationships in the family, among friends, in social and work groups, and in counseling and psychotherapy. Other fields are *education* and *government*. A few examples from each will show how nonscientific preconceptions are affecting our current thinking about human behavior.

Personal Control

People living together in groups come to control one another with a technique which is not inappropriately called "ethical." When an individual behaves in a fashion acceptable to the group, he receives admiration, approval, affection, and many other reinforcements which increase the likelihood that he will continue to behave in that fashion. When his behavior is not acceptable, he is criticized, censured, blamed, or otherwise punished. In the first case the group calls him "good"; in the second, "bad." This practice is so thoroughly ingrained in our culture that we often fail to see that it is a technique of control. Yet we are almost always engaged in such control, even though the reinforcements and punishments are often subtle.

The practice of admiration is an important part of a culture, because behavior which is otherwise inclined to be weak can be set up and maintained with its help. The individual is especially likely to be praised, admired, or loved when he acts for the group in the face of great danger, for example, or sacrifices himself or his possessions, or submits to prolonged hardship, or suffers martyrdom. These actions are not admirable in any absolute sense, but they require admiration if they are to be strong. Similarly, we admire people who behave in original or exceptional ways, not because such behavior is itself admirable, but because we do not know how to encourage original or exceptional behavior in any other way. The group acclaims independent, unaided behavior in part because it is easier to reinforce than to help.

As long as this technique of control is misunderstood, we cannot judge correctly an environment in which there is less need for heroism, hardship, or independent action. We are likely to argue that such an environment is itself less admirable or produces less admirable people. In the old days, for example, young scholars often lived in undesirable quarters, ate unappetizing or inadequate food, performed unprofitable tasks for a living or to pay for necessary books and materials or publication. Older scholars and other members of the group offered compensating reinforcement in the form of approval and admiration for these sacrifices. When the modern graduate student receives a generous scholarship, enjoys good living conditions, and has his research and publication subsidized, the grounds for evaluation seem to be pulled from under us. Such a student no longer *needs* admiration to carry him over a series of obstacles (no matter how much he may need it for other reasons), and, in missing certain familiar objects of admiration, we are likely to conclude that such *conditions* are less admirable. Obstacles to scholarly work may serve as a useful measure of motivation—and we may go wrong unless some substitute is found—but we can scarcely defend a deliberate harassment of the student for this purpose. The productivity of any set of conditions can be evaluated only when we have freed ourselves of the attitudes which have been generated in us as members of an ethical group.

A similar difficulty arises from our use of punishment in the form of censure or blame. The concept of responsibility and the related concepts of foreknowledge and choice are used to justify techniques of control using punishment. Was So-and-So aware of the probable consequences of his action, and was the action deliberate? If so, we are justified in punishing him. But what does this mean? It appears to be a question concerning the efficacy of the contingent relations between behavior and punishing consequences. We punish behavior because it is objectionable to us or the group, but in a minor refinement of rather recent origin we have come to withhold punishment when it

cannot be expected to have any effect. If the objectionable consequences of an act were accidental and not likely to occur again, there is no point in punishing. We say that the individual was not "aware of the consequences of his action" or that the consequences were not "intentional." If the action could not have been avoided—if the individual "had no choice"—punishment is also withheld, as it is if the individual is incapable of being changed by punishment because he is of "unsound mind." In all these cases—different as they are—the individual is held "not responsible" and goes unpunished.

Just as we say that it is "not fair" to punish a man for something he could not help doing, so we call it "unfair" when one is rewarded beyond his due or for something he could not help doing. In other words, we also object to wasting *reinforcers* where they are not needed or will do no good. We make the same point with the words *just* and *right*. Thus we have no right to punish the irresponsible, and a man has no right to reinforcers he does not earn or deserve. But concepts of choice, responsibility, justice, and so on, provide a most inadequate analysis of efficient reinforcing and punishing contingencies because they carry a heavy semantic cargo of a quite different sort, which obscures any attempt to clarify controlling practices or to improve techniques. In particular, they fail to prepare us for techniques based on other than aversive techniques of control. Most people would object to forcing prisoners to serve as subjects of dangerous medical experiments, but few object when they are induced to serve by the offer of return privileges—even when the reinforcing effect of these privileges has been created by forcible deprivation. In the traditional scheme the right to refuse guarantees the individual against coercion or an unfair bargain. But to what extent *can* a prisoner refuse under such circumstances?

We need not go so far afield to make the point. We can observe our own attitude toward personal freedom in the way we resent any interference with what we want to do. Suppose we want to buy a car of a particular sort. Then we may object, for example, if our wife urges us to buy a less expensive model and to put the difference into a new refrigerator. Or we may resent it if our neighbor questions our need for such a car or our ability to pay for it. We would certainly resent it if it were illegal to buy such a car (remember Prohibition); and if we find we cannot actually afford it, we may resent governmental control of the price through tariffs and taxes. We resent it if we discover that we cannot get the car because the manufacturer is holding the model in deliberately short supply in order to push a model we do not want. In all this we assert our democratic right to buy the car of our choice. We are well prepared to do so and to resent any restriction on our freedom.

But why do we not ask *why* it is the car of our choice and resent the forces which made it so? Perhaps our favorite toy as a child was a car, of a very different model, but nevertheless bearing the name of the car we now want. Perhaps our favorite TV program is sponsored by the manufacturer of that car. Perhaps we have seen pictures of many beautiful or prestigeful persons driving it—in pleasant or glamorous places. Perhaps the car has been designed with respect to our motivational patterns: the device on the hood is a phallic symbol; or the horsepower has been stepped up to please our competitive spirit in enabling us to pass other cars swiftly (or, as the advertisements say, "safely"). The concept of freedom that has emerged as part of the cultural practice of our group makes little or no provision for recognizing or dealing with these kinds of control. Concepts like "responsibility" and "rights" are scarcely applicable. We are prepared to deal with coercive measures, but we have no traditional recourse with respect to other measures which in the long run (and especially with the help of science) may be much more powerful and dangerous.

Education

The techniques of education were once frankly aversive. The teacher was usually older and stronger than his pupils and was able to "make them learn." This meant that they were not actually taught but were surrounded by a threatening world from which they could escape only by learning. Usually they were left to their own resources in discovering how to do so. Claude Coleman has published a grimly amusing reminder of these older practices. He tells of a schoolteacher who published a careful account of his services during 51

years of teaching, during which he administered: ". . . 911,527 blows with a cane; 124,010 with a rod; 20,989 with a ruler; 136,715 with the hand; 10,295 over the mouth; 7,905 boxes on the ear; [and] 1,115,800 slaps on the head. . . ."

Progressive education was a humanitarian effort to substitute positive reinforcement for such aversive measures, but in the search for useful human values in the classroom it has never fully replaced the variables it abandoned. Viewed as a branch of behavioral technology, education remains relatively inefficient. We supplement it, and rationalize it, by admiring the pupil who learns *for himself*; and we often attribute the learning process, or knowledge itself, to something *inside* the individual. We admire behavior which seems to have inner sources. Thus we admire one who *recites* a poem more than one who simply *reads* it. We admire one who *knows* the answer more than one who *knows where to look it up*. We admire the *writer* rather than the *reader*. We admire the arithmetician who can do a problem in his head rather than with a slide rule or calculating machine, or in "original" ways rather than by a strict application of rules. In general we feel that any aid or "crutch"—except those aids to which we are now thoroughly accustomed—reduces the credit due. In Plato's *Phaedus,* Thamus, the king, attacks the invention of the alphabet on similar grounds! He is afraid "it will produce forgetfulness in the minds of those who learn to use it, because they will not practice their memories. . . ." In other words, he holds it more admirable to remember than to use a memorandum. He also objects that pupils "will read many things without instruction . . . [and] will therefore seem to know many things when they are for the most part ignorant." In the same vein we are today sometimes contemptuous of book learning, but, as educators, we can scarcely afford to adopt this view without reservation.

By admiring the student for knowledge and blaming him for ignorance, we escape some of the responsibility of teaching him. We resist any analysis of the educational process which threatens the notion of inner wisdom or questions the contention that the fault of ignorance lies with the student. More powerful techniques which bring about the same changes in behavior by manipulating *external* variables are decried as brainwashing or thought control. We are quite unprepared to judge *effective* educational measures. As long as only a few pupils learn much of what is taught, we do not worry about uniformity or regimentation. We do not fear the feeble technique; but we should view with dismay a system under which every student learned everything listed in a syllabus— although such a condition is far from unthinkable. Similarly, we do not fear a system which is so defective that the student must *work* for an education; but we are loath to give credit for anything learned without effort—although this could well be taken as an ideal result—and we flatly refuse to give credit if the student already knows what a school teaches.

A world in which people are wise and good without trying, without "having to be," without "choosing to be," could conceivably be a far better world for everyone. In such a world we should not have to "give anyone credit"—we should not need to admire anyone— for being wise and good. From our present point of view we cannot believe that such a world would be admirable. We do not even permit ourselves to imagine what it would be like.

Government

Government has always been the special field of aversive control. The state is frequently defined in terms of the power to punish, and jurisprudence leans heavily upon the associated notion of personal responsibility. Yet it is becoming increasingly difficult to reconcile current practice and theory with these earlier views. In criminology, for example, there is a strong tendency to drop the notion of responsibility in favor of some such alternative as capacity or controllability. But no matter how strongly the facts, or even practical expedience, support such a change, it is difficult to make the change in a legal system designed on a different plan. When governments resort to other techniques (for example, positive reinforcement), the concept of responsibility is no longer relevant and the theory of government is no longer applicable.

The conflict is illustrated by two decisions of the Supreme Court in the 1930's which dealt with, and disagreed on, the definition of control or coercion. The Agricultural Adjustment Act proposed that the

Secretary of Agriculture make "rental or benefit payments" to those farmers who agreed to reduce production. The government agreed that the Act would be unconstitutional if the farmer had been *compelled* to reduce production but was not, since he was merely *invited* to do so. Justice Roberts expressed the contrary majority view of the court that "The power to confer or withhold unlimited benefits is the power to coerce or destroy." This recognition of positive reinforcement was withdrawn a few years later in another case in which Justice Cardozo wrote "To hold that motive or temptation is equivalent to coercion is to plunge the law in endless difficulties." We may agree with him, without implying that the proposition is therefore wrong. Sooner or later the law must be prepared to deal with all possible techniques of governmental control.

The uneasiness with which we view government (in the broadest possible sense) when it does not use punishment is shown by the reception of my utopian novel, *Walden Two*. This was essentially a proposal to apply a behavioral technology to the construction of a workable, effective, and productive pattern of government. It was greeted with wrathful violence. *Life* magazine called it "a travesty on the good life," and "a menace . . . a triumph of mortmain or the dead hand not envisaged since the days of Sparta . . . a slur upon a name, a corruption of an impulse." Joseph Wood Krutch devoted a substantial part of his book, *The Measure of Man,* to attacking my views and those of the protagonist, Frazier, in the same vein, and Morris Viteles has recently criticized the book is a similar manner in *Science*. Perhaps the reaction is best expressed in a quotation from *The Quest for Utopia* by Negley and Patrick:

"Halfway through this contemporary utopia, the reader may feel sure, as we did, that this is a beautifully ironic satire on what has been called 'behavioral engineering.' The longer one stays in this better world of the psychologist, however, the plainer it becomes that the inspiration is not satiric, but messianic. This is indeed the behaviorally engineered society, and while it was to be expected that sooner or later the principle of psychological conditioning would be made the basis of a serious construction of utopia—Brown anticipated it in *Limanora*—yet not even the effective satire of Huxley is adequate preparation for the shocking horror of the idea when positively presented. Of all the dictatorships espoused by utopists, this is the most profound, and incipient dictators might well find in this utopia a guidebook of political practice."

One would scarcely guess that the authors are talking about a world in which there is food, clothing, and shelter for all, where everyone chooses his own work and works on the average only 4 hours a day, where music and the arts flourish, where personal relationships develop under the most favorable circumstances, where education prepares every child for the social and intellectual life which lies before him, where—in short—people are truly happy, secure, productive, creative, and forward-looking. What is wrong with it? Only one thing: someone "planned it that way." If these critics had come upon a society in some remote corner of the world which boasted similar advantages, they would undoubtedly have hailed it as providing a pattern we all might well follow—provided that it was clearly the result of a natural process of cultural evolution. Any evidence that intelligence had been used in arriving at this version of the good life would, in their eyes, be a serious flaw. No matter if the planner of *Walden Two* diverts none of the proceeds of the community to his own use, no matter if he has no current control or is, indeed, unknown to most of the other members of the community (he planned that, too), somewhere back of it all he occupies the position of prime mover. And this, to the child of the democratic tradition, spoils it all.

The dangers inherent in the control of human behavior are very real. The possibility of the misuse of scientific knowledge must always be faced. We cannot escape by denying the power of a science of behavior or arresting its development. It is no help to cling to familiar philosophies of human behavior simply because they are more reassuring. As I have pointed out elsewhere, the new techniques emerging from a science of behavior must be subject to the explicit countercontrol which has already been applied to earlier and cruder forms. Brute force and deception, for example, are now fairly generally suppressed by ethical practices and by explicit governmental and religious agencies. A similar countercontrol of scientific knowledge in the interests of the group is a feasible and promising possibility. Although we cannot say how devious the course of its evolution may be, a cultural pattern of control and countercontrol will presumably emerge which will be most widely supported because it is most widely reinforcing.

If we cannot foresee all the details of this (as we obviously cannot), it is important to remember that this is true of the critics of science as well. The dire consequences of new techniques of control, the hidden menace in original cultural designs—these need some proof. It is only another example of my present point that the need for proof is so often overlooked. Man has got himself into some pretty fixes, and it is easy to believe that he will do so again. But there is a more optimistic possibility. The slow growth of the methods of science, now for the first time being applied to human affairs, *may* mean a new and exciting phase of human life to which historical analogies will not apply and in which earlier political slogans will not be appropriate. If we are to use the knowledge that a science of behavior is now making available with any hope of success, we must look at human nature as it is brought into focus through the methods of science rather than as it has been presented to us in a series of historical accidents.

If the advent of a powerful science of behavior causes trouble, it will not be because science itself is inimical to human welfare but because older conceptions have not yielded easily or gracefully. We expect resistance to new techniques of control from those who have heavy investments in the old, but we have no reason to help them preserve a series of principles that are not ends in themselves but rather outmoded means to an end. What is needed is a new conception of human behavior which is compatible with the implications of a scientific analysis. All men control and are controlled. The question of government in the broadest possible sense is not how freedom is to be preserved but what kinds of control are to be used and to what ends. Control must be analyzed and considered in its proper proportions. No one, I am sure, wishes to develop new master–slave relationships or bend the will of the people to despotic rulers in new ways. These are patterns of control appropriate to a world without science. They may well be the first to go when the experimental analysis of behavior comes into its own in the design of cultural practices.

II [ROGERS]

There are, I believe, a number of matters in connection with this important topic on which the authors of this article, and probably a large majority of psychologists, are in agreement. These matters then are not issues as far as we are concerned, and I should like to mention them briefly in order to put them to one side.

Points of Agreement

I am sure we agree that men—as individuals and as societies—have always endeavored to understand, predict, influence, and control human behavior—their own behavior and that of others.

I believe we agree that the behavioral sciences are making and will continue to make increasingly rapid progress in the understanding of behavior, and that as a consequence the capacity to predict and to control behavior is developing with equal rapidity.

I believe we agree that to deny these advances, or to claim that man's behavior cannot be a field of science, is unrealistic. Even though this is not an issue for us, we should recognize that many intelligent men still hold strongly to the view that the actions of men are free in some sense such that scientific knowledge of man's behavior is impossible. Thus Reinhold Niebuhr, the noted theologian, heaps scorn on the concept of psychology as a science of man's behavior and even says, "In any event, no scientific investigation of past behavior can become the basis of predictions of future behavior." So, while this is not an issue for psychologists, we should at least notice in passing that it is an issue for many people.

I believe we are in agreement that the tremendous potential power of a science which permits the prediction and control of behavior may be misused, and that the possibility of such misuse constitutes a serious threat.

Consequently Skinner and I are in agreement that the whole question of the scientific control of human behavior is a matter with which psychologists and the general public should concern themselves. As Robert Oppenheimer told the American Psychological Association last year the problems that psychologists will pose for society by their growing ability to control behavior will be much more grave than the problems posed by the ability of physicists to control the reactions of matter. I am not sure whether psychologists generally recognize this. My impression is that by and large they hold a laissez-faire attitude. Obviously Skinner and I do not hold this laissez-faire view, or we would not have written this article.

Points at Issue

With these several points of basic and important agreement, are there then any issues that remain on which there are differences? I believe there are. They can be stated very briefly: Who will be controlled? Who will exercise control? What type of control will be exercised? Most important of all, toward what end or what purpose, or in the pursuit of what value, will control be exercised?

It is on questions of this sort that there exist ambiguities, misunderstandings, and probably deep differences. These differences exist among psychologists, among members of the general public in this country, and among various world cultures. Without any hope of achieving a final resolution of these questions, we can, I believe, put these issues in clearer form.

Some Meanings

To avoid ambiguity and faulty communication, I would like to clarify the meanings of some of the terms we are using.

Behavioral science is a term that might be defined from several angles but in the context of this discussion it refers primarily to knowledge that the existence of certain describable conditions in the human being and/or in his environment is followed by certain describable consequences in his actions.

Prediction means the prior identification of behaviors which then occur. Because it is important in some things I wish to say later, I would point out that one may predict a highly specific behavior, such as an eye blink, or one may predict a class of behaviors. One might correctly predict "avoidant behavior," for example, without being able to specify whether the individual will run away or simply close his eyes.

The word *control* is a very slippery one, which can be used with any one of several meanings. I would like to specify three that seem most important for our present purposes. *Control* may mean: (i) The setting of conditions by *B* for *A*, *A* having no voice in the matter, such that certain predictable behaviors then occur in *A*. I refer to this as external control. (ii) The setting of conditions by *B* for *A*, *A* giving some degree of consent to these conditions, such that certain predictable behaviors then occur in *A*. I refer to this as the influence of *B* on *A*. (iii) The setting of conditions by *A* such that certain predictable behaviors then occur in himself. I refer to this as internal control. It will be noted that Skinner lumps together the first two meanings, external control and influence, under the concept of control. I find this confusing.

Usual Concept of Control of Human Behavior

With the underbrush thus cleared away (I hope), let us review very briefly the various elements that are involved in the usual concept of the control of human behavior as mediated by the behavioral sciences. I am drawing here on the previous writings of Skinner, on his present statements, on the writings of others who have considered in either friendly or antagonistic fashion the meanings that would be involved in such control. I have not excluded the science fiction writers, as reported recently by Vandenburg, since they often show an awareness of the issues involved, even though the methods described are as yet fictional. These then are the elements that seem common to these different concepts of the application of science to human behavior.

1) There must first be some sort of decision about goals. Usually desirable goals are assumed, but sometimes, as in George Orwell's book *1984,* the goal that is selected is an aggrandizement of individual power with which most of us would disagree. In a recent paper Skinner suggests that one possible set of goals to be assigned to the behavioral technology is this: "Let men be happy, informed, skillful, well-behaved and productive." In the first draft of his part of this article, which he was kind enough to show me, he did not mention such definite goals as these, but desired "improved" educational practices, "wiser" use of

knowledge in government, and the like. In the final version of his article he avoids even these value-laden terms, and his implicit goal is the very general one that scientific control of behavior is desirable, because it would perhaps bring "a far better world for everyone."

Thus the first step in thinking about the control of human behavior is the choice of goals, whether specific or general. It is necessary to come to terms in some way with the issue, "For what purpose?"

2) A second element is that, whether the end selected is highly specific or is a very general one such as wanting "a better world," we proceed by the methods of science to discover the means to these ends. We continue through further experimentation and investigation to discover more effective means. The method of science is self-correcting in thus arriving at increasingly effective ways of achieving the purpose we have in mind.

3) The third aspect of such control is that as the conditions or methods are discovered by which to reach the goal, some person or some group establishes these conditions and uses these methods, having in one way or another obtained the power to do so.

4) The fourth element is the exposure of individuals to the prescribed conditions, and this leads, with a high degree of probability, to behavior which is in line with the goals desired. Individuals are now happy, if that has been the goal, or well-behaved, or submissive, or whatever it has been decided to make them.

5) The fifth element is that if the process I have described is put in motion then there is a continuing social organization which will continue to produce the types of behavior that have been valued.

Some Flaws

Are there any flaws in this way of viewing the control of human behavior? I believe there are. In fact the only element in this description with which I find myself in agreement is the second. Its seems to me quite incontrovertibly true that the scientific method is an excellent way to discover the means by which to achieve our goals. Beyond that, I feel many sharp differences, which I will try to spell out.

I believe that in Skinner's presentation here and in his previous writings, there is a serious underestimation of the problem of power. To hope that the power which is being made available by the behavioral sciences will be exercised by the scientists, or by a benevolent group, seems to me a hope little supported by either recent or distant history. It seems far more likely that behavioral scientists, holding their present attitudes, will be in the position of the German rocket scientists specializing in guided missiles. First they worked devotedly for Hitler to destroy the U.S.S.R. and the United States. Now, depending on who captured them, they work devotedly for the U.S.S.R. in the interest of destroying the United States, or devotedly for the United States in the interest of destroying the U.S.S.R. If behavioral scientists are concerned solely with advancing their science, it seems most probable that they will serve the purposes of whatever individual or group has the power.

But the major flaw I see in this review of what is involved in the scientific control of human behavior is the denial, misunderstanding, or gross underestimation of the place of ends, goals or values in their relationship to science. This error (as it seems to me) has so many implications that I would like to devote some space to it.

Ends and Values in Relation to Science

In sharp contradiction to some views that have been advanced, I would like to propose a two-pronged thesis: (i) In any scientific endeavor—whether "pure" or applied science—there is a prior subjective choice of the purpose or value which that scientific work is perceived as serving. (ii) This subjective value choice which brings the scientific endeavor into being must always lie outside of that endeavor and can never become a part of the science involved in that endeavor.

Let me illustrate the first point from Skinner himself. It is clear that in his earlier writing it is recognized that a prior value choice is necessary, and it is specified as the goal that men are to become happy, well-behaved, productive, and so on. I am pleased that Skinner has retreated from the goals he then chose, because to me they seem to be stultifying values. I can only feel that he was choosing these goals for others, not for himself. I would hate to see Skinner become "well-behaved," as that term would be defined for him

by behavioral scientists. His recent article in the *American Psychologist* shows that he certainly does not want to be "productive" as that value is defined by most psychologists. And the most awful fate I can imagine for him would be to have him constantly "happy." It is the fact that he is very unhappy about many things which makes me prize him.

In the first draft of his part of this article, he also included such prior value choices, saying for example, "We must decide how we are to use the knowledge which a science of human behavior is now making available." Now he has dropped all mention of such choices, and if I understand him correctly, he believes that science can proceed without them. He has suggested this view in another recent paper, stating that "We must continue to experiment in cultural design . . . testing the consequences as we go. Eventually the practices which make for the greatest biological and psychological strength of the group will presumably survive."

I would point out, however, that to choose to experiment is a value choice. Even to move in the direction of perfectly random experimentation is a value choice. To test the consequences of an experiment is possible only if we have first made a subjective choice of a criterion value. And implicit in his statement is a valuing of biological and psychological strength. So even when trying to avoid such choice, it seems inescapable that a prior subjective value choice is necessary for any scientific endeavor, or for any application of scientific knowledge.

I wish to make it clear that I am not saying that values cannot be included as a subject of science. It is not true that science deals only with certain classes of "facts" and that these classes do not include values. It is a bit more complex than that, as a simple illustration or two may make clear.

If I value knowledge of the "three R's" as a goal of education, the methods of science can give me increasingly accurate information on how this goal may be achieved. If I value problem-solving ability as a goal of education, the scientific method can give me the same kind of help.

Now, if I wish to determine whether problem-solving ability is "better" than knowledge of the three R's, then scientific method can also study those two values but *only*—and this is very important—in terms of some other value which I have subjectively chosen. I may value college success. Then I can determine whether problem-solving ability or knowledge of the three R's is most closely associated with that value. I may value personal integration or vocational success or responsible citizenship. I can determine whether problem-solving ability or knowledge of the three R's is "better" for achieving any one of these values. But the value or purpose that gives meaning to a particular scientific endeavor must always lie outside of that endeavor.

Although our concern in this symposium is largely with applied science, what I have been saying seems equally true of so-called "pure" science. In pure science the usual prior subjective value choice is the discovery of truth. But this is a subjective choice, and science can never say whether it is the best choice, save in the light of some other value. Geneticists in the U.S.S.R., for example, had to make a subjective choice of whether it was better to pursue truth or to discover facts which upheld a governmental dogma. Which choice is "better"? We could make a scientific investigation of those alternatives but only in the light of some other subjectively chosen value. If, for example, we value the survival of a culture, then we could begin to investigate with the methods of science the question of whether pursuit of truth or support of governmental dogma is most closely associated with cultural survival.

My point then is that any endeavor in science, pure or applied, is carried on in the pursuit of a purpose or value that is subjectively chosen by persons. It is important that this choice be made explicit, since the particular value which is being sought can never be tested or evaluated, confirmed or denied, by the scientific endeavor to which it gives birth. The initial purpose or value always and necessarily lies outside the scope of the scientific effort which it sets in motion.

Among other things this means that if we choose some particular goal or series of goals for human beings and then set out on a large scale to control human behavior to the end of achieving those goals, we are locked in the rigidity of our initial choice, because such a scientific endeavor can never transcend itself to select new goals. Only subjective human persons can do that. Thus if we chose as our goal the state of happiness for human beings (a goal deservedly ridiculed by Aldous Huxley in *Brave New World*), and if we involved all of society in a successful scientific program by which people became happy, we would be locked in a colossal rigidity in which no one would be free to question this goal, because our scientific operations could not transcend themselves to question their guiding purposes. And without laboring this point, I would remark that colossal rigidity, whether in dinosaurs or dictatorships, has a very poor record of evolutionary survival.

If, however, a part of our scheme is to set free some "planners" who do not have to be happy, who are not controlled, and who are therefore free to choose other values, this has several meanings. It means that the purpose we have chosen as our goal is not a sufficient and a satisfying one for human beings but must be supplemented. It also means that if it is necessary to set up an elite group which is free, then this shows all too clearly that the great majority are only the slaves—no matter by what high-sounding name we call them—of those who select the goals.

Perhaps, however, the thought is that a continuing scientific endeavor will evolve its own goals; that the initial findings will alter the directions, and subsequent findings will alter them still further, and that science somehow develops its own purpose. Although he does not clearly say so, this appears to be the pattern Skinner has in mind. It is surely a reasonable description, but it overlooks one element in this continuing development, which is that subjective personal choice enters in at every point at which the direction changes. The findings of a science, the results of an experiment, do not and never can tell us what next scientific purpose to pursue. Even in the purest of science, the scientist must decide what the findings mean and must subjectively choose what next step will be most profitable in the pursuit of his purpose. And if we are speaking of the application of scientific knowledge, then it is distressingly clear that the increasing scientific knowledge of the structure of the atom carries with it no necessary choice as to the purpose to which this knowledge will be put. This is a subjective personal choice which must be made by many individuals.

Thus I return to the proposition with which I began this section of my remarks—and which I now repeat in different words. Science has its meaning as the objective pursuit of a purpose which has been subjectively chosen by a person or persons. This purpose or value can never be investigated by the particular scientific experiment or investigation to which it has given birth and meaning. Consequently, any discussion of the control of human beings by the behavioral sciences must first and most deeply concern itself with the subjectively chosen purposes which such an application of science is intended to implement.

Is the Situation Hopeless?

The thoughtful reader may recognize that, although my remarks up to this point have introduced some modifications in the conception of the processes by which human behavior will be controlled, these remarks may have made such control seem, if anything, even more inevitable. We might sum it up this way: Behavioral science is clearly moving forward; the increasing power for control which it gives will be held by someone or some group; such an individual or group will surely choose the values or goals to be achieved; and most of us will then be increasingly controlled by means so subtle that we will not even be aware of them as controls. Thus, whether a council of wise psychologists (if this is not a contradiction in terms), or a Stalin, or a Big Brother has the power, and whether the goal is happiness, or productivity, or resolution of the Oedipus complex, or submission, or love of Big Brother, we will inevitably find ourselves moving toward the chosen goal and probably thinking that we ourselves desire it. Thus, if this line of reasoning is correct, it appears that some form of *Walden Two* or of *1984* (and at a deep philosophic level they seem indistinguishable) is coming. The fact that it would surely arrive piecemeal, rather than all at once, does not greatly change the fundamental issues. In any event, as Skinner has indicated in his writings, we would then look back upon the concepts of human freedom, the capacity for choice, the responsibility for choice, and the worth of the human individual as historical curiosities which once existed by cultural accident as values in a prescientific civilization.

I believe that any person observant of trends must regard something like the foregoing sequence as a real possibility. It is not simply a fantasy. Something of that sort may even be the most likely future. But is it an inevitable future? I want to devote the remainder of my remarks to an alternative possibility.

Alternative Set of Values

Suppose we start with a set of ends, values, purposes, quite different from the type of goals we have been considering. Suppose we do this quite openly, setting them forth as a possible value choice to be accepted or rejected. Suppose we select a set of values that focuses on fluid elements of process rather than static attributes. We might then value: man as a process of becoming, as a process of achieving worth and dignity through the development of his potentialities; the individual human being as a self-actualizing process, moving on to more challenging and enriching experiences; the process by which the individual creatively adapts to an ever-new and changing world; the process by which knowledge transcends itself, as, for example, the theory of relativity transcended Newtonian physics, itself to be transcended in some future day by a new perception.

If we select values such as these we turn to our science and technology of behavior with a very different set of questions. We will want to know such things as these: Can science aid in the discovery of new modes of richly rewarding living? more meaningful and satisfying modes of interpersonal relationships? Can science inform us on how the human race can become a more intelligent participant in its own evolution—its physical, psychological and social evolution? Can science inform us on ways of releasing the creative capacity of individuals, which seem so necessary if we are to survive in this fantastically expanding atomic age? Oppenheimer has pointed out that knowledge, which used to double in millennia or centuries, now doubles in a generation or a decade. It appears that we must discover the utmost in release of creativity if we are to be able to adapt effectively. In short, can science discover the methods by which man can most readily become a continually developing and self-transcending process, in his behavior, his thinking, his knowledge? Can science predict and release an essentially "unpredictable" freedom?

It is one of the virtues of science as a method that it is as able to advance and implement goals and purposes of this sort as it is to serve static values, such as states of being well-informed, happy, obedient. Indeed we have some evidence of this.

Small Example

I will perhaps be forgiven if I document some of the possibilities along this line by turning to psychotherapy, the field I know best.

Psychotherapy, as Meerloo and others have pointed out, can be one of the most subtle tools for the control of A by B. The therapist can subtly mold individuals in imitation of himself. He can cause an individual to become a submissive and conforming being. When certain therapeutic principles are used in extreme fashion, we call it brainwashing, an instance of the disintegration of the personality and a reformulation of the person along lines desired by the controlling individual. So the principles of therapy can be used as an effective means of external control of human personality and behavior. Can psychotherapy be anything else?

Here I find the developments going on in client-centered psychotherapy an exciting hint of what a behavioral science can do in achieving the kinds of values I have stated. Quite aside from being a somewhat new orientation in psychotherapy, this development has important implications regarding the relation of a behavioral science to the control of human behavior. Let me describe our experience as it relates to the issues of this discussion.

In client-centered therapy, we are deeply engaged in the prediction and influencing of behavior, or even the control of behavior. As therapists, we institute certain attitudinal conditions, and the client has relatively little voice in the establishment of these conditions. We predict that if these conditions are instituted, certain behavioral consequences will ensue in the client. Up to this point this is largely external control, no different from what Skinner has described, and no different from what I have discussed in the preceding sections of this article. But here any similarity ceases.

The conditions we have chosen to establish predict such behavioral consequences as these: that the client will become self-directing, less rigid, more open to the evidence of his senses, better organized and integrated, more similar to the ideal which he has chosen for himself. In other words, we have established by external control conditions which we predict will be followed by internal control by the individual, in pursuit of internally chosen goals. We have set the conditions which predict various classes of behaviors—self-directing behaviors, sensitivity to realities within and without, flexible adaptiveness—which are by their very nature unpredictable in their specifics. Our recent research indicates that our predictions are to a significant degree corroborated, and our commitment to the scientific method causes us to believe that more effective means of achieving these goals may be realized.

Research exists in other fields—industry, education, group dynamics—which seems to support our own findings. I believe it may be conservatively stated that scientific progress has been made in identifying those conditions in an interpersonal relationship which, if they exist in B, are followed in A by greater maturity in behavior, less dependence on others, an increase in expressiveness as a person, an increase in variability, flexibility and effectiveness of adaptation, an increase in self-responsibility and self-direction. And, quite in contrast to the concern expressed by some, we do not find that the creatively adaptive behavior which results from such self-directed variability of expression is a "happy accident" which occurs in "chaos." Rather, the individual who is open to his experience, and self-directing, is harmonious not chaotic, ingenious rather than random, as he orders his responses imaginatively toward the achievement of his own purposes. His creative actions are no more a "happy accident" than was Einstein's development of the theory of relativity.

Thus we find ourselves in fundamental agreement with John Dewey's statement: "Science has made its way by releasing, not by suppressing, the elements of variation, of invention and innovation, of novel creation in individuals." Progress in personal life and in group living is, we believe, made in the same way.

Possible Concept of the Control of Human Behavior

It is quite clear that the point of view I am expressing is in sharp contrast to the usual conception of the relationship of the behavioral sciences to the control of human behavior. In order to make this contrast even more blunt, I will state this possibility in paragraphs parallel to those used before.

1. It is possible for us to choose to value man as a self-actualizing process of becoming; to value creativity, and the process by which knowledge becomes self-transcending.

2. We can proceed, by the methods of science, to discover the conditions which necessarily precede these processes and, through continuing experimentation, to discover better means of achieving these purposes.

3. It is possible for individuals or groups to set these conditions, with a minimum of power or control. According to present knowledge, the only authority necessary is the authority to establish certain qualities of interpersonal relationship.

4. Exposed to these conditions, present knowledge suggests that individuals become more self-responsible, make progress in self-actualization, become more flexible, and become more creatively adaptive.

5. Thus such an initial choice would inaugurate the beginnings of a social system or subsystem in which values, knowledge, adaptive skills, and even the concept of science would be continually changing and self-transcending. The emphasis would be upon man as a process of becoming.

I believe it is clear that such a view as I have been describing does not lead to any definable utopia. It would be impossible to predict its final outcome. It involves a step-by-step development, based on a continuing subjective choice of purposes, which are implemented by the behavioral sciences. It is in the direction of the "open society," as that term has been defined by Popper, where individuals carry responsibility for personal decisions. It is at the opposite pole from his concept of the closed society, of which *Walden Two* would be an example.

I trust it is also evident that the whole emphasis is on process, not on end-states of being. I am suggesting that it is by choosing to value certain qualitative elements of the process of becoming that we can find a pathway toward the open society.

The Choice

It is my hope that we have helped to clarify the range of choice which will lie before us and our children in regard to the behavioral sciences. We can choose to use our growing knowledge to enslave people in ways never dreamed of before, depersonalizing them, controlling them by means so carefully selected that they will perhaps never be aware of their loss of personhood. We can choose to utilize our scientific knowledge to make men happy, well-behaved, and productive, as Skinner earlier suggested. Or we can insure that each person learns all the syllabus which we select and set before him, as Skinner now suggests. Or at the other end of the spectrum of choice we can choose to use the behavioral sciences in ways which will free, not control; which will bring about constructive variability, not conformity; which will develop creativity, not contentment; which will facilitate each person in his self-directed process of becoming; which will aid individuals, groups, and even the concept of science to become self-transcending in freshly adaptive ways of meeting life and its problems. The choice is up to us, and, the human race being what it is, we are likely to stumble about, making at times some nearly disastrous value choices and at other times highly constructive ones.

I am aware that to some, this setting forth of a choice is unrealistic, because a choice of values is regarded as not possible. Skinner has stated: "Man's vaunted creative powers . . . his capacity to choose and our right to hold him responsible for his choice—none of these is conspicuous in this new self-portrait (provided by science). Man, we once believed, was free to express himself in art, music, and literature, to inquire into nature, to seek salvation in his own way. He could initiate action and makes spontaneous and capricious changes of course. . . . But science insists that action is initiated by forces impinging upon the individual, and that caprice is only another name for behavior for which we have not yet found a cause."

I can understand this point of view, but I believe that it avoids looking at the great paradox of behavioral science. Behavior, when it is examined scientifically, is surely best understood as determined by prior causation. This is one great fact of science. But responsible personal choice, which is the most essential element in being a person, which is the core experience in psychotherapy, which exists prior to any scientific endeavor, is an equally prominent fact in our lives. To deny the experience of responsible choice is, to me, as restricted a view as to deny the possibility of a behavioral science. That these two important elements of our experience appear to be in contradiction has perhaps the same significance as the contradiction between the wave theory and the corpuscular theory of light, both of which can be shown to be true, even though incompatible. We cannot profitably deny our subjective life, anymore than we can deny the objective description of that life.

In conclusion then, it is my contention that science cannot come into being without a personal choice of the values we wish to achieve. And these values we choose to implement will forever lie outside of the science which implements them; the goals we select, the purposes we wish to follow, must always be outside of the science which achieves them. To me this has the encouraging meaning that the human person, with his capacity of subjective choice, can and will always exist, separate from and prior to any of his scientific undertakings. Unless as individuals and groups we choose to relinquish our capacity of subjective choice, we will always remain persons, not simply pawns of a self-created science.

III [SKINNER]

I cannot quite agree that the practice of science *requires* a prior decision about goals or a prior choice of values. The metallurgist can study the properties of steel and the engineer can design a bridge without raising the question of whether a bridge is to be built. But such questions are certainly frequently raised and tentatively answered. Rogers wants to call the answers "subjective choices of values." To me, such an expression suggests that we have had to abandon more rigorous scientific practices in order to talk

about our own behavior. In the experimental analysis of other organisms I would use other terms, and I shall try to do so here. Any list of values is a list of reinforcers—conditioned or otherwise. We are so constituted that under certain circumstances food, water, sexual contact, and so on, will make any behavior which produces them more likely to occur again. Other things may acquire this power. We do not need to say that an organism chooses to eat rather than to starve. If you answer that it is a very different thing when a man chooses to starve, I am only too happy to agree. If it were not so, we should have cleared up the question of choice long ago. An organism can be reinforced by—can be made to "choose"—almost any given state of affairs.

Rogers is concerned with choices that involve multiple and usually conflicting consequences. I have dealt with some of these elsewhere in an analysis of self-control. Shall I eat these delicious strawberries today if I will then suffer an annoying rash tomorrow? The decision I am to make used to be assigned to the province of ethics. But we are now studying similar combinations of positive and negative consequences, as well as collateral conditions which affect the result, in the laboratory. Even a pigeon can be taught some measure of self-control! And this work helps us to understand the operation of certain formulas—among them value judgments—which folk-wisdom, religion, and psychotherapy have advanced in the interests of self-discipline. The observable effect of any statement of value is to alter the relative effectiveness of reinforcers. We may no longer enjoy the strawberries for thinking about the rash. If rashes are made sufficiently shameful, illegal, sinful, maladjusted, or unwise, we may glow with satisfaction as we push the strawberries aside in a grandiose avoidance response which would bring a smile to the lips of Murray Sidman.

People behave in ways which, as we say, conform to ethical, governmental, or religious patterns because they are reinforced for doing so. The resulting behavior may have far-reaching consequences for the survival of the pattern to which it conforms. And whether we like it or not, survival is the ultimate criterion. This is where, it seems to me, science can help—not in choosing a goal, but in enabling us to predict the survival value of cultural practices. Man has too long tried to get the kind of world he wants by glorifying some brand of immediate reinforcement. As science points up more and more of the remoter consequences, he may begin to work to strengthen behavior, not in a slavish devotion to a chosen value, but with respect to the ultimate survival of mankind. Do not ask me why I want mankind to survive. I can tell you why only in the sense in which the physiologist can tell you why I want to breathe. Once the relation between a given step and the survival of my group has been pointed out, I will take that step. And it is the business of science to point out just such relations.

The values I have occasionally recommended (and Rogers has not led me to recant) are transitional. Other things being equal, I am betting on the group whose practices make for healthy, happy, secure, productive, and creative people. And I insist that the values recommended by Rogers are transitional, too, for I can ask him the same kind of question. Man as a process of becoming—*what*? Self-actualization—for what? Inner control is no more a goal than external.

What Rogers seems to me to be proposing, both here and elsewhere, is this: Let us use our increasing power of control to create individuals who will not need and perhaps will no longer respond to control. Let us solve the problem of our power by renouncing it. At first blush this seems as implausible as a benevolent despot. Yet power has occasionally been foresworn. A nation has burned its Reichstag, rich men have given away their wealth, beautiful women have become ugly hermits in the desert, and psychotherapists have become nondirective. When this happens, I look to other possible reinforcements for a plausible explanation. A people relinquish democratic power when a tyrant promises them the earth. Rich men give away wealth to escape the accusing finger of their fellowmen. A woman destroys her beauty in the hope of salvation. And a psychotherapist relinquishes control because he can thus help his client more effectively.

The solution that Rogers is suggesting is thus understandable. But is he correctly interpreting the result? What evidence is there that a client ever becomes truly *self*-directing? What evidence is there that he ever makes a truly *inner* choice of ideal or goal? Even

though the therapist does not do the choosing, even though he encourages "self-actualization"—he is not out of control as long as he holds himself ready to step in when occasion demands—when, for example, the client chooses the goal of becoming a more accomplished liar or murdering his boss. But supposing the therapist does withdraw completely or is no longer necessary—what about all the other forces acting upon the client? Is the self-chosen goal independent of his early ethical and religious training? of the folk-wisdom of his group? of the opinions and attitudes of others who are important to him? Surely not. The therapeutic situation is only a small part of the world of the client. From the therapist's point of view it may appear to be possible to relinquish control. But the control passes, not to a "self," but to forces in other parts of the client's world. The solution of the therapist's problem of power cannot be *our* solution, for we must consider *all* the forces acting upon the individual.

The child who must be prodded and nagged is something less than a fully developed human being. We want to see him hurrying to his appointment, not because each step is taken in response to verbal reminders from his mother, but because certain temporal contingencies, in which dawdling has been punished and hurrying reinforced, have worked a change in his behavior. Call this a state of better organization, a greater sensitivity to reality, or what you will. The plain fact is that the child passes from a temporary verbal control exercised by his parents to control by certain inexorable features of the environment. I should suppose that something of the same sort happens in successful psychotherapy. Rogers seems to me to be saying this: Let us put an end, as quickly as possible, to any pattern of master-and-slave, to any direct obedience to command, to the submissive following of suggestions. Let the individual be free to adjust himself to more rewarding features of the world about him. In the end, let his teachers and counselors "wither away," like the Marxist state. I not only agree with this as a useful ideal, I have constructed a fanciful world to demonstrate its advantages. It saddens me to hear Rogers say that "at a deep philosophic level" *Walden Two* and George Orwell's *1984* "seem indistinguishable." They could scarcely be more unlike—at any level. The book *1984* is a picture of immediate aversive control for vicious selfish purposes. The founder of *Walden Two,* on the other hand, has built a community in which neither he nor any other person exerts any *current* control. His achievement lay in his original *plan,* and when he boasts of this ("It is enough to satisfy the thirstiest tyrant") we do not fear him but only pity him for his weakness.

Another critic of *Walden Two,* Andrew Hacker, has discussed this point in considering the bearing of mass conditioning upon the liberal notion of autonomous man. In drawing certain parallels between the Grand Inquisition passage in Dostoevsky's *Brothers Karamazov,* Huxley's *Brave New World,* and *Walden Two,* he attempts to set up a distinction to be drawn in any society between conditioners and conditioned. He assumes that "the conditioner can be said to be autonomous in the traditional liberal sense." But then he notes: "Of course the conditioner has been conditioned. But he has not been conditioned by the conscious manipulation of another *person*." But how does this affect the resulting behavior? Can we not soon forget the origins of the "artificial" diamond which is identical with the real thing? Whether it is an "accidental" cultural pattern, such as is said to have produced the founder of *Walden Two,* or the engineered environment which is about to produce his successors, we are dealing with sets of conditions generating human behavior which will ultimately be measured by their contribution to the strength of the group. We look to the future, not the past, for the test of "goodness" or acceptability.

If we are worthy of our democratic heritage we shall, of course, be ready to resist any tyrannical use of science for immediate or selfish purposes. But if we value the achievements and goals of democracy we must not refuse to apply science to the design and construction of cultural patterns, even though we may then find ourselves in some sense in the position of controllers. Fear of control, generalized beyond any warrant, has led to a misinterpretation of valid practices and the blind rejection of intelligent planning for a better way of life. In terms which I trust Rogers will approve, in conquering this fear we shall become more mature and better organized and shall, thus, more fully actualize ourselves as human beings.

REFERENCES

Rogers, C. R. (1951). *Client centered therapy.* Boston: Houghton Mifflin.

Rogers, C. R., & Dymond, R. (Eds.) (1954). *Psychotherapy and personality change.* Chicago: University of Chicago Press.

Skinner, B. F. (1948). *Walden Two.* New York: Macmillan.

Skinner, B. F. (1953). *Science and human behavior.* New York: Macmillan.

―――――― Questions to Think About ――――――

1. What aspects of this interchange actually reflect a dialogue, in which the participants are responding to one another rather than just taking turns stating their individual positions?

2. Suppose that a successful science of human behavior could be developed that would allow for the prediction and control of people's actions. What would each of these theorists perceive as the risks inherent in such a science and its potential benefits?

3. Rogers acknowledges that, under scientific examination, behavior is best understood as determined by prior causation, and yet he also claims that responsible personal choice is the most essential element in being a person. How can these two ideas be made compatible?

24

Learning: Its Conditions and Principles

NEAL E. MILLER AND JOHN DOLLARD

Neal E. Miller (1909–2002) had a very long and productive career in psychology as a major contributor to multiple fields. After receiving his Ph.D. at Yale University, he spent a year at the Institute of Psychoanalysis in Vienna, exposed to Freud's ideas in their heyday, and then returned to Yale where he was on the faculty for 30 years, followed by 15 more years at Rockefeller University. In his later years, he was best known as a behavioral neuroscientist, but before that he was a pioneer in studies of motivation, learning, and reward. At Yale, Miller began a collaboration with John Dollard (1900–1980), a junior colleague trained in the University of Chicago approach to sociology, which emphasized the social or relative nature of the self. These two researchers brought to their collaboration a rich background in many important approaches to personality—the psychoanalytic and ego aspects, the social and anthropological aspects, and the biological and cognitive aspects, all in the overall context of a learning and behaviorist framework. They developed an approach to personality called social learning theory. This selection, the opening chapter of their book *Social Learning and Imitation,* lays out what they believe to be the fundamental conditions and principles of learning.

Human behavior is learned; precisely that behavior which is widely felt to characterize man as a rational being, or as a member of a particular nation or social class, is acquired rather than innate. To understand thoroughly any item of human behavior—either in the social group or in the individual life—one must know the psychological principles involved in its learning and the social conditions under which this learning took place. It is not enough to know either principles or conditions of learning; in order to predict behavior both must be known. The field of psychology describes learning principles, while the various social science disciplines describe the conditions.

Learning is a fact so familiar to human beings that it often does not receive the attention which it deserves. The difficult learning experiences of early childhood are forgotten by adults, and recalled to attention only by observing the blundering adaptations of children. Everyone at some time has tried to learn a skill and failed, without knowing why; or he has tried to teach and found others slow to understand. Such experiences drive home the fact that learning is not automatic. Where the principles are not understood so that the conditions can be correctly arranged, no learning takes place.

What, then, is learning theory? In its simplest form, it is the study of the circumstances under which a response and a cue stimulus become connected. After learning has been completed, response and cue are bound together in such a way that the appearance of the cue evokes the response. Everyone remembers learning to stop at a red light when driving an automobile. The cue pattern in this case is a simple one: it consists of the red light, the street intersection, and

Source: From Miller, N. E., & Dollard, J. (1941). *Social learning and imitation.* New Haven: Yale University Press. Reprinted by permission. This selection is the first chapter of the book.

perhaps the appearance of other cars moving across the highway. The response is equally simple: the right foot presses on the brake, the left foot on the clutch, and the car is brought to a halt. The cue of the red light has been associated with the response of pressing on pedals. Everyone remembers, similarly, that this response is not learned in one trial. The car must be slowly brought to a halt and stopped at the intersecting street. Errors have occurred, such as pressing too hard on the brake and stopping the car violently. Again, the distance to the intersecting street is badly gauged, and the car is stopped too soon; sometimes other cars are bumped in the process. In any case, after a series of trials, the connection between the light cue and the pressing response is established. The same technique of learning seems to operate in a great variety of situations. Under appropriate conditions the child learns to talk, to have good table manners, and to suppress the naughty words that he hears from his play group. Adults may learn to adapt to another person in the marriage relationship, to teach their children, and to grow old gracefully.

Learning takes place according to definite psychological principles. Practice does not always make perfect. The connection between a cue and a response can be strengthened only under certain conditions. The learner must be driven to make the response and rewarded for having responded in the presence of the cue. This may be expressed in a homely way by saying that in order to learn one must want something, notice something, do something, and get something. Stated more exactly, these factors are drive, cue, response, and reward. These elements in the learning process have been carefully explored, and further complexities have been discovered. Learning theory has become a firmly knit body of principles which are useful in describing human behavior.

Learning principles can, of course, operate only under specific material or social conditions. For human beings these conditions are those imposed by the society in which a particular individual lives. The analysis of social behavior seems to require a knowledge of learning principles, exactly as the analysis of any personality trait requires knowledge of the social conditions under which it was learned. In order to give

point to this contention, the authors will present examples showing the need for learning principles in the analysis of characteristic social facts and, conversely, the necessity of a knowledge of learning conditions in the psychological sphere.

To take first a case from social science. The anthropological theory of diffusion provides the following facts: While the Indians of the eastern woodlands of North America were learning to use the gun which they took over from the whites, the whites in turn were learning a new style of warfare—they discovered the advantage of lying in ambush and shooting at the enemy from behind trees and rocks as the Indians did. While the gun was diffusing to the Indians, a military technique was diffusing to the whites. Is it a matter of chance that the whites did not adopt the bow and arrow and the Indians the close-order drill which was characteristic of the European armies? Seen from the standpoint of learning theory, it can hardly have been accidental. The Indians were heavily punished by the superior striking power of the gun, and to avoid this punishment they copied the use of the musket from the whites. The whites, on the other hand, suffered severely from the ambush techniques of the Indians. Each side, to escape punishment, learned a new set of responses.

To take a second example, the behavior of voters, or at least some voters, in a boss-ridden town has puzzled many observers. They often seem to act in defiance of their own best interests as widely conceived. They may be inordinately taxed to maintain service on a graft-inflated debt; they may be deprived of the best level of services which a city government can render; and they may be ruled and delivered by an arrogant machine. The use of psychological principles may help to explain these apparently irrational loyalties. Many voters in the lower social and income brackets have needs of which the wider society seems to be unaware. These needs are met by the political machine. Through the machine the voter can satisfy some of his urgent wants without seeming to accept charity. The boss, for instance, has jobs to offer—not always big jobs, but ones much appreciated by his constituents. The machine voter feels that he has some control over these jobs and that they offer a less precarious form of security than open competition in the job market. This is a primary reward for taking orders and voting the straight ticket. The ward boss watches the rise of needs among his constituents. If someone dies, he calls to express sympathy, to aid in funeral arrangements, or he offers money to make possible the conventional hospitality; the Christmas basket and ton of coal are sent with his compliments. All of these rewards are immediate and therefore more effective than the delayed consequences of good government. For other voters still, the boss can tear up a parking ticket, overlook the infraction of a fire law, or even induce authorities to ignore an illegal business. It is clear, of course, that all the voters would be better off in the long run if the city administration were honestly and efficiently administered in the interest of the whole community; but the boss's henchmen do not think in terms of the long run. Their loyalty is won by the small but promptly produced favors which they receive from the machine. Political attitudes in such a group will be as stable as the rewards which reinforce them. If the machine loses its power to deliver the coal or the protection, as the case may be, it also loses its power to deliver the vote.

Examples indicating the usefulness of learning principles in solving the problems of social scientists could be selected from a variety of fields. What, for instance, are the mechanisms by which culture is transmitted from one generation to the next? Since such transmission is not instinctive, it can only be that social habits are taught to children by the adults of the culture and learned by children from their elders. The transmission of culture must follow the laws of learning. An adequate understanding of the individual life in terms of acquiring culture by learning is one of the important current problems of social science.

The stability of culture patterns, once they are acquired by the individuals of a given generation, presents likewise an interesting, though still obscure, problem. Are social habits, once acquired through the learning of childhood, fixed and immutable? Do they have a kind of gravitational property which makes it difficult to change them, or do they respond to one of the laws of habit which states that unrewarded habits will disappear? If the habits of adults *are* constantly rewarded, what are the rewards in question? There are

no definitive answers to these questions at the present time, but they seem bound to receive discussion in the future. On a common-sense level, it seems likely that the satisfactions of daily life maintain cultural habit. But rewards there must be—or changes in the learning theory which seems to demand them. In any case, the stability of culture patterns and habits is not to be taken for granted as a matter too obvious and unimportant for close examination.

If social scientists find the knowledge of learning principles valuable in solving problems in their field, psychologists will find it no less useful to emphasize the conditions under which human learning takes place. These conditions for human beings are primarily social and cultural conditions. No psychologist would venture to predict the behavior of a rat without knowing on what arm of a T-maze the food or the shock is placed. It is no easier to predict the behavior of a human being without knowing the conditions of his "maze," i.e., the structure of his social environment. Culture, as conceived by social scientists, is a statement of the design of the human maze, of the type of reward involved, and of what responses are to be rewarded. It is in this sense a recipe for learning. This contention is easily accepted when widely variant societies are compared. But even within the same society, the mazes which are run by two individuals may seem the same but actually be quite different. In our own society, for instance, a person at the top of the social hierarchy may look much like the same American as a person at the bottom of the hierarchy; but actually his life is differentiated from that of a lower-class person by a series of divergent customs and habits. No personality analysis of two such people can be accurate which does not take into account these cultural differences, that is, differences in the types of responses which have been rewarded.

The importance of knowing the conditions of learning can be illustrated from a common personality problem, i.e., that of aggressive individuals. Individual aggressiveness has often been supposed to be natural, or instinctive. In one group of aggressive persons, it is quite clear that social conditions have influenced the development of this personality trait. These are persons who have recently been socially mobile. In the course of struggle for social advancement, these mobile individuals have found frequent occasion for aggressive responses. They have, for instance, competed in business with cut-throat severity, but have been rewarded by success. They have boldly copied the manners and habits of those above them in social position and, though often ridiculed, have often succeeded in achieving higher status. They have learned to strive, compete, and fight, where others have quietly accepted deprivations, and they have lived to see themselves superior. Since competitive and aggressive habits have been so highly and consistently rewarded, it is not surprising to find such persons displaying aggression in a great variety of situations. Seen in this context, the "pushiness" of the mobile person is not mysterious; it seems rather the inevitable result of the learning conditions of his life. The social structure of our society is so designed that it grants rewards to those who fight for them; in the course of so doing, it creates combative individuals. A psychologist understanding these conditions might well go on to make the following prediction: If the aggressive individual achieves status in a social group higher than his own, and if in the higher group his "pushiness" is no longer rewarded but is, on the contrary, punished, such a trait will tend to drop out—although it may distinguish the recently mobile person during the time he is becoming adapted to the superior group.

The importance of social conditions can be further emphasized by considering the different ways in which people use alcoholic drinks at different levels in our society. There are definite social conventions which govern drinking in different social groups, although to state this is not to deny that there are also biological and psychological factors involved. If one did not know the social conditions, however, it would be easy to overestimate the importance of such factors. The matter can be exemplified, though in oversimplified form, from the data gathered on a small American town. In the lower class, both men and women may drink, although the men seem to drink with much more freedom from criticism than do the women. There is little punishment for overindulgence and no urgency to "drink like a gentleman" among lower-class men. Getting drunk is not frowned upon. Lower-class individuals drink episodically—usually when they happen to have the money necessary to buy liquor. If these conditions were unknown, the drinking of a lower-class person might seem to be a very marked personality trait. Lower-middle-class individuals in the very same town drink little or not at all. They have religious scruples against it and are afraid that the habit of drinking would lead to their being confused with lower-class persons. Upper-middle-class people draw a distinction between men and women so far as drinking is concerned. The men drink quite freely, especially in their clubs, but they do not engage in mixed drinking with women. Upper-middle-class wives are expected to refuse alcohol when it is offered. In the upper class, by contrast, both men and women drink, and there is no moral significance attached to drinking. There is, however, a code involved. While an upper-class individual is allowed to drink a good deal, he must "drink like a gentleman." He is punished with social scorn if he allows his drinking to lead to disorderly or aggressive behavior, such as is often characteristic of lower-class people.

If an individual moves from one of these social classes to another, he must change his habits with regard to the use of alcohol. If he moves into the lower-middle class from the lower class, he must learn to stop drinking or he will be thought vulgar. Lower-middle-class men who move into upper-middle class must learn to begin again, at least when they are with men. Upper-middle-class individuals who move into upper class must learn to become very liberal from the standpoint of their former upper-middle-class habits, or they will be thought stuffy. What is rewarded in one social class is punished in the other. It is clear that if a person from the town in question came into the hands of a psychologist in a clinic, it would be absolutely necessary for the latter to know the special social conditions with regard to drinking which were characteristic of the social class of the patient. Without a knowledge of these social conditions, a personality analysis of a given case of drinking would certainly be confused.

A further example from anthropological literature may serve to emphasize the importance of the social environment still more decisively. The Semang people of the Malay Peninsula are known among anthropologists as excessively shy and timid. They are said never to respond to ill treatment with violence or treachery. In the face of hostility from others, they withdraw yet deeper into the jungle area which they inhabit. Is this a personality trait? Are these people naturally deficient in aggressive tendencies and constitutionally prone to flight? The question can be answered only by posing another: Have the conditions of life been such for the Semang that aggressive responses have been punished while escape responses have been rewarded? For some time past, the Semang have been in contact with a more powerful group, the Malays, who have regularly cheated them in trade, occasionally raided them for slaves, and slowly crowded them out of their lands. One may fairly surmise that in former times the Semang attempted resistance, but found it led only to severe punishment. Like a child who is punished first for a naughty act, and then for crying in protest at the punishment, their only resource was muteness and flight. Apparently, also, although aggressive responses were not rewarded, flight tendencies were successful and became stabilized. This stabilization took the form of culture patterns defining flight as the correct response to strangers. It is no longer necessary for each generation of Malays to punish each generation of Semang into learning escape behavior; this teaching is now done by the Semang with their own children. Conditions of learning which formerly taught the whole tribe to avoid contact with the dangerous Malays have now been absorbed into the culture, and form in turn conditions of learning for each Semang child.

In earliest life the conditions of learning and the principles of learning can be sharply and logically marked off one from the other. Social scientists are keenly aware of the rôle of primary drives, such as hunger, which are met by the distinctive conditions of learning characteristic of each society. Hunger, pain, and fatigue are clamorous and distinctive in the infant. The routines of feeding, the type of food offered, and the behavior of the nurse are carefully defined. As time passes in the life of the child, these crude drive tendencies become less visible—although they are never absent—and are replaced by various *social* motivations. These social motivations are variously called *secondary drives, acquired drives,* or *social attitudes.* Upon the primary drive of pain is built the (also painful) secondary drive of anxiety. Upon the

crude hunger drive are built appetites for particular foods. All of these secondary drives are derived by the joint operation of psychological variables under the pressure of social conditions. It is these secondary drives which particularly interest the social scientist, because they form such a large and obvious part of social motivation. In an analogous though more complex manner, there arise also acquired drives toward gregariousness, social conformity, prestige seeking, desire for money, and, most important here, *imitativeness.* It is necessary to notice that once these social drives have been generated, they operate exactly as do the primary drives; but it is also crucial that they never lose their acquired, or dependent, character. A theory of social learning must give a full account of these social motivations, since they are so characteristic of the behavior of human beings.

The joint operation of psychological principles and social conditions will be exemplified by a detailed discussion of imitation. Imitation is a process by which "matched," or similar, acts are evoked in two people and connected to appropriate cues. It can occur only under conditions which are favorable to learning these acts. If matching, or doing the same as others do, is regularly rewarded, a secondary tendency to match may be developed, and the process of imitation becomes the derived drive of imitativeness.

The importance of the study of matched behavior is clearer when one considers the high rewards which attend joint social action. If all pull on the same rope, the cart moves. National unity of thought and action is important in a crisis. Individuals must be trained to pull harder on the rope when others pull and to act more decisively together when others act. Such joint action is often essential to the survival of a society.

Imitation is also important in maintaining social conformity and discipline. Individuals must be trained, in many situations, so that they will be comfortable when they are doing what others are doing and miserable when they are not. The culture patterns of a society have been achieved by many generations of trial-and-error behavior, and they constitute a tested way of life which has long proved its value. Individuals cannot be permitted to deviate too readily from it. This desirable conformity to the social pattern is achieved, in part, by techniques of imitation which individuals acquire during the early years of life. It is important, therefore, to understand just how imitative behavior arises.

There seem to be two important types of action which go under the common name of *imitation*. In *matched-dependent* behavior, the leader is able to read the relevant environmental cues, but the follower is not; the latter must depend upon the leader for the signal as to what act is to be performed and where and when. The follower does not need to be keenly aware that his act is matched. This matched-dependent mechanism apparently plays a considerable rôle in the formation of crowds, and it will be found useful in the analysis of crowd behavior.

The second type of matched behavior is described here as *copying*. The copier must slowly bring his response to approximate that of a model and must know, when he has done so, that his act is an acceptable reproduction of the model act. Copying units are established early in the history of each individual, and appear to play a considerable rôle in all fundamental social learning. For instance, once the child has learned the fundamental phonemes of his speech, it is possible for him to copy any new word in the language. By copying, the correct word can be rapidly and efficiently elicited. Copying itself is, of course, learned only when the appropriate conditions of reward for learning it are present.

The method of this research is exemplified in the order of the chapters which follow. The authors first attempted to get some practice in applying learning theory to social behavior. Then, addressing the inquiry to the imitation problem, they selected and analyzed some examples of imitative behavior which were derived from a study of children. These examples were then discussed and dissected in the search for relevant variables. With a preliminary list of these variables, an attempt was made to manipulate them in experiments. From the experiments, there arose a more systematic statement of a theory of imitative behavior, derived under controlled conditions. Once this theory had been tested, it was applied to several problems of social behavior in order to determine its usefulness. The evidence seems to show that imitative behavior follows the laws of learning and arises under the social conditions which reward it.

REFERENCES

Davis, A., & Dollard, J. (1940). *Children of bondage: The personality development of Negro youth in the urban South.* New York: Harper & Row.

Davis, A., Gardner, B. B., & Gardner, M. R. (1941). *Deep South; a social anthropological study of caste and class.* Chicago, IL: University of Chicago Press.

Whiting, J. W. M. (1941). *Becoming a Kwoma: Teaching and learning in a New Guinea tribe.* New Haven, CT: Yale University Press.

_____ Questions to Think About _____

1. The authors provide a straightforward description of how people learn the accepted behaviors of their cultural environments. How would the authors respond if they were asked whether these behaviors (for example, aggression versus withdrawal in the face of challenge) become, over time, the personality characteristics of each individual in the group?

2. The authors say that in order to learn, one must "want something, notice something, do something, and get something." Is conscious awareness of any of those processes required in order for the learning to occur? Might conscious awareness alter the learning?

3. What roles might be played in learning by characteristics such as insight, self-awareness, reflection, sensitivity, or creativity, which are not included in the model of learning presented here?

25

Personal Construct Theory
and the Psychotherapeutic Interview

GEORGE A. KELLY

George A. Kelly (1905–1966), best known for his psychology of "Personal Constructs," was born in Kansas. After receiving his Ph.D. from Iowa State University, Kelly focused his early work on issues of diagnostic testing. Throughout his career Kelly pursued his interest in training and providing clinical psychological services that utilized his theories.

It was, however, Kelly's personal construct theory that had a large impact on approaches to personality and on clinical practice. Kelly used the model of the scientific method to describe human behavior, claiming that every person is, in his or her own particular way, a scientist. Importantly, Kelly's major work was published in 1955, years before cognitive psychology became firmly established as a field of study within psychology. Nevertheless, Kelly's work helped lay the groundwork for the cognitive social learning theories that followed.

BIOGRAPHY OF A THEORY

A good many years ago when I first set for myself the task of writing a manual of clinical procedures it was with the idea that psychologists needed to get their feet on the ground, and I was out to help them do it. Other scientists had gotten their feet on the ground; why couldn't we? Elsewhere all about us there were those hardy breeds who had penetrated the frontiers of reality with boldness and forthrightness. Practical men they were who, with each bedrock discovery, discredited all those generations of anemic philosophers who never dared venture beyond the comforts of their own redundancies. And yet here was the gloomiest vista of all, the mind of man, only one step away—a deep cavern so close behind our very own eyes and still enshadowed in Delphian mystery. And here we were, psychologists, standing on one foot wanting very much to be scientists—and more than a little

defensive about it, too—chattering away and so frightened of what we might see that we never dared take a close look.

Fancying myself thus as a practical man and seeing science as something which was, above all things, practical, it seemed that whatever I could do to bring psychologists into contact with human beings, novel as that might be, would help extricate psychology from the mishmash of its abstruse definitions. So I proposed to write as much as I knew about how to come to terms with living persons. I took as my prototypes the ones who confided in me, particularly those who were in trouble, because, as I saw it, when a person is in trouble he acts more like what he is and less like something dangling from the strings of social convention. Out of such an undertaking, if enough psychologists were willing to join in, I could envision a gradual awakening of the ancient half-conscious

Source: Kelly, G. A. (1969). Personal construct theory and the psychotherapeutic interview. In B. Maher (Ed.), *Clinical psychology and personality: The selected papers of George Kelly* (pp. 224–232). New York: Wiley. Copyright © 1969, John Wiley & Sons. Reprinted by permission of John Wiley & Sons, Inc. (Original work published 1958.)

mind of man and the ultimate fruition of its vast potentialities. It should be obvious that all this fantasy took place when I was very young.

That manual was never written, at least not that kind of manual. The business of being practical turned out to be not as simple as I thought. After more delay than should have been necessary, even for one short of wits, the notion finally struck me that, no matter how close I came to the man or woman who sought my help, I always saw him through my own peculiar spectacles, and never did he perceive what I was frantically signaling to him, except through his. From this moment I ceased, as I am now convinced every psychotherapist does whether he wants to admit it or not, being a realist. More important, I could now stop representing psychology to clients as packaged reality, warranted genuine and untouched by human minds.

Perhaps "realism" is not a good term for what I am talking about. It is obvious, of course, that I am not talking about Platonic realism. Nobody talks about that any more. The realism from which my clients and I are always trying to wriggle loose might possibly be called "materialistic realism." At least it is the hard-headed unimaginative variety nowadays so popular among scientists, businessmen, and neurotics.

REALISM AND DOGMATISM

What happened was this. Like most therapists with a background of liberal scholarship rather than strictly professional training, I soon became aware that dogmatic interpretations of clients' problems often did more harm than good. It was not only the client who suffered; therapists were affected in much the same way he was. Dogmatism produces a kind of mental rigidity that replaces thoughts with word, stifles the zest for free inquiry, and tries to seal the personality up tight at the conclusion of the last psychotherapeutic interview.

Understand, I am not yet ready to say that dogmatism has no place whatsoever in psychotherapy, especially when weighed against certain grimmer alternatives. It may even prove valuable to all of us as a firm point from which to rebel. But these are other matters.

What actually jarred me loose was the observation that clients who felt themselves confronted with down-to-earth realities during the course of psychotherapy became much like those who were confronted with downright dogmatic interpretations of either the religious or psychological variety. On the heels of this observation came the notion that dogmatism—the belief that one has the word of truth right from the horse's mouth—and modern realism—the belief that one has the word of truth right from nature's mouth—add up to the same thing. To go even further, I now suspect that neither of these assumptions about the revealed nature of truth is any more useful to scientists than it is to clients. But especially I am sure that both assumptions get square in the way of that supreme ontological venture we call psychotherapy and that they serve only to perpetuate its present unhappy captivity to fee-based medical materialism.

While my original views of ontology—and I am insisting that it is the same ontological process that runs its course whether the man is in the role of a client, a psychotherapist, a physicist, or an artist—have changed in some respects with the years, one of my original convictions remains with me. It still seems important for the psychologist to deal directly with persons on the most forthright terms possible. This is why I think of clinical psychology, not as an applied field of psychology, but as a focal and essential area and method of scientific inquiry. On the other hand, traditional psychology, it seems to me, is still much too self-consciously scientific and still much too peripheral to its subject matter. Instead of being so careful to do nothing that a scientist would not do, it would be more appropriate for the psychologist to get on with his job of understanding human nature. To the extent that he is successful, "Science" will eventually be only too glad to catch up and claim his methods as its own.

As for dogmatism, I certainly am not the first to say that it often works badly in therapy. Nor am I the first to recognize that the client has a point of view worth taking into account. But if one is to avoid dogmatism entirely he needs to alert himself against realism also, for realism, as I have already implied, is a special form of dogmatism and one which is quite as likely to stifle the client's creative efforts. A client who is confronted with what are conceded to be stark realities can be as badly immobilized as one confronted with a thickheaded therapist. Even the presumed realism of his own raw feelings can convince a client that he has reached a dead end.

ALTERNATIVISM

As my client's therapist I can temporarily avoid pushing him over the brink of reality by being passive or by accepting as nonjudgmentally as possible anything and everything he says or does. There is no doubt but that in this atmosphere of intimate ambiguity many clients will figure out sensible things to do in spite of a therapist's shortsightedness. This is good and, for a therapist who thinks he has to act like a realist, it is about as far as one can go without betraying the dogmatism implicit in his realism. But I am not a realist—not anymore—and I do not believe either the client or the therapist has to lie down and let facts crawl over him. Right here is where the theoretical viewpoint I call *the psychology of personal constructs* stakes out its basic philosophical claim.

There is nothing so obvious that its appearance is not altered when it is seen in a different light. This is the faith that sustains the troubled person when he undertakes psychotherapy seriously. It is the same as the faith expressed in the *Book of Job*—not so much in the overwritten poetic lines as in the development of the theme. To state this faith as a philosophical premise: *Whatever exists can be reconstrued*. This is to say that none of today's constructions—which are, of course, our only means of portraying reality—is perfect and, as the history of human thought repeatedly suggests, none is final.

Moreover, this is the premise upon which most psychotherapy has to be built, if not in the mind of the therapist, at least in the mind of the client. To be sure, one may go to a therapist with his facts clutched in his hand and asking only what he ought to do with them. But this is merely seeking technical advice, not therapy. Indeed, what else would one seek unless he suspected that the obstacles now shaping up in front of him are not yet cast in the ultimate form of reality? As a matter of fact, I have yet to see a realistic client who sought the help of a therapist in changing his outlook. To the realist, outlook and reality are made of the same inert stuff. On the other hand, a client who has found his therapeutic experience helpful often says, "In many ways things are the same as they were before, but how differently I see them!"

This abandonment of realism may alarm some readers. It may seem like opening the door to wishful thinking, and to most psychologists wishful thinking is a way of coming unhinged. Perhaps this is why so many of them will never admit to having any imagination, at least until after they suppose they have realistically demonstrated that what they secretly imagined was there all the time, waiting to be discovered. But for me to say that *whatever exists can be reconstrued* is by no manner or means to say that it makes no difference how it is construed. Quite the contrary. It often makes a world of difference. Some reconstructions may open fresh channels for a rich and productive life. Others may offer one no alternative save suicide.

A THEORETICAL POSTULATE

Here, then, is where one takes the next step, a step that leads him from a philosophical premise—called *constructive alternativism*—to a psychological postulate. Put it this way: *A person's processes are psychologically channelized by the ways in which he anticipates events.* Next, combining this statement with the gist of some of its ensuing corollaries, we can say simply: *A person lives his life by reaching out for what comes next and the only channels he has for reaching are the personal constructions he is able to place upon what may actually be happening.* If in this effort he fails, by whatever criterion, the prudence of his constructions is laid open to question and his grasp upon the future is shaken.

Let us make no mistake; here we come to the exact point where we all have trouble. If our misleading construction is based on dogmatic belief, that is to say it is held to be true because someone like God or the Supreme Soviet said so, we are not likely to have the audacity to try to revise it. Similarly, if it is believed to have had its origin in nature rather than in our own noggin—the position of "realism" I have been talking about—we are left with no choice except to adjust and make the best of matters as they stand. Or if realizing that it was altogether our own mistaken notions that led us afield, if it seems now that there is nothing left to do except to scrap our convictions, one and all, then utter chaos will start closing in on all sides. Any of these is bad. Fortunately, there are always other alternatives when predictions go awry. For the person who does not see any of them—psychotherapy!

VIEW OF PSYCHOTHERAPY

We have ruled out the notion of psychotherapy as the confrontation of the client with stark reality, whether it is put to him in the form of dogma, natural science, or the surges of his own feelings. Instead, we see him approaching reality in the same ways that all of us have to approach it if we are to get anywhere. The methods range all the way from those of the artist to those of the scientist. Like them both and all the people in between, the client needs to assume that something can be created that is not already known or is not already there.

In this undertaking the fortunate client has a partner, the psychotherapist. But the psychotherapist does not know the final answer either—so they face the problem together. Under the circumstances there is nothing for them to do except for both to inquire and both to risk occasional mistakes. So that it can be a genuinely cooperative effort, each must try to understand what the other is proposing and each must do what he can to help the other understand what he himself is ready to try next. They formulate their hypotheses jointly. They even experiment jointly and upon each other. Together they take stock of outcomes and revise their common hunches. Neither is the boss, nor are they merely well-bred neighbors who keep their distance from unpleasant affairs. It is, as far as they are able to make it so, a partnership.

The psychotherapy room is a protected laboratory where hypotheses can be formulated, test-tube sized experiments can be performed, field trials planned, and outcomes evaluated. Among other things, the interview can be regarded as itself an experiment in behavior. The client says things to see what will happen. So does the therapist. Then they ask themselves and each other if the outcomes confirmed their expectations.

Often a beginning therapist finds it helpful to close his cerebral dictionary and listen primarily to the subcortical sounds and themes that run through his client's talk. Stop wondering what the words literally mean. Try to recall, instead, what it is they sound like. Disregard content for the moment; attend to theme. Remember that a client can abruptly change content—thus throwing a literal-minded therapist completely off the scent—but he rarely changes the theme so easily. Or think of these vocal sounds, not as words, but as preverbal outcries, impulsive sound gestures, stylized oral grimaces, or hopelessly mumbled questions.

But at other times the therapist will bend every effort to help the client find a word, the precise word, for a newly emerged idea. Such an exact labeling of elusive thoughts is, at the proper time, crucial to making further inquiries and to the experimental testing of hypotheses. Particularly is this true when the team—client and therapist—is elaborating personal constructs. But before we can discuss this matter further we need to say something about the nature of personal constructs from the point of view of the theory.

PERSONAL CONSTRUCTS

We have said that a person lives his life by reaching out for what comes next and the only channels through which he can reach are the personal constructions he is able to place upon what appears to be going on. One deals with the events of life, not as entirely strange and unique occurrences but as recurrences. There is a property, a human quality of our own manufacture, that makes today seem like yesterday and leads us to expect that tomorrow may be another such day. To see this is to construe similarity among one's days. Without this view the future would seem chaotic indeed.

But to say that one's days are all alike, and nothing more, is to lose them amidst the hours and the years. What makes days seem alike is also precisely what sets them apart. We construe, then, by ascribing some property that serves both to link an event with certain other events and to set it in contrast to those with which it might most likely become confused. This construed dimension, embodying both likeness and difference, this reference axis, is what we call a construct. And constructs are personal affairs; regardless of the words he uses, each person does his own construing.

In this world—past, present, and future—ordered by each of us in his own way, constructs and events are interwoven so that events give definition to constructs and constructs give meaning to events. Take the client. The events, for example, that he recalls from childhood during the course of a psychotherapeutic interview serve to define the constructs that often he can otherwise express only through "intellectualization" or by "acting out." But constructs, on the other hand, give current meaning both to his memories and to his future plans and, particularly when they are precisely verbalized, they lay the ground for profitable experimentation.

The constructs one applies to himself and his interpersonal relationships have particular importance. Psychotherapy finds itself mainly concerned with them. While always fewer in number than one might wish, they nevertheless set the pattern of human resources available to the client and, when they are applied to his own changes of mood or behavior, they become wide-open pathways for shifting his position and altering the course of his life. Knowledge of them helps the therapist predict and control the client's possible reactions to threat, including the implicit threat that, to some extent, is always implied by psychotherapy itself.

THE VARYING TECHNIQUES OF PSYCHOTHERAPY

The team of client and therapist can go about their task in a variety of ways. Essentially these are the same ways that, on one kind of occasion or another, man has always employed for dealing with perplexities. (1) The two of them can decide that the client should reverse his position with respect to one of the more obvious reference axes. Call this slot rattling, if you please. It has its place. (2) Or they can select another construct from the client's ready repertory and apply it to matters at hand. This, also, is a rather straightforward approach. Usually the client has already tried it. (3) They can make more explicit those preverbal constructs by which all of us order our lives in considerable degree. Some think of this as dredging the unconscious. The figure is one that a few have found useful; but I would prefer not to use it. (4) They can elaborate the construct system to test it for internal consistency. (5) They can test constructs for their predictive validity. (6) They can increase the range of convenience of certain constructs, that is, apply them more generally. They can also decrease the range of convenience and thus reduce a construct to a kind of obsolescence. (7) They can alter the meaning of certain constructs; rotate the reference axes. (8) They can erect new reference axes. This is the most ambitious undertaking of all.

Alteration or replacement of constructs—the last two methods mentioned—is essentially a creative kind of effort. Both involve first a loosening of the client's constructions, either by the use of fantasy, dreams, free association, or the introduction of varied and illusive content into the therapeutic interview. But creativity is not a single mode of thought; it follows a cycle. The second phase of the cycle involves tightening and validation of the newly placed or newly formed constructs.

I have summarized what goes on in therapy under eight headings. More might have been used. It is necessary only that I offer some sketch of how psychotherapy can be envisioned in terms of personal construct theory, that I try to make clear that what I am talking about is not restricted to the process tradition calls "cognition" (a term for which I find little practical use lately), that psychotherapy runs the gamut of man's devices for coming to grips with reality, and that the client and his therapist embark together as shipmates on the very same adventure.

Questions to Think About

1. What is materialistic realism? Why should therapists wriggle loose from this view?
2. What is personal construct theory?
3. Describe the components of the ideal client/therapist relationship from the viewpoint of a theorist.
4. If the therapist is to abandon "realism" so that the client can maintain his or her own reality, then the therapist will no longer be on common ground with the client. Under those circumstances, there is no shared understanding of what the client expresses, so what does it mean for the therapist to "accept" what the client presents?

26

External Control and Internal Control

JULIAN B. ROTTER

Julian Rotter (1916–) was an important bridge between traditional social learning theories and the modern ideas that have come to be called social-cognitive theory. He believes that our behavior depends both on how strongly we expect that our performance will have a positive result and on how much we value the expected reinforcement. Expectancy is key but expectancy is not necessarily so simple.

Rotter was born in New York to Jewish immigrants, and he was influenced by the situational pressures he observed during the Great Depression of the 1930s. Rotter is perhaps best known for his ideas about internal and external locus of control. This has turned out to be a powerful and popular approach to individual differences and he describes it in the following selection.

Some social scientists believe that the impetus behind campus unrest is youth's impatient conviction that they can control their own destinies, that they can change society for the better.

My research over the past 12 years has led me to suspect that much of the protest, outcry and agitation occurs for the opposite reason—because students feel they *cannot* change the world, that the system is too complicated and too much controlled by powerful others to be changed through the students' efforts. They feel more powerless and alienated today than they did 10 years ago, and rioting may be an expression of their hostility and resentment.

Dog. One of the most pervasive laws of animal learning is that a behavior followed by a reward tends to be repeated, and a behavior followed by a punishment tends not to be repeated. This seems to imply that reward and punishment act directly on behavior, but I think this formulation is too simplistic to account for many types of human behavior.

For example, if a dog lifts its leg at the exact moment that someone throws a bone over a fence, the dog may begin to lift its leg more often than usual when it is in the same situation—whether or not anyone is heaving a bone. Adult human beings are usually not so superstitious—a person who finds a dollar bill on the sidewalk immediately after stroking his hair is not likely to stroke his hair when he returns to the same spot.

It seemed to me that, at least with human beings who have begun to form concepts, the important factors in learning were not only the strength and frequency of rewards and punishments but also whether or not the person believed his behavior produced the reward or punishment.

According to the social-learning theory that I developed several years ago with my colleagues and students, rewarding a behavior strengthens an *expectancy* that the behavior will produce future rewards.

In animals, the expectation of reward is primarily a function of the strength and frequency of rewards. In human beings, there are other things that can influence the expectation of reward—the information others give us, our knowledge generalized from a variety of

Source: Rotter, J. (1971). External control and internal control. *Psychology Today, 5* (June), pp. 37, 38, 40, 42, 58–59. Reprinted with permission from Psychology Today, copyright © 1971, www.psychologytoday.com.

experiences, and our perceptions of causality in the situation.

Consider the ancient shell game. Suppose I place a pea under one of three shells and quickly shuffle the shells around the table. A player watches my movements carefully and then, thinking that he is using his fine perceptual skills, he tells me which shell the pea is under. If his choice is correct, he will likely choose the same shell again the next time he sees me make those particular hand movements. It looks like a simple case of rewarding a response.

But suppose I ask the subject to turn his back while I shuffle the shells. This time, even if his choice is rewarded by being correct, he is not so likely to select the same shell again, because the outcome seems to be beyond his control—just a lucky guess.

Chips. In 1957, E. Jerry Phares tried to find out if these intuitive differences between chance-learning and skill-learning would hold up in the laboratory. Phares would give each subject a small gray-colored chip and ask him to select one of 10 standard chips that had exactly the same shade of gray. The standards were all different but so similar in value that discrimination among them was very difficult. Phares told half of his subjects that matching the shades required great skill and that some persons were very good at it. He told the rest that the task was so difficult that success was a matter of luck. Before the experiment began, Phares arbitrarily decided which trials would be "right" and which would be "wrong"; the schedule was the same for everyone. He found that because of the difficulty of the task all subjects accepted his statements of right and wrong without question.

Phares gave each subject a stack of poker chips and asked him to bet on his accuracy before each trial as a measure of each subject's expectancy of success.

The subjects who thought that success depended on their own skills shifted and changed frequently—their bets would rise after success and drop after failure, just as reinforcement-learning theory would predict. But subjects who thought that a correct match was a matter of luck reacted differently. In fact, many of them raised their bets after failure and lowered them after success—the "gambler's fallacy." Thus, it appeared that traditional laws of learning could not explain some types of human behavior.

Guess. Another well-established law of learning states that behavior learned by partial reinforcement takes longer to extinguish than behavior learned by constant reinforcement. In other words, when rewards cease, a behavior becomes weaker and eventually stops—but it takes longer for a behavior to die out if it was learned with intermittent rewards than if it had been rewarded every time it occurred.

William H. James and I tested this proposition. We told some subjects that an ESP guessing task was a matter of skill; we told other subjects that the same task was purely chance. We told some subjects they were correct on half their guesses. At a predetermined point we began to call all guesses incorrect. The subjects who believed they were in a skill task lowered their expectancy of success sooner than the subjects who thought that successful guesses were a matter of luck. Other subjects had been told they were correct on every trial. In this condition it was the chance subjects who lost their expectancy of success soonest.

In these early studies we gave one task to all subjects and told some that it was a skill task and others it was a chance task. To discover how subjects behaved when no such instructions were given, Douglas Crowne, Shephard Liverant and I repeated the study using two different tasks and no special instructions. We found that the "law" of partial reinforcement held true only when subjects thought their successes were the result of chance. Subjects who thought their rewards were due to skill actually took longer to extinguish their responses after constant (100 per cent) reinforcement than after partial (50 per cent) reinforcement. This is the opposite of what one would expect from the laws of animal learning. In this experiment half of the subjects guessed at hidden cards in an ESP test in which cultural expectancies led most of them to assume that success was primarily a matter of luck. The other subjects tried, by pulling a string, to raise a platform with a ball balanced on it—a task that is easily assumed to be a skill.

Actually, the experimenter could control the ball—keep it on the platform or let it fall off—so that both chance and skill subjects had the same sequence of success and failure.

Several other experiments have confirmed that, under skill conditions, constant-reward learning may take longer to extinguish than partial-reward learning. It has become increasingly clear that in chance situations other laws as well are quantitatively and qualitatively different from the laws that apply to skill learning.

I decided to study internal and external control (I-E), the beliefs that rewards come from one's own behavior or from external sources. The initial impetus to study internal-external control came both from an interest in individual differences and from an interest in explaining the way human beings learn complex social situations. There seemed to be a number of attitudes that would lead a person to feel that a reward was not contingent upon his own behavior, and we tried to build all of these attitudes into a measure of individual differences. A person might feel that luck or chance controlled what happened to him. He might feel that fate had preordained what would happen to him. He might feel that powerful others controlled what happened to him or he might feel that he simply could not predict the effects of this behavior because the world was too complex and confusing.

Scale. Phares first developed a test of internal-external control as part of his doctoral dissertation, and James enlarged and improved on Phares' scale as part of his doctoral dissertation. Later scales were constructed with the important help of several of my colleagues including Liverant, Melvin Seeman and Crowne. In 1962 I developed a final 29-item version of the I-E scale and published it in *Psychological Monographs* in 1966. This is a forced-choice scale in which the subject reads a pair of statements and then indicates with which of the two statements he more strongly agrees. The scores range from zero (the consistent belief that individuals can influence the environment— that rewards come from *internal* forces) to 23 (the belief that all rewards come from *external* forces).

A recent bibliography of studies of internal versus external control contains over 300 references. Most of these that deal with high-school or college students or adults use the 29-item scale. This test has also been translated into at least six other languages. Other successful methods of measuring I-E control have been devised and there are now four children's scales in use.

Degree. One conclusion is clear from I-E studies: people differ in the tendency to attribute satisfactions and failures to themselves rather than to external causes, and these differences are relatively stable. For the sake of convenience most investigators divide their subjects into two groups—internals and externals— depending on which half of the distribution a subject's score falls into. This is not meant to imply that there are two personality types and that everyone can be classified as one or the other, but that there is a continuum, and that persons have varying degrees of internality or externality.

Many studies have investigated the differences between internals and externals. For example, it has been found that lower-class children tend to be external; children from richer, better-educated families tend to have more belief in their own potential to determine what happens to them. The scores do not seem to be related to intelligence, but young children tend to become more internal as they get older.

Esther Battle and I examined the attitudes of black and white children in an industrialized Ohio city. The scale we used consisted of five comic-strip cartoons; the subjects told us what they thought one of the children in the cartoon would say. We found the middle-class blacks were only slightly more external in their beliefs than middle-class whites but that among children from lower socioeconomic levels blacks were significantly more external than whites. Herbert Lefcourt and Gordon Ladwig also found that among young prisoners in a Federal reformatory, blacks were more external than whites.

Ute. It does not seem to be socioeconomic level alone that produces externality, however. Theodore Graves, working with Richard and Shirley L. Jessor, found that Ute Indians were more external than a group of Spanish-Americans, even though the Indians had higher average living standards than the Spanish-Americans. Since Ute tradition puts great emphasis on fate and unpredictable external forces, Graves concluded that internality and externality resulted from cultural training. A group of white subjects in the same community were more internal than either the Indians or the Spanish-Americans.

A measure of internal-external control was used in the well-known Coleman Report on Equality of Educational Opportunity. The experimenters found that among disadvantaged children in the sixth, ninth

TABLE 1   Internal Control—External Control, A Sampler

Julian B. Rotter is the developer of a forced-choice 29-item scale for measuring an individual's degree of internal control and external control. This I-E test is widely used. The following are sample items taken from an earlier version of the test, but not, of course, in use in the final version. The reader can readily find for himself whether he is inclined toward internal control or toward external control, simply by adding up the choices he makes on each side.

I more strongly believe that:	**OR**
Promotions are earned through hard work and persistence.	Making a lot of money is largely a matter of getting the right breaks.
In my experience I have noticed that there is usually a direct connection between how hard I study and the grades I get.	Many times the reactions of teachers seem haphazard to me.
The number of divorces indicates that more and more people are not trying to make their marriages work.	Marriage is largely a gamble.
When I am right I can convince others.	It is silly to think that one can really change another person's basic attitudes.
In our society a man's future earning power is dependent upon his ability.	Getting promoted is really a matter of being a little luckier than the next guy.
If one knows how to deal with people they are really quite easily led.	I have little influence over the way other people behave.
In my case the grades I make are the results of my own efforts; luck has little or nothing to do with it.	Sometimes I feel that I have little to do with the grades I get.
People like me can change the course of world affairs if we make ourselves heard.	It is only wishful thinking to believe that one can really influence what happens in society at large.
I am the master of my fate.	A great deal that happens to me is probably a matter of chance.
Getting along with people is a skill that must be practiced.	It is almost impossible to figure out how to please some people.

and 12th grades, the students with high scores on an achievement test had more internal attitudes than did children with low achievement scores.

One might expect that internals would make active attempts to learn about their life situations. To check on this, Seeman and John Evans gave the I-E scale to patients in a tuberculosis hospital. The internal patients knew more details about their medical conditions and they questioned doctors and nurses for medical feedback more often than did the external patients. The experimenters made sure that in their study there were no differences between the internals and externals in education, occupational status or ward placement.

Rules. In another study, Seeman found that internal inmates in a reformatory learned more than external inmates did about the reformatory rules, parole laws, and the long-range economic facts that would help one get along in the outside world. These subjects did not differ from one another in intelligence—only in the degree of belief in internal or external control.

At a Negro college in Florida, Pearl Mayo Gore and I found that students who made civil-rights commitments to march on the state capitol during a vacation or to join a Freedom-Riders group were clearly and significantly more internal than the students who would only attend a rally or who were not interested at all. The willingness to be an activist seems to be related to previous experiences and the generalized expectation that one can influence his environment.

Studying a Negro church group in Georgia, Bonnie Strickland found that activists were significantly more internal than were nonactivists of similar educational and socioeconomic status.

Smoke. Phares wanted to see if internals really were more effective than externals in influencing their environments. He instructed his subjects to act as experimenters and try to change other college students' attitudes toward fraternities and sororities. Using a before-and-after questionnaire to assess these attitudes, Phares found that the internal subjects were much more successful than the external subjects in persuading students to change their minds.

It is not surprising that persons who believe that they can control their environments also believe that they can control themselves. Two studies have shown that nonsmokers are significantly more internal than smokers. After the Surgeon General's report, one study showed that male smokers who successfully quit smoking were more internal than other male smokers who believed the report but did not quit smoking. The difference was not significant with females, who apparently were motivated by other variables including, for example, one's tendency to gain weight after quitting.

Bet. Highly external persons feel that they are at the mercy of the environment, that they are being manipulated by outside forces. When they *are* manipulated, externals seem to take it in stride. Internals are not so docile. For example, Crowne and Liverant set up an experiment to see how readily their subjects would go along with a crowd. In a simple Asch-type conformity experiment in which there is one true

subject plus several stooges posing as subjects, Crowne and Liverant found that neither internals nor externals were more likely to yield to an incorrect majority judgement. But when the experimenters gave money to the subjects and allowed them to bet on their own judgments, the externals yielded to the majority much more often than did the internals. When externals did vote against the majority they weren't confident about their independence—they bet less money on being right than they did when they voted along with the crowd.

Strickland also studied the way people react to being manipulated. In a verbal-conditioning experiment, she handed each subject a series of cards. On each card were four words—two nouns, a verb and an adjective. The subject simply picked one of the words. Strickland would say "good" whenever a subject picked the verb, for example, which was intended as a subtle social reward to get the subjects to pick more verbs.

In a thorough postexperiment interview she found out which subjects had caught on to the fact that she was dispensing praise ("good") systematically. There were no important differences among subjects who said they did not notice her system. But among subjects who were aware of her attempt to manipulate them, those who actually chose the verbs more often tended to be external—the internal subjects actively resisted being conditioned.

TATs. But internals are negative only when they think they are victims of hidden manipulation. If a manipulative system is out in the open—as in a typical student-teacher relationship—internals may choose to go along readily. Gore clarified this issue in a study in which she asked subjects to tell stories about TAT cards. She told them she was trying to test her theory about which cards produce the longest stories. In one group she told each subject which card she thought was best, and in this case there was no significant difference between the stories of internals and those of externals—the stories all tended to be a little longer than those of a control group that was not given biasing instructions.

But with another group she indicated her favorite picture more subtly—when she presented it to a subject she would smile and say, "Now let's see what you do with *this* one." In this condition, the internals made up much shorter stories than did either externals or control subjects who got no special suggestions. Internals actively resist subtle pressure.

Suspicion. Some externals, who feel they are being manipulated by the outside world, may be highly suspicious of authorities. With Herbert Hamsher and Jesse Geller, I found that male subjects who believed that the Warren Commission Report was deliberately covering up a conspiracy were significantly more external than male subjects who accepted the report.

To some degree externality may be a defense against expected failure but internals also have their defenses. In investigating failure defenses, Jay Efran studied high-school students' memories for tasks they had completed or failed. He found that the tendency to forget failures was more common in internal subjects than in external ones. This suggests that external subjects have less need to repress past failures because they have already resigned themselves to the defensive position that failures are not their responsibility. Internals, however, are more likely to forget or repress their failures.

Today's activist student groups might lead one to assume that our universities are filled with internals—

people with strong belief in their ability to improve conditions and to control their own destinies. But scores on the same I-E test involving large numbers of college students in many localities show that between 1962 and 1971 there was a large increase in externality on college campuses. Today the average score on the I-E scale is about 11. In 1962 about 80 per cent of college students had more internal scores than this. The increase in externality has been somewhat less in Midwest colleges than in universities on the coasts, but there is little doubt that, overall, college students feel more powerless to change the world and control their own destinies now than they did 10 years ago.

Clearly, we need continuing study of methods to reverse this trend. Our society has so many critical problems that it desperately needs as many active, participating internal-minded members as possible. If feelings of external control, alienation and powerlessness continue to grow, we may be heading for a society of dropouts—each person sitting back, watching the world go by.

—————————————— Questions to Think About ——————————————

1. What are the various factors that determine whether someone has an internal or external locus of control?

2. Do you think personality differences about issues of control have an effect on social activism and other social movements?

3. To what extent can a person's locus of control be modified by training or experience?

4. In most of the experiments reported here, participants were classified as internal versus external based on a simple median split (where those above the median for the group became the externals and those below the median the internals). Assuming a normally distributed population, most of the participants would have clustered near the median. How might the findings have been different if the comparison had been between highly external (top quartile) and highly internal (bottom quartile) participants?

5. How might the concept of internal versus external locus of control be applied to improve outcomes for self-help groups, drug treatment programs, and the like?

27

Social Foundations of Thought and Action: A Social Cognitive Theory

ALBERT BANDURA

Albert Bandura (1925–) is a social cognitive personality theorist whose work focuses on observational learning processes, including how we interpret what we see. The individual is affected not only by external processes of reinforcement, but also by expectations, anticipated reinforcement, thoughts, plans, and goals. Behavior, cognition, and the environment all affect one another.

Trained in learning theory at the University of Iowa, Bandura first made his mark trying to understand aggression. A psychology professor at Stanford University, Bandura's approach to personality is especially distinctive because it not only accepts the importance of social learning, but also emphasizes that people think about their prospective (future) actions, setting goals and plans for themselves. As this selection illustrates, he widened the learning theory perspective to allow cognitive factors.

In the social cognitive view people are neither driven by inner forces nor automatically shaped and controlled by external stimuli. Rather, human functioning is explained in terms of a model of triadic reciprocality in which behavior, cognitive and other personal factors, and environmental events all operate as interacting determinants of each other. The nature of persons is defined within this perspective in terms of a number of basic capabilities. These are discussed briefly below. . . .

SYMBOLIZING CAPABILITY

The remarkable capacity to use symbols, which touches virtually every aspect of people's lives, provides them with a powerful means of altering and adapting to their environment. Through symbols people process and transform transient experiences into internal models that serve as guides for future action. Through symbols they similarly give meaning, form, and continuance to the experiences they have lived through.

By drawing on their knowledge and symbolizing powers, people can generate innovative courses of action. Rather than solving problems solely by enacting options and suffering the costs of missteps, people usually test possible solutions symbolically and discard or retain them on the basis of estimated outcomes before plunging into action. An advanced cognitive capability coupled with the remarkable flexibility of symbolization enables people to create ideas that transcend their sensory experiences. Through the medium of symbols, they can communicate with others at almost any distance in time and space. Other distinctive human characteristics to be discussed shortly are similarly founded on symbolic capability.

Source: Bandura, A. (1986). *Social foundations of thought and action: A social cognitive theory.* Englewood Cliffs, NJ: Prentice-Hall. Reprinted by permission of Pearson Education, Inc., Upper Saddle River, NJ. (Selection is pp. 18–22.)

To say that people base many of their actions on thought does not necessarily mean they are always objectively rational. Rationality depends on reasoning skills which are not always well developed or used effectively. Even if people know how to reason logically, they make faulty judgments when they base their inferences on inadequate information or fail to consider the full consequences of different choices. Moreover, they often missample and misread events in ways that give rise to erroneous conceptions about themselves and the world around them. When they act on their misconceptions, which appear subjectively rational, given their errant basis, such persons are viewed by others as behaving in an unreasoning, if not downright foolish, manner. Thought can thus be a source of human failing and distress as well as human accomplishment.

FORETHOUGHT CAPABILITY

People do not simply react to their immediate environment, nor are they steered by implants from their past. Most of their behavior, being purposive, is regulated by forethought. The future time perspective manifests itself in many ways. People anticipate the likely consequences of their prospective actions, they set goals for themselves, and they otherwise plan courses of action for cognized futures, for many of which established ways are not only ineffective but may also be detrimental. Through exercise of forethought, people motivate themselves and guide their actions anticipatorily. By reducing the impact of immediate influences, forethought can support foresightful behavior, even when the present conditions are not especially conducive to it.

The capability for intentional and pursive action is rooted in symbolic activity. Future events cannot serve as determinants of behavior, but their cognitive representation can have a strong causal impact on present action. Images of desirable future events tend to foster the behavior most likely to bring about their realization. By representing foreseeable outcomes symbolically, people can convert future consequences into current motivators and regulators of foresightful behavior. Forethought is translated into action through the aid of self-regulating mechanisms.

In analyses of telic or purposive mechanisms through goals and outcomes projected forward in time, the future acquires causal efficacy by being represented cognitively in the present. Cognized futures thus become temporally antecedent to actions. Some writers have misinterpreted the acknowledgment that experience influences thought to mean that thoughts are nothing more than etchings of environmental inputs in the host organism (Rychlak, 1979). When thought is miscast as mechanical mediationism, it is imprinted histories, rather than cognized futures, that impel and direct behavior. This is clearly not the view of cognition and personal agency to which social cognitive theory subscribes. Forethought is the product of generative and reflective ideation.

VICARIOUS CAPABILITY

Psychological theories have traditionally assumed that learning can occur only by performing responses and experiencing their effects. Learning through action has thus been given major, if not exclusive, priority. In actuality, virtually all learning phenomena, resulting from direct experience, can occur vicariously by observing other people's behavior and its consequences for them. The capacity to learn by observation enables people to acquire rules for generating and regulating behavioral patterns without having to form them gradually by tedious trial and error.

The abbreviation of the acquisition process through observational learning is vital for both development and survival. Because mistakes can produce costly, or even fatal consequences, the prospects for survival would be slim indeed if one could learn only from the consequences of trial and error. For this reason, one does not teach children to swim, adolescents to drive automobiles, and novice medical students to perform surgery by having them discover the requisite behavior from the consequences of their successes and failures. The more costly and hazardous the possible mistakes, the heavier must be the reliance on observational learning from competent exemplars. The less the behavior patterns draw on inborn properties, the greater is the dependence on observational learning for the functional organization of behavior.

Humans come with few inborn patterns. This remarkable plasticity places high demand on learning. People must develop their basic capabilities over an extended period, and they must continue to master new competencies to fulfill changing demands throughout their life span. It therefore comes as no surprise that humans have evolved an advanced vicarious learning capability. Apart from the question of survival, it is difficult to imagine a social transmission system in which the language, life styles, and institutional practices of the culture are taught to each new member just by selective reinforcement of fortuitous behaviors, without the benefit of models to exemplify these cultural patterns.

Some complex skills can be mastered only through the aid of modeling. If children had no exposure to the utterances of models, it would be virtually impossible to teach them the linguistic skills that constitute a language. It is doubtful that one could ever shape intricate words, let alone grammatical rules, by selective reward of random vocalization. In other behavior patterns that are formed by unique combinations of elements selected from numerous possibilities, there is little, if any, chance of producing the novel patterns spontaneously, or something even resembling them. Where novel forms of behavior can be conveyed effectively only by social cues, modeling is an indispensable aspect of learning. Even when it is possible to establish new patterns of behavior through other means, the acquisition process can be considerably shortened through modeling.

Most psychological theories were cast long before the advent of enormous advances in the technology of communication. As a result, they give insufficient attention to the increasingly powerful role that the symbolic environment plays in present-day human lives. Indeed, in many aspects of living, televised vicarious influence has dethroned the primacy of direct experience. Whether it be thought patterns, values, attitudes, or styles of behavior, life increasingly models the media.

SELF-REGULATORY CAPABILITY

Another distinctive feature of social cognitive theory is the central role it assigns to self-regulatory functions.

People do not behave just to suit the preferences of others. Much of their behavior is motivated and regulated by internal standards and self-evaluative reactions to their own actions. After personal standards have been adopted, discrepancies between a performance and the standard against which it is measured activate evaluative self-reactions, which serve to influence subsequent behavior. An act, therefore, includes among its determinants self-produced influences.

Self-directedness is exercised by wielding influence over the external environment as well as enlisting self-regulatory functions. Thus, by arranging facilitative environmental conditions, recruiting cognitive guides, and creating incentives for their own efforts, people make causal contribution to their own motivation and actions. To be sure, self-regulatory functions are fashioned from, and occasionally supported by, external influences. Having some external origins and supports, however, does not refute the fact that the exercise of self-influence partly determines the course of one's behavior.

SELF-REFLECTIVE CAPABILITY

If there is any characteristic that is distinctively human, it is the capability for reflective self-consciousness. This enables people to analyze their experiences and to think about their own thought processes. By reflecting on their varied experiences and on what they know, they can derive generic knowledge about themselves and the world around them. People not only gain understanding through reflection, they evaluate and alter their own thinking. In verifying thought through self-reflective means, they monitor their ideas, act on them or predict occurrences from them, judge the adequacy of their thoughts from the results, and change them accordingly. While such metacognitive activities usually foster veridical thought (Flavell, 1978a), they can also produce faulty thought patterns through reciprocal causation. Forceful actions arising from erroneous beliefs often create social effects that confirm the misbeliefs (Snyder, 1980).

Among the types of thoughts that affect action, none is more central or pervasive than people's judgments of their capabilities to deal effectively with different realities. It is partly on the basis of self-percepts of efficacy that they choose what to do, how much effort to invest in activities, how long to persevere in the face of disappointing results, and whether tasks are approached anxiously or self-assuredly (Bandura, 1982a). In the self-appraisal of efficacy, there are many sources of information that must be processed and weighed through self-referent thought. Acting on one's self-percepts of efficacy brings successes or missteps requiring further self-reappraisals of operative competencies. The self-knowledge which underlies the exercise of many facets of personal agency is largely the product of such reflective self-appraisal.

Self-reflectivity entails shifting the perspective of the same agent, rather than reifying different internal agents or selves regulating each other. Thus, in their daily transactions, people act on their thoughts and later analyze how well their thoughts have served them in managing events. But it is the one and the same person who is doing the thinking and then later evaluating the adequacy of his or her knowledge, thinking skills, and action strategies. The shift in perspective does not transform one from an agent to an object. One is just as much an agent reflecting on one's experiences as in executing the original courses of action. The same self performing multiple functions does not require positing multiple selves pursuing different roles.

THE NATURE OF HUMAN NATURE

Seen from the social cognitive perspective, human nature is characterized by a vast potentiality that can be fashioned by direct and observational experience into a variety of forms within biological limits. To say that a major distinguishing mark of humans is their endowed plasticity is not to say that they have no nature or that they come structureless (Midgley, 1978). The plasticity, which is intrinsic to the nature of humans, depends upon neurophysiological mechanisms and structures that have evolved over time. These advanced neural systems for processing, retaining, and using coded information provide the capacity for the very characteristics that are distinctly human—generative symbolization, forethought, evaluative self-regulation, reflective self-consciousness, and symbolic communication.

Plasticity does not mean that behavior is entirely the product of post-natal experience. Some innately organized patterns of behavior are present at birth; others appear after a period of maturation. One does not have to teach infants to cry or suck, toddlers to walk, or adolescents how to copulate. Nor does one have to teach somatic motivators arising from tissue deficits and aversive events or to create somatically-based rewards. Infants come equipped with some attentional selectivity and interpretive predilections, as well (von Cranach, Foppa, Lepenies, & Ploog, 1979). This neural programming for basic physiological functions is the product of accumulated ancestral experiences that are stored in the genetic code.

Most patterns of human behavior are organized by individual experience and retained in neural codes, rather than being provided ready-made by inborn programming. While human thought and conduct may be fashioned largely through experience, innately determined factors enter into every form of behavior to some degree. Genetic factors affect behavioral potentialities. Both experiential and physiological factors interact, often in intricate ways, to determine behavior. Even in behavioral patterns that are formed almost entirely through experience, rudimentary elements are present as part of the natural endowment. For example, humans are endowed with basic phonetic elements which may appear trivial compared to complex acquired patterns of speech, but the elements are, nevertheless, essential. Similarly, even action patterns regarded as instinctual, because they draw heavily on inborn elements, require appropriate experience to be developed. The level of psychological and physiological development, of course, limits what can be acquired at any given time. Because behavior contains mixtures of inborn elements and learned patterns, dichotomous thinking, which separates activities neatly into innate and acquired categories, is seriously inaccurate.

REFERENCES

Bandura, A. (1982). Self-efficacy mechanism in human agency. *American Psychologist, 37,* 747–755.

Flavell, J. H. (1978). Metacognitive development. In J. M. Scandura & C. J. Brainerd (Eds.), *Structural-process theories of complex human behavior* (pp. 213–245). Alphen a.d. Rijn, Netherlands: Sijithoff and Noordhoff.

Midgley, M. (1978). *Beast and man: The roots of human nature.* Ithaca, NY: Cornell University Press.

Rychlak, J. F. (1979). A nontelic teleology? *American Psychologist, 34,* 435–438.

Snyder, M. (1980). Seek, and ye shall find: Testing hypotheses about other people. In E. T. Higgins, C. P. Herman, & M. P. Zanna (Eds.), *Social cognition: The*

Ontario symposium on personality and social psychology (Vol. 1, pp. 105–130). Hillsdale, NJ: Erlbaum.

von Cranach, M., Foppa, K., Lepenies, W., & Ploog, D. (Eds.). (1979). *Human ethology: Claims and limits of a new discipline.* Cambridge, UK: Cambridge University Press.

Questions to Think About

1. Bandura cites the capacity to use symbols as a key element of the social cognitive approach. Why are symbols so important?

2. Bandura is well-known for his emphasis on vicarious learning—the ability to learn through observation. How is this different from more traditional learning approaches?

3. Bandura's theory is full of complex notions like self-regulation, self-efficacy, and planning. Can these concepts be assessed and applied in a clear and meaningful way?

4. Bandura claims that most human behavior is purposive, regulated by forethought. Can this perspective be reconciled with a behaviorist view that claims that all behavior is governed by its reinforcement contingencies?

5. In Bandura's view, people have a self-reflective capability that allows them to derive generic knowledge about themselves and the world around them through analyzing their experiences and thinking about their own thought processes. This claim presupposes that people have substantial introspective access to their own thought processes, and that all the relevant material can be brought into their conscious awareness. Are these reasonable assumptions? Why or why not?

28

Exercise of Human Agency
through Collective Efficacy

ALBERT BANDURA

Albert Bandura (who also authored selection 27 of this reader) is probably best known for his early work on observational learning and aggression. In recent years, he has focused much of his effort on exploring the concept of efficacy. For many years, he worked on self-efficacy—an expectancy or belief about how competently one will be able to enact a behavior in a particular situation—looking at both the processes by which self-efficacy develops and the effects of self-efficacy on various aspects of performance. In the selection below, the concept of self-efficacy is broadened to apply to efficacy as a characteristic of a group rather than of a single individual. In many ways, this represents a return to Bandura's core interest in the social nature of humankind.

People are partly the products of their environments, but by selecting, creating, and transforming their environmental circumstances they are producers of environments as well. This agentic capability enables them to influence the course of events and to take a hand in shaping their lives. A substantial body of literature based on diverse lines of research in varied spheres of functioning shows that, indeed, people motivate and guide their actions partly by their beliefs of personal efficacy (Bandura, 1997).

Perceived efficacy plays a key role in human functioning because it affects behavior not only directly, but by its impact on other determinants such as goals and aspirations, outcome expectations, affective proclivities, and perception of impediments and opportunities in the social environment. Efficacy beliefs influence whether people think erratically or strategically, optimistically or pessimistically; what courses of action they choose to pursue; the goals they set for themselves and their commitment to them; how much effort they put forth in given endeavors; the outcomes they expect their efforts to produce; how long they persevere in the face of obstacles; their resilience to adversity; how much stress and depression they experience in coping with taxing environmental demands; and the accomplishments they realize. Statistical analyses that combine the findings of numerous studies confirm the influential role of perceived self-efficacy in human adaptation and change.

FORMS OF HUMAN AGENCY

Conceptions of human agency have been essentially confined to personal agency exercised individually. But this is not the only form of agency through which people manage events that affect their lives. Social-cognitive theory distinguishes among three different forms of agency—*personal, proxy,* and *collective.*

The theorizing and research on human agency has centered almost exclusively on the direct exercise of personal agency and the cognitive, motivational,

Source: Bandura, A. (2000). Exercise of human agency through collective efficacy. *Current Directions in Psychological Science, 9*(3), 75–78. Reprinted with permission.

Editor's note: All citations in the text of this selection have been left intact from the original, but the list of references includes only those sources that are the most relevant and important. Readers wishing to follow any of the other citations can find the full references in the original work or in an online database.

affective, and choice processes through which it exerts its effects. In many activities, however, people do not have direct control over social conditions and institutional practices that affect their lives. Under these circumstances, they seek their well-being and security through the exercise of proxy agency. In this socially mediated mode of agency, people try to get other people who have expertise or wield influence and power to act on their behalf to get the outcomes they desire. People also turn to proxy control because they do not want to saddle themselves with the arduous work needed to develop requisite competencies, and to shoulder the responsibilities and stressors that the exercise of control entails. These dissuading conditions dull the appetite for personal control.

People do not live their lives in individual autonomy. Indeed, many of the outcomes they seek are achievable only through interdependent efforts. Hence, they have to work together to secure what they cannot accomplish on their own. Social cognitive theory extends the conception of human agency to collective agency. People's shared beliefs in their collective power to produce desired results are a key ingredient of collective agency. A group's attainments are the product not only of shared knowledge and skills of its different members, but also of the interactive, coordinative, and synergistic dynamics of their transactions. For example, it is not uncommon for groups with members who are talented individually to perform poorly collectively because the members cannot work well together as a unit. Therefore, perceived collective efficacy is not simply the sum of the efficacy beliefs of individual members. Rather, it is an emergent group-level property.

The locus of perceived collective efficacy resides in the minds of group members. A group, of course, operates through the behavior of its members. It is people acting coordinatively on a shared belief, not a disembodied group mind that is doing the cognizing, aspiring, motivating, and regulating. There is no emergent entity that operates independently of the beliefs and actions of the individuals who make up a social system. Although beliefs of collective efficacy include emergent aspects, they serve functions similar to those of personal efficacy beliefs and operate through similar processes (Bandura, 1997). People's shared beliefs in

their collective efficacy influence the types of futures they seek to achieve through collective action, how well they use their resources, how much effort they put into their group endeavor, their staying power when collective efforts fail to produce quick results or meet forcible opposition, and their vulnerability to the discouragement that can beset people taking on tough social problems.

MEASURING COLLECTIVE EFFICACY

There are two main approaches to the measurement of a group's perceived efficacy. The first method aggregates the individual members' appraisals of their personal capabilities to execute the particular functions they perform in the group. The second method aggregates members' appraisals of their group's capability operating as a whole. The latter holistic appraisal encompasses the coordinative and interactive aspects operating within groups.

One could also measure perceived collective efficacy by having group members arrive at a concordant judgment. The deliberative approach has serious limitations, however. Forming a consensual judgment of a group's efficacy via group discussion is subject to the distorting vagaries of social persuasion by individuals who command power and by pressures for conformity. Assessment by constructed consensus may itself change the efficacy beliefs. Moreover, a social system is not a monolith. A forced consensus masks the variability in efficacy beliefs among factions within a system.

The two informative indices of perceived collective efficacy differ in the relative weight given to individual factors and interactive ones, but they are not as distinct as they might appear. Being socially situated, and often interdependently so, individuals' judgments of their personal efficacy are not detached from the other members' enabling or impeding activities. For example, in judging personal efficacy, a football quarterback obviously considers the quality of his offensive line, the fleetness and blocking capabilities of his running backs, the adeptness of his receivers, and how well they all work together as a unit. In short, a judgment of individual efficacy inevitably embodies the coordinative and interactive group dynamics. Conversely, in judging the efficacy of their team, members certainly consider how well key teammates can execute their roles. Players on the Chicago basketball team would judge their team efficacy quite differently depending on whether or not Michael Jordan was in the lineup.

Given the interdependent nature of the appraisal process, linking efficacy measured at the individual level to performance at the group level does not necessarily represent a cross-level relation. The two indices of collective efficacy are at least moderately correlated and predictive of group performance. The fact that appraisals of group efficacy embody members' dependence on one another has important bearing on gauging emergent properties. It is commonly assumed that an emergent property is operative if differences between groups remain after statistical methods are used to control variation in characteristics of individuals within the groups. The analytic logic is fine, but the results of such statistical controls can be quite misleading. Because judgments of personal efficacy take into consideration the unique dynamics of a group, individual-level controls can inadvertently remove most of the emergent group properties.

The relative predictiveness of the two indices of collective efficacy will depend largely on the degree of interdependent effort needed to achieve desired results. For example, the accomplishments of a gymnastics team are the sum of successes achieved independently by the gymnasts, whereas the accomplishments of a soccer team are the product of players working intricately together. Any weak link, or a breakdown in a subsystem, can have ruinous effects on a soccer team despite an otherwise high level of talent. The aggregated holistic index is most suitable for performance outcomes achievable only by adept teamwork. Under low system interdependence, members may inspire, motivate, and support each other, but the group outcome is the sum of the attainments produced individually rather than by the members working together. Aggregated personal efficacies are well suited to measure perceived efficacy for the latter types of endeavors.

CONTENTIOUS DUALISMS

Conceptualizations of group functioning are replete with contentious dualisms that social cognitive theory

rejects. They include personal agency versus social structure, self-centered agency versus communality, and individualism versus collectivism. The agency-sociostructural duality pits psychological theories and sociostructural theories as rival conceptions of human behavior or as representing different levels and temporal proximity of influences. In the social cognitive theory of triadic reciprocal causation (Bandura, 1986, 1997), personal agency and social structure operate interdependently. Social structures are created by human activity, and sociostructural practices, in turn, impose constraints and provide resources and opportunities for personal development and functioning.

A full understanding of human adaptation and change requires an integrative causal structure in which sociostructural influences operate through mechanisms of the self system to produce behavioral effects. However, in agentic transactions, the self system is not merely a conduit for external influences. The self is socially constituted but, by exercising self-influence, human agency operates generatively and proactively on social systems, not just reactively.

Nor can sociostructural and psychological determinants be dichotomized neatly into remote and proximate ones. For example, poverty is not a matter of multilayered or remote causation. Lacking the money needed to provide for the subsistence of one's family pervades everyday life in an immediate way. Analyses of paths of influence involving educational, familial, occupational, and political spheres of functioning lend support for a multicausal model that integrates sociostructural and personal determinants. Economic conditions, socioeconomic status, and family structure affect behavior through their impact on people's sense of efficacy, aspirations, and affective self-regulatory factors rather than directly.

Another disputable duality pits self-efficacy, misconstrued as a self-centered individualism and selfishness, against communal attachments and civic responsibility. A sense of efficacy does not necessarily spawn an individualistic lifestyle, identity, or morality. If belief in the power to produce results is put to social purposes, it fosters a communal life rather than eroding it. Indeed, developmental studies show that a high sense of efficacy promotes a prosocial orientation characterized by cooperativeness, helpfulness, and sharing.

Another variant of dualism inappropriately equates self-efficacy with individualism and pits it against collectivism at a cultural level. In fact, high perceived efficacy is vital for successful functioning regardless of whether it is achieved individually or by group members working together. A collective system with members plagued by self-doubts about their capabilities to perform their roles will achieve little. A strong sense of personal efficacy to manage one's life circumstances and to have a hand in effecting societal changes contributes substantially to perceived collective efficacy (Fernández-Ballesteros, Díez-Nicolás, Caprara, Barbaranelli, & Bandura, 1999).

Cross-cultural research attests to the general functional value of efficacy beliefs. Perceived personal efficacy contributes to productive functioning by members of collectivistic cultures just as it contributes to functioning by people raised in individualistic cultures (Earley, 1994). But culture shapes how efficacy beliefs are developed, the purposes to which they are put, and the sociostructural arrangement under which they are best expressed.

Cultures are not monolithic, static entities as stereotypic portrayals indicate. Both individualistic and collectivistic sociocultural systems come in a variety of forms. Moreover, there is substantial heterogeneity in communality among individuals in different cultural systems, and even greater intraindividual variation across different types of social relationships.

IMPACT OF PERCEIVED COLLECTIVE EFFICACY ON GROUP FUNCTIONING

A growing body of research attests to the impact of perceived collective efficacy on group functioning. Some of these studies have assessed the motivational and behavioral effects of perceived collective efficacy using experimental manipulations to instill differential levels of perceived efficacy (Durham, Knight, & Locke, 1997; Earley, 1994; Hodges & Carron, 1992; Prussia & Kinicki, 1996). Other investigations have examined the effects of naturally developed beliefs of collective efficacy. The latter studies have analyzed diverse social systems, including educational systems (Bandura, 1997), business organizations (Earley, 1994; Hodges & Carron, 1992; Little & Madigan, 1994), ath-

letic teams (Carron, 1984; Feltz & Lirgg, 1998; Mullen & Cooper, 1994; Spink, 1990), combat teams (Jex & Bliese, 1999; Lindsley, Mathieu, Heffner, & Brass, 1994), and urban neighborhoods (Sampson, Raudenbush, & Earls, 1997). The findings taken as a whole show that the higher the perceived collective efficacy, the higher the groups' motivational investment in their undertakings, the stronger their staying power in the face of impediments and setbacks, and the greater their performance accomplishments.

The conjoint influence of perceived collective political efficacy and trust in the governmental system predicts the form and level of people's political activity (Bandura, 1997). People who believe they can achieve desired changes through their collective voice, and who view their governmental systems as trustworthy, are active participants in conventional political activities. Those who believe they can accomplish social changes by perseverant collective action, but view the governing systems and officeholders as untrustworthy, favor more confrontive and coercive tactics outside the traditional political channels. The politically apathetic have little faith that they can influence governmental functioning through collective initiatives, and are disaffected from the political system, believing it ignores their interests.

CONCLUDING REMARKS

Significant progress has been made in understanding the nature, structure, and functions of perceived collective efficacy. However, much work remains to be done in evaluating the different ways of gauging collective efficacy, refining analytic procedures for identifying emergent properties arising from the social dynamics of whole systems, and developing socially oriented strategies for enhancing collective efficacy to improve the quality of life and shape the social future.

The revolutionary advances in electronic technologies and economic globalization have transformed the nature, reach, and loci of human influence, and the way people live their lives. These new social realities vastly expand opportunities and create new constraints, often by social forces that know no national borders. People's success in shaping their social and economic lives lies partly in a shared sense of efficacy to bring their collective influence to bear on matters over which they can have some command. With growing international embeddedness and interdependence of societies, the scope of cross-cultural research must be broadened to elucidate how global forces from abroad interact with national ones to shape the nature of cultural life. As globalization reaches ever deeper into people's lives, a resilient sense of shared efficacy becomes critical to furthering their common interests.

REFERENCES

Bandura, A. (1986). *Social foundations of thought and action: A social cognitive theory.* Englewood Cliffs, NJ: Prentice-Hall.

Bandura, A. (1997). *Self-efficacy: The exercise of control.* New York: Freeman.

Hodges, L., & Carron, A. V. (1992). Collective efficacy and group performance. *International Journal of Sport Psychology, 23,* 48–59.

Jex, S. M., & Bliese, P. D. (1999). Efficacy beliefs as a moderator of the impact of work-related stressors: A multilevel study. *Journal of Applied Psychology, 84,* 349–361.

Mullen, B., & Cooper, C. (1994). The relation between group cohesiveness and performance: An integration. *Psychological Bulletin, 115,* 210–227,

Prussia, G. E., & Kinicki, A. J. (1996). A motivational investigation of group effectiveness using social cognitive theory. *Journal of Applied Psychology, 81,* 187–198.

Sampson, R. J., Raudenbush, S. W., & Earls, F. (1997). Neighborhood, and violent crime: A multilevel study of collective efficacy. *Science, 277,* 918–924.

Questions to Think About

1. What is the relationship between the perceived collective efficacy of a group and the personal efficacy of the members of that group?

2. Given Bandura's view of collective efficacy, is the relationship between the efficacy of the whole (the collective efficacy), and the efficacy of parts (the self-efficacy of the individuals in the group) described by a mathematical rule, such as the average, the minimum, or the maximum?

3. What is the impact of high collective efficacy on the performance of a group, and how does that impact differ from the impact of an individual's self-efficacy on his or her performance?

4. In terms of their collective efficacy, how might a group that has been assigned to work together (for example, a team that has been assembled by the instructor for a group project in a course) differ from a group that has voluntarily formed (for example, a team where individuals have chosen to work together on a group project in a course)?

5. The concept of self-esteem is often contrasted with the concept of self-efficacy (at the level of an individual person). What might be the group-level analogue to self-esteem?

29

Catastrophizing and Untimely Death

CHRISTOPHER PETERSON, MARTIN E. P. SELIGMAN, KAREN H. YURKO,
LESLIE R. MARTIN, AND HOWARD S. FRIEDMAN

Christopher Peterson (1950–) is a psychology professor at the University of Michigan. With his colleague Karen H. Yurko, and with Martin E. P. Seligman, a professor at the University of Pennsylvania, Peterson has conducted research on optimism and learned helplessness and their long-term effects. For this study, they joined forces with Leslie R. Martin, a professor at La Sierra University, and Howard S. Friedman, a professor at the University of California, Riverside. Friedman and his team have been studying how personality relates to mortality risk.

The paper that follows illustrates how the social–cognitive approach to personality psychology can be applied to health psychology. The researchers scored people's explanatory style from answers they had given about bad events in 1936 and 1940. These characteristics were used to predict their likelihood of dying each year through 1991.

Explanatory style is a cognitive personality variable that reflects how people habitually explain the causes of bad events (Peterson & Seligman, 1984). Among the dimensions of explanatory style are

- internality ("it's me") versus externality
- stability ("it's going to last forever") versus instability
- globality ("it's going to undermine everything") versus specificity

These dimensions capture tendencies toward self-blame, fatalism, and catastrophizing, respectively. Explanatory style was introduced in the attributional reformulation of helplessness theory to explain individual differences in response to bad events (Abramson, Seligman, & Teasdale, 1978). Individuals who entertain internal, stable, and global explanations for bad events show emotional, motivational, and cognitive disturbances in their wake.

Explanatory style has been examined mainly with regard to depression, and all three dimensions are consistent correlates of depressive symptoms (Sweeney, Anderson, & Bailey, 1986). More recent studies have looked at other outcomes (notably, physical well-being), and researchers have also begun to examine the dimensions separately. Stability and globality—but not internality—predict poor health (Peterson & Bossio, 1991). This is an intriguing finding, but questions remain.

First, do these correlations mean that explanatory styles are risk factors for early death? Previous studies are equivocal either because of small samples or because research participants were already seriously ill.

Second, is the link between explanatory style and health the same or different for males versus females? Again, previous studies are equivocal because they often included only male or only female research participants.

Source: Peterson, C., Seligman, M. E. P., Yurko, K. H., Martin, L. R., & Friedman, H. S. (1998). Catastrophizing and untimely death. *Psychological Science, 9,* 127–130. Reprinted by permission.

Editor's note: All citations in the text of this selection have been left intact from the original, but the list of references includes only those sources that are the most relevant and important. Readers wishing to follow any of the other citations can find the full references in the original work or in an online database.

Third, what mediates the link between ways of explaining bad events and poor health? The path is probably overdetermined, but one can ask if fatalism and catastrophizing predict differentially to particular illnesses. These explanatory styles, as cognates of hopelessness, may place one at special risk for cancer, implying an immunological pathway (Eysenck, 1988). Alternatively, these explanatory tendencies, because of their link with stress, may place one at special risk for heart disease, suggesting a cardiovascular pathway (Dykema, Bergbower, & Peterson, 1995). Or perhaps fatalism and catastrophizing predispose one to accidents and injuries and thus point to an incautious lifestyle as a mediator. Once again, previous studies are equivocal either because illness was deliberately operationalized in nonspecific terms or because only one type of illness was studied.

We attempted to answer these questions by investigating explanatory style and mortality among participants in the Terman Life-Cycle Study (Terman & Oden, 1947). The original sample of more than 1,500 preadolescents has been followed from the 1920s to the present, with attrition (except by death) of less than 10% (Friedman et al., 1995). For most of those who have died (about 50% of males and 35% of females as of 1991), year of death and cause of death are known. In 1936 and 1940, the participants completed open-ended questionnaires about difficult life events, which we content-analyzed for explanatory style. We determined the associations between dimensions of explanatory style on the one hand and time of death and cause of death on the other.

METHOD

Sample

The Terman Life-Cycle Study began in 1921–1922, when most of the 1,528 participants were in public school. Terman's original objective was to obtain a reasonably representative sample of bright California children (IQs of 135 or greater) and to examine their lives. Almost every public school in the San Francisco and Los Angeles areas was searched for intelligent children. The average birth date for children in the sample was 1910 (SD = 4 years). Most of the children were preadolescents when first studied; those still living are now in their 80s. Data were collected prospectively, without any knowledge of eventual health or longevity.

In young adulthood, the participants were generally healthy and successful. In middle age, they were productive citizens, but none was identifiable as a genius. The sample is homogeneous on dimensions of intelligence (above average), race (mostly white), and social class (little poverty).

Content Analysis of Causal Explanations

We scored explanatory style of the responses to the 1936 and 1940 questionnaires using the CAVE (content analysis of verbatim explanations) technique (Peterson, Schulman, Castellon, & Seligman, 1992). A single researcher read through all responses in which bad events were described. Examples of questions that elicited such responses include

> (from 1936): Have any disappointments, failures, bereavements, uncongenial relationships with others, etc., exerted a prolonged influence upon you?

> (from 1940): What do you regard as your most serious fault of personality or character?

When a bad event was accompanied by a causal explanation, the event and the attribution were written down. These events, each with its accompanying attribution, were then presented in a nonsystematic order to eight judges who blindly and independently rated each explanation on a 7-point scale according to its stability, its globality, and its internality. The researchers (supervised by Peterson) who identified and rated attributions were independent of the researchers (supervised by Friedman) who collected and coded mortality information (see the next section).

A total of 3,394 attributions was obtained from 1,182 different individuals, an average of 2.87 attributions per person, with a range of 1 to 13. Each of these attributions was rated by each of the eight judges along the three attributional dimensions. We estimated coding reliability by treating the judges as "items" and calculating Cronbach's (1951) alpha for each dimension; alphas were satisfactory: .82, .73, and .94, for stability, globality, and internality, respectively. Ratings were averaged across raters and across different attributions for the same participant. These scores were intercorrelated (mean $r = .52$), as previous research has typically found (Peterson et al., 1982). The means (and standard deviations) were 4.52 (0.86) for stability, 4.46 (0.64) for globality, and 4.49 (1.29) for internality.

Cause of Death

Death certificates for deceased participants were obtained from the relevant state bureaus and coded for underlying cause of death by a physician-supervised certified nosologist using the criteria of the ninth edition of the International Classification of Diseases (U.S. Department of Health and Human Services, 1980) to distinguish among deaths by cancer, cardiovascular disease, accidents or violence, and other causes. For approximately 20% of the deceased, death certificates were unavailable; whenever possible, cause of death was assigned from information provided by next of kin. Among the 1,182 participants for whom explanatory style scores were available, mortality information was known for 1,179. The numbers of deaths as of 1991 were 148 from cancer (85 men, 63 women), 159 from cardiovascular disease (109 men, 50 women), 57 from accidents or violence (40 men, 17 women), 87 from other (known) causes (50 men, 37

women), and 38 from unknown causes (24 men, 14 women).

RESULTS

Explanatory Styles and Mortality

To investigate the association between explanatory styles and mortality (through 1991), we used Cox Proportional Hazards regressions and checked them with logistic regressions. The Cox approach is nonparametric and assumes that the ratio of hazard functions for individuals with differing values of the covariates (stability, globality, and internality) is invariant over time. We used Tuma's (1980) RATE program for the Cox models, and LOGIST of SAS for the logistic regressions. When all three attributional dimensions were examined simultaneously for the entire sample, only globality was associated with mortality, with a risk hazard (rh) of 1.26 ($p < .01$). Results from the logistic regression analyses (predicting to a dichotomous variable of survival to at least age 65 vs. not) were consistent with this finding; only the odds ratio associated with globality was significant ($rh = 1.25, p < .05$).

Figure 1 depicts the probability of a 20-year-old in this sample dying by a given age as a function of

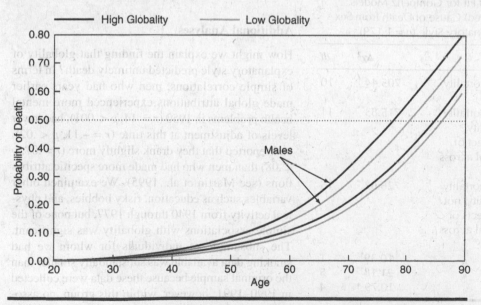

FIGURE 1   Probability of a 20-year-old dying by a given age as a function of sex and globality (upper vs. lower quartiles).

sex and globality (top vs. bottom quartiles of scores). The point at which each curve crosses the .50 probability line represents the "average" age of death of individuals in the group. As can be seen, males with a global explanatory style were at the highest risk for early death.

To test whether the effects of globality were due to individuals being seriously ill or suicidal at the time of assessment, we conducted additional survival analyses that excluded individuals who died before 1945. The effects of globality remained for males.

Globality of Explanatory Style and Cause of Death

Next we investigated whether globality was differentially related to causes of death (cancer, cardiovascular disease, accidents or violence, other, and unknown) by comparing Gompertz models (see Table 1). When comparing a model with both sex and globality as predictors but constraining the effects of globality to predict equally across all causes of death (Model 2) with an unconstrained model in

which globality was allowed to predict differentially to separate causes of death (Model 3), we found that the unconstrained model fit the data better than did the constrained model. This finding was also obtained when participants who did not survive until at least 1945 were excluded, $\Delta\chi^2(4, N = 1, 157) = 13.29, p < .01$.

Globality best predicted deaths by accident or violence ($rh = 1.98, p < .01$) and deaths from unknown causes ($rh = 2.08, p < .01$). The risk ratios associated with other causes were 1.03 for cardiovascular disease (n.s.), 1.18 for cancer (n.s.), and 1.22 for other (known) causes (n.s.).

Finally, we computed a Cox model for prediction from globality specifically to suicide (which had been included in the accident-violence group). The result was marginally significant ($rh = 1.84, p < .06$), but only 25 individuals in the sample with globality scores available were known to have committed suicide. When these 25 individuals were excluded, along with individuals who died of accidents (some of which may have been suicides), and the analyses already described were repeated, the same results were obtained: Globality predicted mortality for the entire sample ($rh = 1.20, p < .05$), especially for males ($rh = 1.31, p < .05$).

Additional Analyses

How might we explain the finding that globality of explanatory style predicted untimely death? In terms of simple correlations, men who had years earlier made global attributions experienced more mental health problems in 1950 ($r = .14, p < .001$), had lower levels of adjustment at this time ($r = -.11, p < .02$), and reported that they drank slightly more ($r = .07, p < .08$) than men who had made more specific attributions (see Martin et al., 1995). We examined other variables such as education, risky hobbies, and physical activity from 1940 through 1977, but none of the simple associations with globality was significant. The subsample of individuals for whom we had smoking data available was substantially smaller than the original sample because these data were collected in 1990–1991; however, within this group, no associations with globality were found.

TABLE 1   Goodness of Fit for Gompertz Models Predicting (Age-Adjusted) Cause of Death from Sex and Globality of Explanatory Style ($n = 1,179$)

MODEL	$\Delta\chi^2$	df
Model 1: predicting mortality from sex	705.44**	10
Model 2: predicting mortality from sex and globality, constraining the effect of globality to be equal across all causes of death	715.83**	11
Model 3: predicting mortality from sex and globality, not constraining the effects of globality to be equal across all causes of death	726.62**	15
Model 2 vs. Model 1	10.39**	1
Model 3 vs. Model 1	21.18**	5
Model 3 vs. Model 2	10.79 *	4

*$p < .05$.   **$p < .001$.

Additional survival analyses were conducted, controlling for mental health and psychological adjustment. In these analyses, the association between globality and mortality risk remained stable and significant. When mental health was controlled, the relative hazard associated with globality was 1.27 ($p < .05$). When level of adjustment was controlled, the relative hazard was 1.29 ($p < .01$). A final model controlling for both mental health and adjustment resulted in a relative hazard of 1.24 ($p < .05$). Globality, although related to these aspects of psychological well-being, was distinct, and its association with mortality was not substantially mediated by these other factors.

Finally, globality of explanatory style was inversely related to a measure of neuroticism constructed from 1940 data ($r = -.15$, $p < .001$) (Martin, 1996). This finding seems to rule out confounding of our measures by response sets involving complaints or exaggeration.

DISCUSSION

The present results extend past investigations of explanatory style and physical well-being. They represent the first evidence from a large sample of initially healthy individuals that a dimension of explanatory style—globality—is a risk factor for early death, especially among males. Because globality scores were the least reliably coded of the three attributional dimensions and had the most restricted range, the present results may underestimate the actual association between globality and mortality. In any event, our findings were not due to confounding by neuroticism, suicide, or psychological maladjustment. Stability per se did not predict mortality, perhaps because it involves a belief that is circumscribed, that is, relevant in certain situations but not others.

In contrast, globality taps a pervasive style of catastrophizing about bad events, expecting them to occur across diverse situations. Such a style can be hazardous because of its link with poor problem solving, social estrangement, and risky decision making across diverse settings (Peterson, Maier, & Seligman,

1993). Supporting this interpretation is the link between globality and deaths due to accident or violence. Deaths like these are often not random. "Being in the wrong place at the wrong time" may be the result of a pessimistic lifestyle, one more likely among males than females. Perhaps deaths due to causes classified as unknown may similarly reflect an incautious lifestyle.

Explanatory style, at least as measured in this study, showed no specific link to death by cancer or cardiovascular disease. Speculation concerning explanatory style and poor health has often centered on physiological mechanisms, but behavioral and lifestyle mechanisms are probably more typical and more robust. We were unable to identify a single behavioral mediator, however, which implies that there is no simple set of health mediators set into operation by globality.

Previous reports on the health of the Terman Life-Cycle Study participants found that childhood personality variables predicted mortality (Friedman et al., 1993). Specifically, a variable identified as "cheerfulness" was inversely related to longevity. Its components involved parental judgments of a participant's "optimism" and "sense of humor." Because a hopeless explanatory style is sometimes described as pessimistic and its converse as optimistic, these previous reports appear to contradict the present results. However, in this sample, cheerfulness in childhood was unrelated to explanatory style in adulthood. If cheerfulness and explanatory style tap the same sense of optimism, then this characteristic is discontinuous from childhood to adulthood. It is also possible, perhaps likely, that these two variables measure different things: An optimistic explanatory style is infused with agency: the belief that the future will be pleasant because one can control important outcomes.

In summary, a cognitive style in which people catastrophize about bad events, projecting them across many realms of their lives, foreshadows untimely death decades later. We suggest that a lifestyle in which an individual is less likely to avoid or escape potentially hazardous situations is one route leading from pessimism to an untimely death.

REFERENCES

Friedman, H. S., Tucker, J. S., Schwartz, J. E., Tomlinson-Keasey, C., Martin, L. R., Wingard, D. L., & Criqui, M. H. (1995). Psychosocial and behavioral predictors of longevity: The aging and death of the "Termites." *American Psychologist, 50,* 69–78.

Peterson, C., & Bossio, L. M. (1991). *Health and optimism.* New York: Free Press.

Peterson, C., Maier, S. F., & Seligman, M. E. P. (1993). *Learned helplessness: A theory for the age of personal control.* New York: Oxford University Press.

Peterson, C., & Seligman, M. E. P. (1984). Causal explanations as a risk factor for depression: Theory and evidence. *Psychological Review, 91,* 347–374.

Terman, L. M., & Oden, M. H. (1947). *Genetic studies of genius: IV. The gifted child grows up: Twenty-five years follow-up of a superior group.* Palo Alto, CA: Stanford University Press.

Questions to Think About

1. How can it be that factors of global attribution (thought) can affect risk of mortality?

2. How does this approach to health differ from our more usual assumptions about health?

3. Why might it be that males show a higher association of globality to mortality than females?

4. What are the possible relationships between explanatory style, depression, and untimely death? What types of data and/or analyses would permit a disentangling of the causal pathways?

30

Traits Revisited

GORDON W. ALLPORT

When he was a young boy, Gordon W. Allport (1897–1967) was accused by callous school-mates of swallowing a dictionary, so enthralled was he with the details of language. This child-hood fascination would later prove crucial when he constructed his trait theories of personality. Allport believed that common traits (general internal organizing structures) and personal dispo-sitions (neuropsychic structures peculiar to the individual) intertwine to shape our lives and direct us to behave the ways we do. He viewed personality as a "dynamic organization within the individual of those psychophysical systems that determine his characteristic behavior and thought."

In this selection, Allport defends the concept of traits from two sorts of attacks. The first criticism is the behaviorist one, which argues that we should not label someone as "aggressive," but rather focus directly on the aggressive acts. The second attack is the interactionist one, which argues that because behavior varies from situation to situation, it is difficult to speak of a stable personality. In response, Allport argues that we do gain tremendous utility in understanding peo-ple's behavior by using a summary concept like traits, and that people do have tendencies to be-have in certain ways, even if they do not always follow these tendencies in every given situation.

Years ago I ventured to present a paper before the Ninth International Congress at New Haven (G. W. Allport, 1931). It was entitled "What Is a Trait of Personality?" For me to return to the same topic on this honorific occasion is partly a sentimental indulgence, but partly too it is a self-imposed task to discover whether during the past 36 years I have learned anything new about this central problem in personality theory.

In my earlier paper I made eight bold assertions. A trait, I said,

1. Has more than nominal existence.
2. Is more generalized than a habit.
3. Is dynamic, or at least determinative, in behavior.
4. May be established empirically.

5. Is only relatively independent of other traits.
6. Is not synonymous with moral or social judgment.
7. May be viewed either in the light of the person-ality which contains it, or in the light of its dis-tribution in the population at large.

To these criteria I added one more:

8. Acts, and even habits, that are inconsistent with a trait are not proof of the nonexistence of the trait.

While these propositions still seem to me defensi-ble they were originally framed in an age of psy-chological innocence. They now need reexamination in the light of subsequent criticism and research.

Source: Allport, G. W. (1966). Traits revisited. *American Psychologist, 21*, 1–10. Copyright © 1966 by the American Psychological Association. Reprinted with permission.

Editor's note: All citations in the text of this selection have been left intact from the original, but the list of references includes only those sources that are the most relevant and important. Readers wishing to follow any of the other citations can find the full references in the original work or in an online database.

CRITICISM OF THE CONCEPT OF TRAIT

Some critics have challenged the whole concept of trait. Carr and Kingsbury (1938) point out the danger of reification. Our initial observation of behavior is only in terms of adverbs of action: John behaves aggressively. Then an adjective creeps in: John has an aggressive disposition. Soon a heavy substantive arrives, like William James' cow on the doorstep: John has a trait of aggression. The result is the fallacy of misplaced concreteness.

The general positivist cleanup starting in the 1930s went even further. It swept out (or tried to sweep out) all entities, regarding them as question-begging redundancies. Thus Skinner (1953) writes:

> When we say that a man eats because he is hungry, smokes a great deal because he has the tobacco habit, fights because of the instinct of pugnacity, behaves brilliantly because of his intelligence, or plays the piano well because of his musical ability, we seem to be referring to causes. But on analysis these phrases prove to be merely redundant descriptions [p. 31].

It is clear that this line of attack is an assault not only upon the concept of trait, but upon all intervening variables whether they be conceived in terms of expectancies, attitudes, motives, capacities, sentiments, or traits. The resulting postulate of the "empty organism" is by now familiar to us all, and is the scientific credo of some. Carried to its logical extreme this reasoning would scrap the concept of personality itself—an eventuality that seems merely absurd to me.

More serious, to my mind, is the argument against what Block and Bennett (1955) called "traitology" arising from many studies of the variability of a person's behavior as it changes from situation to situation. Every parent knows that an offspring may be a hellion at home and an angel when he goes visiting. A businessman may be hardheaded in the office and a mere marshmallow in the hands of his pretty daughter.

Years ago the famous experiment by La Piere (1934) demonstrated that an innkeeper's prejudice seems to come and go according to the situation confronting him.

In recent months Hunt (1965) has listed various theories of personality that to his mind require revision in the light of recent evidence. Among them he questions the belief that personality traits are the major sources of behavior variance. He, like Miller (1963), advocates that we shift attention from traits to interactions among people, and look for consistency in behavior chiefly in situationally defined roles. Helson (1964) regards trait as the residual effect of previous stimulation, and thus subordinates it to the organism's present adaptation level.

Scepticism is likewise reflected in many investigations of "person perception." To try to discover the traits residing within a personality is regarded as either naive or impossible. Studies, therefore, concentrate only on the *process* of perceiving or judging, and reject the problem of validating the perception and judgment. (Cf. Tagiuri & Petrullo, 1958.)

Studies too numerous to list have ascribed chief variance in behavior to situational factors, leaving only a mild residue to be accounted for in terms of idiosyncratic attitudes and traits. A prime example is Stouffer's study of *The American Soldier* (Stouffer et al., 1949). Differing opinions and preferences are ascribed so far as possible to the GI's age, martial status, educational level, location of residence, length of service, and the like. What remains is ascribed to "attitude." By this procedure personality becomes an appendage to demography (see G. W. Allport, 1950). It is not the integrated structure within the skin that determines behavior, but membership in a group, the person's assigned roles—in short, the prevailing situation. It is especially the sociologists and anthropologists who have this preference for explanations in terms of the "outside structure" rather than the "inside structure" (cf. F. H. Allport, 1955, Chapter 21).

I have mentioned only a few of the many varieties of situationism that flourish today. While not denying any of the evidence adduced I would point to their common error of interpretation. If a child is a hellion at home, an angel outside, he obviously has two contradictory tendencies in his nature, or perhaps a deeper genotype that would explain the opposing phenotypes. If in studies of person perception the process turns out to be complex and subtle, still there would be no perception at all unless there were something out there to perceive and to judge. If, as in Stouffer's studies, soldiers' opinions vary with their marital status or length of service, these opinions are still their own. The fact that my age, sex, social status help form my outlook on life does not change the fact that the outlook is a functioning part of me. Demography deals with distal forces—personality study with proximal forces. The fact that the innkeeper's behavior varies according to whether he is, or is not, physically confronted with Chinese applicants for hospitality tells nothing about his attitude structure, except that it is complex, and that several attitudes may converge into a given act of behavior.

Nor does it solve the problem to explain the variance in terms of statistical interaction effects. Whatever tendencies exist reside in a person, for a person is the sole possessor of the energy that leads to action. Admittedly different situations elicit differing tendencies from my repertoire. I do not perspire except in the heat, nor shiver except in the cold; but the outside temperature is not the mechanism of perspiring or shivering. My capacities and my tendencies lie within.

To the situationist I concede that our theory of traits cannot be so simpleminded as it once was. We are now challenged to untangle the complex web of tendencies that constitute a person, however contradictory they may seem to be when activated differentially in various situations.

ON THE OTHER HAND

In spite of gunfire from positivism and situationism, traits are still very much alive. Gibson (1941) has pointed out that the "concept of set or attitude is nearly universal in psychological thinking." And in an important but neglected paper—perhaps the last he ever wrote—McDougall (1937) argued that *tendencies* are the "indispensable postulates of all psychology." The concept of *trait* falls into this genre. As Walker (1964) says trait, however else defined, always connotes an enduring tendency of some sort. It is the structural counterpart of such functional concepts as "expectancy," and "goal-directedness."

After facing all the difficulties of situational and mood variations, also many of the methodological hazards such as response set, halo, and social desir-

ability, Vernon (1964) concludes, "We could go a long way towards predicting behavior if we could assess these stable features in which people differ from one another [p. 181]." The powerful contributions of Thurstone, Guilford, Cattell, and Eysenck, based on factor analysis, agree that the search for traits should provide eventually a satisfactory taxonomy of personality and of its hierarchical structure. The witness of these and other thoughtful writers helps us withstand the pessimistic attacks of positivism and situationism.

It is clear that I am using "trait" as a generic term, to cover all the "permanent possibilities for action" of a generalized order. Traits are cortical, subcortical, or postural dispositions having the capacity to gate or guide specific phasic reactions. It is only the phasic aspect that is visible; the tonic is carried somehow in the still mysterious realm of neurodynamic structure. Traits, as I am here using the term, include long-range sets and attitudes, as well as such variables as "perceptual response dispositions," "personal constructs," and "cognitive styles."

Unlike McClelland (1951) I myself would regard traits (i.e., some traits) as motivational (others being merely stylistic). I would also insist that traits may be studied at two levels: (*a*) dimensionally, that is as an aspect of the psychology of individual differences, and (*b*) individually, in terms of *personal dispositions*. (Cf. G. W. Allport, 1961, Ch. 15.) It is the latter approach that brings us closest to the person we are studying.

As for factors, I regard them as a mixed blessing. In the investigations I shall soon report, factorial analysis, I find, has proved both helpful and unhelpful. My principal question is whether the factorial unit is idiomatic enough to reflect the structure of personality as the clinician, the counselor, or the man in the street apprehends it. Or are factorial dimensions screened so extensively and so widely attenuated—through item selection, correlation, axis manipulation, homogenization, and alphabetical labeling—that they impose an artifact of method upon the personal neural network as it exists in nature?

A HEURISTIC REALISM

This question leads me to propose an eptistemological position for research in personality. Most of us, I suspect, hold this position although we seldom formulate it even to ourselves. It can be called a *heuristic realism*.

Heuristic realism, as applied to our problem, holds that the person who confronts us possesses inside his skin generalized action tendencies (or traits) and that it is our job scientifically to discover what they are. Any form of realism assumes the existence of an external structure ("out there") regardless of our shortcomings in comprehending it. Since traits, like all intervening variables, are never directly observed but only inferred, we must expect difficulties and errors in the process of discovering their nature.

The incredible complexity of the structure we seek to understand is enough to discourage the realist, and to tempt him to play some form of positivistic gamesmanship. He is tempted to settle for such elusive formulations as: "If we knew enough about the situation we wouldn't need the concept of personality"; or "One's personality is merely the way other people see one"; or "There is no structure in personality but only varying degrees of consistency in the environment."

Yet the truly persistent realist prefers not to abandon his commitment to find out what the other fellow is really like. He knows that his attempt will not wholly succeed, owing partly to the complexity of the object studied, and partly to the inadequacy of present methods. But unlike Kant who held that the *Ding an Sich* is doomed to remain unknowable, he prefers to believe that it is at least partly or approximately knowable.

I have chosen to speak of *heuristic* realism, because to me special emphasis should be placed on empirical methods of discovery. In this respect heuristic realism goes beyond naive realism.

Taking this epistemological point of view, the psychologist first focuses his attention on some limited slice of personality that he wishes to study. He then selects or creates methods appropriate to the empirical testing of his hypothesis that the cleavage he has in mind is a trait (either a dimensional trait or a personal disposition). He knows that his present purposes and the methods chosen will set limitations upon his discovery. If, however, the investigation achieves acceptable standards of validation he will have progressed far toward his identification of traits. Please note, as with any heuristic procedure the

process of discovery may lead to important corrections of the hypothesis as originally stated.

Empirical testing is thus an important aspect of heuristic realism, but it is an empiricism restrained throughout by rational considerations. Galloping empiricism, which is our present occupational disease, dashes forth like a headless horseman. It has no rational objective; uses no rational method other than mathematical; reaches no rational conclusion. It lets the discordant data sing for themselves. By contrast heuristic realism says, "While we are willing to rest our case for traits on empirical evidence, the area we carve out for study should be rationally conceived, tested by rational methods; and the findings should be rationally interpreted."

THREE ILLUSTRATIVE STUDIES

It is now time for me to illustrate my argument with sample studies. I have chosen three in which I myself have been involved. They differ in the areas of personality carved out for study, in the methods employed, and in the type of traits established. They are alike, however, in proceeding from the standpoint of heuristic realism. The presentation of each study must of necessity be woefully brief. The first illustrates what might be called *meaningful dimensionalism*; the second *meaningful covariation*; the third *meaningful morphogensis*.

Dimensions of Values

The first illustration is drawn from a familiar instrument, dating almost from the stone age, *The Study of Values* (Allport & Vernon, 1931). While some of you have approved it over the years, and some disapproved, I use it to illustrate two important points of my argument.

First, the instrument rests on an a priori analysis of one large region of human personality, namely, the region of generic evaluative tendencies. It seemed to me 40 years ago, and seems to me now, that Eduard Spranger (1922) made a persuasive case for the existence of six fundamental types of subjective evaluation or *Lebensformen*. Adopting this rational starting point we ourselves took the second step, to put the hypothesis to empirical test. We asked: Are the six dimensions proposed—the *theoretic,* the *economic*, the *esthetic, social, political*, and *religious*—measurable on a multidimensional scale? Are they reliable and valid? Spranger defined the six ways of looking at life in terms of separate and distinct ideal types, although he did not imply that a given person belongs exclusively to one and only one type.

It did not take long to discover that when confronted with a forced-choice technique people do in fact subscribe to all six values, but in widely varying degrees. Within any pair of values, or any quartet of values, their forced choices indicate a reliable pattern. Viewed then as empirical continua, rather than as types, the six value directions prove to be measurable, reproducible, and consistent. But are they valid? Can we obtain external validation for this particular a priori conception of traits? The test's *Manual* (Allport & Vernon, 1931) contains much such evidence. Here I would add a bit more, drawn from occupational studies with women subjects. (The evidence for men is equally good.) The data in Table 1 are derived partly from the *Manual*, partly from Guthrie and McKendry (1963) and partly from an unpublished study by Elizabeth Moses.

For present purposes it is sufficient to glance at the last three columns. For the *theoretic* value we note that the two groups of teachers or teachers in preparation select this value significantly more often than do graduate students of business administration. Conversely the young ladies of business are relatively

more *economic* in their choices. The results for the *esthetic* value probably reflect the higher level of liberal arts background for the last two groups. The *social* (philanthropic) value is relatively low for the business group, whereas the *political* (power) value is relatively high. Just why nurses should more often endorse the *religious* value is not immediately clear.

Another study of external validation, showing the long-range predictive power of the test is an unpublished investigation by Betty Mawardi. It is based on a follow-up of Wellesley graduates 15 years after taking the Study of Values.

Table 2 reports the significant deviations (at the 5% level or better) of various occupational groups from the mean scores of Wellesley students. In virtually every case we find the deviation meaningful (even necessary) for the occupation in question. Thus women in business are significantly high in *economic* interests; medical, government, and scientific workers in *theoretical*; literary and artistic workers in *esthetic*; social workers in *social*; and religious workers in *religious* values.

One must remember that to achieve a relatively high score on one value, one must deliberately slight others. For this reason it is interesting to note in the table the values that are systematically slighted in order to achieve a higher score on the occupationally relevant value. (In the case of social workers it appears that they "take away" more or less uniformly from other values in order to achieve a high social value.)

TABLE 1   Mean Scores for Occupational Groups of Women: Study of Values

	FEMALE COLLEGIATE NORMS N = 2,475	GRADUATE NURSES TRAINING FOR TEACHING N = 328	GRADUATE STUDENTS OF BUSINESS ADMINISTRATION N = 77	PEACE CORPS TEACHERS N = 131
Theoretical	36.5	40.2	37.3	40.6
Economic	36.8	32.9	40.4	29.9
Esthetic	43.7	43.1	46.8	49.3
Social	41.6	40.9	35.0	41.2
Political	38.0	37.2	41.8	39.7
Religious	43.1	45.7	38.7	39.2

TABLE 2   Significant Deviations of Scores on the Study of Values for Occupational Groups of Wellesley Alumni from Wellesley Mean Scores

OCCUPATIONAL GROUPS	N	THEORETICAL	ECONOMIC	ESTHETIC	SOCIAL	POLITICAL	RELIGIOUS
Business workers	64	Lower	Higher				
Medical workers	42	Higher	Lower			Lower	
Literary workers	40	Higher	Lower	Higher			
Artistic workers	37			Higher	Lower		
Scientific workers	28	Higher		Lower			
Government workers	24	Higher				Lower	Lower
Social workers	26				Higher		
Religious workers	11					Lower	Higher

Thus, even at the college age it is possible to forecast in a general way modal vocational activity 15 years hence. As Newcomb, Turner, and Converse (1965) say, this test clearly deals with "inclusive values" or with "basic value postures" whose generality is strikingly broad. An evaluative posture toward life saturates, or guides, or gates (choose your own metaphor) specific daily choices over a long expanse of years.

One reason I have used this illustration of trait research is to raise an important methodological issue. The six values are not wholly independent. There is a slight tendency for theoretic and esthetic values to covary; likewise for economic and political values; and so too with social and religious. Immediately the thought arises, "Let's factor the whole matrix and see what orthogonal dimensions emerge." This step has been taken several times (see *Manual*); but always with confusing results. Some investigators discover that fewer than six factors are needed—some that we need more. And in all cases the clusters that emerge seem strange and unnameable. Here is a case, I believe, where our empiricism should submit to rational restraint. The traits as defined are meaningful, reliably measured, and validated. Why sacrifice them to galloping gamesmanship?

Covariation: Religion and Prejudice

Speaking of covariation I do not mean to imply that in restraining our empirical excesses we should fail to explore the patterns that underlie covariation when it seems reasonable to do so.

Take, for example, the following problem. Many investigations show conclusively that on the broad average church attenders harbor more ethnic prejudice than nonattenders. (Some of the relevant studies are listed by Argyle, 1959, and by Wilson, 1960.) At the same time many ardent workers for civil rights are religiously motivated. From Christ to Gandhi and to Martin Luther King we note that equimindedness has been associated with religious devoutness. Here then is a paradox: Religion makes prejudice; it also unmakes prejudice.

First we tackle the problem rationally and form a hypothesis to account for what seems to be a curvilinear relation. A hint for the needed hypothesis comes from *The Authoritarian Personality* (Adorno, Frenkel-Brunswik, Levinson, & Sanford, 1950) which suggests that acceptance of institutional religion is not as important as the *way* in which it is accepted. Argyle (1959) sharpens the hypothesis. He says, "It is not the genuinely devout who are prejudiced but the conventionally religious."

In our own studies we have tentatively assumed that two contrasting but measurable forms of religious orientation exist. The first form we call the *extrinsic* orientation, meaning that for the churchgoer religious devotion is not a value in its own right, but is an instrumental value serving the motives of personal comfort, security, or social status. (One man said he went to church because it was the best place to sell insurance.) Elsewhere I have defined this utilitarian orientation toward religion more fully (G. W. Allport, 1960, 1963). Here I shall simply mention two items from our scale, agreement with which we assume indicates the extrinsic attitude:

> *What religion offers me most is comfort when sorrows and misfortune strike.*
>
> *One reason for my being a church member is that such membership helps to establish a person in the community.*

By contrast the *intrinsic* orientation regards faith as a supreme value in its own right. Such faith strives to transcend self-centered needs, takes seriously the commandment of brotherhood that is found in all religions, and seeks a unification of being. Agreement with the following items indicates an intrinsic orientation:

> *My religious beliefs are what really lie behind my whole approach to life.*
>
> *If not prevented by unavoidable circumstances, I attend church, on the average (more than once a week) (once a week) (two or three times a month) (less than once a month).*

This second item is of considerable interest, for many studies have found that it is the irregular attenders who are by far the most prejudiced (e.g., Holtzmann, 1956; Williams, 1964). They take their religion in convenient doses and do not let it regulate their lives.

Now for a few illustrative results in Table 3. If we correlate the extrinsicness of orientation with various prejudice scales we find the hypothesis confirmed. Likewise, as predicted, intrinsicness of orientation is negatively correlated with prejudice.

In view of the difficulty of tapping the two complex traits in question, it is clear from these studies that our rationally derived hypothesis gains strong support. We note that the trend is the same when different denominations are studied in relation to differing targets for prejudice.

Previously I have said that empirical testing has the ability to correct or extend our rational analysis of patterns. In this particular research the following unexpected fact emerges. While those who approach the intrinsic pole of our continuum are on the average less prejudiced than those who approach the extrinsic pole, a number of subjects show themselves to be disconcertingly illogical. They accept both intrinsically

TABLE 3 Correlation between Measures of Religious Orientation among Churchgoers and Various Prejudice Scales

DENOMINATIONAL SAMPLE	N	r
Unitarian	50	
Extrinsic—anti-Catholicism		.56
Intrinsic—anti-Catholicism		−.36
Extrinsic—anti-Mexican		.54
Intrinsic—anti-Mexican		−.42
Catholic	66	
Extrinsic—anti-Negro		.36
Intrinsic—anti-Negro		−.49
Nazarene	39	
Extrinsic—anti-Negro		.41
Intrinsic—anti-Negro		−.44
Mixed[a]	207	
Extrinsic—anti-Semitic		.65

[a]From Wilson (1960).

worded items and extrinsically worded items, even when these are contradictory, such as:

> *My religious beliefs are what really lie behind my whole approach to life.*
>
> *Though I believe in my religion, I feel there are many more important things in my life.*

It is necessary, therefore, to inspect this sizable group of muddleheads who refuse to conform to our neat religious logic. We call them "inconsistently proreligious." They simply like religion; for them it has "social desirability" (cf. Edwards, 1957).

The importance of recognizing this third mode of religious orientation is seen by comparing the prejudice scores for the groups presented in Table 4. In the instruments employed the lowest possible prejudice score is 12, the highest possible, 48. We note that the mean prejudice score rises steadily and significantly from the intrinsically consistent to the inconsistently proreligious. Thus subjects with an undiscriminated proreligious response set are on the average most prejudiced of all.

Having discovered the covariation of prejudice with both the extrinsic orientation and the "pro" response set, we are faced with the task of rational explanation. One may, I think, properly argue that these

TABLE 4   Types of Religious Orientation and Mean Prejudice Scores

	Mean Prejudice Scores			
	CONSISTENTLY INTRINSIC	CONSISTENTLY EXTRINSIC	MODERATELY INCONSISTENT (PRORELIGION)	EXTREMELY INCONSISTENT (PRORELIGION)
Anti-Negro	28.7	33.0	35.4	37.9
Anti-Semitic	22.6	24.6	28.0	30.1

Note.—*N* = 309, mixed denominations. All differences significant at .01 level.

particular religious attitudes are instrumental in nature; they provide safety, security, and status—all within a self-serving frame. Prejudice, we know, performs much the same function within some personalities. The needs for status, security, comfort, and a feeling of self-rightness are served by both ethnic hostility and by tailoring one's religious orientation to one's convenience. The economy of other lives is precisely the reverse: It is their religion that centers their existence, and the only ethnic attitude compatible with this intrinsic orientation is one of brotherhood, not of bigotry.

This work, along with the related investigations of Lenski (1963), Williams (1964), and others, signifies that we gain important insights when we refine our conception of the nature of the religious sentiment and its functions. Its patterning properties in the economy of a life are diverse. It can fuse with bigotry or with brotherhood according to its nature.

As unfinished business I must leave the problem of nonattenders. From data available it seems that the unchurched are less prejudiced on the average than either the extrinsic or the inconsistent churchgoers, although apparently more prejudiced on the average than those whose religious orientation is intrinsic. Why this should be so must form the topic of future research.

Personal Dispositions: An Idiomorphic Approach

The final illustration of heuristic realism has to do with the search for the natural cleavages that mark an individual life. In this procedure there is no reference to common dimensions, no comparison with other people, except as is implied by the use of the English language. If, as Allport and Odbert (1936) have found, there are over 17,000 available trait names, and if these may be used in combinations, there is no real point in arguing that the use of the available lexicon of a language necessarily makes all trait studies purely nomothetic (dimensional).

A series of 172 published *Letters from Jenny* (G. W. Allport, 1965) contains enough material for a rather close clinical characterization of Jenny's personality, as well as for careful quantitative and computational analysis. While there is no possibility in this case of obtaining external validation for the diagnosis reached by either method, still by employing both procedures an internal agreement is found which constitutes a type of empirical validation for the traits that emerge.

The *clinical* method in this case is close to common sense. Thirty-nine judges listed the essential characteristics of Jenny as they saw them. The result was a series of descriptive adjectives, 198 in number. Many of the selected trait names were obviously synonymous; and nearly all fell readily into eight clusters.

The *quantitative* analysis consisted of coding the letters in terms of 99 tag words provided by the lexicon of the General Inquirer (Stone, Bales, Namenwirth, & Ogilvie, 1962). The frequency with which these basic tag words are associated with one another in each letter forms the basis for a factor analysis (see G. W. Allport, 1965, p. 200).

Table 5 lists in parallel fashion the clusters obtained by clinical judgment based on a careful reading of the series, along with the factors obtained by Jeffrey Paige in his unpublished factorial study.

In spite of the differences in terminology the general paralleling of the two lists establishes some

TABLE 5 Central Traits in Jenny's Personality as Determined by Two Methods

COMMON-SENSE TRAITS	FACTORIAL TRAITS
Quarrelsome-suspicious ⎫	
Aggressive ⎬	Aggressive
Self-centered (possessive)	Possessiveness
Sentimental	⎧ Need for affiliation
	⎨ Need for family
	⎩ acceptance
Independent-autonomous	Need for autonomy
Esthetic-artistic	Sentience
Self-centered (self-pitying)	Martyrdom
(No parallel)	Sexuality
Cynical-morbid	(No parallel)
Dramatic-intense	("Overstate")

degree of empirical check on both of them. We can say that the direct common-sense perception of Jenny's nature is validated by quantification, coding, and factoring. (Please note that in this case factor analysis does not stand alone, but is tied to a parallel rational analysis.)

While this meaningful validation is clearly present, we gain (as almost always) additional insights from our attempts at empirical validation of the traits we initially hypothesize. I shall point to one instance of such serendipity. The tag words (i.e., the particular coding system employed) are chiefly substantives. For this reason, I suspect, *sexuality* can be identified by coding as a minor factor; but it is not perceived as an independent quality by the clinical judges. On the other hand, the judges, it seems, gain much from the running style of the letters. Since the style is constant it would not appear in a factorial analysis which deals only with variance within the whole. Thus the common-sense traits *cynical-morbid* and *dramatic-intense* are judgments of a pervading expressive style in Jenny's personality and seem to be missed by factoring procedure.

Here, however, the computer partially redeems itself. Its program assigns the tag "overstate" to strong words such as *always, never, impossible*, etc., while words tagged by "understate" indicate reserve, caution, qualification. Jenny's letters score exceedingly high on overstate and exceedingly low on understate,

and so in a skeletonized way the method does in part detect the trait of dramatic intensity.

One final observation concerning this essentially idiomorphic trait study. Elsewhere I have reported a small investigation (G. W. Allport, 1958) showing that when asked to list the "essential characteristics" of some friend, 90% of the judges employ between 3 and 10 trait names, the average number being 7.2. An "essential characteristic" is defined as "any trait, quality, tendency, interest, that you regard as of major importance to a description of the person you select." There is, I submit, food for thought in the fact that in these two separate studies of Jenny, the common-sense and the factorial, only 8 or 9 central traits appear. May it not be that the essential traits of a person are few in number if only we can identify them?

The case of Jenny has another important bearing on theory. In general our besetting sin in personality study is irrelevance, by which I mean that we frequently impose dimensions upon persons when the dimensions fail to apply. (I am reminded of the student who was told to interview women patients concerning their mothers. One patient said that her mother had no part in her problem and no influence on her life; but that her aunt was very important. The student answered, "I'm sorry, but our method requires that you tell about your mother." The *method* required it, but the *life* did not.)

In ascribing a list of traits to Jenny we may seem to have used a dimensional method, but such is not the case. Jenny's traits emerge from her own personal structure. They are not imposed by predetermined but largely irrelevant schedules.

CONCLUSION

What then have I learned about traits in the last 4 decades? Well, I have learned that the problem cannot be avoided—neither by escape through positivism or situationism, nor through statistical interaction effects. Tendencies, as McDougall (1937) insisted, remain the "indispensable postulates of all psychology."

Further, I have learned that much of our research on traits is overweighted with methodological preoccupation; and that we have too few restraints holding us to the structure of a life as it is lived. We find ourselves confused by our intemperate empiricism which often yields unnameable factors, arbitrary codes, unintelligible interaction effects, and sheer flatulence from our computors.

As a safeguard I propose the restraints of "heuristic realism" which accepts the common-sense assumption that persons are real beings, that each has a real neuropsychic organization, and that our job is to comprehend this organization as well as we can. At the same time our profession uniquely demands that we go beyond common-sense data and either establish their validity or else—more frequently—correct their errors. To do so requires that we be guided by theory in selecting our trait slices for study, that we employ rationally relevant methods, and be strictly bound by empirical verification. In the end we return to fit our findings to an improved view of the person. Along the way we regard him as an objectively real being whose tendencies we can succeed in knowing—at least in part—beyond the level of unaided common sense. In some respects this recommended procedure resembles what Cronbach and Meehl (1955) call "construct validation," with perhaps a dash more stress on external validation.

I have also learned that while the major foci of organization in a life may be few in number, the network of organization, which includes both minor and contradictory tendencies, is still elusively complex.

One reason for the complexity, of course, is the need for the "inside" system to mesh with the "outside" system—in other words, with the situation. While I do not believe that traits can be defined in terms of interaction effects (since all tendencies draw their energy from within the person), still the vast variability of behavior cannot be overlooked. In this respect I have learned that my earlier views seemed to neglect the variability induced by ecological, social, and situational factors. This oversight needs to be repaired through an adequate theory that will relate the inside and outside systems more accurately.

The fact that my three illustrative studies are so diverse in type leads me to a second concession: that trait studies depend in part upon the investigator's own purposes. He himself constitutes a situation for his respondents, and what he obtains from them will be limited by his purpose and his method. But this fact need not destroy our belief that, so far as our method and purpose allow, we can elicit real tendencies.

Finally, there are several problems connected with traits that I have not here attempted to revisit. There are, for example, refinements of difference between trait, attitude, habit, sentiment, need, etc. Since these are all inside tendencies of some sort, they are for the present occasion all "traits" to me. Nor am I here exploring the question to what extent traits are motivational, cognitive, affective, or expressive. Last of all, and with special restraint, I avoid hammering on the distinction between common (dimensional, nomothetic) traits such as we find in any standard profile, and individual traits (personal dispositions) such as we find in single lives, e.g., Jenny's. (Cf. G. W. Allport, 1961, Ch. 15, also 1962.) Nevitt Sanford (1963) has written that by and large psychologists are "unimpressed" by my insisting on this distinction. Well, if this is so in spite of 4 decades of labor on my part, and in spite of my efforts in the present paper—I suppose I should in all decency cry "uncle" and retire to my corner.

REFERENCES

Adorno, T. W., Frenkel-Brunswik, E., Levinson, D. J., & Sanford, R. N. (1950). *The authoritarian personality*. New York: Harpers.

Allport, G. W. (1961). *Pattern and growth in personality*. New York: Holt, Rinehart & Winston.

Allport, G. W. (Ed.). (1965). *Letters from Jenny*. New York: Harcourt, Brace & World.

Allport, G. W., & Vernon, P. E. (1931). *A study of values*. Boston: Houghton-Mifflin.

Hunt, J. McV. (1965). Traditional personality theory in the light of recent evidence. *American Scientist, 53*, 80–96.

_____ Questions to Think About _____

1. Why do individuals within particular occupations tend to support certain values?
2. What is the purpose of approaching empirical testing with the common sense of heuristic realism?

3. Which personality theories best allow us to delve into such complexities as those arising from the covariation of religion and prejudice?

4. Allport claims that two very different approaches that were used to analyze "Jenny" (the woman who wrote the letters included in Allport's book *Letters from Jenny*) led to an almost identical set of traits: having multiple judges read the letters and list what they saw as Jenny's essential traits generated a list of traits almost identical to the traits that emerged from a painstaking quantitative content analysis. What are the methodological implications of such a finding?

31

Validation of the Five-Factor Model
of Personality across Instruments and Observers

ROBERT R. McCRAE AND PAUL T. COSTA, JR.

Robert R. McCrae (1949–) received his Ph.D. in personality psychology from Boston University and has worked for many years at the National Institute on Aging, in collaboration with Paul Costa (1942–). Costa received his Ph.D. in human development from the University of Chicago. They have made many distinguished contributions in the field of personality and aging.

McCrae and Costa have provided much significant evidence that personality traits can be best conceived in terms of five basic factors or dimensions. Always concerned with validity, they have gathered relevant information from a wide range of people, measuring instruments, and tasks. In this selection, they lay out the five-factor model of personality and some significant evidence for its validity.

Perhaps in response to critiques of trait models (Mischel, 1968) and to rebuttals that have called attention to common inadequacies in personality research (Block, 1977), personologists in recent years have devoted much of their attention to methodological issues. Lively discussions have centered on the merits and limitations of idiographic versus nomothetic approaches (Kenrick & Stringfield, 1980; Lamiell, 1981), aggregation and its effects on reliability (Epstein, 1979; Rushton, Brainerd, & Pressley, 1983), and alternative methods of scale construction (Burisch, 1984; Wrobel & Lachar, 1982). The veridicality of traits (beyond the realm of cognitive categories) has been tested by examining the correspondence between traits and behaviors (Mischel & Peake, 1982; Small, Zeldin, & Savin-Williams, 1983) and between self-reports and ratings (Edwards & Klockars, 1981; Funder, 1980; McCrae, 1982). As a body, these studies have simultaneously increased the

level of methodological sophistication in personality research and restored confidence in the intelligent use of individual difference models of personality.

In contrast, there has been relatively little interest in the substance of personality—the systematic description of traits. The variables chosen as vehicles for tests of methodolical hypotheses often appear arbitrary. Bem and Allen (1974) gave no rationale for the use of conscientiousness and friendliness in their classic paper on moderators of validity. McGowan and Gormly's (1976) decision to examine activity and Small et al.'s (1983) choice of prosocial and dominance behavior appear to have been made to facilitate their research designs. Indeed, Kenrick and Dantchik (1983) complained that "catalogs of convenience" have replaced meaningful taxonomies of personality traits among "most of the current generation of social/personality researchers."

Source: McCrae, R. R., & Costa, P. T. (1987). Validation of the five-factor model of personality across instruments and observers. *Journal of Personality & Social Psychology, 52,* 81–90.

Editor's note: All citations in the text of this selection have been left intact from the original, but the list of references includes only those sources that are the most relevant and important. Readers wishing to follow any of the other citations can find the full references in the original work or in an online database.

This disregard of substance is unfortunate because substance and method are ultimately interdependent. Unless methodological studies are conducted on well-defined and meaningful traits their conclusions are dubious; unless the traits are selected from a comprehensive taxonomy, it is impossible to know how far or in what ways they can be generalized.

Fortunately, a few researchers have been concerned with the problem of structure and have recognized the need for a consensus on at least the general outlines of a trait taxonomy (H. J. Eysenck & Eysenck, 1984; Kline & Barrett, 1983; Wiggins, 1979). One particularly promising candidate has emerged. The five-factor model—comprising extraversion or surgency, agreeableness, conscientiousness, emotional stability versus neuroticism, and culture—of Tupes and Christal (1961) was replicated by Norman in 1963 and heralded by him as the basis for "an adequate taxonomy of personality." Although it was largely neglected for several years, variations on this model have recently begun to reemerge (Amelang & Borkenau, 1982; Bond, Nakazato, & Shiraishi, 1975; Conley, 1985; Digman & Takemoto-Chock, 1981; Goldberg, 1981, 1982; Hogan, 1983; Lorr & Manning, 1978; McCrae & Costa, 1985b).

Some researchers (Goldberg, 1982; Peabody, 1984) have chiefly been concerned with the representativeness and comprehensiveness of this model with respect to the natural language of traits; others have sought to provide a theoretical basis for the taxonomy (Hogan, 1983). Our major concern has been the convergent and discriminant validity of the dimensions of the model across instruments and observers. If the five-factor model is a reasonable representation of human personality, it should be recoverable from questionnaires as well as from adjectives and from observer ratings as well as from self-reports. This line of research addresses substantive questions from the methodological perspective developed in the past few years.

FIVE FACTORS IN SELF-REPORTS AND RATINGS

One of the strongest arguments in favor of the five-factor model has been its appearance in both self-reports and ratings. Norman (1963) reported the structure in peer ratings. Goldberg (1980) showed parallel structures

in both ratings and self-reports. As early as the 1960s, convergence across observers was also demonstrated (Borgatta, 1964; Norman & Goldberg, 1966). However, with a few exceptions (e.g., Norman, 1969), these studies used only adjective-rating scales, and few attempts were made to compare adjective factors with standardized questionnaires that are more widely used in personality research.

In a recent publication (McCrae & Costa, 1985b), we examined the correspondence between adjective and questionnaire formats to see if the same substantive dimensions of personality would be obtained in each. Our adjective-rating instrument was an extension of one devised by Goldberg (1983); our questionnaire was the NEO Inventory (McCrae & Costa, 1983a), which measures three broad dimensions identified in analyses of standard personality measures. Self reports on five adjective factors were compared with both self-reports and spouse ratings on the inventory dimensions of neuroticism, extraversion, and openness to experience. In brief, the study showed that a version of the five-factor model could be recovered from the adjectives, that there were clear correspondences for neuroticism and extraversion dimensions across the two instruments, that Norman's culture factor was better interpreted as openness to experience, and that validity coefficients above .50 could be obtained with both self-reports and spouse ratings.

Three major questions were left unanswered by that study. As Kammann, Smith, Martin, and McQueen (1984) pointed out, research using spouses as raters differs in some respects from more traditional peer-rating studies. Spouses may "more often disclose their feelings to each other through verbal self-statements," and spouses may be more willing to adopt and support the self-concept thus communicated than would peers. Further, the design of our earlier study allowed comparison only between an observer and a self-report; no comparisons were possible between different external observers. A first question, then, concerned the generalizability of our findings to agreement among peer ratings and between peer ratings and self-reports.

A second question involved the particular five-factor structure observed in our set of 80 adjectives. In most studies the fifth and smallest factor has been labeled *culture* and has been thought to include intelligence, sophistication, and intellectual curiosity. The latter element, in particular, suggested correspondence with the questionnaire factor of openness to experience (McCrae & Costa, 1985a). In Goldberg's 40-item instrument (1983) the terms *curious* and *creative* fell on a factor defined primarily by self-rated intelligence. By adding 40 additional items, including some intended to measure such aspects of openness as preference for variety and imaginativeness, we tested the hypothesis that the fifth factor might better be construed as openness rather than as culture. Results confirmed this expectation by showing a factor with only small loadings from *intelligent* and *cultured* but large loadings from *original, imaginative*, and *creative*, and including other forms of openness (*independent, liberal, daring*) that were clearly distinct from intelligence. This factor correlated .57 with the NEO Inventory Openness scale. Because of the conceptual importance of this reformulation of the Norman model, it was essential to replicate the adjective-factor structure among peer ratings—the data source on which Norman (1963) had originally relied.

Finally, the NEO Inventory included no measures of two of the Norman factors: agreeableness and conscientiousness. These two dimensions have occurred less frequently in questionnaire measures, and they have been thought by some to represent merely the respondent's evaluation of the target. Consensual validation across observers is therefore particularly important for these two dimensions. For that purpose we developed questionnaire measures of agreeableness–antagonism and conscientiousness–undirectedness, and we examined agreement for both dimensions across instruments and observers in the present study.

METHOD

Subjects

Individuals who provided self-reports and who were targets for peer ratings were members of the Augmented Baltimore Longitudinal Study of Aging. The Baltimore Longitudinal Study of Aging (BLSA) sample is composed of a community-dwelling, generally healthy group of volunteers who have agreed to return for medical and psychological testing at regular inter-

vals (Shock et al., 1984). The sample has been recruited continuously since 1958, with most new subjects referred by friends or relatives in the study. Among the men, 93% are high school graduates and 71% are college graduates; nearly one fourth have doctorate-level degrees. The Augmented BLSA sample consists of 423 men and 129 women who participate in the BLSA, and it includes 183 wives and 16 husbands who are not themselves BLSA participants but who have agreed to complete questionnaires at home. Some participants chose not to participate in this study, and some provided incomplete data. Results are based on the 156 men and 118 women for whom complete data were available, except for one subject who scored more than five standard deviations below the mean on the conscientiousness adjective factor and whose adjective data were thrown out. Comparison of individuals who chose to participate in the peer-rating study with others showed no significant differences in age or sex. Somewhat surprisingly, there were also no differences in self-reported personality as measured by the five adjective factors. Participating subjects were slightly more open to experience than were others, $F(1, 634) = 4.15, p < .05$, when NEO Inventory scores were examined. At the time of the peer ratings, ages ranged from 29 to 93 ($M = 59.9$ years) for men and from 28 to 85 ($M = 53.8$ years) for women.

Peer Raters

Subjects were asked to nominate

> *three or four individuals who know you very well* as you are now. *They can be friends, neighbors, or co-workers, but they should not be relatives. These should be people who have known you for at least one year and have seen you in a variety of situations.*

A few subjects nominated more than four raters, and names and addresses for 1,075 raters were obtained, a few of whom were dropped because they were themselves members of the BLSA or had already been nominated by another subject (peers rated only one subject). Of those contacted, 747 (69%) provided rating data. Raters were assured of the confidentiality of their responses and were specifically instructed not to discuss the ratings with the subject.

For purposes of item factor analyses, all rating were pooled. For intraclass and peer/self-report correlations, data were analyzed in four subsamples defined by the number of ratings available for each subject: 49 subjects had exactly one rater, 71 had two raters, 90 had three, and 63 had four or more raters. Too few subjects had five or more raters to allow analyses of these data, and only the first four raters' data were examined in these cases.

A background sheet completed by raters was used to characterize the peers and their relationships to the subjects. As a group, the raters resembled the subjects. They ranged in age from 19 to 87 ($M = 54.2$ years), and the correlation of rater's age with subject's age was 72. Like BLSA participants, the raters were well educated: 78% were high school graduates, 57% were college graduates, and 41% had some graduate or professional education. Most of the raters (91% of the men and 75% of the women) were of the same sex as the subjects they rated. However, when asked if they thought they were similar in "personality, attitudes, temperament, and feelings" to the subject, only 8% of the raters considered themselves very similar, and 51% considered themselves similar; 34% considered themselves different, and 7% considered themselves very different from the subject.

The raters appeared to be well acquainted with the subjects. They reported knowing the subjects for an average of 18.3 years (range = 1 to 74 years). Currently, 57% reported seeing the subject weekly, 27% monthly, and 14% once or twice a year. In addition, 9% of the subjects volunteered the information that they had seen the subject more frequently at some time in the past. Furthermore, raters appeared to have some depth of acquaintance: 61% reported that the subject sometimes shared confidences or personal feelings with them, and 35% said he or she often did. In addition, raters said that the subject sometimes (67%) or often (15%) came to them for advice and support. When asked for their own assessment, 56% said they knew the subject pretty well, 40% said they knew the subject very well.

Most (75%) of the raters described their relationship with the subject as a close personal friend, 29% as a family friend, 28% as a neighbor, and 34% as a coworker. Only 8% listed themselves as an acquaintance. Most raters had seen the subject in a variety of settings: at parties or social events (89%), with same-sex friends (67%), with family (85%), at work (51%), during subject's personal crisis (46%), on vacation (39%), or at religious services (31%).

As a group, these raters seemed particularly well qualified to give personality ratings. They had known the subjects for many years, seen them frequently in a variety of settings, and shared their confidences. The raters themselves believed they could give accurate ratings: 86% believed they were good at understanding others, and 89% thought the subject they rated was straightforward and easy to understand.

Measures and Procedure

Data from two kinds of instruments—adjective-rating scale factors and questionnaire scales—were obtained by mail administration over a period of 4 years. The schedule of administration of the personality measures is given in Table 1.

Adjective factors. On the basis of a series of analyses of English-language trait names, Goldberg (1983) developed a 40-item bipolar adjective-rating scale instrument to measure five major dimensions of personality. In subsequent work (McCrae & Costa, 1985b) we supplemented his list with an additional 40 items. Subjects rated themselves on this 80-item instrument with the use of Goldberg's 9-point scale. Five factors were derived from these self-reports and identified as neuroticism, extraversion, openness,

TABLE 1 Schedule of Administration of Personality Measures

INSTRUMENT	DATE
Self-reports	
NEO inventory	February 1980
Adjective-rating scales,	
agreeableness and	
conscientiousness items	
(preliminary)	March 1983
Peer ratings	
Adjective-rating scales	
NEO Personality Inventory	
(Form R)	July 1983

agreeableness, and conscientiousness. Similar factors were found for men and women. Neuroticism, extraversion, and openness factors were validated against NEO Inventory measures of the same constructs from both self-reports and spouse ratings, with convergent correlations ranging from .52 to .65 (McCrae & Costa, 1985b). To examine the factor structure of this instrument in peer ratings is one of the aims of this article.

NEO Personality Inventory. A questionnaire measure of the five-factor model is provided by the NEO Personality Inventory (Costa & McCrae, 1985), which comprises the NEO Inventory (Costa & McCrae, 1980; McCrae & Costa, 1983a) along with newly developed scales to measure agreeableness and conscientiousness. The original NEO Inventory is a 144-item questionnaire developed through factor analysis to fit a three-dimensional model of personality. Eight-item scales are used for each of six facets or specific traits within each of three broad trait dimensions, and overall scores are obtained by summing the scores of the six facets of neuroticism, extraversion, and openness. Item scoring is balanced to control for acquiescence, and socially desirable responding does not appear to bias scores (McCrae & Costa, 1983b). Internal consistency and 6-month retest reliability for the three global scores range from .85 to .93 (McCrae & Costa, 1983a). A third-person form of the NEO Inventory has been developed for use by raters and has shown comparable reliability and validity when spouse ratings are obtained (McCrae, 1982).

Questionnaire scales to measure agreeableness and conscientiousness were developed as part of the present research. Two 24-item rational scales were created, and joint factor analysis of these items with NEO Inventory items led to the identification of the hypothesized five factors. Ten items loading on the agreeableness and conscientiousness factors were tentatively adopted as measures of those factors. These items also correlated more highly with the appropriate adjective factor than with any of the other adjective factors in self-reports.

When the NEO Inventory Rating Form was administered to peers, 60 items intended to measure agreeableness and conscientiousness were interspersed. These included the best items from the pilot study undertaken on self-reports along with new items written subsequently. Two final 18-item scales

measuring agreeableness and conscientiousness were derived from analyses of these data. Two criteria were used for item selection. First, joint factor analysis with the NEO items in peer ratings again showed five factors that could be identified as neuroticism, extraversion, openness, agreeableness, and conscientiousness. Items selected for the final scales were required to have their highest loadings on their hypothesized factor. Second, scales were created by using the 10-item preliminary scales developed on self-reports. The 60 proposed items were correlated with these two scales as well as with the three domain scores from the NEO Inventory Rating Form. To be included in the final selection, items were required to show higher correlations with the Agreeableness or Conscientiousness scale than with any of the other four scales. Because the final selection included some items written after the self-report data had been collected, the final self-report scales consisted of only 10 agreeableness and 14 conscientiousness items.

Coefficient alpha for the Conscientiousness scale was .91 within peer ratings and .84 within self-reports; for the Agreeableness scale it was .89 within peer ratings but only .56 within self-reports. In part, this low internal consistency was due to the inclusion of only 10 items in the self-report scale; in part, it was due to lower average interitem correlations. Correlations between questionnaire and adjective measures of agreeableness and conscientiousness in self-reports were .48 and .65, respectively; neither scale correlated over .20 with any of the other adjective factors.

It is essential to note that although the development of the Agreeableness and Conscientiousness scales was conducted in parallel on peers and self-reports, correlations across these two methods did not influence item selection in any way. Thus, the correlation between self-reports and ratings was not inflated by the capitalization on chance inherent in some types of item selection.

RESULTS

The results will be considered in three sections. First, we will examine the factor structure of the 80-item adjective-rating scales in peer ratings and validate the factors by correlation with peer ratings on the NEO

Personality Inventory. Second, we will consider agreement among peers on the personality characteristics of the targets they have rated by examining intraclass correlations among raters for both adjective factor and questionnaire measures of the five-factor model. Finally, we will present correlations between self-reports and peer ratings.

Adjective Factors in Peer Ratings

Everett (1983) has recently suggested that the number of factors to be retained and interpreted should be determined by comparing rotated solutions in different samples or subsamples and adopting the solution that can be replicated. Coefficients of factor comparability should be used as the measure of similarity, and Everett suggested that coefficients above .90 be required to consider two factors to be a match. When peer ratings on the 80 adjective scales were submitted to principal components analysis, a scree test suggested that approximately five factors would be needed. Everett's procedure was then used to compare solutions in self-reports and peer ratings for the third through eighth factors. Varimax-rotated three-factor solutions were obtained independently in self-report data from 503 subjects (McCrae & Costa, 1985b) and in ratings from 738 peers. Comparability coefficients were calculated by applying the scoring weights derived from both analyses to the data from peers and by correlating the resulting factor scores. This process was repeated for four-, five-, six-, seven-, and eight-factor solutions (results are shown in Table 2). Only

the five-factor solution showed replication of all factors, and comparabilities were very high in this case, ranging from .95 to .98. This is clear evidence that the five-factor solution, and only the five-factor solution, was invariant across observers.

Table 3 shows factor loadings for the five-factor solution in peers. The factors in Table 3 have been re-ordered, and variables are arranged using the structure observed in self-reports (McCrae & Costa, 1985b) for comparison. The match between factors in the two data sets is clear; the great majority of items loaded on the same factor in peer ratings as they did in self-reports. The most notable difference appeared to be in the peer agreeableness–antagonism factor, which included, as definers of the antagonistic pole, aspects of dominance (e.g., *dominant, bold*) from the extraversion factor and hostility (e.g., *temperamental, jealous*) from the neuroticism factor.

The similarity of structure was particularly important in the case of the openness factor. In peer ratings, as in self-reports, *broad interests, prefer variety, independent,* and *liberal* were among the definers of this factor, *intelligent* and *cultured* showed small loadings. From this set of 80 items in both data sources, a factor emerged in which concern with rich and varied experience was more central than cognitive ability.

The interpretation of the peer-rating factors were [sic] confirmed by correlating factor scores with scale scores from the NEO Personality Inventory ratings. Convergent correlations between adjective factors and corresponding NEO scales were .73 for neuroticism, .70 for extraversion, .70 for openness, .80 for agreeableness,

TABLE 2   Comparabilities for Varimax-Rotated Principal Components in 738 Peers Using Factor-Scoring Matrices from Ratings and Self-Reports

COMPONENTS ROTATED	*Factor Comparabilities after Varimax Rotation*							
	1ST	2ND	3RD	4TH	5TH	6TH	7TH	8TH
8	.94	.87	.85	.73	.72	.70	.68	.14
7	.95	.95	.86	.85	.58	.53	.08	
6	.96	.93	.91	.89	.82	.61		
5	.98	.98	.97	.96	.95			
4	.93	.86	.81	.76				
3	.87	.84	.74					

TABLE 3   Varimax-Rotated Factor Loadings for 80 Adjective Items from Peer Ratings

ADJECTIVES	Factor				
	N	E	O	A	C
Neuroticism (N)					
Calm–worrying	**79**	05	–01	–20	05
At ease–nervous	**77**	–08	–06	–21	–05
Relaxed–high-strung	**66**	04	01	–34	–02
Unemotional–emotional	**44**	**40**	14	03	–03
Even-tempered–temperamental	**41**	01	01	**–56**	–21
Secure–insecure	**63**	–16	–08	–07	–39
Self-satisfied–self-pitying	**53**	–17	–07	03	–17
Patient–impatient	**41**	02	–03	**–57**	02
Not envious–envious/jealous	29	01	–10	**–46**	–19
Comfortable–self-conscious	**57**	–30	–17	–16	–16
Not impulse ridden–impulse ridden	20	26	22	–16	–38
Hardy–vulnerable	**50**	–14	–13	23	–26
Objective–subjective	17	10	–31	–20	–36
Extraversion (E)					
Retiring–sociable	–14	**71**	08	08	08
Sober–fun loving	–08	**59**	12	14	–15
Reserved–affectionate	–01	**65**	12	25	–15
Aloof–friendly	–16	**58**	02	**45**	06
Inhibited–spontaneous	–21	**52**	**49**	01	–02
Quiet–talkative	01	**64**	06	–19	00
Passive–active	–26	**42**	28	–23	37
Loner–joiner	–14	**53**	–08	14	12
Unfeeling–passionate	14	**43**	28	31	09
Cold–warm	–05	**57**	09	**54**	06
Lonely–not lonely	**–49**	30	–01	10	11
Task oriented–person oriented	–04	36	09	35	–29
Submissive–dominant	–16	20	20	**–57**	27
Timid–bold	–21	33	31	**–44**	10
Openness (O)					
Conventional–original	–06	12	**67**	08	–04
Down to earth–imaginative	16	03	**54**	–10	–12
Uncreative–creative	–08	09	**56**	11	25
Narrow interests–broad interests	–15	20	**52**	18	27
Simple–complex	16	–13	**49**	–20	08
Uncurious–curious	00	12	**41**	00	24
Unadventurous–daring	–18	31	**55**	–06	08
Prefer routine–prefer variety	–11	30	**43**	14	–21
Conforming–independent	–22	09	**49**	–14	21
Unanalytical–analytical	–15	–13	**43**	–13	30
Conservative–liberal	04	08	**46**	15	–13
Traditional–untraditional	02	–01	**45**	–05	–36
Unartistic–artistic	10	15	36	21	18

Note. These are varimax-rotated principal component loading for 738 raters. The loadings above .40 given in boldface. Decimal points are omitted.

ADJECTIVES	N	E	O	A	C
Aggreeableness vs. antagonism (A)					
Irritable–good natured	–17	34	09	**61**	16
Ruthless–soft hearted	12	27	–01	**70**	11
Rude–courteous	03	18	09	**55**	36
Selfish–selfless	–07	–02	04	**65**	22
Uncooperative–helpful	–01	23	14	**44**	45
Callous–sympathetic	04	29	11	**67**	20
Suspicious–trusting	–14	19	15	**62**	08
Stingy–generous	02	24	17	**55**	22
Antagonistic–acquiescent	–02	–06	–09	**66**	–02
Critical–lenient	–13	09	00	**65**	–14
Vengeful–forgiving	–15	11	07	**70**	16
Narrow-minded–open-minded	–14	15	**48**	54	16
Disagreeable–agreeable	14	24	06	**59**	26
Stubborn–flexible	–18	08	12	**61**	00
Serious–cheerful	–10	**58**	08	26	02
Cynical–gullible	14	14	–17	**40**	–16
Manipulative–straightforward	–15	06	–02	**47**	31
Proud–humble	01	–18	–09	**45**	13
Conscientiousness vs. undirectedness (C)					
Negligent–conscientious	–01	02	08	18	**68**
Careless–careful	–08	–07	–01	11	**72**
Undependable–reliable	–07	04	05	23	**68**
Lazy–hardworking	–07	17	14	03	**66**
Disorganized–well organized	14	–02	05	–05	**68**
Lax–scrupulous	05	03	03	10	**53**
Weak willed–self-disciplined	26	–01	23	–03	**62**
Sloppy–neat	–01	00	–04	12	**59**
Late–punctual	–05	–09	–05	05	**60**
Impractical–practical	–24	01	–04	05	**54**
Thoughtless–deliberate	–03	–08	05	14	**45**
Aimless–ambitious	–09	12	21	–08	**52**
Unstable–emotionally stable	–57	09	07	27	**45**
Helpless–self-reliant	–29	19	21	–01	**53**
Playful–businesslike	00	–26	–02	–09	**49**
Unenergetic–energetic	–14	34	27	–06	**46**
Ignorant–knowledgeable	–12	–03	**53**	13	43
Quitting–perservering	–09	13	27	00	**62**
Stupid–intelligent	–04	03	**41**	17	44
Unfair–fair	–14	04	19	**59**	33
Imperceptive–perceptive	–16	07	**46**	24	39
Uncultured–cultured	01	00	36	15	33

and .76 for conscientiousness ($N = 722$, $p < .001$). The largest divergent correlation was .33. These findings demonstrate that raters were highly consistent across instruments in the ways in which they described their targets on each of the five dimensions. The findings do not, however, speak to the accuracy of the ratings, as judged against external criteria.

Consensual Validation Across Peer Raters

The extent to which different peers agreed on the attribution of traits to the same individual was calculated by examining the intraclass correlations between factor scores for raters. Intraclass correlations were equivalent to the Pearsonian correlation between all possible pairs of raters (Haggard, 1958). The top half of Table 4 gives intraclass correlations for groups of subjects with two, three, or four raters. All were statistically significant, and values ranged from .30 to .65, with a median of .38. Levels of cross-peer agreement were approximately equal for all five factors. These data provide evidence of consensual validation for all five dimensions in three independent subsamples.

Agreement across observers on questionnaire measures is seen in significant intraclass correlations given in the bottom half of Table 4 for three subsamples. These correlations closely resemble those for adjective factors, and they suggest that peers agreed as well on questionnaire as on adjective checklist descriptions of their friends.

Although the magnitude of correlations seen in Table 4 compares favorably with most in the literature (see McCrae, 1982, for a review), and although virtually all exceed the .3 barrier sometimes thought to set a limit to validity coefficients in personality research, it is also true that there was room for considerable difference of opinion between raters with regard to the same subject.

Agreement Between Self-Reports and Ratings

Agreement among raters was only one piece of evidence for consensual validation. It could be argued that shared stereotypes account for some or all of the agreement among peers (Bourne, 1977). A more rigorous test would compare ratings with self-reports, because it is unlikely that any of the artifacts affecting either of these sources would be shared (McCrae, 1982). The top half of Table 5 presents the correlations between averaged peer ratings and self-reports for each of the five factors. With the exception of conscientiousness among subjects having only a single rater, all the correlations were statistically significant and many were substantial in magnitude.

The bottom half of Table 5 gives corresponding correlations for the NEO Personality Inventory for subjects with complete data. Although several

TABLE 4 Intraclass Correlations for Peer Ratings

NUMBER OF PEER RATERS	N^a	Factor				
		N	E	O	A	C
		Adjective-Factor Scores				
2	146	30	59	65	43	37
3	267	38	37	37	44	36
4	248	30	42	41	36	41
		NEO Personality Inventory				
2	142	53	52	51	38	47
3	270	30	38	39	38	38
4	252	31	43	40	28	40

Note. N = Neuroticism. E = Extraversion. O = Openness. A = Agreeableness. C = Conscientiousness. All correlations are significant at $p < .01$. Decimal points are omitted.

[a]Refers to number of raters.

TABLE 5   Convergent Correlations between Self-Reports and Peer Ratings for Adjective-Factor Scores and NEO Personality Inventory

NUMBER OF PEER RATERS	N^a	Self-Reports					
		N	E	O	A	C
		Adjective-Factor Scores					
1	49	33*	29*	46***	41**	25
2	72	53***	62***	46***	42***	30**
3	85	59***	45***	54***	55***	49***
4	61	51***	48***	52***	59***	50***
		NEO Personality Inventory					
1	45	26	37*	53***	20	21
2	68	47***	60***	53***	34**	33**
3	81	43***	46***	62***	35**	50***
4	54	51***	56***	67***	24	58***

Note. N = Neuroticism. E = Extraversion. O = Openness. A = Agreeableness. C = Conscientiousness. Decimal points are omitted.

[a]Refers to targets, not to raters.

*p < .05. **p < .01. ***p < .001.

correlations were small when only a single rater was used, they increased considerably in magnitude when multiple raters were averaged. Only the Agreeableness scale failed to show the utility of aggregating raters.

Finally, we considered divergent as well as convergent validation of the five factors across instruments and observers. To simplify presentation of the data, the four subsamples were combined by calculating an average peer rating (standardized within subsample) for each adjective-factor and questionnaire scale. Table 6 presents the correlations of mean peer ratings on both adjective factors and questionnaire scales with self-reports on the same variables. Convergent correlations, given in boldface, were invariably larger than divergent correlations, markedly so for all cases except those involving the self-report questionnaire Agreeableness–Antagonism scale. Because there was good agreement across observers when the agreeableness adjective-factor scores were used, it could be inferred that the problem here lay with the questionnaire scale and not with the construct. This was expected given the low reliability of the preliminary Agreeableness scale used in self-reports. For all five dimensions, the median validity

coefficient was .44. When examined by sex, convergent correlations ranged from .19 to .58 for men (median = .35) and from .17 to .56 for women (median = .48).

DISCUSSION

Convergence across Observers and Instruments

This research examined the correspondence between assessments of five major personality dimensions among peer ratings and between peer ratings and self-reports, using both adjective factors and questionnaire scales. The results are straightforward, showing convergent and discriminant cross-observer and cross-instrument validation for all five factors.

The magnitude of the correlations—generally .4 to .6—deserves some comment, because it was larger than typically reported (e.g., Borgatta, 1964). In part, the higher agreement may be due to reliable and well-constructed measures and, in part, to the nature of the raters. On the whole, raters were very well acquainted with the subjects they rated, having seen them frequently in a variety of circumstances over a period of many years. As Table 5 shows, aggregating across

TABLE 6 Correlations of Self-Reports with Mean Peer Ratings for Adjective Factors and Questionnaire Scales

| | Self-Reports | | | | | | | | | |
| | Adjective Factors | | | | | NEO Personality Inventory | | | | |
MEAN PEER RATING	N	E	O	A	C	N	E	O	A	C
Adjective factors										
N	**50*****	00	02	05	−10	**38*****	06	08	01	−09
E	19**	**48*****	01	09	−07	08	**40*****	16*	04	−03
O	01	−01	**49*****	−01	−08	02	11	**43*****	−06	−11
A	−05	−14*	−18**	**49*****	−20***	−08	−26***	−02	**28*****	−19**
C	−09	−08	−12*	−08	**40*****	−11	−02	−09	11	**40*****
NEO Personality Inventory										
N	**44*****	−03	00	−03	−15*	**42*****	02	02	−11	−14*
E	06	**45*****	16**	00	06	−04	**47*****	25***	02	02
O	07	08	**45*****	13*	−07	03	13*	**57*****	02	−13*
A	−06	−11	−15*	**45*****	−10	−12	−25***	−03	**30*****	−12
C	−11	−05	−10	−09	**39*****	−14*	−02	−08	08	**43*****

Note. N = Neuroticism. E = Extraversion. O = Openness. A = Agreeableness. C = Conscientiousness.

N = 255 to 267. Convergent correlations are shown in boldface. Decimal points are omitted.

*p < .05. **p < .01. ***p < .001.

raters also tended to increase agreement. However, as Kammann et al. (1984) noted, there are limits to the improvements in accuracy offered by aggregating. Although the averaged ratings may reflect more accurately the consensus of how the individual is viewed, they may always diverge to some extent from the individual's phenomenological view of himself or herself. Given the qualifications of the raters in this study, it seems likely that the correlations seen here will be near the ceiling for self–other agreement.

It is also worth pointing out that ratings and self-reports differed in another respect as well. When raw scores on the NEO Inventory were compared, ratings were approximately one-half standard deviation higher on extraversion, and one-third lower on neuroticism, than were self-reports. Separate norms would thus be needed to make self-reports and ratings comparable.

The Nature of the Five Factors

These methodological considerations lay the groundwork for the equally important question of substance. A growing body of research has pointed to the five-factor model as a recurrent and more or less comprehensive taxonomy of personality traits. Theorists disagree, however, on precisely how to conceptualize the factors themselves. It seems useful at this point to review each of the factors and attempt to define the clear elements as well as disputed aspects. The factors in Table 3, which so closely parallel factors found in self-reports and which show such clear evidence of convergent and discriminant validity across observers and instruments, can form a particularly useful guide to the conceptual content of the dimensions of personality.

Neuroticism versus emotional stability. There is perhaps least disagreement about neuroticism, defined here by such terms as worrying, insecure, self-conscious, and temperamental. Although adjectives describing neuroticism are relatively infrequent in English (Peabody, 1984), psychologists' concerns with psychopathology have led to the development of innumerable scales saturated with neuroticism. Indeed, neuroticism is so ubiquitous an element of personality scales that theorists sometimes take it for granted.

A provocative view of neuroticism is provided by Tellegen (in press), who views it as negative emotionality, the propensity to experience a variety of negative affects, such as anxiety, depression, anger, and embarrassment. Virtually all theorists would concur in the centrality of negative affect to neuroticism; the question is whether other features also define it. Tellegen himself [1985] pointed out that his construct of negative emotionality has behavioral and cognitive aspects. Guilford included personal relations and objectivity in his emotional health factor (Guilford, Zimmerman, & Guilford, 1976), suggesting that mistrust and self-reference form part of neuroticism. We have found that impulsive behaviors, such as tendencies to overeat, smoke, or drink excessively, form a facet of neuroticism (Costa & McCrae, 1980), and *impulse-ridden* is a definer of the neuroticism factor in self-reports, although not in ratings. Others have linked neuroticism to irrational beliefs (Teasdale & Rachman, 1983; Vestre, 1984) or to poor coping efforts (McCrae & Costa, 1986).

What these behaviors seem to share is a common origin in negative affect. Individuals high in neuroticism have more difficulty than others in quitting smoking because the distress caused by abstinence is stronger for them. They may more frequently use inappropriate coping responses like hostile reactions and wishful thinking because they must deal more often with disruptive emotions. They may adopt irrational beliefs like self-blame because these beliefs are cognitively consistent with the negative feelings they experience. Neuroticism appears to include not only negative affect, but also the disturbed thoughts and behaviors that accompany emotional distress.

Extraversion or surgency. Sociable, fun-loving, affectionate, friendly, and talkative are the highest loading variables on the extraversion factor. This is not Jungian extraversion (see Guilford, 1977), but it does correspond to the conception of H. J. Eysenck and most other contemporary researchers, who concur with popular speech in identifying extraversion with lively sociability.

However, disputes remain about which elements are central and which are peripheral to extraversion. Most writers would agree that sociability, cheerfulness, activity level, assertiveness, and sensation seeking all covary, however loosely. But the Eysencks have at times felt the need to distinguish between sociability

and what they call impulsiveness (S. B. G. Eysenck & Eysenck, 1963; Revelle, Humphreys, Simon, & Gilliland, 1980). Hogan (1983) believed that the five-factor model was improved by dividing extraversion into sociability and assertiveness factors. In Goldberg's analyses, surgency (dominance and activity) were the primary definers of extraversion, and terms like warm–cold were assigned to the agreeableness–antagonism factor. Tellegen (in press) emphasized the complementary nature of neuroticism and extraversion by labeling his extraversion factor positive emotionality.

These distinctions do seem to merge at a high enough level of analysis (H. J. Eysenck & Eysenck, 1967; McCrae & Costa, 1983a), and sociability—the enjoyment of others' company—seems to be the core. What is essential to recall, however, is that liking people does not necessarily make one likable. Salesmen, those prototypic extraverts, are generally happier to see you than you are to see them.

Openness to experience. The reinterpretation of Norman's culture as openness to experience was the focus of some of our previous articles (McCrae & Costa, 1985a, 1985b), and the replication of results in peer ratings was one of the purposes of the present article. According to adjective-factor results, openness is best characterized by original, imaginative, broad interests, and daring. In the case of this dimension, however, questionnaires may be better than adjectives as a basis for interpretation and assessment. Many aspects of openness (e.g., openness to feelings) are not easily expressed in single adjectives, and the relative poverty of the English-language vocabulary of openness and closedness may have contributed to confusions about this domain (McCrae & Costa, 1985a). We know from questionnaire studies that openness can be manifest in fantasy, aesthetics, feelings, actions, ideas, and values (Costa & McCrae, 1978, 1980), but only ideas and values are well represented in the adjective factor. Interestingly, questionnaire measures of openness give higher validity coefficients than do adjective-factor measures—indeed, the correlation of .57 between the self-reported NEO Openness scale and the peer-rated NEO Openness scale is the highest of those shown in Table 6.

Perhaps the most important distinction to be made here is between openness and intelligence. Open individuals tend to be seen by themselves and others as somewhat more intelligent, and there are correlations of .30 between psychometric measures of intelligence and openness. However, joint factor analyses using Army Alpha intelligence subtests and either adjectives (McCrae & Costa, 1985b) or NEO Inventory scales (McCrae & Costa, 1985a) show that intelligence scales define a factor clearly separate from openness. Intelligence may in some degree predispose the individual to openness, or openness may help develop intelligence, but the two seem best construed as separate dimensions of individual differences.

Agreeableness versus antagonism. As a broad dimension, agreeableness–antagonism is less familiar than extraversion or neuroticism, but some of its component traits, like trust (Stark, 1978) and Machiavellianism (Christie & Geis, 1970), have been widely researched. The essential nature of agreeableness–antagonism is perhaps best seen by examining the disagreeable pole, which we have labeled antagonism. As the high-loading adjectives in Table 3 and the items in Table 2 show, antagonistic people seem always to set themselves against others. Cognitively they are mistrustful and skeptical; affectively they are callous and unsympathetic; behaviorally they are uncooperative, stubborn, and rude. It would appear that their sense of attachment or bonding with their fellow human beings is defective, and in extreme cases antagonism may resemble sociopathy (cf. H. J. Eysenck & Eysenck's, 1975, psychoticism).

An insightful description of antagonism in its neurotic form is provided by Horney's account of the tendency to move against people (1945, 1950). She theorized that a struggle for mastery is the root cause of this tendency and that variations may occur, including narcissistic, perfectionistic, and arrogant vindictive types. Whereas some antagonistic persons are overtly aggressive, others may be polished manipulators. The drive for mastery and the overt or inhibited hostility of antagonistic individuals suggests a resemblance to some formulations of Type A personality (Dembroski & MacDougall, 1983), and systematic studies of the relations between agreeableness–antagonism and measures of coronary-prone behavior should be undertaken.

Unappealing as antagonism may be, it is necessary to recognize that extreme scores on the agreeable pole may also be maladaptive. The person high in agreeableness may be dependent and fawning, and agreeableness has its neurotic manifestation in Horney's self-effacing solution of moving toward people.

Antagonism is most easily confused with dominance. Amelang and Borkenau (1982), working in German and apparently unaware of the Norman taxonomy, found a factor they called *dominance*. Among its key definers, however, were Hartnäckigkeit (*stubbornness*) and Erregbarkeit (*irritability*); scales that measure agreeableness and cooperation defined the opposite pole in their questionnaire factor. Clearly, this factor corresponds to antagonism. In self-reports (McCrae & Costa, 1985b), submissive–dominant is a weak definer of extraversion; in Table 3, from the peers' point of view, it is a definer of antagonism. The close etymological relationship of *dominant* and *domineering* shows the basis of the confusion.

Agreeableness–antagonism and conscientiousness–undirectedness are sometimes omitted from personality systems because they may seem too value laden. Indeed, the judgment of character is made largely along these two dimensions: Is the individual well or ill intentioned? Is he or she strong or weak in carrying out those intentions? Agreeableness–antagonism, in particular, has often been assumed to be an evaluative factor of others' perceptions rather than a veridical component of personality (e.g., A. Tellegen, personal communication, March 28, 1984).

However, the fact that a trait may be judged from a moral point of view does not mean that it is not a substantive aspect of personality. The consensual validation seen among peers and between peer-reports and self-reports demonstrates that there are some observable consistencies of behavior that underlie attributions of agreeableness and conscientiousness. They may be evaluated traits, but they are not mere evaluations.

Conscientiousness versus undirectedness. Conscientious may mean either governed by conscience or careful and thorough (Morris, 1976), and psychologists seem to be divided about which of these meanings best characterizes the last major dimension of personality. Amelang and Borkenau (1982) labeled their factor self-control versus impulsivity, and Conley (1985) spoke of impulse control. This terminology connotes an inhibiting agent, as Cattell (Cattell, Eber,

& Tatsuoka, 1970) recognized when he named his Factor G *superego strength*. A conscientious person in this sense should be dutiful, scrupulous, and perhaps moralistic.

A different picture, however, is obtained by examining the adjectives that define this factor. In addition to conscientious and scrupulous, there are a number of adjectives that suggest a more proactive stance: hardworking, ambitious, energetic, persevering. Digman and Takemoto-Chock (1981) labeled this factor *will to achieve*, and it is notable that one of the items in the questionnaire measure of conscientiousness, "He strives for excellence in all he does," comes close to the classic definition of need for achievement (McClelland, Atkinson, Clark, & Lowell, 1953).

At one time, the purposefulness and adherence to plans, schedules, and requirements suggested the word *direction* as a label for this factor, and we have retained that implication in calling the opposite pole of conscientiousness *undirectedness*. In our view, the individual low in conscientiousness is not so much uncontrolled as undirected, not so much impulse ridden as simply lazy.

It seems probable that these two meanings may be related. Certainly individuals who are well organized, habitually careful, and capable of self-discipline are more likely to be able to adhere scrupulously to a moral code if they choose to—although there is no guarantee that they will be so inclined. An undirected individual may have a demanding conscience and a pervasive sense of guilt but be unable to live up to his or her own standards for lack of self-discipline and energy. In any case, it is clear that this is a dimension worthy of a good deal more empirical attention than it has yet received. Important real-life outcomes such as alcoholism (Conley & Angelides, 1984) and academic achievement (Digman & Takemoto-Chock, 1981) are among its correlates, and a further specification of the dimension is sure to be fruitful.

Some personality theorists might object that trait ratings, in whatever form and from whatever source, need not provide the best foundation for understanding individual differences. Experimental analysis of the psychophysiological basis of personality (H. J. Eysenck & Eysenck, 1984), examination of prototypic acts and act frequencies (Buss & Craik, 1983), psychodynamic

formulations (Horney, 1945), or behavioral genetics (Plomin, DeFries, & McClearn, 1980) provide important alternatives. But psychophysiological, behavioral, psychodynamic, and genetic explanations must eventually be related to the traits that are universally used to describe personality, and the five-factor model can provide a framework within which these relations can be systematically examined. The minor conceptual divergences noted in this article suggest the need for additional empirical work to fine-tune the model, but the broad outlines are clear in self-reports, spouse ratings, and peer ratings; in questionnaires and adjective factors; and in English and in German (Amelang & Borkenau, 1982; John, Goldberg, & Angleitner, 1984). Deeper causal analyses may seek to account for the structure of personality, but the structure that must be explained is, for now, best represented by the five-factor model.

REFERENCES

Eysenck, H. J., & Eysenck, M. (1984). *Personality and individual differences*. London: Plenum.

Goldberg, L. R. (1982). From Ace to Zombie: Some explorations in the language of personality. In C. D. Spielberg & J. N. Butcher (Eds.), *Advances in personality assessment* (Vol. 1, pp. 203–234). Hillsdale, NJ: Erlbaum.

Hogan, R. (1983). A socioanalytic theory of personality. In M. M. Page (Ed.), *Nebraska Symposium on Motivation, 1982: Personality—Current theory and research* (pp. 55–89). Lincoln, NE: University of Nebraska Press.

McCrae, R. R. (1982). Consensual validation of personality traits: Evidence from self-reports and ratings. *Journal of Personality and Social Psychology, 43*, 293–303.

McCrae, R. R., & Costa, P. T. (1985). Openness to experience. In R. Hogan and W. H. Jones (Eds.), *Perspectives in personality* (Vol. 1, pp. 145–172). Greenwich, CT: JAI Press.

Mischel, W. (1968). *Personality and assessment*. New York: Wiley.

Norman, W. T. (1963). Toward an adequate taxonomy of personality attributes: Replicated factor structure in peer nomination personality ratings. *Journal of Abnormal and Social Psychology, 66*, 574–583.

Wiggins, J. S. (1979). A psychological taxonomy of trait-descriptive terms: The interpersonal domain. *Journal of Personality and Social Psychology, 37*, 395–412.

Questions to Think About

1. Does it make sense to summarize human personality in terms of five dimensions? Eysenck has argued for three dimensions, and Cattell has argued for sixteen.

2. Although the five factors do a good job in accounting for the data, they are nowhere near perfect. Why might this be?

3. Does it make sense to rely on basic trait dimensions in explaining personality, or do we need to take into account unconscious drives, other motives, perceptions, situations, goals, and other such elements?

4. What evidence supports the five-factor model as appropriate beyond the North American cultural environment? Acknowledging the thorny methodological complexities of translation of instruments between languages, what kinds of data would support the global applicability of the model for all cultural groups?

32

Personality Pinned Down

RAYMOND B. CATTELL

Raymond Cattell, who studied with English and American intelligence researchers, took a mathematical approach to understanding personality. In particular, he used the statistical approach termed "factor analysis" to distill a basic set of dimensions of personality. Factor analysis is a way of reducing or summarizing a large number of correlation coefficients. Cattell's approach was very inductive and data-driven.

Cattell (1905–1998) typically used research designs in which a large number of raters would judge other persons they knew well on a large number of adjectives. Such studies led to what Cattell called "mental factors." Cattell proposed that there are sixteen basic personality traits, which he labeled with letters of the alphabet to be sure that they were objective results of the statistical method, not biased by preconceived notions. In this selection, he describes the Sixteen Personality Factor Questionnaire.

Personality is like love: everyone agrees it exists, but disagrees on what it is. Psychologists have tried to pin down the elusive nature of "personality" in many ways, ranging from the broad intuitive systems of psychoanalysis to the precise but narrow views of behaviorism and learning theory. Still, the substance of personality theory from 1910 to 1960 was Freudian, and novelists and journalists still speak the language of Freud.

In the 1930s, my colleagues and I developed a radical approach to personality based on factor analysis. We discovered that there are certain basic mental factors that can be measured with mathematical precision. Consider the sex drive, presumably an impossible force to quantify (other than "she has a lot of it" or "he has too little of it"). George Kawash and Gerrit De Young used our Motivational Analysis Test to measure the strength of the sex drives of 50 married male graduate students at the University of Illinois. The men rated erotic pictures in terms of how sexually arousing they were. The researchers found that a person's score on our sex drive factor predicted accurately how aroused he would be by the pictures, how much his sex drive would increase after looking at the pictures, and how likely he was to want, or to have, sexual intercourse that evening.

We started our study of personality factors with a conservative goal: to define and measure objectively the basic components of personality before trying to explain, predict, or theorize about them. The history of science demonstrates that breakthroughs always follow this pattern. Isaac Newton pointed out that he could not have tested his theories of motion (forces) if he had not been able to use the exact ways to describe

Source: Cattell, R. B. (1973). Personality pinned down. *Psychology Today, 7* (July), 41–42, 44–46.
Reprinted with permission from Psychology Today, copyright © 1971, www.psychologytoday.com.

moving objects developed by Galileo. Similarly, without accurate measurement of personality, it was virtually impossible to choose between, say, two theories concerning the origin and cure of neurosis.

Clinicians vs. Experimenters.   In the 1930s, when we began our work, many experimental psychologists were turning their attention to the study of reflexes, nerve conduction, laws of perception, and laws of rat-learning. But most clinicians chose to ignore the methods of quantitative science. They felt that the experimental psychologists refused to deal with the full complexity of the mind that they encountered in each patient. To the great clinicians, the experimental psychologist must have seemed like a drunkard who knows that his lost wrist watch is out in the alley but searches for it in the house because there is more light inside.

The approach used by experimental psychologists was based typically on a bivariate (meaning "two-variables" or "two-measurements") design. Two groups use the same toothpaste, for example, which varies only in its amount of fluoride. To assess the effect of that one variable, the experimenter looks at a single second variable, the amount of tooth decay.

Such bivariate methods do not work well for studying the mind because mental traits are broad *patterns* of numerous related behaviors, feelings, and responses. Human beings are so complex, and psychological effects so subtle, that trying to get two groups of persons identical in all respects except one becomes unrealistic. It can be done, at best, only in laboratory settings. Bivariate experimental techniques are about as useful for studying personality as forks are for eating soup.

To get around these complex problems, we turned to a mathematical method called factor analysis, which Charles Spearman and Louis L. Thurstone developed in the '20s and '30s. J. P. Guilford used factor analysis in the '50s to find 15 specific ability factors and John L. Horn and I used it to locate two general intelligence factors that account for a person's performance on ability tests [see "Are I.Q. Tests Intelligent?" PT, March 1968].

Factor analysis allows us to look simultaneously at any number and kind of measures and determine how they reduce to patterns. Out of some 100 test responses, for example, we may find nine underlying factors that influence them. It makes no difference whether the variables we start with are repeated measurements of chemicals in one person's blood, or intelligence test scores taken from thousands of persons, or the distribution of traits in a given group.

The Patterns of Personality.   One of our early factor-analysis experiments used check lists of 171 adjectives. We asked our 208 raters to describe other persons they knew well by checking various adjectives—anxious, friendly, dominating, etc. Any individual who tries to describe a particular person in such words might be substantially off base. But we believed that the patterns of use of the adjectives would point to the mental factors which make-up one's "personality." We believed, to paraphrase Lincoln, that you can fool some of the raters all of the time, and all of the raters some of the time, but you can't fool all the raters all the time. Indeed, our factor analysis showed that when the raters describe other persons they often unknowingly evaluate the strength of some 20 underlying personality factors.

We labeled the resulting factors alphabetically, from A to O. We did not assign them descriptive names for years; in the meantime, we established beyond doubt that they were really mental factors, not mathematical artifacts. We slowly became familiar with the intuitive meanings behind the letters and numbers, and we assigned two names to each: one for a high score and another for a low score. We wanted to emphasize that a low score on factor N (forthrightness), for example, indicated the *presence* of something just as an extremely high score on factor N (shrewdness) does. While the verbal names convey meaning to persons unfamiliar with our tests, we prefer the letter designations. Any verbal label gets tied to a complex of everyday meanings and nuances that are different for different persons; moreover, the labels rarely capture the full meaning and content of the factor.

We also wanted to eliminate any possibility that these factors represented some arbitrary but culturally agreed-upon way of speaking about personalities. If we had found *true* mental factors, whatever their psychological meanings, they should appear when we factor-analyzed *any* measures that personality influences. So next we looked at the way individuals describe themselves.

We asked thousands of persons to answer questions about themselves and again analyzed their responses. We came up with 16 to 20 distinct "introspective" factors; most of them turned out to correspond exactly to the factors that the raters had identified earlier.

The Belated Four.   We were now quite certain that we had found the building blocks of personality. But there were four new factors that the older rating method had not picked up (Q_1, conservative–experimenting; Q_2, group-dependent–self-sufficient; Q_3, uncontrolled-controlled, and Q_4, relaxed–tense). At first we wondered if these were artifacts not really related to personality. But two findings kept us from discarding them. First, they recurred with different persons, different questions, and even with different ways of computing the factors; that is, the new factors were too persistent to ignore. Second, and more important, these factors turned out to have strong correlations with our ultimate validation, real life behavior. For example, persons who score very high on factor Q_4 (tense/driven) tend to be accident-prone, and a high score on factor Q_1 (conservative) or Q_3 (controlled) predicts a tendency to succeed in school. [Editor's note: The sixteen factors are shown in Table 1.]

Apparently, our early belief that the basic personality factors were independent of how they were measured was only partly correct. The four new factors were clearly real, yet undetectable in a factor analysis of raters' descriptions. They were, in a way, the four occasions on which all of the raters were fooled.

Some of the personality traits, as Thomas Klein has shown, are strongly influenced by heredity. One is factor B, general intelligence. Factor C (ego strength), factor F (serious minded–enthusiastic), factor G (superego strength) and factor I (emotional sensitivity) are fairly strongly affected by heredity. Others, such as factor D (calm–excitable), factor E (submissive–dominant), and factor Q (relaxed–tense), are strongly influenced by the way a person is treated in childhood.

A few of the factors are identical to the intuitive concepts that astute clinicians have developed. Factor

TABLE 1   The 16 Personality Factors

A	reserved	outgoing
B	less intelligent	more intelligent
C	affected by feelings	emotionally stable
E	submissive	dominant
F	serious	happy-go-lucky
G	expedient	conscientious
H	timid	venturesome
I	tough-minded	sensitive
L	trusting	suspicious
M	practical	imaginative
N	forthright	shrewd
O	self-assured	apprehensive
Q_1	conservative	experimenting
Q_2	group-dependent	self-sufficient
Q_3	uncontrolled	controlled
Q_4	relaxed	tense

G (expedient–conscientious) corresponds to what Freud called the superego, while factor C corresponds to ego strength. Jung's concept of extraversion/introversion is identical to a "second-order factor"—an influence touching several primary factors—in this case affecting factors A (aloof–warm), F (sober–happy), H (shy–venturesome), and M (practical–imaginative). Factor A is remarkably like the dimension that Ernst Kretschmer described and called "cyclothymia" (warm) on one extreme and "schizothymia" (cold) on the other.

In addition to confirming some clinical concepts, we were able to enlarge upon them. For example, where Jung thought that there were at most four parts to extroversion, our analysis revealed that there are at least five. Further, we found that a true neurotic usually differs from a normal person on five or six personality factors. In particular, neurotics always have a low level of what we call "regression–energy-mobilization." Regression is a lack of psychological energy and a lack of persistence and it includes a tendency to fall back to simple, inadequate, ways of coping.

True and False Neurotics.   By having clinicians diagnose people who have been tested we find that they often diagnose a neurotic person by sensing his high anxiety. As a result they often put the "neurotic"

label on an individual who has high anxiety for reasons not related to any neurosis. He may, for example, be anxious because he has been told that half the employees of his company will be laid off that week. Our regression factor distinguishes persons who have high "situational" anxiety from those who have true neurotic anxiety.

The first general-purpose personality test based on our work is the Sixteen Personality Factor Questionnaire. Its 368 (184 in each of two equivalent forms) multiple-choice questions, selected by factor analysis and not by our subjective choice, measure the level of 16 primary personality factors and eight composite, "secondary," personality factors. This test has very practical, predictive abilities.

For instance, John Nesselroade and I wanted to determine whether "opposites attract" or "like marries like." Some psychologists have proposed that persons with similar temperaments will make compatible marriage partners. Others suggest that persons with different ("complementary") personalities should be more compatible.

We gave our test to two groups of married couples, 100 couples who were stably married, and 80 couples who had come to the counseling center for help with marriage difficulties. We found, basically, that like should marry like if one wants a lasting relationship. Couples in the stable marriages were more likely to have similar personalities than those whose marriages were in trouble.

Several personality factors appear to be especially related to the stability of a marriage: factor A (aloof–warm), factor L (trusting–suspicious), and factor Q (group-dependent–self-sufficient). Persons who are similar in these factors tended to fall in the stably married group. The fourth relevant factor is E (submissive–dominant). Husbands in stable marriages were likely to be more dominant than their wives, but if a husband was *much* more dominant than his wife, that couple generally fell in the unstably married group.

Many researchers have used the Sixteen Personality Factor Questionnaire to explore the relationships between mind and body. A. H. Ismail studied persons in a physical conditioning program and found that exercise is linked with personality changes [see "Jogging the Imagination," PT, March]. A. M. Ostfeld

analyzed the factor scores of nearly 2,000 men between 40 and 55 years old, the age bracket in which most heart attacks occur. Fifty of the men later developed heart disease. Ostefeld found that these 50 men were significantly more likely to be suspicious (factor L), self-sufficient (factor Q_2), and low in superego strength (factor G), than the other men.

The Psychosomatic and Creative Personalities.   In fact, there is a distinct psychosomatic profile that is different from the general neurotic's profile. The person who tends to get psychosomatic ailments has considerable ego-strength (factor C) and self-assurance (factor O); most of all, he is cool, reserved (factor A) and unsentimental (factor I). He also has an atypically high level of a second-order factor called cortical alertness. The psychosomatic person seems to have the psychological resources that make him ready to meet and cope with stress, but he acts out the stress internally instead of anxiously withdrawing like a typical neurotic.

The Sixteen Personality Factor Questionnaire also has been used to study creative people. John Drevdahl and I found that the personalities of prominent artists and writers were more similar to each other than to the general population. And despite the fact that we often think of scientists and artists as opposite types, the profile of a group of creative scientists was very similar to that of the artists and writers. The psychological concomitants of creativity are apparently fairly constant, no matter what the person's creative area is. The composite profile of a creative person partly confirms the popular picture of him, or her, as a sometimes tactless, autonomous, nonconformist who does not always work well with a group.

From this and other related studies, we have extracted an equation that roughly estimates any person's creative potential from his personality factor scores. Our work suggests that there is much more to creativity than intelligence. If we wish to study or nurture creativity, or if we want to avoid screening creative persons out of positions because of their sometimes unpleasant personalities, we now have the means to do so.

Getting out of Introspection.   There are a number of problems with introspective questionnaires. A person can deliberately or unconsciously distort his responses, out of the desire to appear in a particular light. While attempts at distortion rarely achieve the effect that the person desires, there are no perfect ways to unscramble the distortion. Another disadvantage of questionnaire tests is that they can be taken only by persons who can read, or at least talk. Many of the questions that personality researchers want to answer concern young children or persons from other cultures with different languages. The fact that a particular question may be interpreted differently by different persons makes any questionnaire test fall short of perfection.

With those drawbacks in mind, and to show that our factors were properties of the mind rather than of the test, we began to design objective measures. Objective tests are a diverse collection of techniques. We define a test as objective if the person being measured cannot tell what aspect of himself is being evaluated, or, if he can, he has no way to change or distort the outcome of the measurement.

Some objective measures are physiological variables, such as heart rate, metabolism, respiration rate, muscle tension, levels of various biochemicals in the blood, or changes in the electrical resistance of the skin. Other objective measures are psychophysical, such as reaction speed or ability to pick spoken words out of a noisy background. Further, we can measure a person's actual behavior, for example while he is working on pencil and paper maze puzzles. We observe his speed, the amount of time he spends hesitating at intersections, and his persistence on mazes that he does not know are insoluble. We can even extract objective measures from pencil and paper tests, such as the Gottschaldt and the Gestalt Closure Test, in which a person tries to identify the subject of an incomplete but definite line drawing. We can measure such variables as the number of correct guesses or the number of threatening objects he claims to see. Clinicians have used such responses to put the person into one of two intuitively defined categories—"synthetic type" or "analytic type." Instead, we throw these measures into the computer for correlation and let the mathematics of factor analysis tell us whether they can be explained by underlying factor types. In the case of the Gestalt Closure Test, they can.

As evidence that our personality factors are true constructs, we factor-analyzed thousands of responses to more than 2,000 objective tests. The results supported our findings from the previous rater and questionnaire tests.

Most of our personality factors have proved stable, so we call them "source traits," emphasizing that they are steady traits and constant sources of behavior. One's level of ego strength or intelligence, for instance, is usually about the same from month to month. However, when change measures are factored, such dimensions as tension, regression, and anxiety are revealed to fluctuate with time and situation. We may think of them as mood or "state" factors. We later found seven other very changeable mood factors, including excitement, general fatigue, and effort stress. These factors, which make for the ups and downs of daily life, appear most distinctly when we factor-analyze physiological measures such as pulse rate, amounts of hormones and nutrients in the blood, amounts of sleep, goodness of memory, and time of day.

Predictions from Personality.   In predicting behavior, what state a man is in may be as important as what kind of man he is. But practicing psychologists have plenty to do at present in predicting from traits. Personality factors already permit us to calculate equations that predict many behaviors: academic success, the likelihood of being able to tolerate contact lenses, alcoholism or drug addiction, the volume of a salesman's selling. For example, low G (expediency), high M (imaginativeness) and high E (dominance) each contribute to accident proneness. Our tests can identify neurotic or psychotic persons as well as a good team of psychiatrists can, and they do so more consistently than any one psychiatrist.

Clinicians often treat patients with psychoactive drugs, without knowing which patients will experience unexpected and negative reactions. Gary Forrest, Timothy Bortner and Cornelis Bakker found they could use a test of factor E (submissive–dominant) to predict reactions to the tranquilizer chlorpromazine. Highly dominant persons tend to respond to this drug by becoming agitated.

Until 1960 our factors did not include motivations and drives which are different from general personality dimensions, and which, we knew, manifest themselves in a person's attitudes and emotions. Thus, the strength of the person's self-assertion drive might appear in his attitudes toward winning arguments, or toward his salary, or toward leading groups.

Two technical advances need to be emphasized. First, we no longer measure motive strength by check list or subjective appraisal. As psychoanalysis has long known, such methods have been shown to be unreliable. Second, we base the decision as to what human drives actually *exist* on multivariate analysis; we do not postulate X number on an armchair basis, as personality theorists have been wont to do. Unfortunately, most laymen, and even many psychologists untrained in multivariate methods, fail to see that the two procedures (nonarbitrary factor analysis and arbitrary speculation) are as different from each other as modern identification of chemical elements is from the air-earth-fire-water system of the alchemists. The labels and the scales may not look very different superficially, but they belong in a new world relative to previous questionnaire scales.

Ergs and Sentiments. In the realm of dynamic structure factors we soon noticed that we were unearthing two quite distinct kinds of motivational roots:

1) Ergs, which seem to be basic biological drives such as sex, fear (or need for security), parental-prospectiveness, gregariousness, curiosity, self-assertion, and narcissism (self-indulgent sensuality).

2) Sentiments, which are learned drives such as self-sentiment (respect for self-image), career-sentiment, and superego-sentiment (conscience). The sentiments are not distinguishable mathematically from the ergs, but the attitudes that the sentiments affect are directed to cultural objects or events.

Our mathematical analysis showed that each motivation, whether an erg or a sentiment, has two components. One is conscious, and shows up in direct, "inventory" measures of attitudes; the other is unconscious, and shows up in indirect measures, such as word associations, blood pressure, and electrical skin-resistance changes.

Keith Barton, T. E. Dielman and I measured the motivation factors, ability factors and personality factors of 311 sixth- and seventh-grade students. Three

months later the students took Educational Testing Service achievement tests in social science, science, mathematics and reading. We found that our factors were significantly related to the student's achievement in each area. For example, high assertiveness was related to good performance in social studies and reading, but had no relation to performance in science or mathematics. High superego and self-sentiment strengths were positively related to all performances. In contrast, high scores on fear, pugnacity (the hostile-destructive drive), were negatively related to the students' achievement. To our surprise, only the *conscious* component of the motivations affected achievement scores. The unconscious component, if anything, inhibited achievement.

As Freud noted years ago, a person's unconscious motivation can be far different from his conscious motivation. It seemed to us, as to Freud, that such disparities would be a source of psychological conflict. But unlike Freud, we could measure the amount of both components for each motivation factor and get numerical overall conflict scores. In 1959, J. R. Williams measured conflict scores for eight mental hospital patients and found them significantly higher than those of persons from the general population. We may be able to detect mental illness before it develops by measuring a person's conflicts and watching for sudden changes or long-term trends. Similarly, a therapist might be able to use conflict scores to see if a particular technique is working for a particular patient.

Measures of the Mind. We can formulate equations that demonstrate the role of each motive in any action. This permits us to find out which methods of teaching will reinforce or punish which motives. We have already shown that a freshman college student's first motivation to learn psychology is usually curiosity; but within one semester, curiosity defers to self-assertion and insecurity (fear).

After three decades of learning to catalog and measure the dimensions of the mind, we have the tools to give specific answers to complicated and practical questions. The interrelations of the mental factors we find are extremely complex. They are going to involve more intricate but more exact mathematical predictions than have been envisaged in the incomplete intuitive schemes of clinicians, or the fragmented truths that come from bivariate experiments. But our precise and integrating approach permits us to recognize and handle a person's uniqueness as well as his common humanity, in a manner that no single-faceted psychological system can surpass.

Questions to Think About

1. What are the advantages of an inductive, data-driven approach to personality? How is such an approach limited?

2. Other personality psychologists argue that there are three basic trait dimensions, or five basic trait dimensions. What do you think of Cattell's claim that we need sixteen?

3. Does the approach put forward by Cattell make a more convincing case for the reliability of the personality factors that emerge from his analysis or for their validity? How?

4. How (and with what degree of success) does Cattell, steeped in his factor analytic technique, relate his empirically derived dimensions to the more theoretically based constructs proposed by other personality theorists?

33

Personality Dimensions in Nonhuman Animals: A Cross-Species Review

SAMUEL D. GOSLING AND OLIVER P. JOHN

Modern personality research often uses narrower approaches than the grand theories of the past, but often uses innovative tactics in looking for converging lines of evidence. Although most people believe that their animal pets have personality, the topic has drawn relatively little attention from psychologists. Evolutionary theory, however, suggests that we may gain some insights into the structure of human personality by examining individual consistencies in other animals.

Samuel Gosling and Oliver John conducted this research at the Institute of Personality and Social Research, at the University of California, Berkeley. They have conducted considerable work on the Big Five model that asserts that personality can be best summarized in terms of five major personality dimensions. In this selection, they look for evidence of these basic dimensions in nonhuman animals.

In a recent article in the *Los Angeles Times*, Robert Fagen, a professor of biometry, described Susie as irascible, irritable, grumpy, and manipulative. This is hardly newsworthy, except that Susie is a bear. Scientists have been reluctant to ascribe personality traits, emotions, and cognitions to animals, even though they readily accept that the anatomy and physiology of humans is similar to that of animals. Yet there is nothing in evolutionary theory to suggest that only physical traits are subject to selection pressures, and Darwin (1872/1998) argued that emotions exist in both human and nonhuman animals. Thus, personality traits like Extraversion and Agreeableness may not be as uniquely human as once was thought (Buss, 1988). Early attempts to assess animal personality, including the pioneering studies by Stevenson-Hinde, were conducted in the 1970s, and the 1990s have seen

a resurgence of research activity. Our goal in this article is to take stock of what is known about animal personality, focusing on individual differences *within* species. We ask, What are the major dimensions of animal personality?

MAPPING THE LANDSCAPE OF ANIMAL PERSONALITY

Faced with the challenge of integrating the fragmented literature on animal personality, we felt like early cartographers faced with the challenge of constructing a map of the globe. Our task—much like that of the cartographers—was to piece together the isolated reports about the landscape of personality. These reports came in different languages; used a variety of scales, methods, and notations; and varied

Source: Gosling, S. D., & John, O. P. (1999). Personality dimensions in nonhuman animals: A cross-species review. *Current Directions in Psychological Science, 8,* 69–75. Reprinted by permission.

Editor's note: All citations in the text of this selection have been left intact from the original, but the list of references includes only those sources that are the most relevant and important. Readers wishing to follow any of the other citations can find the full references in the original work or in an online database.

in their scope and reliability. Our first task was to select the most trustworthy reports; starting with more than 100 potentially relevant studies, we selected those that had sample sizes larger than 20 animals and a reasonably broad coverage of personality traits.

To integrate the many pieces of information provided by the diverse research reports, we used the most widely accepted and complete map of personality structure: the human Five-Factor Model (FFM; John, 1990). The FFM is a hierarchical model with five broad factors (Table 1), which represent personality at the broadest level of abstraction. Each bipolar factor (e.g., Extraversion vs. Introversion) summarizes several more specific facets (e.g., sociability), which, in turn, subsume a large number of even more specific traits (e.g., talkative, outgoing). Unfortunately, no short labels capture the broad FFM dimensions adequately, so the traditional labels are easily misunderstood; thus, we use the letters N (for *N*euroticism, *N*ervousness, *N*egative affectivity), A (for *A*greeableness, *A*ltruism, *A*ffection), E (for *E*xtraversion, *E*nergy, *E*nthusiasm), O (for *O*penness, *O*riginality, *O*pen-mindedness), and C (for *C*onscientiousness, *C*ontrol, *C*onstraint).

Are there additional dimensions that might be of special importance for describing the personality of nonhuman animals? In adult human personality, Activity and Dominance are part of the E dimension. In children, however, Activity may form a separate dimension (John, Caspi, Robins, Moffitt, & Stouthamer-Loeber, 1994), and temperament models (Buss & Plomin, 1984) also consider it separate. Moreover, many socially living animal species show individual differences related to status in the dominance hierarchy: Individuals with high status can control others

and get their way. To explore whether Activity and Dominance form separate dimensions in animals, we added them to the five FFM dimensions in our preliminary framework (see Table 2).

Our review includes 19 factor analytic studies and represents 12 different species. We reviewed the items defining each personality factor in each study and compared them with the definitions of the seven potential dimensions in Table 2. If there was a match in item content, we classified the animal factor into one of the seven dimensions and included its label (or a short definition) in the appropriate column of Table 2.

Extraversion, Neuroticism, and Agreeableness: Cross-Species Dimensions?

Three human FFM dimensions—E, N, and A—showed considerable generality across species. Of the 19 studies, 17 identified a factor related to E. The factor labels in the E column in Table 2 range from Surgency in chimpanzees to Sociability in pigs, dogs, and rhesus monkeys; Energy in cats and dogs; Vivacity in donkeys; and a dimension contrasting Bold Approach versus Avoidance in octopuses. The particular labels may differ, but they all reflect core features of the broad E dimension (see Table 1). Factors related to N appeared almost as frequently; again, despite the differences in factor labels, these animal factors capture core elements of N, such as Fearfulness, Emotional Reactivity, Excitability, and low Nerve Stability. Factors related to A appeared in 14 studies, with Affability, Affection, and Affinity capturing the high pole of A, and Aggression, Hostility, and Fighting capturing the low pole.

TABLE 1   The Dimensions of the Five-Factor Model (FFM)

FFM DIMENSION LABEL	EXAMPLES OF FACETS
N Neuroticism vs. Emotional Stability	Anxiety, depression, vulnerability to stress, moodiness
A Aggreableness vs. Antagonism	Trust, tendermindedness, cooperation, lack of aggression
E Extraversion vs. Introversion	Sociability, assertiveness, activity, positive emotions
O Open vs. Closed to Experience	Ideas/intellect, imagination, creativity, curiosity
C Conscientiousness vs. Impulsiveness	Deliberation, self-discipline, dutifulness, order

Note. See John (1990) and Costa and McCrae (1992) for details.

TABLE 2 Review of Animal Personality Factors: Factor Labels Organized in Terms of the Five-Factor Model (FFM) Plus Two Potential Additional Dimensions

| SPECIES | Trait Dimensions in the Human FFM | | | | | Additional Dimensions | | STUDY |
	NEUROTICISM	AGREEABLENESS	EXTRAVERSION	OPENNESS	CONSCIENTIOUSNESS	DOMINANCE	ACTIVITY	
Chimpanzee	Emotional Stability	Agreeableness	Surgency	Openness	Dependability	Dominance		King and Figueredo (1997)
	Audiovisual Reactivity		Affect-Extraversion		Task Behavior		Activity	Bard and Gardner (1996)
	Excitability-Agitation	Aggression; Affinity[a]	Social Play	Curious-Playful		Submission		Hooff (1973)
Gorilla	Fearfulness	Understanding	Extroversion			Dominance		Gold and Maple (1994)
Rhesus monkey	Tense-Fearful	Aggressive	Solitary	Curious-Playful		Confidence		Bolig, Price, O'Neill, and Suomi (1992)
	Excitability		Sociability					Stevenson-Hinde and Zunz (1978); Stevenson-Hinde, Stillwell-Barnes, and Zunz (1980)
								Chamove, Eysenck, and Harlow (1972)
Vervet monkey	Fear	Hostility	Affiliation	Curiousity		Social Competence Assertiveness		McGuire, Raleigh, and Pollack (1994)
Hyena	Excitability	Opportunistic-Self-Serving	Playful-Curious[b]	Competence[c]				Gosling (1998)
Dog	Emotional Reactivity	Sociability; Human-Related Agreeableness[a]	Energy	Learning and Obedience Ability[c]				Gosling and John (1998)
	Stability vs. Excitability	Affection	Sociability			Dominance-Territoriality		Coren (1998)
	Nerve Stability	Affability; Aggression[a]	Lively Temperament					Wilsson and Sundgren (1997)

TABLE 2 Review of Animal Personality Factors: Factor Labels Organized in Terms of the Five-Factor Model (FFM) Plus Two Potential Additional Dimensions

| | Trait Dimensions in the Human FFM | | | | | Additional Dimensions | | |
SPECIES	NEUROTICISM	AGREEABLENESS	EXTRAVERSION	OPENNESS	CONSCIENTIOUSNESS	DOMINANCE	ACTIVITY	STUDY
	Reactivity	Aggression (Disagreeableness)	Reactivity (Surgency)	Trainability (Openness)				Hart and Hart (1985) (reanalyzed by Draper, 1995)
Cat	Emotional Reactivity	Affection	Energy	Competence[c]				Gosling and John (1998)
Donkey		Obstinancy	Vivacity					French (1993)
Pig		Aggression	Sociability	Exploration-Curiosity				Forkman, Furuhaug, and Jensen (1995)
Rat	Emotionality	Fighting vs. Timidity; Freezing vs. Aggression[a]						Billingslea (1941)
Guppy	Fear-Avoidance		Approach				Bold vs. Avoiding	Budaev (1997)
Octopus	Reactivity						Activity	Mather and Anderson (1993)

Note. All studies are based on factor analyses of individual animals, except Coren (1998) and Hart and Hart (1985), who analyzed experts' ratings of breeds. Several studies did not include factor labels at all or included labels too brief to understand without further information; for these cases, we used high-loading items to help name the factors.

[a] These four studies yielded two separate factors related to Agreeableness.

[b] This factor combined both social and imaginative elements and thus reflects both Extraversion and Openness.

[c] These factors combined elements from both Openness and Conscientiousness.

237

The evidence indicates that chimpanzees, various other primates, nonprimate mammals, and even guppies and octopuses all show individual differences that can be organized along dimensions akin to E, N, and (with the exception of guppies and octopuses) A. These remarkable commonalities across such a wide range of taxa suggest that general biological mechanisms are likely responsible. The way these personality dimensions are manifested, however, depends on the species. For example, whereas the human scoring low on Extraversion stays at home on Saturday night, or tries to blend into a corner at a large party, the octopus scoring low on Boldness stays in its protective den during feedings and attempts to hide itself by changing color or releasing ink into the water.

Openness: Another Potential Cross-Species Personality Dimension?

Factors related to the O dimension in the FFM were identified in 7 of the 12 species. The two major components defining this dimension were curiosity-exploration (interest in new situations and novel objects) and playfulness (which is associated with E when social, rather than imaginative, aspects of play are assessed). Although these factors are similar to the O dimension known from humans, some core facets are obviously missing; openness to ideas and interest in arts are difficult to observe in animals that lack advanced means of symbolic expression, such as language and music. The O factor in these animal studies resembles the early forms of O observed in human toddlers; lacking advanced language skills, their curiosity is manifested in an intense interest in novel objects and events, and their imagination is shown in perspective taking and role shifts characteristic of pretend play.

The evidence for an O-related factor was not consistent across multiple studies of the same species, pointing to methodological differences, most likely in the traits included in the studies. For example, the two chimpanzee studies that did not find an O factor did not include items clearly relevant to O. Given that forms of curiosity have been observed in a wide range of species, a thorough and focused search should provide more consistent evidence for O.

Conscientiousness: Only in Humans and Chimpanzees?

Although cats and dogs showed a factor that combined C and O, chimpanzees were the only species with a separate C factor. The chimpanzee factor was defined more narrowly than in humans but included lack of attention and goal directedness, as well as erratic, unpredictable, and disorganized behavior—characteristics typical of the low pole of C. Why did we not find separate C factors in any other species? The failure to include relevant items cannot explain this finding: In our own studies of dogs and cats, we included items that define C in humans, but they did not form a separate factor. Considering the "superego" aspects of the C factor (following norms and rules, thinking before acting, and other complex cognitive functions involved in the control of impulses), it may not be surprising that we found a separate C factor only in humans and in humans' closest relatives, chimpanzees. These findings suggest C may have appeared relatively recently in the evolution of Homininae, the subfamily comprising humans, chimpanzees, and gorillas.

Dominance and Activity: Two Additional Dimensions?

Dominance emerged as a clear separate factor in 7 of the 19 studies. Although interpreted as Confidence in rhesus monkeys and Assertiveness in hyenas, the factor was essentially the same, correlating substantially with dominance rank. Across studies, the Dominance factor was typically defined by assertiveness or boldness (high E), physical aggression (low A), and low fearfulness (low N). Thus, dominance had more diverse personality implications in animals than in humans, for whom it is related only to the E dimension. Perhaps these differences arise because humans participate in multiple dominance hierarchies that are less clearly defined and involve widely divergent skills: The class bullies may dominate in the school yard, but the conscientious students will get the grades to advance academically, and the open-minded artists will win prizes for their creations. Future research needs to examine more closely the links between dominance rank and personality traits. Personality may vary even among animals of the same rank, and rather than being viewed as a personality trait, dominance rank may be better conceived as a social outcome determined by both personality and physical traits (Buss, 1988).

Finally, our review uncovered scant evidence for the idea that Activity should be retained as a separate dimension of animal personality, with only 2 of the 19 studies showing support. Of the 3 chimpanzee studies, only the study of infants identified a separate Activity factor. This age difference in chimpanzees parallels findings in humans suggesting that Activity may not become integrated with the E dimension until late adolescence (John et al., 1994).

THE SPECTER OF ANTHROPOMORPHISM

A number of the studies summarized in Table 2 relied on human observers rating animals on trait adjectives defined in brief behavioral terms (e.g., playful was defined as "initiates play and joins in when play is solicited"). Although some researchers argue that observer ratings are the best way to assess personality, others are skeptical and worry that these ratings might be anthropomorphic projections. Three kinds of evidence argue against this concern. First, for a wide range of species, including chimpanzees, rhesus monkeys, and hyenas, studies show that independent observers agree about the relative ordering of individuals on a trait. Second, many of the studies reviewed here used behavioral tests in specific situations or carefully recorded ethological observations. Both types of data yielded similar factors. For example, when piglet behavior was tested in specific situations, the E factor was defined by number of vocalizations, number of nose contacts, and location in the pen; when chimpanzee behavior was observed in naturally occurring settings, the E factor was defined by behavior patterns such as "pull limb" (playful social contact), "grasp and poke" (boisterous but relaxed contact), and "gymnastics" (exuberant locomotory play, such as swinging, dangling, turning somersaults). It is remarkable that such similar factors were discovered using such diverse methods. In fact, studies using multiple methods have demonstrated the validity of trait ratings (Capitanio, 1999). Third, our finding that the factor structures showed meaningful differences across species argues against the operation of general rating

biases in observers. For example, in our own work, we found the familiar FFM dimensions for humans but only four factors for dogs, even when we collected personality ratings using the same instrument for both species; the items defining a clear C factor in humans failed to form a separate factor in dogs (Gosling & John, 1998). These differences show that personality structure depends on the individual rated, rather than on the particular items in the rating instrument.

Sex differences are another domain where cross-species differences in the meaning and implications of personality factors can be illustrated. Research on the human FFM has repeatedly shown that women tend to be more emotional and prone to worry (i.e., higher on N) than men (Costa & McCrae, 1992). Does the same sex difference emerge in other species? Not necessarily. To illustrate this point, we collected observer ratings of humans using items previously used in a study of hyenas (Gosling, 1998). In humans, women were described as somewhat higher on N than men; in hyenas, the sex difference was reversed, with males being considerably more high-strung, fearful, and nervous than females (see Figure 1). What explains this dramatic interaction effect? The key is the difference in social organization: In the hyena clan,

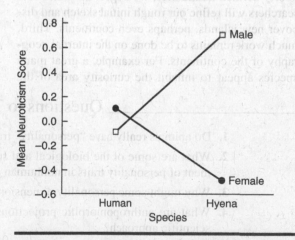

FIGURE 1   Sex differences in standard (z) scores for Neuroticism among humans and hyenas. The ratings for hyenas are from Gosling (1998); the humans (n = 100) were described by peers on the same rating scales used for hyenas.

dominance rank is transmitted through a matrilineal system, and females are larger than males and more dominant. This example suggests that sex differences in personality may be related to the ecological niches occupied by the two sexes in a species, and illustrates how a comparative approach can offer a fresh perspective on the interplay between social and biological factors in personality.

CONCLUSIONS AND FUTURE DIRECTIONS

The cartographic metaphor serves to highlight some limitations of the initial map of animal personality dimensions presented in Table 2. First, Antarctica will be discovered only if one sails south: The lack of evidence for a dimension does not necessarily prove the factor does not exist; studies may not have included the items relevant for the factor. To show that a dimension does not exist in a species requires that future researchers actively search for that dimension. Equipped with our initial map, we can now conduct hypothesis-driven research. For example, we may hypothesize that solitary species (e.g., orangutans) would not show a separate A dimension, or that O occurs only in species that depend on a great variety of food sources. Second, just as early maps look rough by today's standards, with missing land masses and poorly defined boundaries, we expect that future researchers will refine our rough initial sketch and discover new islands, perhaps even continents. Third, much work remains to be done on the internal geography of the continents. For example, a great many species appear to inhabit the curiosity area of the

O continent, but other areas may be inhabited solely by humans and perhaps chimpanzees. Fourth, researchers need to move from mapping personality continents to formulating theories about the movements of tectonic plates, addressing how and why the continents emerged; animal models of personality may be uniquely suited to identify genes for complex traits and to study how these genes work (i.e., functional genomics). Finally, the early sailors knew their maps were not perfect, but imperfect maps were better than no map at all; it is in this spirit that we offer the present classification of animal personality, hoping that future researchers may find this initial sketch helpful in their quest for new discoveries.

REFERENCES

Buss, A. H. (1988). *Personality: Evolutionary heritage and human distinctiveness.* Hillsdale, NJ: Erlbaum.

Darwin, C. (1998). *The expression of emotions in man and animals.* Oxford, England: Oxford University Press. (Original work published 1872).

Draper, T. W. (1995). Canine analogs of human personality factors. *Journal of General Psychology, 122,* 241–252.

King, J. E., & Figueredo, A. J. (1997). The Five-Factor Model plus dominance in chimpanzee personality. *Journal of Research in Personality, 31,* 257–271.

Mather, J. A., & Anderson, R. C. (1993). Personalities of octopuses. (*Octopus rubescens*). *Journal of Comparative Psychology, 107,* 336–340.

McGuire, M. T., Raleigh, M. J., & Pollack, D. B. (1994). Personality features in vervet monkeys: The effects of sex, age, social status, and group composition. *American Journal of Primatology, 33,* 1–13.

Questions to Think About

1. Do animals really have "personality" traits? Why might this be the case?

2. What are some of the biological and social factors that will affect the development of personality traits in nonhuman animals?

3. Why might some personality dimensions appear only in some animal species?

4. What are anthropomorphic projections, and why are they so dangerous for a scientific approach?

5. If we fail to find evidence among nonhuman species for the openness and conscientiousness dimensions (while we do find evidence for extraversion, neuroticism, and agreeableness), how can we determine whether the underlying cause is that these dimensions truly fail to generalize, or that we just do not know how to interpret, measure, and evaluate these dimensions beyond our own species?

34

What Understanding and Acceptance Mean to Me

CARL ROGERS

Carl Rogers (1902–1980) believed that people have an inherent tendency toward growth and maturation, but that this maturation is not inevitable. By emphasizing that each person is responsible for his or her own life, Rogers had a tremendous influence on the development of humanistic approaches to personality as well as on the practice of psychotherapy.

Rogers was raised in a strict religious atmosphere with a strong emphasis on ethics. Like many personality theorists, Rogers was influenced by religious and philosophical ideas and was always concerned with the human spirit. In this selection, Rogers makes one of his central points. He emphasizes the value of learning to accept oneself, of accepting others, of dropping masks, and of becoming more open and self-trusting.

This selection is a transcript of a talk Rogers gave in 1956, and was not published until almost forty years later, long after Rogers had died.

When I was invited to address this conference, I debated for some time before accepting the responsibility. It is difficult for me to know what I can offer to the group at this convention. I am no longer in close contact with classroom teachers in the public schools. My experience along those lines is many years in the past. I feel that I have relatively little knowledge of guidance and personnel work in schools and colleges, even though I blush to admit such ignorance. I do have experience, over many years, in personal counseling; but I believe that only a small fraction of this group is primarily engaged in fulltime counseling.

In addition to these doubts, there is my feeling that almost anything which might be said in regard to understanding and acceptance has already been said in this conference with its theme of "helping people understand themselves." I suspect that by this time many of you share the feeling of the heroine in *My*

Fair Lady when she sings, in the song "Show Me," about how sick she is of words and no action. So it is not without reason that I have questioned myself rather deeply as to what I might have to offer at this point to the conference.

One thing which I fall back upon, one possible point of communication is that we are all individuals who are dealing with people. Each of us is a person dealing with other persons. Furthermore, I suspect that each one of us, in our dealings with these other persons, hopes that as a result of our contact, these individuals will become better informed, more independent, wider, better integrated, and more mature.

This realization that we do have this important area in common makes me feel that perhaps there is something of myself that I might share with you, something which might have meaning to you in your work. I have dealt with individuals over a period of

Source: Rogers, C. (1995). What understanding and acceptance mean to me. *Journal of Humanistic Psychology, 35*(4), 7–22. (Transcript of a talk presented to the Illinois Guidance and Personnel Association 12th Annual Conference in 1956.) Copyright © 1995 by Sage Publications. Reprinted by permission of Sage Publications.

many years and, like you, I have hoped that these relationships would prove constructive. Perhaps then, I can voice some of the lessons which I feel I have learned for myself as I have worked with these individuals.

I would like to say in advance that these statements I am going to make, these learnings that have meaning for me, are not intended to be guides for you or for anyone else. It is my strong belief that each one of us has to work out his own way of dealing effectively with others and that it is of no help to copy or imitate or follow the procedures of another. Yet, the experience of another person and his learnings may have meaning for you and may illuminate some of your own experience, may clarify some of the directions which, as individuals, you are taking.

It is with this hope in mind that I shall try to state as simply as I can some of the learnings that have had meaning for me in my experience with working with people.

In the things that I shall say I suppose I am drawing primarily upon my experiences in working with troubled clients, yet I am also drawing upon my experience in working with graduate students, my experience in workshops, seminars, and other educational enterprises. I might start off these several statements of significant learnings with a negative item. *In my relationships with persons I have found that it does not help, in the long run, to act as though I were something that I am not.* It does not help to behave in an understanding way when actually I am trying to manipulate the other person, not understand him. It does not help to act calm and pleasant when actually I am angry and critical. It does not help to act as though I were permissive when I am really feeling that I would like to set limits. It does not help to act as though I know the answers when I do not. It does not help to act as though I were a loving person when actually I am hostile. It does not help to act as though I were acceptant of another person when underneath that exterior I feel rejection of him. It does not help to act as though I were non-evaluative and non-judgmental, if in fact, I am making judgments and evaluations. It does not help for me to act like a conventional, evaluating teacher if, in fact, I am something quite different. Even on a very simple level I have found that this statement seems to hold. It does not help for me to act

as though I were well when I feel ill. It does not help for me to act fresh when, in actuality, I feel tired. It does not help me to act as though I were full of assurance, when actually I am frightened and unsure.

What I am saying here, put in another way, is that I have not found it to be helpful or effective in my relationships with other people to try to maintain a facade; to act in one way on the surface when I am experiencing something quite different underneath. It does not, I believe, make me helpful in my attempts to build up constructive relationships with other individuals. I would want to make it clear that while I feel I have learned this to be true, I have, by no means, adequately profited from it. In fact, it seems to me that most of the mistakes I make in personal relationships, most of the times in which I fail to be of help to other individuals, can be accounted for in terms of the fact that I have, for some defensive reason, behaved in one way at a surface level, while in reality my feelings run in a contrary direction.

A second thing which I have learned might be stated as follows: *I have found it effective, in my dealings with people, to be acceptant of myself.* I feel that over the years I have learned to become more adequate in listening to myself; so that I know somewhat more adequately than I used to what I am feeling at any given moment—to be able to realize I *am* angry, or that I *do* feel rejecting toward this person, or that I am uninterested in what is going on, or that I am eager to understand this individual. All of these diverse attitudes are feelings which I think I can listen to in myself. One way of putting this is that I feel I have become more adequate in letting myself be what I am. It becomes easier for me to accept myself in the way in which I would like to function.

This must seem to some like a very strange direction in which to move. It seems to me to have value because the curious paradox is that when I accept myself as I am, then I change. I believe that I have learned this from my clients as well as within my own experience— that we cannot change, we cannot move away from what we are, until we thoroughly *accept* what we are. Then change seems to come about almost unnoticed.

Another result which seems to grow out of self-acceptance is that relationships then become real. Real relationships have an exciting way of being vital and meaningful. If I can accept the fact that I am angry or annoyed at this student, then I am also much more likely to be able to accept his feelings in response. I can also accept the changed experience and the changed feelings which are then likely to occur in me and in him. Real relationships tend to change rather than to remain static.

I am not sure that I can make clear what I am trying to say in regard to this matter of self-acceptance. I think of a foreign student, an advanced graduate student who came into one of my courses and she and others asked me a number of questions, to several of which I simply answered that I did not know. For me, this was simply an acceptance of the fact of my ignorance on these points. To her, it was an utterly incredible experience to hear a professor say he did not know. In all her university work in her own country she had never heard such a statement. This experience challenged her interest to a marked degree and helped her to become a person who is seeking for answers, not simply a person who is a passive receptacle for knowledge. Thus, my acceptance of my ignorance established a relationship between us in which she found herself changing.

So I find it effective to let myself be what I am in my attitudes; to know when I have reached my limit of endurance or of tolerance, and to accept that as a fact; to know when I desire to mold or manipulate people, and to accept that as a fact in myself. I would like to be as acceptant of these feelings as of feelings of warmth, interest, permissiveness, kindness, understanding. It is when I do accept all these attitudes as a part of me, then my relationship with the other person becomes what it is and then is able to grow and change most readily.

What I have said up to this point may seem to be somewhat negative in nature, although it does not seem so to me. I come now to a central learning which has had a great deal of significance for me, which I believe comes rather close to the purpose of this conference. I can state this learning as follows: *I have found it of enormous value when I can permit myself to understand another person.*

The way in which I have worded this statement may seem strange to you. Is it necessary to permit oneself to understand another? I think that it is. Our first

reaction to most of the statements which we hear from other people is an immediate evaluation, or judgment, rather than an understanding of it. When a pupil speaks up in class expressing some feeling or attitude or belief, our tendency is, almost immediately, to feel "That's good"; "That's right"; or "That's bad"; "That's incorrect." Very rarely do we permit ourselves to understand precisely what the meaning of his statement is to him. Perhaps I can make this even sharper by suggesting that you imagine yourself in conversation with someone who holds a point of view very different from your own on a topic such as segregation, or politics, or the best means of teaching reading. I believe that if you engage in such imaginary conversations for even a few seconds you will not find yourself endeavoring to understand what the person is saying from his point of view, but immediately forming your own judgment of it, or your own argumentative response to it. So I say, it is not an easy thing to permit oneself to understand an individual, to enter thoroughly and completely and empathetically into his frame of reference. I think of one woman in a seminar when I was counseling a client in front of this group. This woman came up to me excitedly after one of the interviews and said:

> *I realize now for the first time what it means really to listen to another person without trying to judge or evaluate. I felt that I entered into this client's experience, I really* understood *another person for the first time in my life.*

This, I too, have found to be a valuable and rewarding experience.

To understand is enriching in a double way. I find when I am working with clients in distress that to understand the bizarre world of a partially psychotic individual, or to understand and sense the attitudes of a person who feels that life is too tragic to bear, or to understand a man who feels he is a worthless and inferior individual—each of these understandings somehow enriches me in giving a realization and experience of how other individuals face and meet life. Even more important, perhaps, is the fact that my understanding of these individuals permits them to change. It permits them to accept their own fears and bizarre thoughts and tragic feelings and discouragements as well as their moments of courage and kindness and love and sensitivity; and it is their experience as well as mine that once someone has fully understood those feelings, this has enabled them to accept those feelings in themselves. Then, they find both the feelings and themselves changing. Whether it is understanding a woman who feels that very literally she has a hook in her head by which others lead her about, or understanding a man who feels that no one is as lonely, no one is as separated from others as he, I find these understandings to be of value to me. But also, and perhaps even more importantly, to be understood has a very positive value to these individuals.

Here I am going to digress a bit and talk about one practical channel for understanding others which I have found extremely helpful in my experience with classes of students. Because I have wanted to know the personal and individual reactions of students in my classes, I frequently set up the policy of asking for individual weekly reaction sheets, as I call them, on which the student can express any feeling he wishes which is relevant to the course. He may talk about the work he is doing; he may express feelings in regard to the class or the instructor; he may quite literally use it in any way he wishes, and he is given my solemn assurance that what he says on these sheets will have no relationship whatsoever to the grade he receives in the course. The use of this simple device has been one of the most meaningful things I have ever done in my teaching. I would like to talk, at some length, about this simple approach.

In the first place, it has caused me to realize that a course is not a course, it is an assemblage of many highly individual perceptions of experience. For example, during this past summer, I taught a course in Personality. I did certain things, I presented certain materials to the group, such as playing tape recordings of interviews. I facilitated discussions. Anyone looking in on the group as an outside observer would say that this was a definite, describable, given experience in which 30 different people were participating. If you ask for the individual reactions of the students, you find that it is not one thing, it is 30 different experiences. The same class can view so differently one and the same situation. I think I would like to read to you some brief excerpts from the reaction sheets which these students turned in. It may help you to re-

alize why I find it of value for myself to permit myself to understand another person.

Let me, for example, take a few excerpts from the statements that were turned in at the end of the first week. One student says,

> My immediate thoughts were favorable. I prefer discussions to lectures. I have been able to read without specific assignments. Each member of the class seems to be at a different stage of sophistication regarding personality.

As I understand this person, he is saying, "I am quite comfortable in the way in which the course is starting. Everything is fine." Here is another statement:

> I feared that the course might prove too much for a person of my academic standards to cope with. There was only one way that I could find out if this was so; it was necessary for me to register for such a course and find out for myself. I have thus far found the two class sessions interesting, though there were instances that terms referred to were a bit over my head. I keep reminding myself that we all have to start somewhere, and this happens to be that way for me.

Here, if I am understanding him correctly, is a person who is saying, "I feel pretty insecure, but perhaps I can swim in this difficult stream." Here is another reaction:

> The first week of class has been one of uncomfortableness and apprehension. These feelings were heightened even more by Friday's session. Even though theory of personality is not an area that is completely foreign to me, it is an area in which I do not have a strong academic background. As I listened to some of the other class members' purposes, projects, etc. I wondered how I could reconcile my very primary needs in this field with their seemingly strongly defined and explicit needs. One of the ways I can see of somewhat removing this apprehension and uncomfortableness is to do some very concentrated reading and thus be better able to share and contribute to class discussions effectively.

To me it is helpful to understand that for such a student this is a frightening new experience in which the main feeling is one of fear. There are also feelings of criticism. Here is one:

The class seems to be lacking in planning and direction.

Here is another:

Since I had looked forward to a fairly rigorous course in personality theory, the first two class meetings have been disappointing. I am sure that in classes such as the last two, one learns something about conducting a class like this, about how other people and I react; but due to the size of the group, it seems to be a bad example even of these things; and these are not what I am primarily interested in. I keep wishing the course would start.

And then one runs across a reaction like this, which also is a reaction to this same first week of this same course:

I couldn't help hearing words beneath words. Everyone spoke to the instructor. To the instructor only; "I want to know you." "I want you to know me." "See my bright shiny mind; see how sharp and clear it is." "I'm no beginner at this; I know plenty." "I don't know but I want to learn." "I hope you'll help me with this." And one person said, "I want to know myself and other people to know themselves. That seems to me the only human use for a personality theory." I liked listening, liked hearing the voices; I liked watching the instructor; but it seems a very long way away. I felt a terrifying distance. I couldn't stay with the voice or the group long. I kept seceding—to interrogate myself. Why was I here? Did I have a speakable purpose? It's all stiff and formal still. I wished my purposes were as clear and keen as some I heard. And persistently, every few minutes, I thought: We are a room full of strangers.

I am sure that this group of students was not unusual. Here is simply a sample of the wide variety of reactions and feelings which occur in every course— favorable reactions, frightened reactions, critical reactions, sensitive reactions. I feel as though I would like to give you many more of their statements, but let me concentrate on two other samples.

I will take one sampling of reactions during the fourth week of the course. I had been teaching the course in quite a free fashion, with a good deal of discussion, with relatively little direction on my part. Here are some of the reactions by the fourth week of the course. Here is one:

My feeling is one of indefinable revulsion with the tone of indecency. As nearly as I can get it, the answer lies somewhere around my dislike of the fuzzy, and my liking for the clear-cut.

I am sure that reactions just as violently negative occur in almost any class we teach. Yet, by our formal structure, we keep ourselves from knowing these reactions. Personally, I have found it of the utmost value to realize how keenly and sharply and negatively people are responding, as well as to understand those who are responding in a much more positive fashion. Here is another reaction from that fourth week:

I was somewhat disturbed by the discussion session wherein several members of the class expressed a desire for a more directive approach from the instructor. I asked myself the question, "Is the atmosphere of this class, which I find so conducive to thought, really so different from the experience of the other members of the class as they expressed?" I found myself questioning whether or not those who were disturbed by the freedom were here to try to find ways and means of understanding human behavior, or whether they desired repetitions from various texts by you through lectures. I could not help but feel that if they desired the latter that they were in the wrong place. The place for texts is the library. I shall have to admit that I am vain enough to believe that I can direct my own readings at this level of education.

Here is another reaction to this same week:

The past week proved to be the most fruitful one for the birth and development of new ideas in a long, long time. The project which I want to carry out for this course was discussed with various people and many new aspects of the problem involved were discovered. This kind of thing seems to happen every time when you share an idea with other people: the more you think that you really have thought of everything, the more you are surprised to find new facets.

Here is one more reaction written by a foreign student and, therefore, rather clumsily worded. He says:

It seems to me that our class follows the best, fruitful and scientific way of learning. But for people who have been taught for a long, long time, as we have, by the lecture type, authoritative method, this new procedure is ununderstandable. People like us are conditioned to hear the instructor, to keep passively our notes and memorize their reading assignments for the exams. There is no need to say that it takes a long time for people to get rid of their habits regardless of whether or not their habits are sterile, infertile and barren.

Thus, during this one week, in which they were all exposed to the same situation, I found that the reactions ranged from finding the class utterly revolting to finding it exceptionally fruitful, from experiencing it as just what is wanted to finding it a challenge to old but sterile habits.

As the course continues the reactions become more positive in nature. One student who has evidently been infected by the atmosphere of the class says:

I've been caught up by the idea that "listening is contagious." Or maybe what I want to say is that I've been contaminated by the phenomenon of listening in this class. I want to express the strong feeling I have this week: I like us all so much. To the important thing is not just the positive feeling, but the "all of us." And I think that's where listening comes in. It seems to me as if somehow I have shaken off my rigidity in relating to other people in the class. Now, instead of a categorical response, I can listen, and I hear. I'm rarely without emotional response to this or any other group, but lately I've been quite intellectually stimulated. Suddenly, I'm more realistically aware of the paucity of my formal knowledge. And although I have had glimmers of this lack before, and a thousand "good intentions" for repairing it, I now feel a real intellectual hunger. I think it's because I have now experienced the twofoldedness of communication. It's expression, of course; but it's also listening. I listened. And the experience has forced me to revise my feelings about the omniscience of my wisdom. I feel somehow quite humble, and very grateful.

I believe this student has voiced the same values I feel in listening—that it opens up new vistas of knowledge, it makes me realize how much there is that I have not yet learned.

At the risk of continuing this digression too long, I would like to quote several things from a student who was one of the most quietly resentful and rebellious of any in the course. I must say that if I had not had these reaction sheets, I would have simply assumed that here was a calm quiet girl, who came to

nearly all the meetings of the class, sat through them without taking part in the discussion, was quietly learning the material of the course. But her reaction sheets revealed her as being at times almost violently antagonistic. I would like to give three excerpts from her reaction statements toward the end of the course. In one of these reports she says:

Class this last week has not raised my blood pressure quite as much, but I haven't found it as interesting either. All and all, I'm coming to the realization that in spite of myself I'm getting something from the course.

The following week, however, her whole reaction is taken up with a violent attack upon me. I had played a recording of an interview from another therapeutic orientation and commented on it and she says:

Your own remarks, which you so carefully stated as being biased—but you needn't have since the whole presentation was—only showed more clearly the weakness of your position. A theory which rests on attacks against other theories is worthless. Only when a theory can show inner consistency is it valid and worthy. Mud-slinging attacks only indicate the weakness of the adherent to a belief; they weaken immeasurably their own stand.

The rest of the reactions were quite sarcastic and equally antagonistic.

One week later she turned in her final reaction to the course. She says:

This course has been of great interest to me, even though I have maintained a rather consistent silence. I have been angry; I have gone from class filled with fury—fury at first over the fact that the class was so lacking in structure, lacking in unity of purpose, lacking in everything. It all seemed so completely pointless. I would come back solely to see if it actually could go on as it had. Next, I became very angry over your biased presentation of psychoanalytic approaches. (I was biased enough myself pro analysis that I couldn't stand your bias!)

Again and again in my mind these past few days I have found myself thinking about this darn class; I don't seem to be able to escape it. I find myself thinking again and again of a quotation which I cannot remember in its entirety—it's from Walter Whitman, I think, and it goes something like this—"Have you learned lessons only of those who were easy with you . . . have you not also learned great lessons from those who disputed the passionate with you?"

Well, anyway, that seems to be the way I feel at this point about the course. It has been a battle for me, veiled though it has been. I have come up with no world-shaking conclusions. I doubt that I will know for some time just what I have achieved from this, but one thing is certain, I am not the same as I was prior to this experience.

Looking back now, I try to remember just what my original purpose was in taking the course. I think it was to find out whether or not my own psychoanalytic bias was correct in its impression of non-directive procedures, and to find out specifically about client-centered theory and practice—mainly to discredit it, to have information with which to continue my own bias and prejudice, to enable me to argue intelligently against it.

Yet, in my readings, I have found many things which I do like. I have amazed myself. I have come to no final conclusions, however, but, at least the door is open and I have achieved a measure of objectivity about it. Time will tell just what the outcome of this all will be, but no longer is there the closed mind and prejudiced approach. If I gained nothing more from the course, but this standard alone it would be a great contribution to my future learning.

My only regret is that for so long during the quarter I had not the time nor the energy to devote myself to the readings which I would like to have done. Now, however, there will be time to seek some of the answers to the questions raised in my mind. Perhaps, it would seem that there is great merit to this student-centered teaching. I know that I will not be finished with this course for quite some time to come. So thanks a lot for jolting me out of a certain smug lethargy!

To me it is very enriching indeed to permit myself to understand this wide range variety of reactions to what outwardly is but one course. I find that when I can permit myself to understand these extremely varied reactions, that my contributions to the group are so much richer, so much more personal, so much more responsive to the individuals who compose the group. To put it a slightly different way, I have found that when I can permit myself to understand the students in my classes and their real feelings, the whole interactional experience becomes much more valuable for

them and for me. For myself, this is an extension of what I have already learned in counseling with individuals, that to understand another person's private world of feelings is a mutually rewarding experience.

I have talked at considerable length about what understanding another person means to me. There is another very closely related learning which perhaps should already have been part of what I have said. I can voice this learning very briefly: *I have found it highly rewarding when I can accept another person.*

I have found that truly to accept another person and his feelings is by no means an easy thing, any more than is understanding. I think this can be quite well illustrated from the excerpts I have just read to you. Can I really permit a student to feel hostile toward me? Can I accept him when he views life and psychological problems in a way quite different from mine? Can I accept his anger as a real and legitimate part of himself? Can I accept him when he feels very positively toward me, admiring me and wanting to model himself after me?

All this is involved in acceptance and it does not come easy. I believe that it is an increasingly common pattern in our culture for each of us to believe, "Every other person must feel and think and believe the same as I do." We find it very hard to permit our children or our parents or our spouses or other countries to feel differently than we do about particular issues or problems. We cannot permit a student to differ from us or to utilize his experience in his own way and to discover his own meaning in it—the right of the student to enter a course with an instructor and to see it in his own way—this is one of the most priceless potentialities of life. Each of us is an island unto himself, in a very real sense; and he can only build bridges to other islands if he is first of all content to be himself and permitted to be himself. So I find that when I can accept another person, which means specifically accepting the feelings and attitudes and beliefs that he has as a real and vital part of him, then I am assisting him to become a person; and there seems to me great value in this.

All that I have been saying thus far is very much of one piece. It is only when I can be myself, when I can accept myself, that it is possible for me to understand others and accept others. There are plenty of times and plenty of relationships in which I do not achieve this, and then it seems to me life in these relationships is superficial. My relationship with these individuals is not particularly helpful. I tend either to make these people dependent on me or hostile to me. I do not like the results which ensue when I fail to profit from the learning I have mentioned. On the other hand, in the rather rare experience when these learnings do combine when I am able to accept myself as I am, and to be that self; when I am truly understanding of the way life seems to this other person, and when I can accept him as a separate individual who is not necessarily like me in attitudes or feelings or beliefs, then the relationship seems exceptionally profitable; and both the other person and I gain from it in deep and significant ways. We tend, I think, in such experience, to grow towards being more mature persons. So I have come to prize these learnings because they seem to lead to the development of separate, unique, and creatively different personalities.

I would like to go on to two or three additional learnings, which I will try to state much more briefly. *I have found it of value to be open to the realities of life as they are revealed in me and in other people.* To me, this seems such a personal learning that I am not at all sure that I can communicate it to you. Perhaps I can express a part of it by saying simply that life *is*. It is not something I have to feel responsible for. As Eliza points out to Professor Higgins in *My Fair Lady*, the tide comes in without him pulling it and the earth spins without him twirling it. Somehow, when I can take this attitude of being a part of life, but responsible only for my own small portion of it, responsible really only for me and my reactions, then I find that I enjoy it much more. Then I can appreciate something of the incredible complexity of persons, and can realize that though I categorize them in some of my simple-minded and ignorant classifications, they are far more richly differentiated than any of the pigeonholes into which I can put them. I find that I can appreciate both the delicacy and fragile nature of life and of individuals; but I can also appreciate the strength and ruggedness which is equally evident.

Another learning which has had meaning to me, or perhaps it is the same learning voiced in a somewhat different way, is: *The more I am able to under-*

stand myself and others, the more I accept myself and others, the more that I am open to the realities of life, the less do I find myself wishing to rush in.

What I mean by this is that I have become less and less inclined to hurry in to fix things, to set goals, to mold people, to manipulate and push them in the way that I would like them to go. I am much more content simply to be myself and to let another person be himself. I know very well that this must seem like a strange, almost an Oriental point of view. What is life for if we are not going to do things to people? What is life for if we are not going to mold them to our purposes? What is life for if we are not going to teach them the things that *we* think they should learn? How can anyone hold such a static point of view as the one I am expressing? I am sure that attitudes such as these must be a part of the reaction of many of you.

Yet, the paradoxical aspect of my experience is that the more I am simply willing to be myself, in all this complexity of life, and the more I am willing to understand and accept the realities in myself and in other people, the more change seems to be stirred up. It is a very paradoxical thing—that to the degree that each one of us is willing to be himself, then he finds not only himself changing; but he finds that other people to whom he relates are also changing. At least this is a very vivid part of my experience, and one of the deepest things I think I have learned in my personal and professional life.

There is one final learning about which I should like to speak. It is perhaps basic to all of the things I have said thus far. It has been forced upon me by more than 25 years of trying to be helpful to individuals in personal distress. It is simply this: *It has been my experience that persons have a basically positive direction.* In my deepest contacts with individuals in therapy, even those whose troubles are most disturbing, whose behavior has been most antisocial, whose feelings seem most abnormal, I find this to be true. When I can sensitively understand the feelings which they are expressing, when I am able to accept them as separate persons in their own right, then I find that they tend to move in certain directions. What are these directions in which they tend to move? The words which I believe are most truly descriptive are words such as positive, constructive, moving toward self-actualization, growing toward maturity, growing toward socialization. I have come to feel that the more fully the individual is understood and accepted, the more he tends to drop the false front with which he has been meeting life, and the more he tends to move in a direction which is forward.

I would not want to be misunderstood on this. I do not have a Pollyanna view of human nature. I am quite aware that out of defensiveness and inner fear individuals can and do behave in ways which are horribly destructive, immature, regressive, antisocial, hurtful. Yet, one of the most refreshing and invigorating parts of my experience is to work with such individuals and to discover the strongly positive directional tendencies which exist in them, as in all of us, at the deepest levels.

CONCLUSION

I am a little astonished at the highly personal trend which this talk has taken as I have prepared it. I had not quite anticipated that I would reveal so much. I wonder if I will dare to give it.

Does it have anything at all to do with you and the work in which you are engaged? I am not in the least sure. Yet I can think of two possibilities, each of which leaves me somewhat encouraged. You may find yourself inwardly objecting to almost all that I have said.

You may feel, "This is not at all what my experience has taught me." If so, I shall feel that my remarks have been worthwhile because I believe that in that case you will probably be impelled to formulate more clearly for yourself just what you have learned from your dealings with individuals, what you have learned from your relationships with your students and your clients, as well as your supervisors and administrators; and perhaps you can work out more clearly the meanings that your professional experience has had for you and, consequently, the directions you will want to take.

And if, on the other hand, some of the meanings that I have found in understanding and acceptance, in my own experience, resonate or seem to be in tune with some part of your experience in dealing with the many individuals with whom you work, then perhaps that too, will strengthen you in thinking your own thoughts. It may help you in discovering more sharply the meaning of your experience, learning more clearly the ways in which you have found it helpful to relate to your students and to others; and thus finding more definitely the direction which is meaningful to you in your own life. At any rate, that is my hope.

———— Questions to Think About ————

1. How is Rogers's humanistic–existential approach to personality very different from most other personality approaches?

2. Rogers is perhaps best known for emphasizing the importance of "unconditional positive regard." How has this idea been adopted into our common culture?

3. Rogers welcomed systematic testing of his ideas, and in fact demanded evaluations of his type of psychotherapy. How can we validate ideas such as Rogers's notion that a person should "become one's self"?

4. Rogers points out a paradoxical aspect of the relationship between acceptance and change: He claims that accepting himself, including those aspects of himself that fall short of his ideal, leads to greater positive change than he accomplishes by direct attempts to change. That is, flaws and limitations are better overcome by accepting them than by fighting them. Why might this be the case?

35

Love and Its Disintegration
in Contemporary Western Society

ERICH FROMM

Erich Fromm (1900–1980) was born in Frankfurt am Main, Germany, to a father whom he described as a moody businessman and a mother who suffered bouts of depression. Despite this childhood environment, Fromm grew up to pursue a doctorate from the University of Heidelberg, study at the University of Munich and the Psycho-Analytic Institute in Berlin, and become a renowned psychoanalyst. Initially a follower of Freud, Fromm eventually developed his own theories that human behavior stems not from unconscious drives, but rather from the needs of a conscious person existing within a network of societal demands. He is thus one of the founders of the existential and humanistic movement. Fromm also disdained the traditional passive and noncommittal role of the psychoanalyst and encouraged the utilization of a more participatory role in treating patients.

In this selection, Fromm bemoans the loss of true love, and notes that in modern society, too many of us are alienated from ourselves, from others, and from nature. We try to overcome this existential alienation of modern society by "having fun." But, alas, it does not work.

If love is a capacity of the mature, productive character, it follows that the capacity to love in an individual living in any given culture depends on the influence this culture has on the character of the average person. If we speak about love in contemporary Western culture, we mean to ask whether the social structure of Western civilization and the spirit resulting from it are conducive to the development of love. To raise the question is to answer it in the negative. No objective observer of our Western life can doubt that love—brotherly love, motherly love, and erotic love—is a relatively rare phenomenon, and that its place is taken by a number of forms of pseudo-love which are in reality so many forms of the disintegration of love.

Capitalistic society is based on the principle of political freedom on the one hand, and of the market as the regulator of all economic, hence social relations, on the other. The commodity market determines the conditions under which commodities are exchanged, the labor market regulates the acquisition and sale of labor. Both useful things and useful human energy and skill are transformed into commodities which are exchanged without the use of force and without fraud under the conditions of the market. Shoes, useful and needed as they may be, have no economic value (exchange value) if there is no demand for them on the market; human energy and skill are without exchange value if there is no demand for them under existing market conditions. The owner of capital can buy labor and command it to work for the profitable investment of his capital. The owner of labor must sell it to capitalists under the existing market

Source: Fromm, E. (1956). Love and its disintegration in contemporary Western society. In E. Fromm, *The art of loving* (pp. 83–107). New York: Harper & Row. Copyright © 1956 by Erich Fromm. Copyright renewed © 1984 by Annis Fromm. Reprinted by permission of HarperCollins Publishers, Inc. (Selection is pp. 83–94.)

conditions, unless he is to starve. This economic structure is reflected in a hierarchy of values. Capital commands labor; amassed things, that which is dead, are of superior value to labor, to human powers, to that which is alive.

This has been the basic structure of capitalism since its beginning. But while it is still characteristic of modern capitalism, a number of factors have changed which give contemporary capitalism its specific qualities and which have a profound influence on the character structure of modern man. As the result of the development of capitalism we witness an ever-increasing process of centralization and concentration of capital. The large enterprises grow in size continuously, the smaller ones are squeezed out. The ownership of capital invested in these enterprises is more and more separated from the function of managing them. Hundreds of thousands of stockholders "own" the enterprise; a managerial bureaucracy which is well paid, but which does not own the enterprise, manages it. This bureaucracy is less interested in making maximum profits than in the expansion of the enterprise, and in their own power. The increasing concentration of capital and the emergence of a powerful managerial bureaucracy are paralleled by the development of the labor movement. Through the unionization of labor, the individual worker does not have to bargain on the labor market by and for himself; he is united in big labor unions, also led by a powerful bureaucracy which represents him vis-à-vis the industrial colossi. The initiative has been shifted, for better or worse, in the fields of capital as well as in those of labor, from the individual to the bureaucracy. An increasing number of people cease to be independent, and become dependent on the managers of the great economic empires.

Another decisive feature resulting from this concentration of capital, and characteristic of modern capitalism, lies in the specific way of the organization of work. Vastly centralized enterprises with a radical division of labor lead to an organization of work where the individual loses his individuality, where he becomes an expendable cog in the machine. The human problem of modern capitalism can be formulated in this way:

Modern capitalism needs men who co-operate smoothly and in large numbers; who want to consume more and more; and whose tastes are standardized and can be easily influenced and anticipated. It needs men who feel free and independent, not subject to any authority or principle or conscience—yet willing to be commanded, to do what is expected of them, to fit into the social machine without friction; who can be guided without force, led without leaders, prompted without aim—except the one to make good, to be on the move, to function, to go ahead.

What is the outcome? Modern man is alienated from himself, from his fellow men, and from nature. He has been transformed into a commodity, experiences his life forces as an investment which must bring him the maximum profit obtainable under existing market conditions. Human relations are essentially those of alienated automatons, each basing his security on staying close to the herd, and not being different in thought, feeling or action. While everybody tries to be as close as possible to the rest, everybody remains utterly alone, pervaded by the deep sense of insecurity, anxiety and guilt which always results when human separateness cannot be overcome. Our civilization offers many palliatives which help people to be consciously unaware of this aloneness: first of all the strict routine of bureaucratized, mechanical work, which helps people to remain unaware of their most fundamental human desires, of the longing for transcendence and unity. Inasmuch as the routine alone does not succeed in this, man overcomes his unconscious despair by the routine of amusement, the passive consumption of sounds and sights offered by the amusement industry; furthermore by the satisfaction of buying ever new things, and soon exchanging them for others. Modern man is actually close to the picture Huxley describes in his *Brave New World*: well fed, well clad, satisfied sexually, yet without self, without any except the most superficial contact with his fellow men, guided by the slogans which Huxley formulated so succinctly, such as: "When the individual feels, the community reels"; or "Never put off till tomorrow the fun you can have today," or, as the crowning statement: "Everybody is happy nowadays." Man's happiness today consists in "having fun." Having fun lies in the satisfaction of consuming and "taking in" commodities, sights, food, drinks, cigarettes, people, lectures, books, movies—all are consumed, swallowed. The world is one great object for our appetite, a big apple, a big bottle, a big breast; we are the sucklers, the eternally expectant ones, the hopeful ones—and the eternally disappointed ones. Our character is geared to exchange and to receive, to barter and to consume; everything, spiritual as well as material objects, becomes an object of exchange and of consumption.

The situation as far as love is concerned corresponds, as it has to by necessity, to this social character of modern man. Automatons cannot love; they can exchange their "personality packages" and hope for a fair bargain. One of the most significant expressions of love, and especially of marriage with this alienated structure, is the idea of the "team." In any number of articles on happy marriage, the ideal described is that of the smoothly functioning team. This description is not too different from the idea of a smoothly functioning employee; he should be "reasonably independent," co-operative, tolerant, and at the same time ambitious and aggressive. Thus, the marriage counselor tells us, the husband should "understand" his wife and be helpful. He should comment favorably on her new dress, and on a tasty dish. She, in turn, should understand when he comes home tired and disgruntled, she should listen attentively when he talks about his business troubles, should not be angry but understanding when he forgets her birthday. All this kind of relationship amounts to is the well-oiled relationship between two persons who remain strangers all their lives, who never arrive at a "central relationship," but who treat each other with courtesy and who attempt to make each other feel better.

In this concept of love and marriage the main emphasis is on finding a refuge from an otherwise unbearable sense of aloneness. In "love" one has found, at last, a haven from aloneness. One forms an alliance of two against the world, and this egoism à deux is mistaken for love and intimacy.

The emphasis on team spirit, mutual tolerance and so forth is a relatively recent development. It was preceded, in the years after the First World War, by a concept of love in which mutual sexual satisfaction was supposed to be the basis for satisfactory love relations, and especially for a happy marriage. It was believed that the reasons for the frequent unhappiness in

marriage were to be found in that the marriage partners had not made a correct "sexual adjustment"; the reason for this fault was seen in the ignorance regarding "correct" sexual behavior, hence in the faulty sexual technique of one or both partners. In order to "cure" this fault, and to help the unfortunate couples who could not love each other, many books gave instructions and counsel concerning the correct sexual behavior, and promised implicitly or explicitly that happiness and love would follow. The underlying idea was that love is the child of sexual pleasure, and that if two people learn how to satisfy each other sexually, they will love each other. It fitted the general illusion of the time to assume that using the right techniques is the solution not only to technical problems of industrial production, but of all human problems as well. One ignored the fact that the contrary of the underlying assumption is true.

Love is not the result of adequate sexual satisfaction, but sexual happiness—even the knowledge of the so-called sexual technique—is the result of love. If aside from everyday observation this thesis needed to be proved, such proof can be found in ample material of psychoanalytic data. The study of the most frequent sexual problems—frigidity in women, and the more or less severe forms of psychic impotence in men— shows that the cause does not lie in a lack of knowledge of the right technique, but in the inhibitions which make it impossible to love. Fear of or hatred for the other sex are at the bottom of those difficulties which prevent a person from giving himself completely, from acting spontaneously, from trusting the sexual partner in the immediacy and directness of physical closeness. If a sexually inhibited person can emerge from fear or hate, and hence become capable of loving, his or her sexual problems are solved. If not, no amount of knowledge about sexual techniques will help.

But while the data of psychoanalytic therapy point to the fallacy of the idea that knowledge of the correct sexual technique leads to sexual happiness and love, the underlying assumption that love is the concomitant of mutual sexual satisfaction was largely influenced by the theories of Freud. For Freud, love was basically a sexual phenomenon. "Man having found by experience that sexual (genital) love afforded him his greatest gratification, so that it became in fact a prototype of all happiness to him, must have been thereby impelled to seek his happiness further along the path of sexual relations, to make genital eroticism the central point of his life." The experience of brotherly love is, for Freud, an outcome of sexual desire, but with the sexual instinct being transformed into an impulse with "inhibited aim." "Love with an inhibited aim was indeed originally full of sensual love, and in man's unconscious mind is so still." As far as the feeling of fusion, of oneness ("oceanic feeling"), which is the essence of mystical experience and the root of the most intense sense of union with one other person or with one's fellow men, is concerned, it was interpreted by Freud as a pathological phenomenon, as a regression to a state of an early "limitless narcissism."

It is only one step further that for Freud love is in itself an irrational phenomenon. The difference between irrational love, and love as an expression of the mature personality does not exist for him. He pointed out in a paper on transference love, that transference love is essentially not different from the "normal" phenomenon of love. Falling in love always verges on the abnormal, is always accompanied by blindness to reality, compulsiveness, and is a transference from love objects of childhood. Love as a rational phenomenon, as the crowning achievement of maturity, was, to Freud, no subject matter for investigation, since it had no real existence.

However, it would be a mistake to overestimate the influence of Freud's ideas on the concept that love is the result of sexual attraction, or rather that it is the *same* as sexual satisfaction, reflected in conscious feeling. Essentially the causal nexus proceeds the other way around. Freud's ideas were partly influenced by the spirit of the nineteenth century; partly they became popular through the prevailing spirit of the years after the First World War. Some of the factors which influenced both the popular and the Freudian concepts were, first, the reaction against the strict mores of the Victorian age. The second factor determining Freud's theories lies in the prevailing concept of man, which is based on the structure of capitalism. In order to prove that capitalism corresponded to the natural needs of man, one had to show that man was by nature competitive and full of mutual hostility.

While economists "proved" this in terms of the insatiable desire for economic gain, and the Darwinists in terms of the biological law of the survival of the fittest, Freud came to the same result by the assumption that man is driven by a limitless desire for the sexual conquest of all women, and that only the pressure of society prevented man from acting on his desires. As a result men are necessarily jealous of each other, and this mutual jealousy and competition would continue even if all social and economic reasons for it would disappear.

Eventually, Freud was largely influenced in his thinking by the type of materialism prevalent in the nineteenth century. One believed that the substratum of all mental phenomena was to be found in physiological phenomena; hence love, hate, ambition, jealousy were explained by Freud as so many outcomes of various forms of the sexual instinct. He did not see that the basic reality lies in the totality of human existence, first of all in the human situation common to all men, and secondly in the practice of life determined by the specific structure of society. (The decisive step beyond this type of materialism was taken by Marx in his "historical materialism," in which not the body, nor an instinct like the need for food or possession, serves as the key to the understanding of man, but the total life process of man, his "practice of life"). According to Freud, the full and uninhibited satisfaction of all instinctual desires would create mental health and happiness. But the obvious clinical facts demonstrate that men—and women—who devote their lives to unrestricted sexual satisfaction do not attain happiness, and very often suffer from severe neurotic conflicts or symptoms. The complete satisfaction of all instinctual needs is not only not a basis for happiness, it does not even guarantee sanity. Yet Freud's idea could only have become so popular in the period after the First World War because of the changes which had occurred in the spirit of capitalism, from the emphasis on saving to that on spending, from self-frustration as a means for economic success to consumption as the basis for an ever-widening market, and as the main satisfaction for the anxious, automatized individual. Not to postpone the satisfaction of any desire became the main tendency in the sphere of sex as well as in that of all material consumption.

It is interesting to compare the concepts of Freud, which correspond to the spirit of capitalism as it existed, yet unbroken, around the beginning of this century, with the theoretical concepts of one of the most brilliant contemporary psychoanalysts, the late H. S. Sullivan. In Sullivan's psychoanalytic system we find, in contrast to Freud's, a strict division between sexuality and love.

What is the meaning of love and intimacy in Sullivan's concept? "Intimacy is that type of situation involving two people which permits validation of all components of personal worth. Validation of personal worth requires a type of relationship which I call collaboration, by which I mean clearly formulated adjustments of one's behavior to the expressed needs of the other person in pursuit of increasingly identical—that is, more and more nearly mutual satisfactions, and in the maintenance of increasingly similar security operations." If we free Sullivan's statement from its somewhat involved language, the essence of love is seen in a situation of collaboration, in which two people feel: "We play according to the rules of the game to preserve our prestige and feeling of superiority and merit."

Just as Freud's concept of love is a description of the experience of the patriarchal male in terms of nineteenth-century capitalism, Sullivan's description refers to the experience of the alienated, marketing personality of the twentieth century. It is a description of an "egotism à deux," of two people pooling their common interests, and standing together against a hostile and alienated world. Actually his definition of intimacy is in principle valid for the feeling of any cooperating team, in which everybody "adjusts his behavior to the expressed needs of the other person in the pursuit of common aims" (it is remarkable that Sullivan speaks here of *expressed* needs, when the least one could say about love is that it implies a reaction to *unexpressed* needs between two people).

Love as mutual sexual safisfaction, and love as "teamwork" and as a haven from aloneness, are the two "normal" forms of the disintegration of love in modern Western society, the socially patterned pathology of love. . . .

REFERENCES

Fromm, E. (1955). *The sane society.* NY: Rinehart.
Freud, S. (1953). *Civilization and its discontents* (J. Riviere, Trans.). London: Hogarth Press.
Sullivan, H. S. (1953). *The Interpersonal theory of psychiatry.* New York: W. W. Norton.

_____ Questions to Think About _____

1. How might the current socioeconomic structure of Western society interfere with the development of loving relationships? To what extent is capitalism itself part of the problem?

2. In Fromm's view, why does having fun (or maintaining the façade of having fun) actually increase alienation from ourselves, others, and nature?

3. How can it be that retaining a sense of independence (separateness) can encourage the growth of a strong relationship with another person (togetherness)?

4. How does Fromm define "pseudo-love" and how is it different from what Fromm sees as real love?

5. What is the value of experience and knowledge in building a loving relationship?

36

Self-Actualization and Beyond

ABRAHAM H. MASLOW

Abraham Maslow (1908–1970) was born in New York to Russian-Jewish immigrants; he had a difficult childhood with a mother who engaged in bizarre behaviors. As a child, he was shy, bookish, and neurotic. However, he grew up to reach his full potential and become an eminent humanistic psychologist. Maslow believed that the highest form of human need is the need for self-actualization. However, according to his hierarchy of needs, the baser needs such as biological needs, safety needs, belonging, and esteem needs must be met before the higher needs can become important.

Ultimately, as a humanistic psychologist, Maslow expected the best about the potential of human beings, but had to admit that the darker side of humans is perpetually present and cannot be completely eliminated. This selection is an adaptation of an address Maslow delivered at a professional workshop in 1965. It describes some of Maslow's own journey in developing the approach and describes behaviors that can promote self-actualization. Contrary to the psychoanalytic approach, which focuses on unconscious motivations, and contrary to the behaviorist approach, which focuses on conditioning and rewards, the humanistic approach urges people to live in such a way that they bring out the best aspects of themselves.

In this chapter, I plan to discuss ideas that are in midstream rather than ready for formulation into a final version. I find that with my students and with other people with whom I share these ideas, the notion of self-actualization gets to be almost like a Rorschach ink blot. It frequently tells me more about the person using it than about reality. What I would like to do now is to explore some aspects of the nature of self-actualization, not as a grand abstraction, but in terms of the operational meaning of the self-actualizing process. What does self-actualization mean in moment-to-moment terms? What does it mean on Tuesday at four o'clock?

THE BEGINNINGS OF SELF-ACTUALIZATION STUDIES

My investigations on self-actualization were not planned to be research and did not start out as research.

They started out as the effort of a young intellectual to try to understand two of his teachers whom he loved, adored, and admired and who were very, very wonderful people. It was a kind of high-IQ devotion. I could not be content simply to adore, but sought to understand why these two people were so different from the run-of-the-mill people in the world. These two people were Ruth Benedict and Max Wertheimer. They were my teachers after I came with a Ph.D. from the West to New York City, and they were most remarkable human beings. My training in psychology equipped me not at all for understanding them. It was as if they were not quite people but something more than people. My own investigation began as a prescientific or nonscientific activity. I made descriptions and notes on Max Wertheimer, and I made notes on Ruth Benedict. When I tried to understand them, think about them, and write about them in my journal and my

Source: Maslow, A. H. (1967). Self-actualization and beyond. In J. F. T. Bugental (Ed.), *Challenges of humanistic psychology.* New York: McGraw Hill Book Company. Reprinted with permission.

notes, I realized in one wonderful moment that their two patterns could be generalized. I was talking about a kind of person, not about two noncomparable individuals. There was wonderful excitement in that. I tried to see whether this pattern could be found elsewhere, and I did find it elsewhere, in one person after another.

By ordinary standards of laboratory research, that is of rigorous and controlled research, this simply was not research at all. My generalizations grew out of *my* selection of certain kinds of people. Obviously, other judges are needed. So far, one man has selected perhaps two dozen people whom he liked or admired very much and thought were wonderful people and then tried to figure them out and found that he was able to describe a syndrome—the kind of pattern that seemed to fit all of them. These were people only from Western cultures, people selected with all kinds of built-in biases. Unreliable as it is, that was the only operational definition of self-actualizing people as I described them in my first publication on the subject.

After I published the results of my investigations, there appeared perhaps six, eight, or ten other lines of evidence that supported the findings, not by replication, but by approaches from different angles. Carl Rogers's findings (1961, etc.) and those of his students add up to corroboration for the whole syndrome. Bugental (1965, pp. 266–275) has offered confirmatory evidence from psychotherapy. Some of the new work with LSD, some of the studies on the effects of therapy (good therapy, that is), some test results—in fact everything I know adds up to corroborative support, though not replicated support, for that study. I personally feel very confident about its major conclusions. I cannot conceive of any research that would make major changes in the pattern, though I am sure there will be minor changes. I have made some of those myself. But my confidence in my rightness is not a scientific datum. If you question the kind of data I have from my researches with monkeys and dogs, you are bringing my competence into doubt or calling me a liar, and I have a right to object. If you question my findings on self-actualizing people (Maslow, 1954, pp. 203–205; Maslow, 1962), you may reasonably do so because you don't know very much about the man who selected the people on whom all the conclusions are based. The conclusions are in the realm of pre-science, but the affirmations are set forth in a form that can be put to test. In that sense, they are scientific.

The people I selected for my investigation were older people, people who had lived much of their lives out and were visibly successful. We do not yet know about the applicability of the findings to young people. We do not know what self-actualization means in other cultures, although studies of self-actualization in China and in India are now in process. We do not know what the findings of these new studies will be, but of one thing I have no doubt: When you select out for careful study very fine and healthy people, strong people, creative people, saintly people, sagacious people—in fact, exactly the kind of people that I picked out—then you get a different view of mankind. You are asking how tall can people grow, what can a human being become? These are the Olympic gold-medal winners—the best we have. The fact that somebody can run 100 yards in less than ten seconds means that potentially any baby that is born into the world is, in theory, capable of doing so too. In that sense, any baby that is born into the world can in principle reach the heights that actually exist and can be described.

Intrinsic and Extrinsic Learning

When you look at mankind this way, your thinking about psychology and psychiatry changes radically. For example, 99 percent of what has been written on so-called learning theory is simply irrelevant to a grown human being. "Learning theory" does not apply to a human being growing as tall as he can. Most of the literature on learning theory deals with what I call "extrinsic learning," to distinguish it from "intrinsic learning." Extrinsic learning means collecting acquisitions to yourself like keys in your pocket or coins that you pick up. Extrinsic learning is adding another association or another craft. The process of learning to be the best human being you can be is another business altogether. The far goals for adult education, and any other education, are the processes, the ways in which we can help people to become all they are capable of becoming. This I call intrinsic learning, and I am confining my remarks here entirely to it. That is the way self-actualizing people learn. To help the client achieve such intrinsic learning is the far goal of counseling.

These things I *know* with certainty. There are other things that I feel very confident about—"my smell tells me," so to speak. Yet I have even fewer objective data on these points than I had on those discussed above. Self-actualization is hard enough to define. How much harder it is to answer the question: Beyond self-actualization, what? Or, if you will: Beyond authenticity, what? Just being honest is, after all, not sufficient in all this. What else can we say of self-actualizing people?

B-Values

Self-actualizing people are, without one single exception, involved in a cause outside their own skin, in something outside of themselves. They are devoted, working at something, something which is very precious to them—some calling or vocation in the old sense, the priestly sense. They are working at something which fate has called them to somehow and which they work at and which they love, so that the work-joy dichotomy in them disappears. One devotes his life to the law, another to justice, another to beauty or truth. All, in one way or another, devote their lives to the search for what I have called (1962) the "being" values ("B," for short), the ultimate values which are intrinsic, which cannot be reduced to anything more ultimate. There are about fourteen of these B-values, including the truth and beauty and goodness of the ancients and perfection, simplicity, comprehensiveness, and several more. These B-values are described in the appendix to my book *Religions, Values and Peak Experiences* (1964). They are the values of being.

Meta-Needs and Meta-Pathologies

The existence of these B-values adds a whole set of complications to the structure of self-actualization. These B-values behave like needs. I have called them *meta-needs.* Their deprivation breeds certain kinds of pathologies which have not yet been adequately described but which I call *meta-pathologies*—the sicknesses of the soul which come, for example, from living among liars all the time and not trusting anyone. Just as we need counselors to help people with the simpler problems of unmet needs, so we may need

meta-counselors to help with the soul-sicknesses that grow from the unfulfilled meta-needs. In certain definable and empirical ways, it is necessary for man to live in beauty rather than ugliness, as it is necessary for him to have food for an aching belly or rest for a weary body. In fact, I would go so far as to claim that these B-values are the meaning of life for most people, but many people don't even recognize that they have these meta-needs. Part of our job as counselors may be to make them aware of these needs in themselves, just as the classical psychoanalyst made his patients aware of their instinctoid basic needs. Ultimately, perhaps, we shall come to think of ourselves as philosophical or religious counselors.

We try to help our counselees move and grow toward self-actualization. These people are often all wrapped up in value problems. Many are youngsters who are, in principle, very wonderful people, though in actuality they often seem to be little more than snotty kids. Nevertheless, I assume (in the face of all behavioral evidence sometimes) that they are, in the classical sense, idealistic. I assume that they are looking for values and that they would love to have something to devote themselves to, to be patriotic about, to worship, adore, love. These youngsters are making choices from moment to moment of going forward or retrogressing, moving away from or moving toward self-actualization. As counselors, or as meta-counselors, what can we tell them about becoming more fully themselves?

BEHAVIORS LEADING TO SELF-ACTUALIZATION

What does one do when he self-actualizes? Does he grit his teeth and squeeze? What does self-actualization mean in terms of actual behavior, actual procedure? I shall describe eight ways in which one self-actualizes.

First, self-actualization means experiencing fully, vividly, selflessly, with full concentration and total absorption. It means experiencing without the self-consciousness of the adolescent. At this moment of experiencing, the person is wholly and fully human. This is a self-actualization moment. This is a moment when the self is actualizing itself. As individuals, we all experience such moments occasionally. As counselors, we can help clients to experience them more often. We can encourage them to become totally absorbed in something and to forget their poses and their defenses and their shyness—to go at it whole hog. From the outside, we can see that this can be a very sweet moment. In those youngsters who are trying to be very tough and cynical and sophisticated, we can see the recovery of some of the guilelessness of childhood; some of the innocence and sweetness of the face can come back as they devote themselves fully to a moment and throw themselves fully into the experiencing of it. The key word for this is "selflessly," and our youngsters suffer from too little selflessness and too much self-consciousness, self-awareness.

Second, let us think of life as a process of choices, one after another. At each point there is a progression choice and a regression choice. There may be a movement toward defense, toward safety, toward being afraid; but over on the other side, there is the growth choice. To make the growth choice instead of the fear choice a dozen times a day is to move a dozen times a day toward self-actualization. Self-actualization is an ongoing process; it means making each of the many single choices about whether to lie or be honest, whether to steal or not to steal at a particular point, and it means to make each of these choices as a growth choice. This is movement toward self-actualization.

Third, to talk of self-actualization implies that there is a self to be actualized. A human being is not a *tabula rasa*, not a lump of clay or plastocene. He is something which is already there, at least a "cartilaginous" structute of some kind. A human being is, at minimum, his temperament, his biochemical balances, and so on. There is a self, and what I have sometimes referred to as "listening to the impulse voices" means letting the self emerge. Most of us, most of the time (and especially does this apply to children, young people), listen not to ourselves but to Mommy's introjected voice or Daddy's voice or to the voice of the Establishment, of the Elders, of authority, or of tradition.

As a simple first step toward self-actualization, I sometimes suggest to my students that when they are given a glass of wine and asked how they like it, they try a different way of responding. First, I suggest that they *not* look at the label on the bottle. Thus they will not use it to get any cue about whether or not they *should* like it. Next, I recommend that they close their eyes if possible and that they "make a hush." Now they are ready to look within themselves and try to shut out the noise of the world so that they may savor the wine on their tongues and look to the "Supreme Court" inside themselves. Then, and only then, they may come out and say, "I like it" or "I don't like it." A statement so arrived at is different from the usual kind of phoniness that we all indulge in. At a party recently, I caught myself looking at the label on a bottle and assuring my hostess that she had indeed selected a very good Scotch. But then I stopped myself: What was I saying? I know little about Scotches. All I knew was what the advertisements said, I had no idea whether this one was good or not; yet this is the kind of thing we all do. Refusing to do it is part of the ongoing process of actualizing oneself. Does *your* belly hurt? Or does it feel good? Does this taste good on *your* tongue? Do *you* like lettuce?

Fourth, when in doubt, be honest rather than not. I am covered by that phrase "when in doubt," so that we need not argue too much about diplomacy. Frequently, when we are in doubt we are not honest. Our clients are not honest much of the time. They are playing games and posing. They do not take easily to the suggestion to be honest. Looking within oneself for many of the answers implies taking responsibility. That is in itself a great step toward actualization. This matter of responsibility has been little studied. It doesn't turn up in our textbooks, for who can investigate responsibility in white rats? Yet it is an almost tangible part of psychotherapy. In psychotherapy, one can see it, can feel it can know the moment of responsibility. Then there is a clear knowing of what it feels like. This is one of the great steps. Each time one takes responsibility, this is an actualizing of the self.

Fifth, we have talked so far of experiencing without self-awareness, of making the growth choice rather than the fear choice, of listening to the impulse voices, and of being honest and taking responsibility. All these are steps toward self-actualization, and all of them guarantee better life choices. A person who does each of these little things each time the choice point comes will find that they add up to better choices about what is constitutionally right for him. He comes to know what his destiny is, who his wife or husband will be, what his mission in life will be. One cannot choose wisely for a life unless he dares to listen to himself, *his own self*, at each moment in life, and to say calmly, "No, I don't like such and such."

The art world, in my opinion, has been captured by a small group of opinion and taste makers about whom I feel suspicious. That is an *ad hominem* judgment, but it seems fair enough for people who set themselves up as able to say, "You like what I like or else you are a fool." We must teach people to listen to their own tastes. Most people don't do it. When standing in a gallery before a puzzling painting, one rarely hears "That is a puzzling painting." We had a dance program at Brandeis not too long ago—a weird thing altogether, with electronic music, tapes, and people doing surrealistic and Dada things. When the lights went up everybody looked stunned, and nobody knew what to say. In that kind of situation most people will make some smart chatter instead of saying, "I would like to think about this." Making an honest statement involves daring to be different, unpopular, nonconformist. If we cannot teach our clients, young or old, about being prepared to be unpopular, we might just as well give up right now. To be courageous rather than afraid is another version of the same thing.

Sixth, self-actualization is not only an end state but also the process of actualizing one's potentialities at any time, in any amount. It is, for example, a matter of becoming smarter by studying if one is an intelligent person. Self-actualization means using one's intelligence. It does not mean doing some far-out thing necessarily, but it may mean going through an arduous and demanding period of preparation in order to realize one's possibilities. Self-actualization can consist of finger exercises at a piano keyboard. Self-actualization means working to do well the thing that one wants to do. To become a second-rate physician is not a good path to self-actualization. One wants to be first-rate or as good as he can be.

Seventh, peak experiences (Maslow, 1962; Maslow, 1964) are transient moments of self-actualization. They are moments of ecstasy which cannot be bought, cannot be guaranteed, cannot even be sought. One must be, as C. S. Lewis wrote, "surprised by joy." But one can set up the conditions so that peak experiences are more likely, or he can perversely set up the conditions so that they are less likely. Breaking up an illusion, getting rid of a false notion, learning what one is not good at, learning what his potentialities are *not*—these are also part of discovering what one is in fact.

Practically everyone does have peak experiences, but not everyone knows it. Some people wave these small mystical experiences aside. Helping people to recognize these little moments of ecstasy when they happen is one of the jobs of the counselor or meta-counselor. Yet, how does one's psyche, with nothing external in the world to point at—there is no blackboard there—look into another person's secret psyche and then try to communicate? We have to work out a new way of communication. I have tried one. It is described in another appendix in that same book (*Religions, Values and Peak Experiences*) under the title "Rhapsodic Communications." I think that kind of communication may be more of a model for teaching, and counseling, for helping adults to become as fully developed as they can be, than the kind we are used to when we see teachers writing on the board. If I love Beethoven and I hear something in a quartet that you don't, how do I teach you to hear? The noises are there, obviously. But I hear something very, very beautiful, and you look blank. You hear the sounds. How do I get you to hear the beauty? That is more our problem in teaching than making you learn the ABC's or demonstrating arithmetic on the board or pointing to a dissection of a frog. These latter things are external to both people; one has a pointer, and both can look at the same time. This kind of teaching is easy; the other kind is much harder, but it is part of our job as counselors. It is meta-counseling.

Eighth, finding out who one is, what he is, what he likes, what he doesn't like, what is good for him and what bad, where he is going and what his mission is—opening oneself up to himself—means the exposure of psychopathology. It means identifying defenses, and after defenses have been identified, it means finding the courage to give them up. This is painful because defenses are erected against something which is unpleasant. But giving up the defenses is worthwhile. If the psychoanalytic literature has taught us nothing else, it has taught us that repression is not a good way of solving problems.

Desacralizing

Let me talk about one defense mechanism that is not mentioned in the psychology textbooks, though it is a very important defense mechanism to the snotty and yet idealistic youngster of today. It is the defense mechanism of *desacralizing*. These youngsters mistrust the possibility of values and virtues. They feel themselves swindled or thwarted in their lives. Most of them have, in fact, dopey parents whom they don't respect very much, parents who are quite confused themselves about values and who, frequently, are simply terrified of their children and never punish them or stop them from doing things that are wrong. So you have a situation where the youngsters simply despise their elders—often for good and sufficient reason. Such youngsters have learned to make a big generalization: They won't listen to anybody who is grown up, especially if the grown-up uses the same words which they've heard from the hypocritical mouth. They have heard their fathers talk about being honest or brave or bold, and they have seen their fathers being the opposite of all these things.

The youngsters have learned to reduce the person to the concrete object and to refuse to see what he might be or to refuse to see him in his symbolic values or to refuse to see him or her eternally. Our kids have desacralized sex, for example. Sex is nothing; it is a natural thing, and they have made it so natural that it has lost its poetic qualities in many instances, which means that it has lost practically everything. Self-actualization means giving up this defense mechanism and learning or being taught to resacralize.

Resacralizing

Resacralizing means being willing, once again, to see a person "under the aspect of eternity," as Spinoza says, or to see him in the medieval Christian unitive perception, that is, being able to see the sacred, the eternal, the symbolic. It is to see Woman with a capital "W" and everything which that implies, even when one looks at a particular woman. Another example: One goes to medical school and dissects a brain. Certainly something is lost if the medical student isn't awed but, without the unitive perception, sees the brain only as one concrete thing. Open to resacraliza-

tion, one sees a brain as a sacred object also, sees its symbolic value, sees it as a figure of speech, sees it in its poetic aspects.

Resacralization often means an awful lot of corny talk—"very square," the kids would say. Nevertheless, for the counselor, especially for the counselor of older people, where these philosophical questions about religion and the meaning of life come up, this is a most important way of helping the person to move toward self-actualization. The youngsters may say that it is square, and the logical positivists may say that it is meaningless, but for the person who seeks our help in this process, it is obviously very meaningful and very important, and we had better answer him, or we're not doing what it is our job to do.

Put all these points together, and we see that self-actualization is not a matter of one great moment. It is not true that on Thursday at four o'clock the trumpet blows and one steps into the pantheon forever and altogether. Self-actualization is a matter of degree, of little accessions accumulated one by one. Too often our clients are inclined to wait for some kind of inspiration to strike so that they can say, "At 3:23 on this Thursday I became self-actualized!" People selected as self-actualizing subjects, people who fit the criteria, go about it in these little ways: They listen to their own voices; they take responsibility; they are honest; and they work hard. They find out who they are and what they are, not only in terms of their mission in life, but also in terms of the way their feet hurt when they wear such and such a pair of shoes and whether they do or do not like eggplant or stay up all night if they drink too much beer. All this is what the real self means. They find their own biological natures, their congenital natures, which are irreversible or difficult to change.

THE THERAPEUTIC ATTITUDE

These are the things people do as they move toward self-actualization. Who, then, is a counselor? How can he help the people who come to him to make this movement in the direction of growth?

Seeking a Model

I have used the words "therapy," "psychotherapy," and "patient." Actually, I hate all these words, and I hate the medical model that they imply because the medical model suggests that the person who comes to the counselor is a sick person, beset by disease and illness, seeking a cure. Actually, of course, we hope that the counselor will be the one who helps to foster the self-actualization of people, rather than the one who helps to cure a disease.

The helping model has to give way, too; it just doesn't fit. It makes us think of the counselor as the person or the professional who knows and reaches down from his privileged position above to the poor jerks below who don't know and have to be helped in some way. Nor is the counselor to be a teacher, in the usual sense, because what teachers have specialized in and gotten to be very good at is the "extrinsic learning" I described above. The process of growing into the best human being one can be is, instead, intrinsic learning, as we saw.

The existential therapists have wrestled with this question of models, and I can recommend Bugental's book, *The Search for Authenticity* (1965), for a discussion of the matter. Bugental suggests that we call counseling or therapy "ontogogy," which means trying to help people to grow to their fullest possible height. Perhaps that's a better word than the one I once suggested, a word derived from a German author, "psychogogy," which means the education of the psyche. Whatever the word we use, I think that the concept we will eventually have to come to is one that Alfred Adler suggested a long, long time ago when he spoke of the "older brother." The older brother is the loving person who takes responsibility, just as one does for his young, kid brother. Of course, the older brother knows more; he's lived longer, but he is not qualitatively different, and he is not in another realm of discourse. The wise and loving older brother tries to improve the younger, and he tries to make him better than he is, in the younger's own style. See how different this is from the "teaching somebody who doesn't know nothin'" model!

Counseling is not concerned with training or with molding or with teaching in the ordinary sense of telling people what to do and how to do it. It is not concerned with propaganda. It is a Taoistic uncovering and *then* helping. Taoistic means the noninterfering, the "letting be." Taoism is not a laissez-faire philoso-

phy or a philosophy of neglect or of refusal to help or care. As a kind of model of this process we might think of a therapist who, if he is a decent therapist and also a decent human being, would never dream of imposing himself upon his patients or propagandizing in any way or of trying to make a patient into an imitation of himself.

What the good clinical therapist does is to help his particular client to unfold, to break through the defenses against his own self-knowledge, to recover himself, and to get to know himself. Ideally, the therapist's rather abstract frame of reference, the textbooks he has read, the schools that he has gone to, his beliefs about the world—these should never be perceptible to the patient. Respectful of the inner nature, the being, the essence of this "younger brother," he would recognize that the best way for him to lead a good life is to be more fully himself. The people we call "sick" are the people who are not themselves, the people who have built up all sorts of neurotic defenses against being human. Just as it makes no difference to the rosebush whether the gardener is Italian or French or Swedish, so it should make no difference to the younger brother how his helper learned to be a helper. What the helper has to give is certain services that are independent of his being Swedish or Catholic or Mohammedan or Freudian or whatever he is.

These basic concepts include, imply, and are completely in accord with the basic concepts of Freudian and other systems of psychodynamics. It is a Freudian principle that unconscious aspects of the self are repressed and that the finding of the true self requires the uncovering of these unconscious aspects. Implicit is a belief that truth heals much. Learning to break through one's repressions, to know one's self, to hear the impulse voices, to uncover the triumphant nature, to reach knowledge, insight, and the truth—these are the requirements.

Lawrence Kubie (1953–1954), in "The Forgotten Man in Education," some time ago made the point that one, ultimate goal of education is to help the person become a human being, as fully human as he can possibly be.

Especially with adults we are not in a position in which we have nothing to work with. We already have a start; we already have capacities, talents, directions, missions, callings. The job is, if we are to take this model seriously, to help them to be more perfectly what they already are, to be more full, more actualizing, more realizing in fact what they are in potentiality.

REFERENCES

Bugental, J. F. T. (1965). *The search for authenticity.* New York: Holt, Rinehart and Winston.

Kubie, L. (1953–1954). The forgotten man in education. *Harvard Alumni Bulletin,* 56, 349–353.

Maslow, A. H. (1954). *Motivation and personality.* New York: Harper & Row.

Maslow, A. H. (1962). *Toward a psychology of being.* Princeton, NJ: Van Nostrand.

Maslow, A. H. (1964). *Religions, values and peak experiences.* Columbus: Ohio State University Press.

Rogers, C. R. (1961). *On becoming a person.* Boston: Houghton Mifflin.

Questions to Think About

1. Why should being involved with some cause beyond one's self promote self-actualization? How can people improve themselves if much of their energy is being directed elsewhere?

2. Among the behaviors that Maslow says lead to self-actualization, which one would be the easiest for you to incorporate into your own life? If you were to do so, what do you think the outcome would be?

3. According to Maslow, what is the proper role of the therapist in promoting self-actualization among his or her clients?

4. Do you agree with Maslow that almost everyone has peak experiences, but many do not realize it? How might a "peak" experience fail to be recognized?

37

Existential Bases of Psychotherapy

ROLLO MAY

Existential psychologists are willing to consider anxiety, dread, and even despair as core elements of human existence. Anxiety has been a particular focus of the existential psychologist Rollo May (1909–1994), who sees anxiety as triggered by a threat to one's core values of existence. May believed that anxiety could be harnessed and used as a positive force for self-fulfillment.

Sometimes considered the father of existential psychotherapy, Rollo May actually bridges the gap between existential and humanistic approaches to personality because he sees the human journey as a dignifying one, albeit soaked with anxiety. Like many in the existential tradition, May was interested in the ministry before turning to psychotherapy. In this selection, May provides a striking example of his approach to both psychotherapy and human nature.

Though the existential approach has been the most prominent in European psychiatry and psychoanalysis for two decades, it was practically unknown in America until a year ago. Since then, some of us have been worried that it might become *too* popular in some quarters, particularly in national magazines. But we have been comforted by a saying of Nietzsche's, "The first adherents of a movement are no argument against it."

We have no interest whatever in importing from Europe a ready-made system. I am, indeed, very dubious about the usefulness of the much-discussed and much-maligned term "Existentialism." But many of us in this country have for years shared this approach, long before we even knew the meaning of that confused term.

On the one hand this approach has a deep underlying affinity for our American character and thought. It is very close, for example, to William James' emphases on the immediacy of experience, the unity of thought and action, and the importance of decision and commitment. On the other hand, there is among some psychologists and psychoanalysts in this country a great deal of hostility and outright anger against this approach. I shall not here go into the reasons for this paradox.

I wish, rather, to *be* existentialist, and to speak directly from my own experience as a person and as a practicing psychoanalytic psychotherapist. Some fifteen years ago, when I was working on my book *The Meaning of Anxiety*, I spent a year and a half in bed in a tuberculosis sanitarium. I had a great deal of time to ponder the meaning of anxiety—and plenty of first-hand data in myself and my fellow patients. In the course of this time I studied the two books written on anxiety up till our day, the one by Freud, *The Problem of Anxiety*, and the one by Kierkegaard, *The Concept of Dread*. I valued highly Freud's formulations: namely, his first theory, that anxiety is the reemergence of repressed libido, and his second, that anxiety is the

Source: May, R. (1960). Existential bases of psychotherapy. *American Journal of Orthopsychiatry, 30*, 685–695.

ego's reaction to the threat of the loss of the loved object. Kierkegaard, on the other hand, described anxiety as the struggle of the living being against non-being which I could immediately experience there in my struggle with death or the prospect of being a lifelong invalid. He went on to point out that the real terror in anxiety is not this death as such but the fact that each of us within himself is on both sides of the fight, that "anxiety is a desire for what one dreads," as he put it; thus like an "alien power it lays hold of an individual, and yet one cannot tear one's self away."

What powerfully struck me then was that Kierkegaard was writing about *exactly what my fellow patients and I were going through.* Freud was not; he was writing on a different level, giving formulations of the psychic mechanisms by which anxiety comes about. Kierkegaard was portraying what is immediately experienced by human beings in crisis—the crisis specifically of life against death which was completely real to us patients, but a crisis which I believe is not in its essential form different from the various crises of people who come for therapy, or the crises all of us experience in much more minute form a dozen times a day even though we push the ultimate prospect of death far from our minds. Freud was writing on the technical level, where his genius was supreme; perhaps more than any man up to his time, he *knew about* anxiety. Kierkegaard, a genius of a different order, was writing on the existential, ontological level; he *knew anxiety.*

This is not a value dichotomy; obviously both are necessary. Our real problem, rather, is given us by our cultural-historical situation. We in the Western world are the heirs of four centuries of technical achievement in power over nature, and now over ourselves; this is our greatness and, at the same time, it is also our greatest peril. We are not in danger of repressing the technical emphasis (of which Freud's tremendous popularity in this country were proof if any were necessary). But rather we repress the opposite. If I may use terms which I shall be discussing more fully presently, we repress the *sense of being,* the ontological sense. One consequence of this repression of the sense of being is that modern man's image of himself, his experience of himself as a responsible individual, his experience of his own humanity, have likewise disintegrated.

The existential approach, as I understand it, does not have the aim of ruling out the technical discoveries of Freud or those from any other branch of psychology or science. It does, however, seek to place these discoveries on a new basis, a new understanding or rediscovery, if you will, of the nature and image of man.

I make no apologies in admitting that I take very seriously the dehumanizing dangers in our tendency in modern science to make man over into the image of the machine, into the image of the techniques by which we study him. This tendency is not the fault of any "dangerous" men or "vicious" schools; it is rather a crisis brought upon us by our particular historical predicament. Karl Jaspers, both psychiatrist and existentialist philosopher, holds that we in the Western world are actually in process of losing self-consciousness and that we may be in the last age of historical man. William Whyte in his *Organization Man* cautions that modern man's enemies may turn out to be a "mild-looking group of therapists, who . . . would be doing what they did to help you." He refers here to the tendency to use the social sciences in support of the social ethic of our historical period; and thus the process of helping people may actually make them conformist and tend toward the destruction of individuality. We cannot brush aside the cautions of such men as unintelligent or antiscientific; to try to do so would make *us* the obscurantists.

You may agree with my sentiments here but cavil at the terms "being" and "non-being" and many of you may already have concluded that your suspicion was only too right, that this so-called existential approach in psychology is hopelessly vague and muddled. Carl Rogers remarked in his paper at the American Psychological Association convention last September in Cincinnati that many American psychologists must find these terms abhorrent because they sound so general, so philosophical, so untestable. Rogers went on to point out, however, that he had no difficulty at all in putting the existential principles in therapy into empirically testable hypotheses.

But I would go further and hold that *without* some concepts of "being" and "non-being," we cannot even understand our most commonly used psychological mechanisms. Take for example, *repression, resistance* and *transference.* The usual discussions of these terms hang in mid-air, without convincingness or psychological reality, precisely because we have lacked an underlying structure on which to base them. The term "repression," for example, obviously refers to a phenomenon we observe all the time, a dynamism which Freud clearly described in many forms. We generally explain the mechanism by saying that the child represses into unconsciousness certain impulses, such as sex and hostility, because the culture in the form of parental figures disapproves, and the child must protect his own security with these figures. But this culture which assumedly disapproves is made up of the very same people who do the repressing. Is it not an illusion, therefore, and much too simple, to speak of the culture over against the individual in such fashion and make it our whipping boy? Furthermore, where did we get the ideas that child or adult are so much concerned with security and libidinal satisfactions? Are these not a carry-over from our work with the *neurotic, anxious* child and adult?

Certainly the neurotic, anxious child is compulsively concerned with security, for example; and certainly the neurotic adult, and we who study him, read our later formulations back into the unsuspecting mind of the child. But is not the normal child just as truly interested in moving out into the world, exploring, following his curiosity and sense of adventure— going out "to learn to shiver and to shake," as the nursery rhyme puts it? And if you block these needs of the child, you get a traumatic reaction from him just as you do when you take away his security. I, for one, believe we vastly overemphasize the human being's concern with security and survival satisfactions because they so neatly fit our cause-and-effect way of thinking. I believe Nietzsche and Kierkegaard were more accurate when they described man as the organism who makes certain values—prestige, power, tenderness—more important than pleasure and even more important than survival itself.

My implication here is that we can understand repression, for example, only on the deeper level of the meaning of the human being's potentialities. In this respect, "being" is to be defined as the individual's "pattern of potentialities." These potentialities will be partly shared with other persons but will in every case form a unique pattern in each individual. We must ask

the questions: What is this person's relation to his own potentialities? What goes on that he chooses or is forced to choose to block off from his awareness something which he knows, and on another level *knows that he knows?* In my work in psychotherapy there appears more and more evidence that anxiety in our day arises not so much out of fear of lack of libidinal satisfactions or security, but rather out of the patient's fear of his own powers, and the conflicts that arise from that fear. This may be the particular "neurotic personality of our time"—the neurotic pattern of contemporary "outer-directed," organizational man.

The "unconscious," then, is not to be thought of as a reservoir of impulses, thoughts, wishes which are culturally unacceptable; I define it rather as *those potentialities for knowing and experiencing which the individual cannot or will not actualize.* On this level we shall find that the simple mechanism of repression is infinitely less simple than it looks; that it involves a complex struggle of the individual's *being* against the possibility of *non-being;* that it cannot be adequately comprehended in "ego" and "not-ego" terms, or even "self" and "not-self"; and that it inescapably raises the question of the human being's margin of freedom with respect to his potentialities, a margin in which resides his responsibility for himself which even the therapist cannot take away.

Let us now come back from theory to more practical matters. For a number of years as a practicing therapist and teacher of therapists, I have been struck by how often our concern with trying to understand the patient in terms of the mechanisms by which his behavior takes place blocks our understanding of what he really is experiencing. Here is a patient, Mrs. Hutchens (about whom I shall center some of my remarks this morning) who comes into my office for the first time, a suburban woman in her middle thirties who tries to keep her expression poised and sophisticated. But no one could fail to see in her eyes something of the terror of a frightened animal or a lost child. I know, from what her neurological specialists have already told me, that her presenting problem is hysterical tenseness of the larynx, as a result of which she can talk only with a perpetual hoarseness. I have been given the hypothesis from her Rorschach that she has felt all her life, "If I say what

I really feel, I'll be rejected; under these conditions it is better not to talk at all." During this first hour, also, I get some hints of the genetic *why* of her problem as she tells me of her authoritarian relation with her mother and grandmother, and how she learned to guard firmly against telling any secrets at all. But if as I sit here I am chiefly thinking of these *why's* and *how's* concerning the way the problem came about, I will grasp everything except the most important thing of all (indeed the only real source of data I have), namely, this person now existing, becoming, emerging, this experiencing human being immediately in the room with me.

There are at present in this country several undertakings to systematize psychoanalytic theory in terms of forces, dynamisms and energies. The approach I propose is the exact opposite of this. I hold that our science must be relevant to the distinctive characteristics of what we seek to study, in this case the human being. We do not deny dynamisms and forces—that would be nonsense—but we hold that they have meaning only in the context of the existing, living person; that is to say, in the *ontological* context.

I propose, thus, that we take the one real datum we have in the therapeutic situation, namely, the *existing person* sitting in a consulting room with a therapist. (The term "existing person" is used here as our European colleagues use *Dasein*.) Note that I do not say simply "individual" or "person"; if you take individuals as units in a group for the purposes of statistical prediction—certainly a legitimate use of psychological science—you are exactly *defining out of the picture* the characteristics which make this individual an existing person. Or when you take him as a composite of drives and deterministic forces, you have defined for study everything except *the one to whom these experiences happen,* everything except the existing person himself. Therapy is one activity, so far as I can see, in which we cannot escape the necessity of taking the subject as an existing person.

Let us therefore ask, What are the essential characteristics which constitute this patient as an existing person in the consulting room? I wish to propose six characteristics which I shall call principles, which I find in my work as a psychotherapist. Though these principles are the product of a good deal of thought and experience with many cases, I shall illustrate them with episodes from the case of Mrs. Hutchens.

First, Mrs. Hutchens like every existing person *is centered in herself,* and an attack on this center is an attack on her existence itself. This is a characteristic which we share with all living beings; it is self-evident in animals and plants. I never cease to marvel how, whenever we cut the top off a pine tree on our farm in New Hampshire, the tree sends up a new branch from heaven knows where to become a new center. But this principle has a particular relevance to human beings and gives a basis for the understanding of sickness and health, neurosis and mental health. Neurosis is not to be seen as a deviation from our particular theories of what a person should be. *Is not neurosis, rather, precisely the method the individual uses to preserve his own center, his own existence?* His symptoms are ways of shrinking the range of his world (so graphically shown in Mrs. Hutchens' inability to let herself talk) in order that the centeredness of his existence may be protected from threat; a way of blocking off aspects of the environment that he may then be adequate to the remainder. Mrs. Hutchens had gone to another therapist for half a dozen sessions a month before she came to me. He told her, in an apparently ill-advised effort to reassure her, that she was too proper, too controlled. She reacted with great upset and immediately broke off the treatment. Now technically he was entirely correct; existentially he was entirely wrong. What he did not see, in my judgment, was that this very properness, this overcontrol, far from being things Mrs. Hutchens wanted to get over, were part of her desperate attempt to preserve what precarious center she had. As though she were saying, "If I opened up, if I communicated, I would lose what little space in life I have." We see here, incidentally, how inadequate is the definition of neurosis as a failure of adjustment. *An adjustment is exactly what neurosis is; and that is just its trouble.* It is a necessary adjustment by which centeredness can be preserved; a way of accepting *non-being,* if I may use this term, in order that some little *being* may be preserved. And in most cases it is a boon when this adjustment breaks down.

This is the only thing we can assume about Mrs. Hutchens, or about any patient, when she comes in:

that she, like all living beings, requires centeredness, and that this has broken down. At a cost of considerable turmoil she has taken steps, that is, come for help. Our second principle thus, is: *every existing person has the character of self-affirmation, the need to preserve its centeredness.* The particular name we give this self-affirmation in human beings is "courage." Paul Tillich's emphasis on the "courage to be" is very cogent and fertile for psychotherapy at this point. He insists that in man being is never given automatically but depends upon the individual's courage, and without courage one loses being. *This makes courage itself a necessary ontological corollary.* By this token, I as a therapist place great importance upon expressions of the patients which have to do with willing, decisions, choice. I never let little remarks the patient may make such as "maybe I can," "perhaps I can try," and so on slip by without my making sure he knows I have heard him. It is only a half truth that the will is the product of the wish; I wish to emphasize rather the truth that the wish can never come out in its real power except with will.

Now as Mrs. Hutchens talks hoarsely, she looks at me with an expression of mingled fear and hope. Obviously a relation exists between us not only here but already in anticipation in the waiting room and ever since she thought of coming. She is struggling with the possibility of participating with me. Our third principle is, thus: *all existing persons have the need and possibility of going out from their centeredness to participate in other being.* This always involves risk; if the organism goes out too far, it loses its own centeredness—its identity—a phenomenon which can easily be seen in the biological world. If the neurotic is so afraid of loss of his own conflicted center that he refuses to go out but holds back in rigidity and lives in narrowed reactions and shrunken world space, his growth and development are blocked. This is the pattern in neurotic repressions and inhibitions, the common neurotic forms in Freud's day. But it may well be in our day of conformism and the outer-directed man, that the most common neurotic pattern takes the opposite form, namely, the dispersing of one's self in participation and identification with others until one's own being is emptied. At this point we see the rightful emphasis of Martin Buber in one sense and Harry Stack Sullivan in another, that the human being cannot be understood as a self if participation is omitted. Indeed, if we are successful in our search for these ontological principles of the existing person, it should be true that the omission of any one of the six would mean we do not then have a human being.

Our fourth principle is: *the subjective side of centeredness is awareness.* The paleontologist Pierre Teilhard de Chardin has recently described brilliantly how this awareness is present in ascending degrees in all forms of life from amoeba to man. It is certainly present in animals. Howard Liddell has pointed out how the seal in its natural habitat lifts its head every ten seconds even during sleep to survey the horizon lest an Eskimo hunter with poised bow and arrow sneak up on it. This awareness of threats to being in animals Liddell calls *vigilance*, and he identifies it as the primitive, simple counterpart in animals of what in human beings becomes anxiety.

Our first four characteristic principles are shared by our existing person with all living beings; they are biological levels in which human beings participate. The fifth principle refers now to a distinctively human characteristic, self-consciousness. *The uniquely human form of awareness is self-consciousness.* We do not identify awareness and consciousness. We associate awareness, as Liddell indicates above, with vigilance. This is supported by the derivation of the term—it comes from the Anglo-Saxon *gewaer, waer*, meaning knowledge of external dangers and threats. Its cognates are *beware* and *wary.* Awareness certainly is what is going on in an individual's neurotic reaction to threat, in Mrs. Hutchens' experience in the first hours, for example, that I am also a threat to her. Consciousness, in contrast, we define as not simply my awareness of threat from the world, but *my capacity to know myself as the one being threatened*, my experience of myself as the subject who has a world. Consciousness, as Kurt Goldstein puts it, is man's capacity to transcend the immediate concrete situation, to live in terms of the possible; and it underlies the human capacity to use abstractions and universals, to have language and symbols. This capacity for consciousness underlies the wide range of possibility which man has in relating to his world, and it constitutes the foundation of psychological freedom. Thus human freedom has its ontological base and I believe must be assumed in all psychotherapy.

In his book *The Phenomenon of Man,* Pierre Teilhard de Chardin, as we have mentioned, describes awareness in all forms of evolutionary life. But in man, a new function arises, namely, this self-consciousness. Teilhard de Chardin undertakes to demonstrate something I have always believed, that when a new function emerges the whole previous pattern, the total gestalt of the organism, changes. Thereafter the organism can be understood only in terms of the new function. That is to say, it is only a half truth to hold that the organism is to be understood in terms of the simpler elements below it on the evolutionary scale; it is just as true that every new function forms a new complexity which conditions all the simpler elements in the organism. *In this sense, the simple can be understood only in terms of the more complex.*

This is what self-consciousness does in man. All the simpler biological functions must now be understood in terms of the new function. No one would, of course, deny for a moment the old functions, nor anything in biology which man shares with less complex organisms. Take sexuality for example, which we obviously share with all mammals. But given self-consciousness, sex becomes a new gestalt as is demonstrated in therapy all the time. Sexual impulses are now conditioned by the *person* of the partner; what we think of the other male or female, in reality or fantasy or even repressed fantasy, can never be ruled out. The fact that the subjective person of the other to whom we relate sexually makes least difference in *neurotic* sexuality, say in patterns of compulsive sex or prostitution, only proves the point the more firmly; for such requires precisely the blocking off, the checking out, the distorting of self-consciousness. Thus when we talk of sexuality in terms of sexual *objects,* as Kinsey does, we may garner interesting and useful statistics; but we simply are not talking about human sexuality.

Nothing in what I am saying here should be taken as antibiological in the slightest; on the contrary, I think it is only from this approach that we *can* understand human biology without distorting it. As Kierkegaard aptly put it, "The natural law is as valid as ever." I argue only against the uncritical acceptance of the assumption that the organism is to be understood solely in terms of those elements below it on the evolutionary scale, an assumption which has led us to overlook the self-evident truth that what makes a horse a horse is not the elements it shares with the organisms below it but what constitutes distinctively "horse." *Now what we are dealing with in neurosis are those characteristic and functions which are distinctively human.* It is these that that have gone awry in our disturbed patients. The condition for these functions is self-consciousness—which accounts for what Freud rightly discovered, that the neurotic pattern is characterized by repression and blocking off of consciousness.

It is the task of the therapist, therefore, not only to help the patient become aware; but even more significantly to help him to *transmute this awareness into consciousness.* Awareness is his knowing that something is threatening from outside in his world—a condition which may, as in paranoids and their neurotic equivalents, be correlated with a good deal of acting-out behavior. But self-consciousness puts this awareness on a quite different level; it is the patient's seeing that *he is the one who is threatened,* that he is the being who stands in this world which threatens, he is the subject who *has* a world. And this gives him the possibility of *in-sight,* of "inward sight," of seeing the world and its problems in relation to himself. And thus it gives him the possibility of doing something about the problems.

To come back to our too-long silent patient: After about 25 hours of therapy Mrs. Hutchens had the following dream. She was searching room by room for a baby in an unfinished house at an airport. She thought the baby belonged to someone else, but the other person might let her take it. Now it seemed that she had put the baby in a pocket of her robe (or her mother's robe) and she was seized with anxiety that it would be smothered. Much to her joy, she found that the baby was still alive. Then she had a strange thought, "Shall I kill it?"

The house was at the airport where she at about the age of 20 had learned to fly solo, a very important act of self-affirmation and independence from her parents. The baby was associated with her youngest son, whom she regularly identified with herself. Permit me to omit the ample associative evidence that convinced both her and me that the baby stood for herself. The dream is an expression of the emergence and growth of self-consciousness, a consciousness she is not sure is hers yet, and a consciousness which she considers killing in the dream.

About six years before her therapy, Mrs. Hutchens had left the religious faith of her parents, to which she had had a very authoritarian relation. She had then joined a church of her own belief. But she had never dared tell her parents of this. Instead, when they came to visit, she attended their church in great tension lest one of her children let the secret out. After about 35 sessions, when she was considering writing her parents to tell them of this change of faith, she had over a period of two weeks spells of partially fainting in my office. She would become suddenly weak, her face would go white, she would feel empty and "like water inside," and would have to lie down for a few moments on the couch. In retrospect she called these spells "grasping for oblivion."

She then wrote her parents informing them once and for all of her change in faith and assuring them it would do no good to try to dominate her. In the following session she asked in considerable anxiety whether I thought she would go psychotic. I responded that whereas anyone of us might at some time have such an episode, I saw no more reason why she should than any of the rest of us; and I asked whether her fear of going psychotic was not rather anxiety coming out of her standing against her parents, as though genuinely being herself she felt to be tantamount to going crazy. I have, it may be remarked, several times noted this anxiety at being one's self experienced by the patient as tantamount to psychosis. This is not surprising, for consciousness of one's own desires and affirming them involves accepting one's originality and uniqueness, and it implies that one must be prepared to be isolated not only from those parental figures upon whom one has been dependent, but at that instant to stand alone in the entire psychic universe as well.

We see the profound conflicts of the emergence of self-consciousness in three vivid ways in Mrs. Hutchens, whose chief symptom, interestingly enough, was the denial of that uniquely human capacity based on consciousness, namely, talking: 1) the temptation to kill the baby; 2) the grasping at oblivion by fainting, as though she were saying, "If only I did not have to be conscious, I would escape this terrible problem of telling my parents"; and 3) the psychosis anxiety.

We now come to the sixth and last ontological characteristic, *anxiety.* Anxiety is the state of the human being in the struggle against what would destroy his being. It is, in Tillich's phrase, the state of a being in conflict with non-being, a conflict which Freud mythologically pictured in his powerful and important symbol of the death instinct. One wing of this struggle will always be against something outside one's self; but even more portentous and significant for psychotherapy is the inner side of the battle, which we saw in Mrs. Hutchens, namely, the conflict within the person as he confronts the choice of whether and how far he will stand against his own being, his own potentialities.

From an existential viewpoint we take very seriously this temptation to kill the baby, or kill her own consciousness, as expressed in these forms by Mrs. Hutchens. We neither water it down by calling it "neurotic" and the product merely of sickness, nor do we slough over it by reassuring her, "O.K., but you don't need to do it." If we did these, we would be helping her adjust at the price of surrendering a portion of her existence, that is, her opportunity for fuller independence. The self-confrontation which is involved in the acceptance of self-consciousness is anything but simple: it involves, to identify some of the elements, accepting the hatred of the past, her mother's against her and hers of her mother; accepting her present motives of hatred and destruction; cutting through rationalizations and illusions about her behavior and motives, and the acceptance of the responsibility and aloneness which this implies; the giving up of childhood omnipotence, and acceptance of the fact that though she can never have absolute certainty of choices, she must choose anyway. But all of these specific points, easy enough to understand in themselves, must be seen in the light of the fact that *consciousness itself implies always the possibility of turning against one's self, denying one's self.* The tragic nature of human existence inheres in the fact that consciousness itself involves the possibility and temptation at every instant of killing itself. Dostoevski and our other existential forebears were not indulging in poetic hyperbole or expressing the aftereffects of immoderate vodka when they wrote of the agonizing burden of freedom.

I trust that the fact that existential psychotherapy places emphasis on these tragic aspects of life does not at all imply it is pessimistic. Quite the contrary. The confronting of genuine tragedy is a highly cathartic experience psychically, as Aristotle and others through history have reminded us. Tragedy is inseparably connected with man's dignity and grandeur, and is the accompaniment, as illustrated in the dramas of Oedipus and Orestes *ad infinitum*, of the human being's moments of greatest insight.

I hope that this analysis of ontological characteristics in the human being, this search for the basic principles which constitute the existing person, may give us a structural basis for our psychotherapy. Thus the way may be opened for the developing of sciences of psychology and psychoanalysis which do not fragmentize man while they seek to study him, and do not undermine his humanity while they seek to help him.

Questions to Think About

1. For existentialists, the anxiety of being ignored by one's parents or being alienated from one's religion can be the essence of who we are and why we behave as we do. What are the implications of this for understanding human nature?

2. How does the existential explanation of anxiety differ from that offered by other personality psychologists?

3. How can Rollo May's concern with philosophy and existentialism become part of a personality psychology that is heavily scientific?

4. What beneficial purposes are served by neurosis and anxiety? Do these benefits mean that we should not seek to reduce neurosis and anxiety in ourselves and in others?

38

The Will to Meaning

VIKTOR E. FRANKL

Viktor Frankl (1905–1997), in the tradition of existential-humanistic theorists, emphasized the benefits of personal choice. If people choose to grow and develop, the challenge of the unknown produces anxiety; but this anxiety can lead to triumph and self-fulfillment. Frankl was imprisoned in a Nazi concentration camp. He survived psychologically by choosing to find meaning in the suffering, and by adopting the responsibility to control the little bit of his life that was left to him, and not passively accepting and complying with the horrors that surrounded him. Although Frankl's parents and pregnant wife were killed in the camps, he found the strength to go on to become one of the most influential existential psychologists, reaching out to those weighed down with despair or emptiness. He called his approach logotherapy—the search for the meaning of existence. An existential struggle can lead to a triumph of the human spirit. Our modern day heroes are those who can resist the pressures of an authoritarian society run wild. This shows that in many ways the existential and humanistic perspectives are opposite sides of the same coin.

Central to my psychiatric approach known as logotherapy is the principle of the will to meaning. I counterpose it both to the pleasure principle, which is so pervasive in psychoanalytic motivational theories, and to the will to power, the concept which plays such a decisive role in Adlerian psychology. The will to pleasure is a self-defeating principle inasmuch as the more a person really sets out to strive for pleasure the less likely he is to gain it. For pleasure is a by-product or side effect of the fulfillment of our strivings, and it is contravened to the extent that it is made a goal. The more a person directly aims at pleasure, the more he misses it. In my opinion this mechanism underlies most cases of sexual neurosis. Accordingly, a logotherapeutic technique based on this theory of the self-thwarting character of pleasure intention yields remarkable short-term results. Even the psychodynamically oriented therapists on my staff have come to acknowledge the value of logotherapy, and one such staff member has used this technique exclusively in treating sexually neurotic patients.

In the final analysis both the will to pleasure and the will to power are derivatives of the will to meaning. Pleasure is an effect of meaning fulfillment; power is a means to an end. A degree of power—economic power, for instance—is generally a prerequisite of meaning fulfillment. But while the will to pleasure mistakes the effect for the end, the will to power mistakes the means to an end for the end itself.

We are not really justified, however, in speaking of a *will* to pleasure or power in connection with psychodynamically oriented schools of thought, since they assume that man pursues behavior goals unwillingly and unwittingly and that his conscious motivations are not his actual motivations. Thus Erich Fromm in *Beyond the Chains of Illusion* speaks of

Source: Frankl, V. E. (1964). The will to meaning. *The Christian Century, 71,* 515–517. Copyright 1964 Christian Century. Reprinted with permission from the April 22, 1964, issue of the Christian Century.

"the motivating forces which make man act in certain ways, the drives which propel him to strive in certain directions." But to me it is inconceivable that man can really be driven to strivings; either he strives or he is driven. To ignore this difference, to sacrifice one phenomenon to another, is a procedure unworthy of a scientist; to do so is to allow one's adherence to hypotheses to blind one to facts.

Freud and his epigones have taught us always to see something behind or beneath human volitions: unconscious motivations, underlying dynamics. Freud never took a human phenomenon at face value; as Gordon W. Allport states in *Personality and Social Encounter,* "Freud was a specialist in precisely those motives that cannot be taken at their face value." But are there no motives at all which should be taken at face value? Such an assumption is comparable to the attitude of the man who, on being shown a stork, said, "I thought the stork didn't exist!" Does the fact that the stork has been misused to hide the facts of life from children in any way deny that bird's reality?

According to Freud, the reality principle is an extension of the pleasure principle and merely serves its purposes. But one could just as well say that the pleasure principle itself is an extension of the homeostasis principle and serves *its* purposes. Ultimately the psychodynamic approach views man as a being basically concerned with maintaining or restoring his inner equilibium and seeking to do so by gratifying his drives and satisfying his instincts. Even Jungian psychology essentially interprets human motivation thus; the archetypes of Jungian thought are also "mythical beings" (as Freud called the instincts). Both Freud and Jung view man as bent on getting rid of tensions, be they aroused by drives and instincts clamoring for gratification (Freud) or by archetypes urging their materialization (Jung). In either case, reality, the world of beings and meanings, is reduced to instrumentalities for getting rid of unpleasant stimuli. What has been eliminated in this view of man is the fundamental fact that man is a being who encounters other beings, who also reaches out for meanings to fulfill.

This is why I speak of a will to meaning rather than a need for or a drive toward meaning. If man were really driven to meaning he would embark on meaning fulfillment solely to rid himself of this drive in order that homeostasis might be restored; at the same time he would no longer be really concerned with meaning but rather with his own equilibrium and thus with himself.

Nor is the concept of self-actualization or self-realization a sufficient ground for a motivational theory. Self-actualization is another phenomenon which can be realized only as a side effect and which is thwarted precisely to the extent that it is made a matter of direct intention. Self-actualization is of course a desideratum. But man can actualize himself only insofar as he fulfills meaning, in which case self-actualization occurs by itself—automatically, as it were. Like pleasure, self-actualization is contravened when deliberately sought after or made an end in itself.

While lecturing at Melbourne University some years ago, I was given a boomerang as a souvenir. In contemplating this gift I concluded that in a sense it symbolized human existence. One generally assumes that a boomerang returns to the thrower; actually it returns only when the thrower has missed his target. Similarly, man returns to himself, to being concerned with his self, only after he has missed his mission, only after he has failed to find meaning in life.

In his doctoral dissertation Ernest Keen, one of my assistants during a teaching period at Harvard's summer session, seeks to demonstrate that the shortcomings of Freudian psychoanalysis are compensated for by Heinz Hartmann's ego psychology, and the deficiencies of ego psychology in turn by Erikson's identity concept. Keen goes on to contend, however, that despite these correctives there is still a missing link in psychotherapy, and that this link is supplied by logotherapy. It is my conviction that man should not, indeed cannot, struggle for identity in a direct way; rather, he finds identity to the extent to which he commits himself to something beyond himself, to a cause greater than himself. No one has put it as cogently as has Karl Jaspers: What man is he ultimately becomes through the cause which he has made his own.

Rolf von Eckartsberg, also a Harvard assistant of mine, has shown the insufficiency of the role-playing concept by pointing out that it avoids the very problem prompting it—that of choice and value. For the question remains: Which role to adopt, which cause to advocate? The same criticism holds for those who insist that man's primary intention and ultimate goal are to develop his potentialities. One recalls the example of Socrates, who confessed that he had within himself the potentiality to become a criminal but nevertheless decided to turn away from such a potentiality.

What is behind all these arguments that man should try to live out his inner potentialities or—as it is sometimes put—to "express himself"? The hidden motive behind such notions is, I believe, to lessen the tension aroused by the gap between what a man is and what he ought to become, between the actual state of affairs and that which he should help secure, between existence and essence, or being and meaning. To say that man need not worry about ideals and values since they are nothing but "self-expressions" and that he should therefore simply embark on the actualization of his own potentialities is to say that he need not reach out for meaning to fulfill or values to realize, that everything is all right as it is. Pindar's injunction, "Become what you are," is thus deprived of its imperative quality and transmuted into an indicative statement, namely, that man has all along been what he should become and hence need not reach for the stars to bring them down to earth, since the earth is itself a star!

The fact remains, however, that the tension between being and meaning is ineradicable in man, is inherent in his humanness. And that is why it is indispensable for mental well-being. Having started from man's meaning orientation, i.e., his will to meaning, we have now arrived at another problem—his meaning confrontation. The first issue refers to what man basically is: oriented toward meaning; the second refers to what he should be: confronted with meaning.

To confront man with values which are interpreted merely as self-expression will not do. Still less valid is the approach which would have him see in values "nothing but defense mechanisms, reaction formations or rationalizations of his instinctual drives"—to use the definition of two outstanding psychoanalytically oriented therapists. Personally I would not be willing to live for the sake of my defense mechanisms, much less to die for the sake of my reaction formations.

To treat a patient in terms of psychodynamic ideas may very well serve the purpose of what I call existential rationalization. If a person is taught that his concern about ultimate meaning is no more than, say, a way of coming to terms with his early childhood Oedipal situation, then his concern can be analyzed away, along with the existential tension aroused by it. The approach of logotherapy is altogether different. Logotherapy does not spare a patient confrontation with the specific meaning which he must act on—and which the therapist should help him find. In his book *Logotherapy and the Christian Faith* Donald F. Tweedie recounts an incident in which an American visitor to Vienna asked me to tell him in one sentence the difference between logotherapy and psychoanalysis—where upon I invited him first to tell me what he regarded as the essence of psychoanalysis. He replied: "In psychoanalysis the patient must lie down on a couch and tell you things which sometimes are disagreeable to tell." And I quickly responded: "In logotherapy the patient is allowed to sit erect but must hear things which sometimes are disagreeable!"

Erwin Straus has rightly stressed that in existential thinking the otherness of the other should not be attenuated. The same holds true for meaning. The meaning which a person has to fulfill is something beyond himself, never just himself. Only if this meaning retains otherness can it exert upon a person that quality of imperativeness which yields itself to a phenomenological analysis of one's experience of existence. Only a meaning which is not just an expression of the person himself can be a true challenge to him. The Bible tells us that when Israel wandered through the desert God's glory went before in the form of a cloud; only in this way was it possible for Israel to be guided by God. Imagine what would have happened if God had dwelled in the midst of Israel in the form of a cloud: rather than leading the people safely, the cloud would have obscured everything and Israel would have gone astray.

Meaning must not coincide with being; meaning must be ahead of being; meaning sets the pace for being. Existence falters unless lived in terms of transcendence, in terms of something beyond itself. Here we might distinguish between pacemakers and peacemakers: the former confront us with meanings and values, thus supporting our meaning orientation; the latter alleviate the burden of meaning confrontation.

In this sense Moses was a pacemaker; he did not soothe man's conscience but rather stirred it up. Moses with his Ten Commandments did not spare his people a confrontation with ideals and values.

There is also the appeaser type of peacemaker who tries to reconcile others with himself. Let's face facts, he says. Why worry about one's shortcomings? Only a few live up to their ideals. So let's attend to peace of mind or soul rather than those existential meanings which only arouse tensions. What this kind of peacemaker overlooks is the wisdom of Goethe's warning: If we take man as he is, we make him worse; if we take him as he ought to be, we help him become it.

When meaning orientation becomes meaning confrontation, that stage of maturation and development has been reached where freedom becomes responsibleness. An individual is responsible for the fulfillment of the specific meaning of his own life, but he is also responsible *to* something, be it society or humanity or mankind or his own conscience. A significant number of people interpret their own existence not just in terms of being responsible to some*thing* but rather to some*one*—namely, to God. As a secular theory and medical practice logotherapy

must restrict itself to such a factual statement, leaving to the patient the decision whether to interpret his own responsibleness in terms of religion or agnosticism. Logotherapy must remain available to everyone; to this I am obliged to adhere, if for no other reason, by my Hippocratic oath. In any case, logotherapy sees in responsibleness the very essence of human existence, and for that reason the patient must himself decide for what and to what, or to whom, he is responsible.

A logotherapist is not entitled consciously to influence the patient's decision as to how to interpret his own responsibleness or as to what to embrace as his personal meaning. The fact that a person's conscience is subject to error does not release him from his obligation to obey it; existence involves the risk of error. He must risk committing himself to a cause not worthy of his commitment. Perhaps my commitment to the cause of logotherapy is erroneous. But I prefer to live in a world in which man has the right to make choices, even if they are wrong choices, rather than one in which no choice at all is left to him. A world in which both fiends and saints are possible is infinitely preferable to a totally conformist, collectivist world in which man is a mere functionary of the party or the state.

Questions to Think About

1. How is the will to meaning superior in its outcomes to both the will to pleasure and the will to power?

2. Frankl claims that Freudian approaches are oriented toward reducing conflict and removing tension. In what way does the will to meaning attempt to transcend those goals?

3. Why does Frankl choose the term "will to meaning" rather than "need for meaning" or "drive toward meaning"—what special quality is captured by the notion of "will"?

39

The Self in Jung and Zen

ABE MASAO

Abe Masao (1915– .) is a Buddhist philosopher from Japan. Abe (his surname) is interested in bringing the Zen Buddhist perspective to the West. Much of his writing is about Buddhism in relation to Western religions and Western philosophy, as part of an ongoing dialogue with the goal of interreligious understanding. In this selection, he addresses the ways in which the conceptualization of the self in the work of Carl Jung differs from the Zen view. Jung addressed this issue himself, in dialogue at his home in Switzerland with a leading professor of Buddhism from Kyoto University, Hisamatsu Shin'ichi, who was Jung's contemporary. This article reports on that dialogue and then offers some interpretation.

The most conspicuous difference between Buddhism and Western psychology is perhaps found in their respective treatments of the concept of "self." In Western psychology, the existence of a "self" is generally affirmed; Buddhism denies the existence of an enduring "self" and substitutes instead the concept of *anātman*, "no-self."

In Western spiritual traditions one of the classical examples of the affirmation of an enduring self is Plato's notion of the immortal soul. The basis of the modern Western conception of the self was established by Descartes' *cogito ergo sum*, which led to a dualistic interpretation of mind as thinking substance and matter as extended substance. Christianity, which is not based on human reason but divine revelation, emphasizes man's self-denial or self-sacrifice in devotion to one's God and fellow human beings. Even so, as a responsible agent in an I-Thou relationship, the human self is affirmed as something essential. Although it is a relatively new scientific discipline, modern Western psychology shares with older Western spiritual traditions the affirmation of the existence of a self.

In ancient India, the Brahmanical tradition propounded the idea of atman or the eternal, unchanging

self which is fundamentally identical with Brahman, the ultimate Reality of the universe. The Buddha did not accept the notion of atman and discoursed instead about anātman, no-self. As Walpola Rahula states:

> *Buddhism stands unique in the history of human thought in denying the existence of such a Soul, Self, or Atman. According to the teaching of the Buddha, the idea of self is an imaginary, false belief which has no corresponding reality, and it produces harmful thoughts of 'me' and 'mine', selfish desire, craving, attachment, hatred, ill-will, conceit, pride, egoism, and other defilements, impurities and problems. It is the source of all the troubles in the world from personal conflicts to wars between nations. In short, to this false view can be traced all the evil in the world.*

Throughout his life, the Buddha taught the means to remove and destroy such a false view and thereby enlighten human beings.

To those who desire self-preservation after death, the Buddhist notion of no-self may sound not only strange but frightening. This was true even for the ancient Indians who lived in the time of the Buddha. A bhikkhu once asked the Buddha: "Sir, is there a case

Source: Abe, M. (1985). The self in Jung and Zen. *The Eastern Buddhist, 18*(1), 57–70. Reprinted with permission.

where one is tormented when something permanent within oneself is not found?" Not unaware of such fear, the Buddha answered, "Yes, bhikkhu, there is." Elsewhere the Buddha says: "O bhikkhus, this idea that I may not be, I may not have, is frightening to the uninstructed worldling." Nevertheless, the Buddha preached the notion of no-self tirelessly until his death, simply because the doctrine is so essential to his teaching: to emancipate human beings from suffering and to awaken them to the fundamental reality of human existence.

To properly understand the Buddhist notion of no-self, it would be helpful to consider the following five points:

First, the doctrine of no-self is the natural result of, or the corollary to, the analysis of the five skandhas or five aggregates, that is, matter, sensation, perception, mental formations, and consciousness. According to Buddhism, human beings are composed of these five aggregates and nothing more.

Second, the notion of no-self, that is, the notion of no substantial unchanging own-being, is applied not only to human beings, but also to all beings. This is why one of the three essentials peculiar to Buddhism is that "all dharmas [i.e., all entities] are without self." Thus, not only conditioned, relative things, but also unconditioned, absolute things are understood to be without self, without their own-being. Accordingly, not only samsara, but also nirvana, not only delusion, but also enlightenment, are without own-being. Neither relative nor absolute things are self-existing and independent.

Third, the notion of no-self entails, therefore, the denial of one absolute God who is self-existing, and instead forwards the doctrine of dependent origination. That is, in Buddhism, nothing whatever is independent or self-existing; everything is dependent on everything else. Thus, all unconditioned, absolute, and eternal entities such as Buddha or the state of nirvana co-arise and co-cease with all conditioned, relative, and temporal entities, such as living beings or the state of samsara.

Fourth, in accordance with these teachings, the ultimate in Buddhism is neither conditioned nor unconditioned, neither relative nor absolute, neither temporal nor eternal. Therefore, the Buddhist ultimate is called *śūnyatā*, that is, "Emptiness." It is also called the "Middle Way," because it is neither an eternalist view which insists on the existence of an unchanging eternal entity as the ultimate, nor an annihilationist view which maintains that everything is null and void.

Fifth, if one clearly understands that the Buddhist notion of no-self is essentially connected with its doctrine of dependent origination and *śūnyatā* or Emptiness, one may also naturally understand that the Buddhist notion of no-self does not signify the mere lack or absence of self, as an annihilationist may suggest, but rather constitutes a standpoint which is beyond both the eternalist view of self and the nihilistic view of no-self. This is forcefully illustrated by the Buddha himself when he answered with silence both the questions "Is there a self?" and "Is there no-self?" Keeping silence to both the affirmative and negative forms of the question concerning the "self," the Buddha profoundly expressed the ultimate Reality of humanity. His silence itself does not indicate an agnostic position, but is a striking presence of the true nature of human being which is beyond affirmation and negation.

In the light of these five points, I hope it is now clear that the Buddhist notion of no-self does not signify a mere negation of the existence of the self, but rather signifies a realization of human existence which is neither self nor no-self. Since the original human nature cannot be characterized as self or no-self, it is called No-self. Therefore, No-self represents nothing but the true nature or true Self of humanity which cannot be conceptualized at all and is beyond self and no-self.

In the Buddhist tradition, Zen most clearly and vividly emphasizes that the Buddhist notion of No-self is nothing but true Self. Rinzai's phrase, the "true man of no rank" serves as an example. "No rank" implies freedom from any conceptualized definition of human being. Thus the "true man of no rank" signifies the "true man" who cannot be characterized either by self or no-self. "True man of no rank" is identical with the true nature of human being presenting itself in the silence of the Buddha. Unlike the Buddha who emphasizes meditation, however, Rinzai is an active and dynamic Zen master, directly displaying his own "true Self" while demanding his disciples to actively demonstrate this "true Self" in themselves. The following exchange vividly illustrates this dynamic character:

One day Rinzai gave this sermon: "There is the true man of no rank in the mass of naked flesh, who goes in and out from your facial gates [i.e., sense organs]. Those who have not testified [to the fact], look! look!"

A monk came forward and asked, "Who is this true man of no rank?"

Rinzai came down from his chair and, taking hold of the monk by the throat, said, "Speak! Speak!"

The monk hesitated.

Rinzai let go his hold and said, "What a worthless dirt-stick this is!"

In this exchange, "true man of no rank" represents a living reality functioning through our physical body. Furthermore, Rinzai is asking his audience to notice the living reality functioning in himself by saying "Look! Look!" and demanding from the monk a demonstration of his own true nature, taking him by the throat and saying "Speak! Speak!" Zen does not intend to provide an explanation or interpretation of the nature of true Self, but rather to precipitate a direct and immediate testimony or demonstration of it through a dynamic encounter between master and disciple.

In seeking to point out the similarities and dissimilarities between modern Western psychology and Buddhism, especially Zen, with regard to their understanding of the concept of the "self," let us examine a dialogue between Hisamatsu Shin'ichi (1889–1980) and Carl Gustav Jung (1875–1961).

Hisamatsu Shin'ichi was a professor of Buddhism at Kyoto University. He is regarded as one of the outstanding Zen thinkers of contemporary Japan. But Hisamatsu was also a Zen layman who had attained a very profound, clear-cut Zen awakening, and his subsequent thinking and way of life were deeply rooted in this awakening. He was an excellent calligrapher, tea master, and poet as well. In all, he was a real embodiment of the Zen spirit, outstanding even among contemporary Zen masters in Japan. This dialogue with Carl Jung took place at Jung's home at Küsnacht, on the outskirts of Zurich, on May 16, 1958. While there were many stimulating exchanges and many interesting points raised in the course of the dialogue, I would like to focus here on the issue of self as understood by Jung and Hisamatsu.

After a discussion about the relation between consciousness and the unconscious, Hisamatsu asked, "Which is our true Self, 'the 'unconscious' or 'conscious'?" Jung replied,

The consciousness calls itself 'I', while the 'self' is not 'I' at all. The self is the whole, because the personality—you as the whole—consists of the 'conscious' and the 'unconscious'. That is the whole, or the 'self'. But 'I' know only the consciousness. The 'unconscious' remains to me unknown."

This is Jung's well known distinction between I or ego, and self. To Jung, "ego" is the center of the field of consciousness and the complex entity to which all conscious contents are related, whereas "self" is the total personality which, though always present, cannot fully be known.

Later in the dialogue, the following exchange occurs:

HISAMATSU: "Is the 'I-consciousness' (ego-consciousness) different from the 'self-consciousness' or not?"

JUNG: "In the ordinary usage, people say 'self-consciousness', but psychologically it is only 'I consciousness'. The 'self' is unknown, for it indicates the whole, that is, the conscious and the unconscious . . ."

HISAMATSU: "What! The 'self' is not known?"

JUNG: "Perhaps only the half of it is known and it is the 'I'. It is the half of the 'self'."

Hisamatsu's surprise is understandable, because in Zen practice the self is to be clearly known. Satori is "self-awakening," that is, the self awakening to itself. The awakened self is characterized as *ryōryōjōchi*, that is, "always clearly aware."

Here we can see an essential difference between Jung and Zen. In Jung, self as the total personality consists of the consciousness as "I" or "ego," which is known to itself, and the unconscious, which remains unknown. Furthermore, the unconscious includes the personal unconscious which owes its existence to personal experience, and the collective unconscious, the content of which has never been conscious and which owes its existence exclusively to heredity. Whereas the personal unconscious can sooner or later present itself to consciousness, the collective unconscious, being universal and impersonal, consists of pre-existent forms, or archetypes, which give definite form to certain psychic contents, but which can only become conscious secondarily. It would therefore be appropriate to say that in Jung, the collective unconscious, as the depth of the self, is seen from the side of the conscious ego as something beyond, or as something "over there," though not externally but inwardly. It is in this sense that the unconscious is unknown. In contrast to this, according to Zen, the self is not the unknown, but rather the clearly known. More strictly speaking, the knower and the known are one, not two. The knower itself is the known, and vice versa. Self is not regarded as something existing "over there," somewhere beyond, but rather is fully realized right here and now.

We must therefore recognize clearly that although both Jung and Zen discuss the concept of the self, the entity of the self is understood by them in fundamentally different ways. According to Zen, in order to awaken to the true Self, it is necessary to realize No-self. Only through the clear realization of No-self can one awaken to the true Self. And the realization of No-self in Zen would reflect the realization of the non-substantiality of the unconscious self as well as the conscious ego, to use Jungian terminology. In Jung, self is the total personality which cannot be fully known. It consists of the conscious and the unconscious. But in Zen the true Self is awakened to only through overcoming or breaking through the self in the Jungian sense. I will try to clarify later how this process can occur, but at this point I would merely like to observe that there is no suggestion of the realization of the No-self in Jung. Since the No-self, that is the nonsubstantiality of self, is not clearly realized in Jung, it therefore remains as something unknown to the ego.

The dialogue now turns to the case of a patient's mental suffering and the method of curing the infirmity. Hisamatsu asked, "How is the therapy connected with the fundamental 'unconscious'?" Jung replied, "When a disease is caused by things which we are not conscious of, there is the possibility that it might be cured by making these causes conscious. While the cause does not always exist in the 'unconscious', there are cases where the symptoms show that the psychic causes have existed [in the 'unconscious']." Emphasizing the existence of the worries and difficulties in our daily life, Hisamatsu then raises several other ques-

tions. "If the essence of cure is freedom from worry, what sort of changes in the sphere of the 'unconscious' correspond to this freedom?" "Is it possible or not possible for psychotherapy to shake off the thousand and one worries of human life all at once?"

JUNG: "How can such a method be possible? A method which enables us to free ourselves from suffering itself?"

HISAMATSU: "Doesn't psychotherapy emancipate us from suffering all at once?"

JUNG: "Free man from his suffering itself? What we are trying to do is to reduce the suffering for human beings. Still some suffering remains."

At this point in the conversation, Jung's reaction to the possibility of sudden emancipation from suffering itself was quite negative. Referring to Jesus Christ and Gautama Buddha, Hisamatsu says, "The intention of these religious founders was to emancipate us from our fundamental suffering. Is it really possible for such great freedom to be achieved by psychotherapy?" Jung's response to this question is not simply negative.

JUNG: "It is not impossible if you treat your suffering not as a personal disease but as an impersonal occurrence, as a disaster or an evil . . . Patients are enmeshed by *klesha* (passion) and they are able to be freed from it by their insight. What [psychotherapy] aims at is all the same with the aim of Buddhism."

This leads to a crucial point in the dialogue:

HISAMATSU: "The essential point of freedom [from suffering] is how we can be awakened to our fundamental Self. That fundamental Self is the one which is no more confined by a myriad of things. To attain this Self, is the essential point of freedom. It is necessary, therefore, to free oneself both from the 'collective unconscious' and from the bondage caused by the 'collective unconscious'."

JUNG: "If someone is enmeshed by a myriad of things and confined in them, it is because he is caught in the 'collective unconscious' at the same time. He can be freed only when he is emancipated from both of them. . . . After all, man must reach, to the degree that he is able, freedom both from 'he must', being obligated to chase after things, and from being obligated inconveniently to be ruled by the 'unconscious'. Both are radically the same and nirvana."

HISAMATSU: "In what you have just said before about the 'unconscious', Professor Jung, do you mean that the 'collective unconscious' is something from which, in its nature, we can free ourselves?"

JUNG: "Yes, it is."

HISAMATSU: "What we generally call self is the same as the "self" characterized by Professor Jung. But it is only after the emancipation of the self that the 'Original Self' of Zen emerges. It is the true Self of *dokudatsu mue*, absolute freedom, independent from everything."

At this point, Jung answered affirmatively Hisamatsu's question as to whether the collective unconscious is something from which one must be emancipated for real freedom. Earlier in the dialogue, he answered negatively a question concerning the possibility of gaining freedom from suffering all at once. Towards the end of the conversation, however, Jung clearly agreed with Hisamatsu on the need of overcoming even the collective unconscious for a complete cure of the patient. According to Tsujimura Kōichi, who acted as interpreter for the dialogue, Jung's affirmative response surprised people in the room, for if the collective unconscious can be overcome, then Jung's analytical psychology must be fundamentally reexamined.

Looking back over the dialogue, I would like to make three remarks:

First, the psychotherapeutic method of relieving a patient's suffering and the Zen method of dissolving a student's suffering are different. In Jungian psychotherapy, to cure a patient's suffering, the analyst tries to help the patient become aware of the causes of his suffering, which previously had been unconscious, or he tries to help the patient realize the aim or meaning of his life, or he tries to help change the patient's attitude towards psychic worry and make him more accepting and positive. But as Jung says in the conversation, there is no universal rule or method for the cure. There are only individual cases, and in psychotherapy the analyst must cure the patient's worries as fully as possible in each individual case. As Hisamatsu points out in his additional note, however, "If each disease is cured separately and individually, we shall not be completely

cured of disease, for when one disease is gone, another disease comes. This in itself may be said to be a disease in a very profound sense."

Hisamatsu calls this "the vicious endlessness" of psychoanalytic therapy. Unless the root of all possible diseases is dug out and cut away, the vicious endlessness of psychoanalytic therapy will not be overcome. What, then, is the root of all possible psychic diseases? According to Jung it is the collective unconscious or the unknown self which is responsible for hindering us psychically. Instead of analyzing psychic diseases one by one, Zen tries to dig out and cut away the very root of the human consciousness beyond consciousness, including the Jungian or any other hypothesized realm of an unconscious. Zen insists that only then can complete emancipation from human suffering be achieved and the true Self be awakened. The realization of No-self, which is indispensible for the awakening to true Self, is simply another way of describing "cutting away" the root of human consciousness.

Second, in Jung, the collective unconscious is something unknown which must be intensively analyzed to discover the cause of a patient's suffering, but it is at the same time a realm that can never be completely known. By definition, the collective unconscious remains an unknown "*x*" for both analyst and analysand. In Zen, through zazen and koan practice with a Zen master, the Zen student not only digs out the root of the unknown "*x*" but also becomes one with it. For the Zen student the unknown "*x*" is not something "over there." It comes to be realized as "here and now." In other words, it is totally, completely and experientially realized by the student as *the unknown* "*x.*" In this total, experiential realization, it ceases to be an *object* to the student, and instead the two become one with each other. Now, the student *is* the unknown "*x*" and the unknown "*x*" *is* the student. Only in this way can the student overcome the unknown "*x,*" "cut off" its root, and awaken to his true Self.

This event can be illustrated by a *mondō* (a question and answer exchange) between Bodhidharma, the first patriarch in the Zen tradition, and Hui-ko, who later became the second patriarch. In deep anguish and mental perplexity after many years of inner struggle, Hui-ko approached Bodhidharma and asked him:

"My mind is not yet pacified. Pray, Master, pacify it."

"Bring your mind here and I will pacify it," said Bodhidharma. "I have sought it for many years," Hui-ko replied, "I am still unable to take hold of it. My mind is really unattainable."

"There! Your mind is pacified once and for all," Bodhidharma confirmed.

Instead of analyzing the causes of Hui-ko's suffering, Bodhidharma asked Hui-ko to bring forth his mind. Confronted with this straightaway command, Hui-ko, who had sought after his mind for many years, clearly realized that the mind is unattainable. Suddenly, he totally and experientially realized the mind to be the unattainable and the unattainable to be the mind; there was no longer even the slightest gap between himself and the unattainable. His internal perplexity was resolved in this existentially complete realization of the mind as the unattainable. Recognizing this, Bodhidharma immediately said, "There! Your mind is pacified once and for all."

In Jung, the depth of mind is *objectively* regarded from the side of the conscious "I" as the unknown collective unconscious. In contrast, by overcoming such an objective approach, Zen straightforwardly enters into the depth of mind and breaks through it by becoming completely identical with it. In Zen, this breaking through is called the Great Death—because it signifies the complete denial of human consciousness, including any such Jungian notion of the collective unconscious. And yet the Great Death in Zen is at one and the same time a resurrection in the Great Life—because in this breaking through of mind, not only is the realization that mind is unattainable or unknowable included, but also the realization that the unattainable or the unknowable is precisely the true Mind or true Self. This is why 'No mind' in Zen is not a negative but a positive entity. That is to say, unlike the Jungian unconscious, No-mind in Zen is not an extra-conscious psyche, but rather is the true Mind or Original Mind which is realized beyond Jung's framework of the mind.

A significant aspect of Zen in this connection is perhaps the emphasis in koan practice on the Great Doubt. Most koans, such as Joshu's *Mu* and Hakuin's "Listen to the sound of the single hand," are designed to drive a Zen student into a mental corner, to break

through the wall of the human psyche, and to open up an entirely new spiritual dimension beyond analytic or dualistic thinking. For example, the koan, "Show your Original Face before your parents were born," does not refer to one's pre-existence in a temporal sense, but rather asks of a student to demonstrate his or her original nature which can be *immediately* realized at the depth of existence. Only when the student demonstrates it can he or she break through the framework of a self-centered psyche. The phrase, "Original Face *before your parents were born*" can be understood to refer to that which lies beyond even the hypothesized collective unconscious and which is impersonal, universal, and yet is the root-source of your own being and which is unknown to the "I" which is limited by time and space.

Zen emphasizes the importance for a Zen student to become a "Great Doubting Mass": "At the base of Great Doubt lies Great Awakening." This emphasis on Great Doubt implies that a Zen student must dig up and grapple with the unknown "x" so thoroughly that he turns into the unknown "x" itself. To become a Great Doubting Mass is to turn into the unknown "x." To turn into the unknown "x" is to come to know existentially that the unknown "x" is nothing but the true Self. And that knowing is the Great Awakening to the true Self, characterized as *ryōryōjōchi*, "always clearly aware." Koan practice has proved an effective way to lead a student to the Great Awakening through Great Doubt.

Third, despite the essential differences between Zen and Jungian psychology in their understandings of self and their respective methods of curing human suffering, I believe there are also points at which these two disciplines can profitably learn from each other, although the scope and depth of their mutual learning may perhaps not be equal. Since Zen is so overwhelmingly concerned with cutting off the root of the human consciousness in order to attain No-self as true Self, or to attain No-mind as true Mind, it tends on the whole to neglect psychological problems that occur sometimes in the process of Zen practice, in particular the delusory apparitions known as *makyō*. But if Zen learns from Jungian psychology about the theory of the archetype as an unconscious organizer of human ideas, and the process of individuation, it might help the Zen practicer to better understand such mental fabrication.

Modern Western psychology, and particularly Freudian and Jungian psychology, have claimed to discover the existence of a psyche outside consciousness. With this discovery the position of the ego, until then absolute as the center of human consciousness and the active source of man's spiritual act, was relativized. In Jung, the ego is no longer identical with the whole of the individual but is a limited substance serving as the center of non-unconscious phenomena. If this relativization of the ego is strengthened, that is, the substance of the ego is understood to be even more limited, it could help open the way to the realization of No-self. But in Jung, instead of a relativization of the position of ego, the position of the self as the total personality based on the collective unconscious is strongly maintained. If the collective unconscious is something ultimate in which human suffering is rooted, then, as Hisamatsu suggests in his dialogue with Jung, Jungian psychotherapy may not be free from an inevitable "vicious endlessness," because even though it can relieve a particular disease separately and individually, other forms of psychic disease may recur endlessly. Only when the true source is reached beyond such possible psychological realms as the collective unconscious, can

human beings go beyond the root of suffering itself and be released from the "vicious endlessness" of particular manifestations of suffering. Zen offers a way to break through even the collective unconscious and similar theories about the structure of the mind.

In this respect, it is extremely significant that in his dialogue with Hisamatsu, Jung seemed eventually to agree with the possibility and necessity of freedom from the collective unconscious. Ultimately, Jung and Zen seem to agree that there is hope for human beings to be emancipated from suffering itself, rather than their being destined to remain in a samsaric cycle, finding relief from one suffering only to be faced with another.

REFERENCES

Jung, C. G. (1959). *Archetypes and the collective unconscious.* New York: Pantheon Books.

Rahula, W. (1959). *What the Buddha taught.* New York: Grove Press.

Suzuki, D. T. (1949). *Essays in Zen Buddhism.* London: Rider.

Suzuki, D. T., Fromm, E., & DeMartino, R. (1960). *Zen Buddhism and psychoanalysis.* London: George Allen & Unwin.

Questions to Think About

1. Is the Buddhist ideal of "no-self" possibly attainable by any person? Is it attainable by any Westerner whose culture is centered on the self?

2. In what way does Jung's distinction between the conscious portion of the psyche (the ego) and the unconscious portions (the personal unconscious and the collective unconscious) relate to the Buddhist notion of the fundamental Self?

3. What level of mutual understanding could Jung and the Zen master aspire to, given the gulf between their backgrounds, cultures, and goals?

40

Hope and Happiness

DAVID G. MYERS

David Myers (1942–), a social psychologist who has spent his career at Hope College in Michigan, is a prominent figure in the movement called "positive psychology." As Abraham Maslow and Carl Rogers had proposed many years earlier, this movement looks at the positive forces of life. Rather than focusing on aggression, weakness, and pathology (as much of the field of psychology still does), positive psychology is concerned with creativity, hope, wisdom, and spirituality. Many researchers identified with the positive psychology movement are interested specifically in happiness (its causes, characteristics, and effects), and Myers is among those. In this chapter, Myers examines what factors do and do not correlate with self-reported happiness.

During much of its first century, psychology has focused on negative emotions: on aggression more than love, on conflict more than peace, on fear more than courage. A PsycInfo electronic search of *Psychological Abstracts* since 1967 reveals 5,548 articles mentioning anger, 41,416 on anxiety, and 54,040 on depression, but only 415 on joy, 1,710 on happiness, and 2,582 on life satisfaction. In all, there are 21 articles on negative emotions for every article on positive emotions.

But the tide is changing. During the 1980s, articles mentioning well-being, life satisfaction, or happiness quadrupled from 200 to 800 annually. This new scientific pursuit of happiness and life satisfaction (together called "subjective well-being") has asked: How happy are people? And who is happy?

ARE ONLY A FEW PEOPLE HAPPY?

We are "not born for happiness," observed Samuel Johnson. Modern books for the would-be happy,

written by clinicians who spend their days with the unhappy, agree. "One-third of all Americans wake up depressed every day," says Father John Powell in *Happiness Is an Inside Job*. Professionals estimate that only 10% to 15% of Americans think of themselves as truly happy. But when asked about their happiness, random samples of people paint a brighter picture. In National Opinion Research Center surveys, three in ten Americans say they are "very happy"; only one in ten say "not too happy"; and the rest, six in ten, describe themselves as "pretty happy." Diener (Myers & Diener, 1996) has assembled data from 916 surveys of 1.1 million people in 45 nations representing most of the human population. He recalibrated the self-reported well-being on a 0 to 10 scale (where 0 is the low extreme, such as reporting oneself "very unhappy" or "completely dissatisfied," 5 is neutral, and 10 is the high extreme). The average human, as shown in Figure 1, responded at a moderately positive 6.75.

Source: Myers, D. G. (2000). Hope and happiness. In J. E. Gilham (Ed.), *The science of optimism and hope*. Philadelphia: Templeton Foundation Press. Reprinted with permission.

Editor's note: All citations in the text of this selection have been left intact from the original, but the list of references includes only those sources that are the most relevant and important. Readers wishing to follow any of the other citations can find the full references in the original work or in an online database.

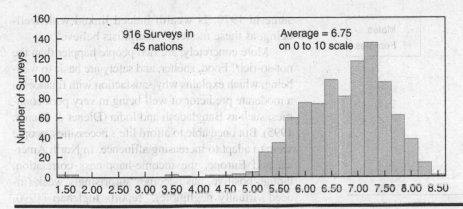

FIGURE 1   Subjective well-being, as self-reported in 916 surveys of 1.1 million people in 45 nations (with answers calibrated to a 0 to 10 scale, with 5 neutral). (From Myers & Diener, 1996.)

The set point for happiness, therefore, appears to be set slightly to the positive side of neutral. This serves to give the occasional stone in the emotional shoe signal value. When something goes awry, it alerts the organism to do something to alleviate the negative mood.

WHO IS HAPPY?

By searching for predictors of subjective well-being, psychologists and sociologists have exploded some myths. Consider some illustrative findings (see Myers, 1993, Myers & Diener, 1995, for further evidence).

Are There Happy and Unhappy Times of Life?

Many people believe so with the stress-filled teen years, the midlife crisis years, and the declining years brought on by old age representing major episodes. But as illustrated by one 16-nation survey of 170,000 people (Figure 2), no time of life is notably happier and more satisfying. In every age group, there are many happy and some unhappy people.

Does Happiness Favor One Gender?

Are men happier, because of their greater incomes and social power? Are women happier because of their reportedly greater capacity for intimacy and so-

cial connection? Despite gender gaps in misery—women are much more vulnerable to disabling depression and anxiety, and men to alcoholism and antisocial personality disorder—gender gives no clue to subjective well-being. Men and women are equally likely to declare themselves "satisfied" or "very happy" (Figure 3).

Percent "Satisfied" or "Very Satisfied" with Life as a Whole

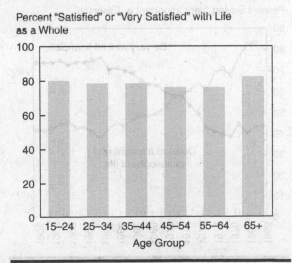

FIGURE 2   Age and well-being in 16 nations. Data are from 169,776 people representatively sampled from 1980 to 1986, as reported by Inglehart (1990).

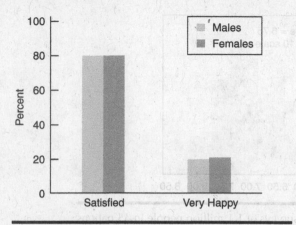

FIGURE 3   Gender and well-being in 16 nations. Data are from 169,776 people representatively sampled from 1980 to 1986, as reported by Inglehart (1990).

Does Money Buy Happiness?

In 1997, 74% of entering American collegians declared that a "very important" or "essential" life goal was "being very well off financially." As Figure 4 shows, that was nearly double the 39% who said the

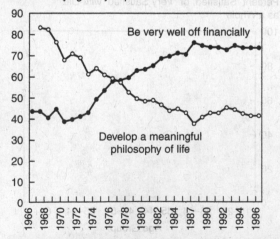

FIGURE 4   Changing materialism. Annual surveys of more than 200,000 entering American collegians revealed an increasing desire for wealth from 1970 to the late 1980s (Dey et al., 1991; Sax et al., 1997).

same in 1970. Is wealth indeed linked with well-being, as these modern materialists believe?

More concretely, are rich people happier than the not-so-rich? Food, shelter, and safety are basic to well-being, which explains why satisfaction with finances is a moderate predictor of well-being in very poor countries, such as Bangladesh and India (Diener & Diener, 1995). But once able to afford life's necessities, people seem to adapt to increasing affluence. In North America and Europe, the income-happiness correlation, though positive, has become "surprisingly weak (indeed virtually negligible)," reports Inglehart (1990, p. 242). Even the super rich and state lottery winners express only slightly greater than average happiness (Brickman, Coates, & Janoff-Bulman, 1978; Diener, Horwitz, & Emmons, 1985). Although its utter absence can breed misery, wealth does not guarantee happiness.

If even a *little* more money would buy a *little* more happiness, then has happiness grown over time as income has increased? In 1957, as economist John Galbraith was about to describe the United States as *The Affluent Society,* Americans' per person income, expressed in today's dollars, was about $9,000. Today, it is about $20,000, defining a doubly affluent society—with double what money buys. We own twice as many cars per person and eat out two and a half times as often. Home air conditioning, dishwashers, and clothes dryers have become common-place instead of rare.

So, are we happier than forty years ago? Apparently, we are not. As Figure 5 indicates, the percentage of Americans who report they are "very happy" has declined slightly since 1957, from 35% to 30%. Meanwhile, the divorce rate doubled. The teen suicide rate tripled. Arrests for juvenile crime quadrupled. Depression rates have soared. Much the same story can be told of many other industrialized nations. Although people in affluent countries enjoy better nutrition, health care, education, science—and are somewhat happier than people in very poor countries—increasing real incomes has not been accompanied by increasing happiness. Simply said, *economic growth in affluent countries has not boosted human morale.*

THE TRAITS OF HAPPY PEOPLE

If happiness is similarly available to those of any age or gender, and to people at all but the lowest income

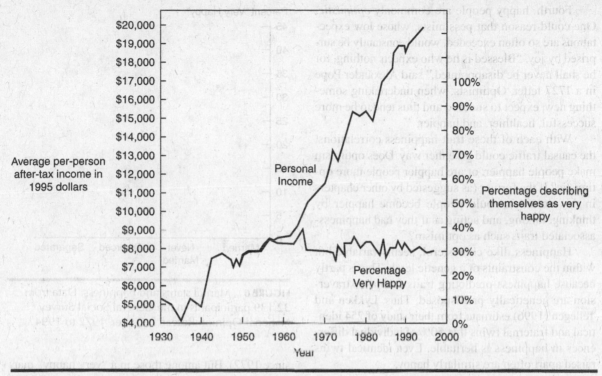

FIGURE 5 Does economic growth boost human morale? Inflation-adjusted income has risen, happiness has not. Income data from Bureau of the Census (1975) and Economic Indicators. Happiness data from the periodic General Social Survey, National Opinion Research Center, University of Chicago.

levels, then who are the very happy people? Through life's ups and downs, some people's capacity for joy persists. In one National Institute of Aging study of five thousand adults, the happiest of people in 1973 were still relatively happy ten years later, despite changes in their work, their residence, and their family status (Costa, McCrae, & Zonderman, 1987).

Across many studies, four positive traits have marked happy lives (Myers & Diener, 1995). First, happy people like themselves. Especially in individualistic countries, they exhibit high *self-esteem,* by agreeing with statements such as: "I'm a lot of fun to be with" and "I have good ideas." Perhaps not surprisingly, given the moderately happy human condition, most people do report positive self-esteem. They not only score above the scale midpoint on self-esteem tests, but also exhibit a self-serving bias, by believing themselves more ethical, intelligent, unprejudiced,

sociable, and healthier than the average person (Myers, 1999).

Second, happy people tend to be *extroverted.* Although we might have expected that introverts would live more contentedly in the serenity of their unstressed contemplative lives, the consistent finding is that whether alone or with others, whether working in solitary or social occupations, extroverts are usually happier.

Third, happy people typically feel *personal control.* Feeling empowered rather than helpless, capable rather than victimized, they also perform better in school, achieve more at work, and cope better with stress. Deprived of control over one's life, as happens when in prison, in nursing homes, or when living under totalitarian regimes, people suffer lowered morale and worsened health. Severe poverty demoralizes people when it erodes their sense of control.

Fourth, happy people are commonly *optimistic*. One could reason that pessimists, whose low expectations are so often exceeded, would constantly be surprised by joy. "Blessed is he who expects nothing, for he shall never be disappointed," said Alexander Pope in a 1727 letter. Optimists, when undertaking something new, expect to succeed and thus tend to be more successful, healthier, and happier.

With each of these trait-happiness correlations, the causal traffic could go either way. Does optimism make people happier, or are happier people more optimistic? If the former (as suggested by other chapters in this volume), could people become happier by thinking, talking, and acting as if they had happiness-associated traits such as optimism?

Happiness, like cholesterol, seems variable but within the constraints of a genetic leash. This is partly because happiness-predicting traits such as extraversion are genetically predisposed. Thus, Lykken and Tellegen (1996) estimate from their study of 254 identical and fraternal twins that 50% of individual differences in happiness is heritable. Even identical twins raised apart often are similarly happy.

THE RELATIONSHIPS OF HAPPY PEOPLE

Close, supportive, committed relationships also mark happy lives. Despite Sartre's surmise that "Hell is other people," and despite all the stresses that mark our close relationships, those who can name several soul-mate friends are healthier and happier than those lacking such close relationships (Burt, 1986; Cohen, 1988; House, Landis, & Umberson, 1988). Our honoree, Martin Seligman (1991), contends that today's epidemic depression stems partly from impoverished social connections in increasingly individualistic Western societies. Individualistic societies offer personal control, harmony between the inner and outer person, and opportunity to express one's feelings and talents, but with the risks of a less embedded, more detached self.

For more than nine in ten people, one significant alternative to aloneness is marriage. Broken marital relationships are a source of much misery. Among Americans saying their marriage is "not too happy," a mere 3% live very happy lives (among 32,139 people sampled by the National Opinion Research Center

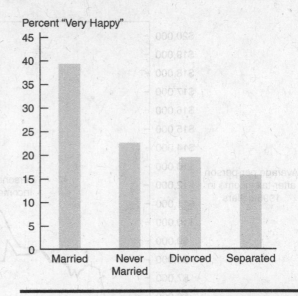

Percent "Very Happy"

FIGURE 6   Marital status and happiness. Data from 32,139 participants in the General Social Survey, National Opinion Research Center, 1972 to 1994.

since 1972). But among those in a "very happy" marriage, 57% declare their lives as "very happy." Most currently married people do report their marriages as happy, which helps explain why 40% of married adults, compared to 24% of never married adults, declare they are "very happy." Even slightly less happy are the divorced and separated (see Figure 6).

THE FAITH OF HAPPY PEOPLE

Although the accumulating studies of religiosity and happiness cannot speak to the truth of the claims of any religion, they do help us sort among conflicting opinions over whether religious faith is conducive or corrosive to a sense of well-being. Is religion, as Freud believed, an obsessional neurosis entailing guilt, repressed sexuality, and suppressed emotions? Or was C. S. Lewis right to presume that "Joy is the serious business of heaven"?

In Europe and North America, religiously active people report higher levels of happiness and satisfaction with life. Consider a Gallup Organization (1984) national survey. Those responding with the highest spiritual commitment (agreeing, for example, that "my religious faith is the most important influence in my life") were twice as likely, as compared to those lowest in spiritual commitment, to declare themselves "very happy" (Figure 7). In National Opinion Research Center surveys of 32,000 Americans since 1972, religious attendance also predicts self-reported happiness. One meta-analysis of research on elderly people found that the two best predictors of life satisfaction were health and religiousness (Okun & Stock, 1987).

Other studies have probed the connection between faith and coping with a crisis. Compared to religiously inactive widows, recently widowed women who worship regularly report more joy in their lives (Harvey, Barnes, & Greenwood, 1987; McGloshen & O'Bryant, 1988; Siegel & Kuykendall, 1990). Compared to irreligious mothers of disabled children, those with a deep religious faith are less vulnerable to depression (Friedrich, Cohen, & Wilturner, 1988). Those with a strong faith also recover greater happiness after suffering divorce, unemployment, serious illness, or bereavement (Ellison, 1991; McIntosh, Silver, & Wortman, 1993)

Researchers seek to explain these positive links between faith and well-being: Is it the supportive, close relationships often enjoyed by those in faith communities (of which there are some 350,000 in the United States alone)? Is it the sense of meaning and purpose that many people derive from their faith? Is it the motivation to focus beyond self (as reflected in the Gallup Organization's consistent finding of doubled rates of volunteerism and quadrupled rates of charitable giving among weekly church and synagogue attendees compared to nonattendees)?

Supportive evidence exists for each of these conjectures. Pertinent to this volume (and to my writing from a place called Hope), there remains also another possibility: that religious worldviews, by offering answers to some of life's deepest questions, encourage a more optimistic appraisal of life events; in addition, a sense of hope emerges when confronting what Solomon, Greenberg, and Pyszczynski (1991) call "the terror resulting from our awareness of vulnerability and death." Different faiths offer varied paths, but each offers its adherents a sense that they, or something meaningful in which they participate, will survive their deaths. Aware of the great enemies, suffering and death, religious faith offers a hope that in the end, the very end, "all shall be well and shall be well and all manner of things shall be well" (Julian of Norwich).

This hope-filled perspective on the fragility of life emboldens some to think that life has value. What is worth preserving, forever, must be of ultimate value. Moreover, a hope-filled utopian vision of peace, justice, and love can direct one's involvement in the here and now. It defines an ideal world—a back-to-the-present vision—and fuels courage to pursue it. Thus Martin Luther King (1964) could declare, "I have a dream," a vision of a future reality, of a world liberated from oppression, suffering, and death. With a dream worth dying for and a hope that even death could not kill it, he could also declare, "If physical death is the price I must pay to free my white brothers and sisters from a permanent death of the spirit, then nothing can be more redemptive." As Reubem Alves (1972) stated, "Hope is hearing the melody of the future. Faith is to dance to it."

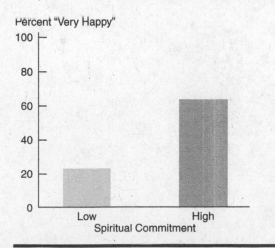

FIGURE 7 Spiritual commitment and happiness. Data from Gallup (1984).

REFERENCES

Costa, P. T., Jr., McCrae, R. R., & Zonderman, A. B. (1987). Environmental and dispositional influences on well-being: Longitudinal follow-up of an American national sample. *British Journal of Psychology, 78,* 299–306.

Diener, E., & Diener, M. (1995). Cross-cultural studies of life satisfaction and self-esteem. *Journal of Personality and Social Psychology, 68,* 653–663.

Ellison, C. G. (1991). Religious involvement and subjective well-being. *Journal of Health and Social Behavior, 32,* 80–99.

Lykken, D., & Tellegen, A. (1996). Happiness is a stochastic phenomenon. *Psychological Science, 7,* 186–189.

Myers, D. G. (1993). *The pursuit of happiness.* New York: Avon.

Myers, D. G., & Diener, E. (1995). Who is happy? *Psychological Science, 6,* 10–19.

Myers, D. G., & Diener E. (1996, May). The pursuit of happiness. *Scientific American,* 54–56.

Questions to Think About

1. Why do so many people in our society seem unshakable in their belief that more money would buy them more happiness, when the evidence is that more money doesn't seem to contribute much to increasing happiness, except for those who are truly poor?

2. Why might there be an asymmetry in the effects of the quality of one's marriage on happiness? People in "very happy" marriages only have a 57% rate of "very happy" lives (that is, 43% of people in "very happy" marriages do not have "very happy" lives), but of people in marriages that are "not too happy," 97% do not have "very happy" lives.

3. What are the implications of the estimate that 50% of individual differences in happiness is heritable? Should people who are not currently happy conclude that they are likely doomed by their genes to unhappiness?

41

A Note on Formulating the Relationship
of the Individual and the Group

HARRY STACK SULLIVAN

Harry Stack Sullivan (1892–1949) believed that the essence of personality involves enduring patterns of human relationships. Life is a series of interpersonal processes. Influenced by social psychology and the idea of the social self, Sullivan took issue with the idea that each person has a single, fixed personality. Rather, we have as many personalities as we have recurring interpersonal situations.

Sullivan was born in upstate New York, was trained in medicine, and spent much time dealing with people with psychiatric problems. Because people need to learn healthy interpersonal interactions, Sullivan thought that it was often more harmful than helpful to lock away the mentally "ill" in mental sanitariums. Because of this belief, Sullivan often spent time interacting with his patients as chums.

We think conventionally of ourself as a person and of others as individual persons or individuals. This is a convention of reference strongly entrenched in our language and widely disseminated in our culture. It seems to derive immediately from our observations of gross biological phenomena, and any other view would seem to be nothing short of absurd. I am here and not elsewhere. This is my hand, the expression of my thought. It is true that I must maintain recurrent communion with the environing supply of oxygen, water, and other substances. It may even be true that I cannot continue very long to manifest essentially human traits unless I maintain recurrent communion with other people. But my individuality as a concrete human being does not seem to be impaired by these perduring necessities which affect everyone in exactly the same way and to much the same degree that they affect me.

I may go farther and describe myself in generic terms: white, American, denizen of the Western culture in its transitional phase from the Industrial Era. I agree that I would not be myself if I were a Negro—American or African. I have no difficulty in understanding that as I, myself, I am largely a product of acculturation and as such not particularly different in many culturally controlled respects from a great many white Americans of approximately my somatic age and educational background. But, I shall insist that, however like some average people I may be in many respects, I am nonetheless the product of a unique course of acculturation; I have undergone a unique series of events many of which have left their impress in my own personal memory. I know that I have come to have a relatively durable congeries of traits or characteristics (which I call my personality) which singles me out from everyone else. In a word, I am a person of some, however little, distinction; and there are at least a few other people who would be emphatic in supporting this judgment. They know me; they can tell you exactly

Source: Sullivan, H. S. (1939). A note on formulating the relationship of the individual and the group. *American Journal of Sociology, 44,* 932–937. Copyright © 1939 University of Chicago Press. Reprinted by permission of The University of Chicago Press, publisher.

what to expect if you have dealings with me. Should you confuse me with some other stranger about whom you have been told, you will gradually realize your error as you talk with me. You will see that my personality is different from the one with which you erroneously believed yourself to be dealing.

One may pause here to consider how often one has actually failed to observe these presumably specific differences of personality, has carried on serious conversation with the wrong person without any realization of the error in identification. These instances may not seem to have been at all numerous; this, however, in all likelihood is sheer illusion of memory. Most people would learn a great deal if they could study the negative instances of their identifying a stranger in terms of his reputed personality. So strongly ingrained in us is the conviction that we ought to be able to perceive the "personal traits" of other people that our feeling of personal security is involved in this norm of the "knower of men." In fact, the less secure one feels, the greater a comfort one derives from a facile classifying of other people among various patterns of projection of one's own presumptively static traits—and their verbal opposites.

From infancy each of us is trained to think in this way. If one was fortunately born, the parents have been fairly consistent in their expressed appraisals, and one has elaborated a dependable self. However absurdly it may be related to one's manifest behavior, one is relatively secure in dealing with others. If one's parents have been less reassuring or if experience subsequent to childhood has demonstrated the serious deficiency of a once-trusted illusion as to one's personality, the case is quite otherwise. "I did not think you were *that* kind of a person" comes to be a very painful remark the deeper implications of which do not engage one's attention. One becomes as realistically as possible a member of the group made up of the right kind of people and acts as rightly as possible in those restricted interpersonal contexts in which one still has freedom to participate.

The traits with which one believes one's self characterized are often amazingly fluid, if one's serious statements are to be taken as evidence. Discussing one's self with one person, one reports one perhaps only moderately consistent set. In an equally serious

discussion with a different auditor the account is different. Some people are consistent in referring to certain outstanding traits about which a consensus could be obtained; some are consistent only in the breach—the traits that they generally claim are those which come near being merely ideal; the statements express wishful rather than factual data. Some know that their accounts vary with different auditors and can even rationalize noted differences—usually on the basis of the attitude of the auditor and one's wanting to make as good an impression as possible. The traits with which we endow others are also of varying certainty and sometimes subject to radical change under pressure of divergent opinion. The shift may not appear in the course of the particular controversy but may become evident in subsequent discussions. About all that seems perfectly certain about personal traits as subjects of opinion is that the having of such opinions seems important.

The interpretation of behavior is generally regarded as of a higher probability than is the analysis of conversation about one's self. It is easier to say the right thing than to keep on doing the right thing. This truism is not to be taken too seriously, however, for some people show high consistency over long periods in behavior that expresses a role which they feel is incongruous to them but demanded by the other person. Success in "acting like" this incongruous person does not excite them to much speculation about their "real" personality, perhaps for the good reason that it is but a particular, a clearly noticed, instance of something that has been going on from very early years.

The psychiatrist has to regard each personality (individual, unique person) as an indeterminate entity some significant characteristics of which may be inferred from the processes that occur in the group of persons—real and fantastic—in which the subject-individual participates. Participation is a pattern of processes and, in seeking to delimit the universe of interpersonal relations, the psychiatrist may begin with those psychobiological states in which interpersonal processes do not occur. These are chiefly two: deep sleep and panic. Panic is that condition which is beyond or in excess of complete insecurity. Deep sleep is antithetic in that it can appear only in the absence of insecurity or after neutralization of all insecurity-provoking factors. Behavior is impossible in either state, and the appearance of implicit (mental) activity marks the change alike from panic or from deep sleep toward a more characteristically human condition. Panic is the extreme of a series of states that grades through insecurity and fear to mild anxiety. Deep sleep is the extreme of a series including various levels of what may be called "active" sleep, somnolent detachment, and inattentive reverie states.

The reality of relevant other people is vestigial in severe insecurity and in all the sleep-states. Interpersonal phenomena are present, but the people concerned are largely fantastic, complexly related to real people. Characteristics of related real people have been magnified or minimized, moved from one personality to another, combined in poignantly artificial patterns. Experiences from long ago involving people but remotely related to those seemingly involved contribute elements to the fantastic personalizations. The novel and unreal are created out of items of actual experience, but the items are combined into patterns that reveal little about anyone except the subject-individual, himself in a state bordering on the primitive, if not, in fact, on the infra-human, type of integration.

These are the minimal limits of interpersonal relations. What are the maximal? To find these limits of his field, the psychiatrist organizes his observations of the most durable and the most effective interpersonal situations. Duration is a directional function in time. Effectiveness is less easy to define but must, too, have some reference to vector quality. Remembering that only interpersonal phenomena can be observed, an effective situation must be one that shows directional change in the interpersonal processes and hence in the series of interpersonal situations in which the subject-individual is involved. Maximal interpersonal relations must then be those that approach the span of a lifetime in duration and those that most powerfully alter the integrating tendencies of the person chiefly concerned.

Integrating tendencies are conceived to be the psychobiological substrata of the corresponding integrated interpersonal situations. Person A tends to integrate with Person B a situation to the more or less clearly envisaged end of improving his social status, thus relieving felt insecurity. Provisionally, we assume that, if any incipent A-B situation appears, Person B

also tended to integrate a situation with a person such as Person A is apprehended to be. We need not assume that the integrating tendencies respectively of A toward B and of B toward A are in any sense complementary. If they happen to be complementary—if B tends to integrate a situation of the vassalage type with A—and if there are no stronger integrating tendencies that conflict, the A-B situation is consolidated and endures until its tensional aspect shall have been resolved. If the integrating tendencies that coincided in the incipient A-B situation are not complementary, B's integrating tendency is powerful, and there is no strong conflicting tendency, there will develop a B-A situation which will have value to A, but is not likely to relieve the insecurity about status and deference. The incipient A-B situation will in any other case disintegrate promptly, generally with increased feeling of insecurity on the part of A, who will tend somewhat more urgently to integrate a presumably reassuring situation with some other person apprehended by him as in the same class as B; that is, useful in improving A's status. The B-A situation, on the other hand, may be effective in significantly changing this particular integrating tendency in A, so that his insecurity about status disappears.

One must observe that interpersonal situations may have multiple integration, and that durable situations may include more transient multiply integrated phases. Love situations often show recurrent episodes of lust and are not quite the same when there is mutual sexual excitement, "untimely" excitement of one partner, and in the intervals. The tendencies to integrate lustful-erotic situations should not be confused with those which eventuate in love situations. The latter may survive indefinitely the loss of prospective sexual satisfactions or the integration of sexual situations with persons not in the love relationship.

I have now presented in extreme abstract the conceptual framework of the psychiatric study of interpersonal relations, which would seem to have relevance to the sociopsychological study of the relations of the individual and the various groups with which he is more or less identified. I hope that it is clear that the psychiatrist must usually confine his exploration to (1) situations in which he himself takes part—in which his trained alertness may help him to analyze the incipient situations—and (2) those other situations concerned in the life of his subject-individual which have been either very durable or clearly effective in changing the course of the individual's manifest interpersonal living. Verbal report and collateral evidence are useful in establishing the second category of data. In actual practice certainty is greatest in working back from the first type of data through the second. Without what we may call the immediate experimental situation and the historic view it is often extremely difficult to get access to a particular group relationship. Durable associations in the general interest of beauty, truth, or humanity—security, love, lust, income, deference—may readily be mistaken one for another by the investigator. The subject-individual, if the relationship to the psychiatrist is not explicit, may also "mislead himself" almost endlessly.

It is clear that the study of interpersonal relations in contrast to the study of persons and group has

validity. The demarcation of the field is made difficult by the conventions of speech and thought and by other aspects of the controlling culture. The new type of orientation that can be obtained by this type of approach is quite certain to be fruitful both in social theory and practice. It has some fundamental implications for the field of education.

REFERENCES

Sullivan, H. S. (1937). A note on the implications of psychiatry, the study of interpersonal relations, for investigations in the social sciences. *American Journal of Sociology, 42,* 848–861.

Sullivan, H. S. (1938). Psychiatry: Introduction to the study of interpersonal relations. *Psychiatry, 1,* 121–134.

Sullivan, H. S. (1939). Intuition, reason, and faith. *Psychiatry, 2,* 129–132.

Questions to Think About

1. If the focus of personality study should be on the interpersonal situation, not on the person, then how could we go about assessing personality?

2. It is clear that the individual has some self-contained psychobiological characteristics. How can this fact be integrated with the idea that personality involves enduring patterns of relationships?

3. Is it only an illusion that a person has a single, fixed personality?

4. When a psychiatrist wants to understand the interpersonal relations of his patient, Sullivan claims, the best source of data is interpersonal situations in which the psychiatrist can see the patient interacting with the groups with which the patient is identified. Is this a practical strategy, and what effect might such a strategy have on the confidentiality of the patient's treatment?

42

The Social Self

GEORGE HERBERT MEAD

George Herbert Mead (1863–1931), was a psychologist and philosopher who played an important role in both disciplines (much like William James, who was one of Mead's mentors). In philosophy, he was a prominent figure in the pragmatist movement at the turn of the twentieth century. In psychology, he is considered as a founder of social psychology. While psychoanalytic theory was focusing on the internal struggles and conflicts of the individual, Mead found a richer source in looking at a person's ongoing social interaction with significant others. The selection below was published in 1913 in *The Journal of Philosophy, Psychology and Scientific Methods*, demonstrating the close ties that the disciplines of philosophy and psychology shared in that era.

Recognizing that the self can not appear in consciousness as an "I," that it is always an object, *i.e.*, a "me," I wish to suggest an answer to the question, What is involved in the self being an object? The first answer may be that an object involves a subject. Stated in other words, that a "me" is inconceivable without an "I. "And to this reply must be made that such an "I" is a presupposition, but never a presentation of conscious experience, for the moment it is presented it has passed into the objective case, presuming, if you like, an "I" that observes—but an "I" that can disclose himself only by ceasing to be the subject for whom the object "me" exists. It is, of course, not the Hegelism of a self that becomes another to himself in which I am interested, but the nature of the self as revealed by introspection and subject to our factual analysis. This analysis does reveal, then, in a memory process an attitude of observing oneself in which both the observer and the observed appear. To be concrete, one remembers asking himself how he could undertake to do this, that, or the other, chiding himself for his shortcomings or pluming himself upon his achievements. Thus, in the redintegrated self of the moment passed, one finds both a subject and an object, but it is a subject that is

now an object of observation, and has the same nature as the object self whom we present as in intercourse with those about us. In quite the same fashion we remember the questions, admonitions, and approvals addressed to our fellows. But the subject attitude which we instinctively take can be presented only as something experienced—as we can be conscious of our acts only through the sensory processes set up after the act has begun.

The contents of this presented subject, who thus has become an object in being presented, but which still distinguish him as the subject of the passed experience from the "me" whom he addressed, are those images which initiated the conversation and the motor sensations which accompany the expression, plus the organic sensations and the response of the whole system to the activity initiated. In a word, just those contents which go to make up the self which is distinguished from the others whom he addresses. The self appearing as "I" is the memory image self who acted toward himself and is the same self who acts toward other selves.

On the other hand, the stuff that goes to make up the "me" whom the "I" addresses and whom he observes, is the experience which is induced by this

Source: Mead, G. H. (1913). The social self. *The Journal of Philosophy, Psychology and Scientific Methods, 10*(4), 374–380.

action of the "I." If the "I" speaks, the "me" hears. If the "I" strikes, the "me" feels the blow. Here again the "me" consciousness is of the same character as that which arises from the action of the other upon him. That is, it is only as the individual finds himself acting with reference to himself as he acts towards others, that he becomes a subject to himself rather than an object, and only as he is affected by his own social conduct in the manner in which he is affected by that of others, that he becomes an object to his own social conduct.

The differences in our memory presentations of the "I" and the "me" are those of the memory images of the initiated social conduct and those of the sensory responses thereto.

It is needless, in view of the analysis of Baldwin, of Royce and of Cooley and many others, to do more than indicate that these reactions arise earlier in our social conduct with others than in introspective self-consciousness, *i.e.,* that the infant consciously calls the attention of others before he calls his own attention by affecting himself and that he is consciously affected by others before he is conscious of being affected by himself.

The "I" of introspection is the self which enters into social relations with other selves. It is not the "I" that is implied in the fact that one presents himself as a "me." And the "me" of introspection is the same "me" that is the object of the social conduct of others. One presents himself as acting toward others—in this presentation he is presented in indirect discourse as the subject of the action and is still an object,—and the subject of this presentation can never appear immediately in conscious experience. It is the same self who is presented as observing himself, and he affects himself just in so far and only in so far as he can address himself by the means of social stimulation which affect others. The "me" whom he addresses is the "me," therefore, that is similarly affected by the social conduct of those about him.

This statement of the introspective situation, however, seems to overlook a more or less constant feature of our consciousness, and that is that running current of awareness of what we do which is distinguishable from the consciousness of the field of stimulation, whether that field be without or within. It is this "awareness" which has led many to assume that it is the nature of the self to be conscious both of subject

and of object—to be subject of action toward an object world and at the same time to be directly conscious of this subject as subject,—"Thinking its non-existence along with whatever else it thinks." Now, as Professor James pointed out, this consciousness is more logically conceived of as sciousness—the thinker being an implication rather than a content, while the "me" is but a bit of object content within the stream of sciousness. However, this logical statement does not do justice to the findings of consciousness. Besides the actual stimulations and responses and the memory images of these, within which lie perforce the organic sensations and responses which make up the "me," there accompanies a large part of our conscious experience, indeed all that we call self-conscious, an inner response to what we may be doing, saying, or thinking. At the back of our heads we are a large part of the time more or less clearly conscious of our own replies to the remarks made to others, of innervations which would lead to attitudes and gestures answering our gestures and attitudes towards others.

The observer who accompanies all our self-conscious conduct is then not the actual "I" who is responsible for the conduct in *propria persona*—he is rather the response which one makes to his own conduct. The confusion of this response of ours, following upon our social stimulations of others with the implied subject of our action, is the psychological ground for the assumption that the self can be directly conscious of itself as acting and acted upon. The actual situation is this: The self acts with reference to others and is immediately conscious of the objects about it. In memory it also redintegrates the self acting as well as the others acted upon. But besides these contents, the action with reference to the others calls out responses in the individual himself—there is then another "me" criticizing approving, and suggesting, and consciously planning, *i.e.,* the reflective self.

It is not to all our conduct toward the objective world that we thus respond. Where we are intensely preoccupied with the objective world, this accompanying awareness disappears. We have to recall the experience to become aware that we have been involved as selves, to produce the self-consciousness which is a constituent part of a large part of our experience. As I have indicated elsewhere, the mechanism for this reply to our own social stimulation of others follows as a natural result from the fact that the very sounds, gestures, especially vocal gestures, which man makes in addressing others, call out or tend to call out responses from himself. He can not hear himself speak without assuming in a measure the attitude which he would have assumed if he had been addressed in the same words by others.

The self which consciously stands over against other selves thus becomes an object, an other to himself, through the very fact that he hears himself talk, and replies. The mechanism of introspection is therefore given in the social attitude which man necessarily assumes toward himself, and the mechanism of thought, in so far as thought uses symbols which are used in social intercourse, is but an inner conversation.

Now it is just this combination of the remembered self which acts and exists over against other selves with the inner response to his action which is essential to the self-conscious ego— the self in the full meaning of the term—although neither phase of self-consciousness, in so far as it appears as an object of our experience, is a subject.

It is also to be noted that this response to the social conduct of the self may be in the role of another— we present his arguments in imagination and do it with his intonations and gestures and event perhaps with his facial expression. In this way we play the rôles of all our group; indeed, it is only in so far as we do this that they become part of our social environment— to be aware of another self as a self implies that we have played his role or that of another with whose type we identify him for purposes of intercourse. The inner response to our reaction to others is therefore as varied as is our social environment. Not that we assume the roles of others toward ourselves because we are subject to a mere imitative instinct, but because in responding to ourselves we are in the nature of the case taking the attitude of another than the self that is directly acting, and into this reaction there naturally flows the memory images of the responses of those about us, the memory images of those responses of others which were in answer to like actions. Thus the child can think about his conduct as good or bad only as he reacts to his own acts in the remembered words of his parents. Until this process has been developed into the abstract process of thought, self-consciousness remains dramatic, and the self which is a fusion of the remembered actor and this accompanying chorus is somewhat loosely organized and very clearly social. Later the inner stage changes into the forum and workshop of thought. The features and intonations of the *dramatis personae* fade out and the emphasis falls upon the meaning of the inner speech, the imagery becomes merely the barely necessary cues. But the mechanism remains social, and at any moment the process may become personal.

It is fair to say that the modern western world has lately done much of its thinking in the form of the novel, while earlier the drama was a more effective but equally social mechanism of self-consciousness. And, in passing, I may refer to that need of filling out the bare spokesman of abstract thought, which even the most abstruse thinker feels, in seeking his audience. The import of this for religious self-consciousness is obvious.

There is one further implication of this nature of the self to which I wish to call attention. It is the manner of its reconstruction. I wish especially to refer to it, because the point is of importance in the psychology of ethics.

As a mere organization of habit the self is not self-conscious. It is this self which we refer to as character. When, however, an essential problem appears, there is some disintegration in this organization, and different tendencies appear in reflective thought as different voices in conflict with each other. In a sense the old self has disintegrated, and out of the moral process a new self arises. The specific question I wish to ask is whether the new self appears together with the new object or end. There is of course a reciprocal relation between the self and its object, the one implies the other and the interests and evaluations of the self answer exactly to content and values of the object. On the other hand, the consciousness of the new object, its values and meaning, seems to come earlier to consciousness than the new self that answers to the new object.

The man who has come to realize a new human value is more immediately aware of the new object in his conduct than of himself and his manner of reaction to it. This is due to the fact to which reference has already been made, that direct attention goes first to the object. When the self becomes an object, it appears in memory, and the attitude which it implied has already been taken. In fact, to distract attention from the object to the self implies just that lack of objectivity which we criticize not only in the moral agent, but in the scientist.

Assuming as I do the essentially social character of the ethical end, we find in moral reflection a conflict in which certain values find a spokesman in the old self or a dominant part of the old self, while other values answering to other tendencies and impulses arise in opposition and find other spokesmen to present their cases. To leave the field to the values represented by the old self is exactly what we term selfishness. The justification for the term is found in the habitual character of conduct with reference to these values. Attention is not claimed by the object and shifts to the subjective field where the affective responses are identified with the old self. The result is that we state the other conflicting ends in subjective terms of other selves and the moral problem seems to take on the form of the sacrifice either of the self or of the others.

Where, however, the problem is objectively considered, although the conflict is a social one, it should not resolve itself into a struggle between selves, but into such a reconstruction of the situation that different and enlarged and more adequate personalities may emerge. A tension should be centered on the objective social field.

In the reflective analysis, the old self should enter upon the same terms with the selves whose roles are assumed, and the test of the reconstruction is found in the fact that all the personal interests are adequately recognized in a new social situation. The new self that answers to this new situation can appear in consciousness only after this new situation has been realized and accepted. The new self can not enter into the field as the determining factor because he is consciously present only after the new end has been formulated and accepted. The old self may enter only as an element over against the other personal interests involved. If he is the dominant factor it must be in defiance of the other selves whose interests are at stake. As the old self he is defined by his conflict with the others that assert themselves in his reflective analysis.

Solution is reached by the construction of a new world harmonizing the conflicting interests into which enters the new self.

The process is in its logic identical with the abandonment of the old theory with which the scientist has identified himself, his refusal to grant this old attitude any further weight than may be given to the other conflicting observations and hypotheses. Only when a successful hypothesis, which overcomes the conflicts, has been formulated and accepted, may the scientist again identify himself with this hypothesis as his own, and maintain it *contra mundum*. He may not state the scientific problem and solution in terms of his old personality. He may name his new hypothesis after himself and realize his enlarged scientific personality in its triumph.

The fundamental difference between the scientific and moral solution of a problem lies in the fact that the moral problem deals with concrete personal interests, in which the whole self is reconstructed in its relation to the other selves whose relations are essential to its personality.

The growth of the self arises out of a partial disintegration,—the appearance of the different interests in the forum of reflection, the reconstruction of the social world, and the consequent appearance of the new self that answers to the new object.

Questions to Think About

1. Mead claims that self-consciousness (in the sense of awareness of the self) arises only in the presence of conflict that causes disintegration of the organization of habit. Does this imply that, without conflict in social interaction, a person stagnates in his or her existing state?

2. To what extent do Mead's views of "the social self" correspond to the object relations approach of some neoanalytic theorists? Where are the major differences between these approaches?

3. Mead's article appeared in a periodical called *The Journal of Philosophy, Psychology and Scientific Methods*. To what extent is it a psychology paper, and in what ways a philosophy paper?

43

Continuity and Change in Personality

WALTER MISCHEL

Walter Mischel (1930–) has long been interested in the interactionist approach to personality. Not believing that personality could be broken into broad personality traits, he argued that personality was much more complicated than that. Since a person's behavior varies so much from situation to situation, it may not make sense to think in terms of broad personality traits. Rather, a person's cognitive personality characteristics are learned during experiences with situations and their rewards.

Mischel, born in Vienna, was an undergraduate at City College of New York, and a graduate student in clinical psychology at Ohio State University, where he worked with psychologists who took both a cognitive and a learning approach to personality. He worked for many years at Stanford University, where he was influenced by the social learning theories of Albert Bandura, and he then moved to Columbia University in New York. In this selection, he explains his approach to taking both the person and the situation into account.

The question of continuity and change in personality has enduring importance, and the position that one takes on this topic profoundly influences one's approach to most other issues in personality psychology. Almost no psychologist, myself included, would argue with the basic and widely shared assumption that continuity does exist in personality development (e.g., Kagan, 1969). Indeed, few other phenomena seem to be so intuitively self-evident. The experience of subjective continuity in ourselves—of basic oneness and durability in the self—is perhaps the most compelling and fundamental feature of personality. This experience of continuity seems to be an intrinsic feature of the mind, and the loss of a sense of felt consistency may be a chief characteristic of personality disorganization.

Clinically, it seems remarkable how each of us generally manages to reconcile his seemingly diverse behaviors into one self-consistent whole. A man may steal on one occasion, lie on another, donate generously to charity on a third, cheat on a fourth, and still construe himself readily as "basically honest and moral." Just like the personality theorist who studies them, our subjects also are skilled at transforming their seemingly discrepant behavior into a constructed continuity, making unified wholes out of almost anything.

It might be interesting to fantasize a situation in which the personality theorist and his subjects sat down together to examine each subject's data on behavioral consistency cross-situationally or over time. Actually it might not even be a bad idea for psychologists to enact such a fantasy. In inspecting these data

Source: Mischel, W. (1969). Continuity and change in personality. *American Psychologist, 24*(1), 1012–1018. Copyright 1969 by the American Psychological Association. Reprinted with permission.

Editor's note: All citations in the text of this selection have been left intact from the original, but the list of references includes only those sources that are the most relevant and important. Readers wishing to follow any of the other citations can find the full references in the original work or in an online database.

the theorist would look for genotypic unities that he is sure must be there; his subject would look for genotypic unities and be even more convinced that they exist and would proceed to find his own, often emerging with unities unknown to the theorist. But the consistency data on the IBM sheets, even if they reached statistical significance, probably would account for only a trivial portion of the variance, as Hunt (1965) has pointed out. A correlation of .30 leaves us understanding less than 10% of the relevant variance. And even correlations of that magnitude are not very common and have come to be considered good in research on the consistency of any noncognitive dimension of personality.

How does one reconcile our shared perception of continuity with the equally impressive evidence that on virtually all of our dispositional measures of personality substantial changes occur in the characteristics of the individual longitudinally over time and, even more dramatically, across seemingly similar settings cross-sectionally? I had the occasion to broadly review the voluminous evidence available on this topic of consistency and specificity (Mischel, 1968). In my appraisal, the overall evidence from many sources (clinical, experimental, developmental, correlational) shows the human mind to function like an extraordinarily effective reducing valve that creates and maintains the perception of continuity even in the face of perpetual observed changes in actual behavior. Often this cognitive construction of continuity, while not arbitrary, is only very tenuously related to the phenomena that are construed.

To understand continuity properly it is necessary to be more specific and to talk about types of variations and the conditions that regulate them. In this regard it may be useful to distinguish between consistency in various types of human activity.

There is a great deal of evidence that our cognitive constructions about ourselves and the world—our personal theories about ourselves and those around us (both in our roles as persons and as psychologists)—often are extremely stable and highly resistant to change. Data from many sources converge to document this point. Studies of the self-concept, of impression formation in person perception and in clinical judgment, of cognitive sets guiding selective attention—all these phenomena and many more document the consistency and tenacious continuity of many human construction systems (Mischel, 1968). Often these construction systems are built quickly and on the basis of little information (e.g., Bruner, Olver, & Greenfield, 1966). But, once established, these theories, whether generated by our subjects or ourselves, become exceedingly difficult to disconfirm.

An impressive degree of continuity also has been shown for another aspect of cognition: These are the features of problem solving called cognitive styles. Significant continuity often has been demonstrated on many cognitive style dimensions (e.g., Kagan, 1969; Witkin, Goodenough, & Karp, 1967). The current prolific cognitive style explorations on this topic provide excellent evidence of developmental continuity. In this case the research also reveals a welcome continuity in our professional developmental history. Research into consistent individual differences in cognition has had deep roots and a long and distinguished history in experimental psychology. Simple cognitive measures like reaction time and response speed and duration have intrigued psychologists since the earliest laboratory work on mental measurement began more than 70 years ago. Individual differences on specific measures of problem solving, such as speed of reaction time and weight judgments, began to be explored in 1890 by James McKeen Cattell and others. Their studies of responses on specific cognitive and ability measures in the early laboratories were neglected when the development of practical intelligence testing started in this century. At that time, Binet and Henri shifted attention to the measurement of generalized intelligence by studying individual differences in more complex global tasks. Now it is refreshing to witness the reawakened interest in such enduringly important topics as reaction time and "conceptual tempo" and it is good to see sophisticated consistency evidence for it (Kagan, 1969). The generality and stability of behaviors assessed by these cognitive measures often have been found to be among the best available in personality research.

Some puzzling problems may arise, however, from the correlations found between some of the most promising new cognitive style measures and the traditional measures of generalized intelligence such as the performance IQ on the WISC. That is, correlations between measures of generalized intelligence and cognitive style such as Witkin's field dependence raise the question of the degree to which the consistency of cognitive styles may be due to their associations with intellectual abilities. The obtained generality and stability, as well as the external personality correlates, of at least some cognitive style measures thus may rest in part on their sizable correlations with indexes of more generalized intelligence and achievement behavior, as has been found in other studies (e.g., Crandall & Sinkeldam, 1964; Elliott, 1961). To illustrate, the Witkin measures of cognitive style are strongly related to performance IQ ability indexes. Indeed the relationship between the Witkin Embedded Figures Test and the Wechsler Intelligence Block Design subtest is so strong that Witkin (1965) has indicated be is willing to use Block Design scores when available as a substitute for other field-dependence measures. When such cognitive styles as field independence and such coping patterns as "intellectualization" are substantially correlated with IQ then the stability reported for them and their correlates (e.g., by Schimek, 1968) may partly reflect the stability of the IQ.

This issue might also constitute a problem in interpreting such cognitive styles as Kagan's conceptual tempo. To the extent that conceptual tempo involves reaction time, and fast reaction time is a determinant of generalized performance IQ, one would have to be alert to their interrelations, as has been pointed out by Campbell and Fiske (1959). It will be interesting to continue to explore exactly how conceptual tempo and other cognitive styles based on performance indexes such as response speed and accuracy take us beyond generalized ability measurement and into the domain of personality traits. Ultimately research on cognitive styles surely will provide a clearer analysis of intellective behavior. The implications of cognitive styles for the concept of general intelligence (as well as the reverse relation) should then become more explicit than they are now. In the course of these explorations the meaning of intercorrelations among diverse cognitive style measures—such as conceptual tempo, field dependence-independence, leveling-sharpening, and so on—will become clearer. At the same time our understanding of the interactions among cognitive and non-cognitive personality dimensions hopefully will improve.

When we turn away from cognitive and intellective dimensions to the domain of personality and interpersonal behavior, consistency evidence is generally much harder to establish, at least whenever we use conventional tactics and the correlation coefficient (e.g., Maccoby, 1969). On the basis of past literature on this topic, one should no longer be surprised when consistency correlations for social behavior patterns turn out to be quite low. Theoretically, in my view, one should not expect social behavior to be consistent unless the relevant social learning and cognitive conditions are arranged to maintain the behavior cross-situationally. On theoretical as well as on empirical grounds, much of the time there is no reason to expect great consistency in the social behaviors comprising most of our personality dimensions.

It is not possible to even begin to cite here the extensive evidence that I believe supports this point, namely, that noncognitive global personality dispositions are much less global than traditional psychodynamic and trait positions have assumed them to be (Mischel, 1968). A great deal of behavioral specificity has been found regularly on character traits such as rigidity, social conformity, aggression, on attitudes to authority, and on virtually any other non-intellective personality dimension (Mischel, 1968; Peterson, 1968; Vernon, 1964). Some of the data on delay of gratification with young children, emerging from our current studies at Stanford, are illustrative. In an ongoing longitudinal study on this problem we have obtained evidence that delay of gratification has some developmental consistency and increases with age, up to a point. Much more impressive in my view, however, is our finding that within any child there exists tremendous variability on this dimension. Now we are studying how long preschool children will actually sit still alone in a chair waiting for a preferred but delayed outcome before they signal to terminate the waiting period and settle for a less preferred but immediately available gratification. We are finding that the same $3\frac{1}{2}$-year-old child who on one occasion may terminate his waiting in less than half a minute may be capable of waiting by himself up to an hour on another occasion a few weeks earlier or later, *if* cognitive and attentional conditions are appropriately arranged. Our conclusion is that some significant predictions of length of voluntary delay of gratification certainly can be made from individual differences data; but the most powerful predictions by far come from knowledge of the cognitive and incentive conditions that prevail in the particular situation of interest.

These results are not at all atypical. A tribute to the interaction of person and environment is usually offered at the front of every elementary textbook in the form of Kurt Lewin's famous equation: Behavior is a function of person and environment. In spite of such lip service to the stimulus, most of our personality theories and methods still take no serious account of conditions in the regulation of behavior. Literally thousands of tests exist to measure dispositions, and virtually none is available to measure the psychological environment in which development and change occurs.

Evidence on observed instability and inconsistency in behavior often has been interpreted to reflect the imperfections of our tests and tools at the resulting unreliability and errors of our measurements, as due to the fallibility of the human clinical judge and his ratings, and as due to many other methodological problems. Undoubtedly all these sources contribute real problems. Some of these have been excellently conceptualized by Emmerich (1969). His emphasis on the need to considering rate and mean changes over age if one is to achieve a proper understanding of continuity, growth, and psychological differentiation is especially important. Likewise, his call for longitudinal, multimeasure, and multivariate studies needs to be heeded most seriously.

I am more and more convinced, however, hopefully by data as well as on theoretical grounds, that the observed inconsistency so regularly found in studies of noncognitive personality dimensions often reflects the state of nature and not merely the noise of measurement. Of course, that does not imply a capriciously haphazard world—only one in which personality consistencies seem greater than they are and in which behavioral complexities seem simpler than they are. This would, if true, be extremely functional. After all, if people tried to be radical behaviorists and to describe each other in operational terms they would

soon run out of breath and expire. It is essential for the mind to be a reducing valve—if it were not it might literally blow itself!

Perhaps the most widely accepted argument for consistency in the face of seeming diversity is the one mentioned so often, the distinction between the phenotypic and the genotypic. Thus most theorizing on continuity seems to have been guided by a model that assumes a set of genotypic personality dispositions that endure, although their overt response forms may change. This model, of course, is the one shared by traditional trait and dynamic dispositional theories of personality. The model was well summarized in the example of how a child at age 12 may substitute excessive obedience to a parent for his earlier phobic reaction as a way of reducing anxiety over parental rejection (Kagan, 1969). At the level of physical analogy Kagan spoke of how the litre of water in the closed system is converted to steam and recondensed to liquid.

This type of hydraulic Freudian-derived personality model, while widely shared by personality theorists, is of course not the only one available and not the only one necessary to deal with phenomena of continuity and change. Indeed, in the opinion of many clinical psychologists the hydraulic phenotypic-genotypic model applied to personality dynamics, psychotherapy, and symptom substitution has turned out to be a conceptual trap leading to some tragic pragmatic mistakes in clinical treatment and diagnosis for the last 50 years (e.g., Mischel, 1968; Peterson, 1968). I am referring, of course, to the unjustified belief that seemingly diverse personality problems must constitute symptoms of an underlying generalized core disorder rather than being relatively discrete problems often under the control of relatively independent causes and maintaining conditions.

The analysis of diverse behaviors as if they were symptomatic surface manifestations of more unitary underlying dispositional forces also is prevalent in our theories of personality development (e.g., Kagan, 1969; Maddi, 1968). But while diverse behaviors often may be in the service of the same motive or disposition, often they are not. In accord with the genotype-phenotype distinction, if a child shows attachment and dependency in some contexts but not in others one would begin a search to separate phenotypes from genotypes. But it is also possible that seeming inconsistencies, rather than serving one underlying motive, actually may be under the control of relatively separate causal variables. The two behavior patterns may not reflect a phenotype in the service of a genotype but rather may reflect discrimi- nation learning in the service of the total organism. Likewise, while a child's fears sometimes may be in the service of an underlying motive, most research on the topic would lead me to predict it is more likely that the fear would involve an organized response system with its own behavioral life, being evoked and maintained by its own set of regulating conditions (e.g., Bandura, 1969; Paul, 1967).

When we observe a woman who seems hostile and fiercely independent some of the time but passive, dependent, and feminine on other occasions, our reducing valve usually makes us choose between the two syndromes. We decide that one pattern is in the service of the other, or that both are in the service of a third motive. She must be a really castrating lady with a facade of passivity—or perhaps she is a warm, passive-dependent woman with a surface defense of aggressiveness. But perhaps nature is bigger than our concepts and it is possible for the lady to be a hostile, fiercely independent, passive, dependent, feminine, aggressive, warm, castrating person all-in-one. Of course which of these she is at any particular moment would not be random and capricious—it would depend on who she is with, when, how, and much, much more. But each of these aspects of her self may be a quite genuine and real aspect of her total being. (Perhaps we need more adjectives and hyphens in our personality descriptions. That is what is meant, I think, by "moderator variables.")

I am skeptical about the utility of the genotype-phenotype distinction at the present level of behavioral analysis in personality psychology because I fear it grossly oversimplifies the complexity of organized behavior and its often nonlinear causes. The genotype-phenotype oversimplification may mask the complex relations between the behavior and the organism that generates it, the other behaviors available to the organism, the history of the behavior, and the current evoking and maintaining conditions that regulate its occurrence and its generalization.

The question of the nature of the similarity or dissimilarity among the diverse responses emitted by a person is one of the thorniest in psychology. Even when one response pattern is not in the service of another the two of course may still interact. No matter how seemingly separated the various branches of behavior may be, one can always construe some common origins for them and some current interactions. At the very least, all behavior from an organism, no matter how diverse, still has unity because it is all generated from the same source—from the same one person. At the other extreme, incidentally, few response patterns are ever phenotypically or physically identical: Their similarity always has to be grouped on some higher-order dimension of meaning. To make sense of bits of raw behavior one always has to group them into larger common categories. The interesting theoretical issue is just what the bases of these groupings should be. Dispositional theories try to categorize behaviors in terms of the hypothesized historical psychic forces that diverse behaviors supposedly serve; but it is also possible to categorize the behaviors in terms of the unifying evoking and maintaining conditions that they jointly share.

Moreover, few potent response patterns can occur without exerting radical consequences for the other alternatives available to the person. Thus an extremely "fast-tempo" child may be so active that, in addition to fatiguing his parents, he may as Kagan (1969) found, smile less. Perhaps that happens because he is too busy to smile. My comment about how fast-tempo children may be too busy to smile is not really facetious. One of the intriguing features of any strong response syndrome is that it soon prevents all kinds of other intrinsically incompatible behaviors. If a child darts about a lot and is fast there are all sorts of other things he automatically cannot do. His speed in living, his pace, not only automatically influences his other possible behavior, it also soon starts to shape his environment. I now expect my fast-tempo children to be fast tempo, and currently it takes almost no cues from them to convince me I am right about them.

It would have been relatively simple to assess and predict personality if it had turned out to consist mainly of stable highly generalized response patterns that occur regularly in relation to many diverse stimulus constellations. The degree and subtlety of discrimination shown in human behavior, however, is at least as impressive as is the variety and extensiveness of stimulus generalization. What people do in any situation may be altered radically even by seemingly minor variations in prior experiences or slight modifications in stimulus attributes or in the specific characteristics of the evoking situation. From my theoretical perspective this state of affairs—namely, the enormously subtle discriminations that people continuously make, and consequently the flexibility of behavior—is not a cause of gloom. Instead, the relative specificity of behavior, and its dependence on environmental supports, is the expected result of complex discrimination learning and subtle cognitive differentiation. When the eliciting and evoking conditions that maintain behavior change—as they generally do across settings—then behavior surely will change also. While the continuous interplay of person and condition may have been a surprise for faculty and trait psychology it should come as no upset for us now. If one pays more than verbal tribute to the dependency of behavior on conditions, and to the modification of behavior when situations change, then the so-called negative results of dispositional research on behavioral continuity appear attributable largely to the limitations of the assumptions that have guided the research. From the viewpoint of social behavior theory the findings of behavioral specificity, rather than primarily reflecting measurement errors, are actually congruent with results from experimental research on the determinants and modification of social behavior (Mischel, 1968). When response consequences and valences change so do actions; but when maintaining conditions remain stable so does behavior.

The last decade has seen an exciting growth of research on cognitive styles and many researchers, have begun to study the person as an information-processing and problem-solving organism. Generally, however, these processes have been viewed in dimensional and dispositional terms and quickly translated back to fit the consistency assumptions of traditional global trait and psychodynamic theory. Individual differences on dimensions such conceptual tempo, field dependence, leveling-sharpening, and so on, have been

isolated with some promising results. Less progress has been made in applying the concepts and language of information processing and cognitive styles to forming a better theoretical conception of personality structure itself. It has become fashionable to speak of the organism as creating plans, generating rules, and, depending on his needs and situations, devising strategies. These tactics yield payoffs and consequences, and in light of these the person modifies his plans accordingly. But when contingencies change stably, what happens? For example, what happens when the mother-dependent child finds that his preschool peers now consistently have little patience for his whining, attention-getting bids, and instead respect independence and self-confidence? Generally the child's behavior changes in accord with the new contingencies, and if the contingencies shift so does the behavior—if the contingencies remain stable so does the new syndrome that the child now displays. Then what has happened to the child's dependency trait?

One might argue that the basic genotype remained but its manifestation phenotypically has altered. But is this just a "symptom" change leaving unaffected the psyche that generated it and the life space in which it unfolds? A vigorous "No!" to this question comes from much research on behavior change in the last few years (e.g., Bijou, 1965; Fairweather, 1967; Mischel, 1966; Patterson, Ray, & Shaw, 1969).

What would happen conceptually if we treated the organism as truly active and dynamic rather than as the carrier of a stable dispositional reservoir of motives and traits? Might one then more easily think of changes in the developing organism not as phenotypic overlays that mask genotypic unities but as genuinely new strategies in which many of the person's old plans are discarded and replaced by more appropriate ones in the course of development? (Perhaps Gordon Allport's idea of functional autonomy needs to be rethought.) Can the person even become involved in plans to change what he *is* as well as what he does? George Kelly and the existentialists in their search for human nature noted that existence precedes essence. According to that position, to find out what I *am* I need to know what I *do*. And if my actions change do they leave me (the "real me") behind? Or perhaps they just leave some of my discarded psychological genotypes behind?

A search for a personality psychology that has conceptual room for major variability and changes within the individual's dispositions can easily be misinterpreted as undermining the concept of personality itself. That would be an unfortunate misconstruction. Instead, we do need to recognize that discontinuities— real ones and not merely superficial or trivial veneer changes—are part of the genuine phenomena of personality. If one accepts that proposition, an adequate conceptualization of personality will have to go beyond the conventional definition of stable and broad enduring individual differences in behavioral dispositions. We may have to tolerate more dissonance than we like in our personality theory. To be more than nominally dynamic our personality theories will have to have as much room for human discrimination as for generalization, as much place for personality change as for stability, and as

much concern for man's self-regulation as for his victimization by either enduring intrapsychic forces or by momentary environmental constraints.

REFERENCES

Bandura, A. (1969). *Principles of behavior modification.* New York: Holt, Rinehart & Winston.

Bruner, J. S., Olver, R. R., & Greenfield, P. M. (1966). *Studies in cognitive growth.* New York: Wiley.

Hunt, J. McV. (1965). Traditional personality theory in the light of recent evidence. *American Scientist, 53,* 80–96.

Mischel, W. (1968). *Personality and assessment.* New York: Wiley.

Vernon, P. S. (1964). *Personality assessment: A critical survey.* New York: Wiley.

Witkin, H. A., Goodenough, D. R., & Karp, S. A. (1967). Stability of cognitive style from childhood to young adulthood. *Journal of Personality and Social Psychology, 7,* 291–300.

_____ Questions to Think About _____

1. What is the ideal balance between continuity and change in personality, avoiding the extremes of stagnation and volatility?

2. If instability and inconsistency of behavior is found through the repeated use of some measurement instrument (test) or scheme for scoring behavior, how can we distinguish true instability from unreliable measurement?

3. Is continuity in personality (the absence of change) a desirable characteristic, or is it rather evidence that there is inadequate opportunity for growth?

4. How should modern personality psychology conceptualize consistency of behavior, given that the situation in which a behavior is observed can have such a great impact?

44

Global Traits: A Neo-Allportian
Approach to Personality

DAVID C. FUNDER

David C. Funder (1953–) focuses his research on personality judgment. He also considers the process by which people come to those judgments on personality. His focus combines psychologists' judgments about personality with personality assessment done by everyday people. That is, he studies a variety of influences on personality assessment. He is also interested in finding out how people acquire the personalities that they have.

Funder received his Ph.D. from Stanford University and was a psychology professor at the University of Illinois and Harvard University before joining the University of California, Riverside. Growing out of the "person-situation controversy," this selection lays out a case for the validity of global personality traits, along with a series of caveats.

But let us not join the camp of skeptics who say an individual's personality is "a mere construct tied together with a name"—that there is nothing outer and objectively structured to be assessed. No scientist, I think, could survive for long if he heeded this siren song of doubt, for it leads to shipwreck. (Allport, 1958, p. 246)

One of the most widely used concepts of intuitive psychology is the global personality trait. Almost everyone is accustomed to thinking about and describing the people one knows using terms like "conscientious," "sociable," and "aggressive." Traits like these are *global* because each refers not just to one or a few specific behaviors, but to *patterns* of behavior presumed to transcend time and specific situations. Historically, the global trait used to be an important part of formal psychological theory as well. Gordon Allport (1931, 1937) wrote extensively about traits

more than a half century ago, and for a time many research programs either developed general trait theories (Cattell, 1946), or investigated in detail specific traits (Witkin et al., 1954).

In recent years, however, theorizing about dispositional constructs such as global traits has been at a relative standstill. As Buss and Craik (1983) pointed out, "the field of personality appears to have set its theoretical gears into neutral" (p. 105). One cause of this inactivity may have been the field's two decades of immersion in a distracting debate over whether significant individual differences in social behavior exist at all (Mischel, 1968). Although, in the end, the existence of important individual regularities was reaffirmed (Kenrick & Funder, 1988), a lingering effect of the controversy seems to be an image of traits—most especially global ones—as old-fashioned, rather quaint ideas not relevant for modern research in personality.

Source: Funder, D. C. (1991). Global traits: A Neo-Allportian approach to personality. *Psychological Science, 2,* 31–38. Reprinted by permission.

Editor's note: All citations in the text of this selection have been left intact from the original, but the list of references includes only those sources that are the most relevant and important. Readers wishing to follow any of the other citations can find the full references in the original work or in an online database.

Indeed, when global traits do appear in the literature nowadays, it is usually to play the role of straw man. The recent literature has seen a plethora of "reconceptualizations" of personality each of which begins, typically, by announcing its intention to replace global traits.

Modern reconceptualizations differ from global traits in at least three ways. First and most obviously, many constructs of the new personality psychology go out of their way not to be global. The range of life contexts to which they are relevant is specified narrowly and specifically, and this narrowness is touted as an important virtue. For instance, the recently promulgated "social intelligence" view of personality "guides one away from generalized assessments . . . towards more particular conclusions about the individual's profile of expertise in the life-task domains of central concern at that point in time" (Cantor & Kihlstrom, 1987, p. 241).

Second, and just as importantly, many modern personality variables are relatively *esoteric*—they are deliberately nonintuitive or even counterintuitive. For instance, in the place of trait terms found in ordinary language, one prominent investigator has offered person variables such as "self regulatory systems," "encoding strategies," and the like (Mischel, 1973).

Third, some modern reconceptualizations go so far as to eschew an explanatory role for personality variables altogether. For instance, the act frequency approach treats personality dispositions as little more than frequency counts of "topographically" (i.e., superficially) similar acts (Buss & Craik, 1983).

The intent of these reconceptualizations is laudable. Each is designed to correct one or more of the problems of overgenerality, vagueness, and even philosophical confusion to which trait psychology has sometimes been prone. The present article, however, is motivated by a belief that the movement away from global traits, however fashionable it may be, entails several dangers that are not usually acknowledged.

Briefly, the dangers are these. First, when we use dispositional terms that are framed *narrowly,* we discard any possibility of generating statements about individual differences that have real explanatory power. Second, when we use dispositional terms that are *esoteric,* we fail to make contact with traits as used in everyday social discourse, lose any basis for understanding and evaluating lay trait judgments, and discard the vast lore of common sense and wisdom that they embody. And third, when we are content to define traits as *frequencies* of superficially similar behaviors, we run the risk of being fundamentally deceived when, as often happens, the causes of behavior turn out to be complex. Each of these points will be expanded later in this article.

What follows is a brief outline of a modern, *neo-Allportian* theory of global traits, presented in the form of 17 assertions. The term "neo-Allportian" is meant to emphasize that this approach to personality is fundamentally based on the seminal writings of Gordon Allport (especially Allport, 1937), but also to acknowledge that his basic theory was published more than a half-century ago and so is ripe for updating and reinvigoration (Zuroff, 1986). As it turns out, Allport's basic ideas look remarkably sound even with 53 years of hindsight, and yield a large number of implications for conceptualization and research in modern personality psychology.

DEFINITIONAL ASSERTIONS

Traits Are Real

This assertion is the most fundamental of Allport's assumptions, one he believed was essential for subsequent research to be meaningful. He held this position in the face of objections that it was philosophically naive and arguments (still heard today) that traits should be regarded not as entities that have objective reality, but merely as hypothetical constructs (Carr & Kingsbury, 1938). Allport believed that this idea made about as much sense as astronomers regarding stars as hypothetical constructs rather than astronomical objects. He failed to see how any science, including personality psychology, could proceed without assuming its subject of study to be real.

More specifically, Allport (1931, 1966) said traits are "neurodynamic structures" (1966, p. 3) that have "more than nominal existence" (1966, p. 1). If it is obvious that all behavior originates in the neurons of the brain, and that does seem obvious, then it follows that stable individual differences in behavior—to the extent they exist—must similarly be based on stable individual differences in neural organization.

Unfortunately, a method to assess the neural basis of personality is not yet in sight. The presence of a trait can only be inferred on the basis of overt behavior. For all practical purposes, therefore, a global trait must refer to two things at the same time: (a) a complex pattern of behavior from which the trait is *inferred,* and (b) the psychological structures and processes that are the source of the pattern. When we call someone "friendly" or "aggressive" or "generous," we are saying something both about how the person behaves (or would behave) in certain kinds of situations *and* about the functioning of his or her mind. The next assertion follows as a consequence.

Traits Are More than Just Summaries

A viewpoint prominently expressed in recent years is that "dispositions" (a.k.a. traits) should be considered as no more than summaries of behavioral frequencies, or "act trends" (Buss & Craik, 1983). An individual's generosity then becomes the frequency, over a specified unit of time, of his or her superficially generous acts.

This definition deliberately abdicates any explanatory role. Dispositions are treated as circular constructs in which a generous act implies generosity, and the attribution of generosity is used to predict future generous acts *solely* "on actuarial grounds" (Buss & Craik, 1983, p. 106).

However, the appearance of behavior can be misleading (Block, 1988). As Allport pointed out:

A bearer of gifts may not be, in spite of all appearances, a truly generous person: he may be trying to buy favor. . . . Pseudo-traits, then, are errors of inference, misjudgments that come from fixing attention solely upon appearances. The best way to avoid such errors is to find the genotype that underlies the conduct in question. What is the individual trying to do when he brings his gifts? (Allport, 1937, p. 326)

The Meaning of a Behavior Depends on Two Kinds of Context

A single behavior, considered out of context, is frequently ambiguous. Depending on the intention with which the act was performed, there may be multiple possible and plausible alternatives for the traits that might be relevant. This is not to deny that there are interpretational defaults. The act of gift-giving might be interpreted as generous, all other things being equal. All other things are seldom equal, however, so the gift-giving might also reflect insecurity, Machiavellianism, or even anger, depending on the situational circumstances, the gift-giver's behavior in other situations, and what together they imply about the gift-giver's inner state and motives.

Two kinds of context help disambiguate an act. The first is the immediate situation. The giving of a gift becomes more interpretable if one knows whether it was given to a subordinate who performed a job well, or to a superior considering the promotion of the gift-giver. The usefulness of this kind of situational information has been discussed in detail by attribution theorists within social psychology (Heider, 1958; Kelley, 1967), but has been taken into account less often by personality psychologists.

The other kind of context is just as important, but is mentioned even more rarely. Acts become less ambiguous to the extent they fit into a pattern of the individual's other acts. A consistent pattern of generous behavior provides a more plausible context in which to infer that generosity is the trait underlying the gift-giving than does a consistent pattern of mean, nasty, and sneaky behavior. (Indeed, an act that seems inconsistent with the actor's past patterns of behavior is commonly called suspicious.) A pattern of sneaky behavior might lead to an attribution of Machiavellianism that would explain, in turn, why the person gave a lavish gift to his worst enemy.

DEVELOPMENTAL ASSERTIONS

Traits Are Learned

Global traits are manifest by patterns of perception and action in the social world; therefore, they must be a product of how one has learned to interact with that world. The process of learning that produces a trait almost certainly involves an interaction between one's experience (in one's particular social environment) and one's genetic endowment (Scarr & McCartney, 1983). Thus, two people with identical environments, or two people with identical genes, could and often do have very different traits.

Because traits are learned, they are not necessarily immutable. Anything learned can in principle be unlearned. Global trait theory is not necessarily pessimistic about possibilities for either personal or social change.

However, traits are relatively stable. Presumably, the difficulty in unlearning a trait (the amount of retaining or new experience required) will be proportional to the amount and salience of the experience through which it was learned in the first place. Genetic predispositions, and perhaps even species-specific characteristics, may also make some traits easier to learn and harder to unlearn than others (Buss, 1984). But the present analysis asserts that because all traits are, in the final analysis, learned, all traits can, in theory if not always in practice, be unlearned.

The Process of Learning a Trait is Complex

Such learning is far more than a simple matter of reward and punishment or S and R. That simple kind of learning can produce, at most, the narrow patterns of behavior that Allport (1931) called "habits." Traits are the result of complex patterns of experience and of higher-order inductions the person makes from that experience. Kelly (1955) believed that *any* pattern of experience could lead a person to any of at least a large number of behavioral outcomes (just as any pattern of data can always lead a scientist to more than one interpretation). Kelly believed that the ability to choose between these alternative outcomes provided a basis for free will. The comedian Bill Cosby has described his childhood neighborhood as a place where adolescents were all on the verge of deciding whether to be killers or priests. The point is that similar patterns of past experience do not necessarily produce similar outcomes.

When *fully* analyzed, every person's pattern of behavior will be every bit as complex as the unique pattern of endowment and experience that produced it. Again, in Allport's (1937, p. 295) words: "Strictly speaking, no two persons ever have precisely the same trait. . . . What else could be expected in the view of the unique hereditary endowment, the differ-

ent developmental history, and the never-repeated external influences that determine each personality?"

But there are commonalities among people that are useful for characterizing individual differences. A trait like sociability is relevant to behavior in a set of situations regarded as functionally equivalent by people in general: specifically, situations with other people in them. Hence, it is *generally* meaningful to rank-order people on their overall sociability. Allport acknowledged this point as well: "The case for the ultimate individuality of every trait is indeed invincible, but . . . for all their ultimate differences, normal persons within a given culture-area tend to develop a limited number of roughly comparable modes of adjustment" (1937, pp. 297–298).

Still, the list of social situations that are functionally equivalent for people in general is unlikely to fully capture the situations that are regarded as functionally equivalent by any *single* individual. To capture general trends or gists, and to detect things that are true of people in general, one always loses the details of each individual case. This tradeoff between nomothetic and idiographic analyses can be and often has been lamented, but it is inevitable.

FUNCTIONAL ASSERTIONS

A Behavior May Be Affected by Several Traits At Once

The chief danger in the concept of trait is that, through habitual and careless use, it may come to stand for an assembly of separate and self-active faculties, thought to govern behavior all by themselves, without interference. We must cast out this lazy interpretation of the concept. . . . The basic principle of behavior is its continuous flow, each successive act representing a convergent mobilization of all energy available at the moment. (Allport, 1937, pp. 312–313)

The fact that every behavior is the product of multiple traits implies that disentangling the relationship between a given trait and a given behavior is extremely difficult. It also implies that the ability of any particular trait to predict behavior by itself is limited. Ahadi and Diener (1989) showed that if a behavior is totally caused by only four traits whose influence combines additively, the maximum correlation between any one trait and behavior that could be expected is .45. If different traits combine multiplicatively, which seems plausible, the ceiling is even lower.

A third implication is that modern research on traits should conduct a renewed examination of the way traits combine in the determination of behavior. Investigators should more often look beyond the traditional research question of how single traits affect single behaviors, to how multiple traits interact within persons (Carlson, 1971).

Traits Are Situational Equivalence Classes

In a trenchant phrase, Allport wrote that traits have the capacity "to render many stimuli functionally equivalent" (1937, p. 295). The tendency to view different situations as similar causes a person to respond to them in a like manner, and the patterns of behavior that result are the overt manifestations of traits.

The template-matching technique (Bem & Funder, 1978) provides one empirical approach to the study of situational equivalence classes. The technique looks for empirical ties between behavior in real-life situations that subjects' acquaintances have viewed and interpreted, and laboratory situations in which subjects' behavior is measured directly. To the extent higher-order similarity or functional equivalence exists, correlations will be found. The experimental situations are then interpreted, or in Bem and Funder's words, the subjects' "personalities assessed," based on the equivalence classes thus established.

For instance, in one of Bem and Funder's first studies (1978), the parents of nursery school children provided judgments of the degree to which their children were cooperative with adults. These ratings of cooperativeness turned out to correlate highly with minutes and seconds of delay time measured directly in our delay-of-gratification experiment. We inferred that our experimental situation must have been in some way functionally equivalent to the situations at home from which the parents had judged cooperativeness. Our final conclusion was that delay time in our experiment was a symptom of such cooperativeness as much as it was of self control or anything like it. The equivalence class to which the delay experiment seemed to belong consisted of other cooperation situations, not necessarily other self-control situations.

Access to One's Own Traits Is Indirect

The interpretation of a trait as a subjective, situational-equivalence class offers an idea about phenomenology—about what it feels like to have a trait, to the person who has it. It doesn't feel like anything, directly. Rather, the only subjective manifestation of a trait *within* a person will be his or her tendency to react and feel similarly across the situations to which the trait is relevant. As Allport wrote, "For some the world is a hostile place where men are evil and dangerous; for others it is a stage for fun and frolic. It may appear as a place to do one's duty grimly; or a pasture for cultivating friendship and love" (1961, p. 266).

Certainly a friendly person (ordinarily) does nothing like say to him- or herself, "I am a friendly person; therefore, I shall be friendly now." Rather, he or she responds in a natural way to the situation as he or she perceives it. Similarly, a bigoted person does not decide, "I'm going to acted [sic] bigoted now." Rather, his or her bigoted behavior is the result of his or her perception of a targeted group as threatening, inferior, or both (Geis, 1978).

But on reflection one can indeed begin to come to opinions about one's own traits (Bem, 1972; Thome, 1989). One might realize that one is always happy when there are other people around, or always feels threatened, and therefore conclude that one must be "sociable" or "shy," respectively. But again, this can only happen retrospectively, and probably under unusual circumstances. Psychotherapy might be one of these: when "on the couch," one is encouraged to relate past experiences, and the client and therapist together come up with interpretations. Whether called that or not, these interpretations often involve the discovery of the client's situational equivalence classes, or traits. Certain profound life experiences might also stimulate conscious introspection.

In rare cases, explicit, volitional self-direction toward a trait-relevant behavior might take place. For example, one might say to oneself (before going to an obligatory party attended by people one detests), "now, I'm going to be *friendly* tonight," or, before asking one's boss for a raise, self-instruct "be *assertive*." As a matter of interesting psychological fact, however, in such circumstances the resulting behavior is *not* authentically a product of the trait from which it might superficially appear to emanate. The other people at the party, or the boss, probably would interpret the behavior very differently if they knew about the individual's more general behavior patterns and certainly would interpret it differently if they knew about the self-instruction.

Traits Influence Perceptions of Situations Through Dynamic Mechanisms

Different situations may be rendered functionally equivalent through at least three kinds of mechanism. One kind is *motivational*. A person who is hungry arranges situations along a continuum defined by the degree to which food is offered. A person who is dispositionally fearful sees situations in terms of potential threat. A person with a high degree of sociability approaches most situations where other people are present in a positive frame of mind. Another way to say this is that one's perception of the world is partially structured by one's goals (Cantor & Kihlstrom, 1987).

A second kind of mechanism concerns *capacities* and *tendencies*. A person with great physical strength will respond to the world in terms of situational equivalence classes that are different than those experienced by one who is weak. Situations containing physical obstacles may appear interesting and challenging rather than discouraging. Similarly, a person with a tendency to overcontrol motivational impulses will behave differently across a variety of motivationally involving situations than a person whose tendency is towards undercontrol. The overcontroller will restrain his or her impulses, whereas the undercontroller will tend to express them (Funder & Block, 1989).

A third kind of mechanism is *learning*. Perhaps one has been rewarded consistently in athletic settings. Then one will approach most new athletic-like settings with an expectation of reward, with direct consequences for behavior. (This learning experience might itself be a function of one's physical prowess, an example of how these mechanisms can interact.) Perhaps one has been consistently punished for risk-taking. Such an individual is likely to perceive situations involving risk as threatening, and behave across them in a consistently cautious manner.

An important direction for future research is to specify further the dynamic mechanisms through which global traits influence behavior. Several modern approaches bypass trait concepts on the way to examining goals, perceptions, or abilities. Instead, or at least additionally, it might be helpful to ascertain how people with different traits perceive and categorize situations. In turn, it might be useful to explore how these perceptions and categorizations can be explained through motivational mechanisms, abilities and capacities, and learning.

ASSESSMENT ASSERTIONS

Self-Report Is a Limited Tool for Personality Assessment

Because people are not directly aware of the operation of their own traits, their self-reports cannot always be taken at face value. Such reports might be wrong because of errors in retrospective behavioral analysis—including failures of memory and failures of insight. Both kinds of failure are very common. Self-reports are also subject to self-presentation effects, the desire to portray oneself in the most favorable possible light.

This is one point where the present analysis diverges from previous and traditional presentations of trait theory. Self-reports have been and continue to be the most widely used tool for trait measurement (see McClelland, 1984, and Block & Block, 1980, for notable exceptions). This is unfortunate because, according to the present analysis, the person is in a relatively poor position to observe and report accurately his or her own traits, except under exceptional circumstances. Indeed, certain important traits may be almost invisible to the persons who have them. Imagine a chronic repressor asked to rate him- or herself on the item, "tends to deny one's own shortcomings."

This analysis helps account for one of the best known findings of attribution research. Observers of a person's behavior are more likely to report that it was influenced by traits than is the person him- or herself. Traditional accounts of this finding have assumed this is because the observers are, simply, wrong (Jones & Nisbett, 1972). The present analysis views the actor–observer effect as a natural result of the person being

310 UNIT EIGHT PERSON-SITUATION INTERACTIONIST ASPECTS OF PERSONALITY

in a relatively poor position to observe his or her own traits. A more objective, external point of view is necessary. This leads to the next assertion.

The Single Best Method of Trait Assessment Is Peer Report

As was discussed above, traits are manifest by complex patterns of behavior the precise nature of which have by and large gone unspecified, as personality psychologists focused their attention elsewhere. However, our intuitions daily utilize complex *implicit* models of how traits are manifest in behavior. Making explicit these implicit understandings is an important but almost untouched area for further research. In the meantime, such intuitions are there to be used.

The intuitions available are those of the person being assessed, and those of the people who know him or her in daily life. Self-judgments of personality are easy to gather, and research suggests that by and large they agree well with judgments by peers (Funder & Colvin, [1997]). Nonetheless, self-reports are also suspect for a number of reasons, as was discussed earlier.

The impressions a person makes on those around him or her may provide a more reliable guide for how he or she can be accurately characterized. Peers' judgments have the advantage of being based on large numbers of behaviors viewed in realistic daily contexts, and on the filtering of these behavioral observations through an intuitive system capable of adjusting for both immediate situational and long-term individual contexts (Funder, 1987). Moreover, as Hogan and Hogan [1991] have observed, "personality has its social impact in terms of the qualities that are ascribed to individuals by their friends, neighbors, employers, and colleagues" (p. 12). For social traits at least, it is hard to imagine a higher court of evidential appeal that could over-rule peers' judgments, *assuming the peers have had ample opportunity to observe the target's behavior in daily life.* If everyone you meet decides you are sociable, for instance, then you are (Allport & Allport, 1921).

This assertion implies that an important direction for future research is to find out more about how judges of personality perform (Neisser, 1980). A better understanding of the cues that are used by every-

day acquaintances in judging personality, and the circumstances under which those cues are accurate, will lead to progress regarding two important issues: (a) how personality is manifest in behavior, and (b) how personality can most accurately be judged. My own current research focuses on these topics (Funder, 1987, 1989).

EPISTEMOLOGICAL ASSERTIONS

For Purposes of Explanation, the Most Important Traits Are Global (but for Purposes of Prediction, the Narrower the Better)

It appears to have become fashionable in the personality literature to eschew generality by constructing individual difference variables that are as narrow as possible. Cantor and Kihlstrom (1987) espouse a theory of "social intelligence" that regards the attribute as central to personality but *not* a general individual difference. Rather, it is viewed as a collection of relatively discrete, independent, and narrow social capacities, each relevant to performance only within a specific domain of life. A related viewpoint is that of Sternberg and Smith (1985), who suggest that different kinds of social skill are relevant only to extremely narrow classes of behavior, and that as a general construct "social skill" has little or no validity (but see Funder & Harris, 1986).

The use of narrow constructs may well increase correlations when predicting single behaviors, just as at the same time (and equivalently) it decreases the range of behaviors that can be predicted (Fishbein & Ajzen, 1974). But beyond whatever predictive advantages narrowly construed variables may have, they are often presented as if they were somehow *conceptually* superior as well. They are not. Indeed, explaining behavior in terms of a narrow trait relevant to it and little else represents an extreme case of the circularity problem sometimes (unfairly) ascribed to trait psychology in general. If "social skill at parties" is a trait detected by measuring social skill at parties, and is then seen as a *predictor* or even *cause* of social skill at parties, it is obvious that psychological understanding is not getting anywhere.

Global traits, by contrast, have real explanatory power. The recognition of a pattern of behavior is a *bona fide* explanation of each of the behaviors that comprise it. Indeed, the more global a trait is, the more explanatory power it has. Connections between apparently distal phenomena are the most revealing of the deep structure of nature. For instance, if a general trait of social skill exists (see Funder & Harris, 1986), then to explain each of various, diverse behavioral outcomes with that trait is not circular at all. Instead, such an explanation relates a specific behavioral observation to a complex and general pattern of behavior. Such movement from the specific to the general is what explanation is all about.

This is not to say the explanatory task is then finished—it never is. These general patterns called traits should be the targets of further explanatory effort. One might want to investigate the developmental history of a trait, or its dynamic mechanisms, or its relationships with other traits, or the way it derives from even more general personality variables. But traits remain important stopping points in the explanatory regress. To *any* explanation, one can always ask "why?" (as every 4-year-old knows). Still, between each "why" is a legitimate step towards understanding.

The Source of Trait Constructs Should Be Life and Clinical Experience, as Filtered by Insightful Observers

It has often been argued that personality constructs should be formulated independently of, or even in explicit avoidance of, the constructs used by ordinary intuition. Indeed, this is one point upon which investigators as diverse as R. B. Cattell and Walter Mischel have found common ground. Often, mechanical procedures (e.g., factor analysis, behavioral analysis) have been touted as ways to construct personality variables uncontaminated by erroneous preconceptions. The results can be quite esoteric, having ranged from Cattell's (1946) favored variables of "alexia," "praxernia," and the like, to Mischel's (1973) cognitive social-learning variables of "subjective expected values," "encoding strategies," and so forth.

However, the theory of global traits asserts that trait constructs *should* be intuitively meaningful, for

three reasons. First, intuitively discernible traits are likely to have greater social utility. Many global traits describe directly the kinds of relationships people have or the impacts they have on each other. More esoteric variables, by and large, do not.

Second, psychology's direct empirical knowledge of human social behavior incorporates only a small number of behaviors, and those only under certain specific and usually artificial circumstances. Restricting the derivation of individual difference variables to the small number of behaviors that have been measured in the laboratory (or the even smaller number that have been measured in field settings) adds precision to their meaning, to be sure, but inevitably fails to incorporate the broader patterns of behaviors and contexts that make up daily life. Our intuitions, by contrast, leapfrog ahead of painstaking research. The range of behaviors and contexts immediately brought to mind by a trait like "sociable" goes far beyond anything research could directly address in the foreseeable future. Of course, our intuitions are unlikely to be completely accurate, so traits as we think of them informally and as they actually exist in nature may not be identical. However, to be useful in daily life our intuitions must provide at least roughly accurate organizations of behavior, and provide a logical starting point for research (Clark, 1987). Corrections and refinements can come later, but to begin analysis of individual differences by eschewing intuitive insight seems a little like beginning a race before the starting line.

Third, the omission of intuitively meaningful concepts from personality psychology makes study of the *accuracy* of human judgments of personality almost meaningless. People make global trait judgments of each other all the time, and the accuracy of such judgments is obviously important (Funder, 1987). However, unless one wishes to finesse the issue by studying only agreement between *perceptions* of personality (Kenny & Albright, 1987), research on accuracy requires a psychology of personality assessment to which informal, intuitive judgments can be compared. Gibson (1979) has persuasively argued that the study of perception cannot proceed without knowledge about the stimulus array and, ultimately, the reality that confronts the perceiver. This point applies equally to person perception. A theory of personality will be helpful in understanding judgments of people for the same reason that a theory of the physics of light is helpful in understanding judgments of color.

EMPIRICAL ASSERTIONS

Global Traits Interact with Situations in Several Ways

Every global trait is situation specific, in the sense that it is relevant to behavior in some (perhaps many), but not all, life situations. Sociability is relevant only to behavior in situations with other people present, aggressiveness when there is the potential for interpersonal confrontation, friendliness when positive interaction is possible, and so forth. Our intuitions handle this sort of situational delimitation routinely and easily.

The delimitation of the situational relevance of a trait is sometimes called a "person-situation interaction." The empirical and conceptual development of this idea is an important achievement of the past two decades of personality research, and a valuable by-product of the consistency controversy (Kenrick & Funder, 1988). The kind of interaction just described has been called the ANOVA or "passive" form (Buss, 1977). All that is meant is that different traits are relevant to the prediction of behavior in different situations. A child whose cooperativeness leads her to delay gratification in a situation with an adult present may be the first to quit if left alone (Bem & Funder, 1978).

At least two other, more active kinds of interaction are also important. The first is situation selection. Personality traits affect how people choose what situations to enter (Snyder & Ickes, 1985). A party might contain strong, general pressures to socialize, pressures that affect the behavior of nearly everyone who attends. But sociable people are more likely to have chosen to go the party in the first place. Thus, the trait of sociability influences behavior in part by affecting the situational influences to which the individual is exposed.

Traits can also magnify their influence on behavior through another kind of interaction. Most situations are changed to some extent by the behavior of the people in it. The presence of a sociable person can cause a situation to become more sociability-inducing. An aggressive child can turn a previously peaceful playground into a scene of general mayhem.

However, certain situations are *not* freely chosen, being imposed arbitrarily, and some situations will *not* change, no matter what the people in them may do. By short-circuiting the two kinds of person-situation interactions just discussed, such situations limit severely the influence traits can have on behavior. A prototypic example is the psychological experiment. Experiments assign subjects to conditions randomly, and the experimenter works from a set script. The subject's personality then cannot influence which situation he or she is exposed to, nor can his or her actions change the nature of the situation into which he or she is thrust (Wachtel, 1973).

But even in experiments like this, the influence of global traits is frequently detected; many examples could be cited. Consider the delay-of-gratification experiment already discussed (Bem & Funder, 1978). Nearly all the children who happened to be enrolled in a certain nursery school class entered this situation, and the experimenter worked from a set script that did not vary as a function of what the child did. Even so, the children's delay-of-gratification behavior had many and meaningful ties to their global personality traits, as assessed by their parents.

Evidence Concerning Personality Correlates of Behavior Supports the Existence of Global Traits

Findings such as those summarized in the preceding paragraph have been obtained again and again. Numerous studies report correlations between behavior in arbitrarily imposed, implacable situations, and personality traits judged on the basis of behavior observed in real life. These correlations constitute powerful evidence of the important influence of personality traits on behavior, even under circumstances where one would expect their influence to be weakened.

Most of this evidence has accumulated since 1937, and so was not available to Allport, but has been summarized many times in the course of the person-situation debate. Reviews can be found in articles by Funder (1987), Kenrick and Funder (1988), and many others.

Evidence Concerning Interjudge Agreement Supports the Existence of Global Traits

Another form of evidence for the existence of global traits is the good agreement that can be obtained between judgments of traits rendered by peers who know the subject in diverse life situations, and between such judgments and the subject's own self-judgments. Allport regarded evidence of this sort as especially persuasive:

> What is most noteworthy in research on personality is that different observers should agree as well as they do in judging any one person. This fact alone proves that there must be something really there, something objective in the nature of the individual himself that compels observers, in spite of their own prejudices, to view him in essentially the same way. (Allport, 1937, p. 288)

Fifty-three years later, the evidence is even stronger. Acquaintances who are well-acquainted with the people they judge can provide personality ratings that agree with ratings provided by other acquaintances as well as by the targets themselves (see Funder & Colvin, [1997], for a review). This issue being settled, more recent work has focused on the circumstances that make interjudge agreement higher and lower, including level of acquaintanceship and the nature of the specific trait being judged (Funder, 1989).

Evidence Concerning the Stability of Personality across the Lifespan Supports the Existence of Global Traits

Allport lacked access to well-designed longitudinal studies that examined the stability of personality over time. Today, a vast body of research convincingly demonstrates that general traits of personality can be highly stable across many years. Data showing how behaviors can be predicted from measures of traits taken years before, or "post-dicted" by measures taken years later, have been reported by Funder, Block, and Block (1983), Funder and Block (1989), and Shedler and Block (1990). Similar findings from other longitudinal studies have been reported by Block (1971), Caspi (1987), McCrae and Costa (1984), and others.

DIRECTIONS FOR RESEARCH

As a fruitful theory should, the theory of global traits raises a host of unanswered questions that deserve to be the focus of future research. They include matters of definition, origin, function, and implication.

Definition. How many global traits are there? Allport (1937, p. 305) reported finding 17,953 terms in an unabridged dictionary. Fortunately, these can be partially subsumed by more general constructs. Personality psychology seems to be achieving a consensus that most trait lists boil down to about five overarching terms (Digman, 1990). This does not mean there are "only" five traits, but rather that five broad concepts can serve as convenient, if very *general*, summaries of a wide range of the trait domain. They are Surgency (extraversion), Neuroticism, Openness (or culture), Agreeableness, and Conscientiousness.

Global traits may also be partially reducible to more narrow constructs. Perhaps friendliness is a blend of social potency and positive affect, for instance. The reduction of global traits into more specific (and possibly more factorially pure) constructs is a worthwhile direction for research. But the position taken here is that the appropriate level of analysis at which investigation should *begin,* and which more specific investigations should always remember to *inform,* is the level of intuitively accessible, global traits.

Origin. Developmental psychology has been dominated in recent years by studies of cognitive development, with the term "cognitive" sometimes construed rather narrowly. The theory of global traits draws renewed attention to the importance of investigations, especially longitudinal investigations, into the genetic and environmental origins of personality traits.

Function. The dynamic mechanisms through which global traits influence behavior remain poorly understood. As Allport hinted, they seem to involve the way individuals perceive situations and group them into equivalence classes. But the exact learning, motivational, and perceptual mechanisms involved, the way that different traits interact within individuals, and the circumstances under which a person can become consciously aware of his or her own traits are all issues needing further empirical examination.

Implication.   Given that a person has a given level of a global trait, what kinds of behavioral predictions can be made accurately, into what kinds of situations? This *deductive* question will require further and more detailed examination of person-situation interactions. And, given that a person has performed a certain pattern of behavior across a certain set of situations, what can we conclude about his or her global traits? This *inductive* question will require close attention to the behavioral cues that laypersons use in their intuitive judgments of personality, and an empirical examination of the validity of these cues. Progress toward answering this question will help to provide a valid basis by which human social judgment can be evaluated and, therefore, improved (Funder, 1987).

In the current literature, these issues receive much less attention than they deserve. A Neo-Allportian perspective may lead not only to a renewed examination of these central issues, but to progress in the study of personality's historic mission of integrating the various subfields of psychology into an understanding of whole, functioning individuals.

REFERENCES

Allport, G. W. (1931). What is a trait of personality? *Journal of Abnormal and Social Psychology, 25,* 368–372.

Allport, G. W. (1937). *Personality: A psychological interpretation.* New York: Henry Holt & Co.

Allport, G. W. (1958). What units shall we employ? In G. Lindzey (Ed.), *Assessment of human motives* (pp. 239–260). New York: Rinehart.

Cantor, N., & Kihlstrom, J. F. (1987). *Personality and social intelligence.* Englewood Cliffs, NJ: Prentice-Hall.

Funder, D. C. (1987). Errors and mistakes: Evaluating the accuracy of social judgment. *Psychological Bulletin, 101,* 75–90.

Funder, D. C. (1989). Accuracy in personality judgment and the dancing bear. In D. M. Buss & N. Cantor (Eds.), *Personality psychology: Recent trends and emerging directions* (pp. 210–223). New York: Springer-Verlag.

Zuroff, D. C. (1986). Was Gordon Allport a trait theorist? *Journal of Personality and Social Psychology, 51,* 993–1000.

Questions to Think About

1. How might Allport have viewed the Neo-Allportian approach to personality?

2. Global traits have a central role in everyday, intuitive understanding of personality. Does the field of personality psychology benefit from this, or suffer because of it?

3. What are some dangers in moving away from global traits? How do these dangers affect our view of people and their behaviors?

4. What is the role of learning in the development of personality traits in Funder's view?

5. Do global traits have better explanatory power than narrower dispositional terms? How can global traits be used to explain situations, personalities, and behavior?

45

Gender Differences in Personality Traits across Cultures: Robust and Surprising Findings

PAUL T. COSTA, JR., ANTONIO TERRACCIANO, AND ROBERT R. McCRAE

Paul Costa, Antonio Terracciano, and Robert McCrae are all researchers at the National Institute on Aging, part of the United States National Institutes of Health. Costa and McCrae have been closely associated with work on the Big Five model of personality for many years, contributing both to the theoretical development of the approach and to the literature on its assessment. In this selection, gender differences in personality are the focus, and the nature of those gender differences is examined across multiple cultures.

Gender differences in personality traits have been documented in many empirical studies. Maccoby and Jacklin (1974) conducted the first major review of research on sex-related differences in cognition, temperament, and social behavior in children and adults. They concluded that men are more assertive and less anxious than women; no differences were found for two other traits analyzed, locus of control and self-esteem.

Feingold (1994) used meta-analysis to confirm the gender differences in adult personality traits reported by Maccoby and Jacklin (1974) and explored other gender differences in normative data from the most widely used personality inventories. He concluded that women scored lower than men on assertiveness and higher on gregariousness (extroversion), anxiety, trust, and tender-mindedness (nurturance).

Feingold (1994) organized his review in terms of the five broad factors and 30 specific facets of the

Revised NEO Personality Inventory (NEO-PI-R; Costa & McCrae, 1992). As a comprehensive guide to personality traits, that model can provide the basis for a systematic examination of gender differences in personality. Unfortunately, from the available data, Feingold was only able to conduct reviews of nine traits. In this article, we provide new data that allow an examination of gender differences in all 30 traits assessed by the NEO-PI-R, and thus offer a more complete account of gender differences in personality.

BROAD THEMES IN GENDER DIFFERENCES

The NEO-PI-R is an operationalization of the Five-Factor Model (FFM), which structures specific traits in terms of five broad factors. It is possible to summarize known gender differences in terms of the FFM, although the summary is not completely straightforward. Previously reported gender differences appear

Source: Costa, P. T., Jr., Terracciano, A., & McCrae, R. (2001). Gender differences in personality traits across cultures: Robust and surprising findings. *Journal of Personality and Social Psychology, 81*(2), 322–331.

Editor's note: All citations in the text of this selection have been left intact from the original, but the list of references includes only those sources that are the most relevant and important. Readers wishing to follow any of the other citations can find the full references in the original work or in an online database.

to be associated with Neuroticism (N), the dimensions of the Interpersonal Circumplex (Wiggins, 1979), and variations within the domain of Openness to Experience (O).

Neuroticism (N)

N is a broad domain of negative affect, including predispositions to experience anxiety, anger, depression, shame, and other distressing emotions. Gender differences on traits related to N have been consistently reported, with women scoring higher than men (Lynn & Martin, 1997). Feingold (1994) found that women scored higher in anxiety; Nolen-Hoeksema (1987), in a review of general population surveys, reported that women scored higher in symptoms of depression; and Kling, Hyde, Showers, and Buswell (1999) found that women scored lower than men on measures of self-esteem. Neuroticism predisposes individuals to a wide range of psychiatric disorders, and gender differences in N are reflected in the epidemiology of major psychopathology. Generalized anxiety disorder, panic disorder with or without agoraphobia, phobias, major depression, dysthymic disorder, and borderline personality disorder are all diagnosed substantially more often in women than in men (American Psychiatric Association, 1994).

A possible exception to the generalization that women score higher in traits related to N is anger. Some studies have found that men report higher levels of hostility than women (Scherwitz, Perkins, Chesney, & Hughes, 1991). Others, however, have reported that women score higher in anger (Ross & Van Willigen, 1996), or that there is no difference (Averill, 1982). These different results may be due to different operationalizations, some of which emphasize the experience of anger, whereas others focus on antagonistic attitudes (cf. Costa, Stone, McCrae, Dembroski, & Williams, 1987). Women should score higher on the former, men on the latter.

Interpersonal Traits

One of the most influential approaches to the study of gender differences was offered by Bern (1974), whose Sex Role Inventory included orthogonal scales mea-

suring masculinity and femininity. As Wiggins and Broughton (1985) showed, Bem's masculinity scale is essentially a measure of dominance, whereas Bem's femininity is strongly related to the orthogonal dimension of love. Feingold's (1994) conclusion that men are high in assertiveness and women are high in nurturance is consistent with this distinction, as is Eagly and Wood's (1991) summary of the literature in terms of communal and agentic qualities.

Dominance and love are the axes of the Interpersonal Circumplex, and have been shown to be rotations of the FFM dimensions of Extraversion (E) and Agreeableness (A; McCrae & Costa, 1989); that is, E combines dominance and love, whereas A combines submission and love. It is clear from this analysis that women should score higher on measures of A (because they are both more submissive and more loving), and this has in fact been reported (Budaev, 1999). However, it is less clear whether and how E should be related to gender, because it combines both masculine and feminine traits. It is thus perhaps not surprising that the literature is inconsistent: Feingold (1994) concluded that women are slightly higher in E, and Lynn and Martin (1997) that they are lower. From the perspective of the NEO-PI-R, it would be expected that clear gender differences would be found in specific facets of E: Men should score higher on Assertiveness, women on Warmth.

Openness to Experience (O)

Men and women are often characterized in terms of differing cognitive styles. Winstead, Derlega, and Unger (1999) noted that Western philosophers have frequently characterized men as "guided by 'reason' and women by reason's opposites—including emotion" (p. 264). Within the framework of the FFM—and less pejoratively—this might be seen in terms of aspects of O. Although there is no reason to think that men and women differ in overall O, they might differ in the aspects of experience to which they are preferentially open. It might be hypothesized that women should score higher in Openness to Aesthetics and Feelings, and men, who are more intellectually oriented, should score higher in Openness to Ideas.

There is considerable empirical evidence for the view that women are more sensitive to emotions. Eisenberg, Fabes, Schaller, and Miller (1989) found evidence of greater facial expression of emotion in women, and the ability to decode nonverbal signals of emotion is consistently found to be more developed in adult women than in men (McClure, 2000). Fujita, Diener, and Sandvik (1991) reported that, at least in the United States, women experience positive and negative emotions more intensely and vividly than men do (cf. Grossman & Wood, 1993).

It has recently been hypothesized that gender differences in depression and other negative affects might be due to the greater sensitivity on the part of women to these states (Rossy & Thayer, 2000). In the present study we tested the hypothesis that gender differences in depression, anxiety, and other facets of N are attributable solely to greater emotional sensitivity—Openness to Feelings—among women.

Conscientiousness (C)

Gender differences in aspects of C have rarely been examined. Feingold (1994) found seven studies relevant to the trait of order, which yielded a median d of −.07, suggesting that women scored very slightly higher than men on this trait. The present study assesses gender differences in six facets of C.

EXPLANATIONS OF GENDER DIFFERENCES

Two classes of theories, biological and social psychological, have tried to explain these gender differences in personality traits. The biological theories consider sex-related differences as arising from innate temperamental differences between the sexes, evolved by natural selection. Evolutionary psychology (Buss, 1995) predicts that the sexes will differ in domains in which they have faced different adaptive problems throughout evolutionary history. For example, for biological reasons, including pregnancy, childbirth, and lactation, women have more invested than men do in relations with children. Women who were more agreeable and nurturing may have promoted the survival of their children and gained evolutionary advantage.

Other biological theories have been proposed to account for gender differences in depression, and by extension, N in general. These explanations point to hormonal differences and their effects on mood and personality, and to sex-linked differences in genetic predispositions to psychopathology. In a 1987 review, Nolen-Hoeksema considered that evidence in support of these explanations was inconclusive; however, more recent studies (Berenbaum, 1999; Berenbaum & Resnick, 1997) suggest that sex differences in androgens during early development do affect interests, activities, and aggression.

Social psychological theorists argue for more proximal and direct causes of gender differences. The social role model (Eagly, 1987) explains that most gender differences result from the adoption of gender roles, which define appropriate conduct for men and women. Gender roles are shared expectations of men's and women's attributes and social behavior, and are internalized early in development. There is considerable controversy over whether gender roles are purely cultural creations or whether they reflect preexisting and natural differences between the sexes in abilities and predispositions (Eagly, 1995; Geary, 1999).

A rather different example of a social psychological approach is the artifact model (Feingold, 1994) that explains gender differences on personality scales in terms of method variance. Social desirability bias may lead men and women to endorse gender-relevant traits, and some traits (such as fearfulness) may be less undesirable for women than for men.

These explanations are not mutually exclusive. It is entirely possible that social roles and other environmental influences can modify a biologically based pattern, and there is always a danger that findings from any single method of measurement will be biased.

CROSS-CULTURAL PERSPECTIVES

Pancultural Patterns of Gender Differences

Cross-cultural studies can provide crucial evidence on the relative importance of biological versus cultural factors in gender differences in personality traits. If they are in fact biologically based, the same differences ought to be seen in all cultures, so pancultural gender differences would provide evidence for a biological basis. This might consist of direct effects on personality traits, mediated through neurological or hormonal differences between the sexes. But it is also possible that pancultural gender differences result from universals in learned gender roles. For example, because men in all cultures are physically stronger than women, they may universally be assigned roles as leaders, and in these roles may learn to become more assertive than women. Cross-cultural studies would be most revealing if they showed no consistency in gender differences; strictly biological explanations would essentially be ruled out by such findings.

Relatively few cross-cultural data are currently available. Feingold (1994) examined normative data from the Personality Research Form (Jackson, 1974) to explore gender differences in seven personality traits across six nations. He concluded that differences were generally invariant across nations. Lynn and Martin (1997) examined gender differences in N, E, and Psychoticism (Eysenck, 1978) in 37 countries. They found that men were consistently lower than women in N and generally higher on Psychoticism and E. Nolen-Hoeksema (1987) found that women were more likely than men to be depressed across a range of countries, although the magnitude of the sex difference ratio varied markedly.

Williams and Best (1982, 1990) conducted an extensive cross-cultural investigation of gender stereotypes; that is, characteristics generally attributed to men or to women (regardless of empirical accuracy). University students in 30 different countries judged each of 300 items of the Adjective Check List (ACL; Gough & Heilbrun, 1983) as to whether, in their culture, it was more frequently associated with women or men (or neither). Within each country, Williams and Best determined the frequency with which each item was identified as male associated. These frequencies were converted to an M% score, defined as M% = [male frequency/(male frequency + female frequency)] × 100. High M% values thus indicated that an item was mainly associated with men, whereas low values indicated that an item was associated with women. Williams and Best found substantial similarities across genders and countries for the psychological characteristics associated with male and female pancultural

gender stereotypes—and these stereotypes by and large were consistent with reported gender differences. For example, in a subsample of 14 countries, the word *aggressive* had M% scores ranging from 62 to 99, whereas *affectionate* had M% scores from 1 to 34.

All these studies suggest that gender differences are likely to be widespread, if not universal. In the present article we examined NEO-PI-R data from 26 cultures, including eleven not included in the Feingold (1994) or Lynn and Martin (1997) reviews (see Table 1). We did not conduct traditional meta-analyses of these data because our interest is not in estimating a single effect size, but in examining patterns of cultural similarities or differences.

Gender Differentiation across Cultures

Even if all cultures show the same pattern of gender differences, they may show variations in the magnitude of differences seen. In some cultures, gender differences may be exaggerated; in others, they may be masked. There are several reasons to expect such variation, but the literature to date is somewhat puzzling.

Cultures vary in the degree to which sex roles are emphasized. Williams and Best (1990) administered a Sex Role Ideology scale in 14 cultures and confirmed that men and women in traditional cultures (e.g., Pakistan, Nigeria) emphasized sex role differences, whereas those in modern cultures (e.g., the Netherlands, Finland) minimized them. According to the social role model (Eagly & Wood, 1991), such differences in prescribed values and behaviors should lead to differences in personality traits.

Lynn and Martin (1997) provided a test of that hypothesis. They reasoned that gender differences in personality traits might be greater in less developed countries where differences in norms for sex roles are generally greater and there is less equality between the sexes. They used per capita income as an index of development, but found no statistically significant correlation of this index with gender differences in N, E, or Psychoticism.

The magnitude of gender differences might also be related to a dimension of culture Hofstede (1980) called *masculinity*. This dimension was derived from

TABLE 1   Characteristics of the Samples

| COUNTRY | LANGUAGE | Sample Size | | | | SOURCE |
| | | College Age | | Adult | | |
		MEN	WOMEN	MEN	WOMEN	
Hong Kong	Chinese	60	62			McCrae et al., 1998
Taiwan[a]	Chinese	173	371			Chen, 1996
Croatia	Croatian	233	233	123	133	Marušić, Bratko, & Eterović, 1997
The Netherlands	Dutch	615	690			Hoekstra, Ormel, & De Fruyt, 1996
Belgium[a]	Dutch/Flemish	34	68	527	490	F. De Fruyt
United States	English	148	241	500	500	Costa & McCrae, 1992
South Africa (Blacks)[a]	English	19	46			W. Parker
South Africa (Whites)[a]	English	41	168			W. Parker
Estonia[a]	Estonian	119	398	189	331	J. Allik
The Philippines[a]	Filipino	134	375			G. del Pilar
	English	152	236			A. T. Church
France	French	54	338	279	395	J. P. Rolland; Rolland, 1998
Germany	German	290	454	1,185	1,801	F. Ostendorf
Indonesia[a]	Indonesian	34	138			L. Halim
Italy	Italian	26	41	315	308	G. V. Caprara
Japan	Japanese	176	177	164	164	Shimonaka, Nakazato, Gondo, & Takayama, 1999
South Korea	Korean (1)	1,257	1,096			Lee, 1995
	Korean (2)			278	315	R. L. Piedmont
Malaysia[a]	Malaysian	124	327			Mastor, Jin, & Cooper, 2000
India	Marathi	107	107			S. Deo
Norway	Norwegian (1)	74	18	397	295	H. Nordvik
	Norwegian (2)			148	210	Ø. Martinsen
Portugal	Portuguese	205	253	606	816	M. P. de Lima
Zimbabwe[a]	Shona	36	35	135	106	R. L. Piedmont
United States[a]	Spanish	24	49			Psychological Assessment Resources, 1994
Peru[a]	Spanish	274	165			Cassaretto, 1999
Spain	Spanish			89	107	M. Avia
Yugoslavia	Serbian	72	547	256	245	G.Knežević
Russia	Russian	26	91	201	192	T. Martin

Note. From "Trait Psychology and Culture: Exploring Intercultural Comparisons," by R. R. McCrae (2001). *Journal of Personality.* In the public domain. Where no reference is given, data were provided by the individual listed.

[a]New cultures not included in the Feingold (1994) or Lynn and Martin (1997) reviews.

contrasting work values: In masculine cultures (like Japan and Austria), emphasis is placed on occupational advancement and earnings; in feminine cultures (like Costa Rica and Sweden), cooperation with coworkers and job security are valued. Hofstede (1998) argued that gender differences are accentuated in masculine countries. For example, fathers in masculine cultures are said to deal with facts, mothers with feelings, whereas both fathers and mothers deal with feelings in feminine cultures. Both boys and girls are allowed to cry in feminine countries, but only girls may cry in masculine countries. Presumably such values could affect the development of gender differences in personality traits.

Some empirical data also point to cultural variations in the extent of gender differentiation. In their study of gender stereotypes, Williams and Best (1990) examined variance in M% scores across the 300 ACL items in different countries. High variance scores occur when many adjectives are clearly ascribed to men or to women, but not both, suggesting strong gender differentiation. Curiously, these variance scores were strongest in modern, not traditional, countries: "In more developed countries with more individualistic value systems, the two sexes were viewed as more differentiated in terms of their psychological makeup than in less developed countries with more communal value systems" (p. 27).

That difference in stereotypes between more and less developed countries is also mirrored in epidemiological data on gender differences in depression. As Nolen-Hoeksema (1987) reported, most Western nations showed higher rates of depression in women, but "a number of the studies conducted in less modern cultures did not find significant sex differences" (p. 262).

It is possible that gender differentiation varies with the specific trait examined. For example, men and women in traditional cultures may not differ in N, leading to equivalent rates of clinical depression, but they may differ sharply in A, leading to marked differences in work values. In the present study, use of the full NEO-PI-R allowed us to ask whether gender differentiation is common across a range of traits or specific to individual factors. We examined associations of gender differentiation with several culture-level variables, including M% variance and Hofstede's masculinity index.

METHOD

Literature Search

The data analyzed were provided by colleagues from a variety of countries who had translated the NEO-PI-R and collected data for their own research projects. As a requirement of licensing, translators are obliged to submit an independent back-translation to the test authors (Paul T. Costa and Robert R. McCrae) for review and approval. In consequence, the authors are aware of all versions of the instrument. They also maintain a current bibliography of publications using the NEO-PI-R, based in part on periodic examinations of the PsycINFO database and the Social Sciences Citation Index. Drawing on these resources, McCrae [2001] prepared the present dataset for another article concerned with mean level differences among cultures. Although it would be possible to include additional samples from the United States, the data appear otherwise to exhaust available information on gender differences on the NEO-PI-R as of March 2000. More recent data are considered in the Discussion.

Samples

Table 1 summarizes characteristics of the samples. Participants in all these studies were volunteers; clinical and occupational selection samples were excluded. Samples were stratified by age and gender; in addition to American samples, college-age samples were available for 24 cultures and adult samples for 14 cultures. The samples represent five continents and several different language families. Note that gender differences in the American samples have been previously published (Costa & McCrae, 1992).

Measure

The NEO-PI-R (Costa & McCrae, 1992) assesses 30 specific traits, or facets, that define the five basic factors of personality: N, E, O, A, and C; factor scores use weighted combinations of all 30 facets (see Costa & McCrae, 1992, Table 2). Information on the reliability and validity of the American version of the NEO-PI-R is summarized in the manual (Costa & McCrae, 1992).

The instrument has been translated into over 30 languages, with back-translations into English reviewed by the original test authors. In general, these translations have shown adequate reliabilities, and all have satisfactorily replicated the original factor structure (see McCrae, [2001]). Some of the translations are well validated, others have only preliminary supporting data.

Because previous research has shown age differences within cultures for all five factors (Costa et al., 2000; McCrae et al., 1999), samples were divided into subsamples of college age (generally age 18–21, but varying somewhat across cultures) and adult (age 22 or above), the age division used in norming the American version of the NEO-PI-R. When raw scores from the adult subsamples were compared with the college-aged subsamples, the expected differences were seen: Adults were lower in N, E, and O and higher in A and C across the 26 cultures (all $p < .01$).

To obtain a common metric across all cultures, we converted raw facet scores to z scores by subtracting the mean and dividing by the standard deviation for the subsample, and we computed factor scores from these z-scored facets. Differences between women's and men's z scores provide the familiar d metric of effect size. Raw facet and factor scores for men and women reflect cultural differences as well as any artifacts introduced by translation and adaptation, but the ds analyzed here subtract out most cultural and artifactual effects, and are directly comparable across cultures.

Culture-Level Variables

To help interpret cultural variations in gender differences, we related data in the present study to culture-level variables (i.e., variables that characterize a culture rather than an individual). Mean levels of NEO-PI-R factors from the same samples studied here are reported in McCrae [2001]. In addition, we examined correlations of gender differentiation with the culture-level dimensions identified by Hofstede (1994; Peabody, 1999). These are Power Distance, found in cultures in which status differences are the accepted norm; Uncertainty Avoidance, high in cultures that seek to reduce ambiguous situations; Individualism, characteristic of cultures in which each person is oriented toward his or her own interests instead of those of the group; and Masculinity, high in cultures that value ego goals of achievement and material advancement over social goals like cooperation. Hofstede ratings were available for 23 of the 26 cultures. Finally, Williams and Best (1990) reported variance in masculinity ratings across the 300 ACL adjectives; high variances suggest strong gender stereotype differentiation. M% ratings were available for only 10 of the 26 cultures.

In addition, we examined some national statistics as indicators of the status of women in the 26 cultures (United Nations Statistics Division, 2000). These included gross domestic product (GDP), fertility rate, and women's life expectancy. We also examined illiteracy rates; these were not provided for Japan, Taiwan, Hong Kong, Germany, Spain, Norway, the United States, France, the Netherlands, or Belgium, presumably because "illiteracy is believed to have been reduced to minimal levels" (United Nations Statistics Division, 2000). We assigned values of 0% to these 10 countries. We also calculated the difference between illiteracy rate in women and men as an index of the status of women relative to national development as a whole.

RESULTS

Cross-Cultural Similarities in Gender Differences

Table 2 summarizes analyses of NEO-PI-R facet scales. The first column reports individual-level gender differences in the U.S. adult normative sample (Costa & McCrae, 1992). The second and third columns report culture-level analyses across the 25 other cultures included in Table 1, grouped by age. Because the focus here was on patterns across cultures, not individuals, unweighted means were used, giving equal weight to each culture.

The first notable feature of the Table is the magnitude of gender differences. None of the effects in Table 2 is as large as one-half standard deviation; most are closer to one-quarter standard deviation. Gender differences, although pervasive, appear to be relatively subtle compared with the range of individual differences found within each gender (cf. Williams & Best, 1990).

A second point is that individual differences in the United States closely mirror the average effects seen across a range of other cultures. Correlations between the three columns in Table 2 ranged from .84 to .91. Additional analyses of the eleven cultures not included in reviews by Feingold (1994) and Lynn and

TABLE 2   Mean z-Score Differences (d) between Women and Men on Revised NEO Personality Inventory (NEO-PI-R) Facets in the United States and 25 Other Cultures

NEO-PI-R FACET	U.S. ADULTS	Other Cultures	
		COLLEGE AGE	ADULT
N1: Anxiety	.40***	.32***	.43***
N2: Angry Hostility	.09	.16***	.19***
N3: Depression	.24***	.17**	.29***
N4: Self-Consciousness	.30***	.22***	.23***
N5: Impulsiveness	.23***	.16**	.11*
N6: Vulnerability	.44***	.28***	.36***
E1: Warmth	.33***	.24***	.23***
E2: Gregariousness	.21***	.20***	.14***
E3: Assertiveness	−.19**	−.10*	−.27***
E4: Activity	.11**	.04	.11*
E5: Excitement Seeking	−.31***	−.18***	−.38***
E6: Positive Emotions	.29***	.27***	.16***
O1: Fantasy	−.16**	.12**	.06
O2: Aesthetics	.34***	.40***	.35***
O3: Feelings	.28**	.33***	.31***
O4: Actions	.19***	.11**	.17**
O5: Ideas	−.32***	−.17***	−.16*
O6: Values	−.07	.15**	.01
A1: Trust	.19**	.10*	.17***
A2: Straightforwardness	.43***	.34***	.32***
A3: Altruism	.43***	.25***	.25***
A4: Compliance	.38***	.03	.17***
A5: Modesty	.38***	.22***	.22***
A6: Tender-Mindedness	.31***	.26***	.28***
C1: Competence	−.20***	−.09	−.10
C2: Order	.05	.09	.10**
C3: Dutifulness	.00	.18***	.13*
C4: Achievement Striving	.08	.06	−.04
C5: Self-Discipline	−.02	.09*	.04
C6: Deliberation	−.12	−.04	−.06

Note. Ns = 1,000 U.S. adults; 10,952 college age, other cultures; 10,690 adults, other cultures. t tests were used to compare U.S. men and women; paired t tests were used to compare means for men and women across cultures. N = Neuroticism; E = Extraversion; O = Openness to Experience; A = Agreeableness; C = Conscientiousness.

*p < .05. **p < .01. ***p < .001.

Martin (1997) showed the same patterns there. It appears that self-reported gender differences, like gender stereotypes, are pancultural.

Third, the differences seen are generally consistent with previous literature and with some theoretical predictions. In particular, women were consistently higher in facets of N and A. They showed a more var-

ied pattern with the other three domains, how ever. Women in most cultures were higher than men in Warmth, Gregariousness, and Positive Emotions, but lower in Assertiveness and Excitement Seeking. These associations are predictable from the placement of these traits within the Interpersonal Circumplex (McCrae & Costa, 1989). Women scored higher than men in Openness to Aesthetics, Feelings, and Actions, but lower in Openness to Ideas, consistent with pervasive stereotypes that associate women with feeling and men with thinking. There are no consistent gender differences on Openness to Fantasy or Values. In most cultures, women were more dutiful than men, but there are few other consistent differences in facets of C.

To test the hypothesis that gender differences in N facets were attributable to greater sensitivity to emotional experiences among women, we conducted analyses of covariance contrasting men and women on the six N facets, controlling for O3: Feelings. As hypothesized, there was a reduction in the magnitude of gender differences, although women remained significantly higher on N1: Anxiety, N4: Self-Consciousness, and N6: Vulnerability. Further, there is reason to think that the effects are not specific to emotional sensitivity: When A2: Straightforwardness is used as the covariate, a similar attenuation of gender differences in N facets is seen. Removing the influence of any variable on which there are marked gender differences may attenuate any other gender differences. Such an overall variation in gender differentiation is discussed below.

Effects on the five factors themselves are largely predictable from the facet results. Among U.S. adults, there are strong effects (ds = .51 and .59, respectively) for N and A, and a moderate effect (d = .29) for E; there are no significant differences for O or C. The effects for N, A, and E are replicated in culture-level analyses of both college-age and adult samples (ds = .28 to .50). In addition, however, there are smaller (ds = .11 to .16) but significant effects in both age groups showing women higher than men in O and C factors.

Cross-Cultural Variation in Gender Differences

Although the general pattern of gender differences is similar across cultures, there is also variation across cultures, especially in the magnitude of gender differences. Before attempting to interpret such differences, it is necessary to show that they are reliable, and not simply the result of sampling error. With the available data, the clearest evidence of reliability comes from a comparison of college-age and adult samples: Do cultures in which there are strong gender differences

among college students tend to show the same strong differences among adults? Complete data were available for 14 cultures; gender differences for college-age samples were significantly correlated with differences in the corresponding adult samples for N, E, and A (rs = .75, .73, and .61, respectively, ps < .05); correlations were not significant for O or C.

For N and A domains it is reasonable to consider gender differentiation at the factor level, because all the facets in these domains show the same direction of gender differences. For E and O, however, there are distinct patterns at the facet level. To represent gender differences in these domains, we created two new variables that summarize consistent gender differences. Feminine extraversion/introversion (F-Ex/In) was calculated as (E1: Warmth + E2: Gregariousness – E3: Assertiveness – E5: Excitement Seeking + E6: Positive Emotions)/5, because these five facets show significant gender differences across samples (see Table 2). High scorers on this composite are loving, sociable, submissive, cautious, and cheerful. Similarly, feminine openness/closedness (F-Op/Cl) was calculated as (O2: Aesthetics + O3: Feelings + O4: Actions – O5: Ideas)/4, and reflects a preference for feelings and novelty over intellectual interests. These two composites showed marginally significant correlations across age groups in 14 cultures (r = .48, p < .10; r = .53, p < .05). No facets of C showed consistent gender differences, so no composite was created for that domain.

To quantify gender differences in each culture, we calculated a mean score by averaging the subsamples across age groups in the 26 cultures. Differences in z scores (women – men) are reported in Table 3 for N and A factors and F-Ex/In and F-Op/Cl composites. All but two of the entries in the table are positive, emphasizing the universality of gender differences.

Although the five factors themselves are orthogonal, gender differences on the factors are not. Correlations across the four columns in Table 3 show that all variables are strongly intercorrelated (rs = .52 to .81, n = 26, p < .01). These associations show a generalized pattern of gender differentiation, as if some cultures emphasized the universal pattern of gender differences, whereas other cultures minimized it. Summing differences across the four variables gives an index of the extent to which gender differences are

TABLE 3   Mean z-Score Differences (d) Between Women and Men in 26 Cultures on Revised NEO Personality Inventory Factors or Composites

CULTURE	N	A	F-Ex/In	F-Op/Cl
Zimbabweans	−.02	−.05	.10	.12
Black South Africans	.08	.05	.05	.12
South Koreans	.20	.18	.11	.16
Japanese	.09	.39	.17	.19
Malaysians	.44	.16	.10	.15
Indians	.15	.34	.20	.19
Taiwan Chinese	.16	.39	.17	.21
Indonesians	.33	.37	.09	.17
Filipinos	.34	.45	.16	.18
Hong Kong Chinese	.44	.43	.21	.17
Peruvians	.41	.43	.19	.25
Portuguese	.54	.45	.17	.16
White South Africans	.50	.46	.19	.27
Russians	.46	.27	.28	.43
Yugoslavians	.58	.46	.19	.21
Germans	.51	.41	.28	.33
Spaniards	.55	.50	.24	.24
Estonians	.42	.51	.26	35
Norwegians	.65	.38	.24	.27
Italians	.70	.47	.23	.25
Americans	.55	.57	.25	.29
Hispanic Americans	.68	.53	.27	.19
French	.71	.43	.29	.29
Dutch	.63	.49	.23	.39
Croatians	.75	.54	.28	.32
Belgians	.69	.55	.36	.40

Note. N = Neuroticism; A = Agreeableness; F-Ex/In = feminine extraversion/introversion; F-Op/Cl = feminine openness/closedness.

emphasized, and the cultures in Table 3 are ranked from least gender differentiated to most. Zimbabweans show little difference between men and women in any of the variables, whereas Belgians show strong gender effects for all of them.

An inspection of Table 3 shows an unmistakable pattern: Gender differences are most marked among European and American cultures and most attenuated among African and Asian cultures. Correlations of the ranking with mean levels of personality factors (McCrae, [2001]), shows that gender differentiation is associated with higher levels of E ($r = .69$, $p < .001$) and O ($r = .43$, $p < .05$). Correlations with the four Hofstede dimensions show that gender differentiation

is associated with Individualism ($r = .71$, $n = 23$, $p < .01$). Western nations with individualistic values and with inhabitants who are more assertive and progressive have greater gender differences in self-reported personality traits than non-Western, collectivistic cultures. The correlation of gender differentiation rank with Hofstede Masculinity did not approach significance, $r = -.21$. Gender differentiation was also unrelated to Power Distance and Uncertainty Avoidance and to M% variance in the small subsample with values for that variable ($r = .27$, $n = 10$, ns).

Finally, we examined rank-order correlations between gender differentiation and national statistics in the 22 cultures for which data were available. Gender differentiation was positively associated with GDP ($r = .47$, $p < .05$) and women's life expectancy ($r = .57$, $p < .01$), and negatively associated with fertility rate ($r = -.56$, $p < .05$), women's illiteracy rate ($r = -.46$, $p < .05$), and women's illiteracy rate relative to men's ($r = -.48$, $p < .05$). Gender differences in self-reported personality traits are largest in prosperous and healthy cultures where women have greater educational opportunities.

DISCUSSION

The present results extend to a wider range of cultures and a broader selection of personality traits conclusions reached by Feingold in his 1994 review of gender differences in personality. In brief, gender differences are modest in magnitude, consistent with gender stereotypes, and replicable across cultures. Substantively, most of the gender differences we found can be grouped in four categories: Women tend to be higher in negative affect, submissiveness, and nurturance, and more concerned with feelings than with ideas.

The elevation of N facets among women in the present study is consistent with the conclusions of previous reviews that have assessed general anxiety or neuroticism (Feingold, 1994; Lynn & Martin, 1997). It is also consistent with pancultural gender stereotypes. For example, Williams and Best (1990, Appendix A) reported M% scores across 14 cultures averaging 15 for *fearful* and 14 for *complaining*. These gender differences in susceptibility to negative affect are not attributable solely to differential sensitivity to emotional experience, because many of them remained significant even when Openness to Feelings was statistically controlled. Nor is an artifactual explanation likely: Researchers in the United States have failed to find evidence that men are more reluctant than women to report distress (Fujita et al., 1991), and even if they were, one would then need to explain why this gender-linked bias is found in virtually every culture.

As in previous studies and reviews (Feingold, 1994), men were found to be higher in assertiveness and women higher in nurturance, with the net effect that women scored substantially higher than men on A. These findings, again, are consistent with pancultural gender stereotypes: mean M% scores for *adventurous* and *dominant* were 94 and 87, whereas mean M% scores for *affectionate* and *sentimental* were 10 and 12, respectively.

Because E combines aspects of dominance and nurturance (McCrae & Costa, 1989), gender differences in E vary by facet, with men higher in E3: Assertiveness and E5: Excitement Seeking, and women higher in E1: Warmth, E2: Gregariousness, and E6: Positive Emotions. Because Extraversion scales vary in the ratio of dominant to nurturant content, the direction of gender differences may also vary. It seems likely that women scored lower than men on Extraversion in Lynn and Martin's (1997) review but higher here because the NEO-PI-R E factor emphasizes warmth more than assertiveness, whereas the opposite may be true for the Eysenck scale.

The difference in experiential preference for feelings versus ideas found here is also reflected in gender stereotypes. *Emotional* has a mean M% of 12, whereas *logical* has a mean M% of 80 across the 14 cultures studied by Williams and Best (1990). These effects have not often been reported in the literature, however, because relatively few personality instruments assess different facets of O. Perhaps the strongest support for this effect is found in the literature on vocational interests, in which men score higher in investigative interests and women higher in artistic interests. These two types of interest are differentially associated with Openness to Ideas and Aesthetics, respectively (Costa, McCrae, & Holland, 1984).

Some Possible Limitations

The present dataset is less than optimal in several respects. The range of cultures is limited, with only one

Latin American and two Black African cultures. Few of the samples can be considered nationally representative, and in most, women are overrepresented. Some of the subsamples are quite small. Yet the overall patterning of the data seems to emerge despite these limitations.

The subsamples differ in age distributions, especially for adults. For example, the Russian adults were considerably younger than the Japanese adults (cf. Costa et al., 2000). It is possible that the present results were distorted by age differences or cohort effects. Yet differences between college-age and adult samples were fairly modest, as Table 2 shows, and an Age × Gender analysis of variance in the American normative sample showed no significant interaction. It seems likely that any maturational or cohort effects on gender differences after age 18 are modest.

The data analyzed here were collected at different times, and it is possible that period effects might have biased results (cf. Twenge, 1997). Date of data collection was not recorded; however, all translations were begun after publication of the NEO-PI-R in 1992, and the literature search was completed in 2000, leaving a fairly narrow window. Future reviews should deal more explicitly with period effects.

Finally, questions remain about how well each culture is represented by results from a single study and investigator. For three of the cultures, new data have since become available. Samples of Taiwan Chinese high school students (1,497 men and 1,898 women aged 17 to 19; personal communication, K. Wu, March 8, 2001), Italian college students and adults (214 men and 355 women; personal communication, A. Terracciano, March 10, 2001), and Belgian junior and senior high students (325 boys and 402 girls; personal communication, F. De Fruyt, December 8, 2000) were examined. Values of *d* for the four indicators in Table 3 (N, A, F-Ex/In, and F-Op/Cl) were calculated for these three samples. For Taiwan they were .23, .32, .10, and .23, respectively; for Italy, .62, .39, .26, and .37, respectively; and for Belgium, .54, .67, .37, and .38, respectively. These values are very close to those seen in Table 3, and, summed to estimate overall gender differentiation, they would show identical ranks for all three cultures. If these three cultures are representative, then the present results are likely to be generalizable across different studies and samples within cultures.

Cultural Differences in Gender Differentiation

Of particular interest in the present study was the puzzling finding that self-reported gender differences are more pronounced in Western, individualistic countries. These countries tend to have more progressive sex role ideologies, endorsing such items as "A woman should have exactly the same freedom of action as a man" and "Swearing by a woman is no more objectionable than swearing by a man" (Williams & Best, 1990, p. 89). The social role model would have hypothesized that gender differences would be attenuated in progressive countries, when in fact they are magnified. Evolutionary theory also appears to be unable to account for this pattern; evolved species-wide characteristics ought to be uniform across cultures.

Analyses of cultural variation in gender differences showed that differentiation is both reliable and general. College-age men and women from each culture show the same magnitude of gender differences as do their adult counterparts, and cultures that show large differences on one variable tend to show large differences on others.

That fact makes some explanations unlikely. Differences across cultures in the frequency of psychiatric diagnoses might be due to differential access to health care (Nolen-Hoeksema, 1987), but that could not easily explain differences in A. Yet the same cultures that find little difference between the sexes in N also find little difference in A, and in composites of facets from E and O. Some broader explanation seems to be needed.

One possible explanation is that these results are artifactual. Perhaps in traditional cultures, where clear sex role differences are prescribed, self-descriptions are based on comparisons of the self with others of the same gender. For example, when asked if she were kind, a traditional woman might rank herself relative to women she knows, but not to men. In that case, gender differences would be eliminated, just as they are eliminated by the use of within-gender norms. By contrast, in modern cultures men and women may compare themselves with others of both genders, and thus reveal true gender differences. If respondents in traditional cultures were explicitly instructed to compare themselves with both men and women, larger gender differences might be found.

However, if cultural differences in gender differentiation were due solely to the adoption of different standards of comparison, then gender stereotypes would not be affected, because questions about stereotypes require the respondent explicitly to contrast the sexes. Yet Williams and Best (1990) also found that gender stereotypes were most differentiated in Western, individualistic cultures.[1]

Another possibility is that personality traits in general are less relevant to members of collectivist cultures (Cross & Markus, 1999), and thus relatively subtle gender differences may simply not be noticed. Church and Katigbak (2000), however, in their review of trait psychology in one collectivist culture, the Philippines, disputed that claim. Observer-rating data, particularly from observers outside the culture, might help resolve this issue.

It is possible that gender differences in personality are genetically determined, and that variations in gender differentiation are a result of differences in gene pools between European and non-European countries. Such a possibility might be tested in acculturation studies (McCrae, Yik, Trapnell, Bond, & Paulhus, 1998). For example, if culture dictates the degree of gender differentiation, one would expect U.S.-born African Americans and Asian Americans to show the same pronounced gender differentiation as Americans of European descent. Curiously, a preliminary study (McCrae, Herbst, & Masters, 2001) of African American samples instead showed small gender differences that more closely resembled those of Asian and African cultures than of European cultures. However, it is possible that the relatively traditional sex role ideology of African American subculture (Levant, Majors, & Kelley, 1998) is responsible for this effect.

A final, and perhaps most plausible, explanation relies on attribution processes (Weiner, 1990). In individualistic, egalitarian countries, an act of kindness by a woman may be perceived (by her and others) as

---

[1]The co-occurrence of highly differentiated gender stereotypes with large gender differences in personality is consistent with social role theory, which holds that traits and behaviors follow socially inculcated beliefs and expectation. What is not clear from social role theory is why extreme gender stereotypes would be found in countries with progressive sex role ideologies.

a free choice that must reflect on her personality. The same act by a woman in a collectivistic, traditional country might be dismissed as mere compliance with sex role norms. Thus, real differences in behavior might be seen everywhere, but would be attributed to roles rather than traits in traditional cultures. Note that such a process would affect not only the self-reports with which the present study was concerned, but also the gender stereotypes studied by Williams and Best (1990). In traditional cultures, perceived differences between men and women in general might be attributed to role requirements rather than to intrinsic differences in personality traits.

The present study relied exclusively on the use of self-reports to assess personality traits. Many of the difficulties in interpreting cultural differences in gender differentiation are due to this mono-method approach. The attribution argument, for example, assumes a discrepancy between behavior (in which the same gender differences are found everywhere) and questionnaire responses; clearly, it would be useful to observe behaviors in both controlled and natural settings to test that assumption. Again, the attribution hypothesis could be tested by comparing observer ratings of personality made by judges from within and outside a traditional culture. Even when judging the same targets (perhaps on videotape; cf. Funder & Sneed, 1993), traditional judges should perceive less evidence of gender differences in personality than would egalitarian judges. The future of research on gender differences in personality lies beyond self-reports.

REFERENCES

Budaev, S. V. (1999). Sex differences in the Big Five personality factors: Testing an evolutionary hypothesis. *Personality and Individual Differences, 26,* 801–813.

Buss, D. M. (1995). Psychological sex differences: Origins through sexual selection. *American Psychologist, 50,* 164–168.

Costa, P. T., Jr., & McCrae, R. R. (1992). *Revised NEO Personality Inventory (NEO-PI-R) and NEO Five-Factor Inventory (NEO-FFI) professional manual.* Odessa, FL: Psychological Assessment Resources.

Cross, S. E., & Markus, H. R. (1999). The cultural constitution of personality. In L. A. Pervin & O. P. John (Eds.), *Handbook of personality: Theory and research* (2nd ed., pp. 378–396). New York: Guilford Press.

Eagly, A. H., & Wood, W. (1991). Explaining sex differences in social behavior: A meta-analytic perspective. *Personality and Social Psychology Bulletin, 17,* 306–315.

Feingold, A. (1994). Gender differences in personality: A meta-analysis. *Psychological Bulletin, 116,* 429–456.

Maccoby, E. E., & Jacklin, C. N. (1974). *The psychology of sex differences.* Stanford, CA: Stanford University Press.

McCrae, R. R., Yik, M. S. M., Trapnell, P. D., Bond, M. H., & Paulhus, D. L. (1998). Interpreting personality profiles across cultures: Bilingual, acculturation, and peer rating studies of Chinese undergraduates. *Journal of Personality and Social Psychology, 74,* 1041–1055.

Twenge, J. M. (1997). Changes in masculine and feminine traits over time: A meta-analysis. *Sex Roles, 36,* 305–325.

Questions to Think About

1. What are some of the methodological challenges of adapting a measurement instrument for use in different languages and in different cultural environments?

2. If gender differences are, on average, small relative to within-gender variation, does that necessarily mean that the between-gender differences are unimportant?

3. The authors discuss possible explanations for the finding that gender differences in personality were greatest in the United States and Europe, where gender roles are least divergent. Can you think of other explanations for the finding?

46

Psychosocial and Behavioral Predictors of Longevity: The Aging and Death of the "Termites"

*HOWARD S. FRIEDMAN, JOAN S. TUCKER, JOSEPH E. SCHWARTZ,
CAROL TOMLINSON-KEASEY, LESLIE R. MARTIN,
DEBORAH L. WINGARD, AND MICHAEL H. CRIQUI*

Howard S. Friedman (1950–) is professor of psychology at the University of California, Riverside. He is the recipient of the career award for "Outstanding Contributions to Health Psychology" from the American Psychological Association. He has authored or edited many books and articles in health psychology and in personality. Co-editor of this readings book and co-author of the textbook, *Personality: Classic Theories and Modern Research,* Professor Friedman is also a recipient of UCR's Distinguished Teaching Award.

For many years, Friedman and his associates have been studying the psychosocial predictors of longevity among 1,538 participants first studied by psychologist Lewis Terman in 1922. Joan Tucker completed her doctoral work with Friedman working on this longevity project. Joseph E. Schwartz is a sociologist and biostatistician at the State University of New York at Stony Brook. Carol Tomlinson-Keasey was a professor of developmental psychology at the University of California, Riverside, when this project began, and became the founding Chancellor of the University of California, Merced. Leslie Martin also completed her doctoral work at the University of California, Riverside, on this project and became a professor at La Sierra University. Deborah Wingard and Michael Criqui are professors at the University of California, San Diego Medical School.

In 1921, Lewis Terman began one of the most comprehensive and best-known studies in psychology. To investigate his genetic theories of intelligence, Terman recruited 1,528 bright California boys and girls, intensively studied their psychosocial and intellectual development, and followed them into adulthood. These clever participants nicknamed themselves the "Termites." About half of the Termites are now dead, and we have gathered most of their death certificates and coded their dates and causes of death. These life span data provide a unique opportunity to address intriguing questions about the role of psychosocial variables in physical health and longevity through a life span prospective design.

Source: Friedman, H. S., Tucker, J. S., Schwartz, J. E., Tomlinson-Keasey, C., Martin, L. R., Wingard, D. L., & Criqui, M. H. (1995). Psychosocial and behavioral predictors of longevity: The aging and death of the "Termites." *American Psychologist, 50,* 69–78. Copyright © 1995 by the American Psychological Association. Reprinted with permission.

Editor's note: All citations in the text of this selection have been left intact from the original, but the list of references includes only those sources that are the most relevant and important. Readers wishing to follow any of the other citations can find the full references in the original work or in an online database.

Although there is little doubt that psychosocial factors such as stress and coping play some role in the development or progression of many chronic diseases and in premature death, there is quite a bit of uncertainty about the nature of the causal pathways. Are aspects of personality and social stress related to longevity in general and to heart disease or cancer in particular across the life span? If so, what is the nature of the links? To address these matters, we studied Terman's archives and our new follow-up data to focus on psychosocial disturbance and mortality. We considered three types of variables. First, we examined two major sources of social stress: the divorce of one's parents (during childhood) and the instability of one's own marriage. Second, we looked at patterns of personality evident in childhood and general psychological stability in adulthood. Finally, we considered the possible role of certain unhealthy habits in mediating the influence of stress and personality on longevity. This article integrates the key findings uncovered thus far, in a search for synthesis. A common thread does indeed emerge—a psychosocial risk pattern for premature mortality. Our more technical articles should be consulted for details that cannot be included here.

THE "TERMITES"

The Terman Life-Cycle Study (formerly called the Genetic Studies of Genius or Gifted Children Study) began in 1921–1922, when most of the children were preadolescents (Terman & Oden, 1947). Terman's aim was to secure a reasonably random sample of bright California children, and so most public schools in the San Francisco and Los Angeles areas were searched for bright kids, nominated by their teachers and tested by Terman to have an IQ of at least 135. There were 856 boys and 672 girls in the study; they have been followed at 5- to 10-year intervals ever since. In addition to Terman, many other researchers, including Melita Oden and Robert Sears (himself a Termite), contributed heavily to the archives, and we are certainly in their debt. Our own contribution has been to gather and code death certificates, to gather and refine certain data about smoking, and to develop the many new indexes necessary for studying longevity and cause of death effects.

In this remarkable study, only small percentages (fewer than 10%) of participants are unaccounted for. (Size varies somewhat with the subsample of each analysis.) We generally restricted our analyses to those who were of school age in 1922 ($M = 11$ years old), who lived at least until 1930, and for whom there were no substantial missing data. Our childhood personality measures were derived from information obtained by Terman in 1922, and our adult health behaviors, adult marriage information, and adult adjustment measures derived from midlife follow-ups (usually 1950, but ranging from 1940–1960). This typically resulted in a sample size of between 1,100 and 1,300. Analyses by Terman's researchers as well as our own comparisons indicated that those lost from study did not differ systematically.

In our sample, women significantly outlived men. As of 1991, 50% of the men but only 35% of the women were known to have died. Statistical survival analyses produce a ratio called a relative hazard, which is the relative probability that a person will die at any given time. The hazard rate for women was more than one third lower than that for men, confirming what is of course generally true in the population. Because women in this sample live about six years longer than men, all our analyses examined or controlled for gender differences.

The Termites were a bright, well-educated group, integrated into American society (but none grew up to win a Nobel prize or to be identified as an obvious genius). They had regular contact with Stanford University. Certain confounds common to other psychosocial health studies are therefore not likely in this sample. The Termites could understand medical advice and prescription, had adequate nutrition, and had access to medical care. Explanations of poor health involving poverty, ignorance, or discrimination are generally not applicable to this sample, and so the sample is valuable for focusing on certain personality and social stress variables. The Termites were successful in public school, at least to the extent that they made it through teachers' nominations and Terman's tough screening for intellectual talent; this is important to keep in mind because it helps rule out certain competing explanations for longevity. The sample is certainly not, however, representative of the U.S. population as a whole (e.g., it contains less than 1% Asian, African, or Native Americans); results are not necessarily generalizable to subpopulations that are different on health-relevant dimensions.

During the past several years, we have hunted down and gathered up hundreds of death certificates for the dead Termites, often from resistant state bureaucracies (Friedman, Tucker, & Martin, 1994). Following established epidemiologic procedures, we coded underlying cause of death according to the *International Classification of Diseases* (9th rev., U.S. Department of Health and Human Services, 1980), with the assistance of a certified nosologist supervised by our team's physician–epidemiologist. As in the general population, the leading cause of death was cardiovascular disease, followed by cancer.

DIVORCE

Divorce of Parents

It has been well established that the divorce of one's parents during childhood can have ill effects on one's future mental health. Although some questions remain about the causal processes, there is good longitudinal evidence that children of divorce, especially boys, are at greater risk for observable behavior and adjustment problems (Amato & Keith, 1991; J. Block, Block, & Gjerde, 1988; J. H. Block, Block, & Gjerde, 1986; Hetherington, 1991; Jellinek & Slovik, 1981; Shaw, Emery, & Tuer, 1993; Zill, Morrison, & Coiro, 1993). Most of the conceptual analyses concern a lack of social dependability or ego control (i.e., impulsivity and nonconformity), although neuroticism or low emotional stability have also often been implicated.

There has never before been a lifelong prospective study of family stress predictors of mortality and cause of death. Even physical health effects of family stress have been the object of little research attention, although some physiological differences among children have been documented (e.g., Gerra et al., 1993; Weidner, Hutt, Connor, & Mendell, 1992). Family stress (particularly parental divorce) has been found

to predict unhealthy behaviors such as smoking and drug use in adolescence as well as poor psychological adjustment (Amato & Keith, 1991; Chassin, Presson, Sherman, Corty, & Olshavsky, 1984; Conrad, Flay, & Hill, 1992; Hawkins, Catalano, & Miller, 1992), but the further consequential links to physical health have rarely been studied from long-term longitudinal data. Can these detrimental effects of parental divorce reach across the life span and affect longevity? Do they differentially affect cause of death?

We looked at the children ($N = 1,285$) whose parents either did or did not divorce before the child reached age 21, who were of school age in 1922, and who lived at least until 1930 (Schwartz et al., [1995]). We used hazard regression analyses (survival analyses) to predict longevity, controlling for gender.

Children of divorced parents faced a one third greater mortality risk than people whose parents remained married at least until they reached age 21 ($p < .01$). Among men whose parents divorced while they were children, the predicted median age of death was 76 years old; for men whose parents remained married, the predicted age of death was 80 years old. For women, the corresponding predicted ages of death were 82 and 86 years (Schwartz et al., [1995]).

This striking finding raises many important questions about causal mechanisms. Only 13% of the people in the Terman sample had faced the divorce of their parents during childhood, a situation different from that faced by children today. The estimates of the size of the effects on mortality may not be directly comparable for today's children. Still, in light of the overwhelming evidence from other studies indicating damaging psychological effects of parental divorce, this finding does provoke serious concern. Death of a parent had very little effect, consistent with other research indicating that parental strife and divorce is a greater influence on subsequent psychopathology than is parental death (Tennant, 1988). In the Terman sample, our analyses suggested that parental divorce was the key early social predictor of premature mortality, throughout the life span.

We used the information we gathered and coded from the death certificates to examine whether divorce of one's parents related differentially to cause of death. We found that parental divorce was not associated with whether one is more likely to die of cancer or heart disease or other disease. Also, the overall higher mortality risk cannot be explained away by a higher injury rate, although the possibility of an especially increased risk of injury death cannot be ruled out, because of the small sample.

Instability of One's Own Marriage

There is substantial epidemiological evidence that marriage is correlated with longer life (e.g., House, Robbins, & Metzner, 1982; Hu & Goldman, 1990; Kotler & Wingard, 1989). This is often viewed as a protective effect of the social support of marriage. "Get married" appears on pop lists of health recommendations. However, embedded in this relation are several distinct issues too rarely discussed. Should we assume that it is the marriage itself that is protective? Marriage brings the risk of marital dissolution. Death of spouse, divorce, and marital separation are the top three most stressful events on the classic Social Readjustment Rating Scale (Holmes & Rahe, 1967), and there seems little doubt that marital dissolution is the most significant common social stressor in American society (with the possible exception of abject poverty). Furthermore, is it possible that an unstable marital history is the result of other psychological and behavioral problems rather than itself being a primary cause of premature mortality?

As of 1950 (when they were about 40 years old), the vast majority of the Termites were alive, mature, and had married if they were ever going to marry. We classified them as currently and steadily married ($N = 829$), married but not in their first marriage (inconsistently married; $N = 142$), never married ($N = 102$), or currently separated, widowed, or divorced ($N = 70$). Very few Termites had been widowed by this point. Controlling for gender and self-reported health, we found (in survival analyses) that the inconsistently married people were at higher risk for premature mortality than the steadily married people and that the currently separated, widowed, or divorced people were at even higher risk. Inconsistently married men had a relative hazard of mortality of almost 1.4 (40% greater risk), and separated or divorced men had a relative hazard of 2.2. For women, the relative hazards were

1.4 and 1.8, respectively. Those who had never married had less of an increased risk and resembled the steadily married when their other social ties were taken into account (men's relative hazard = 1.05 and women's relative hazard = 1.00 when controlling for social ties; Tucker, 1993; Tucker, Friedman, & Wingard, 1994). This last finding concerning the long life of the never marrieds may be particular to the bright, career-oriented nature of the sample. Note that we have purposely considered marital history at a relatively stable, healthy, and mature time of life; the effects might be different in the very young or in much older people.

The steadily married people and the inconsistently married people were all married in 1950, yet they had significantly different life expectancies. This dramatic finding suggests that it may not be marriage's effect as a buffer against stress that is always important. Rather, there seems to be a detrimental effect of previous divorce that is not eliminated when the individuals remarry. Furthermore, additional analyses revealed that part of the association between marital status and mortality risk seems to be due to a selection into steady marriages—Termites who were impulsive children grew up both more likely to be inconsistently married and more likely to die younger ($p < .05$; Tucker, 1993).

Parental Divorce and One's Own Divorce

Is the increased mortality risk of children of divorce due in part to these people's own subsequent divorce? People whose parents divorced were indeed more likely to face divorce themselves ($p < .05$). Furthermore, individuals who were divorced or remarried reported that their childhoods were significantly more stressful than did those who stayed married ($p < .05$). In other words, Terman study participants who experienced a marital breakup were more likely to have seen the divorce of their own parents, and they were more likely to report having experienced a stressful home environment as children, such as marked friction among family members.

Given that parental divorce is associated with one's own future divorce, and given that one's divorce is predictive of increased mortality risk, it is indeed the case that one's unstable adult relations "explain" some of the detrimental effects of parental divorce. However, after controlling for one's (adult) divorce, parental divorce during childhood remained a significant predictor of premature mortality ($p < .05$), suggesting that it has additional adverse consequences in adulthood.

In summary, in this sample, marriage itself was not fully health protective. On the other hand, a stable marriage history was indeed predictive of increased longevity. Advice to get married to promote health seems unjustified. Advice to stay in a satisfactory marriage seems somewhat better, as there are hints of negative health consequences of divorce. Most surprising in light of previous research is the appearance of a psychosocial selection factor: Some people make poor marriage partners and are also prone to die prematurely (Tucker, 1993; Tucker, Friedman, & Wingard, 1994). All in all, family instabilities—parental and one's own divorce—are clearly predictive of premature mortality.

PERSONALITY AND ADJUSTMENT

Childhood Personality

There is a long history of research and theory arguing that certain patterns of psychological responding are damaging to physical health—that is, that certain personalities are disease-prone or self-healing (see overviews by Friedman, 1990, 1991, 1992; Pennebaker, 1990). The theorists and researchers have generally argued that resilient personalities—high in stability, sociability, and optimism—are prone to health, whereas aggressive, excitable, impulsive, and neurotic people are prone to disease and mortality.

In 1922, Terman collected trait ratings about the participants from their parents and teachers. The scales he used were remarkably modern in their appearance and provide a better assessment than the primitive personality tests that were available at the time. It is reasonable to expect that parents and teachers have a good idea of whether an 11-year-old child is sociable, popular, conscientious, self-confident, and so on. We constructed six personality dimensions and used them to predict longevity and cause of death

through 1986, using survival analyses (see Friedman et al., [1995]; Friedman et al., 1993). We used both Cox proportional hazards and Gompertz regressions; they yielded the same results.

Did childhood personality predict premature mortality decades later? The most striking finding in these and follow-up analyses was that childhood social dependability or conscientiousness predicted longevity. Children, especially boys, who were rated as prudent, conscientious, truthful, and free from vanity (four separate ratings, which we averaged, $\alpha = .76$) lived significantly longer. They were about 30% less likely to die in any given year.

The finding that certain aspects of personality predicted survival across the life span raises many fascinating questions concerning causal mechanisms. Why are conscientious, dependable children who live to adulthood more likely to reach old age than their less conscientious peers? Our survival analyses ($N = 1,215$) suggested that the protective effect of conscientiousness was not primarily due to a reduction in the risk of injury: Although there is some tendency for the unconscientious to be more likely to die a violent death, conscientiousness is also protective against early death from cardiovascular disease and cancer. A focus on unhealthy behaviors showed them to be somewhat relevant as explanatory mechanisms (see below), but a significant effect of conscientiousness remained after controlling for drinking ($p < .01$) and for smoking and other aspects of personality ($p < .05$; Friedman et al., [1995]).

We have found no evidence so far that the personality trait of sociability or other elements of extraversion were strongly related to health and longevity in this sample. This is somewhat surprising, given that biological and social theories of psychosocial factors and health generally predict such effects. Rather, the locus of health-relevant effects seems to be centered in such traits as impulsivity, egocentrism, toughmindedness, and undependability. For example, childhood ratings on such variables as popularity and preference for playing with other people did not predict longevity. To further explore the lifelong effects of sociability, we followed up on Terman's (1954) study of scientists. Terman had found that the Termites who grew up to be scientists (broadly construed) were much less sociable early in life than the nonscientists. (Terman studied only male scientists.) In fact, Terman considered the differences in sociability to be quite remarkable. Using the Stanford archives, we recreated Terman's groups (*Ns* 288 and 326) and compared their longevity through 1991. However, our survival analyses found that the scientists did not die at a younger age. In fact, the scientists tended to live longer (relative hazard = 1.26, *p* < .09; Friedman et al., 1994).

What about neuroticism? Although the traits of neuroticism—emotional instability, depression, and hostility—are thought to be correlated with poor health, we have found mixed results in this sample. On the childhood measures, there is some hint that neuroticism may be unhealthy. For example, for men, permanency of mood (as rated in childhood) tended to be associated with increased longevity. Effects of maladjustment appeared in adulthood (see the following section). In general, it has proved challenging to create valid measures of neuroticism because it is desirable to take various elements of the Termites' reaction patterns into account. This is a focus of our ongoing efforts.

Finally, we have been examining childhood cheerfulness—rated optimism and a sense of humor. Contrary to our expectations, we have found that childhood cheerfulness is inversely related to longevity. Survival analyses showed that the cheerful kids grew up to be adults who died younger (about 22% increased risk, *p* < .01; Friedman et al., 1993). Puzzled, we followed up on those Termites rated as cheerful in childhood. We found that they grew up to be more likely to smoke, drink, and take risks (all *p*s < .05, comparing upper and lower quartiles), although these habits do not fully explain their increased risk of premature mortality (Martin et al., 1994). It might be the case that cheerfulness is helpful when facing a stress such as surgery, but harmful if it leads one to be careless or carefree throughout one's life (Tennen & Affleck, 1987; Weinstein, 1984). In other words, the health relevance of such traits as optimism may need to be more carefully conceptualized (cf. Wortman, Sheedy, Gluhoski, & Kessler, 1992).

Personality, Parents' Divorce, and Longevity

Children of divorced parents were somewhat less likely to have been seen as conscientious children,

$r(1283) = -.14$, but controlling for parental divorce did not change the relations between childhood personality and longevity. Other correlations of parental divorce with personality characteristics were even smaller. In our sample, personality and parental divorce are independent predictors of longevity (Schwartz et al., [1995]).

Survival functions for a 20-year-old Termite are shown in Figure 1. It shows the probability of death as a function of age. The top four curves are for males in the sample. The topmost curve is for men who were rated as unconscientious in childhood and whose parents divorced during childhood; their probability of dying by age 70 was 40%. In contrast, for conscientious males whose parents did not divorce, the probability of dying by age 70 was less than 30%.

The bottom curve shows the longest-living women—those rated as conscientious and whose parents did not divorce. The difference between this curve and the bottom curve for men represents the gender effect—the longer lives of women. Note that the difference between these two curves at age 70 is smaller than the difference between the highest and lowest male curves. This means that the combined effect of the two psychosocial variables is greater than the well-known major effect of gender on longevity. Although we have purposely selected these two strong psychosocial predictors for this figure, there is (as noted above) excellent theoretical and empirical reason to believe that these childhood factors are highly relevant to subsequent unhealthy psychological functioning and behavior. The fact that childhood psychosocial information about personality and family stress does as well as gender in predicting longevity is dramatic evidence of the importance of psychosocial factors for understanding premature mortality.

Adult Psychosocial Adjustment

The relation between psychological adjustment and premature mortality has not been much studied in long-term prospective population research. Although special groups such as the clinically depressed or criminals are more likely to face early death (e.g., from suicide or homicide), the more general question has received surprisingly little study. It could be argued that psychosocial maladjustment is implicit in the Type A

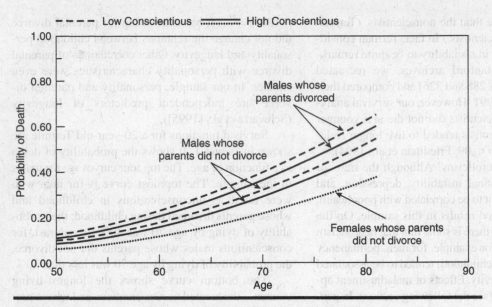

FIGURE 1   Survival Functions for a 20-year-old, by Conscientiousness and Parental Divorce
Note. High and low conscientiousness represent the 75th versus the 25th percentiles. Fitted curves were based on Gompertz hazard function estimates. Copyright 1994, Joseph E. Schwartz and Howard S. Friedman.

disease-prone pattern, but only the psychosomatic theorists have focused intensively on psychotherapy as a means of promoting general physical health (Dunbar, 1943; see also Berry & Pennebaker, 1993).

In 1950, the Termites were asked about tendencies toward nervousness, anxiety, or nervous breakdown; there had also been personal conferences with participants and with family members. On the basis of this and previous related information in the files dating back a decade, Terman's team then categorized each on a 3-point scale of mental difficulty: *satisfactory adjustment, some maladjustment, or serious maladjustment.* (Almost one third experienced at least some mental difficulty by this stage.) Survival analyses show that for men, mental difficulty as of 1950 significantly predicted mortality risk through 1991, in the expected direction (relative hazard = 1.30, *p* < .01, for men and 1.12, *ns,* for women). Similar results were found on a measure we constructed of poor psychological adjustment as self-reported in 1950 on six

11-point scales that included items like *moodiness* (significant risk for men, *p* < .05, but not for women).

Further analyses revealed that the consistently married Termites had the fewest mental difficulties; alternatively, this could be stated as a finding that those with the fewest mental difficulties were most likely to remain married. It is interesting that controlling for mental difficulty weakened but did not eliminate the relation between marital history and longevity. In other words, although mental distress seemed to play the expected role in poor health, a significant detrimental effect of divorce remained, even after taking psychological health in 1950 into account.

In analyses thus far on cause of death, there have been no dramatic differences as a function of psychological adjustment. A general survival analysis model testing for differences among cause of death (cardiovascular disease, cancer, injury, and other diseases) has shown no significant difference. That is, poorly adjusted men are more likely to die from all causes. There is some indication that poorly adjusted participants are especially more likely to die from injury (including suicide), as would be expected. However, because so few people died from injury in this sample, such differences cannot (and do not) account for the main effect of adjustment on longevity. There is also a hint that poorly adjusted men may have an extra risk of dying from cardiovascular disease.

HEALTH BEHAVIORS

Cigarette smoking and heavy use of alcohol (which often occur together) are well established as behavioral causes of significant morbidity and premature mortality. Thus, it is of significant interest to ascertain the extent to which such behaviors can be predicted from childhood and the extent to which they might account for differences in longevity. It is important, however, to keep in mind the time periods in which the various predictors were measured as well as the nature of the Terman sample. We deem it inadvisable to attempt precise effect size comparisons; rather, these data are best suited for uncovering stable, robust patterns.

Terman collected very good contemporaneous data on alcohol consumption. We used information collected in 1950 and 1960 to classify the Termites as heavy drinkers ($N = 226$ men and 87 women), as moderate drinkers (seldom or never intoxicated; $N = 339$ men and 302 women), or as rarely (or never) taking a drink ($N = 99$ men and 128 women). Alcohol use was quite stable across decades. Because moderate drinking may be protective of heart disease, we also looked for U-shaped effects on mortality, but none were found. Information about smoking was poorly documented in the files, so we collected as much smoking information as possible during 1991–1992. We contacted those Termites who could be found, and we attempted to contact relatives of the rest. We gathered smoking data on over 900 Termites, but some of them were missing data on other key variables. Unlike the other measures, there was some evidence of bias in this subsample. Those who died young seemed more likely to have had very unhealthy behaviors and also were less likely to have locatable

families. Thus, the mediating effect of smoking may be underestimated.

As expected, smoking and drinking each predicted premature mortality. Did they mediate the relations reported above? Conscientious children grew up to drink and smoke less, but cheerful kids grew up to drink and smoke more (all $ps < .05$; Tucker et al., 1994; cf. J. Block, Block, & Keyes, 1988). However, conscientiousness remained a strong predictor of longevity in various survival analyses, controlling for smoking and drinking (decreased hazard of 20%–30%). Cheerfulness remained predictive when alcohol use was controlled, but the effects of cheerfulness changed when smoking was controlled; because the sample size dropped by one third, what this means is problematic. Termites (especially girls) who faced parental divorce grew up to smoke a little more ($p < .05$), but not drink more (possibly due to Prohibition during adolescence).

Analyses of obesity (body mass index in young to mid-adulthood) showed little systematic relationship to either psychosocial variables or mortality in this intelligent sample, perhaps because obesity was measured in 1940, when few participants were heavily overweight, or because obesity was unusual in bright people of this cohort. What about exercise, hobbies, and other such potentially important mediators? Although there is of course no simple exercise variable per se among the thousands of variables in the data set, information on activity levels and hobbies at various ages is scattered throughout and can eventually be pieced into the puzzle.

It might be the case that psychosocial factors affect a whole host of health behaviors in addition to drinking and smoking—exercise patterns, diet, use of prophylactics, adherence to medication regimens, avoidance of environmental toxins, and more—which, when put together, may explain most of the associations between psychology and longevity. Surprisingly, there has been little prospective study of psychosocial predictors of unhealthy lifestyle patterns across long time periods and how they subsequently and consequently affect health, longevity, and cause of death.

In summary, the data concerning unhealthy behaviors are tantalizing but not definitive. Personal and social factors evident in childhood were predictive of smoking and excessive drinking in adulthood, and these unhealthy behaviors predicted premature mortality in this sample. Yet these behaviors did not come close to fully accounting for the effects of childhood predictors on longevity. It may be the case that more reliable and more extensive measurement of health behaviors could have a major impact in explaining the psychosocial predictors of longevity, without resorting to psychosomatic explanations involving stress. Given the documented associations of stress with both cardiovascular disease mechanisms and suppression of the immune system, however, it is likely that there are multiple pathways linking psychosocial factors to longevity. Our guess is that personality and stress variables have both direct (psychosomatic) and behaviorally mediated effects on health, but ascertaining their relative importance is a difficult empirical question.

DISCUSSION

A number of intriguing new findings have emerged from efforts thus far in studying longevity and cause of death in the Terman cohort. These enduring patterns could emerge only from a lifelong comprehensive study such as the one that Terman and his colleagues worked so hard to establish.

First, and most basically, the results leave little doubt that aspects of individual psychology are significantly linked to longevity, across the life span. In particular, we found confirmation in the physical health arena of the importance of what psychologists have typically seen as ego strength—dependability, trust, and lack of impulsivity. This pattern of results unites and extends the various related sorts of findings by other researchers.

Second, we found evidence that both personality and social stress factors are independent predictors of longevity. Past findings of psychopathological sequelae of divorce and family conflict can now be extended to the arena of long-term health effects. In both childhood and adulthood, the trauma of divorce clearly predicted premature mortality—but so did personality. Yet the effect of each was substantially independent of the other. Further examination of Figure 1 reveals that unconscientious males whose parents divorced crossed the 50th percentile of survival at (i.e., lived on

average to) 74 years. For conscientious males from stable families, the average survival was to 81 years. (The figures were analogous for females.) Although these numbers probably represent the maximum size of effect that is likely to be found in such a sample, their dramatic nature nevertheless should promote substantial future research focused on this area.

Third, we have not, as yet, found striking associations with specific disease causes of death. Our careful, physician-supervised collection and coding of underlying cause of death from death certificates makes us confident of the reliability of this variable. The fact that personality and social factors predicted all causes of death suggests either that a general homeostasis is critical to good health (Selye, 1976) or that a group of unhealthy behaviors mediates a wide variety of health problems. This is not to say that a specific psychosocial influence cannot further raise the risk of a particular disease. However, to the extent that specific disease-prone patterns do exist (such as a coronary-prone personality), they probably depend on the co-occurrence of more than one factor; in other words, interaction effects are likely involved. This could explain why such phenomena have proved so hard to capture.

How large are these effects? Because genetic hardiness, exposure to microbes and toxins, and many random factors affect longevity, researchers should not normally expect an overwhelming effect of psychosocial influences. Yet, where life and death are concerned, an influence that leaves 55% of the people alive compared with only 45% alive in an uninfluenced comparison group is of great interest. The effects discussed would generally translate into a relative hazard of between 1.2 and 1.5, a correlation of between 0.1 and 0.2, or a decreased life expectancy of two to four years (comparing upper and lower quartiles; cf. Friedman & Booth-Kewley, 1987; Lipsey & Wilson, 1993; Rosenthal, 1991; Schwartz et al., [1995]). These effects are smaller than the influences of gender or smoking on longevity, but comparable to common biological risk factors such as systolic blood pressure and serum cholesterol and to common behavioral risks such as exercise and diet, as they affect all-cause mortality. Nevertheless, caution should be used in making inferences about the magnitude of the effects in other socioeconomic groups and in other historical times; the Terman data are best suited for uncovering robust psychosocial variables that predict longevity rather than for ruling out complex pathways or explicating a full causal model.

Women significantly outlive men in this sample. Consistent with previous research, most of the psychosocial effects were more pronounced for the men (e.g., greater effects for childhood conscientiousness, adult mental difficulties, and self-reported early family stress). Like other researchers (Wingard, 1984), we have not yet been able to account for the gender differences in longevity, nor for the greater psychological effects in males, but this is a focus of ongoing efforts.

As in the general population, the significant mortality in this sample occurs after age 55. The important questions that remain unanswered revolve around the mechanisms that lead from seemingly physically healthy but psychosocially impaired middle-aged adulthood to premature mortality. We have seen that smoking and excessive drinking likely play some causal role, but perhaps not a dominant role. Our analyses of cause of death have thus far not provided any dramatic insights into this question. We of course are studying this matter in the Terman sample, but insights will also be gleaned from cross-sectional and other shorter-term studies that now can be focused on these issues.

Especially interesting is the importance of stable individual patterns of responding. In light of the current findings, a model that focused on socioenvironmental stress would be clearly inadequate. It is not the case that most people are equally likely to die prematurely until some of them happen to encounter divorce, job loss, or other unexpected stress. Although such factors do play a significant role, it is also the case that personality—a stable individual pattern of responding—is highly relevant. Furthermore, this effect of personality was maintained when we controlled for childhood socioeconomic status and for childhood health (i.e., parents' reports of health and illnesses in infancy and childhood).

Could it be the case that biological factors are a primary cause of both personality and health, as Eysenck (1985, 1991) has argued? At this point, the evidence is not totally inconsistent with such an explanation. Surprisingly, however, it is what Eysenck

termed *psychoticism,* not neuroticism or introversion, that seems most relevant. (People high on psychoticism are impulsive, cruel, hostile, foolhardy, impersonal, and troublesome.) That is, the unhealthy patterns that have emerged thus far in our study predominantly involved being impulsive, imprudent, and arrogant rather than anxious, shy, pessimistic, and unsociable. This may change somewhat as more complex approaches are taken to these data; there is of course good evidence from other studies that the latter traits are indeed also relevant. More complex models of causality are also plausible. In addition to underlying biology predisposing an individual to both certain styles of behaving and excessive sympathetic reactivity, individuals undoubtedly play some role in selecting their own healthy or unhealthy environments (Magnus, Diener, Fujita, & Payot, 1993; Scarr & McCartney, 1983; also see work on testosterone, Dabbs & Morris, 1990).

Previous notions of a disease prone personality (Friedman & Booth-Kewley, 1987) and a self-healing personality (Friedman, 1991) seem viable in light of the current findings. Indeed, the long-term predictive value of psychosocial factors, across decades, confirms the utility of thinking in terms of stable individual differences. The past emphasis on emotional reaction patterns, however, must be supplemented by significantly increased attention to behavioral correlates and mediators. For those researchers with a psychodynamic bent, the healthy pattern might be termed *mature ego defenses* (Vaillant, 1993). For those more focused on behavior, key issues may involve dependability and addictions. In either case, the same sorts of variables emerge—the destructiveness of impulsiveness and substance abuses, and the healthiness of maturity and social stability.

The longitudinal design of the present study points out the importance of not focusing too heavily on short-term coping with stress to the exclusion of lifelong habits and patterns. Although other research gives reason to believe that aspects of personality such as sociability and optimism are related not only to feelings of psychological well-being but also to good health, such influences may be heavily context dependent. For example, it may be helpful to be optimistic when one is facing trauma and it may be helpful to have friends when one is bereaved, but these things may not necessarily be generally health protective by themselves across the life span. Impaired social support can sometimes occur as a result of (as well as be a cause of) psychological maladjustment.

This line of thinking points to the fascinating speculation that problems in psychosocial adjustment that revolve around an egocentric impulsivity are a key general risk factor for all-cause mortality. In terms of healthy aspects of the so-called "Big Five" dimensions of personality, this would probably involve elements of Agreeableness such as trust and straightforwardness, and elements of Conscientiousness such as achievement striving, competence, and deliberation (see McCrae & Costa, 1991; Ones, Viswesvaran, & Schmidt, 1993; Watson & Clark, 1992); closely related are stable interpersonal ties. It has been pointed out that such a pattern might be seen to define "character" (Costa, McCrae, & Dembroski, 1989). Although common wisdom might argue that a selfish, self-indulgent boor may prosper by stepping on others, this does not seem to be the case. Nor do we find a triumph of the lazy, pampered dropout. In terms of the rush toward death, the encouraging news may be that good guys finish last.

The size of the effects we have uncovered, their fit with previous theory, and their support by ancillary lines of research point to the possibility of major public health implications for these psychosocial variables. Although bright children growing up in California in the 1920s obviously faced some unique challenges and one should not carelessly generalize the results to other groups of people in other historical contexts, it is also the case that the findings fit quite well with what is already known about the correlates of better or worse mental health. Indeed, if such patterns of findings were found concerning toxic associations with insecticides, electromagnetic fields, or diets (even in a nonrandom sample), it is likely that a public health emergency would be perceived.

Although improvements in longevity are often assumed to be a function of medical technology, a good case can be made that most of the increase has come from changes in public health—sewage handling, food supply, inoculation, lessened crowding,

and so on (McKeown, 1979, makes a cogent case; of course, there are many particular exceptions where medical cures have been discovered). The psychosocial and behavioral variables we have been discussing fit well into such a public health framework—major, lifelong, psychosocial patterns seem highly relevant to longevity. On the other hand, the effects of successful social intervention are not necessarily so clear, as the casual pathways have not been proved. For example, the effects of early psychological and social interventions on subsequent longevity have not been studied, much less documented. Still, given the other known benefits of a society with socially dependable individuals and stable families, the findings of significant relations with longevity should lend a new sense of urgency to addressing these complex issues.

Terman died in 1956. He was almost 80. His wife had died earlier that same year, after more than 50 years of marriage. Terman had set out in 1921 to study the simple bases of intelligence and success, but he came to recognize that it was much more complicated than he had imagined. The same might now be said about our understanding of the psychosocial bases of longevity.

REFERENCES

Amato, P. R., & Keith, B. (1991). Parental divorce and the well-being of children: A meta-analysis. *Psychological Bulletin, 110,* 26–46.

Block, J. H., Block, J., & Gjerde, P. F. (1986). The personality of children prior to divorce: A prospective study. *Child Development, 57,* 827–840.

Eysenck, H. J. (1991). Personality, stress, and disease: An interactionist perspective. *Psychological Inquiry, 2,* 221–232.

Friedman, H. S. (1990) (Ed.). *Personality and Disease.* New York: Wiley & Sons.

Friedman, H. S. (1991). *The Self-Healing Personality: Why Some People Achieve Health and Others Succumb to Illness.* New York: Henry Holt. (Republished by <Iuniverse.com>, 2000).

Friedman, H. S., & Booth-Kewley, S. (1987). The "disease-prone personality": A meta-analytic view of the construct. *American Psychologist, 42,* 539–555.

Hetherington, E. M. (1991). Families, lies, and videotapes: Presidential Address of the Society for Research in

Adolescence. *Journal of Research on Adolescence, 1,* 323–348.

Magnus, K., Diener, E. Fujita, F., & Payot, W. (1993). Extraversion and neuroticism as predictors of objective life events: A longitudinal analysis. *Journal of Personality & Social Psychology, 65,* 1046–1053.

Tennant, C. (1988). Parental loss in childhood: Its effect in adult life. *Archives of General Psychiatry, 45,* 1045–1050.

Vaillant, G. E. (1993). *The wisdom of the ego.* Cambridge: Harvard University Press.

Questions to Think About

1. Because no single approach to personality and longevity seems adequate, which combinations of personality perspectives and theories are most likely to prove suitable for understanding the complex relations between personality and health?

2. Why should such issues as conscientiousness, mature ego defenses, lack of impulsiveness, and social stability prove so important to health and longevity?

3. Should efforts to promote health focus primarily on changing the individual (as is now often done), or should significantly more attention be given to changing the society and culture?

4. Longitudinal studies provide unique opportunities for research on predictors of longevity. What are some of the limitations that arise from following a single cohort of participants for scores of years?

47

The Roots of Evil: Social Conditions, Culture, Personality, and Basic Human Needs

ERVIN STAUB

Ervin Staub (1938–) is a psychology professor at the University of Massachusetts who studies the psychology of good and evil. He applies theories and research from personality and social psychology to the understanding of hate, mass violence, and genocide. He is also interested in exploring methods of raising nonviolent children.

Staub's interest in evil (and especially in genocide) becomes more understandable in the context of his own life experiences. As a young child in Hungary in the 1940s, he and his family—all Jews—barely escaped death at the hands of the Nazis. When Staub later moved to the United States and completed his doctorate at Stanford, he remained fascinated by both the genocidal evil of the Nazis and the failure of many millions of ordinary citizens to oppose the killing of their neighbors.

In this selection, Staub addresses how individuals and groups become genocidal and the influence and status of those who could intervene but do not.

The focus of this article is on the origins of evil, in several domains. An important domain is *genocide,* the attempt to exterminate a whole group of people. This is a form of violence that seems "obviously" evil. Another domain is individual violence. What are the origins of aggression in children, and how does the kind of violence that may be regarded as evil develop out of it? A number of elements in the generation of evil are evident as these two domains are explored: the system in which individuals operate—whether constituted by a culture and social conditions, the nature of a family or a classroom, and relationships among people; personal characteristics and the behavior of bystanders; the evolution of increasingly harmful acts over time; and the frustration of basic human needs and their "destructive" fulfill-

ment. To exemplify further how these elements operate, father–daughter incest and, very briefly, bullying in schools also are discussed. Space limitations do not allow a detailed examination of "cures" or prevention, but the discussion of origins at times implies, and at other times I briefly explore ways to stop or prevent evil.

IS EVIL A USEFUL CONCEPT FOR PSYCHOLOGISTS?

One focus of my work for many years has been the exploration of the roots of violence, especially of genocide and mass killing, which I referred to as *evil* (Staub, 1989). How does a group, a culture, as well as a person evolve so that they come to engage in "evil"

Source: Staub, E. (1999). The roots of evil: Social conditions, culture, personality, and basic human needs. *Personality and Social Psychology Review, 3,* 179–192. Reprinted by permission.

Editor's note: All citations in the text of this selection have been left intact from the original, but the list of references includes only those sources that are the most relevant and important. Readers wishing to follow any of the other citations can find the full references in the original work or from an online database.

actions or even develop a tendency for them? In recent years, I have also been greatly concerned with the prevention of genocide (Staub, 1996b, 1998b, 1999). Genocide and mass killing may seem obviously evil to most of us. However, because the concept of evil is becoming increasingly used in the social-psychological literature (Baumeister, 1997; Darley, 1992; Staub, 1989), it is important to ask whether it has useful meaning for psychologists. How would the meaning of evil be differentiated from the meaning of "violence"? Is evil the end point in the evolution of violence? In genocide, a plan is formulated to destroy a group. Usually, a decision is made to do this. Reactions to events and psychological and social processes turn into a plan. However, a conscious intention of extreme destructiveness does not seem a necessary aspect of evil. The real motivation is often unconscious, and a group's or person's habitual, spontaneous reactions to certain kinds of events can become highly destructive.

Evil has been a religious concept. The word also has been used as a secular term to describe, explain, or express aversion to certain actions and the human beings or natural forces from which they originate. The notion of a nonhuman force and origin often has been associated with evil, such as the devil, Satan, or Mephistopheles. Some have seen the forces of nature, when manifested in the destruction they sometimes bring, as evil. From a psychological standpoint, the forces of nature are surely neutral: They do, at times, cause harm but without conscious or unconscious intention.

The word *evil* is emotionally expressive for people: It communicates horror over some deed. People often romanticize evil. They want to see the abhorrent acts or events to which the word refers as having mythic proportions. Designating something as evil is sometimes used to suggest that the actions are not comprehensible in an ordinary human framework: They are outside the bounds of morality or even of human agency. However, evil is the outcome of basic, ordinary psychological processes and their evolution. Arendt's (1963) concept of the "banality of evil" seems to recognize this. However, the notion of the banality of evil also makes it seem as if its ordinariness diminishes the significance of evil.

I originally used the term *evil* to denote extreme human destructiveness, as in cases of genocide and mass killing (Staub, 1989), but evil may be defined by a number of elements. One of these is *extreme harm*. The harm can be pain, suffering, loss of life, or the loss of personal or human potential. Violent actions tend to arise from difficult, threatening circumstances and the psychological reactions of people to them. They are elicited by varied instigators, such as attack, threat, or frustration. Not all people react to such conditions with violence, but some do. Some individuals or groups engage in extremely harmful acts that are not commensurate with any *instigation* or *provocation* (Darley, 1992), another defining element of evil. Finally, some individuals, groups, or societies evolve in a way that makes destructive acts by them likely. The repetition or *persistence of greatly harmful acts* may be another defining element of evil. It is most appropriate to talk of evil when all these defining elements are present: intensely harmful actions, which are not commensurate with instigating conditions, and the persistence or repetition of such actions. A series of actions also can be evil when any one act causes limited harm, but with repetition, these acts cause great harm.

An important question, which this article in part addresses, is what might be the nature of the actor, whether a society or a person, that makes such acts probable. By "nature of the actor," whether a person or society, I do not refer to psychopathology. The evil I focus on and explore in this article arises out of ordinary psychological processes and characteristics, although usually extreme forms or degrees of them: seeing people as hostile, devaluing certain groups of people, having an overly strong respect for authority, and others.

When a person or group is attacked, they have a right to defend themselves. If someone begins to shoot at me and I pull out a gun and kill the person, my action is not evil. Whether self-defense is justified can get complicated very fast, however. What if someone has threatened me, and I then lie in wait for him and shoot him when he leaves his house? If this person in a moment of anger has threatened to kill me, most of us would not see this as sufficient provocation to justify killing him, unless perhaps we know that this person has threatened other people in similar ways and then actually killed them.

A particular person, at a particular time, for idiosyncratic reasons, may take a threat extremely seriously and respond by killing another. This extremely violent act may not be evil: It may be peculiar to the circumstances and emotional state of the person at that time. Not arising from this person's personality, or from a combination of personality and the ongoing of circumstances, it is unlikely to be repeated. Evil usually has a more enduring quality. Thus, it might be best not to regard as evil a single act of intense harm that is out of balance with provocation. However, violence evolves, and individuals and groups change as a result of their actions (see subsequent discussion). As a person or group commits an intensely harmful act, there is an increased likelihood that they will do so again.

As well as action, omission may be evil, especially when it causes extreme harm, there is no strong justification for it in circumstances (such as lack of clarity of events or very high cost of action), and when it persists. Consider an extreme example: A person standing at the edge of a lake, taking no action while witnessing a child drowning in shallow water. Passivity in such an extreme situation is likely to arise from this person's nature, predicting other evil acts (or from this person's relationship to that particular child).

Evil acts are mainly directed at other human beings, although the destruction of animals or nature may also be considered evil. These actions often cause material harm: death, injury, pain, or severe deprivation and injustice. Persistent neglect or belittling of a child that causes physical harm, psychological pain, or psychological injury that diminishes the capacity for growth and satisfaction are also appropriately regarded as evil.

It may be most appropriate to regard it evil when destructive actions are intentional. However, intention is highly complicated psychologically because a person's real motive is often unconscious; individuals and groups tend to justify their actions, even to themselves; and various belief systems develop that propagate harmful actions in the service of some presumed good. Persons or groups who act destructively

tend to claim self-defense or to claim that their victims are morally bad and dangerous or stand in the way of human betterment and, therefore, deserve suffering or death. They may simply use this as justification or may genuinely believe it even when it is completely untrue.

An example of a belief system leading people to act cruelly in the service of what they see as a good cause is the way children were treated in many societies (Greven, 1991; Miller, 1983). In many places, including Germany, England, and the United States, children were seen as inherently willful. Obedience by them was seen as a high virtue and important goal and it was believed that children's will had to be broken early if they were to become good people. Such thinking often had religious roots (Greven, 1991). Any and all means, such as threatening children with the devil and in other ways scaring them, as well as physically punishing them or depriving them, were seen appropriate to break their will and teach them obedience and respect (Miller, 1983).

In the case of genocide, it is usually clear to outside observers that it is not justified by provocations even if it is a response to real violence by the other group. However, frequently the victim group has done nothing to justify violence against them, except in the perpetrators' minds. The Jews engaged in no destructive actions against Germans. Many of the intellectuals and educated people in Cambodia who were killed or worked to death by the Khmer Rouge did no harm that would justify such actions in the minds of most people. According to the Khmer Rouge ideology, however, these intellectuals had participated in an unjust system that favored them at the expense of others and were incapable of participating in a system of total social equality. To fulfill a "higher" ideal, to create total social equality, was the motivation to kill them or to reduce them to slaves working in the "killing fields" (Staub, 1989).

There is the same absence of provocation in many cases of recurrent violence against a spouse, or severe neglect, harsh verbal and physical treatment, and persistent physical violence against children. Some parents blame their children all the time: for having been noisy, thereby causing the car accident in which the parents were involved; for needing things that cost money, thereby depriving the family of other things; for anything and everything (L. Huber, school psychologist, personal communication, June 1997). Peck (1983) gave this as a primary example of evil. Such parents may completely lack awareness of what in themselves leads to their blaming and scapegoating, seeing their actions as justifiable reactions to the child.

Frequently, there are two levels of motivation in harmful behavior, including evil acts. One is to "harm" a person or a group, and another is to fulfill some goal that the harmful act supposedly serves. Perpetrators may present and often actually see their actions as in the service of higher ideals and of beneficial outcomes, even to the victims themselves (raising a good child), to society (creating social equality), or to all of humanity (creating a better world).

My discussion of the concept of evil suggests that it could be a useful concept for psychologists. It could lead, for example, to more focused exploration of the characteristics of persons, cultures, and situations that lead to harmdoing that represents an overreaction to circumstances (provocation), is extreme and/or recurrent. It also could lead to more focused work on how cultures that promote such responses and who respond in these ways develop. Time will tell whether evil will be a comfortable concept for psychologists and whether it will become used.

Although the starting point for evil is usually the frustration of basic human needs (see subsequent discussion), evil actions are made possible by some or all of the following: lack or loss of concern with the welfare of other people; a lack of empathy with people, both lack of empathic feelings and lack of understanding how others feel; lack of self-awareness, the ability to understand one's own motives; having a negative view of others; a sense of entitlement, a focus on one's own rights; and devaluation, fear of, and hostility toward some or all human beings. How do the psychological tendencies that contribute to evil actions come about? How do motivations to intensely harm others arise? How do inhibitions decline?

THE ORIGINS OF EVIL

Both in groups and individuals, the evolution of evil starts with the frustration of basic human needs and

the development of destructive modes of need fulfillment. Evil usually begins when profoundly important needs of human beings are not fulfilled, either in the course of growing up or later in life, and especially when early frustration of basic needs is combined with later frustration. We human beings have certain shared psychological needs that must be fulfilled if we are to lead reasonably satisfying lives: We need to feel secure; we need to develop a positive identity; we need to feel effective and to have reasonable control over what is essential to us; we need both deep connections to other people and autonomy or independence; we need to understand the world and our place in it (see Staub, 1989, 1996b, 1998a; for additional views on basic needs, see Burton, 1990; Kelman, 1990; Maslow, 1971).

Basic needs press for satisfaction. If people cannot fulfill them constructively, they will engage in destructive psychological processes and actions to satisfy them. Destructive need satisfaction means one of two things. First, people will satisfy some basic need in ways that in the long run interfere with the satisfaction of other needs. One example is a child who blames himself for harsh parental treatment, in part at least because this increases a sense of security: "If I am at fault, I have a chance to avoid punishment by acting differently." This self-blaming, however, interferes with the need for a positive identity, as well as the ability to create positive connections. Another example is a person who so intensely focuses on the satisfaction of one need, such as feeling effective and being in control, that in the process alienates other people and has difficulty fulfilling the need for positive connection. Second, people may satisfy needs in ways that interfere with the fulfillment of other people's needs or harm others. The need for security, a feeling of effectiveness, or a positive identity may be satisfied by power over other people and the use of force.

EVIL IN GROUPS: GENOCIDE AND MASS KILLING

I start with an exploration of group behavior, particularly genocide and mass killings, as manifestations of evil. This exploration is relevant to the understanding of lesser harmdoing within societies, such as discrimination. The conception that I briefly describe has been applied to and supported by an examination of the Holocaust, the genocide of the Armenians, the "autogenocide" in Cambodia, and the disappearances in Argentina (Staub, 1989); by a brief examination of the mass killing in Bosnia (Staub, 1996b) and the genocide in Rwanda (Staub, 1999); and by a brief exploration of the mass killing of native Americans in the United States (Staub, 2000). Its description (see subsequent discussion) draws on all of these sources, but especially on Staub (1989).

In understanding violence in a group, whether the group is a society or a smaller community such as a school, gang, or family, it is important to consider both influences at the level of the group (culture, political system and processes, the role of leaders, group psychological processes) and individual psychology. The abstract identification of relevant social and psychological or other principles has somewhat limited value. The specification of how psychological and social processes arise from societal conditions and culture and how they join is required. In other words, the generation of violence in the group is best studied and understood as a systemic process.

Instigating Conditions and the Psychological and Social Processes They Give Rise To

Difficult conditions of life in a society are one important starting point for the evolution of mass killing and genocide. Intense economic problems or political conflict, great social changes, or their combination profoundly frustrate basic needs. People usually do not know how to deal with the material deprivation, chaos, and social disorganization these conditions create. They do not join together to deal with them effectively. Instead, the life problems in society give rise to psychological and social processes that turn subgroups of society against each other.

Individuals, feeling helpless on their own, turn to their group for identity and connection. They scapegoat some other groups. They adopt or create destructive ideologies—hopeful visions of social arrangements but visions that also identify enemies who supposedly stand in the way of the fulfillment of these visions. Such psychological and social processes help affirm identity and connection within the group, offer the possibility of effectiveness and control, and provide a new understanding of reality. Ideological movements are especially effective vehicles for the fulfillment of basic needs. Ideologies are almost always part of the generation of genocide and other collective violence.

Other instigators include real conflicts of interest, of varied kinds. These can be conflicts of vital interests, such as the need for living space, as between the Israelis and the Palestinians. However, these real conflicts are intractable because they have essential psychological and cultural components, such as attachment to a territory that is part of the self-definition of a group, or mistrust and fear of the other. Conflict between dominant groups and subordinate groups with little access to resources, power, or privilege, can also instigate violence.

In the latter instances as well, the issue of frustration of basic needs and psychological reactions to their frustration are important, so is the presence, almost invariably, of ideology. When subordinate groups demand more, they threaten not only privilege but also the feeling of security, identity, and worldview of dominant groups. They threaten the "legitimizing ideologies" (Sidanius, 1998) that such groups have long employed. When dominant groups engage in increasingly harsh acts to defend their dominance, one of the primary sources of genocide since World War II (Fein, 1993), they usually are guided by such ideologies.

The Evolution of Collective Violence

Great violence, and certainly group violence, usually evolves over time. Individuals and groups change as a result of their own actions. Acts that harm others, without restraining forces, bring about changes in perpetrators, other members of the group, and the whole system that makes further and more harmful acts probable. In the course of this evolution, the personality of individuals, social norms, institutions, and culture change in ways that make further and greater violence easier and more likely.

People justify their actions by blaming the victims. As their initial devaluation intensifies, they come to see their victims as less than human and to exclude them from the moral realm (Opotow, 1990; Staub, 1990). The usual moral principles and values that prohibit violence and protect people from being harmed become inapplicable to the victims. They are replaced by higher values derived from an ideology, such as protecting the purity, goodness, life, and well-being of one's own group and creating a better society or improving all of humanity by destroying the victims.

Progressively, the norms of the group change. Behavior toward the victims that would have been inconceivable becomes accepted and "normal." Institutions are changed or created to serve violence. The society is transformed. In the end, there may be a *reversal of morality*. Killing the victims becomes the right, moral thing to do. This has been advocated and has become accepted by at least some of the perpetrators, and often by many in the society, in many instances ranging from Nazi Germany to Rwanda (Gourevich, 1998). As violence evolves, it frequently expands to include other groups as victims.

Often, this process takes place over a long historical period. For example, in Turkey, Armenians were persecuted for a long time, with occasionally intense violence against them, long before the government that perpetrated the genocide came to power (Staub, 1989). At times, the process seems to unfold fast, but there are usually significant cultural and historical elements that prepare the ground. Past violence between groups and unhealed wounds in perpetrators may be especially likely to contribute to a speedy evolution, as they did in Bosnia. Intense propaganda by leaders and the creation of paramilitary groups also facilitate a speedy evolution to intense violence (Staub, 1999).

Cultural Preconditions

Evil is the outcome of normal psychological processes in groups (and individuals): the frustration of basic needs, scapegoating and ideologies that serve to fulfill these needs, harming others and the evolution that follows from this. This evolution normally has begun long before a group (or individual) engages in extreme,

persistently destructive acts. In the end, a society (or person) may become evil, in the sense that its characteristics make intensely harmful actions probable. Often, groups develop cultures and social institutions that are not themselves evil, but they create the preconditions or enhance the potential for the generation and speedy evolution of evil.

Cultural Devaluation

Perhaps the most important source of evil is the way the "other" is seen, or the devaluation of others. The devaluation of certain groups and their members often becomes part of a culture. Devaluation can vary in form and intensity (Staub, 1989). A milder form is not liking the other, seeing the other as lazy, unintelligent, and generally inferior. A more intense form—which often arises when a devalued group is relatively successful, such as the Jews in Germany, the Armenians in Turkey, or the Tutsis in Rwanda—is to see the other as manipulative, exploitative, dishonest, and generally morally deficient, characteristics that are claimed to have brought members of that group wrongful gains at the expense of the dominant group. This latter form of devaluation easily evolves into seeing the other as a threat to the survival of one's own group, as Hitler (1923/1943) saw the Jews, an especially intense form of devaluation.

The human tendency to differentiate between ingroup and outgroup, us and them, has been extensively demonstrated. The devaluation of a whole group arises out of this tendency. It has several origins (Staub, 1996b). One of them is social stratification: A subgroup of society has become poor or less privileged, which is justified by devaluation. The differentness of a group that may create discomfort or fear or may threaten identity is another source. A further source is exploitation of a group, which may result from prior devaluation but is then justified by further devaluation, as in the case of African Americans.

The need to create a separate identity is a further origin. This seems to have played a role in giving rise to Christian anti-Semitism (Staub, 1989) and may have played a role among Serbs, Croats, and Muslims in Yugoslavia. Difficult life conditions that require a scapegoat, the strengthening of identity and connection within a group through enmity, and real conflicts of interest all can lead to intense devaluation of another that becomes part of a group's culture.

A past history of conflict, antagonism, and violence between two groups can give rise to an especially intense form of devaluation, which I have called an *ideology of antagonism*. This is a perception of the other as an enemy and a group identity in which enmity to the other is an integral component. When an ideology of antagonism exists, anything good that happens to the other inflames hostility. The ideology makes the world seem a better place without the other.

Once devaluation becomes part of a culture, its literature, art, and media are perpetuated in social institutions, and, especially once it gives rise to discrimination or other institutionalized forms of antagonism, it becomes highly resistant to change. Even when its public expression is relatively quiescent for a period of time, as it was in the first decade of this century in Germany or during the Tito era in the former Yugoslavia, it often remains part of the deep structure of the culture and can reemerge when instigating conditions for violence are present.

Orientation to Authority

All societies foster some degree of respect for and obedience to authority. Without that, group life is impossible. However, when respect and unquestioning obedience are overemphasized, the potential for destructive social processes intensifies. Observation and research indicate that, in many cases of genocide or mass killing, the society has been characterized by strong respect for authority (Gourevich, 1998; Kressel, 1996; Staub, 1989).

Such an orientation to authority has at least three problematic consequences. First, when instigation to violence arises, such as difficult life conditions or group conflict, people who have relied on leaders for guidance and protection will find it more difficult to bear the threat, anxiety, and frustration of basic needs they experience. Second, when policies and practices are instituted in a group that harms others, people will be less willing to speak out to oppose the authorities and the rest of the group. As a result, the evolution is

less likely to stop. Third, such strong respect for authority makes obedience to immoral orders by authorities more likely.

Other Cultural Characteristics

There are several other predisposing cultural characteristics. One is a pluralistic rather than monolithic culture. Well-established democracies (Rummel, 1994; Staub, 1999) that are genuinely pluralistic are unlikely to engage in genocide. Pluralistic societies not only allow a broad range of beliefs and views but are likely to be more self-correcting. Societal self-concepts—both of superiority and of weakness or inferiority—are also important.

I recently suggested "unhealed wounds" in a society as an important predisposing characteristic. When a group has experienced great suffering, especially due to persecution and violence at the hand of others, and is therefore deeply wounded, it is more likely to respond to a renewed threat with violence. People who experience trauma are deeply affected (Janoff-Bulman, 1992; McCann & Pearlman, 1990). The resulting self-focus makes it difficult for them to consider the needs of others in case of conflict. Their feeling of insecurity in the world will make members of victimized groups see the world as a dangerous place and experience threat as more intense than it is. They are more likely to engage, therefore, in what they see as defensive aggression (Staub, 1998b).

Healing following victimization makes it less likely that a group turns against another and perpetrates violence. Others acknowledging the group's suffering, expressing caring and empathy, providing emotional and material support, all contribute to healing. The group engaging with its past experience, including certain kinds of memorials and rituals of mourning and remembrance, also can promote healing (Staub, 1998b).

Followers, Leaders, and the Elite

Milgram's (1974) research on and theorizing about obedience has implicated obedience as an important contributor to genocide. I suggested previously the wide-ranging implications of a group's orientation to authority on the evolution of genocidal processes, as well as the importance of direct obedience by perpetrators. Reports from Rwanda indicate that orders by authorities to kill had a powerful influence (Gourevich, 1998).

However, obedience is not a primary cause of genocide. The conception advanced here suggests that instigating conditions and cultural preconditions lead people to be open to, join, and even seek and create leadership that turns the group against others. It suggests that the inclinations of followers are extremely important in a genocidal process.

Still, except under the most extreme conditions, leaders and the elite in a society have some latitude in the direction they take. The political leadership and economic elite of a country, or a segment of them, frequently spearhead the evolution toward violence. They propagate a destructive ideology, intensify historical antagonisms, work to maintain differences in power and status, and create organizations that are potential instruments of violence. Paramilitary-type organizations, broadly defined, have become in many instances tools of collective violence in Rwanda, Argentina and other South American countries, Turkey, Germany, and elsewhere.

Such behavior by leaders frequently is interpreted as the desire to gain followers, to maintain power and influence with followers, or both. These can be and often are part of leaders' motives. However, leaders are also members of their groups and are affected by instigating conditions and culture. Their own basic needs are frustrated; they and their families have unhealed wounds. A more complex psychology of leaders is important both for understanding the origins and developing effective methods of preventing group violence.

Bystander Actions

The passivity of bystanders allows the continued evolution that ends in intense collective violence. Passivity by internal bystanders, by members of the population where the violence is occurring, and by external bystanders, outside groups, and nations, encourages perpetrators. Such passivity is common (Staub, 1989, 1993). External bystanders frequently continue commercial, cultural, and other relations with a country that engages in violence against an internal group, thereby expressing tacit acceptance. Often, some external bystanders actively support the perpetrator group. When instigators and predisposing cultural characteristics have existed but violence has remained limited in scope, as in South Africa, Israel, or Northern Ireland, usually bystanders have taken an active role (Cairns & Darby, 1998; Staub, 1999).

BYSTANDERS AS EVIL: THE EXAMPLE OF RWANDA

I return to the question of whether bystanders can be seen as evil and examine bystander actions in Rwanda and some complexities surrounding bystander behavior. The circumstances bystanders face in a situation such as Rwanda are different from those of witnesses who see in front of them a person who is in great distress and needs help (DesForges, 1999). Even then, circumstances are usually ambiguous: There is pluralistic ignorance, diffusion of responsibility, and the diffidence of many people to step forward (Latane & Darley, 1970; Staub, 1974). However, circumstances preceding collective violence are often more ambiguous. Perpetrators usually claim self-defense or other good reasons for what they do. When there is mob violence against a victim group, which often is instigated by authorities, participants and the authorities usually claim that it was the spontaneous response of the population to threat, danger, and violent actions by others.

In this spirit, perhaps, France sent troops to help the Rwandan government in 1990, when a small rebel group that called itself the Rwandan Patriotic Front (RPF) entered the country from Uganda. This group consisted primarily of Tutsi refugees who had lived in Uganda since they escaped earlier waves of violence against Tutsis, beginning in 1959. The French help temporarily stopped the RPF, but its activities intensified again after massacres of Tutsi peasants by Hutus, who make up about 85% of the population in Rwanda. France did not complain to the government about these massacres and continued to help militarily (Gourevich, 1998; Prunier, 1995). In 1993, the government and the RPF agreed, in the Arusha accords, to a multiparty government that would include the RPF. The accord prohibited the acquisition of more arms by the parties, but France continued to send arms to the government.

Bystanders often respond to events on the basis of a history of relationships they have had with the parties involved. They refrain from assessing and making decisions on the basis of actual events, moral principles, and human suffering. They either do not exercise prudence or good judgment, which the ancient Greeks regarded an essential element of morality (Staub, 1978), or they act on the basis of sentiments and what they regard as their interests. France may have acted as it did, in part, because of a friendship between President Mitterand of France and the President of Rwanda, Habyarimana. France also may have acted as it did because the RPF came from Uganda, which in the colonial era was ruled by England, and France feared that an Anglophile influence would spread into an area of Africa they considered their domain (Gourevich, 1998; Prunier, 1995).

However, France was not the only culprit. Information about impending violence and later about the ongoing genocide against Tutsis had come to the rest of the world from many quarters. Human Rights Watch issued alarming reports. The commanding general of the United Nations peacekeeping force, Major General Dallaire, received information from a person within the Rwandan president's circle of plans for a genocide against the Tutsis. He was not allowed to take action but was told by his superiors within the United Nations to communicate this information to President Habyarimana, whose circle prepared the plans for genocide (DesForges, 1999).

As the violence began in April 1994, some Belgian peacekeepers were killed. Belgium withdrew its contingent of peacekeepers, and the United Nations followed, withdrawing most of them. As the genocidal proportions of this violence emerged, General Dallaire claimed, and many now believe, that he could have stopped it all with 5,000 troops. However, no one was interested in such action. Within a few months as many as 800,000 people were killed (some estimate 1 million; see Gourevich, 1998), most of them Tutsis, but also more than 50,000 Hutus who were seen as politically "moderate" or who were

from the South in contrast to the group in power, which came from the Northwest. (For an application of the conception of the origins in genocide to Rwanda, see Staub, 1999.)

The United States was a passive bystander but also acted in ways that made a response by others less likely. The United Nations, other nations, and the United States resisted calling the violence genocide, so that the genocide convention, which requires or at least creates strong pressure for a response, would not be invoked. The United States resisted and slowed down a vote in the Security Council on sending back peacekeepers, even though U.S. troops were not required. The United States refused to provide equipment but insisted on leasing it to the United Nations. The United States and the United Nations haggled over the amount to be paid for the equipment, while every day many thousands of people were killed (Gourevich, 1998).

Does it make sense to call the passivity and at times complicity by bystander nations "evil" in the face of information about impending violence, and especially in the face of actual, very large-scale violence? The previous analysis suggests both that such passivity (and, of course, even more support or complicity) makes the evolution toward genocide more likely by encouraging and affirming perpetrators and that bystander nations have great potential influence in inhibiting this evolution. In addition, at times, the need for action is clear and there are low-cost ways to at least attempt to exert influence (see also Staub, 1989, 1996b, 1996c, 1999, 2000).

Passivity and various forms of support for perpetrators by outside nations contributes to extreme harm. Often, there is no provocation to justify even limited violence against the victims, much less genocide—or passivity in the face of it. The passivity and complicity often persist. In its physical properties, the situation is highly dissimilar from allowing a young child to drown while one is watching, but in its meaning, it is similar. Perhaps it is also like passively watching while someone is drowning the child, without even calling out to the person to stop. Although passivity is different from action, in terms of the definition of evil offered previously, the kind of passivity and complicity I discuss here is comparable in its effects to the actions that may be called evil. Even passivity in this case involved action—as torturous contortions by a spokeswoman for the U.S. State Department in avoiding the use of the term *genocide* in relation to Rwanda indicated, together with other actions to stop the international community from responding. Calling certain kinds of passivity and especially complicity evil might have influence on the behavior of nations, which is important for the prevention of future genocides.

Highly questionable actions on the part of international humanitarian organizations and the United Nations followed the genocide. The RPF defeated the government army and stopped the genocide. Elements of this army, together with paramilitary groups—the *interahamwe*—were the prime perpetrators of the genocide. These "genocidaires," together with huge numbers of Hutus—who either participated in the genocide, were pressured or forced by the genocidaires, or frightened by the propaganda about the Tutsis' murderous intentions—fled into neighboring countries. The 1.5 million to 2 million refugees lived in camps, the largest ones in Zaire, very near the Rwandan border. These camps were run by the former army and the *interahamwe*. They ruled over the refugees, stopped those who were so inclined from returning home, used the aid they received as a source of income, and bought large shipments of arms that were delivered to the camps. After awhile, they began incursions into Rwanda, killing many Tutsis and some Hutus who were regarded as sympathetic to Tutsis, and destroying and stealing property. The humanitarian organizations and international community did nothing to deal with this situation, allowing not only ongoing violence but the buildup of the capacity for continuing the genocide. Although some humanitarian organizations, aware of what was happening, pulled out, others immediately took their place.

Part of the problem seemed to be systemic. Humanitarian organizations have a mandate, which is to provide assistance. They do not ask why people need help or make policy judgments as to who should or should not receive help. Under these circumstances, a split self may develop, as in the hero of George Orwell's *1984* (1949) who opposes the totalitarian system and understands the absurdity of the government

declaring the friend of yesterday an enemy and the enemy of yesterday a friend, but nonetheless goes about his job with great enthusiasm, erasing written information about the past and replacing it with a false history that is consistent with current circumstance (Staub, 1989). However, part of the problem also may have been what Gourevich (1998) described as a well-known syndrome, "clientitis," the tendency by humanitarian organizations to see only, and be taken in by, the perspective of their client.

The reason for the United Nations and the international community to do nothing about the situation in the camps may have been similar to their usual reasons for inaction: a difficult situation, the absence of clear national interest to motivate action, and a disregard of the human costs of passivity. Besides, action was already taken—people in the camps were being helped. Perhaps there is also some truth to more sinister motives seen by Kegame, the vice president of Rwanda (Gourevich, 1998): Africans, like the Tutsi-led RPF, took events into their own hands, in Rwanda and in Zaire, without guidance and influence by the international community. Moreover, these actions defeated the aims of major international actors, particularly France, who supported the Hutu genocidaires until the very end.

Passivity was certainly not all due to blindness. In the first few months after the genocide, there was discussion within the United Nations of assembling an international force to disarm the "militants" in the camp and separate out from the rest of the refugees the criminal elements and the political forces planning a continuation of the genocide. However, in response to a request for volunteers by the United Nations Secretary-General, no country was willing to provide troops.

The Individual in Group Violence

I address, briefly, the question of the characteristics of participants in group violence at this point, rather than earlier, for two reasons. First, although past study of instances of group violence has provided substantial information of the roots of such violence, individual perpetrators have relatively rarely been studied. Second, the discussion of individual perpetrators relates to the next topic. However, this is not a simple relation: Group violence is a societal process, and some of those who are perpetrators of it would be unlikely to become violent as individuals.

In the conception I advanced, the personalities of people who, in the course of the evolution of group violence become perpetrators, are likely to be primarily the expression of the culture. They may carry the cultural characteristics identified previously, perhaps to a greater extent than the rest of the population. For example, members of the paramilitary group important in bringing the Nazis to power were probably about as anti-Semitic as the German people in general. However, those in leadership positions were intensely anti-Semitic (Merkl, 1980).

The limited evidence also indicates that perpetrators of the Holocaust (Steiner, 1980) and of torture in Greece (Haritos-Fatouros, 1988) were strongly authority-oriented (Staub, 1989). People who have developed strong respect for authority usually like to be part of a hierarchical system. They enjoy being led as well as having authority over others lower in the hierarchy. They prefer order and predictability. Their preference for and reliance on authority, hierarchy, and structure make social conditions under which effective leadership and the protective role of the leaders break down, and when uncertainty about the future and about how to deal with the present is great (Soeters, 1996), it makes it especially difficult for them.

People whose basic needs in childhood were frustrated to a greater extent also may be especially affected by social conditions and group conflict that frustrate basic needs. Individuals with personal wounds, or with hostility toward other people that is kept in check under normal conditions, or both, may be activated by conditions that instigate group violence. All such persons may find a clear and well-defined ideology and involvement with an ideological movement highly appealing. Perpetrators tend to show early ideological affinity with the violent groups they come to serve (Lifton, 1986).

Personality appears to be a source of selection of people by those in authority for perpetrator roles. It also seems to be a source of "self-selection," not initially for destroying others but for roles that later may become violent. Needs for identity and connection,

low self-esteem (as in the case of hate groups in the United States; Staub, 2000), the desire to find leaders, and the need for a clear-cut ideological vision, all may lead people to "join." However, once a group is formed, a system of *careerism*—the desire to advance in the system—can also enter (Steiner, 1980). To gain respect from like-minded others, to be a good member of the group, is probably also an important motivation.

Once they are part of an ideological-perpetrator group and participating in behavior that harms others, important changes seem to take place in people, including a progressive desensitization to others' suffering. This might develop into pleasure in harming others. The boundaries of the self are loosened and the usual internalized prohibitions and controls are lost, as in mobs (Staub & Rosenthal, 1994), but also progressively in individual conduct in relation to devalued others.

THE DEVELOPMENT OF AGGRESSION IN CHILDREN AND ADOLESCENTS

In discussing collective violence, I have focused on instigating conditions, already existing characteristics of the culture and psychological and social processes in the course of the evolution of increasing violence. In exploring the origins of aggression in youth and then commenting on an evolution toward evil, I start with socialization and experience that develops certain characteristics in children.

Neglect and harsh treatment are probably the primary source of aggression in children and youth (Coie & Dodge, 1997; Staub, 1996a, 1996b). When children are neglected and harshly treated, all their basic needs are frustrated. As a result, they come to fear, mistrust, and dislike people. At the least, these feelings easily arise in them in response to threat or the stresses of life (Staub, 1998a).

Children who are treated harshly also learn that aggression is normal, acceptable, or even right, rather than deplorable or unacceptable (Huesmann & Eron, 1984). In addition to experiencing aggression against themselves, they often see it among the adults in their lives, whether it is in their homes or the community around them. This further shows that the world is dangerous and people are hostile. It further models aggression as a way of dealing with conflict and acting in interpersonal situations.

Boys who grow up in such environments are also likely to watch a substantial amount of aggressive television, which provides information consistent with their already evolving understanding of the world and of how to behave in it (Eron, Walder, & Lefkowitz, 1971; Huesmann & Eron, 1984). The experiences of such boys limit opportunities for learning social skills (Weiss, Dodge, Bates, & Pettit, 1992), especially prosocial modes of connecting to and engaging with their peers (Friedrich & Stein, 1973).

Aggressive boys see other people as hostile, especially to themselves. They see others as intending to harm. For example, when they see pictures showing boys playing and one boy kicking another while trying to get the ball away from the him, they interpret this as intentional harmdoing (Coie & Dodge, 1997). Aggressive adults, both college students and prison inmates, also see other people as hostile (Galvin & Spielman, 1999). However, intentional rather than accidental harm caused by others is especially likely to provoke retaliatory aggression (Mallick & McCandless, 1966). Boys who are not aggressive assume that such acts are accidental. Some children who are badly treated, given their specific circumstances, may come to feel hostility and even hatred toward people. However, the need for connection to other people is profound, and even such children and the adults they grow into will desire and seek connection to some others.

Negative beliefs and hostility, as they come to be expressed in behavior, create a self-fulfilling prophecy. Reacting to others as if they had aggressed against us makes them respond aggressively. A group of unfamiliar boys, after spending a period of time with an aggressive boy, becomes aggressive toward him (Dodge, 1980). Our early experiences shape us, but we, in turn, tend to create circumstances that further develop our personalities in the same direction, a form of "self-socialization."

Both in youth and later in life, the characteristics such boys develop lead to expressively violent behavior, apart from any tendency for instrumental violence they may develop. Later in life, they also

aggress against their children (Huesmann, Eron, Lefkowitz, & Walder, 1984). It is estimated that about 30% of children who have received harsh physical punishment treat their children the same way, in contrast to 2% to 3% of physical abuse in the general population (Ziegler, Taussig, & Black, 1992).

Harsh treatment also leads to difficulty in liking and accepting oneself. As Freud has proposed, rather than seeing, examining, and accepting conflicting, problematic aspects of oneself, one projects them into other people. Alternatively, it becomes extremely important to affirm one's own value, relative to other people. Because in many parts of our society and in the world men are supposed to be strong and powerful, affirming one's value becomes showing that one is strong and powerful. Many men who have been imprisoned for violent crimes report that they used to pick fights either to feel good about themselves or to look good in others' eyes (Toch, 1969).

Self-Esteem and Aggression

How does this picture fit the recent evidence and debate on self-esteem and aggression in youth? Olweus (1979, 1993) found that bullies, who tend to pick on and repeatedly victimize other children, do not have low self-esteem. Coie and Dodge (1997), in reviewing research on aggression in children, reported that aggressive boys do not have low self-concepts and that they tend to blame others rather than themselves for "negative outcomes." Baumeister (1997) proposed that it is high self-esteem and injured narcissism that are associated with aggression.

However, the background and experience of boys I described make it unlikely that they have "genuinely" high self-esteem, as does further information I describe later. How might we understand the evidence, then? First, such boys, and later the men they become, may compensate for their sense of vulnerability and social and academic difficulties by proclaiming their own worth, thereby affirming themselves to others and even themselves. Related to such a compensatory self-esteem may be projection, seeing weakness, vulnerability, and various bad qualities in others, rather than themselves, and blaming others for negative outcomes.

Second, there may be important, alternative avenues in the development of aggression. One of these is permissiveness and lack of punishment for aggression. Another is an environment that may or may not be harsh and punitive but encourages aggression, so that children, youth, and the adults they grow into feel when they aggress that they are doing the right thing. In fact, although many aggressive children are ineffective, and although their aggressive behavior is disorganized, with limited self-control and easy flare-up of anger (Rausch, 1965), others are effective aggressors. Although the former are unpopular among their peers, among the latter, aggression is unrelated to popularity (Coie & Dodge, 1997).

A group of peers, for example, antisocial friends or members of a gang, may also help to maintain self-esteem. Often a seeming focus in such groups, and probably the most important function of the group for its members, is to help create and maintain positive identity and connection to like-minded others. Thus, members of such groups would have a heightened sense of self, at least while they are members.

Perhaps another important issue is not simply the level of self-esteem but what it is based on and how stable and reliable rather than how fragile it is. Many boys who become aggressive do not have the socially valued means to gain a positive image through competence and good performance in school and good relationships with peers. Therefore, they organize their self-esteem around strength, power, and physical superiority over others. Their early experiences as victims, the models of aggression around them, and the culture's focus on male strength and superiority all facilitate this. It is how self-esteem is constituted, what self-esteem is based on, that may matter. However, the self-esteem of aggressive boys and of aggressive men (Baumeister, 1997) appears to be very vulnerable and fragile. Its maintenance may require the continued feeling of and perhaps use of strength and power over others.

Thus, the level of self-esteem, how it is constituted, and its fragility and sources may all matter. As I have written elsewhere

In groups and in individuals very high self-evaluation often masks self-doubt. Persistent life difficulties may contradict the high self-evaluation and bring self-doubt to the surface. Even when there is no underlying self-doubt, a very high self-evaluation may be associated with limited concern for others. Among individuals, a moderately positive self concept is most strongly associated with sensitivity and responsiveness to other people. (Staub, 1989, p. 55; see also Jarymowitz, 1977; Reese, 1961)

People have to value themselves to value other people, but not value themselves so strongly that others do not matter.

"High self-esteem" for some people (but not for many others) may include a sense of superiority that must be defended. When it is frustrated, it is likely to lead to aggression. Low self-esteem may lead some people to affirm themselves in their own and others' eyes by aggression or to have a greater sense of insecurity in the world and feel that they must defend themselves. I have suggested that both "group self-concepts" of superiority and of weakness and vulnerability (and sometimes their combination) are cultural elements that may make genocide more likely (Staub, 1989).

However, in many instances of violence or with many actors, self-esteem may not have a primary role. Instead, orientations to people and the world—perceptions of hostility, valuing or devaluing people, and feelings of hostility—may have strong influence, even though the experiences that have affected these orientations also have had an impact on self-esteem.

The Evolution of Evil

I have implied and partially described an evolution of aggressive children. Such children and the adults they become see others as hostile, and many of them may come to feel hostile toward people. They develop a cognitive structure, internal dialogue, and behavioral skills (Meichenbaum, 1980) that move them to aggressive actions. The reactions they receive further shape them.

Given their limited social skills and aggressive behavior, they are often unpopular with their peers. However, they lack self-awareness. They do not know that they are unpopular. Nonaggressive kids who are unpopular tend to know this, which makes it more likely that they will change their behavior and become more popular over time (Zakriski, Jacobs, &

Coie, 1997). Aggressive boys often have academic difficulties as well. They are, on the whole, disconnected from peers and from school in general, a disconnection that seems to increase over time. Their aggressive behavior tends to deteriorate and become more intense (Coie & Dodge, 1997). All along, they tend to have a few other antisocial youth as associates. Over time, they may join a gang.

As a result of this evolution, some of them may come to engage in persistently aggressive behavior that creates great harm to others. They may become highly and predictably reactive in their aggression. Given such an evolution, it is reasonable to assume that some youth, as they grow into adults, develop the intention to harm others. Harming others may be a way for them to affirm their identity, to gain a feeling of security, to feel effective and in control, to develop and maintain connections with aggressive peers or associates, and to maintain the understanding of the world they have developed. In other words, they come to fulfill their basic needs in aggressive ways (Staub, 1998a).

Preventing Violence and Evil in Youth: The Case of Bullying

Warm, affectionate parenting, positive guidance, leading children and youth to learn caring and helping by engaging in such behavior, make the development of aggression unlikely and the development of caring about others' welfare probable (Eisenberg, 1992; Staub, 1979, 1996a). However, children who have had harsh, punitive experiences at home or other experiences that create aggression need not continue to develop in the direction they started. Research on resilience shows, for example, that significant human connections—to teachers, counselors, relatives outside the home, friends of the family (Butler, 1997) and, I believe, to peers as well (Staub, 1979, 1999)— can ameliorate the effects of negative experiences.

Schools can be important places for either allowing and furthering or preventing the evolution of violence. Substantial recent evidence indicates that there is a tremendous amount of bullying or repeated victimization of students in schools by physical or verbal means or by exclusion (Farrington, 1993;

Olweus 1993). Such victimization starts in the earliest school years. Some of the victims are themselves not aggressive. Others are aggressive; they also bully, although usually not those who have bullied them (Farrington, 1993).

Bullying contributes to the evolution of perpetrators into even more aggressive people. Although various characteristics of bullies as well as victims have been identified (Farrington, 1993; Olweus, 1993), bullying is not simply a matter of personality, but also of culture and system. Although not well explored as yet, the frequency of bullying differs by school and neighborhood. Variation in the "climate" of the classroom and school, the extent of guidance, and fairness in contrast to punitiveness contribute to school violence (Goldstein & Conoley, 1997) and are likely to contribute to bullying as well.

Teachers are frequently passive, as are peers, in the face of bullying. As with other forms of violence, this affirms perpetrators and must contribute to a feeling of insecurity and mistrust by victims. Bullying and aggression in school may be diminished by creating a community in the classroom that includes all students, a community in which students are participating members and in which respecting others is an important value and harming others is not accepted (Staub, 1999).

Bullying may help us further examine the meaning of the concept of evil. Extensive bullying creates significant harm. In recent years, I have been asking students to write about their personal experiences in relation to theory and research they read and discuss in my classes. The most frequent topic is the experience and painful effects of taunting, exclusion, and being picked on. Although some children and youth who bully may realize how much pain they create, many probably do not. Their motivation may be to get something from the other person, to look good in front of others, to create an alliance with others to feel powerful, or to respond to a differentness in another child that makes them uncomfortable. However, even though they lack awareness, their repeated actions, usually without provocation, create severe psychological pain, with long-term effects. If we are to use the concept, the identification of actions as evil cannot depend on the intentions or motivation of the actors.

Sexual Abuse in the Home: Revisiting Personality and System

A parent or parent substitute sexually engaging the child may be seen as evil, even if there is no physical force or overt intimidation. A child cannot freely give or withdraw consent. Engaging sexually with a child is a form of abuse that involves breaking a moral barrier and, in a large percentage of cases, creates significant long-term harm (McCann & Pearlman, 1990).

I analyze the influences that lead to such behavior with one type of perpetrator I call *needy–dependent* (Staub, 1991). The purpose of this analysis is to clarify further the origins of violence, to show how personality and system join in leading to the destructive fulfillment of basic needs. The analysis that follows is an application of the approach presented for group violence to a form of individual violence.

Gelinas (1983) described the kind of perpetrator I focus on here as a person who has difficulty acting in the world and taking care of his needs. Such a person meets a woman who was a "parentified child," someone who was put into the role of a caretaker of parents and siblings in her family of origin. As a good caretaker, she is good at responding to the needs of this man. They marry and have children. However, at some point, her long history of taking care of others catches up with her. She begins to withdraw. She may become ill or find other ways to pull back from physical and emotional caretaking of her family. She also pulls back from her sexual relationship with her husband. A daughter progressively becomes the parentified child in this family, assuming the burdens of physical as well as emotional caretaking.

In the course of this, warmth and affection may grow between the father and this daughter. They may watch television or do other things together. The father does not have the personal strength and skills needed to take action and satisfy his needs for connection or to feel worthwhile and significant and fulfill other emotional and sexual needs in legitimate ways. Instead, he breaks the moral barrier and sexually engages his daughter. The withdrawal and passivity of his wife also means that she is likely to remain passive as a bystander.

In the case of such a needy–dependent perpetrator, the family system as it interacts with personality

is very important. In contrast, there is another type of perpetrator in which personality seems to have primary importance. He treats his family as his property, as chattel. His sexual abuse of his children is one expression of his personality and orientation to his family (Staub, 1991).

Sexually abusing fathers often rationalize and justify their actions. Therapists report absurd claims, such as having sexually engaged a daughter to protect her from the sexual dangers of the outside world (Staub, 1991).

CONCLUSIONS

Even evil actions by individuals are often the joint outcome of culture, whether of the society or a family; of a system of relationships among individuals including the passivity or encouragement of bystanders; of specific or nonspecific (systemic) instigators; and of the personality of perpetrators. Culture, social conditions, and how the system functions are more important in the case of group violence. Attention to the levels of influence, of predisposing conditions, instigators, and personality, are essential both to understand and prevent such violence, whether we call it evil or not.

Considering both individuals and collections of individuals, evil is usually the end result of an evolution. This is not necessarily a smooth, continuous evolution. It can progress to a point, halt, and then evolve further. Depending on where the evolution has progressed, individuals or groups may respond to "instigation" with intense violence. Alternatively, once the evolution has been set into motion, it may continue and lead to intense violence without further instigation.

Evil actions may serve the satisfaction of basic, profound, human needs that have an imperative character. When such needs are frustrated in the life of individuals and groups, destructive modes of need satisfaction are likely to develop. The nature of the individual or of the culture and social system of a group may lead to a heightened probability of violence by them. At the extreme, such individuals and groups also may develop the intention to harm or destroy others that habitually expresses itself in action. The absence of consideration for others' welfare also allows intense instrumental violence as well as wanton, seemingly motiveless violence. Further research and theory are needed on these developed forms of evil.

REFERENCES

Baumeister, R. F. (1997). *Evil: Inside human violence and cruelty.* New York: Freeman.

Latané, B., & Darley, J. (1970). *The unresponsive bystander: Why doesn't he help?* New York: Appleton-Century-Crofts.

Lifton, R. J. (1986). *The Nazi doctors: Medical killing and the psychology of genocide.* New York: Basic Books.

Milgram, S. (1974). *Obedience to authority: An experimental view.* New York: Harper & Row.

Staub, E. (1989). *The roots of evil: The origins of genocide and other group violence.* New York: Cambridge University Press.

Staub, E. (1993). The psychology of bystanders, perpetrators and heroic helpers. *International Journal of Intercultural Relations, 17,* 315–341.

Steiner, J. M. (1980). The SS yesterday and today: A sociopsychological view. In J. Dimsdale (Ed.), *Survivors, victims and perpetrators: Essays on the Nazi Holocaust* (pp. 405–457). Washington, DC: Hemisphere.

Questions to Think About

1. What social conditions in present-day society might encourage violence and evil? How might our society change, so as to reduce violence?

2. Consider some of the roots of evil that Staub talks about in this article. How can family, peers, and society in general create an "evil" individual?

3. Staub goes into detail about the development of aggression in children, particularly boys. How should we change the way boys are raised?

4. What does Staub mean by a needy–dependent perpetrator? What kind of people fall into this category? What personality characteristics do people of this category have? How do they acquire these personality characteristics?

48

Birth Cohort Changes in Extraversion:
A Cross-Temporal Meta-Analysis, 1966–1993

JEAN M. TWENGE

Jean Twenge is a psychology professor at San Diego State University. She has done research in the areas of gender roles, effects of social rejection, and birth cohort differences. This selection combines her methodological interest in meta-analysis (a statistical technique for combining the results of many separate studies) with her interest in birth cohort changes (differences between groups born at different times, such as Baby Boomers and Generation Y). Developments over the last several years in techniques for meta-analysis have enabled many new questions to be answered by looking at existing data sets—questions that might not have been thought of at the time the data were originally collected.

1. INTRODUCTION

Many personality measures still popular today were written in the late 1960s and early 1970s. Yet a vast amount of social change has occurred since this time, change that may have affected personality traits and/or self-reports of these traits (Baltes & Nesselroade, 1972; Duncan & Agronick, 1995; Dyer, 1987; Twenge, 1997a; Woodruff & Birren, 1972). This paper uses meta-analytic techniques to investigate birth cohort differences in one of the most-studied personality traits (extraversion) as measured by two of the most popular personality inventories [the Eysenck Personality Inventory (Eysenck & Eysenck, 1968) and the Eysenck Personality Questionnaire (Eysenck & Eysenck, 1975)]. In short, have college students' self-reports of extraversion changed over time? Is birth cohort (as a proxy for the larger sociocultural environment) a significant influence on the personality trait of extraversion?

These questions are important for both theoretical and practical reasons. First, change over time (here

referred to as birth cohort differences) provides a unique view of the effects of the larger sociocultural environment—a possible "third influence" on personality beyond genetics and family environment. A large body of research has convincingly established that genetics account for about 40 to 50% of the variance in extraversion, and family environment only about 5% (Bergeman, Plomin, McClearn, Pedersen & Friberg, 1988; Langinvaionio, Kaprio, Koskenvuo & Lonngvist, 1984; Loehlin, 1989, 1992; Rowe, 1990; Shields, 1962). If genetics explain about 45% of the variance in extraversion, and family environment about 5%, that still leaves 50% of the variance unexplained. It is difficult (as well as distressing) to believe that half of the variance in personality is error variance. Yet little research has explored possible third influences on personality such as the environment outside the family (including birth cohort effects).

This is partially due to the particular assumptions made by this type of research; as Eysenck and

---

Source: Twenge, J. M. (2001). Birth cohort changes in extraversion: a cross-temporal meta-analysis, 1966–1993. *Personality and Individual Difference, 30,* 735–748. Reprinted with permission from Elsevier.

Editor's note: All citations in the text of this selection have been left intact from the original, but the list of references includes only those sources that are the most relevant and important. Readers wishing to follow any of the other citations can find the full references in the original work or in an online database.

Eysenck (1985) point out, heritability is a population statistic, one that does not apply to other cultures and other times (p. 90). In addition, birth cohort is necessarily equivalent in twins (either fraternal or identical); thus twin studies effectively control for birth cohort. This means that birth cohort does not confound the results of twin studies, but it also means that it cannot be studied as a source of variance in personality in these studies. Given how birth cohort has been ignored, it is not surprising that, in a review of personality research, Matthews and Deary (1998) discuss only two types of environmental influences: "those shared by family members and those unique to the individual" (p. 106). Such statements are true only if we consider genetics and family or individual environment to be the *only* two variables influencing personality. However, each birth cohort (or, to take a broader view, each generation) effectively grows up in a different society; these societies vary in their social relationships, attitudes, environmental threats, complexity, and in many other ways (Caspi, 1987; Elder, 1981a; Mannheim, 1952; Ryder, 1965; Stewart and Healy, 1989; Strauss & Howe, 1991). Although it is also possible for the genetic makeup of a population to change across time, most researchers agree that such an evolution is unlikely to occur over time spans of only 20 or 30 years (Klerman & Weissman, 1989).

Investigating change over time in self-reports of extraversion is also important for methodological and practical reasons. Many researchers compare the mean scores of their samples to means from original test manuals; in many cases, they are comparing subjects who may differ in birth year by 30 years or more. Although newer measures avoid this problem, older versions of measures, including the Eysenck scales, are still very popular (and rightly so, because their longevity demonstrates their dependability and usefulness). In addition, any linear trends observed in one scale are likely to affect every scale eventually, regardless of its age. Thus if any changes occur, this paper will provide estimates of the likely norms for a given year and how much they must be adjusted. This analysis will focus on American college students.

Addressing the question of changes in extraversion requires two theoretical discussions: one, theories of change over time (i.e., birth cohort differences) in general, and two, environmental influences on

extraversion in general. The first helps explain why we would expect any personality trait to differ between birth cohorts; the second provides reasons for the mechanisms behind any changes in extraversion specifically.

1.1.   Birth Cohort and Change over Time

Many theorists and researchers have noted the influence of historical change on individuals (Caspi, 1987; Elder, 1981a; Gergen, 1973; Kertzer, 1983; Lambert, 1972; Nesselroade & Baltes, 1974; Ryder, 1965; Schaie, 1965; Sloan, 1996; Stewart & Healy, 1989; Woodruff & Birren, 1972). This influence occurs not just by living through a certain historical era, but by experiencing it at a certain age; the same event or environment means different things to individuals of different ages (Elder, 1979, 1981a, 1981b; Mannheim, 1952; Ryder, 1965; Stewart & Healy, 1989). The existence of many such birth cohort effects has led some authors to describe American society as shaped by a succession of distinctive generations, each characterized by its common experiences and ethos (Holtz, 1995; Howe & Strauss, 1993; Jones, 1980; Ryder, 1965; Strauss & Howe, 1991). These differences are not merely perceived ones. Previous empirical studies have found strong cohort effects on a number of personality, attitude, psychopathology, and life outcome variables (Duncan & Agronick, 1995; Dyer, 1987; Klerman & Weissman, 1989; Lewinsohn, Rohde, Seeley & Fischer, 1993; Sherman & Spence, 1997; Stewart & Healy, 1989; Twenge, 1997a,b; Woodruff & Birren, 1972). As Gergen (1973) noted, conceptions and levels of personality traits are likely to change over time, and researchers must be aware of these changes or risk invalid results.

As discussed above, however, birth cohort differences have not been studied extensively, despite critiques of psychological research for being ahistorical (Elder, 1981a; Caspi, 1987). In fact, as two examples will illustrate, birth cohort has often been ignored completely even when it might be influential. First, a striking paradox can be found in the literature on personality traits: longitudinal studies have often found remarkable consistency in personality traits as people age (Conley, 1984; Costa & McCrae, 1988; Costa, McCrae & Arenberg, 1980; Finn, 1986; Kelly, 1955), while cross-sectional studies purporting to measure age differences have often showed large effects (Bendig, 1960; Calden & Hokanson, 1959; Costa et al., 1986; Eysenck & Eysenck, 1969, 1975; Gutman, 1966). Cohort differences may partially explain this contradiction: in a cross-sectional study, the individuals of different ages also belong to different birth cohorts (Baltes & Nesselroade, 1972; Buss, 1974; Nesselroade & Baltes, 1974; Schaie, 1965; Woodruff & Birren, 1972). Thus at least some of the conflict between the results of longitudinal and cross-sectional studies may be explained by birth cohort differences in personality traits. The contradiction between these studies suggests that birth cohort differences in personality are widespread.

Second, as noted above, many researchers examining the origins of personality have concentrated on genetic and individual or family environment effects, without examining or acknowledging cohort or larger environment influences (Bergeman et al., 1988; Bouchard, 1994; Loehlin, 1989, 1992; Pedersen, Plomin, McClearn & Fridberg, 1988; Shields, 1962). Given that many researchers have found the effects of family environment to be very small (Loehlin, 1992; Rowe, 1990) or even negative (Shields, 1962), birth cohort (as a proxy for the larger sociocultural environment) should be considered as an additional environmental influence.

1.2. Influences on Extraversion Affected by Birth Cohort

Western societies have undergone many changes between the 1960s and the 1990s. Many of these changes can be described as a decrease in social capital or social integration, and an increase in individualism (Fukuyama, 1999). Most important for changes in extraversion are the following: mobility increased, day care became more common, parenting was less rule-bound, and the economy increasingly moved toward service and away from industry. These changes most likely affected levels of extraversion. Increased family mobility (Packard, 1972; Whyte, 1956) may have increased extraversion in children and adolescents who had to learn how to interact with more and different people. Day care may have had much the

same effect. In addition, philosophies of child-rearing changed; in general, child-raising became progressively more permissive, allowing children to speak their minds, in contrast to the earlier doctrine of being "seen and not heard" (McCrae & Costa, 1990; Ehrenreich & English, 1978, p. 215). This change most likely encouraged extraversion in children. In fact, Bergeman et al. (1988) showed that low controlling family environments led to higher EPI extraversion scores in a sample of twins.

Shifts in the economic structure may also be important. For example, Whyte (1956) argues that Baby Boom children (who would become the college students of the late 1960s, 1970s, and early 1980s) were actively encouraged to be outgoing and extraverted by their teachers and parents, perhaps in an effort to prepare them for the new, service-oriented economy. During the second half of the century, schools increasingly emphasized group work and social skills, recognizing that there are few jobs in the new economy that do not involve dealing with people. Sloan (1996) theorizes that extraverts are better adapted to contemporary society; "an active, extroverted, gregarious temperament," he writes, tends to "incline a person towards the exciting pace of modern lifestyles" (p. 30).

In addition, the role of women has changed tremendously over the time period in question; women are more likely to work than in previous decades, and they are more likely to obtain professional degrees. Extraversion is often considered to be similar to assertiveness, dominance, or surgency, and is highly correlated with these traits (Costa & McCrae, 1992; John, 1990). Previous evidence suggests that women have increased in self-reports of these traits, most likely in response to their role changes (Twenge, 1997a). Thus women's self-reports of extraversion are likely to increase along with assertiveness. These changes and those described previously suggest that extraversion will increase between the late 1960s and early 1990s.

1.3. Previous Empirical Evidence

As noted previously, very little research has examined birth cohort differences. However, the research that exists corroborates the cultural influences that predict increases in extraversion over time. Baltes and Nesselroade (1972) studied students in an American high school between 1970 and 1972; they found that the younger birth cohorts (even though they differed by only a few years) scored higher on the extraversion scale of the High School Personality Questionnaire. Following the students longitudinally as well, they found that this was true even when the cohorts were tested at the same age. Dyer (1987) examined two samples of incoming college students on the California Psychological Inventory (CPI) sociability scale: one collected in 1970 and the other in 1980. He found that the 1980 cohort scored higher on sociability, a trait with similarities to EPI and EPQ extraversion. The changes in women's roles may also have produced increases in extraversion; O'Connell (1980) found that housewives scored significantly lower than employed women on the CPI sociability scale.

Cross-sectional studies of personality traits may also suggest changes in extraversion. These studies (Bendig, 1960; Calden & Hokanson, 1959; Costa et al., 1986; Eysenck & Eysenck, 1969, 1975; Gutman, 1966) consistently showed that younger age groups were more extraverted. Although some of these differences may of course be due to age, the usual consistency of personality found in longitudinal studies suggests that at least some of it is due to birth cohort. Unless there are negative interactions occurring, these cross-sectional studies also indicate that extraversion should increase progressively with birth year. Overall, the few previous studies suggest that extraversion should increase over the time period studied here.

1.4. Overview and Hypotheses

This paper uses meta-analytic techniques to examine birth cohort differences in extraversion on the EPI and EPQ. Because few individual studies include samples collected at different times, birth cohort differences must be analyzed across (rather than within) studies, comparing the mean scores across studies from different years. Thus this study differs from most meta-analyses: it will not report a mean d for all studies, but instead the relationship between mean scores on personality trait scales and the year of measurement. I have used this cross-temporal meta-analysis method

in three previous studies (Twenge, 1997a,b; Twenge & Campbell, 2000). This method requires a somewhat restricted sample to ensure that the results are not confounded by other variables. First, any time-lag analysis (like this one) must sample one age group to investigate birth cohort differences; here, I studied college students because they are the most common subjects in psychological research. Second, the study needed to be limited to one country, since changes in the sociocultural environment over time will necessarily differ between countries, as will mean scores (Jamison, 1984). I limited the data collection to samples collected in the United States because there were a large number of samples collected there and the culture was best understood by the researcher.

The cultural influences and empirical evidence discussed above all suggest that extraversion scores should increase over the time period. Thus it was expected that mean scores on both measures of extraversion should demonstrate positive correlations with the year the data were collected. The analyses will show a linear upward trend in scores, with significant change from the late 1960s to the early 1990s.

2. METHOD

2.1. Locating Studies

The search technique attempted to locate all studies that administered the EPI or EPQ to samples of American college students. The primary source of studies was the Social Sciences Citation Index (SSCI), which provides a list of all studies that cite certain articles. I searched this database for studies citing the sources for the EPI and EPQ (Eysenck & Eysenck, 1968, 1975, 1985). In addition, I searched PsycInfo using the keywords "Eysenck Personality Inventory" and "Eysenck Personality Questionnaire."

As a major source of unpublished data, I relied on Dissertation Abstracts, which catalogs master's theses and dissertations from 1861 to the present. I searched this database using the same keywords used for PsycInfo. Because Dissertation Abstracts does not include abstracts before 1979, many fewer dissertations appeared in the scale keyword searches before this time. To supplement the number of dissertations before 1979, I searched the University of Michigan library database for Michigan dissertations using the keywords extraversion, extroversion, and personality.

2.2.   Inclusion Rules

Possible studies for the analysis were included or excluded based on specific inclusion rules. To be included in the analysis, a study had to meet the following criteria: (1) participants were undergraduates at conventional four-year institutions; (2) participants were attending college in the United States; (3) the study included at least 20 male or 20 female participants; (4) participants were not clients at a counseling center or any other group singled out for being maladjusted; (5) means were reported for unselected groups of students, not groups that were extremely high or extremely low on a measure; and (6) means were broken down by sex.

A large number of studies did not provide means for the personality measures they used; most studies excluded were eliminated for not including means rather than for violating any other criterion. The breakdown of means by sex was important given possible sex differences in extraversion and the changing numbers of women in psychology samples. In addition, the direction and magnitude of any personality change may differ for men and women. Thus simply controlling for the number of women in the sample might not illustrate the true nature of the personality change. Those studies meeting the requirements were recorded for the analysis. Unless another date was mentioned in the article, year of data collection was coded as two years prior to publication, a common technique (Oliver & Hyde, 1993).

These data collection and inclusion strategies yielded 59 studies that administered the EPI and EPQ (a list of the studies included in the meta-analysis is available from the author). In total, these studies included 16,846 college students (8903 women and 7943 men).

2.3.   Control Variables and Limitations

It is possible that samples may differ in region and type of college in a way that confounds with year. These two variables were recorded for each datapoint when available. Region was coded as East, Midwest, South, or West according to the US Census designations, and three dummy variables were used for the regression analyses. Type of college was coded as public or private according to a list of US colleges and universities and thus formed a single dichotomous variable. Most studies did not report information on the racial or socioeconomic status composition of their samples; thus it was not possible to use these variables as controls.

Another possible limitation was changes in the American college population over the time period studied here. One measure of this might be the median income of college students' parents; this statistic was available beginning in 1966 (Dey, Astin & Korn, 1992). This survey found that the median income did not change very much over this time period when adjusted for inflation. At least in terms of income, it appears that the socioeconomic status of American college students did not vary much since the mid-1960s. As for the racial composition of college samples, this did not change very much either (US Bureau of the Census, 1998). The percentage of American college students who are black did not change from 1970 to 1993 (at both times it was 10%). The percentage of Asian and Hispanic students did changed only slightly: Asians increased from 2 to 5%, and Hispanics increased from 5 to 7%. Thus any change in scores probably cannot be traced to changing racial composition.

One statistic that has changed more is the number of people going to college. However, this change was not linear during the time period in question (US Bureau of the Census, 1998). In 1967, the percentage of high school graduates enrolled in college was 53%; this declined during the 1970s and did not consistently stay above 53% again until 1984. After that time enrollment increased, reaching 62% in 1993. The small size of this change (9%) and its non-linear nature suggested that it was not likely to be a strong influence on extraversion scores. In addition, because the median family income of students has not changed, it is unclear what effects higher college enrollment would have on extraversion scores.

3.   RESULTS

Have American college students' self-reports of extraversion changed over time? As shown in Table 1 and

TABLE 1 Weighted Least Squares Regressions between Year of Scale Administration and American College Students' Extraversion Scores, 1966–1993[a]

	Men's Extraversion		Women's Extraversion	
	WITHOUT CONTROLS	**WITH CONTROLS**	**WITHOUT CONTROLS**	**WITH CONTROLS**
Eysenck Personality Inventory Extraversion	0.75*** (28)	0.72*** (28)	0.65** (27)	0.71*** (27)
Eysenck Personality Questionnaire Extraversion	0.65*** (26)	0.66*** (26)	0.65*** (23)	0.53*** (23)
Z-scored composite	0.76*** (54)	0.78*** (54)	0.71*** (50)	0.68*** (50)

[a]n of groups is shown in parentheses. ** = $P < 0.01$, *** = $P < 0.001$.

Figures 1 and 2, men's and women's scores on the EPI and EPQ extraversion scales were positively correlated with the year they completed the measure. The correlations without controls represent weighted, bivariate least squares regressions weighted by sample size; thus the larger samples, which are better estimates of the population mean, are given more weight in the regression. This statistic differs from simple bivariate correlations only in the weighting by n. Regressions including the control variables for region and type of college produced only small changes in the correlation between year and extraversion scores; the largest

change between controlled and non-controlled correlations was for women's EPQ extraversion scores (Table 1).

To combine the results for both measures, means for the EPI and EPQ were converted to Z-scores within each measure. I then computed the regressions between these scores and year. These analyses again showed positive and very strong correlations between year and extraversion scores (Table 1, Figures 1 and 2).

Extraversion scores increased in a very linear manner, with all correlations 0.53 or over, and all but

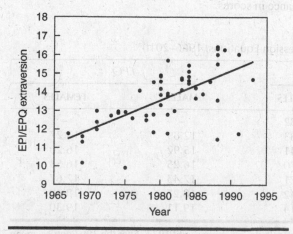

FIGURE 1   Men's EPI/EPQ extraversion scores over time

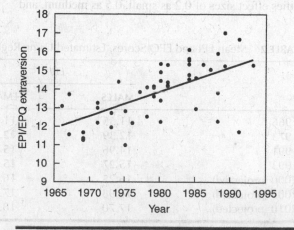

FIGURE 2   Women's EPI/EPQ extraversion scores over time

one 0.65 or over. Thus birth cohort (here, year of data collection in a sample of like-aged subjects) explained between 28 and 61% of the variance in extraversion means. However, this estimate of the variance is based on group means rather than individual scores, so it is necessarily an overestimate. If every individual in each study were a datapoint (rather than the mean for each study), there would be greater spread around the regression line, a lower correlation, and thus a lower percentage of variance explained.

Thus it is necessary to examine the magnitude of the birth cohort effect: that is, how much the mean extraversion score changed over the years. To measure the magnitude of the change, I used the weighted regression equations to calculate the average score for each measure by sex for various years (Table 2; these means differ slightly from the figures because the figures are based on regressions unweighted for sample size). The first datapoint for the EPI was collected in 1966 and the last in 1991. Using the average SD for the EPI (obtained from the studies that reported it; see Table 2), I calculated the change in EPI scores from 1966 to 1991 in terms of SDs (sometimes called d, or an effect size). According to these calculations, men's extraversion scores increased 0.94 SDs, and women's have increased 0.97 SDs. The first and last datapoints for the EPQ were collected in 1973 and 1993; men's extraversion scores increased 0.80 SDs over this time, and women's increased 0.79 SDs. Cohen (1977) classifies effect sizes of 0.2 as small, 0.5 as medium, and 0.8 as large; the effect sizes here, ranging from 0.79 to 0.97, are thus large effect sizes. If these effect sizes are converted to r and then to the percentage of variance explained, birth cohort explains between 14 and 19% of the variance in extraversion scores over this time period. (Clearly, the longer the time period, the greater the effect size attributable to birth cohort; thus the percentage of variance explained must be calculated for a specific period of time only—for example, 20 or 30 years).

The regression equation also allowed the prediction of scores for present and future years if extraversion continues to increase in a linear manner, with the regression line at about the same slope (a debatable point). If we make this assumption, the mean scores for the EPI and EPQ will rise about 0.65 SDs more by 2010, a total of around 1.55 SDs over four decades.

4. DISCUSSION

This cross-temporal meta-analysis demonstrates a large birth cohort effect for extraversion among American college students. This effect holds for both the EPI and EPQ, for both men and women, and for analyses including controls for region and type of college. Extraversion scores shift between 0.79 and 0.97 SDs from the late 1960s/early 1970s to the early 1990s, explaining between 14 and 19% of the variance in scores.

TABLE 2 Mean EPI and EPQ Scores, Estimated Using Regression Equations, 1966–2010[a]

	EPI		EPQ	
	MALES	**FEMALES**	**MALES**	**FEMALES**
1966	11.36	11.82	–	–
1973	12.39	12.83	12.89	13.27
1991	14.96	15.41	15.92	16.20
1993	15.27	15.70	16.25	16.53
2000 (projected)	16.25	16.71	17.43	17.67
2005 (projected)	16.98	17.42	18.27	18.48
2010 (projected)	17.70	18.14	19.11	19.30

[a]EPQ scores are not estimated for 1966 because datapoints for this scale do not appear until 1973. After the 1993 entries, mean scores are projections. The SDs, obtained from the weighted average of studies in the analysis, were: EPI males = 3.85, EPI females = 3.70, EPQ males = 4.21, and EPQ females = 4.14.

As noted in the Introduction, this time period witnessed large changes in the larger sociocultural environment. During this time, mobility and day care increased encounters with strangers and casual acquaintances, parenting became more permissive, and the economy shifted toward service rather than industry. All of these changes could plausibly lead to an increase in extraversion, thus demonstrating the effect of the larger sociocultural environment on personality—a third influence outside genetics and family environment. If these trends continue (and every indication is that they have), then extraversion should continue to rise. However, it is also possible that these environmental changes have already exacted all of their change on extraversion. If this is the case and the ceiling of their effect has been reached, extraversion scores could plateau during the late 1990s and early 2000s.

One alternative explanation for these results lies in measurement; the EPI and EPQ are both self-report measures. Thus change over time on the scales could reflect either true shifts in extraversion or the respondents' willingness to describe themselves as more extraverted, perhaps due to changes in the social desirability of extraversion (Edwards, 1957). Johnson (1981) presents some indirect evidence to suggest that self-presentation (the way we would like to appear to others) may be more accurate in describing respondents' answers on self-report personality measures. Thus men and women completing personality measures may be influenced by self-presentation demands. This possibility is more difficult to test. However, correlations between EPQ and EPQ-R extraversion and the measures' Lie scales are generally low (Eysenck & Eysenck, 1975, 1994). Thus it is unlikely that socially desirable responding is responsible for the changes in extraversion scores. However, *both* interpretations suggest that social change occurred. Whether college students really are more extraverted, or they feel they need to present themselves as more extraverted, both represent change in the environment. In addition, it is unlikely that any gap between reported extraversion and "actual" extraversion would stay that way for long. The experienced self will likely change to meet the expressed self (Tice, 1994). In other words, if the individuals examined in this research repeatedly presented themselves as more extraverted, they would eventually act more extraverted. Furthermore, personality psychologists rely heavily on self-report measures of personality; if these are changing in important ways, it seems wise to recognize the change.

Another alternative explanation might be that samples of college students have changed over the years in characteristics other than birth cohort. As discussed in the methods section, the median family income of American college students has not changed over this time (Dey et al., 1992), and the racial composition of college students has not changed very much (and in fact African-Americans, the largest minority, have not changed in enrollment at all). More high school graduates do attend college, but this change is relatively small (9 percentage points) and has not been linear. The change in extraversion scores has been extremely linear, and it seems unlikely that the small uptick in enrollment would cause a shift of one SD.

The necessity of limiting studies to one age group led to the choice of college students, who are not a random sample of the population. Thus the respondents in the studies gathered here are more likely to be white and from higher socioeconomic backgrounds. These similarities may have increased the percentage of variance explained by birth cohort. However, although these samples may come from a somewhat restricted range of socioeconomic status and family background, there is no evidence to suggest that they come from a restricted range for genetic influences on extraversion. This is important because previous research suggests that genetics seem to be a much stronger influence on personality than family environment (Bergeman et al., 1988; Langinvaionio et al., 1984; Loehlin, 1992; Rowe, 1990; Shields, 1962); thus socioeconomic status is unlikely to affect extraversion scores. The limitation of the samples to Americans also means that only one country was studied; other countries might have undergone changes over this time as well. Future research should determine if other countries also showed changes in extraversion over the same time.

However, this analysis also has clear strengths. First, the data used here represent respondents' concurrent self-reports of their personality traits. Unlike studies of changes in depression rates (Klerman & Weissman, 1989; Lewinsohn et al., 1993) this study does not depend on unreliable retrospective accounts. Second, the increase in extraversion replicated across both measures and in samples of men and women. Last, as a meta-analysis the study incorporates a large number of respondents. The sample of studies also included both published and unpublished datapoints, one guard against bias in meta-analysis.

5.   IMPLICATIONS AND CONCLUSIONS

This study has meaningful implications for several areas of psychology. First, it provides evidence of a previously ignored "third influence" on personality: birth cohort, as a proxy for the larger sociocultural environment. In their review of research on the origins of personality, Matthews and Deary (1998) note that "with so much good evidence for broad heritability effects, the onus is on environmentalists to make clear hypotheses about the effects of specific environmental factors on personality and test them" (p. 120). This meta-analysis tests a broader (rather than specific) environmental effect, but it does provide strong evidence for the influence of a specific ascribed variable (birth cohort) that has clear environmental links.

Second, it is now very clear that cross-sectional studies hopelessly confound age and cohort differences, and that this confounding has serious consequences. Several authors have made such points before (Nesselroade & Baltes, 1974; Woodruff & Birren, 1972), but many researchers have continued to interpret cross-sectional differences as age differences. The results help resolve the contradiction between the large age differences found in these cross-sectional studies (Bendig, 1960; Costa et al., 1986; Eysenck & Eysenck, 1969, 1975; Gutman, 1966) compared to the apparent stability of personality traits over the life course in most longitudinal studies (Conley, 1984; Costa & McCrae, 1988; Costa et al., 1980; Finn, 1986; Kelly, 1955). These two results can be reconciled by realizing that birth cohorts may differ markedly in their responses to personality inventories.

Next, the striking cohort differences found here verify the theories of authors such as Gergen (1973), Caspi (1987), and Stewart and Healy (1989): the historical era and social context have a strong influence on the psychology of individuals. As these and other authors (Elder, 1981a) note, however, few psychologists consider historical and cohort effects in their research and theorizing. As a result, many psychological studies conducted at a particular time are assumed to apply to all times and social contexts (Gergen, 1973). The existence of strong cohort differences suggests that these generalizations cannot and should not be made. If college students have become more extraverted, their behavior in many laboratory situations might be very different now than in the 1970s. Correlational studies may also be affected: How accurate are their conclusions now that average scores have risen almost a full SD? The results also imply that longitudinal studies of development should not be generalized beyond the cohort they study, since age-graded development may differ markedly by cohort (Baltes & Nesselroade, 1972). In addition, these results provide a possible area of inquiry for researchers conducting twin studies. Although birth cohort is necessarily the same in twin pairs, researchers with large datasets might consider comparing the mean extraversion scores for samples collected in different years. If extraversion has risen on average, the mean scores of twin pairs collected earlier should be lower than more recent samples. A comparison could also be made between subjects of different ages, but this would necessarily confound age and cohort as cross-sectional studies traditionally do. These types of analyses might demonstrate the effect of birth year on shared environmental estimates.

On a practical level, the clear changes in personality traits over time suggest that inventory test norms should be used with caution. Many researchers use the norms reported in the original test manuals for the EPI and EPQ (Eysenck & Eysenck, 1968, 1975) to establish the validity and normality of their samples. Many researchers will find that their current samples are very different from the norms reported in the test manual. This does not mean that the original norms are useless, but simply that they need to be adjusted or renormed according to birth cohort.

In conclusion, this study documents clear birth cohort differences in extraversion as measured by the EPI and EPQ. The results demonstrate the importance of birth cohort as an influence on personality. Thus far, environmental explanations for personality have proved disappointing; this may be because researchers were examining only the family environment. Although we may not immediately notice the culture of our times, this Zeitgeist shifts with the years, creating profound social change and, with it, changes in the personality traits of those born to the time.

REFERENCES

Buss, A. R. (1974). Generational analysis: Description, explanation, and theory. *Journal of Social Issues, 30,* 55–71.

Elder, G. H. (1979). Historical change in life patterns and personality. In P. Baltes, & O. Brim (Eds.), *Life-span development and behavior, Vol. 2.* New York: Academic Press.

Flnn, S. E. (1986). Stability of personality self-ratings over 30 years: Evidence for an age/cohort interaction.

Journal of Personality and Social Psychology, 50, 813–818.

Lambert, T. A. (1972). Generations and change: Toward a theory of generations as a force in historical process. *Youth and Society, 4,* 21–46.

Lewinsohn, P., Rohde, P., Seeley, J., & Fischer, S. (1993). Age-cohort changes in the lifetime occurrence of depression and other mental disorders. *Journal of Abnormal Psychology, 102,* 110–120.

Nesselroade, J. R., & Baltes, P. B. (1974). Adolescent personality development and historical change, 1970–1972. *Monographs of the Society for Research in Child Development, 39* (1, Serial No. 154).

Ryder, N. B. (1965). The cohort as a concept in the study of social change. *American Sociological Review, 30,* 843–861.

Woodruff, D. S., & Birren, J. E. (1972). Age changes and cohort differences in personality. *Developmental Psychology, 6,* 252–259.

--- **Questions to Think About** ---

1. What are some of the methodological challenges of looking at different birth cohorts? In comparing studies of college students conducted up to 30 years apart, how might differences in the nature of the overall population (such as changes in the number of immigrants or non-native speakers), and changes in patterns of college attendance (by age, gender, and social class) affect the outcomes?

2. What factors (in domains such as technology, government, economics, family patterns, culture) might account for the substantial increase observed over time in the average extraversion levels?

3. What role might be played by increases in the average age of college students over the decades studied, or a reduction in the average age of onset of puberty?

49

Bicultural Identities:
The Interface of Cultural, Personality, and Socio-Cognitive Processes

JANA HARITATOS AND VERÓNICA BENET-MARTÍNEZ

Jana Haritatos and Verónica Benet-Martínez are current researchers interested in many aspects of cultural identity. Unlike cultural psychology researchers who are focused on understanding the values or behaviors of a specific bicultural community (such as Vietnamese immigrants, for example, or Mexican-Americans), they are instead interested in the underlying structures and processes of biculturalism. The selection here focuses on how the two cultural identities of a bicultural individual can function either compatibly (in a way that is fluid and complementary) or in opposition (in a way that is conflicting and disparate). The study of bicultural identity brings together the fields of cultural psychology and personality psychology.

1. INTRODUCTION

Being 'bicultural' makes me feel special and confused. Special because it adds to my identity: I enjoy my Indian culture, I feel that it is rich in tradition, morality, and beauty; Confused because I have been in many situations where I feel being both cultures is not an option. My cultures have very different views on things like dating and marriage. I feel like you have to choose one or the other.

19-year-old 2nd generation Indian-American (source: Benet-Martínez & Haritatos, 2002).

A large portion of the work done in cross-cultural and cultural psychology has focused on cross-cultural comparisons, seeking to identify differences between distinct (and supposedly homogeneous) cultural groups on a particular variable or construct. However, in today's exceedingly global world, it is increasingly common for individuals to have internalized more than one culture, speak multiple languages, live in culturally mixed environments, and maintain transnational ties. In short, there is an increasing need for psychological work on the experiences of multi-cultural or bicultural individuals. At the same time, the study of biculturalism is relatively new and there is little consensus among researchers about how bicultural identities are cognitively and interpersonally negotiated, and what impact this process has on individuals' lives (LaFromboise, Coleman, & Gerton, 1993). For instance, although some studies suggest that biculturalism brings positive outcomes for the individual (e.g., Lang, Munoz, Bernal, & Sorenson, 1982; Szapocznik & Kurtines, 1980), others

Source: Haritatos, J., & Benet-Martínez, V. (2002). Bicultural identities: The interface of cultural, personality, and socio-cognitive processes. *Journal of Research in Personality, 36,* 598–606. Reprinted with permission from Elsevier.

Editor's note: All citations in the text of this selection have been left intact from the original, but the list of references includes only those sources that are the most relevant and important. Readers wishing to follow any of the other citations can find the full references in the original work or in an online database.

indicate that this type of identity is often filled with contradiction, tension, and social strain (e.g., Lee & Cochran, 1988; Vivero & Jenkins, 1999). One possible reason behind these mixed reports may be the lack of consensus among researchers about how to conceptualize and measure biculturalism. However, these contradictory findings may also reflect unrecognized complexity and variation in the way bicultural individuals experience and organize their cultural identities, variations that themselves may be associated with positive or negative affective experiences.

As the opening quote illustrates, biculturalism can involve feelings of pride, uniqueness, and a rich sense of community and history, while also bringing identity confusion, dual expectations, and value clashes. In this paper we show that, far from falling into simple categories, bicultural individuals differ considerably in the way they subjectively organize their dual cultural orientations, and that these variations are associated with different patterns of contextual, personality, and performance variables. We first introduce the construct of Bicultural Identity Integration (BII) as a framework for organizing and understanding individual differences in the way biculturals perceive the intersection between their mainstream and ethnic cultures. We then report experimental and structural equation modeling findings that elucidate the role of BII in the acculturation process, as well as some of BII's psychosocial antecedents.

2. BICULTURAL IDENTITY INTEGRATION (BII)

Traditionally, the acculturation literature has failed to recognize that while a person may *desire* to maintain positive ties with both cultures (i.e., may support an 'integrative' or bicultural acculturation strategy; Berry & Sam, 1996), particular psychosocial pressures (e.g., national/regional assimilationist vs multi-culturalist policies, racial/cultural make-up of one's living community, personal experiences of discrimination) and individual variables (e.g., personality dispositions, linguistic proficiency, etc.) may lead to significant variations in the process, meanings, and outcomes associated with this effort. Benet-Martínez, Leu, Lee, and Morris (2002) recently conducted a review of the limited (and mostly qualitative) literature on bicultural

identity and introduced the construct of BII as a framework to organize the different meanings and experiences associated with being bicultural. Specifically, individuals high on BII perceive their cultural identities as generally compatible, tend to view themselves as part of a combined, or "third" emerging culture, and find it relatively easy to integrate both cultures into their everyday lives. Biculturals low on BII, on the other hand, report difficulty in incorporating both cultures into a cohesive sense of identity, tend to perceive the two cultures as highly distinct and oppositional, and frequently describe feeling as if they should just choose one culture over the other.

Recently, Benet-Martínez and her colleagues (Benet-Martínez et al., 2002) have investigated the impact of BII on behaviors for which there is strong evidence of cultural effects, namely social attributions. This study and its conclusions are discussed next.

3. BICULTURAL IDENTITY DYNAMICS AND CULTURAL FRAME-SWITCHING: A PRELIMINARY EXPLORATION OF BII

Extensive research has shown that Westerners are more inclined to explain social events in terms of internal, stable causes (e.g., traits, attitudes, etc.), whereas East Asians are more likely to explain such events in terms of external factors such as social roles, group pressures, and cultural expectations (Norenzayan & Nisbett, 2000). Recently Hong, Morris, Chiu, and Benet-Martínez (2000) have extended this work to biculturals, demonstrating that Hong Kong and Chinese-American biculturals make characteristically Western attributions when shown, or "primed with" Western cultural cues, and characteristically East Asian attributions when primed with East Asian cues. This study provides compelling evidence that cultural meaning systems guide socio-cognitive processes, and that biculturals can move between different interpretative lenses rooted in their dual cultural backgrounds, a process that Hong and her colleagues call *cultural frame-switching*.

Given the previously discussed differences in bicultural identity, a natural next step was to explore whether individual differences in BII moderated the processes involved in cultural frame-switching. Using a priming methodology similar to that used in Hong et al.'s (2000) study, Benet-Martínez et al. (2002) conducted a series of three studies in which first-generation Chinese-American biculturals were randomly assigned to one of three priming conditions: an American condition which used American cultural icons as primes (e.g., pictures of the Statue of Liberty, Mickey Mouse, etc.); a Chinese condition which used Chinese cultural icons as primes (e.g., pictures of the Great Wall of China, Chinese dragon, etc.); or a neutral condition which used non-cultural primes (e.g., pictures of natural landscapes). Shortly after seeing these pictures, participants were shown an ambiguous social display of a single fish swimming in front of a group of fish, and asked to explain why the single fish and the group of fish were swimming apart—participants were asked to provide both open ended explanations and ratings on scales tapping internal and external attributions (e.g., internal: the one fish is swimming ahead because of some personal trait such as independence, personal objective, or leadership; external: the one fish is being chased, teased, or pressured by the others). Finally, participants' degree of Bicultural Identity Integration was assessed with a preliminary, single-item scale developed for this study (Bicultural Identity Integration Scale-Pilot, BIIS-P; Benet-Martínez et al., 2002).

Benet-Martínez and her colleagues predicted that biculturals high on BII, by virtue of being unconflicted about their two cultural orientations and seeing them in fluid, non-oppositional terms, would provide prime-consistent attributions to the ambiguous social display (i.e., give stronger internal attributions in the American condition and stronger external attributions in the Chinese condition). Biculturals low on BII, on the other hand, who perceive their two cultural orientations in opposition to each other, were expected to provide prime-inconsistent attributions to the social display (i.e., give stronger internal attributions in the Chinese condition and stronger external attributions in the American condition); in other words, low BIIs were expected to exhibit a contrast effect. In justifying this hypothesized pattern for low BIIs, Benet-Martínez et al., (2002) argued that the cultural conflict and opposition that underlies low BII leads to specific perceptual and cognitive processes (e.g., hyper-vigilance about cultural cues, seeing cultural cues as highly valenced) which themselves are

commonly associated with reverse-priming or contrast effects (Stapel & Winkielman, 1998). Benet-Martínez et al.'s (2002) reasoning for the hypothesized contrast effect among low BIIs was also based on their review of the popular media and literature on topics such as immigration, cultural clash, and biculturalism (e.g., Chavez, 1994; Mehta, 1996; O'Hearn, 1998; Roth, 1969), where inner cultural conflict is often described as leading to behavioral and/or affective "reactance" against the cultural expectations embedded in particular situations (e.g., in Roth's novel, the protagonist finds himself feeling and acting particularly Jewish when traveling to the Midwest, and feeling/acting conspicuously American when visiting Israel).

The findings from Benet-Martínez et al.'s (2002) research consistently supported the above hypotheses and showed that BII is a stable individual-difference moderator of the process of cultural frame-switching. Interestingly, the hypothesized trends for high and low BIIs were not apparent for neutral (non-cultural) primes, indicating that low BIIs' reactance is specific to culture-laden situations.

The studies described above were useful in identifying BII as a key moderator of the acculturation process and raised interesting questions regarding the possible multi-dimensional nature of BII, the kinds of contextual and individual factors that predict variations in BII, and the possible impact of BII on overall adjustment. To address these issues, Benet-Martínez and Haritatos (2002) conducted a series of studies that examined the structure, antecedents, and consequences of BII. This work, which relied on correlational and structural equation modeling methodology, is described in the next section.

4. BII: COMPONENTS, DYNAMICS, AND PSYCHOSOCIAL CORRELATES

Benet-Martínez and Haritatos (2002) studied five different bicultural samples varying in ethnic composition, professional/educational status, geographic location in the US, and generational status. Participants provided detailed demographic information on their familiarity and competence with both American and ethnic cultures (e.g., years lived in the US and other countries, linguistic proficiency, etc.), as well as self-reports on the following measures: acculturation attitudes (preference for integration, separation, assimilation, or marginalization strategies; Berry & Sam, 1996); identification with mainstream and ethnic culture; Big Five personality dimensions (Benet-Martínez & John, 1998); and overall adjustment (anxiety and depression), among others. Participants also completed new multi-item measures of BII and acculturation stress (the later tapped the following domains: discrimination, work and linguistic strains, conflict in intercultural relations, and cultural isolation) developed for the purposes of this study (see Benet-Martínez & Haritatos, 2002; for detailed information on these two measures).

Factor analysis of the new BII measure yielded two orthogonal and reliable dimensions: cultural conflict (vs harmony) and cultural distance (vs blendedness), each representing different aspects of the dynamic intersection between mainstream and ethnic cultural identities in bicultural individuals. As the items defining each dimension in Table 1 reveal, *cultural conflict* captures the experience of feeling torn between two cultural orientations, and encompasses a more emotion-based, subjective element of bicultural identity dynamics than is typically described in the acculturation literature. *Cultural distance,* on the other hand, taps the perception of having non-overlapping, compartmentalized cultural identities. Interestingly, the psychometric independence of cultural conflict and distance suggests that BII is not a uniform and linear process where perceptions of clash and dissociation (vs harmony and overlap) with regard

to one's two cultures go hand-to-hand. Rather, this pattern suggests that a bicultural individual could perceive his/her ethnic and mainstream cultural orientations to be relatively dissociated but not feel that they clash with each other; or alternatively, subscribe to a combined or hyphenated identity but also feel that the two identities are somewhat conflictual.

Figure 1 summarizes the main results from a series of path analyses conducted to explore the unique contribution of some of our acculturation (bicultural competence), personality (Big Five), and contextual (acculturation stress) variables in predicting BII. As the figure indicates, BII's cultural conflict and distance components have a unique pattern of antecedents, which helps explain why very different phenomenological experiences of biculturalism are possible. Cultural conflict is heightened by having an anxious disposition (high neuroticism), and by experiencing three specific types of acculturative threats: discrimination, strained intercultural relations (e.g., being described by ethnic peers as being too American and vice versa), and linguistic concerns (e.g., being self-conscious about one's accent). Cultural distance, on the other hand, is heightened by having a close-minded disposition (i.e., low openness), low levels of bicultural competency, and two acculturative threats: linguistic concerns and living in an environment that is culturally limited, particularly with regard to one's ethnic group (i.e., feeling culturally isolated).

Several personality variables, most notably neuroticism and openness to experience, emerged as antecedents of BII's cultural distance and conflict, as well

TABLE 1   Factorial Structure of the Bicultural Identity Integration Scale-Version 1 (BIIS-1)

	Cultural	
	DISTANCE	CONFLICT
I am simply a Chinese who lives in North America	.72	−.03
I keep Chinese and American cultures separate	.58	−.13
I feel Chinese-American	−.73	−.04
I feel part of a combined culture	−.79	−.03
I am conflicted between the American and Chinese ways of doing things	.04	.66
I feel like someone moving between two cultures	.18	.64
I feel caught between the Chinese and American cultures	.00	.76
I do not feel trapped between the Chinese and American cultures	.09	−.78

Note. N = 133 first-generation Chinese-Americans. Source: Benet-Martínez and Haritatos (2002).

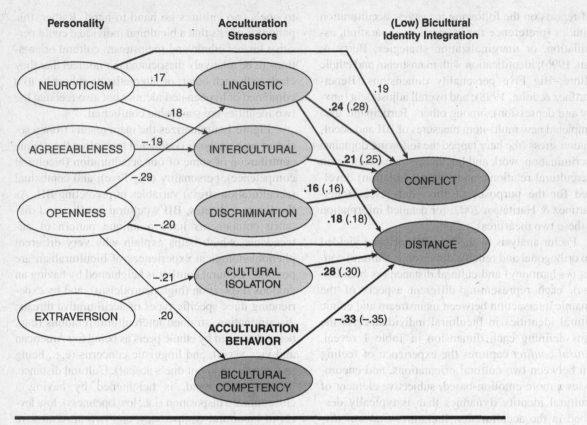

FIGURE 1 Bicultural Identity Integration (BII): components (cultural distance and conflict) and antecedents (personality dispositions, acculturation orientation, and acculturation stressors); $N = 133$ first-generation Chinese-American biculturals; all path coeficients were significant at a p value of .05 or lower; numbers in parenthesis are path coeficients obtained when the Big Five personality dispositions were not included in the model. Fit statistics for the model: $\chi^2/df = 1.65$, CFI = .99, RMSEA = .07 Source: adapted from Fig. 1 in Benet-Martínez and Haritatos (2002).

as other variables in the model. Overall, neuroticism and low openness appear to put bicultural individuals at risk of experiencing the negative aspects of acculturation. Neurotic biculturals (probably because of their higher levels of vulnerability, rumination, and emotional rigidity) were more likely to feel caught between their two cultural identities, and also more prone to experience stress in the linguistic and intercultural relations domains (experiences that, in turn, predicted conflict). Closed-minded biculturals, on the other hand, were more likely to see their identities as dissociated, and also more prone to experience linguistic stress and be less biculturally competent (variables that, in turn,

predicted cultural distance). Perhaps the experiential rigidity of low openness makes biculturals both less willing to acknowledge the flexible boundaries between cultures and less 'permeable' to new cultural ideas and life styles, characteristics that, in turn, may lead to the belief that their two identities cannot "come together" (i.e., high cultural distance), as well as lower levels of bicultural competence.

The interpersonal traits of agreeableness and extraversion also played a role in the acculturation processes depicted in Figure 1. Agreeable biculturals, probably because of their easy-going nature, were less likely to experience and/or report stress in their intercultural relationships. Extraverted individuals, perhaps because of their interpersonal resources and the gains associated with being sociable and outgoing, were less likely to feel strained in culturally isolated (i.e., non-multicultural) social environments. Lastly, conscientiousness had no effects in our model, a finding that suggests that this personality disposition does not play an important role in the present acculturation and identity processes. Overall, the pattern of relationships depicted in Figure 1 highlights the complex, multi-dimensional nature of BII, and suggests that variations in this construct, far from being purely subjective identity representations, are psychologically meaningful experiences linked to specific dispositional factors and contextual pressures.

5. CONCLUSION

As cultural and cross-cultural psychology moves beyond a focus on documenting cultural differences toward an interest in how culture and the psyche mutually constitute each other (Markus & Kitayama, 1998), the need for complex and process-oriented studies that acknowledge the interplay between cultural, socio-cognitive, personality, and adjustment variables has become more critical. The present research applied such an integrative approach to the understanding of individual variations in bicultural identity integration or BII. We hope that this work has demonstrated the importance of studying biculturalism for the understanding of how culture (and multiple cultures) affects individual behaviors and adjustment outcomes. We also hope to raise a broader point about the need to integrate work on personality and cultural psychology and move away from the idea that these two disciplines represent independent forces on the individual. Rather, these disciplines can inform each other about the different ways in which individuals construct meaningful identities as members of their (often complex) cultural, national, and local communities.

REFERENCES

Benet-Martínez, V., & John, O. P. (1998). "Los Cinco Grandes" across cultures and ethnic groups: Multitrait-multimethod analyses of the Big Five in Spanish and English. *Journal of Personality and Social Psychology, 75,* 729–750.

Benet-Martínez, V., Leu, J., Lee, F., & Morris, M. (2002). Negotiating biculturalism: Cultural frame-switching in biculturals with 'oppositional' vs. 'compatible' cultural identities. *Journal of Cross-Cultural Psychology, 33,* 492–516.

LaFromboise, T., Coleman, H., & Gerton, J. (1993). Psychological impact of biculturalism: Evidence and theory. *Psychological Bulletin, 114,* 395–412.

Markus, H. R., & Kitayama, S. (1998). The cultural psychology of personality. *Journal of Cross-Cultural Psychology, 29,* 63–87.

Norenzayan, A., & Nisbett, R. E. (2000). Culture and causal cognition. *Current Directions in Psychological Science, 9,* 132–135.

Questions to Think About

1. The original task from which the data for this study were gathered involved showing Chinese-Americans a picture of a single fish swimming in front of a group of fish, and asking them (in multiple ways) to explain why the single fish was swimming separately from the group of fish. If the participants were of a different cultural group, would the same image and questions necessarily be appropriate? How would a researcher know?

2. For bicultural individuals, what life experiences or personality characteristics might make it more likely that their two cultural identities would be compatible?

3. Does research on biculturalism appear to take a position on whether maintaining a cultural identity in addition to one's mainstream identity is fundamentally desirable or undesirable?